1,000,000 Books

are available to read at

www.ForgottenBooks.com

Read online
Download PDF
Purchase in print

ISBN 978-1-333-10757-4
PIBN 10468717

This book is a reproduction of an important historical work. Forgotten Books uses state-of-the-art technology to digitally reconstruct the work, preserving the original format whilst repairing imperfections present in the aged copy. In rare cases, an imperfection in the original, such as a blemish or missing page, may be replicated in our edition. We do, however, repair the vast majority of imperfections successfully; any imperfections that remain are intentionally left to preserve the state of such historical works.

1 MONTH OF
FREE
READING

at

www.ForgottenBooks.com

By purchasing this book you are eligible for one month membership to ForgottenBooks.com, giving you unlimited access to our entire collection of over 1,000,000 titles via our web site and mobile apps.

To claim your free month visit:

www.forgottenbooks.com/free468717

English
Français
Deutsche
Italiano
Español
Português

www.forgottenbooks.com

Mythology Photography **Fiction**
Fishing Christianity **Art** Cooking
Essays Buddhism Freemasonry
Medicine **Biology** Music **Ancient
Egypt** Evolution Carpentry Physics
Dance Geology **Mathematics** Fitness
Shakespeare **Folklore** Yoga Marketing
Confidence Immortality Biographies
Poetry **Psychology** Witchcraft
Electronics Chemistry History **Law**
Accounting **Philosophy** Anthropology
Alchemy Drama Quantum Mechanics
Atheism Sexual Health **Ancient History**
Entrepreneurship Languages Sport
Paleontology Needlework Islam
Metaphysics Investment Archaeology
Parenting Statistics Criminology
Motivational

CLASSICAL GREEK LITERATURE

VOL. I.

LONDON : PRINTED BY
SPOTTISWOODE AND CO , NEW-STREET SQUARE
AND PARLIAMENT STREET .

A HISTORY

OF

CLASSICAL GREEK LITERATURE

BY THE

REV. J. P. MAHAFFY, M.A.

KNIGHT OF THE ORDER OF THE SAVIOUR
FELLOW AND PROF. OF ANCIENT HISTORY, TRIN. COLL. DUBLIN
HON. FELLOW OF QUEEN'S COLL. OXFORD
AUTHOR OF 'SOCIAL LIFE IN GREECE' 'PROLEGOMENA TO ANCIENT HISTORY' ETC.

IN TWO VOLUMES

VOL. I.

THE POETS

WITH AN APPENDIX ON HOMER, BY PROF. SAYCE

SECOND EDITION

REVISED THROUGHOUT

LONDON

LONGMANS, GREEN, AND CO.

1883

'Αλλὰ γὰρ οὐκ ἐν τοῖς λόγοις χρὴ τούτοις τῶν ἐπιτηδευμάτων ζητεῖν τὰς καινότητας, ἐν οἷς οὔτε παράδοξον οὔτ' ἄπιστον οὔτ' ἔξω τῶν νομιζομένων οὐδὲν ἔξεστιν εἰπεῖν, ἀλλ' ἡγεῖσθαι τοῦτον χαριέστατον, ὃς ἂν τῶν διεσπαρμένων ἐν ταῖς τῶν ἄλλων διανοίαις ἀθροῖσαι τὰ πλεῖστα δυνηθῇ καὶ φράσαι κάλλιστα περὶ αὐτῶν.—ISOCRATES.

PREFACE

TO

THE FIRST VOLUME.

————◆◇◆————

I⊤ is the author's first duty, in committing this second edition
to the public, to thank those kindly and sympathetic critics who
have not only encouraged him by general approbation, but
sought to improve the book by many corrections and suggestions. Similar obligations are due too even to the most adverse
reviewers, who, while they have said many unjust things, have
generally been able to lay their fingers on some distinct blot.
Wherever manifest mistakes were thus pointed out, whether
from good will or the reverse, they have been corrected. But
it is well to say a word here on points which are maintained
against the critics, if it were only to show respect to the
strictures of learned men not here adopted. Many notes are
added in each volume, indicating materials which have since
accrued for the study of particular authors, and which could
not conveniently be embodied in the text.

An incautious reader of reviews might have imagined this
book to be the work of a paradoxical person, who despised the
existing lights, and set up his own, often crude, opinions against
all authority. Nothing could be further from the truth. It was
rather from a wide and laborious survey of the recent literature
in this field, that opinions were gathered and set down without
any pretence to originality, which appeared new to those who
had never searched for them. Unlike the lot of other authors
in the same field, who fret over their unrecognised or refuted
claims to originality, it was my fortune to have far too much

ascribed to me, when I was really selecting from and supporting what the learning or the acuteness of others had discovered.

The reason of this is not far to seek. While it is a usual fashion among authors to affect the modesty of concealing their personal opinions—a fashion very convenient for those who have no personal opinions, or who are afraid to state them—it is surely far more honest, and more modest too, that in disputed questions a man should label the opinion he adopts, not as an universal truth, but as that which he himself has preferred. Thus, when a critic stated that I had been 'unfair to Pindar,' this is itself unfair in the face of the statement (i. p. 225), 'I am bound to say that they (the critics) show a general agreement against the view I have taken of the poet's position in his age.' What more could be expected than that an author should warn his readers not to accept what he said as more than a particular conviction? This personal element in a book has surely its value as well as its weakness.

Passing to more definite criticisms, it may be observed, in answer to those who complained of the omission of Plutarch and Lucian, while Apollonius Rhodius and Babrius were included, that a History of Greek Classical Literature was promised, and nothing more. If, therefore, any classical author had been omitted, it would be a decided defect. But if a few poetical authors outside that category were added, the reader only got more than his bargain, and had no reason to grumble. The principle on which these few authors were added was this very distinct one : that they are read for their form's sake, and are so far classical.

So also the division into poets and prose writers, one now general in Germany, was adopted not merely for its intrinsic value, but to enable each volume to stand alone, and be sold separately. The few repetitions complained of were for this reason unavoidable, and appear, moreover, to have been of special service to those who could find out no more serious faults.

This last advantage also belongs to the spelling of Greek proper names, in which everyone attempts some compromise, and no one satisfies his neighbour. Censures on this head are

therefore of little importance, unless the method adopted produces ambiguity and confusion. And now at last we see our
way to a settlement of this vexed question, by means of the
new pronunciation of Latin. It is hardly possible that the
English schools will keep up the old absurdities of Greek pronunciation ; but even if they do, our obvious course is to print
our Greek names in Latin orthography, and tell our readers
to pronounce them as they pronounce Latin. Thus we shall
banish from our classical books such monstrous forms as
Aischulos, *Lukourgos*, &c., which represent no known utterance,
and have no earthly claim to respect or endurance. Had the
adoption of new Latin speaking been already universal, I
should now have gone back to the Latin orthography of Greek
names. In a few years let us hope that no other course will
even seem tolerable.

It is worth recording as a curious fact, that there is hardly
a chapter, or indeed a general feature in these volumes, which
has not been by some praised as their strongest, by others
censured as their weakest point. This applies, for example, to
the bibliographical notes, which the special student of any one
author often found defective, while the general student, who
sought starting points for study, found them of great assistance.
Of course they could not be, and were not meant to be, complete. They only professed to give the reader some idea of what
amount of special literature he would find on each great Greek
writer, and those works were specially selected which would at
once give him fuller information when he turned to them.
Much additional matter of this kind has been added ; but even
now the critics may possibly find more than one omission of
the name of some learned editor, whose repute, like some very
loud voices, has not reached so far as might be judged from
the noise it made close around him.

The student who desires general directions on the whole
subject, is referred (as was done in my former edition), for
general sketches of the whole course of Greek literature, to
Müller and Donaldson's 'Greek Literature' (if he can procure
it), a work of genius on Müller's part, of vast erudition on
Donaldson's. There are also easily accessible, in French,

E. Bournouf's book, in German, Munk's and Nicolai's, the latter particularly useful for its bibliography, and Mr. Jebb's *Primer*, which gives a good chronological index. The larger and deeper books are partial or unfinished : Bernhardy's and Bergk's Histories, the former on all the poets, the latter (as yet) on the Epic authors ; Patin on the Greek tragedians and Meineke on the comedians, Klein (*Gesch. des Dramas*) on both. Since my first edition appeared, the Fragments of the Old Comedy have been splendidly re-edited by Th. Kock. I will speak of the principal authorities on Greek prose authors in the Preface to the Second Volume.

From all these I have borrowed freely, and far more than can possibly appear from special acknowledgments. There must be added those numerous and invaluable periodicals in which the Germans and French prosecute philological discovery : the Transactions and Proceedings of the many Academies— Berlin, Leipzig, Munich, Göttingen, Vienna, &c. ; the Philologus, Neue Jahrbücher, Hermes, Bursian's Jahresbericht, the Rhein. Museum, the Revue Critique, Journal des Savants, &c., &c., as well as the many Programs, with which the press of Germany teems. For it is not enough now-a-days to know the texts thoroughly, or even the standard commentaries. The historian must take account of the theories of many specialists, who ventilate them in monographs, or in scattered articles throughout various journals. It is only those who have attempted to put together and systematise such materials, who will make due allowance for the mistakes and the inconsistencies, sometimes real, which cannot but creep into so vast a scheme. The existence of such defects may surely be predicted, and should be condoned. It is only their number and quality which can make them the object of fair censure. To delay the publication of this work until all such flaws were removed, would be to postpone it, if not indefinitely, at least till some remote period, and to sacrifice any freshness or vigour it possesses for no certain equivalent.

Homeric Literature in England has since been enriched by Mr. D. B. Monro's *Homeric Grammar*, his article *Homer* in the *Encyclopædia Britannica*, and by an attack on Prof. Sayce's

Appendix to this volume, to which Mr. Sayce has replied—both in the *Journal of Philology*. As regards the general review in the *Homer*, there is nothing special to remark about it, save that the author has regarded Nutzhorn's book as of greater authority than it deserves. This is specially the case in the criticism of the legends about the Peisistratic Commission, which he is disposed to reject, as having no basis in fact. But on all critical questions Mr. Monro expresses himself with an amount of caution which precludes decided views. In his controversy with Mr. Sayce he adopts the more conservative view of the antiquity of the poems, even in language, whereas Mr. Sayce is tending more and more to become a disciple of Mr. Paley, and to assert the Periclean age as that in which *our* Homer assumed its present form. Mr. Paley has himself added another tract to his many declarations on the subject. He has unwittingly classed me among the old conservatives, whereas the view deliberately preferred in this book is that which attributes a moderate antiquity to the completed poems. But I still think the seventh century B.C. nearer the mark than the fifth, though the traces of an Attic recension are very deep and often startling.

The decisions of recent German criticism have been distinctly in Mr. Sayce's direction, though I am glad to see that in a recent remarkable transcription of some of the Iliad into its supposed older or Æolic form, Aug. Fick, while holding the present text to be a *Mischmasch*, does not place the recasting of it later than 700 B.C., so far agreeing with me. The real points of issue between Mr. Sayce and me are this question of date (700 or 450 B.C. for the recension), and also whether the recasting was only linguistic, or affected the plan and substance of the poems. He thinks it must have done both, but has so far failed to persuade me.

I add a few notes on other authors by way of supplement.

The first scrap of an actual MS. of Sappho, though but a scrap, has found its way last year from Egypt to Berlin (cf. Blass' interesting account in the *Rhein. Mus.* xxxv. p. 287, sq.). This raises strange hopes that we may yet recover an unique treasure in Greek Literature.

In discussing the choric art of Pindar, I should have mentioned the curious theory propounded as regards his odes, in connection with those of Æschylus, by R. Westphal (*Prolegg. zu Æsch. Trag.* 1869). This theory has been further expanded and strongly asserted in the case of Pindar by Mezger in his German Commentary on Pindar (Leipzig, 1880). It has received very little attention in Germany, none in England, even in the most recent studies on Pindar, and is nevertheless well worthy of further examination. Westphal asserts that both Pindar and Æschylus (discounting his amœbean *commoi*) composed their odes on the plan of the Terpandrian nome (cf. below, p. 168). If so, the full form of the ode was as follows : first, a προοίμιον (or ἐπαρχά), passing into the ἀρχά (μεταρχά of Pollux). This was followed by the κατατροπά, which introduced, as a transition piece, the ὀμφαλός or main body of the hymn, in which (in Pindar's case) we always find a mythical narrative. A second transition, the μετακατατροπά, corresponding closely to the κατατροπά, leads to the σφραγίς, and the ode ends with the ἐπίλογος. Pindar occupies his ἀρχά and σφραγίς with the praise of the victor and his family, and the transition movements contain some personal remark, often repeating the same metaphor, and *in the same words,* by way of index. Thus the full Pindaric or Æschylean ode might be compared in its grouping to that of the pediments of the Greek temples, which decrease symmetrically, so that the several members correspond according to their respective distances from the great figures in the centre. The correspondences of Greek art dispose us to consider this attractive theory very seriously, especially as both Pindar and Æschylus certainly do not bind themselves (like Euripides and Sophocles) to the divisions of strophe and antistrophe in the *matter* of their odes. The end of a strophe is often with them no halting-point in either the construction or the sense. But if this was more than a mere license, if it was a principle to divide their odes differently, is it not strange that they should universally have adopted a strophic form calculated to mislead and bewilder the hearer ? Why should the rythm of the figures of the dance have violated the deeper meaning of the poem ? This appears to me an unanswered difficulty,

though it is quite true that the later poets were far more
obedient to the form indicated by responsive verses In addition to this formal objection, it may be argued against Mezger,
in the case of Pindar, that the members do not correspond in
length, the ἀρχά and σφραγίς, for example, being seldom of
equal compass. This is a serious objection in a symmetrical
work of art, whose very beauty consists in its symmetry. Lastly,
when we come to Mezger's analysis of individual odes, we find
the seven members hardly ever clearly marked, and in most of
them some subordinate member omitted. These mutually
corroborative objections are decisive against accepting the
theory without further support, even if the speculations he
hazards on the central thought of each ode were not as vague
and uncertain as those of his predecessors. The strength of the
theory is best seen in Ol. vi., where his division happens nearly
to coincide with the strophic arrangement, viz. προοίμ., 1–7 ;
σφραγίς, 78–100 ; μετακατ., 71–7 ; ὀμφαλός, 29–70 ; καταρχά,
22–8 ; ἀρχά, 8–21 ; ἐπίλογ., 100–5.

In the case of Æschylus, the speculations of Westphal will
be read with great profit, as often suggesting an underlying
idea, which explains apparent neglect of strophic form. I have
added a note to the chapter, pointing out the general lines of
this theory. As regards the bibliography of both Æschylus
and Sophocles, general editions are so much more common, if
we except the *Agamemnon,* than special commentaries on single
plays, that their bibliography is placed at the conclusion. The
larger compass of Euripides has made editions of single plays,
in his case, the general rule, and accordingly the best editions
are specified under each. This will account for an apparent
inconsistency, which may thus be fairly vindicated.

Another question as regards the estimate of Sophocles' art
has been raised by my acute but superficial critic in the *Atlantic
Monthly* (November 1880). He has picked out an apparent
inconsistency in the criticisms of the *Œdipus Rex* and *Antigone*
of Sophocles, compared with the praise of Æschylus' chief
merits in tragedy. Though my statements were fairly open to
his censures, the idea suggested was nevertheless true and important. Hamlet and Orestes are far grander tragic figures

than Œdipus or Antigone. For in the former the very character of the actor, as well as his acts, is part of the problem,
and he is placed between conflicting obligations, each of them
holy and awful, to choose his alternative. In Sophocles, on
the other hand, we have the very obvious problem of a lofty
character, with an independent free-will, knowing how to per·
form an act of duty, in spite of tragic difficulties. Œdipus
is no doubt a nobler personage than Orestes, but by no means
so tragic a character. His story shocks us with the odious
tyranny of destiny, while that of Orestes exalts us to speculate
on great ethical world-problems.

Many corrections have been introduced into the account of
the Comic Fragments from the edition of Theodor Kock, as
well as from some valuable private communications, for which I
here return him my sincere thanks. This edition has received
similar help from Prof. Lewis Campbell as regards the MSS. of
Sophocles, and in many places my own studies have taught me
to modify or emend what was amiss.

TRINITY COLLEGE, DUBLIN:
November 1882.

CONTENTS

APPENDICES.

HISTORY

OF

GREEK LITERATURE.

——◆◆◆——

CHAPTER I.

INTRODUCTION.

§ 1. It has been the usual practice with historians of Greek Literature to begin with a survey of the character and genius of the race, the peculiar features of the language, and the action which physical circumstances have produced upon the development of all these things. In the case of many German books these discussions are so long and so vague that the student is wearied before he arrives at a single fact in literature. It is furthermore necessary for the proper understanding of generalities that the reader should be intimate with the details which are postponed to a later part of the book. This appears to me so unpractical a method that I have abandoned it, and will not attempt any broad survey of the subject in a work devoted to the discussion of details, except in immediate connection with these details. In the present day, when so much is taught, and talked, and read about Greek history and art and poetry, the readers of such a book as this cannot but have enough acquaintance with the subject to permit them to dispense with any general introduction.

§ 2. When we come to inquire what were the earliest products of Greek Literature, we turn of course to Greek poetry, for it is a well-known law of human progress, that long before the discovery or use of writing, and long before men care to read or hear simple prose statements, they delight in rythmical song, which strikes their imagination with greater force, and is more easily retained in their memory. This may be seen among us in the education of children, who pass in a few years through successive stages not unlike those of humanity at large in its progress from mental infancy to mature thought. We know that little children can be taught to repeat and remember rimes long before they will listen to the simplest story in prose. We must therefore expect to find the earliest efforts among the Greeks in their poetry. This is of course the case, and the poems of Homer and Hesiod are manifestly older, even as they stand, than any other books the Greeks have left us. For though we should concede to certain modern sceptics that the arrangement, or bringing into large unities, of these poems was not completed till pretty late in their history—even this extreme theory must admit and require that the *materials* of the poems, the short lays from which they were put together, are older than any other species of Greek literature. It must also be admitted that the number and extent of these shorter poems, which may have been worked into what we call Homer, was very considerable, and that only a very small portion of this literature has been transmitted to us.

When, therefore, we go back as far as we can, in our search for the earliest specimens of Greek poetry, we find ourselves in the presence of a very large body of what is called Epic poetry, all of which in early days passed under the name of Homer. The noblest and best of this poetry is in the opinion of all critics, ancient and modern, the *Iliad* ; a poem of great length, of a definite plan and purpose, and composed with a perfect mastery both of style and language. The characters are pretty consistently drawn, and our general impression of the whole work suggests (a) that its author was one master hand, using both the legends of his people, and his own studies in human nature, to produce a dramatic picture not since surpassed or perhaps equalled. If this be so, we may safely assert, that such a piece of work cannot be the first hesitating attempt of any people, however gifted, at literary composition.

But throughout the various shorter episodes of which the Iliad may be composed, there is such a harmony in the drawing of the various heroes who appear on the scene, that (*b*) even if one great master did not sketch them all, they must have been recognised types, which had long since assumed a definite and fixed shape for a school or series of poets, each of whom was able to express this type with adequate consistency. Either theory implies long and gradual preparation, many lesser attempts which have failed, and many faulty pictures which have disappeared, because they departed from the once fixed and recognised features of known characters.

§ 3. The ambitious and elaborate structure of these epics will clearly appear when we come to discuss them more fully in detail. It is here sufficient to insist that such compositions can in no wise represent the first attempts of the nation to frame a literature. In all the other fine arts, which the Greeks cultivated with equal success, they began with rude and even childish efforts, which possessed no beauty, and were evidently the work of artists who had as yet obtained but little control over the material with which they worked. We have still remaining archaic specimens of architecture and of sculpture, which strike us as almost ludicrous; nor do the various accounts of early painting and music handed down to us leave a shadow of doubt that these arts went through a similarly gradual development. The use of harmony in music was a late discovery, after many generations had been content with an accompaniment played note for note with the voice. The laws of perspective were not made out and introduced into painting until the exigencies of theatrical scene-painting had reacted upon the higher branches of the art. Thus everywhere in the history of Greek culture we find the same rude beginnings and gradual growth in grace and power. It is only a false and random metaphor when older critics speak of epic poetry springing like Athene full grown and in panoply from the brain of a single Homer.

§ 4. But if the Iliad is far too great and too perfect for a first attempt in literature, its vast superiority over what went before is, on the other hand, the main cause of our being so badly informed about earlier and ruder efforts. When any people are feeling their way in art, it is but natural that the first work of real genius should eclipse and supersede all its rivals, so as to become the model for succeeding ages. The great popularity and thorough nationality of Homer not only made him supplant earlier epics, but even made epic poetry supplant the earlier and simpler forms of poetry which had existed among the people; and so for some generations in Greek literature we hear of nothing but epic poets, hexameter verse, and legendary subjects.

§ 5. Yet there can be no doubt that the earliest forms of song among the Greeks, as among all other people, were not epic but lyric. The very Linus song mentioned by Homer, and the choral dances accompanied by singing, as well as the vintage songs, and other such national poetry—all these were distinctly of a lyric character. There is no reason to believe that these, though eclipsed by the splendour of epic poetry, ever ceased to exist, and we must rather conceive that the feelings of the common people satisfied themselves in these songs, while the nobles sat in state at their feasts, and even paid a bard to compose and recite the praise of gods and men. But it was not till this more artificial and elaborate school had worked itself out along with the society which produced and fostered it, it was not till the old aristocracies and kingdoms had broken down, and the epic poets became shallow and pedantic, that the lyric instincts began to assert themselves in literature Then it was that great men went back to the people, who alone can originate a really fresh and lasting current in poetry, and borrowed from them the various forms of iambic, elegiac, and lyric proper which form the so-called lyric age of poetry in Greece.

It is a great and general mistake to set down this lyric poetry as the invention or product of a later age; it is merely the revival, and the drawing from obscurity, of the oldest form of Greek national song, modified and varied no doubt by literary genius, but with its root deep-set in the hearts of the people.[1]

When in process of time this lyric poetry became in its turn frigid and over-wrought, when it passed into the pay of despots or Olympic victors, and the people felt the want of some more national literature, the great poets of Athens again went back to the people. They adopted from the rude merry-makings of Dionysus and the boisterous vintage-feasts the popular elements of dramatic poetry, which when ennobled by the heritage of epic and lyric forms took its place as the last and perhaps the greatest branch in the rich growth of Greek national life. For from this day onward, and with a reading public, a national efface-ment and decay, a political ruin, a social decadence made parti-cularism and not nationalism the feature of Greek poetry. Yet even when the centre of gravity of Greek culture had passed from Hellas to the East, Theocritus and his school found in Sicilian pastoral life a pure vein of gold, which has made his bucolics, written among the bookworms of the sandhills of Egypt, an independent and fresh development in Greek Literature. These songs had existed in the uplands of Sicily, as we know, for centuries. They had attracted the genius of the great Stesichorus, who had treated some of their pastoral stories with his elaborate art. But the day of bucolic poetry had not come, or rather the great lyric outburst was just then carrying with it all the higher spirits of the nation; and so the attempt of Stesichorus, though known and approved, did not find any followers.

§ 6. This brief sketch of the periods of Greek poetry is drawn here only so far as to make it appear that all the so-called new kinds of verse, all the revolutions in taste which are so definite and plainly dated in Greek literary history, were simply reversions to the only true and pure source of inspiration in old days—the untutored songs of the people. It is in the

---

[1] This reasonable theory, based on the nature of things, and supported by good scholars, such as Theodor Bergk, is rejected by Bernhardy (*Hist. Lit.* vol. ii. pp. 576, 589, 602) merely because he thinks our positive evidence for it insufficient. I feel bound to note his disapproval, though it does not shake my conviction.

nature of any cultivated school of poetry to grow gradually
more laboured and artificial, until at last it ceases to appeal to
the public taste, and becomes a mere exercise and amusement
for the student and for learned audiences. This was plainly
the case with the later epic poets who were called *Cyclical*, and
whose laboured accounts of the wars of gods, giants, and bygone men, roused the ire and fed the satire of Xenophanes
and his contemporaries. It is perhaps not so easily proved,
and will not be so readily admitted, that the lyric poetry of
Pindar and Simonides, which was eclipsed by the rise of
tragic poetry, showed plain traces of the same defects. The
epitaphs of Simonides are indeed very striking, clear, and
devoted to great national subjects ; but these can hardly be
called a separate school of poetry, and were written with equal
beauty and effect by many poets not exclusively lyric. What
really damaged the national position of Simonides, with all his
merits, was the feeling that he was a poet for pay—a poet of
courts and despots, at a time when courts and despots were
rapidly passing out of all favour and becoming the objects of
a great national hate. The poetry of Pindar laboured under
the same disadvantages. He celebrated, indeed, victories at
the national games, but celebrated them for pay, and was
ready to write for pay in honour of anybody—of Sicilian tyrants
or Corinthian courtesans. There was, moreover, strongly
marked in Pindar's poetry another quality, which we do not
meet in the extant fragments of Simonides, and which heralds
the decadence of lyric poetry—I mean that obscurity and
elaborate richness which made him quite unintelligible to
the masses. Literary men studied him, and admired him for
these bold and daring flights ; but the mass of the Greek public
had forgotten him and laid him aside in the very next generation, as we hear from Cratinus. Of course lyric poetry could
not die in a moment ; but even as epic poetry had been
transformed rather than destroyed in the odes of Stesichorus
and Pindar, and in the dialogues of tragedy, so lyric poetry
passed into the humbler sphere of being the handmaid of the
drama, and filling up the gaps in the action of the piece.
Whatever purely lyrical drama and dithyrambs existed were

never successful, and have left only faint traces in the history of literature.

§ 7. The later fortunes and decay of tragedy, which occurred in a very advanced civilisation and among a reading public, are a more complicated history.   When the majority of people begin to read, poetry loses its hold upon the public, and the prose writer, who composes with greater simplicity and less labour, at last obtains an advantage over his rival the poet, who is put into competition with all the older poets now circulating among a more learned public.   It is here sufficient to repeat, as an additional illustration of the principle, that although in the Alexandrine epoch there were learned and even brilliant imitations of all species of old Greek poetry—the epics of Apollonius, the elegiacs of Callimachus, the lyrics of a false Anacreon, the tragedies of the Pleiad—one kind only of the varied products of that wonderfully prolific and greatly under-rated age has held its place with all the critics and admirers of pure Greek poetry.   This is the bucolic poetry of Theocritus, imitated, not from earlier literature, but from the people's songs, from the shepherds' pipe and ditty, from the fresh feelings of untutored hearts.   It is indeed beyond the scope of the present work, but it is worthy of suggestion, that the history of the fine arts generally, nay even the political history of the world, shows perpetual examples of the same principle.   The tendency of all human invention is to become conventional, then cramped, and then effete.   It is to be revived only by breaking with venerable traditions, and going back to nature, to natural men and natural things, for new inspiration.

CHAPTER II.

THE TRACES OF POETRY BEFORE HOMER.

§ 8. When we endeavour to discover the preliminary stages through which Greek poetry reached the perfect condition which produced the great epics, we find ourselves reduced to doubtful inferences and conjectures. The Homeric poems themselves tell us almost nothing on the subject. Apart from the two bards in the Odyssey—Demodocus at the Phæacian court, and Phemius among the suitors—who are distinctly epic singers of the same style and class as the author or authors of our remaining epics, we have only an allusion to one person, Thamyris, and to various choral songs of a lyric kind, sung at marriages and vintage scenes, or on other occasions of great grief or joy. We have also several earlier legends mentioned in such a way as to suggest that they had already been treated by bards such as Phemius and Demodocus.

§ 9. The facts which may with certainty be inferred from these allusions are: (1) that poets were common before the composition even of the Iliad, or oldest of the poems; (2) that the earlier poems were both lyric and epic in character; and (3) that there existed a feeling of rivalry, if not regular contests, in poetry. These latter are indeed openly asserted to have taken place in the old account of the contest between Homer and Hesiod, but are implied also in the reference to Thamyris (B 594),[1] 'who boasted that he would conquer even were the Muses, the daughters of Zeus, to contend against him; but they in anger made him blind (πηρόν), and took away his

---

[1] The books of the Iliad are indicated in capitals, those of the Odyssey in small letters.

godlike song, and caused him to forget his cunning upon the lute.'

This famous passage occurs, it is true, in the *Catalogue*, which is perhaps the most suspicious part of the Iliad. But, on the other hand, it occurs in the account of the forces of Nestor from Pylus, and there is evidence that many other poetic legends were in vogue about this kingdom—legends perpetually cited in the reminiscences of the aged Nestor himself, whose very age seems to imply that he had been the subject of earlier ballads. This justifies the opinion that the mention of Thamyris [1] is really old, and points to the age before the composition of the Iliad. But, unfortunately, there is no hint as to the nature of his poetry. We cannot tell whether he composed lyric pieces such as the old dirges and marriage-songs, or whether he was an epic singer like Demodocus, or whether, again, he was an author of that early religious poetry, which was by later writers ascribed to the age before Homer.

After the days of Herodotus, we hear constantly of this religious poetry, which was of a mystical or symbolical character, and certainly of a very different type from the worldly Homer. But as to its antiquity, our authorities are not very encouraging. The first and most important is Herodotus, who says in a famous passage (ii. 50–4) in which he discusses the origin and names of the Hellenic gods : ' Whence the gods severally sprang, whether or not they had existed from all eternity, what forms they bore—these are questions of which the Greeks knew nothing till the other day, so to speak. For Homer and Hesiod were the first to compose Theogonies, and give the gods their epithets, to allot to them their several offices and occupations, and describe their forms ; and they lived about 400 years before my time, and not more, as I believe. As for the poets who are thought by some to be earlier than these, they are, in my judgment, decidedly later.' And he adds presently : ' What I have said of Homer and Hesiod is my own opinion, and not borrowed from the priestesses of Dodona.'

I should consider this judgment as to the relative age of the

---

[1] Also called *Thamyras*, especially in a comedy of Antiphanes.

old Orphic and other religious poems (to which he clearly alludes) as of the greatest weight, were it not evident that Herodotus is here sustaining a favourite theory of his own, viz. that almost all the Greek religion, and especially all the mystic part of it, was borrowed from Egypt. Thus he says (ii. 81) : ' Here their (the Egyptian) practice resembles the rites which are called Bacchic and Orphic, but which are in reality Egyptian and Pythagorean ; ' and it was a necessary part of this theory that these rites, and the poems belonging to them, should not be very ancient. I do not, therefore, think that the sceptical judgment of Herodotus, which he, with his usual honesty, confesses to be a peculiar opinion of his own, can be here decisive.[1] The frequent poetical allusions of Euripides to a collection of Orphic poems of pious and philosophic import can, on the other hand, afford no secure evidence of their antiquity,.for we know that the school of Onomacritus, in the sixth century B.C., added considerably to the old religious poems, if it did not forge them wholesale. But the very fact of the forging of the name of Orpheus, Musæus, and others proves clearly the antiquity of these names, and that the poetry ascribed to them was of a character quite different from that of the Epos. The very frequent allusions of Plato, on the other hand, who even in three places quotes the words of Orpheus,[2] show clearly that he accepted Orpheus and Musæus, whom he usually co-ordinates, as ancient masters of religious song, and on a par with Homer and Hesiod. This general acceptance of Orpheus as a real personage, with no less frequent suspicions as to the genuineness of the current Orphic books, appears in other Greek writers ; e.g. Aristotle[3] cites the so-called Orphic poems, just as he cites the so-called Pythagorean books. Apart from these casual allusions, our really explicit authorities are the antiquaries of

----

[1] We might just as well accept the almost unanimous verdict of older tradition, and believe the Greek race to be autochthonous, and their civilisation perfectly original ; whereas their eastern origin can be clearly demonstrated, quite apart from the discoveries of Herodotus and his school, from the surer evidence of architecture and the plastic arts, and from the results of comparative Linguistic.

[2] *Crat.* 402 B, *Phileb.* 66 C, *Legg.* 669 D.

[3] *De Anima*, i. 5, 410 b ; and elsewhere.

later days, to whom we owe almost all the definite knowledge we possess. Pausanias, in particular, not only speaks constantly of these poets, but refers to some of their hymns, which he had heard, and it is he and Strabo who afford us the materials for constructing a general theory about them.

§ 10. It is remarkable that the two races which tradition consistently asserts to have been the first civilisers of Greece are known in history as barbarians—the Pelasgi and the Thracians. Herodotus (i. 57) found remnants of the Pelasgi still living at Creston, Scylace and Placia, and he characterises their language as that of barbarians. The savagery of the Thracians was proverbial all through Hellenic history, and yet among the various obscure and doubtful statements of the legends, these are the only neighbouring peoples of which we can affirm with tolerable certainty that they were the forerunners of the Hellenes in culture. With the Pelasgi we are not much concerned. They were great builders and great reclaimers of land. They settled all over Greece, and especially in such rich plains as those of Thessaly and of Argos. But their literary character is nowhere attested. Nor have we remaining any certain trace of their language, save the words Argos and Larissa, which (as interpreted to mean *plain* and *fortress*) point to these very tastes. They seem to have been a peace-loving, quiet people ; and if they built everywhere great forts, such as was the Pelasgic ring wall of the Acropolis at Athens, they were not, like the Leleges or Minyans, famed for pillage and war. They must have been a settled and agricultural race, opposed to the roving pirates, whom they doubtless dreaded.

One fact connected with literature, and one only, may be traced to them. It was they who received from the Phœnicians the letters of the alphabet, adapted from the Egyptian hieratic character by these traders. The varying appellations of *Cadmean, Phœnician,* and *Pelasgic letters* seem clearly to attest this. Despite Herodotus' condemnation of their language, they were doubtless of Aryan descent [1] ; and one thing is clear, that the change of Greece from its Pelasgic to its Hellenic state was no

---

[1] Émile Burnouf believes them to have been akin to the present Albanians, whom later invasions have reinstated in many parts of Greece.

sudden revolution or conquest, but a gradual absorption of the older and weaker in the new. The most venerable elements in the Hellenic religion were adopted from them, and there is no nobler invocation in the Iliad than that of Achilles to the old Pelasgic Zeus of Dodona that ruled in the heavens.[1] This appeal agrees well with the interesting notice of Herodotus, that they worshipped their gods, but without names or divers functions, in simple and silent adoration. Hence it came that they were reverenced by the Romans for their religion.

§ 11. The legends about the Thracians are of quite a different order. This remarkable people appear from the notices of the Iliad to have been allied rather to the Phrygians than to the western Greeks. The Phrygians have been proved from the extant words of the language to be not only Aryans, but Aryans of the European branch ; and thus we can conceive an early culture among the great Phrygio-Thracian tribes extending to the borders of Thessaly. However this may be, we hear of a school of Thracian minstrels, of whom Orpheus is the best known name, which is associated with the district of Pieria—a region not very clearly defined, and apparently moving gradually southward, till we find it about the slopes of Mount Olympus.[2]

These singers were specially devoted to the worship of the Muses—three goddesses who are always associated with wells and water-springs, and who were the special patronesses and inspirers of poetry.[3] There are traces of these Thracian bards

[1] Cf. Π 233. Ζεῦ ἄνα, Δωδωναῖε, Πελασγικὲ, τηλόθι ναίων,
Δωδώνης μεδέων δυσχειμέρου κ. τ. λ.

[2] It has been well pointed out by many scholars that the legendary Thracians of Attica and the historical Thracians have nothing in common, and that not impossibly the mythical Thracians were pure Ionian Greeks (cf. Petersen in *Ersch und Gruber's Encyclop.* vol. lxxxv. p. 271) ; at all events, they were a distinct people, with a distinct religion and polity.

[3] The names for them at Helicon were, in Pausanias' day, μνήμη, μελέτη· and ἀοιδή ; at Delphi, according to Plutarch, ὑπάτη, μέση, and νήτη, from the principal strings of the lyre. The three Charites of Orchomenus seem to correspond to them (Paus. ix. 35). In later days the number was nine, and the names quite different. Bergk absurdly suggests the Lydian μωυ = water, as the origin of Μοῦσα, which is rather = μοντ-ja, and connected with the root of μάντις.

down through the mountains of Phocis to Delphi and round about Parnassus; and still more certainly are they, and with them the worship of the Muses, associated with the northern slopes of Helicon. There is no range through all Greece so rich in springs and tumbling brooks as the northern slopes of Helicon, and men might well imagine it a favourite abode of goddesses, who loved this most speaking voice in nature. It is here that the author of the *Theogony*, ascribed to Hesiod—possibly Hesiod himself—fixes their abode, when he calls them to come from Pieria at the opening of his didactic poem. The establishment of the worship of the Muses, which the Thracian school had introduced from Pieria, is perfectly demonstrated by its persistence up to the days of Hesiod, and the so-called didactic and genealogical epics.

Attic legends seem to indicate that the Thracians were not mere singers, and that they sought to extend their influence still further. The legend of the war of Eumolpus, the Thracian warrior, king and bard, against Erechtheus, king of Athens, implies that the Thracians extended their power from the slopes of Helicon across the glades and gorges of Cithæron to its last spur—the citadel of Eleusis. This approach so threatened Athens, that the legends represent Erechtheus engaged in a desperate struggle with Eumolpus, and victorious only by the aid of human sacrifices—the voluntary death of his own daughters. This legend, now glorified by Mr. Swinburne's splendid drama, may have real facts underlying it; and it is, in any case, in consonance with the other hints collected by Strabo and Pausanias. Certain it is that the mysteries of Demeter and Persephone, celebrated by the Athenians at Eleusis all through history, were under the special direction of the clan of the Eumolpidæ, who professed to trace their origin to this Thracian ancestor. His name, like that of Musæus, shows clearly enough his connection with the old worship of the Muses, and their poetic inspiration.

§ 12. Our oldest direct evidence for Orpheus is the fact that in Peisistratus' day his name was sufficiently venerable to produce and protect extensive forgeries; but it is probable that Heracleitus, who could hardly have been deceived by Onomacritus,

believed not only in Orpheus, but in some of the extant writings
attributed to him.[1]   The mention of his poems by Pausanias is
very interesting. 'Whoever,' says he, 'has made a critical
study of poetry, knows that the hymns of Orpheus are each
composed in the briefest form, and are altogether very few in
number.   The Lycomidæ (an Attic clan) know them and sing
them in accompaniment to the ceremonies (of the mysteries).
In elegance they would rank second after the hymns of Homer,
at any rate, but they are more highly honoured than these on
account of their religious spirit.'   In another place (i. 14, 3),
he distinctly rejects poems attributed to Orpheus, and doubtfully
to Musæus.   This Musæus was supposed to have been a pupil
or successor to Orpheus.

There are other names which Pausanias considers still
older—Linus, the personification of the Linus song mentioned
by Homer, and from early times identified more or less with the
Adonis song of the Phœnicians and the Maneros of the Egyptians. After Linus came the Lycian Olen, the oldest composer of
Greek hymns known (Paus. ix. 27, 2), whose style was adopted
by Orpheus, and also by Pamphos, the oldest hymn-poet among
the Athenians.   A hymn of this Pamphos to Eros was sung at
the mysteries by the Lycomidæ, along with those of Orpheus.
Several of his hymns are referred to by Pausanias.   With the
old Delphic contests in music and poetry were connected
Chrysothemis, Philammon, and his son Thamyris, who were
said to be the first three victors recorded at these contests.
Orpheus and Musæus were distinctly reported to have abstained from contending, as being of too great fame, and also
connected with a different worship.[2]   The names of Bakis and

---

[1] Bergk calls attention to Euripides' *Alcestis* (v. 967) and the scholia.
Cf. for the following statement, Pausanias, ix. 30, 12.

[2] The various relations or genealogies of these poets referred to by
Pausanias, Diodorus, and Suidas are irreconcilable, and are, indeed, not
worth reconciling.   Some called Thamyris the eighth poet before Homer,
some the sixth.   Charops, Œagrus, Orpheus, Musæus, Eumolpus, Philammon, Thamyris, is one suggested order.   The object of these legends is
various : first, to account for the transference of the mysteries and their
poetical rites from Thrace to Athens ; secondly, to bring the Delphic oracle

Lycus were known as the authors of antique oracles, all of them probably spurious. This only is to be observed about the old responses of the Delphic oracle, that while the extant *rhetra* of Lycurgus seems to be literally an oracular response in the Delphic dialect, we are told that the hexameter verse was first invented at Delphi, either by Phemonoe, the first priestess, or by Olen, when he founded the prophetic shrine.

This inquiry into the poetry of the Greeks before Homer leads us to some very natural and some very strange results. In the first place, no educated Greek, except perhaps Herodotus, seems to have denied the existence of poems, far less of poets, anterior to Homer. The tradition about these poets is all the more trustworthy, because they are not represented in any sense as forerunners of Homer. For, in the second place, all the poems attributed to these men were either lyrical or oracular; they were all short, and they were all strictly religious.[1] In these features they contrasted broadly with the epic school of Homer. Even the hexameter metre seems not to have been used in these old hymns, and was called a new invention of the Delphic priestess. Still further, the majority of these hymns is connected with mysteries apparently ignored by Homer, or with the worship of Dionysus, which he hardly knew.

§ 13. Indeed the Homeric poems seem to ignore all Pelasgian religion (save in a single appeal to Zeus); they seem to ignore the Thracian bards and their Muse-worship; they speak of the rich shrine of Delphi without even naming an oracle. It is therefore plain that if these early bards were really the forerunners of Homer in time, they can in nowise be called his teachers or forerunners in poetry. He seems to start from quite a fresh commencement, like Archilochus, like Æschylus, like Theocritus, and to start up among a people who knew poetry, but of a different sort.

What, then, were the real beginnings of Epic poetry, and who prepared the way for the great Iliad as we have it? To

—really a different religion—into relation with them; and, lastly, to satisfy the universal desire of bringing great men of old into near relationship.

[1] Thus of Thamyris the lexicographers say: ἔγραψε μέλη καὶ ᾄσματα.

this question we can only answer by a probable theory, which now indeed has been accepted by many competent critics, which is however not based directly on positive facts, but on reasonable inferences.   The hexameter verse was commonly attributed to the Delphic priests, who were said to have invented and used it in oracles.   In other words, it was early used in religious poetry.   If we examine its structure, as opposed to the shorter and more varied lyric measures, it is evidently composed and intended for sustained narrative, and for poems of considerable length.   There is no doubt that the priests did compose such works for the purpose of teaching the attributes and adventures of the gods, and bringing into harmony the various local myths concerning them.   These genealogies of the gods were called *Theogonies,* and we have still under the name of Hesiod a poem of this class, which, though later than Homer, appears to have been composed upon a far earlier model, and affords an example of these didactic religious works.   It may be that the earlier lyric hymns contained short descriptions, such as we find them—an epic element—in the remains of Pindar and Stesichorus; but the superior evenness and calm of the hexameter must soon have made this species of verse generally preferred for narrative purposes.

§ 14. With the gods were closely connected the heroes, who ruled over the tribes in these old feudal days, and it was impossible to treat of the descendants of the gods without recording the legends of older days in the history of the nation.   So the genealogies and acts of demigods and of men came to be treated in connection with the Theogonies of the priests. Such old genealogical epics were said to have survived long among the Peloponnesians.   But the secular element gradually gained ground, especially among the luxurious and worldly Ionians, and a class of bards who were not priests began to treat the histories of the heroes and their adventures, in fact, the κλέα ἀνδρῶν [1] of Homer, which delighted the Ionic chiefs and their

---

[1] This phrase—the acts of renowned men—seems almost a technical one. Achilles (I 189) ἄειδε δ' ἄρα κλέα ἀνδρῶν, in his tent, evidently older heroes; so again, v. 524, οὕτω καὶ τῶν πρόσθεν ἐπευθόμεθα κλέα ἀνδρῶν κ. τ. λ.   Again (θ 73), Μοῦσ' ἄρ' ἀοιδὸν ἀνῆκεν ἀειδέμεναι κλέα ἀνδρῶν; and so Hesiod,

courts. Thus epic poetry, from having been purely religious, became purely secular. After having treated men and heroes in subordination to the gods, it came to treat the gods in relation to men. Indeed it may be said of Homer, that in the image of man created he God.[1] The statement of Herodotus, that Homer and Hesiod—the poet of adventure and the genealogist—made the religion of the Greeks, and assigned to the gods their epithets and functions, is apparently true, and full of import.[2]

We must take care not to understand him as if these poems had created or even commenced this transformation. It is plain enough that Homer and Hesiod represent, both theologically and socially, the *close* of a long epoch, and not the youth of the Greek world, as some have supposed. The real signification of many myths is lost to them, and so is the import of most of the names and titles of the elder gods, which are archaic and strange, while the subordinate personages generally have purely Greek names. Such epithets as *Argeiphontes, Tritogeneia,* and *Philommeides* (laughter-loving) seem purely traditional; indeed, the latter is wrongly interpreted by Hesiod (*Theog.* 198) from μήδεα. Speculations about these words were common in the Bœotian school. Some picturesque epithets, such as νὺξ θοή, which seem to indicate the first surprise of northern tribes at the rapid sunsets in southern Greece, may be also traditional, and derived from old hieratic poetry. .

But in Homer's time the whole character of popular

Theog. 99, who shows the combination of the gods and heroes in this sort of poetry,

αὐτὰρ ἀοιδὸς
Μουσάων θεράπων κλεῖα προτέρων ἀνθρώπων
ὑμνήσῃ μάκαράς τε θεοὺς οἳ Ὄλυμπον ἔχουσιν.

Cf. also the *Hymn to Del. Apollo,* 160. These passages are collected by Bergk, *Literaturgeschichte,* i. p. 347.

[1] Cf. Aristotle, *Pol.* i. 1 (p. 1252 b) for this oft-repeated idea.

[2] Bernhardy (*Hist. Lit.* ii. 1, 78) cautions us against exaggerating the words of Herodotus so as to comprise the whole religion of the Greeks. He believes that real faith and religious feeling were strong in the race, and kept up by cults, and by simple prayer and devotion, very generally. It was the combination of plastic art with epic poetry which made the mythological notions of Homer and Hesiod so prominent.

religion had become altered and humanised ; the wars, and adventures, and passions of men had become the centre of interest
among the poets. We must not imagine that the older and
simpler religion wholly disappeared. As the common people
went on singing their Linus and Ialemus, and jesting at their
marriage and vintage feasts, so schools of priests and didactic
bards kept up the old genealogical epics about the gods and
their human descendants, especially in the poorer Peloponnesus, and in Bœotia, while the rich and prosperous Ionians
revelled in the glories of Homer. But so strongly was the
predominance of the Ionic epos felt, that the Ionic dialect
was universally adopted in didactic poems ; and genealogical
poems, nay, even the responses of the Delphic oracle, were
composed in this dialect, which was widely different from most
of those spoken in Greece proper.

The great brilliancy of Homer has completely eclipsed all
the earlier stages of the Epos. He alludes to many stories
which appear to have been treated before him in shorter lays ;
he speaks of the hunt of Calydon, of the exploits of Nestor, of
the labours of Heracles, of the good ship Argo, as well known ;
he alludes to the wars of the gods, and cites a Catalogue of
famous women. It may be well not to conclude this preliminary sketch without noting these epic subjects referred to in
the Iliad and Odyssey, as well as the chief popular songs
which Homer mentions, and which have left some traces even
in historical times.

§ 15. Taking the Iliad separately, as the older of the poems,
and therefore furnishing the clearest evidence as to what earlier
epic lays must have existed, we find a considerable body of
stories mentioned in such a way as to make it extremely probable that they were no mere current popular tales, but had
been poetically treated. This is surely the case with the
legends of the wars and conflicts among the gods in A 396 sq.,
E 380 sq., Z 130 sq., O 10 sq. Some of these are conflicts for
supremacy among the gods ; others are quarrels about or with
men. Both are quite foreign to popular poetry, and show the
influence of a school of priests or theologians who were rapidly
becoming secular. The actual battle of the gods in Φ is a speci-

men of this sort of work. There is less obvious, but still distinct mention of genealogical epics in Σ 38 sq. and Ξ 201, 246.
But the great mass of legends alluded to are the adventures of
earlier heroes, such as Tydeus, Meleager, Heracles, and Bellerophon; as well as of celebrated wars, such as those with the
Amazons and Centaurs. There are even earlier legends about
heroes at the Trojan war presupposed, as is the case with
Achilles and Hector among those present, and Philoctetes and
Protesilaus, among those absent or dead. Even should it be
held that some of these were mere current talk, preserved
among the people as oft-told tales, yet such is the number of
them, and such the character of some of them, that no fair
critic could possibly deny the existence of a large number of
shorter lays of an epic character earlier than the Iliad, and
even presupposed by it.

§ 16. Let us pass to the popular poems alluded to in the
same way. Euripides, who was something of an antiquary,
draws a picture of women at the loom, like Calypso and Circe
in the Odyssey, singing epic lays to the sound of the plying
shuttle.[1] In his day no such custom existed; whether he is
correct in drawing this picture, we cannot now tell; he is
certainly the best authority we could have in his own time.

As Linus and Ialemus were afterwards personified as sons
of the Muses, the subjects of sad ditties sung on various occasions among the people, so Hymenæus was the personified
marriage song, of which we find distinct mention in Homer.[2]
All these were evidently choral performances, accompanied by
pipes and harps, as well as by a dancing chorus of youths, and

οὔτ' ἐπὶ κερκίσιν,
οὔτε λόγοις
φάτιν ἄιον εὐτυχίας μετέχειν
θεόθεν τέκνα θνατοῖς,

says his chorus (*Ion*, v. 506). And again, v. 196 of the same play,

ὃς ἐμαῖσι μυ-
θεύεται παρὰ πήναις
ἀσπιστὰς 'Ιόλαος.

[2] The scholiast on Σ 570 gives the following specimen of the Linus

the last was sung during the procession of the bride to her new home.   So the Threnus or funeral dirge seems a choral song, but with solos interspersed, as may be inferred from the descriptions in the last books of the Iliad and Odyssey.   Hecuba, Helen, and Andromache each make a separate lament over the body of Hector, and this seems an expansion of the simpler and shorter account.[1]   In the Odyssey the nine Muses lead

song, which has been variously emended and restored.   I quote it according to Bergk's version (*Fragg. Lyr.* p. 1297)—

.ὦ Λίνε πᾶσι θεοῖσιν
τετιμένε, σοὶ γὰρ ἔδωκαν
·πρώτῳ μέλος ἀνθρώποισιν
φωναῖς λιγυραῖς ἀεῖσαι·
Φοῖβος δὲ κότῳ σ' ἀναιρεῖ,
Μοῦσαι δέ σε θρηνέουσιν.

Probably the dialect of this song has been considerably modernised, but the metre seems very primitive, and is probably that from which the hexameter was formed.   The lines vary in pairs, and may be called either logocedic or dactylic, with or without an anacrusis, thus : ◡ |‒◡◡|‒◡̆◡̆|‒◡.   Leaving out the first anacrusis, we find that each pair of these lines, with at times the slightest alteration, can form an hexameter.   This origin would also account for the importance of the strong cæsura in hexameters, which was, in fact, the old point of junction of separate lines.   We have fragments of Hymenæal hymns by Sappho (*Fragg.* 91 sq., Bergk), of which the first may possibly be an imitation of the old popular form :—

ἴψοι δὴ τὸ μέλαθρον
'Υμήναον
ἀέρρετε τέκτονες ἄνδρες
'Υμήναον
γάμβρος ἔρχεται ἴσος "Αρευῖ
'Υμήναον
ἄνδρος μεγάλω πόλυ μείζων
'Υμήναον.

Here the metre is apparently the same as in the Linus song.   It is not probable that the beautiful chorus of Euripides' *Phaethon*, beginning ὑμὴν, ὑμὴν, is meant for a hymenæus, it seems rather an ode to Aphrodite.   This would most appropriately be sung by the chorus, while the real procession was supposed to have gone to the bridegroom's house.

[1] Ω 720 : παρὰ δ' εἶσαν ἀοιδοὺς,
        θρήνων ἐξάρχους, οἵτε στονόεσσαν ἀοιδὴν
        οἱ μὲν ἄρ' ἐθρήνεον, ἐπὶ δὲ στενάχοντο γυναῖκες.

the Threnus, supported by the Nereids.　If we are to trust the descriptions of the Iliad, the Threnus was not a fixed formula, but a rehearsal of the virtues of the dead—a form of lament common to almost all ages and nations.　But of course the epic poet must have modified the original metre, which can hardly have been hexameter.

The rest of the fragments of that Greek popular poetry which may have been in vogue before Homer, but which is not actually mentioned in the poems, will be better discussed in connection with the origin of lyric poetry.　The comic or lighter poems ascribed to Homer, such as the *Margites* and *Eiresione,* which show peculiarities in metre and style of great interest, will be treated after the Homeric hymns.　Enough has here been quoted to prove the widespread practice of dancing and playing together with lyric singing, partly religious, like the pæan of supplication or of victory,[1] partly secular, such as war-dances and dances at feasts.　We have also shown the almost certain existence of shorter epics, both heroic and genealogical.　Such were the conditions of literature from which Homer or the Homeric poems sprang.

[1] A 473, X 391.

CHAPTER III.

THE HOMERIC POEMS.—HISTORY OF THEIR TRANSMISSION
FROM THE EARLIEST DAYS.—EDITIONS, SCHOLIA, ETC.

§ 17. THE first great problem which meets us when we approach this subject is that of the origin and composition of the Homeric poems. Was this wonderful species of Greek literature created by the transcendent genius of a single man, or was it the outgrowth of a series of lesser men and lesser poems? Is Homer a real and historical person, or is he only the imaginary author to whose single genius was ascribed the combined excellence of many men, together with the organising and combining talent of later hands? Were the Iliad and Odyssey handed down from prehistoric days substantially in the form which they now present, and did the arrangers (διασκευασται) of Solon's and later days only restore the original order, or were the elements of these works lying in their original disorder and confusion when Onomacritus, or Theagenes, or Antimachus brought them into unity, thus creating an Iliad and an Odyssey which had never before existed?

This is the first great problem on which an historian of Greek literature must make up his mind. It is not to be expected that he will now be able to discover a new theory, seeing that all possible hypotheses have already been suggested. It is not to be expected that he will reconcile the majority of scholars, who, having long since compromised themselves by declaring for various solutions, will not desire, or indeed be able, to shake off their long-adopted and cherished convictions. But what is fairly to be demanded from him is a critical estimate of the controversy up to its latest stage, and a survey of how much certainty has been attained, and how much doubt still remains, in the present state of Homeric controversy. Nor is it fair to the student that this survey should be concluded without the critic's venturing to express his own convictions on the subject.

Perhaps the best way of approaching these complicated and difficult problems is, in the first instance, to dispose of the external history of the poems. .

§ 18. We need but cast a passing glance at the legends current among the Greeks about Homer as a person, and as the author of the great epics. It is quite certain that the extant lives of Homer, attributed to Herodotus and to Plutarch, have no authority, and that even the most critical inquirers of an earlier age could find out nothing trustworthy about him.[1] The very name of the poet has been variously explained, and has given rise to long controversies. The older meanings of *hostage, companion,* or *blind* have given way before the theory that the name is somehow compounded with ὁμοῦ. Welcker suggested ὁμοῦ and ἄρω, in the sense of 'connector of lays.' Upon this G. Curtius observes that the root ἀρ had originally an intransitive sense, so that with this derivation the word would mean the 'bond of union,' or centre-point of the legends.[2]

---

[1] See the critical discussion of these lives, eight in number, in Sengebusch's *Hom. Diss. prior*, pp. 1 sq. Four are anonymous, another attributed to Porphyry, and one of the fullest is in Suidas' *Lexicon*. None of them seems to be older than the age of Augustus, and some of them are certainly as late as the 2nd century A.D. That attributed to Plutarch (who had really written upon Homer) is not more genuine than that ascribed to Herodotus. The extant ἀγών, or contest of Homer and Hesiod, though it may preserve old legends, mentions Hadrian, and is therefore not prior to his reign. Modern critics refer its origin to Alkidamas.

[2] But, as Sengebusch and others observe, this derivation would imply among Æolians and Dorians a form Ὅμαρος, which never occurs. All the Doric citations agree in the form Ὅμηρος. This seems to show that the original form was not Ὅμαρος, but Ὅμερος or Ὅμαρος, and this not formed from ὁμοῦ and εἴρω (which would give as dialectical forms Ὅμιρος and Ὅμερρος), but from ὁμοῦ, with a mere suffix, in the sense of 'the harmonious.' This is the derivation preferred by Düntzer and Sengebusch. Upon this theory it may be identified with the Ὀμύρης, and the more celebrated Θάμυρις,

§ 19. The still wider controversies as to the age and the birthplace of the poet were idle and resultless, till new light came to be thrown upon the causes of the variations among the ancients, first by the researches of Carl Müller, and more recently by Sengebusch. We will consider the dates first. These may be fairly divided into those of conjecture, and those of tradition. Thus, among the former, Crates placed Homer 60 years after the Trojan war ; Philochorus 180 years ; Eratosthenes 240 years ; others in Archilochus' or Lycurgus' times. Müller was the first to show that in these chronological speculations the learned Greeks used astronomical cycles, particularly that of sixty solar years, which corresponded to sixty-three lunar. Hence the apparently precise number of years *post Troica* merely mean the number of cycles, or multiples of sixty, which were supposed to have elapsed, of which the seventh coincided with Lycurgus, and the eighth with Archilochus.

These speculations were, however, suggested by the traditional dates asserted in sundry towns, which laid claim to have been the poet's birthplace or residence, and the dates vary from the Athenian tradition, which places him at the supposed time of the Ionic migration (circ. 1043 B.C.), to the Cretan, which places him in the days of Thaletas (625 B.C.). The particular dates variously assigned during this period by the cities are shown with great probability to be determined by genealogical if not by astronomical reasons. In the genealogies preserved by the Ionic clans or *gentes* in the Asiatic towns, the generation was specified in which Homer was born. Three generations were allowed for a century. Hence the Colophonians placed his birth at Colophon, 132 years before the first Olympiad ; the first year of which, being included, makes up four generations. The 400 years which Herodotus (cf. above, p. 9) mentions as the interval between himself and Homer means twelve generations, perhaps in the genealogies of the Samians, to which he attached great importance. We thus obtain a logical reason for the apparent precision in the numbers of the years assigned as the dates of Homer's birth.

who are mentioned as related to the poet. The whole matter is carefully argued by Sengebusch (*Diss. Hom. prior*, pp. 89-100).

§ 20. How shall we account for the extraordinary divergence of place and of date? From a careful comparison of
these legends Sengebusch was led to the important result
that they severally note the establishing of a Homeric school
of rhapsodes in the various cities, and from this evidence
he endeavours to construct a history of the spread of epic
schools of poetry through Greece. Thus, starting from
the tradition of the Athenians, which Aristarchus adopted
(possibly from Theagenes), that Homer was an Athenian, he
holds him, or his poetry, to have migrated with the Ionic
settlers, first to the island of Ios (according to the tradition of
that people), then to Smyrna, at the time when the Kymæans
sent a colony there. These earliest notices may possibly
refer to a personal Homer. The traditions of the Chians,
Colophonians, Samians, Milesians, as well as of the Cyprians,
Cretans, and Lacedæmonians, he interprets as simply the
recollection of the first settlement of epic schools—that of
Crete by Thaletas. When poems with local allusions (such as
the Chian Hymn to Apollo) came to be composed by succeeding poets, these allusions were ascribed to the original
Homer, and his birthplace asserted in accordance with them.
It is a remarkable corroboration of this theory, that the successive dates assigned by the various towns correspond to
the natural spread of the Ionic race in the Eastern Levant—
Cyprus and Crete being the latest points (with the latest
traditional dates) ; Ios and Smyrna the earliest, and directly
attached to the Athenian date, which asserts Homer to have
gone out with the Ionic migration.

§ 21. There are many traces that the poems early attained
a great and widespread reputation. Midas, king of Phrygia, and
Gyges, king of Lydia, who lived shortly after the year 700 B.C.,
are said to have patronised Greek rhapsodists at their courts, as
we hear from Nicolaus of Damascus. But whatever doubts
may be entertained about these kings, it is probable that the
prominent place given to Lycian, Rhodian, and Cretan heroes
points to recitation in these countries, a long way from the
original home of the poems. The enumeration in the *Catalogue* of Rhodes, Cos, and other adjoining islands, on the

Greek side, though their situation would naturally place them with the Mysian cities, among the allies of the Trojans, is a clear evidence how strong an interest was taken in the poems by the chiefs of these islands. This far-reaching influence is also proved by the adoption of both metre and dialect of the Ionic epos by the Delphic oracle, and by the Bœotian school of Hesiod. It is further proved by the consistent avoidance of Homer's subjects in the cyclic poems, or by other epic composers, who flourished during an epoch reaching back from Solon's day for a long period. Lastly, the legend that Lycurgus brought the poems to Sparta, though perhaps a mere copy of the more authentic stories of Solon's care to preserve them, points to the belief that they were early known and prized in the Peloponnesus. This is corroborated by Herodotus' story (v. 67), that Cleisthenes forbad poetic contests in reciting Homer at Sicyon, on account of the prominence the poet had given to Argos. The chest of Cypselus, an old work of art described by Pausanias, had among its pictures scenes from both Iliad and Odyssey.

§ 22. The first difficulty which arises, if we admit this early date for the composition of the Iliad, is to account for its preservation and transmission up to the time of Solon, who began that careful study of the old epics which was continued by Peisistratus and Hipparchus, and to which we doubtless owe the present form and completeness of both Iliad and Odyssey. It was believed in old times that both poems were written down by Homer, and then transcribed and preserved by schools of rhapsodists. This opinion was exploded as soon as any close criticism was brought to bear upon them, and has never been maintained since Wolf's refutation, till resuscitated by Bergk, who endeavours to prove that writing, even general writing, was much older in Greece than has been supposed, and, though he still maintains that the composition [1] of a great epic such as the Iliad is impossible without writing,

---

[1] I am convinced that it is rather the *composition* than the *transmission* of the great epics which postulates the use of letters. It is the planning and executing the structure, not the remembering of it, which seems almost unattainable without writing.

holds that it probably marks the very time when this instrument of literature first came into use, and was applied to perpetuate the passing thoughts of men. But when he fixes this epoch as the tenth century B.C., we may well hesitate and wonder, in spite of the ingenuity of his arguments. He has indeed established one thing, or rather recent discoveries have established one thing, that the first common use of writing was generally fixed at too late a date. An inscription scrawled by Greek mercenaries under Psamatichus, in Upper Egypt, has proved that some of this class [1] could write easily about the year 600 B.C. —probably fifty years sooner.[2]

This discovery makes it almost certain that the Homeric poems were, or could have been, written down [3] about 700 B.C., and thus they may have been preserved orally only for a very short time. The analogy of early French and German epics is quoted to prove that even when writing exists and is known, very long poems are preserved and recited orally without seeking aid from this invention. But there existed in the early Middle Ages a severance between the bard and the literary classes quite foreign to Greek life, and I am convinced that the rhapsodists did not delay to seize the advantage offered to them.

§ 23. As to the oral preservation and transmission before the art of writing, many scholars have cited cases of extraordinary memory in bards and strolling minstrels, and there

---

[1] It is usual to say 'even such hirelings' could then write ; and this argument is employed both by Bergk and Professor Geddes to argue a wide and therefore not recent diffusion of writing. Both of them forget that it was often the highest classes—exiled nobles like Alcæus and Antimenidas —who served as mercenaries, and on account of their literary talents, which raised up enemies against them at home. Indeed, at no epoch of Greek history did the higher classes despise mercenary service.

[2] This depends upon whether we take the Psammetichus then reigning to be the first or the second of the name. Cf. Kirchhoff, *Studien zur Gesch. des griech. Alphabets,* Wiedemann (*Gesch. Egypt.*) argues for the second.

[3] The reader who desires to see this question more fully discussed may consult my articles in *Macmillan's Magazine* for October 1878, and February 1879, with Mr. Paley's reply and my rejoinder in the succeeding numbers.

is no impossibility in the Iliad or Odyssey having been so preserved, especially by such schools or guilds of rhapsodists as certainly existed in Greece.   In fact, in addition to Creophylus of Samos and Cynæthus of Chios, both of whom are mentioned as friends of Homer, or early preservers of his poetry, the main source of early traditions about Homer seems to be among the clan of Homeridæ, at Chios, who claimed him as their founder, and who recited his epics through Greece.   In the Hymn to the Delian Apollo one of these bards speaks of himself, and we know of contests being held among them, such as are described in the alleged contest between Homer and Hesiod.   So little difficulty, indeed, does there appear to have been in preserving the poems, that a quantity of epic songs came down to historical times along with the Iliad and Odyssey, and was even generally referred to Homer, until a more critical taste separated the wheat from the chaff, and acknowledged the two great poems only.   And not only were there many additional poems, and many additions made within the poems by the rhapsodists, but owing to the fact that they were usually recited in cantos or separate unities, they were remembered in fragments, and these fragments handed down in loose and uncertain order.

§ 24. Thus we must conceive *Homer* as reaching the first *literary* epoch in Greece in some such condition.   With the studies of Solon, and the foundation of the greatness of Athens, a new stage begins in the history of the poems.   There seems little doubt of the fact, hinted at by Pausanias and Plutarch, but explicitly stated only in late scholia—that not only did Peisistratus and his son Hipparchus take every pains to circulate the old epics, by establishing or encouraging musical and poetical contests, at which recitations took place, but that there was even a sort of literary commission appointed to re-arrange and edit the poems.[1] This commission consisted of Orpheus of

[1] Mr. D. B. Monro has adopted from Nutzhorn's work his doubts about the whole story, which he regards as a late fabrication. I acknowledge the frequent absurdities of our accounts, which mix up Zenodotus and Aristarchus with Peisistratus, but still I shall believe in there being an authentic tradition, until he gives us his disproof in a more explicit form.

Croton, Zopyrus of Heraclea, Onomacritus of Athens, and of a fourth, whose name is not to be made out, owing to a corruption of the text of the scholion. No doubt these men did very important work, but what work they did is not easy to discover. It is asserted that the version or edition of the poems which they sanctioned rapidly superseded all others ; that it was the archetype from which the well-known *city editions* were long afterwards copied, and we know that these were the oldest and most trustworthy materials which the Alexandrine critics used. At the same time, we have distinct tradition that Onomacritus, apparently for political purposes, interpolated lines of his own, and this raises a suspicion that the commission may have handled the great epics with somewhat reckless hands.

§ 25. There are modern critics who think that to Onomacritus we owe the whole unity and structure of the great epics, which had never been before united, and that ne not only brought together the separate lays, but welded them together artistically, so as to produce the poems as we now have them. This opinion, which must be discussed at greater length hereafter, is, in the first place, in distinct conflict with our tradition, which states that he *restored* unity to the poems which had been so composed, but separated and corrupted by recitation.[1] There are also clear evidences of a conservative spirit in the old arrangers of the Iliad and Odyssey ; for they left in the poems a number of repetitions and inconsistencies, which

---

[1] It is reported (Diog. Laert. i. 57, and Plato's *Hipparch.* 228 B) that Solon ordered the poems to be recited by the rhapsodes ἐξ ὑποβολῆς and ἐξ ὑπολήψεως. These expressions are anything but clear to us, and have afforded the Germans scope for endless discussions. It results, I think, from the researches of Nitzsch that ὑποβολή means probably a *text*, or authoritative list of lays, to which the rhapsodists were ordered to adhere. Ἐξ ὑπολήψεως is by no means so clear, but is fairly explained by Bernhardy as implying fixed divisions or lays in the poems, which were to be sung entire, and each of which was matched against other similar divisions in the contests. Perhaps it does not differ materially from the other phrase, with which it is not, I think, used in common (cf. Sengebusch, ii. p. 111). In the Teian Inscr. (C. I. G. 3088) ὑποβολή is a subject of competition for boys, and means *recitation*. In Xenophon it means *prompting*.

they could have easily removed, had they intended to produce a new and harmonious whole. What is more important, there is no attempt traceable to interfere with the Homeric gods, and to substitute for them a more moral and philosophic religion ; still less any allusion to the Orphic ideas and mysteries, which had in Onomacritus' day become very prevalent in Greece. There is also no attempt to magnify the glories of Athens. It may be held certain that changes in this direction could not but have been attempted, had the commission of Peisistratus not confined themselves to arranging and sifting extant materials. This, then, was the earliest literary criticism on the Iliad and Odyssey, and all the rhapsodising of the poems of which we are told was at Athens, and in connection with this edition, though it was merely the continuance of an old and widespread fashion.

There seems little doubt that the early critics did not confine themselves to the Iliad and Odyssey, but embraced all the cyclic epics which were at that time, or perhaps after that time, indiscriminately ascribed to Homer.[1] It is probable that the commission did not attempt any critical severance of the wheat from the chaff, and that in the course of succeeding studies these inferior poems were condemned one after another to lose their high claims to the name of Homer.

§ 26. Thus the gradual sifting of the large body of old epic poetry appears to have begun by the gathering and ordering of all the materials by Onomacritus. In the next generation Theagenes of Rhegium was the first professedly critical writer about the Iliad whom the Greeks knew. Then comes Stesimbrotus of Thasos, towards the latter half of the

---

[1] The list given by Suidas shows to what extent this was done : ἀναφέρεται δὲ εἰς αὐτὸν καὶ ἄλλα τινα ποιήματα· ᾿Αμαζονία, ᾿Ιλιὰς μικρὰ, Νόστοι, ᾿Επικιχλίδες, ᾿Ηθιέπακτος ἤτοι ῎Ιαμβοι Μυοβατραχομαχία, ᾿Αραχνομαχία, Γερανομαχία, Κεραμεῖς, ᾿Αμφιαράου ἐξέλασις, Παίγνια, Σικελίας ἅλωσις, ᾿Επιθαλάμια, Κύκλος, ῞Υμνοι, Κύπρια. Of these some are completely unknown, and none have maintained their claim even in old Greek days. It does not include the *Margites*, which was acknowledged genuine by Aristotle.

fifth century B.C. ; and he again is followed by his pupil
Antimachus of Colophon, during the Peloponnesian war—himself an unsuccessful epic poet, but the critical editor of a
text of Homer.   Thus every generation since Solon had its
Homeric studies.   Indeed, at the time of the middle comedy
these critics were so prominent as to be ridiculed upon the
stage.   We know that Aristotle discussed the poems, and
is even said to have prepared a special edition for Alexander.
The copy thus prepared was carried in a precious Persian
casket, and hence known as ἡ ἐκ τοῦ νάρθηκος.   The quotations
from Homer to be found through Aristotle are numerous, and
differ remarkably from our texts, while those made by Plato
are according to our texts.   Ammonius wrote a book about
Plato's citations, and yet all the critics are silent about Aristotle's text, which had been lost when the school of Alexandria
began its labours.   But there remain fragments of his six
books of problems about Homer, and his school busied themselves with these questions also.   We find that Aristotle used
a worse text, and was a worse Homeric critic, than Plato.

The series of Attic editors and critics concludes with
Demetrius Phalereus, who wrote on both the epics.

§ 27. In addition to the professed criticisms on the text,
which were not many, there were endless allusions to, and
discussions about, Homer all through the course of Greek
history. 1. (α) Among the early *poets* Hesiod, though intentionally silent about the Ionic epic,[1] was noted in the scholia
as implying in many places a knowledge of the Iliad.[2] Similar
allusions are found to Archilochus, Alcman, Stesichorus, in fact,
in all the older poets.   Simonides of Ceos seems the earliest who
mentioned Homer himself as distinguished from his poems.[3]
He also seems to refer the Theban cycle of poems to Homer.
Bacchylides is quoted as referring Homer's birthplace to Ios.
Pindar calls him both a Chian and a Smyrnæan, and comments
on the morality of his praise of Odysseus.   He furthermore

---

[1] I agree with Sengebusch (ii. 11) that the three passages in which he
is supposed to mention Homer are spurious.

[2] Twenty places are cited by Sengebusch, *D. H.* ii. 8.

[3] He calls him a Chian poet, quoting Z 146.

seems to have referred the *Cypria* to Homer. (β) As regards
the tragic poets, not only did Æschylus profess his tragedies
to be morsels (τεμάχη) from the mighty banquets of Homer,
but Sophocles 'copied the Odyssey in many dramas,' and
his vulgar admirers were wont to call him *the tragic Homer.*
(γ) Passing on to satyric and comic poetry, we still have the
Cyclops of Euripides, many Homeric titles of other satyric
dramas from Æschylus, and the rest, and indeed the *Margites*
is named in the *Poetics* as the direct forerunner of comedy.
This is especially true of the middle comedy, in which types of
character were ridiculed. The learned epics of the fourth
century B.C. will be considered hereafter.

2. (a) The early *logographers*, who wrote much on genealogies, were often cited by after critics both for differing on such
points from Homer, and also for their pedigrees of Homer and
the other ancient poets. (β) The allusions to Homer in Herodotus and Thucydides are frequent and highly interesting. On
the whole, Herodotus seems the more critical, as he rejects the
Cypria, while Thucydides accepts the *Hymn to the Delian
Apollo*, though well disposed to reject the legends of 'the
old poets.' It is also to be remarked that their references show
considerable variations from the present text. It is discussed
by Greek grammarians and by Germans whether Herodotus or
Thucydides resembled Homer more closely in style and tone
of thought—a ridiculous debate, seeing that Herodotus was
both by temper and by education steeped in epic poetry and
ways of thinking, to which Thucydides was in most respects
antagonistic. Both these authors, however, as they treated
a definite portion of later history, only mention Homer inci-
dentally. (γ) Later historians, such as Ephorus, who gave a
general history of Greece from the earliest times, naturally paid
him more attention.

3. All the *philosophers* were obliged to consider Homer
as the source of the popular notions, not only in theology
and in morals, but also in physics. They may be divided
either into *opponents* of Homer, as an immoral and false teacher,
which was the opinion of Heracleitus, Xenophanes, Pythagoras
and Plato ; or allegorising *interpreters*, such as Anaxagoras,

Metrodorus of Lampsacus, and Democritus, the last being the author of the earliest Homeric *glossary*.   The Homeric style and language of Plato, and his constant citation of the author whom he banishes from his *Republic*, has excited much attention from critics.   It would almost seem that Aristarchus had Plato's very copy of Homer before him, so accurately do Plato's citations agree with the final Alexandrian text.   Antisthenes the Cynic, whose style and tastes were by no means so poetical, wrote a number of tracts on special Homeric points, and indeed Plato's attack on Homer gave rise to a controversial literature.[1] The special studies of the Stoics, Cleanthes and Chrysippus, were developed by the school of Pergamus, which adopted their views.   Aristotle's studies on Homer, which were various, led the way for a whole series of Peripatetic commentators.

4. I will but add a word on the *Sophists*, who constantly used Homeric subjects for declamation, and from whom we still possess *Encomia of Helen* ; there are also allusions to Apologies for Paris, Encomia on Polyphemus, and other paradoxes.

5. Among the *orators*, Demosthenes, like every great Greek writer, is said to have imitated Homer, but we see less Homeric influence in his than in Lycurgus' and Æschines' speeches, both of whom cite passages, though with considerable variants from our texts.

This mere skeleton of the facts shows how constant and familiar was the reading of Homer in classical days.   We might as well attempt to enumerate the biblical phrases and influences in our own standard English authors.

§ 28. Such were the preliminary studies on Homer when he passed into the hands of Zenodotus at Alexandria. While he found many city editions, and private texts representing recensions like that of Rhianus,[2] as well as many additional essays or problems, such as those of Antimachus or Aristotle,

---

[1] Cf. the titles cited by Sengebusch, *Diss. Hom. prior*, p. 119.

[2] It may be inferred that critics of this period, and even Apollonius Rhodius and Aratus, of Alexandrian days, were very reckless in correcting the text.   Timon the Sillograph is said to have told Aratus, when the latter asked his advice to procure a good text, that he would do so, εἰ τοῖς ἀρχαίοις ἀντιγράφοις ἐντυγχάνοι, καὶ μὴ τοῖς ἤδη διωρθωμένοις (Diog. Laert. ix. 12, 6).

we can hardly say that much thorough criticism had been done before his day.   The grammatical or philological side was probably quite obscured by the philosophical and moral, and lines or books were rejected rather as being unworthy of the great poet than as violating epic usage or the traditions of the old epic dialect.   For we must remember that Homer, especially after the rejection of the inferior works once attributed to him, became literally the Bible of the Greeks. All religion and philosophy were supposed to be contained in his poems, and of course, when men were determined to find these things, they easily found them.   As Seneca tells us, some made him a Stoic, some a Peripatetic, some an Epicurean, some even discovered him [1] to be the father of the Sceptics.   Nevertheless the good homely orthodox Greeks of earlier days had attached all their moral teaching of youth to the examples and advices given in the Iliad and Odyssey.

A good deal of adverse criticism had been expended upon this way of looking at Homer by Plato, in the wake of Heracleitus, Xenophanes, and others; but of these Zoilus, a rhetorician of the fourth century B.C., the pupil of Socrates and said to be a teacher of Demosthenes, has gained the chief notoriety. This was because he did not recognise, like Plato, the poetic excellence of the poems, but attacked them æsthetically and even grammatically, as well as morally.   He wrote nine books against Homer.   His name might probably have been forgotten, but for the fancy of some Roman emperors, such as Caligula and afterwards Hadrian, for depreciating Homer. Of course they revived and favoured whatever adverse criticism could be discovered.   But it may fairly be said that, except the work of Zoilus, which was probably more a rhetorical exercise than a serious attempt to destroy Homer's influence,[2] all the criticism which was handed down to the school of Alexandria was rather troublesome from its consistent panegyric, and even superstitious reverence for Homer, than instructive from its severity or justice.

---

[1] Diog. Laert. ix. 71.

[2] γυμνασίας ἕνεκα, εἰωθότων καὶ τῶν ῥητόρων ἐν τοῖς ποιηταῖς γυμνάζεσθαι (Schol. K. 274).

§ 29. It seems that the Alexandrian critics, when they came to sift all these materials, and were unable to reach back even so far as Peisistratus, laid most stress on the *old editions*, of which seven city editions were then extant,[1] and seven κατ' ἄνδρα, or recensions by individual scholars, which had been prepared from the recension of Onomacritus. It would be most interesting to know at what exact time during the present period these copies were taken. Seeing that epical recitation went out of fashion when lyric and dramatic poetry was developed, and seeing that these copies were thought older and better than those of the earliest critics, they cannot have been later than the middle of the fifth century B.C., and possibly somewhat earlier.

§ 30. When we speak of the Alexandrian critics we almost exclude the poets, such as Philetas, Aratus, Apollonius Rhodius, &c., and confine ourselves strictly to the grammarians, who brought the accumulated treasures of the great library to bear upon the study of the text of Homer. It may indeed be said that all philology among the Greeks, all textual and grammatical criticism, arose from the desire to purify and to understand the text of Homer, and then of other old poets.

The glories of the great school of Alexandria cluster about three names—the successive leaders of the school, the two latter each rivalling and opposing his master. Zenodotus [2] was the first who rejected as spurious all but the Iliad and Odyssey, and

---

[1] An edition in those days meant a single official copy, preserved by authority, from which private copies were made. The civic editions were the Massaliotic, Sinopic, Chian, Cyprian, Argive, Cretan, and Æolic (Lesbian). The four first were Ionic, the rest Æolic. The Massaliotic is far most frequently quoted (twenty-nine times), the Chian next (fifteen times). The Æolic editions seem to have been specially intended to preserve the Ionic dialect of the poems among an Æolic population. The quotations from these do not give us a very high idea of them, nor, indeed, were the private editions much better, that of Antimachus being noted for wild conjectures. Nevertheless, Aristarchus seems never to have opposed them, when they all agreed (cf. Sengebusch, *Diss. Hom. prior*, 185–200).

[2] He was an Ephesian, and flourished 300–250 B.C. The second Ptolemy made him librarian at Alexandria, and he undertook the task of critically revising the epic and lyric poets.

undertook a thorough revision of the text, which attained such a reputation that it soon obscured all others. We unfortunately know hardly anything of his work, and what we know is from the criticisms of his successors.[1] It seems probable that he had before him no sufficient materials, or sufficient preliminary discussion, to afford a really clear and scientific method of establishing the text. He therefore was guided partly by æsthetical and moral considerations, partly by a love of archaisms and rare forms. He seems to have laid special stress on Ionic forms, if we may judge from the occasional references to him in the scholia. But he rejected and altered with great boldness, and so incurred the grave censure of his successors.

Before proceeding further we may notice that one of his pupils, Hellanicus, revived the doctrine of an unknown Xenon, and asserted the separate authorship of the Odyssey. This was the natural and logical outcome of the criticism which had abjudicated the Cyclic poems successively, and we may well wonder that this final step had not been taken long before. Hellanicus appears to have had a following—the χωρίζοντες (*Separatists*), and their view might have prevailed but for the determined hostility of Aristarchus, who crushed it completely till the present century. It is now accepted by the majority of critics.

§ 31. The famous successor and pupil of Zenodotus, Aristophanes (of Byzantium), re-edited Homer from a more conservative as well as critical point of view. Here again we can only speak from the hints left us by the criticisms of Aristarchus. He checked the boldness of Zenodotus in rejections and alterations, and based his labours on a careful comparative study of all the best texts, especially the city texts, which were then being acquired for the Alexandrian library. Though

---

[1] His critical edition first separated the poems into books, noted by the letters of the alphabet. He first used the obelus, to distinguish suspicious lines, whereas the manifestly spurious were ejected. These proceedings are respectively called ἀθέτησις and τὸ οὐδὲ γράφειν. He also published a glossary of obscure Homeric words, and a computation of the days of the action of the poems, of which a fragment is published by Lachmann (*Betrachtungen*, p. 90).

defended by his pupil Callistratus against the attacks of Aristarchus, he did not maintain his ground, and we must deeply regret that the labours of so careful and candid a writer have been almost totally lost to us.[1] Thirdly comes Aristarchus, a sort of king or infallible guide to later grammarians, whose opinions were adopted by the scholiasts even when they were aware, as they tell us, that Zenodotus or Aristophanes appeared more reasonable.

§ 32. Aristarchus was not only a remarkable critical scholar, but must have been a man of strong and commanding personality, that swayed all those who came in contact with him. He again edited the Homeric poems as well as the principal lyric and dramatic authors, and besides these editions published commentaries (ὑπομνήματα) and dissertations (συγγράμματα). Moreover, his oral lectures were attended by a crowd of eager hearers. Thus even the unwritten opinions of Aristarchus, taken down by his numerous pupils, became widely known. He analysed carefully the epic use of words and phrases as well as the epic forms of the myths, and based most of his rejections from the text on the violation of these criteria. He indicated his opinions by a famous series of critical marks, which are preserved to us in the old Marcian MS. at Venice.[2]

---

[1] He rejected the end of the Odyssey from ψ 297, and used the stigme and antisigma, as well as the κεραύνιον, Τ, to mark a spurious passage, whereas Aristarchus preferred to append an obelus to each line. But his glossary seems to have been of peculiar value, and he seems also to have composed a formal commentary on Homer.

[2] They were as follows : (1) Zenodotus' *obelus,*—, a sign universally accepted from the terrible grammarian as a mark of spuriousness, and commonly to be found in the margin of German texts now-a-days. (2) Leogoras' *diple,* ⊢ (called διπλῆ καθαρά, or ἀπερίστικτος), used rather for exposition, or to show a line which told against the Separatists, or an ἅπαξ λεγόμενον, or an Attic construction ; in Aristarchus' second edition it seems to have called attention to the notes of the earlier editions. (3) The *dotted* (περιστιγμένη) *diple,* ⊱, to denote the variants from the edition of Zenodotus, and afterwards from that of Crates also. (4) The *asterisk,* ✳ , to mark the genuine verses, in case of repetitions, whereas the rejected duplicates were marked with both asterisk and obelus. (5) The *antisigma* and the *stigme,* ⊃ and . , were used to mark repetitions of the same idea. It seems that Aristarchus' earlier edition was accompanied by

There is great difference of opinion as to the real merits of Aristarchus. Some of the Germans are disposed to raise him above all Homeric critics and submit to his authority absolutely. Others, such as Buttmann, think he was a pretentious and shallow critic, if not an impostor. As he has simply superseded all the older texts, so that all we know of Homer, saving stray quotations, comes from his recension, we have not sufficient materials to judge him. If we may form a conjecture from the extreme arrogance of the man and his absolute dogmatism, we shall not be disposed to rate him too highly; and though he certainly surpassed most men in real grammatical knowledge and familiarity with epic diction, it is to be feared that he was often led by traditional reasons, and even by mere caprice, in default of, or in opposition to, solid grounds. On one question certainly he seems to me to have shown great prejudice—his rejection of the Separatist theory. He based this, we are told, on no more sustainable argument than supposed anticipations of the Odyssey which he found in the Iliad, as well as on the admitted discrepancies within the Iliad itself, and on these points he wrote a special treatise.

All three critics were too straitly bound by tradition to venture on the theory of large interpolations in the text, if we except the sound judgment of Aristophanes, that the end of the Odyssey from ψ 297 was added by another hand. They contented themselves with frequent rejection of what they considered spurious lines—in all 1160 were thus rejected—and this is commonly called *athetising* (ἀθετεῖν). But possibly Aristarchus did this too often, rejecting the genuine, and sparing the spurious. Constant reference to his opinion is preserved in the Venetian scholia on the Iliad.

a commentary, but that the second was not so, the critical marks referring to his own and others' commentaries. His special essays were probably appended, or to be read in relation, to the later text. All these matters are subject to doubt, and are inferred from hints in the scholia and lexica. Lehrs' book *De Studiis Hom. Aristarchi*, and Sengebusch's *First Homeric Dissertation*, may be consulted for full and learned details. On the critical signs, the best book is now Gardthausen's *Palæographie*, p. 288 (Leipzig, 1879). Cf. also Dindorf's prefaces to vols. i. and iii. of the scholia.

§ 33. But whatever faults we may attribute to Aristarchus, his criticism seems sober and practical beside that of Crates, who founded the rival school of Pergamus, and who, under the influence of Stoic philosophy, endeavoured to thrust in allegory where Aristarchus would only allow ordinary inter-pretation. Still the establishment of a rival school, with its controversies, is a fortunate circumstance, since it has preserved for us in our scholia sundry notes, and allusions to Aristarchus' opponents, which had else been lost. It is also to the treasures of this school that the Alexandrian scholars owed the replace-ment of some of their MSS., when the fire of 47 B.C. destroyed the authentic copies of their great recensions—a loss, how-ever, but ill compensated by transfers from the Pergamene library.

· It would require a long and tedious enumeration to give an account of the various grammarians who carried on the work of the great masters. I will mention but a few leading names. Demetrius of Scepsis discussed with prejudiced acuteness the geography in the Iliad, and especially of the Troad. It is to Didymus' book on Aristarchus' recension that we owe almost all our knowledge of that scholar's work. There seems no doubt that this Didymus was copied, perhaps carelessly, by the scholiasts of the Venetian codex. Aristonicus, about the same time, explained the marks of Aristarchus, which were evidently becoming ill-understood. Nicanor on the punctuation of Homer (Hadrian's time), and Herodian on his prosody and accents (M. Aurelius), are well spoken of, though the fashion in Hadrian's day was to slight and even to revile Homer. From a compendium of these four works, Herodian's *Homeric prosody*, Nicanor *on Homeric punctuation*, Didymus' account of Aristarchus' *recension*, and Aristonicus' *critical marks*, is drawn the best body of scholia found in the Marcian codex A at ·Venice, and excerpted in inferior MSS. At the end of the second century A.D., independent criticism, if we except Porphyry's, ceased, and people began to make compendiums and excerpts of previous works. Porphyry seems to have gone carefully into the artistic merits of the poems, but on the somewhat absurd ground that they were to be treated as tragedies. Hence he applied to them the laws laid down in Aristotle's *Poetic* concerning that kind of poetry.[1] A mere compilation from various works, ascribed by Eustathius to Apion, is still extant, though in a bad and incomplete condition.

§ 34. This review has brought us down to the verge of the dark ages. If we ask what the actual materials are which modern scholars can use in reconstructing the texts of the Iliad and Odyssey, we must separate these materials into commentaries, scholia, and texts. Our oldest and best *commentary* is that of Eustathius, Archbishop of Thessalonica, who wrote in the end of the twelfth century in Constantinople a careful Greek commentary on both Iliad and Odyssey. He used not only the same sources as the extant scholia, but had access to many others since lost, and his book is valuable, though he adopted the allegorical interpretation of the Stoics and the Pergamene school, in preference to the Alexandrian. We have besides the beginning of Tzetzes' commentary on the Iliad, Manuel Moschopulos on the first two books of the Iliad, and a prose paraphrase. A little Homeric lexicon by Apollonius has survived,[2] and there are explanations of Homeric words and phrases in the dictionaries of Hesychius and Suidas.

We now come to the *scholia.* These are short notes (ὑπομνήματα) added in the margin of our MSS., and are the work of different hands and ages. They are meant for commentaries on the text. It may fairly be said that some authors, such as Homer and Aristophanes, would be often unintelligible but for these explanations, which were added at a time when the learning of Alexandria yet survived, at least in excerpts and compendia. We must separate here for the first time the Iliad and Odyssey, as the value of the scholia of the former is far superior to that of the latter. For a

---

[1] Cf. the curious details brought together on this question in Trendelenburg's *Gram. Græc. de arte trag. judiciorum Reliqq.*, p. 73, sqq. He shows that the quotations from Porphyry are contained in the scholia on the exterior margin of the cod. Ven. B, while those of the interior margin are mere compendia of these and of the far better scholia of cod. A.

[2] Edited by Villoison (Paris, 1768), and again by Tollius (Leyden, 1788). We have now an Ed. of Porphyry on the Iliad by Schrader (Leipzig, 1880).

long time, indeed, the only scholia known on the Iliad were those called *brevia* or Didymic scholia, which were taken from various fourteenth-century MSS. and first printed by Lascaris (Rome, 1517), and then more completely with those of the Odyssey by Aldus (1521–8). These notes seem merely such as might be of service in school teaching, and are very short and simple.

The discovery of the Marcian codex of the Iliad at Venice, by Villoison, and the publication of its text and scholia (Venice, 1778), known as Schol. Ven. A, form an epoch in the history of Homeric studies. It is from these notes that we derive all our information about the several old editions used or produced by the Alexandrian critics. The text is also furnished with the critical marks (σημειώσεις) of Aristarchus and his pupils, which are explained in a prefatory note.[1]

The best edition of the Venetian scholia A, together with the scholia B, which are not unique, but of the same origin as the Townleiana (Brit. Mus.), Lipsiensia, Leidensia, and Mosquensia, was till lately Bekker's (Berlin, 1825). We have at last from Cobet and D. B. Monro, collating for Dindorf (Oxon. 1877), a thoroughly critical and, I suppose, final revision of the text. La Roche and C. Wachsmuth have written short essays on the critical marks of the margin, and the value of the whole collection has been sifted in the essays of Sengebusch and Lehrs.[2]

It is probable that there was a copy of the Odyssey corresponding to the old Marcian Iliad at Venice also ; but all efforts to find it have been in vain. Apart from the scholia brevia, which extend to the Odyssey, and which were long since

[1] Villoison's text, and his Prolegomena, though perpetually referred to, are now seldom read. As most academic libraries contain the book, a fresh perusal of this great monument of diligence and learning may be strongly recommended. The style of the Prolegomena is very ponderous, and the author is perpetually digressing into all manner of collateral subjects ; but he is always instructive. The account of the dangers he incurred in his voyage from Upsala to Venice, and of his stay there, is very amusing, and almost rivals the famous enumeration of persecutions by S. Paul.

[2] The analysis of this vast body of scattered notes is a very difficult task, and requires the study of an elaborate special literature on the subject.

known, Cardinal Mai published, from the Ambrosian Library
at Milan, older and fuller scholia, which, with some additions
from Palatine and a Harleian MS., were first edited by Buttmann (1821), and now, as fully and completely as the materials
will allow, by G. Dindorf (Oxon. 1855).

§ 35. As to the condition of our *texts*, it seems that the
early mediæval grammarians contented themselves with critical
notes and commentaries, and were not desirous to revise,
so that what has come down to us is a sort of eclectic vulgar
text, with a general adherence to Aristarchus, but fortunately
giving a good many readings from previous editors. We have,
indeed, interesting remains of an older date. In Egypt three
fragments on papyrus were found, dating not later than the
first century after Christ, and probably earlier. They contain part of Ω and part of Σ. There is among the papyri of the
Louvre a similar fragment of N found at Elephantine. These
very early texts offer no remarkable variations from our mediæval MSS., and thus supply a strong argument in favour of the
general trustworthiness of the transmission of our Greek classics.
Next in age come fifty-eight pages of very curious pictures from
an old copy of the fifth or sixth century, containing on the
back of each picture fragments of the poem in capital letters,
very like in character to the oldest New Testament MSS.
These pictures, together with the *tabula Iliaca*,[1] the Odyssey
scenes of the Vatican (just published by Karl Woermann), and
some Pompeian frescoes, show how widely illustrations of the
Homeric poems were circulated. The pictures of the Ambrosian codex (published by A. Mai, Milan, 1819) are very
remarkable, as being perhaps the last really *classical* pictures
before the advent of the lower mediæval type. The text offers
no variants of importance in the 800 lines it contains ; it was
merely added by way of explaining the pictures. Next in age
is the Syriac palimpsest edited by Cureton (London, 1851),
containing several thousand verses. All these fragments are
greatly inferior in critical value to the Marcian codex A in
Venice, which dates from the eleventh century, but is one of

---

[1] A marble relief with illustrations of the Iliad, now in the Capitoline
Museum.

the most precious and carefully prepared in all the range of our Greek classics. The Townley and Harleian seem to rank next in value. From the fourteenth century we possess a great many inferior MSS., which have no independent value.

§ 36. *Bibliographical.* The *editio princeps* of Chalcondylas (Florence, 1488) is a very splendid book, containing the lesser works attributed to Homer as well as the Iliad and Odyssey. It is produced in a type unfortunately abandoned since Aldus began to print,[1] and is now one of the rare ornaments of a few great libraries. The two Aldine editions which follow (Venice, 1504, 1517) are not to be named in comparison with it. Except the first attempt at a commentary by Camerarius, there is no edition of note till the very fine *Heroic Poets of Greece* of Stephanus (1554). Passing by Schrevelius' edition, with scholia and indices (Amsterdam, 1655), we come to Josh. Barnes (1711) and S. Clarke (1724–40), with good notes, and then to Villoison's learned and valuable Iliad from the Marcian codex (1788). Wolf (1794), Heyne (1802–22), and Porson (1800) were the most noted editors at the opening of this century. In our own day the text has been further analysed and fixed by the labours of Bekker (1858), La Roche, and Dindorf. The best annotated editions are, in German, those of La Roche, Faesi, Ameis and Düntzer; in English, Paley's Iliad, Hayman's and Merry's Odyssey—Nitzsch's elaborate commentary on the first twelve books of the latter had led the way (1826-40)—in French, A. Pierron's Iliad (Hachette), with a translation of Wolf's *Prolegomena*, and good notes. Ebeling's elaborate, and at last finished, *Lexicon Homericum* is full of materials; Autenrieth's is shorter, and a mere handbook. The very complete *Indices* of Seber (1604), reprinted with Clarke's Ed. (Oxon., 1780), and Mr. Prendergast (Iliad only), also deserve mention. Commentaries and special tracts on portions of the poems are a library in themselves.

Translations into all manner of tongues, and in every

[1] The earlier Greek types were on the model of the older and finer MSS. of the tenth and eleventh centuries. Aldus unfortunately took the fourteenth century writing as his model, and so permanently injured Greek printing.

variety of style, are even still pouring from the press, though every generation since the Revival of learning has been supplying them.   The literature of these translations has become a special study, as may be seen from Bernays' *Bonn Programm* (1850) on the early Latin ones, and Penon's *Versiones Homeri Anglicæ inter se comparatæ* (Bonn, 1861), in German, W. Henkel on the English, and W. Müller on the German versions ; and Mr. Arnold's Oxford Lectures *on translating Homer* (Longman, 1861).   As has been well said by the last, and, perhaps, best translators of the Odyssey, Messrs. Butcher and Lang (1879), every age has its own way of looking at these immortal epics.   Chapman satisfied the Elizabethan age, while Pope breathed the spirit of Queen Anne's period into his version ; so that these poems, though permanent English works, are translations ' from a lost point of view.'[1] Hence we may expect no version to be final, and so long as Greek letters are studied, and the great poems of Homer read, countless hands will repeat the same fascinating, but never ultimately satisfying experiment.   The *Faust* of Goethe, which already can boast of forty English versions, and the *Divina Commedia* of Dante, seem to possess the same curious and distinctive feature of the highest productions of human genius. I will only specify a few of the successive attempts.

The barbarous version of the Odyssey into Saturnian verse by Livius Andronicus, in the days of the first Punic war, stands alone in its antiquity.   It was long a Roman school-book, though the style shocked literary men of succeeding generations, and, if extant, would be a curious and interesting relic of early Roman education.

After the Revival of letters there were several Latin and hexameter versions, from Valla's (1474) to Cunichius' (1776), in Italy.   The Dutch produced a metrical Odyssey by Cornhorst (1593), then Van Manders' Iliad (1611), a whole prose Homer (1658), and sundry other attempts, ending with the recent hexameter poem of C. Vosmaer.   The French, besides older and now little known versions, have Madame Dacier's (1711) and many others in the present century, ending with

---

[1] Cf. also Arnold, *op. cit.* p. 29.

some remarkable prose translations. The Germans contribute Voss, Donner, and A. Jacob. England has been the most prolific, owing to a longer and more thorough study of Greek. First comes Chapman, then Thos. Hobbes, Pope, MacPherson's prose Iliad, then Cowper. In our own day it is almost hazardous to assert that any scholar has not, at least in part, translated Homer. The catalogue of those which occur in any library is indeed curious. If we include short pieces, Tennyson and Gladstone may be added to F. W. Newman, Lord Derby, Sir J. Herschel, Dean Merivale, J. S. Blackie, Worsley, Wright, Musgrave, Brandreth, and many others. The Odyssey of Messrs. S. H. Butcher and A. Lang deserves special note as a remarkable attempt to render Homer into antique prose. Even the modern Greeks are now producing paraphrases in their language, of which two (Christopoulos' and Loukanis', both Paris, 1870) are cited as of merit.

The reader who has looked through this mere skeleton list will doubtless excuse me from attempting the task of criticising or comparing these myriad reproductions.

Having thus traced the external history of the preservation of the poems down to our own day, we shall proceed to a brief sketch of the Homeric controversy in modern times as based upon the materials set forth in this chapter.

CHAPTER IV.

HISTORY OF THE HOMERIC CONTROVERSY FROM THE REVIVAL OF LEARNING TO THE PRESENT DAY.

§ 37. AFTER the discovery of printing, and the dissemination of copies through Europe, the history of the poems concerns itself no longer with their preservation, now assured, but rather with their general reputation and the criticism of their composition. The scholars of the Renaissance could not but revere the man whom they found celebrated in all Greek literature as by far the first and greatest of poets; but owing partly to the better knowledge they possessed of Latin, partly to the influence of Dante, partly to the artificial nature of their culture and their ignorance of spontaneous art, Homer was not greater in their eyes than Virgil—nay rather with many decidedly inferior. He was praised as the rival and fellow of Virgil, but not studied with any real care. Voltaire, indeed, seems to have appreciated the perfection of the details of the Iliad as compared with its deficiency in plot; and still earlier, Vico had made some bold and curious guesses about the mythical character of Homer himself as the ideal representative of Greek epic poetry, and had been followed by Zoega and Wood. But these isolated judgments are of no importance.

§ 38. The first move in modern Homeric criticism was the discovery and publication of the older Venetian scholia by Villoison. The second and greatest was the *Prolegomena* of F. A. Wolf (1795), based upon this discovery ; for the scholia showed plainly the doubts and difficulties of the Alexandrian editors, who were obliged to accept and reject passages, not on the authority of well-authenticated manuscripts, but according to laws of criticism established among themselves, and based on taste, and on

minute study of epic diction. It was plain that the manuscripts which we possess represent nothing older or purer than
the Alexandrian texts, it was equally plain that the Alexandrians
had before them no text approaching the age of the composition of the poems. Their best authorities were the *city* copies,
which were posterior to the age of Peisistratus, and none of them
written in the older alphabet. As for Peisistratus' copy, not
only had it disappeared (possibly in the Persian destruction of
Athens), but there was no city copy professing to represent it
better than the rest.

Accordingly, Wolf held that we had no evidence for the
writing down of the poems earlier than the commission of
Peisistratus. He showed that the writing down of these long
poems required not merely knowledge, but expertness in
writing, and presupposed a reading public to take advantage of
it.[1] This was not the condition of early poetry in Greece, as
may be seen from the brief and fragmentary remains of early
hymns and of Hesiodic teaching. The poetry of the nation
was rather that of wandering rhapsodes, who composed short
poems for special occasions, and trusted to a well-trained
memory and to a traditional style for their preservation. In the
days of Wolf there was a strong reaction in taste from learned
and artificial composition to folk-song and primitive simplicity.
Hence the rhapsodes were to him no mere repeaters or preservers
of Homer, but gifted natural poets, each pouring out his pure
and fresh utterance to a simple and receptive audience. The
shortness and independence of these several rhapsodies were
proved, in Wolf's mind, by the many discrepancies and contradictions which a careful examination could show in the Iliad.
He would not, in fact, admit in it any conscious or deliberate
plan of composition.

From these premises he drew the conclusion that one
Homer could not be the author of the Iliad and Odyssey,

---

[1] To this last statement I demur. A listening public, with a taste for
poetry, is quite sufficient, provided there exist a literary class who can use
writing in the composition of their works. Cf. my arguments on the question in *Macmillan's Magazine* for February and April, 1879, in answer to
Mr. Paley.

but that **our** Iliad in particular is a mere aggregate of materials, which were accumulating for generations, until the artists of an advanced literary epoch took it in hand to combine and set in order these scattered fragments. This redaction removed many traces of suture and of discrepancy, but left a large number, and especially the conclusions of both poems, which had been suspected and condemned even at Alexandria. Peisistratus completed the work by authentic written copies and orderly recitations. Homer, then, was merely the symbol of this long, secret, national activity among the Ionians, and does not represent an individual genius.

No work on Greek philology ever created such a stir in the world as this short book. All the German poets, philosophers, and critics discussed it. Schiller, on æsthetic grounds, declared it barbarous. Goethe wavered, and having adopted it in his youth recanted in old age. W. von Humboldt declared his assent; and Fichte even pronounced it, in truly German style, to be a conclusion he had himself attained metaphysically and *à priori*. On the whole, with the aid of Niebuhr, the two Schlegels, and G. Hermann, the new theory may be said to have taken Germany by storm. Nothing independent was done, either in France or England, on this question till the nations had settled down after their great war.

§ 39. The Germans consider G. Hermann as the principal writer on the subject in the period following upon Wolf's; but his theories are not so much based on historical data as on probable assumptions, and have therefore been without lasting effect. His main merit was to see the great difficulties in parts of Wolf's theory, and the necessity of not resting content with his book as if it were a Homeric gospel. He pointed to the absurdity of the Homeric bards confining themselves to so small a portion, not only of Greek legend, but even of the Trojan war; then the apparent sudden silence of all these bards in the period between the composition of Homer and that of the Cyclic poems, which were decidedly later; lastly, he pointed to the universal feeling of the unity and excellence of the Iliad and Odyssey as based on the interest and excellence of their matter, rather than on exceptional treatment.

Hence he assumed, what is probable enough, that the didactic epic poetry, like that of Hesiod, is really older in Greek literature ; that Homer was the first bard who struck out a new path, and created a school of imitators and rivals who confined themselves, as he had done, to a small portion of the existing legends. Hermann assumed no pre-Homeric materials in Homer, but supposed him to be a great and original genius whose work, as we have it, is enlarged and deformed by long and disturbing interpolations. He thought the same poet had composed a short Iliad and Odyssey, and that these were the basis of the succeeding poems. But he confessed himself unable to explain the gap or silence in epic poetry from the old Homer to the later Cyclic poems.

The point in favour of this theory, as compared with Wolf's, is that the general plan in the poems is regarded as not the accidental result of their aggregation, but an original outline sketched by a master hand, and gradually filled in by expanding episodes.

§ 40. On the other hand, Lachmann was led by Wolf's work to apply similar reasonings to the old German epic, the *Nibelungen-lied*, which he examined for the purpose of discovering its claim to unity in the relation of its component parts. The result of this comparative study was a more advanced and thorough-going scepticism concerning the unity of the Iliad. He denies, indeed, that the Iliad is a mere aggregate of rudely joined poems without any deliberately composed transitions ; but, nevertheless, he believes that he has found so many inconsistencies and contradictions that he distinctly asserts the plan of the Iliad to be the afterthought of a clever arranger, and not an original feature in the poem.

The views of Hermann and Lachmann may be said to comprise under them all the various theories, or modifications of theories, with which the classical press of Germany is teeming, and which have caused angry controversies.

§ 41. No notable German scholar of the present day ventures to hold the substantial unity and purity of either the Iliad or Odyssey in the sense received at Alexandria, and still not

VOL. I.   E

unfrequent in England. The so-called advocates of the unity of the Iliad—Nitzsch, Bernhardy, Bergk, and a few others—advocate it in a sense which would astonish any ancient critic, or any modern enthusiast for a single Homer. Instead of obelising here and there a line, or pair of lines, as Zenodotus and Aristarchus had done—a proceeding which, with all the old critics together, only affected some 1160 lines in the two poems—these defenders of the unity of the Iliad reject books, and parts of books, with a readiness which almost destroys their own argument. It is, in fact, no more than the theory of Hermann, that there was a short, simple nucleus, enlarged and injured by great and often inconsistent additions.

Thus Bergk, the latest of them, rehandles the Iliad in a manner more arbitrary than has been done by advanced advocates of the theory of aggregation. He assumes that the original Homer, a personage of stern and grand temper, living in the tenth century B.C., composed a short, simple epic of such merit that all additions can be detected by their style. Then there are the imitators, of undetermined number, one of whom certainly possessed much grace and elegance, and was a true poet, though far removed from the grandeur of the real Homer. These have composed the famous dialogue of Priam and Helen on the walls, the parting of Hector and Andromache, the funeral games, and the ransoming of Hector—all unworthy of the stern original poet. It verily requires some assurance to assert that in a great literary artist sternness and tenderness are inconsistent, and to found upon it a difference of authorship! But this is not all.

In addition to the real Homer, and the gifted but weaker imitators, comes the 'impertinent diaskeuast,' who re-arranged, altered, and greatly injured the poems in reducing them to their present form. To this man he attributes all passages in which the Cretan chiefs, Idomeneus and Meriones, appear on the scene. The diaskeuast had probably been hospitably treated in Crete, was very fond of eating and drinking; and so he glorifies Lemnos for its wine and Crete for its valour. He also inserted all the eating and drinking scenes which are so prominent in the Iliad, besides many other narratives, or parts of narratives, which are in Bergk's judgment flippant and vapid in tone, though good literary judges have read and admired them without any suspicion of such late and unworthy origin.

§ 42. Nothing can prove more completely how the views of Wolf and Lachmann have affected even their bitterest adversaries in Germany. There is, in fact, no writer of any note for the last generation in that country who has ventured to uphold the real unity of the Iliad even in the most modest way. On the other hand, the professed followers of Lachmann are numerous, and loud in proclaiming their victory. His attempt to separate part of the Iliad into the original songs of which it was composed has been followed up by Köchly—who has also published an Iliad in sixteen or seventeen separate songs—by Lehrs, by Bonitz, and by many others. They differ, as I have said, from the pretended advocates of unity, by denying that there is any plan in the patchwork of the Iliad beyond what was brought into it by the commission of Peisistratus. Lachmann even declares such a notion of place as ridiculous. Bonitz thinks that all the admiration excited in modern poets and men of critical taste is really produced by the excellence of the details, and that this feeling is fallaciously transferred to the plot, which has no such merit.

All these critics have fixed their attention so firmly on prying after discrepancies, they are so outraged by inconsistencies of the most trifling sort, by mistakes in the names of heroes, by the re-appearance of slain heroes, by the inaccuracies of chronology in the days and nights of the action, that they have lost all sense or appreciation for the large unity of plan which has conquered and fascinated the literary world for more than twenty centuries.

§ 43. Thus the controversy about the Iliad has narrowed itself in Germany to a very definite issue. All critics allow that there is considerable patchwork in the poem, that but a small part of it comes from a single author, that there are evidences of the incorporation of various independent lays. There is, of course, great diversity of opinion among these subtle and dogmatic sceptics concerning the merit of the individual pieces and their fitness for their place. What one considers splendid old poetry the next considers foolish and vapid ; what one holds to be so out of place as to prove manifest patchwork, the next proves necessary to the march of the action. Yet upon many passages they are agreed, and have brought in a verdict of incongruity. The great question still at issue is this : Were these separate poems brought together before the plot or after it ? Were they connected by a poet who conceived a large plan, and who desired to produce a great work on the wrath of Achilles, or were they a mere aggregate brought together for the sake of preserving and publishing old and beautiful lays, which by their mere cohesion formed a sort of loose irregular plot, and by their several excellence imposed a belief in their unity upon an uncritical age?

§ 44. While this has been the general course of the Homeric question as regards the Iliad in Germany, scholarship in England has followed quite a different and isolated path. I will not say that our English writers on the Homeric question are ignorant of the labours of the Germans, especially of the earlier labours, which are for the most part written in Latin. On the contrary, some of them—as, for instance, Mure—show a very wide acquaintance with this literature. But I cannot help thinking that none of them, except Grote, has been familiar with German philology from his youth. They have read the Germans for the sake of the controversy, and when their minds were made up ; so that both Colonel Mure and Mr. Gladstone study the Germans in order to refute them, while Mr. Paley is so carried away by their arguments that he outruns even their wildest scepticism.

§ 45. I will give a very brief sketch of the principal points in the English history of this controversy. The arguments of Wolf had their effect upon Payne Knight, whose *Prolegomena* to his curious edition (with the digamma introduced), while asserting very conservative views as to interpolations or aggregation of parts in the Iliad, advocated the separate origin of the two poems. He urged the usual grounds for a difference of authorship—differences of language, of mythology, and of general treatment—sustaining them with profound learning and great acuteness.   This theory was submitted to an elaborate examination and refutation by Colonel Mure, in his very erudite *History of Greek Literature*—a book which has not received a tithe of the attention it deserved, and which the German writers on the subject pass over with a single sentence, as a retrograde British work a generation behind the attitude of Wolf.

Mure is, indeed, the most determined advocate of the unity of authorship of the whole Iliad and the whole Odyssey.   He will hardly allow even the ψυχαγωγία of the last book in the Odyssey to be interpolated, and will only submit to the obelus of Aristarchus where there is authority for it in the old editions —not where the æsthetical taste of the Alexandrian school was offended.   But he holds this view with his eyes open, and after a careful perusal of all that the Germans up to his day had written upon the subject.   Moreover, he makes good the great standpoint of English criticism as opposed to them : it is the principle that a large quantity of inconsistencies, and even con-tradictions, are perfectly compatible with single authorship.

This principle has been further worked out by Mr. Glad-stone,[1] who has added many illustrations and much ingenious pleading to the position of Mure.   He, too, holds the person-ality of Homer, his historical reality, and that both the Iliad and Odyssey are the offspring of his genius.   He has exhausted his great ability in showing, as Mure had before done, deli-cate touches of character consistently applied to the same individuals all through the poems.   It is well known that Aristarchus refuted the Separatists by a tract proving antici-pations of the Odyssey in the Iliad.   This argument has not been pressed of late years ; but every casual conformity is urged as a proof of unity, while all inconsistencies and diffi-culties are explained as the natural imperfections of a long work composed without writing, in an uncritical age, and addressed to uncritical hearers.   The beauty and perfection of the suspected books of the Iliad (I, Ω, and others) are cited as proving their genuineness ; it is assumed that no

---

[1] *Homer and the Homeric Age* (3 vols., 1858) : *Iuventus Mundi* (1869), and in many short articles in the *Contemporary* and *Nineteenth Century*.

number of different poets could possibly be so excellent. Even the Alexandrian rejection of the conclusions of both poems is disallowed. In fact, the attitude of Mure and Mr. Gladstone is not only behind Wolf, it is distinctly behind Aristarchus and Zenodotus. There is, I think, no other question in Greek literature where England and Germany appear to me to have travelled so long on such different lines ; nor do I know any controversy where the attitude of the two nations is more separate and isolated, in spite of numerous quotations from one another's writings.

§ 46. But while these respectable scholars were advocating the vulgar beliefs of an uncritical age, Mr. Grote, with a complete study, and, still more, with a thorough appreciation of German philology, matured his great chapter[1] on the Homeric poems, which contains (in my opinion) more good sense and sound criticism than all else that has been written on the subject either in England or Germany ; for, in addition to his great natural ability, he combined English good sense, and correct literary taste, with German thoroughness of erudition. He agrees with Payne Knight on the divided authorship of the Iliad and Odyssey, but does not separate them in age by any serious interval. He advances beyond him by admitting what the Germans had unanimously accepted—the want of connection of parts in the Iliad. The arguments of W. Müller, G. Hermann, and Lachmann forced him to see the inconsistencies of the Iliad to be more than mere forgetfulnesses. But he does not admit the necessity of supposing more than two authors—one of an *Achilleis*, the other of an *Iliad*. He constructs an ingenious theory about the piecing together of these poems, and the possibility of resolving the Iliad into its component parts. As to the hypothesis of an aggregation of independent lays, mechanically combined in the time of Peisistratus, he refutes it by arguments so strong that I can hardly conceive them else than final. Whatever doubts may remain as to his positive theory on the construction of the Iliad, his general review of the German authorities up to the year 1854 is of inestimable value to the English reader.

[1] *Hist. of Greece*, part i. chap. xxi.

The theory of Grote, received with great respect and considerable adhesion in Germany, has not yet triumphed among us over the old-fashioned views advocated by Mr. Gladstone— not at least generally, for there are many English scholars who have of late shown tendencies towards a critical attitude.

§ 47. But after many years Grote's labours have borne their fruit in the learned work of Professor Geddes, of Aberdeen, who has taken up and expanded them into a peculiar and ingenious theory of his own.[1] Accepting the severance of the Iliad into an *Achilleis* and an *Iliad*, he spends much ingenuity in showing that the *Achilleis* is by a different and an earlier poet, whose psychology, mythology, and personal character are ruder and less artistic than those of the later poet, but who possesses certain massiveness and fierceness which are very striking. The tastes and the beliefs of this poet point, he thinks, to a Thessalian origin ; and this accounts for such features as his love of the horse, an animal common only in a few parts of Greece, and his limited geographical knowledge, which is well-nigh confined to the northern Ægean.   But as to the rest of our Iliad, Professor Geddes advances a long way beyond Grote, and, indeed, opposes him, holding that it was not only the work of one poet, but that this poet was also the author of the Odyssey, and the real Homer.   This conclusion he seeks to establish by showing that the strong contrasts between the *Achilleis* and the rest of the *Iliad* are all contrasts carried out in the Odyssey as compared with the *Achilleis*.   He is, in fact, a *chorizontist*, or separator, but draws his line through the middle of the earlier poem and not at its close.   In mythology, in manners and customs, in the use of peculiar words and epithets, he draws out tables to show that the Odyssey and the Odyssean cantos of the Iliad agree, and are opposed to the Achilleid.

With his separatist arguments I am perfectly satisfied, and think he has brought valuable evidence in detail to show the critical sagacity of Grote in guessing the truth on general grounds ; but his positive theory is vitiated by accepting what Grote and all the men of his day accepted—the unity of the

---

[1] *The Problem of the Homeric Poems* (1879).

Odyssey. Writing, though in 1878, without regard to Kirchhoff's work, he thinks that any likeness in the 'Ulyssean' cantos
of the Iliad to any part of the Odyssey proves unity of authorship in these cantos. This evidence rather proves that the
same school of poets was at work on both poems, and that
the framers of the Odyssey were either contemporaneous with
the completers of the Iliad, or copied closely the Ionic features
which appear in the 'Ulyssean' cantos. I am still disposed to
place the Odyssey as a whole later than the Iliad, and 'in
the old age of Homer,' as the Greek tradition expresses it ; but
no doubt some books of the Iliad, such as K, Ψ, and Ω, may
be as late as the lays of the Odyssey.[1]

---

[1] This theory of Professor Geddes receives curious corroboration from a
German source which he never quotes, and which may therefore be looked
on as supporting him on perfectly independent grounds. Sengebusch, in his
monumental *Dissertationes Homericæ* (prefixed to Dindorf's Teubner text
of Homer) developes a most important Homeric theory, altogether in pur-
suance of the remaining fragments of Aristarchus' criticism, which is to him
the infallible guide in these matters. Adopting from Aristarchus the Attic
origin of the Homeric epic, he believes the tradition that Homer, or his
parents, or at any rate his poetry, passed with the Ionic migration to Ios,
then to Smyrna, and that there, in the new Ionic home, the Iliad and
Odyssey saw the light. But he also holds that epic poetry in Athens was
not indigenous, and came with Eumolpus, as the legend says, from Pierian
Thrace or Thessaly, the original home of the Olympian worship of the
Muses. These Thracian singers separated into Heliconian (Bœotian)
and Attic, and from the latter arose the poet or the school which passed
into Ionia. Moreover, Sengebusch rejects all arguments to prove that
the Odyssey is younger than the Iliad, or by a different school of poets
—here, too, following in the wake of Aristarchus. In all its main features
this theory of Sengebusch, which is sustained with masterly ability, and
with a knowledge of the Homeric scholia such as few possess, is upon the
same lines as Professor Geddes' book, though Sengebusch divides his
homage for Aristarchus with his homage for his master Lachmann so far
as to admit against Aristarchus that a school of bards working together may
have composed the poems, but within a very few years, as the *Nibelungen-
lied* is said to have been put together between 1190 and 1210 A.D. Thus
Sengebusch would hold that the earlier epics composed in Thrace or Attica
had disappeared, while Professor Geddes holds that they have distinctly
survived in the Achilleid. If our English scholars would but acquaint
themselves with the rest of European study on their subjects, some general
agreement might not be impossible.

§ 48. The atomistic theory of both Iliad and Odyssey has, moreover, received unexpected support from the rise of comparative mythology into philological importance. For upon this theory the legends of the siege of Troy are mere echoes of immensely older solar myths; the names of the heroes are adapted from those of solar phenomena; and extreme easiness of belief on this point is compensated by a corresponding scepticism as to the age of their combination into larger unities. The most prominent advocate of this view is Mr. F. A. Paley, who not only accepts the destructive criticism of Wolf, Lachmann, and all the Germans, but even refuses to the commission of Peisistratus the fabrication of the poems, and believes that the Iliad and Odyssey did not receive their present form till the time of Plato.[1] He bases this judgment on the facts (1) that the quotations from Homer in earlier authors do not correspond with our text; (2) that the earlier art of the Greeks in sculpture, vase painting, and tragedy seems to have borrowed very little from our present text, though perpetually reproducing other Trojan legends; (3) that there are late forms of language in the poems, and blundering archaisms; (4) that the common use of writing, required for the composition and dissemination of the poems, cannot be proved earlier than the days of Pericles. He advances to the position that possibly Antimachus of Colophon, or some obscurer contemporary, put our Iliad and Odyssey together from loose materials—in the words of Dio Cassius, 'having got rid of Homer, he introduces to us instead Antimachus of Colophon, a poet whose very name we hardly knew.' What we do hear of Antimachus is this: that he was a notably frigid and unsuccessful epic poet, contemporary with Plato; that his poems were extant, and are quoted in the Venetian scholia by the Alexandrian critics; that he prepared an edition of the Iliad, which is quoted constantly in the same scholia as one of those κατ' ἄνδρα, and as inferior to and more recent than the city

---

[1] The following tracts contain Mr. Paley's various restatements of his theory : *On Quintus Smyrnæus &c.* (1876) ; *Homerus Periclis ætate, &c.* (1877) ; *Homeri quæ nunc extant, &c.* (1878) ; and his article in *Macmillan's Magazine* for March, 1879.

editions, when it differs from them.   These facts surely dispose
of the claim of any such new Homer, if it were not already
sufficiently absurd to imagine the noiseless and unnoticed birth
of the two great epics in a literary and critical age.

It is moreover only by inventing an impossible epoch that
Mr. Paley has found a date for the composition of the poems.
He places it *after the Tragic poets and before Plato*, who knows
and quotes our text.   But Sophocles and Euripides were composing tragedies until Plato was of age, and the latest of these
plays show no greater familiarity than those of Æschylus with
our Homer.   This silence then of the dramatists must have
been intentional, and proves nothing for Mr. Paley.[1]

Again, the absence of reference in Greek tragedy to the
subjects of the Iliad and Odyssey cannot be explained by their
non-existence as epics, for it would equally demonstrate the
non-existence of the separate lays which compose them, and
would thus prove infinitely too much, as not even Mr. Paley
will assert that the *materials* of the epics were not old.   If they
existed as separate lays, their excellence would have secured
their frequent imitation, but for the only tenable reason—the
conscious abstaining of later Greek art from touching these great
masterpieces.   Thus the Odyssey carefully avoids all iteration
of, or even allusion to, the Iliad.

The assertion of the late dissemination of writing in Greece
has been disproved by the actual existence of old inscriptions.

I cannot here turn aside to discuss the linguistic arguments
of Mr. Paley, but will only refer to Mr. Sayce's supplementary
chapter in this volume, where it is shown, with a full appreciation of Mr. Paley's objections, that no really recent origin can
be inferred from the grammatical complexion of our text.   I
will add, moreover, that the newer researches into Homeric
language prove in many respects not its recent, but its exceedingly ancient complexion.   This is, I believe, more strictly the
case with Homeric syntax, so far as it has been examined.

§ 49. The history of criticism on the Odyssey, which has

---

[1] The reasons of Æschylus, the father of tragedy, for preferring other
legends than Homer's are well explained by Nitzsch in the second volume
of his *Sagenpoesie der Griechen.*

been necessarily touched in the foregoing sketch, is somewhat simpler than that of the Iliad.   Wolf, who felt so strongly the piecemeal character of the Iliad, declares himself as struck at every fresh perusal with the harmony and unity of the Odyssey. Grote, who wonders that critics have commenced with the more complicated and difficult poem, asserts that the question of unity would never have been raised had the Odyssey alone been preserved.   The most trenchant dissectors of the Iliad, and those who stoutly maintain it to be an aggregate without any presiding plan among the authors of its fragments, confess that the Odyssey differs in the much greater method and clearness of its structure, and at least represents the work of a far more experienced arranger.   Nevertheless, the Germans could not but admit large interpolations.   Even Nitzsch, Bäumlein, Schömann, Bergk, and other defenders of its unity, admit this, nor do any of them maintain the conclusion (from ψ 296 to the end) which Aristophanes had already rejected.

But the effect of pulling to pieces the Iliad at last began to tell on the Odyssey.   The task of hunting for supposed discrepancies and the sutures of divers accounts is too congenial to the German analyst, and too well suited to his tone of thinking, to permit so large and complicated an epic as the Odyssey to escape his censure.   So, beginning from Spohn's tract (1816), and Kayser's Program of 1835, a series of acute monographs have assailed the consistency of the Odyssey, and endeavoured to show that this poem also is made up of several special songs, at least four in number, with interpolations besides.   By far the ablest of these critics and their acknowledged master is A. Kirchhoff,[1] whose views are now generally adopted and developed by the Atomistic school.

While this writer shares with his countrymen their oversubtlety, and not very convincing æsthetical judgment as to what is good and bad, or as to what is excusable or inexcusable, in an old poet reciting to an unlettered and uncritical audience, he nevertheless shows with real force many evidences of patching in the Odyssey which had hitherto escaped other scholars.   He makes it very probable that the advice of

---

[1] *Die Composition der Odyssee* (Berlin, 2nd ed., 1879).   Cf. Appendix B.

Athene to Telemachus in α is made up not very skilfully from
the subsequent narrative. Still more clearly he shows how the
action is too manifestly delayed by the absence of any direct
reply of Odysseus to the point-blank question of Arete as to
his name and family.[1] He also shows grounds for asserting
that the long narrative (κ–μ) put into the first person in Odysseus'
mouth was adopted from older narratives in the third person.
He discovers two inconsistent reasons, one natural and the
other miraculous (ν 429), for the non-recognition of Odysseus.
He believes therefore that the old *nostos* of Odysseus was
greatly enlarged, and endeavours to show, on various grounds,
that this took place somewhere about Ol. 30. His theory
seems very parallel to that of Grote on the Iliad, who holds
the shorter, and I think older, *Wrath of Achilles* to have been
expanded by the borrowing of whole books from a longer
Iliad (cf. below p. 524.)

§ 50. The examination of particular passages throughout the
Odyssey has not yet been carried out by the Germans with
their accustomed detail, but enough has been done to bring
the latest advocates of its unity, Bergk and Faesi, to admit
large interpolations. I do not think the theory of a mechanical aggregation by Peisistratus is now held by any man
of sense in Germany; it being universally allowed that the
plan is an essential part of the composition, and that it is
considerably older than the famous commission. Mr. Paley
alone ventures to class it in this respect along with the Iliad,
and bring down its compilation to those well-known and critical
days when every new poem was named and claimed by a jealous
author.

The controversy concerning the composition of the Odyssey
is growing hot in Germany, and is likely to occupy a leading
place for some years to come; but, as well as I can make
out, the main point at issue is not quite the same as in the
case of the Iliad. The theory of aggregation of short lays
being very improbable, and that of a plan guiding the composition or adaptation of the lesser unities being generally

---

[1] Cf. the interpolation α 270–97 with β 209, sq.; and η 238, to which
no answer is vouchsafed until ι 19.

accepted, it remains to account for the numerous passages which are, in the opinion of German critics, out of harmony with this plan, and so inconsistent with it that they cannot have been composed by the poet who framed the general narrative. On the one hand, the school of Kirchhoff, represented by Friedländer, Bonitz, Hartel, and others, hold that these passages [1] are vamped together, or arranged by the poet who was uniting the adventures of Telemachus with the return of Odysseus, and who framed the main narrative of Odysseus' travels as a recital by the hero himself. They hold that original passages were deliberately left out, or changed into the form in which we now have them, and that the unskilfulness with which this has been done lets us see when and why it has been undertaken. Kirchhoff rejects altogether as unscientific the assumption of interpolations, unless a distinct reason can be assigned which prompted such interpolation.

This great principle, which ought to become a canon in criticism, is a terrible blow to the speculations of his opponents, who accordingly attack him vehemently. Of these Düntzer, Heimreich, Kammer, and Bergk maintain that they can restore the primitive form of the Odyssey by merely extending the proceeding of Aristarchus, and rejecting as interpolations such passages as are inconsistent in thought, or unworthy in style, when compared with the genuine poetry of the Odyssey. They allow large room for critical taste, and accordingly differ widely as to the merit or demerit of sundry suspected passages. To assert the unity of the Odyssey in any honest or real sense is now nearly as obsolete in Germany as it is to assert the unity of the Iliad. It is even very unusual to find competent critics, like Sengebusch, who will assert that the Odyssey and the Iliad even in part come from one poet or from poets of the same age and school. Professor Geddes is led to this view by assuming the Odyssey to be one and indivisible, and finding close correspondences in certain parts of the Iliad ; Sengebusch evidently by the authority of Aristarchus, who asserted

---

[1] Such as α 269–302, μ 370–390, ν 94 compared with ο 50 (the same day).

the author of the Iliad to have anticipated the Odyssey in many of his allusions.[1]

§ 51. A calm review of this long controversy suggests several curious reflections, which have so large an application that they can hardly be here out of place. The first point which strikes us is the remarkable contrast of attitude between the English and German critics. The Germans, one and all, lay the greatest stress on matters of detail; and it is quite an admitted axiom among them that any passage inconsistent with the general argument, or illogical, or merely repeating a previous idea, *cannot be genuine.* Of course they quarrel violently over their facts, some declaring against passages which others assert to be necessary to the text and of the highest importance. Secondly, it is generally asserted among them, though not universally admitted, that passages of inferior merit come from the hand of interpolators, and are also to be rejected; but as the question of poetic merit is purely subjective, and as the Germans are not over-competent, though very positive as regards it, the admission of this principle necessarily destroys all chance of ultimate agreement. Thirdly, it seems tacitly assumed by them all, that all the interpolators or imitators, or later poets, if such there were, must be inferior to the older and more original bards. Without this assumption, the second. principle is in absolute jeopardy; and yet why may it not constantly be false? Thus the poet of the last book of the Iliad, generally believed to be later than the rest, is surely a poet of the very first order, and in the opinion of any fair critic this book must be held superior to many of those which precede it. It is even highly conceivable that the very excellence of a later lay might be the cause of its reception in an older and poorer composition.

The English, on the other hand, are all impressed with the fact that no large plan can be carried out without a great deal of inaccuracy in the details, even in critical days; they cite modern poets and novelists who have been guilty of the grossest blunders of this kind; they maintain that such things are abso-

---

[1] All the works of the German authors mentioned will be found enumerated in the notes to Bonitz' fourth edition of his excellent pamphlet *On the Origin of the Homeric Poems.*

lutely to be predicted in long poems, composed without writing, for an uncritical audience, in an uncritical age. They regard all the dissection of details by the Germans as the result of irrelevant subtlety, provided a general harmony of plan, of diction, and of character can be established. They have taken great pains to show such harmony, especially in the characters, and have even applied psychological subtleties to explain away great inconsistencies, as in the cases of Agamemnon and Hector.

This contrast of attitude is so strong that it has blinded each nation to the' importance of what has been said by the other, unless we admit the explanation that few scholars of either nation are able to appreciate accurately the force of an argument in the tongue of the other. They read, indeed, and quote each other; but it is certain that to apprehend and weigh the force of an intricate and tedious polemical statement, the reader must be able to run along quite easily in the language of the writer. It is the absence of this facility which produces both the general contempt and the occasional veneration shown by the two nations for each other's work. The natural results have followed. Each side spoils by exaggeration a very strong case. While the Germans exhibit a ridiculous pedantry in many of their criticisms, and often rouse the astonishment of the reader by the dulness of their literary judgments, they have certainly made good too many flaws and contradictions to be overlooked and explained away. While the English are, on their side, too subtle in discovering harmonies, and over-generous in condoning blunders, they have certainly made a strong case for a general unity of plan in both poems, and their arguments on this point, if read with any care, might have made the Germans less confident in their assumptions. There is but one critic—Grote—who seems really at home in the writings of both sides; accordingly he has propounded an intermediate theory on the Iliad, which is, I conceive, not far from the truth. Had he continued to study the question after Kirchhoff's analysis of the Odyssey became known, he might have modified his views on this poem. The absence of all reference in his notes to the work of Kirchhoff makes it plain that he had not followed up the controversy beyond the date of his fourth edition.

CHAPTER V.

GENERAL REMARKS UPON THE ORIGIN AND THE CHARACTER OF THE HOMERIC POEMS.

§ 52. It will not be here necessary to give a formal analysis of the Iliad and Odyssey, inasmuch as the texts are in every scholar's hands, and even those who are not familiar with Greek can study them in many excellent English translations. For our purpose it will be sufficient to sum up the general results attained by the long controversy on their origin, and offer some suggestions as to the points decided, and the points still in doubt. It is hardly requisite to add a word on the literary aspects of the poems, or to undertake to assist the student in his survey and his appreciation of them.

Looking in a broad way at the arguments for and against the unity of each poem, as bearing upon the unity or diversity of authorship, we may say that there is no controversy in which each side has been more successful in proving its case, and yet has more signally failed to overthrow its opponents. This is the impression which the controversy will make upon most unbiassed readers. As long as we study the advocates of the single author, so many undesigned coincidences, so many hidden harmonies, such consistency in the drawing of character, such uniformity in diction—in fact, such a cloud of witnesses are adduced, that the poem seems certainly the plan of a single mind. On the other hand, when we turn to the subtler analyses of destructive critics, they show us such a crowd of inconsistencies, such wavering in the drawing of character, such forgetfulness of any general plan, such evident traces of suture and agglomeration, that the poem falls in sunder, and discloses a series of ill-matched fragments. But, as the advocates of unity are unable to smooth over these breaks and haltings, so the advocates of plurality are unable to destroy the strong impression produced in favour of a fairly consistent and harmonious plan. In fact, I am distinctly of opinion, that the moderate and critical advocates of the general unity even of the Iliad, as conceived and carried out by a single genius, hold the strongest and the most durable position. But hitherto, and especially in England, they have ruined their case by wild exaggerations, and by putting a greater strain upon our faith than it will bear.

§ 53. Thus, for example, they not only insist upon the unity of authorship of each poem separately, but that both are the work of the same man. This is one of the points which modern criticism has, in my opinion, finally decided in the negative. In the absence of any good evidence for the common authorship of the poems, the differences are quite sufficient to prevent us from assuming so improbable a hypothesis. The whole tone of the Iliad and Odyssey is, to my thinking, contrasted. The poet of the Odyssey is more quiet and reflective; he writes as a poet by pro-fession, and alludes to others of his class as attached to various courts. He lives and moves not in Asia Minor, and close to the Mount Olympus of Bithynia, but in western Greece, and with his interests turning towards the fabled wealth of the western Mediterranean.[1] To him Mount Olympus is not a snow-clad visible peak, but a blessed habi-tation of the gods, where frost and storm are unknown. The lions that are so perpetually stalking through the coverts and prowling about the folds in the Iliad, are only described five

---

[1] On the other hand, Bergk (*LG.* i. p. 741) acutely points out that the troubles of the city of Erythræ, which are repeated from the history of Hippias by Athenæus (vi. 259), have so marked an analogy to the proceed-ings of the suitors in Ithaca—even the name of Irus recurring—that he believes the poet of the Odyssey to have lived in the neighbouring and closely connected Chios, and to have painted his scenes from contem-porary history. But a temporary sojourn would have been sufficient to suggest the subject, and hence Bergk's argument can only prove that the poet knew Erythræ, not that he lived at Chios.

separate times in the Odyssey, and once at least with a complete ignorance of their habits.[1]   Above all, there is a careful
avoidance of all direct allusion to the Iliad, which seems
nevertheless distinctly presupposed by the poet.   This is hardly
explicable if both proceeded from the same hand, but is easily
reconcilable with the attitude of a conscious rival and follower.   But all these details are as nothing when compared
with the difference of tone, which is perfectly convincing to
those who feel it.

The arguments adduced against these reasons are, in my
opinion, either of no intrinsic weight, or based upon a grave
misstatement of evidence.   First comes the *à priori* assertion,
that the coexistence or close succession of two poets of such
genius is inconceivable.   But we may reply, that the composition of the Odyssey is perhaps a century or more subsequent
to that of the Iliad, and, in any case, whatever the law of the
appearance of poetic genius may be, history shows that the coexistence of the greatest poets is rather the rule than the exception.

§ 54. Next comes the confident assertion, that the consistent
tradition of the Greeks assigned the two poems to the same
author.   This is a serious misstatement, and the more likely to
mislead because it is not absolutely false.   The real state of
the facts is as follows.   When we examine the traditions of the
earliest historical age in Greece, we find ascribed to Homer,
not the Iliad and Odyssey alone, but a vast body of epic
literature, including a collection of *Hymns*, and several comic
poems, in some of which there are even passages in iambic
metre alternating with hexameters.   Above all, let it be remembered that some of the cyclic epics, then commonly attributed
to Homer, were composed by known poets, and within historical times.   The name of Homer was, therefore, used in the
same general way as we usually speak of the *Psalms of David*,
though many of them not only make no claim to be composed
by David, but are even distinctly assigned to other authors.   In
Greek literature the names of Hesiod and of Hippocrates were

---

[1] Cf. δ 791, ζ 130, ι 292, χ 402, with δ 335, repeated in ρ 126, where
a doe is represented as leaving her young in a lion's lair—a perfect absurdity.   Lions are simply mentioned a few times in addition (κ 212-8,
ℓ 456, λ 610).

used in the same manner to denote a whole school of a peculiar kind.

This simple and uncritical attitude reaches down to the
days of Pindar, who seems to. ascribe all the cyclic epics to
Homer, and recognises no other early poet except Hesiod.
The critical labours of the commission of Peisistratus, and of
such men as Theagenes of Rhegium, began to open men's eyes
to the impossibility of holding this view.   Herodotus questions
the Homeric authorship of the *Cypria* and the *Epigoni.*   Plato
only once cites the *Cypria*, and as the work of an unknown poet.
He appears from his other numerous quotations to have recognised only the Iliad and Odyssey as genuine ; whereas Thucydides had still acknowledged the *Hymns* as such, and still later
Aristotle quotes the *Margites* as a poem of Homer.

It appears, then, that of all our authorities on this question,
down to the Alexandrian epoch, there is only one (Plato) who
seems to hold that the Iliad and Odyssey, *and these alone*,
were the work of a single Homer.   Nor is even this to be
asserted positively, but merely as an inference from his silence
on the *pseudo-Homerica*, or, where he notes the existence of
such apocryphal poems.   We rather find successive critics disallowing work after work which had been attributed to the
author of the Iliad, and we find that the two poems which
resisted this disintegrating process longest were the Odyssey
and *Margites*.   It is even quite possible that the earliest attacks
on the Odyssey may have preceded Aristotle's time.

But it must be kept in mind that those who may have
allowed the Homeric authorship of the Iliad and Odyssey,
after rejecting the rest, were opposing a feeling the very reverse
of that which they are now quoted as opposing.   They protested against too many works being ascribed to the poet; they
are now quoted as if they had protested against too few being
ascribed to him.   This is a totally different question, and one
which they did not examine.   The so-called consistent evidence
of all old tradition as to this unity of authorship is really only
the evidence of those who believed that every epic came
from Homer ; then of those who believed that a great many
epics and other poems came from Homer ; finally, of those who

were so occupied in rejecting other weaker claims upon his name, that they had not yet thought of discussing the claims of the Odyssey.

§ 55. That day, however, did come at last, and there was a school whose members carried their scepticism to this point. What its fate would have been is hard to say, had not the great Aristarchus crushed it by his authority. He was determined to put down the advance of this scepticism, which would doubtless have next assailed portions of the Iliad ; and he succeeded. But the importance of the controversy is proved by his having written a special treatise against the Chorizontes, in which he sought to prove the common authorship of the two poems. It is very creditable to his sagacity that he endeavoured to prove it by the only argument which could become conclusive —by showing anticipations of the Odyssey implied in the Iliad. All other harmonies can be explained as the result of conscious agreement on the part of the later poet. A large body of unde-signed anticipations in the older poem might indeed convince us. But Aristarchus' book is lost, and his modern followers have not attempted to sustain his position with reasonable evidence. Until, therefore, some new evidence is produced, which is well-nigh impossible, there seems no reason whatever for assuming the Iliad and Odyssey to be the product of a single mind.

§ 56. Having thus disposed of the arguments in favour of this larger unity, we must approach the exaggerated attempts to show that each of the poems as a whole, with the exception of a stray line here and there, and perhaps the end of the Odys-sey, is the work of a single poet developing a logical plot. Here the advocates of unity have really the verdict of antiquity to some extent with them, for although the *Doloneia* (κ) in the Iliad and the last book were much suspected, the sceptics of those days did not venture on the hypothesis of the absorption of lesser poems in the texture of the whole, and Aristarchus believed that all the difficulties could be removed by obelising inconsistent lines or sentences.

But here, again, I protest *in limine* against the evidence of the Greek public, or of any other public, being called in to settle a question of which no public can be a competent judge. What higher authority upon poetry, say our opponents, can you have than the consent of ages? What more infallible verdict than that of successive nations and centuries? All these have felt the Iliad and Odyssey to be unities, and shall not this evidence outweigh the doubts of critics and the subtleties of grammarians? All this plausible talk is founded upon a capital *ignoratio elenchi.* It is perfectly true that the public is the ultimate and best judge of literature in one sense—that of its excellence—and that there is no instance of a bad work surviving for ages in public esteem. But surely it is absurd to set up the public as a judge of the unity of a plot, or the exact composition of an intricate system. On the contrary, uncritical readers are quite certain to imagine unity and consistency in any work handed down to them as one, however incongruous or contradictory its details. Thus the Psalms of David strike the average reader as the effusions of a single bard, in spite of headings asserting the contrary. Thus too the Book of Common Prayer would pass for the work of a single school, if not of a single pen, though there are plain traces of compromise between parties all through it. And so with a thousand other instances. The public, then, is no judge whatever of the unity of a poem, though an excellent judge of poetic merit.

§ 57. Let us now examine the alleged unity of the Iliad more in detail. The arguments advanced by such men as Colonel Mure and Mr. Gladstone, both expert controversialists, are of this kind—general uniformity of diction, general and even minute consistency in the characters, general sameness of style. They urge that when the poem is handed down by tradition as a single whole, these additional marks of design and unity are conclusive against attributing it to various poets. What they say, even though greatly exaggerated, has much weight against the advocates of an aggregation of shorter poems by a subsequent arranger, but has no force against the advocates of an original Iliad of moderate dimensions dilated by successive additions or interpolations. For in this case the enlargers or interpolators would take what care they could to observe harmonies of character and diction, and would do so sufficiently to satisfy the vulgar, though unable to deceive accurate criticism.

This is in fact exactly the case. The unity which strikes every-one at first reading gradually breaks up when we are brought to reflect upon the logical coherence of the parts.

I am very far indeed from asserting the critical principle assumed as obvious by many Germans, that wherever there is plain violation of logical consistency, we have not the work of a single poet telling his own story. The history of modern literature, even in a critical age, shows ample instances of direct contradictions in the undoubted works of the greatest authors. But all these cases, so far as I know, arise from forgetfulness of details, and cannot be adduced to excuse such large improbabilities as we encounter through the Iliad. Yet, even in detail, I know not whether any parallel could be found (among great writers) to the narrative from H 313 to Θ 252, during which at least two days and nights elapse, and a series of inconsistent events—among others the building of a great fortification with gates—are crowded together, while the dead are being buried. Both Hermann and Lachmann[1] have brought out the details. Thus the fact that the same heroes are killed two or three times over may pass as unimportant, but how shall we defend the utter confusion of motives in the second book, the *first* view of the Greek chiefs by Priam from the wall in the tenth year of the war, the fear of Diomede to meet some god in the form of Glaucus, when on the same day and in the same battle he has by divine instigation attacked and wounded both Ares and Aphrodite? How shall we defend the complete forgetfulness through all the rest of the poem of two great scenes —the single combat of Hector and Ajax, and the capture of the horses of Rhesus by Diomede? In the perpetual encounters between Hector and Ajax all through the battle at the ships, Ajax never once alludes to his success in the single combat, though it was the common habit of Homer's heroes to boast of such things. In the races of the twenty-third book, Diomede contends with the horses he took from Æneas in the fifth book, and no mention is made of the much finer horses which he carried off in the tenth. Some allusion to them here was not only natural, but necessary, if a single poet had been thinking

[1] *Betrachtungen zur Ilias,* p. 24.

out his story.   More generally, the promise of Zeus that by
the retirement and wrath of Achilles defeat and ruin shall come
upon the Greeks, is followed in the Iliad by a series of brilliant
victories on the part of the Greeks ; and we are well-nigh tired
of the slaughter of the Trojans, before the least ray of success
dawns upon them.   This is not the work of a single poet carrying out a definite plan, but the work of later hands enlarging,
and even contradicting, the original intentions of the author.

§ 58. But what was this plan, and what the work of the original author?   I will endeavour briefly to sketch what seems to
me the most probable theory, though it is obvious that no con-
structive criticism can be so safe or convincing as the mere
exposure of flaws and defects.

It has already been shown that allusion is made by the
authors to many earlier lays as in existence, and even as presupposed by the Iliad.   There are endless details about the
earlier history of the heroes, about their genealogies, and about
the adventures of the gods, which are referred to as well known
and current.   It is almost certain that there were some lays on
the actual subjects of the Iliad which were adopted or worked
in by the poet.   Every early poet makes free use of earlier
materials, nor is there in the history of primitive literature any
instance where the first great advance was not based on previous
work.   The attempt to discover and to sever out these primitive elements of the Iliad has been prosecuted by the Germans
long and laboriously enough to show its utter futility.   No two
of the dissenters can agree, and if they did, they would fail to
convince any candid critic that their results were more than
guesswork.   But they have undoubtedly shown many sutures
and joining lines, so that, while failing in detail, they may fairly
be said to have established their principle.

But all these debts of Homer to earlier lays are held to
be debts of detail, and it is asserted, with good reason, that
the new feature in the Iliad, and a principal cause of its success, was its splendid plan.   Instead of singing the mere
prowess of special heroes, or chronicling the events of a war,
the great poet who struck out the Iliad devised a tragic plot,
into which he could weave character and incident, thus actually

anticipating, as Aristotle clearly saw, the glories of Æschylus and his successors. The wrath of Achilles equalises the forces on either side, so that the characters and prowess of the lesser heroes appear ; the friendship of Patroclus, his death and the fury of Achilles, the death of Hector—all these events are brought out under one idea—the wrath of Achilles.

§ 59. While agreeing with this view, and convinced as I am that this working in of details under a plot was the secret of the Iliad's greatness, I must insist upon two reservations : first, the plot was not absolutely original; secondly, it was unusually capable of extension.

It has not been remarked by any of the critics, that among the earlier lays mentioned in the Iliad, there is one which is of a far larger and more epic character than the rest—I mean that briefly told by Phœnix in the ninth book concerning the Life and Death of Meleager. There are here the materials for a splendid epic—the anger of Artemis, the ravages of the wild boar, his pursuit and death, the quarrel about his spoils, the consequent war of Curetes and Ætolians, the mother's curse on Meleager, his sullen refusal to help his country, the supplications of all his kindred, the storming of his city, his wife's prayers, his sudden reappearance and victory, his untimely death—all this (except the end) is told by Phœnix with a direct application to the wrath and sullen inaction of Achilles. Though this part of the ninth book probably did not belong to the original poem, it seems so early an addition, that its evidence as to the diffusion of the Legend of Meleager is to be trusted, and that the wrath and refusal of Meleager to help his country may have been the spark which kindled in the mind of Homer the plot of the *Achilleis*. There are ample differences and ample originalities in the Iliad to remove all pretence for asserting any plagiarism. I merely mean to say that if the short epic about Meleager was, as it seems to be, older than the Iliad, its leading idea is reproduced in the later poem.

§ 60. We come to the second and more important feature above mentioned, the elastic nature of the plot. When the wrath of Achilles withdrew him from the field, and the Greeks began the struggle without him, it was quite natural that other heroes should endeavour to supply his place, and to avert the defeat which ultimately showed him to be necessary to his country-men. But though the original poet may have designed and carried out some such extension, especially where Patroclus comes out to fight, still the present extensions of the plot are so distinctly at variance with the main idea, that we must at once admit the interpolation of considerable portions of the present text. Thus the long section which embraces books B–H is plainly foisted in by successive bards, when they sang the epic among Greeks who felt a national jealousy for the prowess of their ancestors, and who would not tolerate their defeat without inflicting greater loss upon the Trojans. This is really carried to an absurd length. The Greeks without Achilles are far more than a match for the Trojans. For every Greek that is slain at least two Trojans fall, and so we are brought to feel that these books were composed by poets actually contradicting the idea of the great tragic master who framed the plot.

It is likewise remarkable that these portions of the Iliad refer to events which are misplaced in the tenth year of the war, but highly suitable at its commencement. Such are the Catalogue, the viewing of the Greek heroes by Priam and Helen, the single combats of Paris and of Hector with Mene-laus and Ajax. All these matters, as Grote clearly saw, belong to an Iliad, but not to an Achilleis, and an Achilleis the origi-nal poem must have been most indubitably. When Mure says, in support of the unity of the poem, that it is inconceivable how all the greatest poets of separate lays should have confined themselves to the events of a few days in the tenth year of the war, he simply assumes an absurdity, and argues from it as a fact. The events just mentioned, and the *aristeiæ* of most of the heroes, will suit any earlier period in the war, and even needed a little adjustment, a few omissions and additions, to make them fit their place as indifferently as they now do.

The second, third, and seventh books were perhaps adapted from an earlier Iliad for mere expansion's sake, or to transfer to a nobler place poetry which was being lost by the growing splendour of a newer Iliad. The *aristeia* of Diomede is probably due to the recitation of the Iliad at Argos, where the poem was

very popular, and where the national hero must be made to play
a prominent part. Thus a kingdom is made for him in the
Catalogue, which is simply cut out of the empire of Agamemnon, though plainly inconsistent with it, and the hero himself is
drawn quite as fearless and as invincible as Achilles. But in
the later books (except the twenty-third) he almost completely
disappears.

The arming and acts of Agamemnon, in the eleventh book,
appear to me another such interpolation, probably for the purpose of recitation at Mycenæ, for in the original plot the King
of Men seems to be a weak, chicken-hearted creature, always
counselling flight, or finding fault with his inferiors, and not
the almost superhuman being he is here represented. In the
same way I cannot believe that the acts of Patroclus are in the
least consistent with his character and reputation all through
the real *Achilleis.* He is nowhere spoken of as a wonderful
hero, inferior only to Achilles in valour, but as an amiable
second-rate personage, who keeps on good terms with everyone,
and who obtains leave to bring out the Myrmidons to battle.
I believe that in the original *Achilleis* he made but a poor
diversion, and was presently slain in fair fight at the ships by
the great Hector, as indeed the later books distinctly imply.
But the subsequent poets who recited in the interests of Greek
vanity made him slaughter Trojans all day, and at last robbed
Hector of his glory by introducing Apollo and Euphorbus to
help him.

§ 61. This brings me to the strongest and clearest inconsistency in the whole of our present Iliad—the character and
position of Hector. It has been common among the English
conservatives to boast of the wonderful harmony and accuracy
of each character in the Iliad, and they quietly assume the
whole of their facts as incontrovertible. But surely we need
not trouble ourselves about their arguments, if we can deny and
disprove their preliminary facts. That there are many subtle
and striking harmonies I will not deny, but will assert what
has hardly been yet touched upon in this country, that there
are abundant and striking inconsistencies also. I have alluded
to some of these—the fear of Diomede on meeting Glaucus,

the various pictures of Agamemnon, the sudden splendour of Patroclus ; but all these are nothing when we come to the case of Hector.

Critics, old and new, have felt the remarkable contradictions in the drawing of this famous hero, and yet none of them have ventured to suggest the real explanation. Even Mure and Mr. Gladstone confess that in our Iliad he is wholly inferior to his reputation ; 'he is paid off,' say they, 'with generalities, while in actual encounter he is hardly equal to the second-rate Greek heroes.'[1] Yet why is he so important all through the plot of the poem ? Why is his death by Achilles made an achievement of the highest order ? Why are the chiefs who at one time challenge and worst him, at another quaking with fear at his approach ? Simply because in the original plan of the Iliad he *was* a great warrior, and because these perpetual defeats by Diomede and Ajax, this avoidance of Agamemnon, this swaggering and 'hectoring' which we now find in him, were introduced by the enlargers and interpolators, in order to enhance the merits of their favourites at his expense.

It seems to me certain that originally the Hector of the Iliad was really superior to all the Greeks except Achilles, that upon the retirement of the latter he made shorter work of them than the later rhapsodists liked to admit, that he soon burst the gates and appeared at the ships, that Patroclus was slain there after a brief diversion, and that in this way the whole catastrophe was very much more precipitated than we now find it. I suppose that even when Achilles returns to the field, these interpolations continue, that the battle of the gods comes from quite a different sort of poetry than the worldly epic, and that possibly the book of the games, and the last book, were added to the shorter plot. But it is likely that these additions must have been made very early, and by very splendid poets, for I cannot think with the Germans that such poetry as the ninth and twenty-fourth books of the Iliad is one whit

---

[1] I should not fail to add that Mr. Gladstone finds no difficulty in reconciling all these inconsistencies, and even attacks the dissectors of the hero, in an article entitled *The Slicing of Hector* (*Nineteenth Century* for Oct. 1878).

inferior to the best parts of the original poem.   It also appears
to me that the interpolators must have handled both the original
poem and their additions or adaptations very freely ; for if my
view of Hector be correct, they must have taken out achievements of his, and put in those of Greek heroes instead, at the
same time adapting stories from the earlier history of the war
to suit the altered time and circumstances.

§ 62. No doubt the strongest objection to this theory of
the formation of our Iliad in most people's minds will be, not the
groundless assertion about so many great poets having confined
themselves to so short a period of the war, which I have set
aside, but rather the assumption of the mere existence of more
than one poet of such eminence, not to say of several, or even
of a school of such splendour.   I think this argument, which at
first sight appears strong, depends upon a want of appreciation
of the varying state of society, and its effects upon literature.   There are ages, sometimes primitive, sometimes simple,
where a school or habit of thinking will produce from a number
of men what another age will only attain in high individual
exceptions.

Here are two well-known instances.   It is impossible for
all our divines in the present day to produce prayers written
in the pious English of our Book of Common Prayer.   There
is a certain depth of style, a certain ' sweet-smelling savour '
about it which is almost unique in our language, and now
unapproachable.   But this book is not the work of a single
man, or even perhaps of a few, but of a considerable number,
who have nevertheless attained such unity or harmony in their
way of thinking and of translating (from the Latin), that it is
not easy to find the least inequality or falling off in any part
These men were not all Shakespeares and Miltons, but they
were men who belonged to a school greater than any individual
can ever be.

Let us consider another case not very dissimilar.   The age
of the Reformation produced in Germany an outburst of devotional poetry, which is preserved in the countless collections
of old hymns still sung in the Protestant churches.   Many
of these hymns are assigned to well-known and celebrated

authors, such as Martin Luther, some to men otherwise un-known, others again are anonymous.   But in literary merit there is a curious evenness about them.   They do not differ in any way as the poetry of great and little poets does in our day. The same lofty tone, the same simple faith, the same pure lan-guage pervades them almost all.   And yet both these examples are from ages very literary and developed as compared to the age of the epic bards in Greece. I conceive, therefore, that this evenness of production, this prevalence of a dominating tone, has made it possible for the work of several hands to coalesce into a great unity, in which the parts are all great, and, in the opinion of many, all worthy of the whole.

§ 63. But the destructive critics would not have recourse to this argument, because they deny the fact which I have assumed. Many Germans find parts of the Iliad wholly unworthy of the rest ; they will even tell you the line where a worse poet began, and where the greater poet takes up the thread again.   This criticism is so completely subjective, so completely dependent upon the varying taste and judgment of the critic, that I for-bear to enter upon it.   Many passages which they think un-worthy seem to me the finest poetry ; and if I were to select a specimen of what seems to me an evident and most disturbing interpolation, I should choose the lines Ω 527–52, which dilute a splendid scene, but which are nevertheless accepted as belong-ing to their present place by Aristarchus, and even by all the destructive critics of late days.

§ 64. The theory which I advocate has many points of resemblance with that of Grote.   But I do not think all the books which disturb the *Achilleis* belong to *one* other poem, or *Ilias*, as he does.   I think they were separate lays, perhaps composed, perhaps adapted, for their place.   It seems too that the part of Hector in the tragedy has been tampered with more seriously than he suspected.   I further agree with Voltaire and the best destructive critics in Germany in thinking, that though the Iliad has a distinct plot, and though this plot was the direct cause of its several lays attaining to their present fame in the world, yet the pleasure which educated men now take in the Iliad is not in its plot, but in its details.   It is for splendid scenes, for touching episodes, for picturesque similes, that we love the Iliad most, and not for its economy or structure.

The successive events are sometimes so loosely connected that we come to suspect the commission of Peisistratus of having found many diverging versions, and of having co-ordinated them, in preference to suppressing them all save one. This is more particularly the case with the similes, with which the Iliad abounds. In spite of the ingenuity and the reverence of critics in defending them, these similes are often excessive and disturbing to the narrative, they often repeat the same facts with hardly any variation, and when we find two or three co-ordinated without adequate reason, it seems as if different reciting rhapsodes had composed them separately, and then the commission included them all in their comprehensive edition.[1]

§ 65. These are the principal reflections which suggest themselves upon a critical survey of the Iliad. It would be idle in this place to rehearse again the centuries of praise which this immortal poem has received from all lovers of real poetry. While the historian and the grammarian will ever find there subjects of perplexity and doubt, every sound nature, from the schoolboy eager for life to the old man weary of it, will turn to its pages for deep human portraits of excitement and of danger, of friendship and of sympathy. So purely and perfectly did the poet of that day mirror life and character, that he forgets his own existence, and leaves no trace of himself upon the canvas which he fills with heroes and their deeds. He paints what he conceives an ideal age, older and better than his own, but paints too naturally not to copy from real life enough to let us look through the ideal to the real beneath. The society thus revealed I have already elsewhere described.[2]

§ 66. We turn to consider the Odyssey. Though there was controversy in old days about the priority of the Iliad, it seems quite settled now[3] that we must look upon the Odyssey as a later poem—how much later it is impossible to say. The limits assigned have varied from those who believed it the work of

[1] Cf. especially B 55–83. [2] *Social Life in Greece,* chaps. i. and ii.
[3] Schömann alone suggests (*Jahn's Jahrb.* vol. lxix. p. 130) that the Odyssey may have been the model for the framers of the Iliad.

the same author in old age, to those who place it two centuries later (as M. É. Burnouf does), owing to the difference of its plan and style. But, as Bonitz says,[1] if not composed in the old age of Homer, it was composed in the old age of Greek epic poetry, when the creative power was diminishing, but that of ordering and arranging had become more developed. The plot of the Odyssey is skilfully conceived, and on the whole artistically carried out, even though modern acuteness has found fault with its sutures. But critics seem agreed that the elements of the Odyssey were not short and disconnected lays, but themselves epics of considerable length, one on the Return of Odysseus, another on the adventures of Telemachus, and these the chief.

The drawing of the characters is perhaps less striking, but more consistent than in the Iliad. The whole composition is in fact tamer and more modern. The first faint pulse of public opinion apart from the ruling chiefs is beginning to be felt; the various elements of society are beginning to crystallise. The profession of poet, which was either unknown or does not chance to be mentioned in the Iliad, is made one of importance, which the author strives consciously to magnify. Instead of constant battles, and perpetual descriptions of blood and wounds, we find that mercantile enterprise and the adventure of discovery are awakening in the Greek mind. Luxury seems increased; and the esteem for chivalry retires before the esteem for prudence and discretion. The gods, who still act, and perpetually interfere in the life of men, are beginning to act upon more definite principles, and with somewhat less caprice and passion. The similes, with which the Iliad abounds, and which even there are less frequent in the later books, become almost exceptional.

§ 67. It has been said, with a good deal of force, by the advocates of the unity of the two poems, that all these differences may be accounted for by the difference of the subjects; that in a poem of travel and adventure we must expect these very variations. But even granting this, the choice of the subject seems rather the consequence than the cause of the altered feelings

---

[1] *Der Ursprung der Homerischen Gedichte*, 4th ed. p. 39.

and customs.   With the blood and wounds, and the rude camp
life of the Iliad before him, the poet who ventured upon a competition with so great a forerunner deliberately set himself to
find contrasts, not only in treatment, but in plan.   He may
fairly claim to have surpassed the Iliad in the latter feature ;
and even in the former, there is more charm about the Odyssey
to a calmer and more reflective age, than about the fiercer
Iliad.   The Greeks of historical times, who were always trying
to stimulate in their citizens military valour—a quality in which
most Greeks were deficient enough—taught their children the
warlike poem with this intent, and praised it above all others
for this reason.   Their approval was taken up by the grammarians, and handed on to modern critics ; but it seems to
me doubtful whether it is not founded wholly upon the educational feeling among the Greeks.   Unbiassed critics will now-
a-days read the Odyssey oftener, and with greater pleasure.
Most of the Germans think that there is a marked falling
off in the second half of the poem ; that the character of the
hero becomes exaggerated, and the narrative generally confused
and injured by repetitions of the same idea.   It would not be
difficult to defend many of the points they have attacked, and
to maintain that the trials of the unrecognised Odysseus in his
own palace among the dissolute suitors are most artistically
varied and prolonged in order to stir the reader with impatience for the thrilling catastrophe.   It is generally agreed
that there are spurious additions at the end.   Again, Kirchhoff
has argued that the double reproof of Penelope's incredulity by
Telemachus and by Odysseus is not consistent, and shows signs
of patching.   Again—and this is no matter of detail—it is clear
that there are in the poem two distinct reasons to account for
the non-recognition of Odysseus on his return home : first, the
natural changes of twenty years' toil and hardship ; secondly,
the miraculous transformation effected by Athene for the purpose of disguise.

These and other similar objections to the original unity of
the Odyssey are not likely to occur to the general reader, or to
disturb him, seeing that they had never occurred to the acutest
critics before Kirchhoff.   Thus Sengebusch, whose writings

(so far as they are known to me) date prior to Kirchhoff's book, is very severe on the Chorizontes, and ridicules all their attempts to prove the Odyssey younger than the Iliad, or made up of parts various in age. His arguments, however, though very strong against the minor points urged, do not touch the later and more serious attack.[1] Professor Geddes is content, with Wolf and Grote, to assume the unity of the Odyssey as unquestioned, and the whole of his Homeric theory is based upon this assumption. These critics have the authority of Aristarchus. But his assumption of the unity of the Iliad must have vitiated his great argument about its anticipations of the Odyssey. If several hands contributed to each poem, it was certain that some of the later Ilian poets knew the Odyssey, at least in part ; nay, it is very likely that the same poets contributed to both, as has been shown by the researches of Professor Geddes. Hence, harmonies of this kind between the Iliad and Odyssey would only prove a gradual construction of both in a school with fixed traditions and intent on avoiding manifest contradictions.

§ 68. It may be fairly expected that I should not conclude the subject without giving a brief summary of the general results attained by this long controversy.

We may assume it as certain that there existed in Ionia schools or fraternities of epic rhapsodists who composed and recited heroic lays at feasts, and often had friendly contests in these recitations. The origin of these recitations may be sought in northern Greece, from which the fashion migrated in early days to Asia Minor. We may assume that these singers became popular in many parts of Greece, and that they wandered from

---

[1] His most ingenious point is his escape from the difficulty about the *Kimmerians*, whose mention in λ 14 is held to prove that that passage was composed after the appearance of the nation in Asia Minor, *circ.* 700 B.C. Sengebusch notes that there were Χειμέριοι in Epirus ; that Aristarchus probably on this account rejected the variant Κερβερίων, but preserved the Ionic form Κιμμερίων, as the home of the legend came from that country ; finally, that this very passage suggested the name which the Ionian Greeks gave to the devastating invaders who overran Asia Minor, and who were not really so called. Cf. *Jahn's Jahrbücher*, vol. lxvii. p. 414. But all this seems *argutius quam verius*.

court to court glorifying the heroic ancestors of the various chiefs. One among them, called Homer, was endowed with a genius superior to the rest, and struck out a plot capable of nobler and larger treatment. It is likely that this superiority was not recognised at the time, and that he remained all his life a singer like the rest, a wandering minstrel, possibly poor and blind. The listening public gradually stamped his poem with their approval, they demanded its frequent recitation, and so this Homer began to attain a great posthumous fame. But when this fame led people to inquire into his life and history, it had already passed out of recollection, and men supplied by fables what they had forgotten or neglected. The rhapsodists, however, then turned their attention to expanding and perfecting his poem, which was greatly enlarged and called the Iliad. In doing this they had recourse to the art of writing, which seems to have been in use when Homer framed his poem, but which was certainly employed when the plan was enlarged with episodes. The home of the original Homer seems to have been about Smyrna, and in contact with both Æolic and Ionic legends. His date is quite uncertain; it need not be placed before 800 B.C., and is perhaps later, but not after 700 B.C.

When the greatness of the Iliad had been already discovered, another rhapsodist of genius conceived the idea of constructing a similar but contrasted epic from the stories about Odysseus and Telemachus, and so our Odyssey came into existence—a more carefully planned story, but not so fresh and original as the older Iliad. Both poets lived at the time when the individual had not asserted himself superior to the clan or brotherhood of bards to which he belonged, and hence their personality is lost behind the general features of the school, and the legendary character of their subjects. An age of rapid and original production is not unlikely to produce this result. Thus Shakespeare, among a crowd of playwrights, and without any prestige, did not become famous till the details of his life were well-nigh forgotten. The controversies concerning his plays have many points of analogy to the disputes about Homer.

When the name of Homer became famous, all epic compositions pretended to be his work, and he gradually became the hero *eponymos* of the schools of rhapsodists.   Hence the first critics began by disallowing the Homeric origin of various inferior and later compositions.   This process had in later classical times gone so far as to reject all but the Iliad and Odyssey. With an attempt to reject even the Odyssey, ancient scepticism paused.   No Greek critic ever thought of denying that each poem was the conception and work of a single mind, and of a mind endowed with exceptional genius.   The attempt of the Wolfian school to prove them mere conglomerates has failed. They have proved that there was extensive interpolation, but all attempts to disengage the original nucleus have failed.

§ 69. It is indeed sad that the historian of Greek literature must devote all his attention to these dry discussions when he comes to treat of the most charming among Greek books, the oldest and the most perfect romance in European society. All the characters of the Odyssey live before us with the most wonderful clearness.   Even the old servants, and the dogs, are life-portraits; and Plato has not attained to a more delicate shading of character than may be found in the drawing of the various ladies, or of the insolent suitors, who crowd upon the scene.   When we hear that Sophocles took whole dramas from the Odyssey, we rather wonder that Euripides did not do so also ; nor can we allege the imaginary reason in Aristotle's *Poetic,.* that the plot was too simple and well-articulated to afford more than one drama.   For it is really very complex and ingenious.   The gradual approach of the catastrophe after Odysseus' return in disguise is wonderfully exciting, and thrills the mind at the twentieth perusal as at the first.   The portrait of the hero is an essentially Greek ideal, with the ingrained weaknesses of the Hellenic character fully expressed in him, yet, on the whole, superior to the fierce and obstinate Achilles.   But the outspoken admission of guile and deceit in Odysseus produced a gradual degradation of his character in the cyclic poets, in Epicharmus, and in tragedy, while Achilles escaped. In fact, *educational* tendencies censured the general inclination to knavery, and exalted the somewhat deficient quality of physical courage, wherever they were found described in the

Bible of the Greeks.   Nevertheless, Odysseus was the Jacob of the nation, the real type and patriarch of the Ionic race.

I will conclude by pointing out a peculiarly poetical trait in the character of Penelope, which seems to me to speak a long world-experience, and very little of that buoyant simplicity of early times and primitive manners which are usually lauded in Homer.   Nothing is at first sight stranger than the obstinate scepticism of Penelope at the end of the story.   She who had for years sought out and given credence to every strolling vagabond's report about her husband, cannot persuade herself, when he actually returns, to accept him !   And yet, nowhere has any modern poet given us truer and deeper psychology.   To a nature like Penelope's, the longing for her husband had become so completely the occupation of her life—'grief filled the room up of her absent lord'—had so satisfied and engrossed her thoughts that, on his return, all her life seemed empty, all her occupation gone, and she was in that blank amazement which paralyses the mind.   For after a great and sudden loss, we know not how to prepare ourselves for a change, however happy, in our daily state, and our minds at first refuse to accept the loss of griefs which have become almost dear to us from their familiarity.   Such a conception we might expect from Menander or from Shakespeare.   In Homer it is indeed passing strange.

CHAPTER VI.

THE CYCLIC POETS AND THE BATRACHO-MYO-MACHIA.—
ÆSOP AND BABRIUS.

§ 70. IT is not the plan of this book to notice the lost works in Greek literature, except so far as it is necessary for the understanding of the remaining treasures. Those who desire to see all that can be said on the obscure subject of the cyclic poets may consult Welcker's *Epischer Cyclus*, where the greater part of three volumes is devoted to the discussion of notices and fragments in themselves of little value, and to an estimate of the genius of poets whom the ancients neglected or despised. The few facts elicited by his very long discussion are easily summed up.

It is a salient fact in Greek literature that originality in each kind of composition was exhausted when the next in order sprang up. Thus, the long period which elapsed from the first outburst of epic poetry to the rise of iambic and lyric poetry, as well as the earlier epochs of these species, was filled with a series of epic writers who treated subjects similar to those of the Iliad and Odyssey. But we are told that no later poet whatever covered this particular ground, owing, it is said, to the great excellence of the real Homer, who far distanced and silenced all competition. It would be safer to assert that all the poets who did sing of these subjects were either embodied in the Homeric poems, or, if not, were immediately thrown aside and forgotten. I have already shown (p. 73) that the earlier lays discernible in the Iliad were by no means confined to the tenth year of the war, but may have suited any period subsequent to the landing or before the death of Hector. To us, however, no separate poet remains who is known to have trodden on the ground of Homer.

It was once commonly believed that the remaining epic poets equally avoided touching upon one another, that they composed their poems upon a fixed chronological plan, each resuming where the other had finished, and so completing an account of what is called the Epic cycle, from the birth of Aphrodite in the *Cypria* down to the conclusion of the *Nostoi,* or *Telegonia,* of Eugammon. But it seems clearly made out now that no such fixed system of poems existed ; that the authors, widely separated in date and birthplace, were no corporation with fixed traditions ; that they did overlap in subject, and repeat the same legends ; and that the epic cycle does not mean a cycle of *poems,* but a cycle of *legends,* arranged by the grammarians, who illustrated them by a selection of poems, or parts of poems, including, of course, the Iliad and Odyssey, and then such other epics as told the whole story of the Theban and Trojan wars, down to the conclusion of the heroic age.

§ 71. We owe chiefly to the summary of the grammarian Proclus,[1] which is preserved to us, the following list of the poems and subjects. (1) The *Cypria,* in early days attributed to Homer himself, then denied to him by Herodotus (ii. 117) and other sound critics on account of variations from the Iliad and the Odyssey in its legends, was generally cited anonymously, as in the Schol. Ven. on the Iliad. Later on, Athenæus and Proclus speak of Stasinus, or Hegesias, or Hegesinus as the author. It was called *Cypria,* either because the author of the poem came from Cyprus, or because it celebrated the Cyprian goddess Aphrodite, and detailed from the commencement her action in the Trojan war. This fact of itself shows a standpoint quite foreign to the Iliad. The poem was, however, an introduction to the Iliad, telling a vast number of myths, and leading the reader from the first causes of the war up to the tenth year of its duration. It is easy to see that such a vast subject loosely connected must have failed to afford the artistic unity which underlies the course of the Iliad. (2) The

---

[1] Cf. Dindorf's *Schol. Græc. in Iliadem,* vol. i. (Pref.) p. xxxi, sq.

Æthiopis, in five books, by Arctinus of Miletus, the oldest certainly known epic poet, who is generally placed about the 1st Olympiad (776 B.C.), and called a pupil of Homer. This poem reached from the death of Hector to that of Achilles, · and told of the arrival of the Amazons and the Æthiopians to aid Troy. It was even tacked on to the Iliad by a modification of the last line. Achilles was the central figure of the poem, and appears to have been treated with breadth and power. He slays Penthesilea, and then feels a pang of remorse on beholding her beauty. This is ridiculed by Thersites, whom he kills in a fit of passion. Antilochus, who seems in some sort to have been the Patroclus of the poem, is slain by Memnon while endeavouring to save his father, Nestor. Achilles then slays Memnon, and is himself slain, in his pursuit of the Trojans, by Paris. The contest for the arms of Achilles, and the suicide of Ajax, concluded the *Æthiopis,* if, indeed, the poem called the *Sack of Ilium,* by the same author, in two books, was not originally connected with the *Æthiopis.* (3) But the arrangers of the mythical cycle preferred, on the Sack of Troy, a poem of Lesches called the *Little Iliad,* by Pausanias also the Sack of Ilium. This Lesches was a Lesbian, and contemporary with Archilochus (about Ol. 30). He related, apparently in more of a chronicler's than a poet's spirit, the events from the contest about Achilles' arms to the actual fall of Troy. Odysseus was his principal hero. (4) The *Nostoi,* in five books, by Agias of Trœzen, but often quoted anonymously. He sang of the adventures of the heroes apart from Odysseus, especially the Atreidæ, and described the regions of the dead in a passage referred to by Pausanias. (5) The *Telegonia,* by Eugammon of Cyrene, who is placed about the 53rd Ol. He described the adventures of Odysseus, Telemachus, and of Telegonus, son of Odysseus and Circe, and thus completed the Trojan cycle. It is hardly necessary to give similar details about the Theban cycle which has no interest to us except that the tragic poets borrowed largely from it.[1]

---

[1] The principal poems of which we have any report are the epic of Œdipus, ascribed to Kinæthon, then an old *Thebais* by an unknown poet, followed by the *Epigoni* of Antimachus of Teos. The capture of Œchalia, and the epics on the Minyans, lie outside this series, but akin to it.

§ 72. Unfortunately, the extant fragments of these poems are so trifling—amounting in all to some sixty lines—as to afford us in themselves no adequate means of judging their authors' merits.   They are all quoted in the appendix to Welcker's *Epischer Cyclus*, and the main body of that work is an ingenious attempt to vindicate the old cyclic poets against the systematic neglect or even disparagement of classical days—I mean the neglect of them as literature, though they were the great mine from which the tragic poets drew their plots.   On the other hand, Colonel Mure, in his excellent second volume, has put together all that can be learned from analysing the extant fragments, and has based an adverse verdict strictly on two famous judgments preserved to us in the *Poetic*, of which this is the substance.   Aristotle compares the nature of the *unity* requisite for history, which he calls merely chronological, and that for poetry, which must be logical ; nor is it enough that the action should be laid in one division of time, or centred about one hero.   He further distinguishes in poetry the epic and the tragic unity, of which the former is the larger, and admits of episodes, while the latter is shorter and stricter.   But in speaking generally of the unity of story in both epic and tragic poetry, he asserts that almost all epic poets had been content with a mechanical unity, whereas Homer, with superior tact, whether instinctive or acquired, had chosen subjects of which the parts are easily comprehended and naturally grouped under a real and logical unity.   In this he contrasts him especially with the authors of the *Cypria* and the *Little Iliad*, and observes that only one, or at most two, tragedies can be derived from the Iliad or from the Odyssey, whereas many can be derived (and indeed were derived) from the *Cypria*, and at least eight, which he mentions, from the *Little Iliad*.   Unfortunately, this latter passage in the *Poetic* (c. 23) is hopelessly corrupt, and conflicts not only with the plain facts of the history of tragedy, but with other statements in this very treatise.   It is said to be absurd (c. 18, § 4) to work the whole Iliad into one tragedy ; it is further asserted (c. 27, § 13) that from any epic poem many tragedies may be formed—an obvious fact, and in accordance with actual literary history.   No doubt ingenious critics have found means of reconciling these inconsistencies; they make Aristotle speak at one time of the central plot only of the Homeric poems; at another of the whole poems, including the episodes; they emend the text, and by these and other contrivances devise a theory which they endeavour to force upon the facts.

I prefer to set aside the criticisms of the *Poetic*, either as not being the genuine text and sense of Aristotle, or else, as showing in that great man such a traditional reverence for the Homeric poems as made him an unsafe critic when they were concerned. The unity of the Iliad is not adequately sustained or highly artistic. Many tragedies could be, and have been, legitimately constructed from it. As far as we can see, the poem of Arctinus was similarly grouped about a central figure —Achilles, whose death was the climax—but introduced important and striking episodes. It is therefore better to refrain from using the so-called authority of Aristotle in this matter.

Colonel Mure, however, arguing from this, and from the low esteem shown by the rest of our authorities, degrades the epic cycle to a series of metrical chronicles maintaining no proper unity, and dealing, moreover, not unfrequently in low and disgusting details. He is no doubt right in showing that the portraiture of many of the tragic heroes, especially of Menelaus and Ulysses, which is so different from that of Homer, comes from the cyclic poems; when he asserts that the poets put themselves forward too prominently, as compared with the self-effacement of Homer, he says what is probable with later poets, but not provable from our fragments. I need not prosecute the matter further, but will conclude by observing that several good critics, such as Welcker and Bernhardy, place Arctinus above the others. They attribute to him the origination of the Amazonian and Ethiopian legends; they see in his fragments seriousness and tragic gloom as compared with the lighter and less dignified Lesches. Beyond this cautious thinkers are now slow to venture. The rest of the cyclic poets are hidden from us in a gloom which only the discovery of a new MS. may some day dispel. Even Quintus Smyrnæus, whose *Posthomerica* cover much of the ground occupied by them, seems not to

have used them diligently, or to have reproduced their treatment.

§ 73. The present place seems the most proper to give an account of the *Batracho-myo-machia* (often cited as μυομαχία for
shortness), or 'Battle of the Frogs and Mice,' which is the only
mock epic remaining to us in early Greek literature, and which,
though it excited little attention of old, has given rise to many
translations and imitations among the Italians and French
since the Renaissance. The poem, as it now exists, consists of 316 hexameters, and though far removed from the
style and power of Homer, to whom it was generally attributed in uncritical days, has more merit than is conceded to
it by recent commentators. By some authorities Pigres, the
son of Artemisia, to whom the *Margites* is also ascribed, is
named as the author—a theory adopted by Baumeister, and
to which I should unhesitatingly subscribe, as the most unlikely tradition in the world to be false, were not Pigres already
reported the author of the *Margites*. This obscure poet may
have been suggested by critics who felt that the work was
not Homer's, and could find no more likely person than the
accredited author of another sportive poem, once called Homeric also. This consideration makes the authorship of Pigres
not improbable, but rather doubtful. There is evidence—from
the familiar allusion to writing at the opening, from the
mention of the cock (v. 193), from the Attic use of the article,
and the frequent shortening of vowels before mute and liquid
(*Atticæ correptiones*, as they are called)—that in the present
form the poem cannot date from a time much earlier than
Æschylus, and that it is, besides, corrupted and interpolated
considerably by far later hands.

The plot is witty, and not badly constructed. A mouse,
after escaping from the pursuit of a cat, is slaking its thirst at a
pond, when it is accosted by a frog, King Puff-cheek, the son
of Peleus (in the sense of muddy), who asks it to come and see
his home and habits. The mouse consents, but the sudden
appearance of an otter terrifies the frog, and makes him dive,
leaving the mouse to perish, after sundry epic exclamations and
soliloquies. A bystanding mouse brings the tidings to the tribe,

who forthwith prepare for war, and arm themselves, sending a formal declaration to the frogs. The deliberations of Zeus and Athena,[1] as to what part they will take in the war, are really comic, and a very clever parody on Homer. Then follows quite an epic

[1] vv. 160–200:

Ὡς ἄρα φωνήσας ὅπλοις ἐνέδυσεν ἅπαντας.
φύλλοις μὲν μαλαχῶν κνήμας ἐὰς ἀμφεκάλυψαν,
θώρηκας δ' εἶχον καλῶν χλοερῶν ἀπὸ σεύτλων,
φύλλα δὲ τῶν κραμβῶν εἰς ἀσπίδας εὖ ἤσκησαν,
ἔγχος δ' ὀξύσχοινος ἑκάστῳ μακρὸς ἀρήρει,
καὶ τὰ κέρα κοχλιῶν λεπτῶν ἐκάλυπτε κάρηνα.
φραξάμενοι δ' ἔστησαν ἐπ' ὄχθης ὑψηλῇσιν,
σείοντες λόγχας, θυμοῦ δ' ἔμπληντο ἕκαστος.

Ζεὺς δὲ θεοὺς καλέσας εἰς οὐρανὸν ἀστερόεντα,
καὶ πολέμου πληθὺν δείξας, κρατερούς τε μαχητάς,
πολλοὺς καὶ μεγάλους ἠδ' ἔγχεα μακρὰ φέροντας,
οἷος Κενταύρων στρατὸς ἔρχεται ἠὲ Γιγάντων,
ἡδὺ γελῶν ἐρέεινε· τίνες βατράχοισιν ἀρωγοὶ
ἢ μυσὶν ἀθανάτων; καὶ 'Αθηναίην προσέειπεν·

Ὦ θύγατερ, μυσὶν ἦ ῥ' ἐπαλεξήσουσα πορεύσῃ;
καὶ γάρ σου κατὰ νηὸν ἀεὶ σκιρτῶσιν ἅπαντες,
κνίσσῃ τερπόμενοι καὶ ἐδέσμασιν ἐκ θυσιάων.

Ὡς ἄρ' ἔφη Κρονίδης· τὸν δὲ προσέειπεν 'Αθήνη·
ὦ πάτερ, οὐκ ἂν πώποτ' ἐγὼ μυσὶ τειρομένοισιν
ἐλθοίην ἐπαρωγός, ἐπεὶ κακὰ πολλά μ' ἔοργαν,
στέμματα βλάπτοντες καὶ λύχνους εἵνεκ' ἐλαίου.
τοῦτο δέ μου λίην ἔδακε φρένας, οἷά μ' ἔρεξαν.
πέπλον μου κατέτρωξαν, ὃν ἐξύφανα καμοῦσα
ἐκ ῥοδάνης λεπτῆς, καὶ στήμονα λεπτὸν ἔνησα,
τρώγλας τ' ἐμποίησαν· ὁ δ' ἠπητής μοι ἐπέστη,
καὶ πράσσει με τόκον· τούτου χάριν ἐξώργισμαι.
χρησαμένη γὰρ ὕφανα, καὶ οὐκ ἔχω ἀνταποδοῦναι.
ἀλλ' οὐδ' ὡς βατράχοισιν ἀρηγέμεν οὐκ ἐθελήσω.
εἰσὶ γὰρ οὐδ' αὐτοὶ φρένας ἔμπεδοι· ἀλλά με πρώην
ἐκ πολέμου ἀνιοῦσαν, ἐπεὶ λίην ἐκοπώθην,
ὕπνου δευομένην, οὐκ εἴασαν θορυβοῦντες,
οὐδ' ὀλίγον καμμῦσαι· ἐγὼ δ' ἄϋπνος κατεκείμην,
τὴν κεφαλὴν ἀλγοῦσα, ἕως ἐβόησεν ἀλέκτωρ.
ἀλλ' ἄγε, παυσώμεσθα, θεοί, τούτοισιν ἀρήγειν,
μή κέ τις ἡμείων τρωθῇ βέλει ὀξυόεντι,
μῆτις καὶ λόγχῃφι τυπῇ δέμας ἠὲ μαχαίρῃ·
εἰσὶ γὰρ ἀγχέμαχοι, καὶ εἰ θεὸς ἀντίος ἔλθοι·
πάντες δ' οὐρανόθεν τερπώμεθα δῆριν ὁρῶντες.

battle, with deliberate inconsistencies, such as the reappearance of several heroes already killed. The frogs are worsted,
and the victorious mice are not even deterred by the thunder
of Zeus, but are presently put to flight by the appearance of an
army of crabs to assist the defeated frogs.

The German destructive critics think the extant poem was
put together from fragments of earlier mock epics of the same
kind. But of this we have no evidence. The opening invocation is that of a Hesiodic bard (addressing the choir of the
Muses from Helicon), and not of a Homerid. Hence it is
not impossible that the idea of such a mock epic originated in
Bœotia (where both frogs and mice must always have been
particularly abundant), and was intended by the didactic and
practical school of Hesiod as a moral reproof of the lighter
and more superstitious Ionic singers. But this is only a conjecture ; the general complexion of the poem, as we have it,
being certainly Attic. The earliest allusion to it in Greek
literature seems to be a sarcasm of Alexander the Great, quoted
by Plutarch in his *Life* (cap. 28). The Alexandrian critics are
silent about it, so far as we know. Several Roman poets under
the Empire—Statius, Martial, and Fulgentius—allude to it as a
relaxation of the great author of the Iliad and Odyssey.

Bibliographical. Our MSS. seem all copied from one archetype of the Byzantine period, ignorantly and carelessly written.
From this Baumeister has shown two families of MSS. to be
derived, one represented by two Bodleian (cod. Baroc. 46 and
64), which are by no means the oldest, but which are tolerably
faithful copies of the archetype, even in its blunders. The
other family is very numerous, and comprises our oldest MSS.,
viz. the Bodleian cod. Baroc. 50 (fol. 358) of the tenth century,
the Laurentian (Plut. xxxii. 3) of the eleventh, a Palatine (at
Heidelberg) of the twelfth, and an Ambrosian (i. 4, super) of
the thirteenth. There are many of the fourteenth century.
These are deliberately interpolated and emended by scribes
endeavouring to restore or improve the original. Some twenty
have been collated, and at least thirty more still await investigation. This family of MSS. shows a decomposition of the
text almost without parallel, as may be seen from a glance at

Baumeister's edition. Most of them have copious scholia and notes by Byzantine grammarians. Those of Moschopulos, if they indeed exist (cf. Baumeister, p. 10), are as yet un-published. The earliest translation is by Sommariva, dated Verona, 1470, but the date is rejected as spurious by Giuliari, the learned historian of Veronese typography. There is a translation into low Greek by Demetrius Zenas, in 1534 (re-printed in Ilgen, and by Mullach, Berlin, 1837), which shows the text he used to be not different from ours. The book was first printed, in alternate black and red lines, at Venice in 1486 [1] —the first Greek classic ever printed—and this very rare edition was imitated (only as to colours) by Mich. Mattaire, in his edition with notes (London, 1721). The Florentine Homer of 1488 is the basis of most following editions, e.g. those of Ilgen (with the Hymns, 1796), Matthiæ, F. A. Wolf, who asserted our text to be a mere conglomerate, Bothe, Frank, and, lastly, Baumeister (Göttingen, 1852), whose little book is a model of care and diligence, and whose account of the text seems very complete, except that he does not specify the age of any of the MSS. which he discusses. Since the Renaissance the poem has excited a good deal of attention, Melanchthon and others imagining a hidden political or moral import under its parody. There is a spirited old translation by George Chapman, re-printed by J. Russell Smith (London, 1858).

§ 74. The 'beast-epic' we have been considering suggests naturally a more general inquiry into the occurrence of beast-fables in Greek literature. This form of imagination was, on the whole, foreign to the Greeks, and there are many indications that the supposed father of fable, Æsop, was a Syrian, Phrygian, or Æthiopian. Some have argued that he was an Egyptian. Nevertheless the fable, originally called αἶνος, though not fre-quent, is found at intervals in various kinds of Greek poetry. We have in Hesiod the fable of the falcon and dove ; in Stesi-chorus, that of the horse and his rider ; in Archilochus, stories

---

[1] Per *Leonicum Cretensem.* There is a beautiful copy in Earl Spencer's library at Althorp. The grammar of Lascaris, the Milan Æsop, and a Greek and Latin Psalter of 1481 are the only earlier books (not *quotations*) in Greek type which I can find. They are all to be seen in the Althorp library.

about the fox ; in the elder Simonides, sketches of character
derived from various animals ; in Æschylus, the Libyan fable
which Byron has so well adapted in his lines *on Kirke White.*

Though Hesiod was named as the earliest poet who used
this form of apologue, its invention was systematically attributed to Æsop, an obscure and perhaps mythical figure, whose
historical reality is now generally rejected since the searching
article on this subject by Welcker.[1] Nevertheless, Herodotus
speaks of him as a slave at Samos in the sixth century. Aristophanes and Plato both speak of Æsopic jokes as a distinct
kind of fun, and Aristotle tells of his murder by the Delphians
having been atoned with great difficulty by the special command of the oracle. It was added that Æsop came to life again,
owing to his piety.[2] In spite of these definite allusions, the
list of which is by no means complete, we cannot fix either the
age or nationality of this strange personage, whom later art
represented a hideous and deformed creature, perhaps to
indicate his nearer approach to the lower animals, and his
peculiar sympathy for their habits. Such is the conception of the
famous statue now in the Villa Albani at Rome.

This side of literature, however, long remained a mere
amusement in society, or among the ignorant classes, nor can
we regard such a literary work as Aristophanes' *Birds* or the
Myomachia in any other light than a most exceptional product.[3]
When original power was failing, and men began to collect the
works of their predecessors, we hear that Demetrius Phalereus
made the first written *corpus* of these popular stories, no doubt
in their rude prose form. Then we find that Callimachus
sought to give them a literary tone by adapting them in choli-
ambic metre, no doubt the best metrical form which could
have been selected.

But so little prominence did he give to this side of his

[1] *Rhein. Mus.* vi. 366, sq.

[2] Cf. Herodotus, ii. 134; Aristoph. *Vesp.* 1258, 1437, and schol.; Plato,
Phædo, 60 D, Aristotle, *Frag.* 445; Æschylus, *Frag.* 129.

[3] Our early allusions seem to distinguish Libyan, Sybaritic, Syrian,
&c. from Æsopic, but ultimately λόγος Αἰσώπειος becomes the recognised
expression for a beast fable.

multiform literary activity, that Babrius, who came much later, was justly regarded as the originator of the metrical fable. This remarkable author, of unknown date,[1] and not cited by early grammarians, was only known by Suidas' fragmentary quotations until the discovery of two MSS. of his works at Mount Athos by Minas, about 1840. The name of the discoverer naturally suggested doubts as to the genuineness of the discovery, but according to Dindorf (*Philol.* xvii. pp. 321, sq.) there is no mistake about the first; the second is probably a compilation by Minas from preexisting fragments. Both texts were printed by Sir G. Lewis (Oxon. 1846 ; London, 1859), but Boissonade's (Paris, 1844) is the *editio princeps*, and Lachmann's the best, at least of the former MS. The literary merit of Babrius is very considerable, though he does not belong to the classical period. As for the Æsopic fables, they were variously collected in later days, and are preserved in many MSS. throughout Europe. The collection of the monk Planudes, with a life of Æsop, was printed among the very earliest Greek books (Milan, Bonus Accursius, perhaps as early as 1479); the latest is Klotz's (Leipzig, 1810). There are besides de Furia's, Coraes' and Schneider's collections, all printed about 1810. There is a new edition of Babrius announced by Mr. W. G. Rutherford, but it has not yet appeared.

---

[1] Otto Crusius (*Leipzig. Stud.* ii. 2, p. 125) has argued that he was a Roman, and that he lived in the 3rd cent. A.D.

CHAPTER VII.

THE DIDACTIC EPOS.   HESIOD—THE EARLY PHILOSOPHERS.

§ 75. GREAT as is the divergence of critics about the Homeric poems, it seems almost unanimity when we come to study the modern Hesiodic literature. Every possible theory, every possible critical judgment has been upheld and refuted; so that, after toiling through wildernesses of German books, and tracts, and programs, one comes to the conclusion that nothing has been gained, nothing proved, and that the field is still open to plain common sense, as well as to new flights of fancy.

The home of this distinct kind of epic poetry, called *Didactic*, because of its occasionally moral and instructive tone, was not originally[1] a sea-coast, with bays, and promontories, and rocky islands, but the inland of Bœotia, surrounded on all sides by mountain chains, with rich arable soil in the plain, and light pastures on the higher slopes; with great sedgy sheets of still water about the lowlands, and streams tumbling from the hills. It was a climate, says the poet of the *Works and Days*, bad in winter, trying in summer, never good; and this he says, contrasting it, I suppose, with what his father told him, or what he himself remembered of Æolic Kyme, upon the rich shore of Asia Minor, where the climate of old was wonderful even to the Greeks. But he has certainly exaggerated the faults of the weather, and said nothing of the richness of the soil.[2] Yet no doubt the extremes of cold and heat were

---

[1] I say *originally*, because Bergk follows the traditions of the poet's death, so far as to hold his ultimate settlement at Naupactus, and to call his school the Locrian School, of which the ἔπη Ναυπάκτια were a further development.

[2] It is worthy of note that Archilochus, with similar injustice, reviles

then greater than they now are, for in our time Bœotia is one of the loveliest and most fertile parts of Greece. The inhabitants came to be ridiculed in the days of Attic greatness for heavy eating, and for their dulness and stupidity—consequences attributed to their moist and foggy climate. Such Attic jibes have been repeated with too much seriousness. The ancient worship of the Muses throughout Bœotia, the splendour of the art and culture of the old Minyans of Orchomenus, the great burst of lyric poetry in the days of the Persian wars, the broad culture of Epaminondas, and through him of Philip, and lastly, the martinmas summer[1] of Greek literature in Plutarch—all these facts, apart from the poetry now before us, show that Bœotia, as we might expect from its rich and well-watered soil, was not only an early home of wealth and civilisation, but sustained its intellectual reputation all through Greek history.

Assuming the *Works and Days* to be the product of the genuine Hesiod, we look in vain for any certain clue to the exact period of the poet's life. The only direct allusion is to his having journeyed to Chalcis in Eubœa for a poetical contest at the funeral games given for Amphidamas, at which he claims to have carried off the prize.[2] But the only clue to the date of Amphidamas is that he was an active leader in the

the climate and soil of Thasos (fr. 21, ed. Bergk), for Plutarch says :—
καθάπερ 'Αρχίλοχος τῆς Θάσου τὰ καρποφόρα καὶ οἰνόπεδα παρορῶν διὰ τὸ τραχὺ καὶ ἀνώμαλον διέβαλε τὴν νῆσον, εἰπών·

"Ἥδε δ' ὥστ' ὄνου ῥάχις
ἕστηκεν ὕλης ἀγρίης ἐπιστεφής·
οὐ γάρ τι καλὸς χῶρος οὐδ' ἐφίμερος
οὐδ' ἐρατός, οἷος ἀμφὶ Σίριος ῥοάς.

Plutarch might have said the very same thing of Hesiod, unless, indeed, we hold that the plain of Thebes was covered with forest in old times, as is described in the Homeric Hymn to the Pythian Apollo.

[1] Cf. Archbp. Trench's *Plutarch and his Age*, p. 11, from whom I gladly borrow the expression. Thus also Mr. Symonds aptly calls the *Hero and Leander* of Musæus the fair November day of Greek poetry.

[2] This contest is apparently transferred to Delos, and described as consisting in singing hymns to Apollo, in frag. 227. We shall return to this point when speaking of the Hymns.

tedious war against the Eretrians about the Lelantine plain.[1]
This passage about the poetical tournament at Chalcis is
accordingly declared spurious by most critics, and referred to
some later Hesiodic bard, who was confused with his great
predecessor, just as the blind old poet of Chios (in the Hymn
to the Delian Apollo) was commonly confused with Homer.
Setting aside, therefore, this hint, they are thrown back upon
vaguer inferences.

The poet describes no monarchy, but an aristocratical
government, as ruling over his native place.   This Ascra was
probably under the sway of Thespiæ, which maintained its
aristocratical government up to late days, so as to be even in
Aristotle's time a remarkable example for citation.   It is said
that royalty was abolished at Thebes about the middle of the
eighth century B.C.; but it is doubtful whether Thebes then
controlled a large district.   The fact that Hesiod's father [2]
came back from the Æolian settlements in Asia Minor—and
on account of poverty—suggests that the colonies had been
some time sent out; yet not so long that discontented colonists
had forgotten the way home, or their sense of unity with the
motherland.   But the poem is so full of evident interpolations,
that many critics reject even this personal statement about the
poet's parentage, and think that a later bard inserted it, in
order to inform the readers of the poem about the supposed
author's life.

§ 76. From a conservative point of view, the following
seems to me the most reasonable theory as to the composition
and date of the *Works and Days.*

It is an admitted fact, that about the beginning of the
seventh century, B.C., the heroic epics of the Greeks were
being supplanted by the poetry of real life—iambic satire,
elegiac confessions, gnomic wisdom, and proverbial philo-

---

[1] Cf. Göttling's Pref., p. xxiii, who quotes Plutarch's *Convivium* (c. 10),
with additional details.   But the genuineness and authority of this tract
is denied by F. Nietzsche (*Rhein. Mus.* vol. xxvi.) in his critical examination of the legends of Hesiod's life.

[2] That his name was Dius seems more than doubtful.   Cf. H. Flach
in *Hermes* for 1874, p. 358.

sophy. The Greeks grew tired of all the praise of courts and ladies and bygone wars, and turned to a sober—nay even exaggerated—realism, by way of reaction from the worship of Homeric rhapsody. The father and forerunner of all this school is clearly Hesiod, to whom the critics have found strong family likenesses in Archilochus, Simonides of Amorgos, and Hipponax, and stronger evidences of imitation in Alcæus and Theognis. The Odyssey, on the other side, both in the society which it describes—the lawless rule of an aristocratic oligarchy; in its catalogue of fair women, the prototype, or antitype, of the Hesiodic *Eoiai;* still more, in the sober tone of its diction, and in its enumerations of names, the Ἡσιόδειος χαρακτὴρ κατ' ὄνομα of the Alexandrian critics—seems the foretaste, or perhaps the heroic expression, of this changing temper in the public mind. The decisive turning point, to my mind a marked epoch in the history of Greek literature, is the great poetical contest at the funeral games of Amphidamas of Chalcis, when the Hesiodic poetry defeated its Homeric rival. This fact seemed so extraordinary to later critics, that, when they wrote the life of Hesiod, and the *Contest of Homer and Hesiod,* they sought to invent reasons—and very absurd ones they were—for such a result, and the judges (whose names were remembered) were held up to ridicule.[1]

Yet a more philosophical review of the development of Greek poetry shows such a result to be natural and necessary. The Greek public was presented with so many weak and watery epics, with so many faint imitations of the great originals, that even these lost their charm, and were a weariness to them. Then it was that a truly original poet again turned his attention to the only real source of life in any literature—the songs and shrewd sayings of the people. He found old gnomes and advices about practical life, rules of agriculture and of morals fused like the Roman lady's distaff and her chastity.[2] He recast them in an artistic form, retaining suffi-

---

[1] Πανείδου ψῆφος was a proverb for a foolish judgment, Paneides, the brother of Amphidamas, being named as the judge on the occasion.

[2] This we find in many Roman epitaphs, e.g. those quoted by Mommsen, *Rom. Hist.* vol. I. p. 61, *note* (Eng. Trans.).

cient flavour of their rudeness to preserve their charm for audiences weary of heroic refinement.   Thus arose the famous *Works and Days*, the homely rival of Homeric song, the parent of Greek gnomic poetry, the great hand-book of moral teaching among Greek educators.   The man who gathered and systematised this old folk lore and folk wisdom— who combined Ionic treatment with a Bœotian subject—who tamed the rude dialect of the farmers on Helicon into an almost epic style—who carried back Ionic memories to his rugged home—who won the tripod at the national contest of Chalcis—who then settled near Naupaetus, and died there— this was the real Hesiod.   He was not removed by centuries from the poetry which directly followed his lead.   He was rather the first of a close and continuous series of poets who took up his realism, though they freed it from its 'Helot' flavour, left out his husbandry and his addresses to rustics, and gave his ethics an aristocratic tone.

Even as to the Hesiod whom we possess, I cannot be-lieve that he was the poet of the lower classes, and that his great originality was to address the people.   No doubt many of the old proverbs and agricultural advices he gathered were current among the people ; but it is to be remarked that the poet distinctly addresses princes also, and gives them a moral lecture (vv. 248, sq.) ; he looks upon their justice and good conduct as essential to the people, not only because they are its judges, but because their sins are visited by Zeus upon the whole people.   This view is to be found in the Iliad.   Neither does Hesiod speak more harshly of these princes than does the poet of the Odyssey in his picture of the suitors.   No princes are attacked or lightly spoken of except for their injustice.   All this is consistent with an age when an increasing population made agriculture more im-portant, and when the better members among the ruling aris-tocrats wished to encourage justice and diligence, not only in their subjects, but in their thoughtless or dissipated equals. The high and noble view of the unity and justice of the Supreme Governor of the world—to the complete exclusion of lesser deities—is the most striking feature of the poem, and its most curious contrast to the *Theogony*. The shepherd class, by the way, is there treated with contempt.

§ 77. The poet of the *Works* seems to me to have lived about the middle of the seventh century, B.C. Here are my reasons :—

The return of his father from Kyme—from a rich and fertile sea-coast to a poor and barren upland farm—can only be accounted for by some grave misfortune or decay in the prosperity of the Asiatic colonies. This is most easily to be found in the rise of the Lydian power under Gyges, after the opening of the seventh century. According to Strabo and Nicolaus Damasc.,[1] this king possessed the whole Troad as far as Abydos, and therefore must have possessed the intermediate territory, which included the inland country round Kyme. The father of the poet seems to have taken at first to sea traffic, but with little satisfaction; and thus, as his agricultural prospects were spoiled by the Lydian conquest, he would ultimately return to Bœotia, from which we may conceive his forefathers to have originally set out.

This chronological argument is evidently strengthened by the further allusion to the games at Chalcis—probably near the conclusion of the Lelantine war. Chalcis and Eretria, which contended for the possession of the disputed plain, were then by their commerce two of the leading cities of Greece Proper. They were founding colonies all over the northern Ægean and the Hellespont. Their war became so important, that all mercantile Greece, especially Samos and Miletus,[2] joined in the fray. These facts have led historians to see in this war a great commercial conflict ; and therefore to place it in the days of the great Hellenic colonisation—about the beginning of the seventh century. If my argument be correct, we must bring it down some fifty years, or at least we must bring down the death of Amphidamas, the 'king' of Chalcis, to a period after the Lydian pressure had been for

---

[1] Quoted by Grote, iii. p. 303 (orig. ed.). Gyges reigned about 680 B.C.

[2] Herodotus says (bk. v. 99) that the Eretrians were repaying (in 500 B.C.) a debt to the Milesians for helping them previously. It seems absurd to imagine this obligation incurred more than 200 years before.

some time felt.[1]   But there is no difficulty in doing so, and
E. Curtius' date for the Lelantine war (704 B.C.) is only, I
should think, a tentative one, and based on the received dates
for the principal colonies, which are all, I suspect, at least a
generation too early.   But to prove this would lead us too far
from our literary history.[2]

It remains to notice what can be said against this theory,
which brings down the date of Hesiod so low, and what evidence there is of his greater antiquity.   I pass by the argument of Bergk,[3] who says that Hesiod must have preceded
the 1st Olympiad in date, because Eumelus of Corinth, who
is said to have been active about Ol. 10, would else be the
leader of this school of poetry, whereas he clearly follows
Hesiod.   This argument contains nothing but ungrounded
assumptions.   We know nothing of Eumelus, except that all
the works attributed to him (save one lyric *prosodion*)—that
is to say, the only works which may have been Hesiodic in
character—were thought spurious by Pausanias.   His date is
unknown ; his very personality hazy and doubtful.

§ 78.   There is indeed a general belief in the primitiveness of
Hesiod, and a desire to place him far anterior to the historical
poets of the seventh century ; but this also rests on no basis of
any value, except the statement of Herodotus, whose real intention was not to raise, but to lower, the date of Homer and Hesiod.   They lived, says he, four hundred years before my time,
and *not more*.   But unfortunately he made them contemporary,
and this takes greatly from his authority about Hesiod : for it
has been made quite plain by modern criticism that Hesiod presupposes Homer, and is therefore posterior.   Of this there is

---

[1] I think the allusion in Theognis (v. 891) to the ravaging of the Lelantine plain must refer to this Lelantine war as contemporary, and must
be an older fragment transferred to the conglomerate which now passes
under his name.   Indeed, the date of Theognis is not very certain;
but most critics place him about 560 B.C.   The lines make the war
contemporary with the Cypselids, and therefore not concluded before
657 B.C.

[2] See the evidence for the Lelantine war brought together and discussed
in the Appendix to my article on Hesiod in *Hermathena*, No. IV. p. 325.

[3] *LG.* i. p. 937.

one clear proof.   I put no stress on the shortening of syllables, or other linguistic evidences, as the dialect of Hesiod is not the same as that of the Ionic School, and therefore what seem later modifications may be original differences.   But in the description of the Four Ages of Man—the Gold, the Silver, the Bronze, and the Iron—the gradual decadence is broken in upon (after the Bronze) by a fifth race, apparently better than two of its predecessors—that of the heroes who fought and died at the wars of Thebes[1] and Troy.   It is evident that no historical place could be found for them, nor were they admitted in the legend which compared the succeeding races of men to the metals.   But so powerful was the effect of the Heroic epics, that the shrewd poet of the *Works* thought it necessary to find a niche for this race in his Temple of Fame ; and so the legend was distorted to admit them as a fifth race, created out of due time by the Father of gods and of men.[2]   This fact in itself would prove that Homer was considerably anterior to Hesiod, if it were not already perfectly plain to anyone who has studied the logical development of Greek literature.   If any critic urges the primitive complexion of many of the saws of Hesiod in defence of his antiquity, I will remind him that my theory postulates this very thing—the adoption, by the historical Hesiod of the seventh century, of all the fine old sayings which floated among the people.   I will even concede that there was an earlier collection[3] : but it seems to me impossible

[1] This seems to imply that the epics based on the Theban cycle of myths were already composed, and widely celebrated—a condition of things pointing to a date after 700 B.C.   But the passage *may* be interpolated.

[2] It is to be noted that the old legends of both Iranians and Indians contain accounts of *five* races of anterior men, and it is not difficult to find a similar division underlying the Semitic history in Genesis.   It is, therefore, probable enough that the oldest Greek legends told of *five* races, and that the number was no novelty invented by the poet.   But admitting this, the distortion of the legend to suit the glories of the epic heroes of Troy and Thebes is the more remarkable, and an even clearer proof of the reputation of Homer and his school.   In all the other legends of five races the decline of excellence seems to be gradual.

[3] The enigmatical epitaph ascribed (on Aristotle's authority) to Pindar,

χαῖρε δὶς ἡβήσας καὶ δὶς τάφου ἀντιβολήσας
'Ησίοδ', ἀνθρώποις μέτρον ἔχων σοφίης,

to detect it and separate it from the later materials.   It is also clearly to be admitted that when the poems came to be used as handbooks of education, many wise and useful proverbs were foisted in, some from later, some from earlier, authors.   There is evidence of distinctly inconsistent proverbs being thus brought together, as we find it perpetually the case in the very similar poet, Theognis.   The very best lines of this kind being probably those chosen for the purpose, it is surely a perfectly idle proceeding to endeavour to restore the original poem by picking out the good lines, and rejecting what appears to be inferior or weak.   The taste of the German critics who have attempted this is not beyond cavil, and they, of course, differ widely from one another in their æsthetic judgments ; but, without disputing these, we may hold fairly that many a line may be interpolated, *because* it is good and striking, and that many a line has held its place, in spite of its weakness, because it was acknowledged by tradition as genuine. Nothing can be more absurd than to argue that, because a poet is a great poet, all that he composes must be great, or even consistent with itself.   If, as I believe, the original Hesiod compiled from older materials, perhaps not very easily fused ; and if most of the interpolations which the critics allege are by them admitted to be so ancient, that the poems were not much different in Plato's day from their present form, it is surely idle to attempt the separation of these various strata.   The procems of both *Works* and *Theogony* may be rejected on fair evidence, and I think there has been patching clearly detected in the long procem of the latter ; but beyond this we can reject with certainty only a very few passages.   We may suspect a great many, but have no sufficient evidence to condemn them.

§ 79. Before proceeding to an analysis of the extant works of Hesiod, a word should be said about the legends of his death,

---

is only explicable, according to Göttling (pref. ad Hes. p. 13), by assuming two Hesiods, of whom two tombs were shown.   The Orchomenians admitted this, but said that the bones had been transferred from Naupactus (or from Ascra), owing to an oracle.   But as Aristotle is speaking only of a second tomb, I suspect ἡβήσας, in spite of the fitness in form, to be a spurious word, concealing some quite different sense.

preserved at length in the γένος Ἡσιόδου of Tzetzes, and the ἀγών. After his alleged victory at Chalcis he went to Delphi, where the oracle told him to avoid the fair grove of Nemea, where the goal of death was destined for him.[1] Accordingly, avoiding the Nemea in Peloponnesus, he went to live at Œnoe in Locris, near Naupactus, with Amphidamas and Ganyctor, sons of Phegeus. The coincidence of name with the king of Chalcis at the games is curious. These men, accusing him of having seduced their sister Clymene, murdered him, and threw him into the sea ; but the body came to land on the shore between Locris and Eubœa (apparently a confusion between the two separate countries called Locris), and was buried at the sacred grove of Nemea in Œnoe. The people of Orchomenus afterwards removed the body, by advice of an oracle, and buried it in the middle of their *agora*. The epitaph on this tomb has been quoted above.[2] I should not mention these apparently late fables, but that they were (partly at least) known and alluded to by Thucydides.[3]

§ 80. The Ἔργα of Hesiod, as it seems to have been once called, without the addition of ἡμέραι, comprises ethics and husbandry in about equal portions, including husbandry under what the Greeks called *Œconomics* ; it directs the choice of a wife, the management of the house, and the observation of

[1]
ὄλβιος οὗτος ἀνὴρ ὃς ἐμὸν δόμον ἀμφιπολεύει
Ἡσίοδος, Μούσῃσι τετιμένος ἀθανάτῃσι·
τοῦ δή τοι κλέος ἔσται ὅσην ἐπικίδναται Ἠώς.
ἀλλὰ Διὸς πεφύλαξο Νεμείου κάλλιμον ἄλσος·
κεῖθι δέ τοι θανάτοιο τέλος πεπρωμένον ἐστίν.

[2] The age and character of these legends has been carefully discussed by F. Nietzsche in his second article on the ἀγών (*Rhein. Mus.* vol. xxvi.), but without any important positive result, except that of sustaining the ἀγών against the *Convivium* (of Plutarch ?) where they differ.

[3] iii. 96. He says of Demosthenes, αὐλισάμενος δὲ τῷ στρατῷ ἐν τοῦ Διὸς τοῦ Νεμείου τῷ ἱερῷ, ἐν ᾧ Ἡσίοδος ὁ ποιητὴς λέγεται ὑπὸ τῶν ταύτῃ ἀποθανεῖν, χρησθὲν αὐτῷ ἐν Νεμέᾳ τοῦτο παθεῖν. Pausanias also mentions that it was doubted in his day whether Hesiod was falsely accused of the crime or not. Aristotle is referred to in his πολ. Ὀρχ. (Müller, FHG. ii. p. 144) as stating (though perhaps only as a tradition) that Stesichorus was his son by Clymene—a legend which certainly brings the date of Hesiod near the very time here suggested.

ordinary morality and superstition. The first ten lines of the exordium were rejected even by the ancients.[1] The address to the *Princes* about their injustice (248–73) is the only part of the poem which could possibly be classed under the head of *politics*, and I think improperly; it is strictly ethical, but not addressed, like the rest, to Perses. The œconomics, on the choice of a wife (695–705), are trifling compared to the advices on husbandry (383–617), from which the whole poem took its name. Then follow advices on coast-trading (618–94), and a calendar of lucky and unlucky days (v. 765 to the end). In addition to these principal parts, there are three remarkable episodes—that of Pandora (47–105); that which immediately follows, on the Five (or Four?) Ages of Man; and, lastly, the picturesque description of winter (524–58), which many of the Germans consider a very late and Ionic addition to the grave soberness of the *Works*, breathing a spirit of levity and of display. In these three episodes, Perses is not addressed, nor is he mentioned in the calendar. This latter portion, especially, which consists of brief, disconnected sentences, shows evidence of much interpolation, though it is impossible to expose it. As to the larger episodes opinions vary considerably, each of them being attacked and defended by able scholars. The *proverbial* character of the whole composition is clear from (*a*) its many short and disconnected sentences, which are in one passage (vv. 300, sq.) only strung together because of the recurrence in them of the root ἐργ in various forms.[2] This attention to sound has been shown to exist all through the Hesiodic poems by Göttling, in the form of (β) alliteration. Many of the successive advices are, furthermore, plainly (γ) inconsistent, as is always the case with proverbial collections of wisdom.

On my theory, this question of genuineness will assume a somewhat different form. The Hesiod of the seventh century—

---

[1] The strictly *ethical* parts are vv. 11–46, 202–47, 274–382, 708–64. I quote from the text of Göttling, who also gives this analysis.

[2] The same peculiarity is to be observed, however, without any such cause, or without the word being of much importance, in the Homeric Hymn to Aphrodite (6–16). Cf. Göttling's Preface, p. 33.

bringing together older materials, loosely and without strict logical nexus—would not be very nice in selecting fragments of
precisely the same age and character ; he would naturally adorn
the dry and sour apophthegms of the Bœotian farmers with episodes of semi-ethical, semi-mythological import. The description of winter is most likely his own, and a most natural description for any man who remembered, or had heard of, the splendid
climate of Asia Minor, and who suffered from the severity of
his adopted home. But the search after special interpolations
is rather a matter of caprice, and of ingenuity, than of literary
history ; and I therefore refer the reader to the special tracts
on the subject.[1]

§ 81. The general character of the *Works* is that of a
shrewd and somewhat mean society, where private interest is the
paramount object, and the ultimate test of morals ; but where
the poor and undefended man sees plainly that religion
and justice, however in themselves respectable, are of value
as affording his only chance of safety. The attainment of
comfort, or of wealth, seems the only object in view—the
distrust of kinsmen and friends seems widely spread—the
whole of the social scheme seems awry, and in a decaying
condition. All the faults of the Greek character, which come
out so strongly in after history, are there, and even obtrusive.
The picture of the Iron Age (vv. 180, sq.) contains every one
of the features so striking in Thucydides' famous picture (iii.
82) of the fourth century Greeks. Nevertheless, the poet
strongly asserts the moral government of the world, and his
Zeus is an All-wise and All-knowing Ruler, far removed from
the foibles and the passions of the Homeric type. While he
mentions the usual evils of poverty—mendicancy and nightly
thieving—it is remarkable that he never alludes practically to the horrors of war, or the risk of slavery, from either

---

[1] Viz. :—A. Twesten, *Comm. Crit. de O. et D.* (Kil., 1815).

F. Thiersch, *De Gnom. Carm. Græc.* (*Abh. Bair. Akad.* iii. p. 391).

C. Lehrs, *Questiones Epicæ* (Königsberg, 1837).

T. L. Heyer, *De Hes. O. et D.* (Schwerin, 1848).

J. Hetzel. *De Carm. Hes. Disp.* (Weilburg, 1860).

A. Steitz, *Die Werke, &c., des Hesiodos* (Leipzig, 1869).

this cause or from piracy.   It is, indeed, doubtful whether any of the farm-servants mentioned are slaves, and not rather hired labourers, working for the owner of a freehold farm.[1]

The poetical merit of the work has generally been under-estimated, owing to a tacit comparison with Homer.   In the epi-sodes on the Ages of Man, and the description of winter, there is much fine and vigorous painting, and even in the homely parts there are quaint and happy thoughts, expressed in terse and suitable words.   I would specially point to the picture (v. 448) of the farmer hearing the annual scream of the crane in the clouds, and feeling a pang at his heart if he has no oxen to begin his ploughing.[2]

There is no advice upon wheat-growing, and little on vine-yards, though the making of wine is assumed as an ordinary thing among the Bœotian farmers (vv. 611–4) ; nor is there a word about horses, which were kept only by the nobles.   The

---

[1] I have no doubt about the meaning of the disputed lines (600, sq.) :

$$\text{αὐτὰρ ἐπὴν δὴ}$$
$$\text{πάντα βίον κατάθηαι ἐπάρμενον ἔνδοθι οἴκου,}$$
$$\text{θῆτά τ' ἄοικον ποιεῖσθαι, καὶ ἄτεκνον ἔριθον}$$
$$\text{δίζεσθαι κέλομαι· χαλεπὴ δ' ὑπόπορτις ἔριθος.}$$

Most of the critics translate, 'Procure a day-labourer who has no house [and family],' and as they cannot see why such a servant should be sought when the main work is over, they proceed to strike out the lines, or transfer them elsewhere.   This seems to me a good instance of rash scepticism. Hesiod throughout supposes that the farmer has one or more farm-servants (cf. vv. 441, 503, 608).   There is always work to be done, as appears from the succeeding verses.   The line must, therefore, be taken strictly with the preceding, and rendered, ' When you have brought all your stores into the house, you must turn your man-servant out of it, and look out for a woman servant (who still sleeps within) who has no child to feed.'   The repetition of οἶκος, which here means *barn*, appears conclusive, and so is the different verb used for the change of residence in one servant, and the pro-curing of another.   This proceeding is, furthermore, recommended *at the beginning of the hot weather*, when sleeping in the open air, or under any natural shelter, is in the climate of Greece no hardship, and not unusual.

[2] The terms φερέοικος, ἡμερόκοιτος, πέντοζος, ἀνόστεος, are noted by the commentators, with a few similar formations in Æschylus, as evidences of what they consider an oracular or religious style.

absence of all advice on manuring struck even the Romans,[1] and can hardly be explained by the causes which permit the same omission in the present farming of Bœotia, where the population is so sparse that the land is not occupied, and the husbandman can shift his crop yearly to a piece of ground which has lain fallow the previous season. Such a state of things could hardly have escaped mention through so many details as we find in the *Works*.

§ 82. The *Theogony*, also called the *Genealogy* of Hesiod, and really an abstract of cosmogony, was acknowledged by all antiquity, including Heracleitus and Plato, as the work of Hesiod, until it was called in question by Pausanias, who states that the Bœotians about Helicon admitted the genuineness of the *Works* only, excluding the preface. He himself, in various places, adopts this opinion as his own, but his reasons, or those of his authorities, are nowhere given. It seems very remarkable (as Göttling notes), that in the list of Greek rivers no mention is made of any Bœotian rivers, even of the Cephissus, which is an important stream, and which was mentioned repeatedly in other poems attributed to Hesiod.[2] Thus the special legends of Bœotia would seem strangely neglected by its national poet.

A careful comparison of the two poems will, however, incline us, if we abandon the preface of the *Theogony*, along with that of the *Works*, to pronounce both poems the work of the same author. The subjects are so diverse that constant similarities are hardly to be expected. Nevertheless, Steitz has carefully collected[3] so many natural and undesigned likenesses in expression, as almost to persuade himself, in spite of his very sceptical turn of mind. There are, in addition, whole passages of still stronger resemblance. The story of Prometheus and Pandora is told in both poems, but with such variations that it is not possible to determine which is the original, so that we must regard them as independent copies of an older account. There is added in the *Theogony*

---

[1] In Xenophon's *Œconomicus* this essential point is duly discussed.
[2] Cf. vv. 343, sqq. ; fragg. 201-3, Gött.
[3] *Op. cit.* pp. 37, sq.

a satirical picture of the female sex, which is exactly in the tone and spirit of the *Works*. Both poems further agree in their piecemeal character, and seem to be the production of the same sort of poet—a man of considerable taste for collecting what was old and picturesque, but without any genius for composing from his materials a large and uniform plan.

These general features, when corroborated by the tradition of the Greeks so far back as Heracleitus, seem to me stronger than the objections brought by modern critics from contrasts rather in subject than in style.

There seems, in fact, an argument in favour of unity of authorship from the very contrast of subject. The *Works*, a purely ethical and practical poem, intentionally avoids theology, and treats of the Deity in the vaguest and broadest sense, as a single consistent power, ruling the world with justice. The loves and foibles of the gods, as portrayed in Homer and the Hymns, are evidently distasteful to the poet, and opposed to his notions of pure and practical ethics. In his second poem, on the contrary, he goes at length and in detail into the wars, alliances, and other relations of the gods, but distinctly in the sense of a *cosmogony*, not as the prototype of a human society. The violences which Homer attributed to the gods, as beings of like passions with men, are felt vaguely but strongly by the poet of the *Theogony* to be great convulsions of physical nature—such as the early eruption of Ætna, which he pictures under the form of the revolt of Typhœus against Zeus (vv. 820, sq.). We can conceive him then composing the *Theogony* as a sort of supplement to the *Works;* but a supplement already showing the changing attitude of Greek religion, by which it was ultimately dissociated from ethics, and gradually reduced to a mere collection of dogmas and of ritual.

§ 83. The poem begins with 115 lines of invocations to the Muses, which are not well put together, and show clear traces of being a *cento* from various older Procemia, or introductory Hymns, but which contain many passages of considerable beauty. The personal passage about Hesiod himself (vv. 22–35) has been very generally suspected by the critics, but assuredly represents a very old tradition, that he was a shepherd

on the slopes of Helicon.   The Bœotian Muses here distinctly
contrast the lying epics of the Ionic bards with the sober truth
of the school of Helicon (26–7).   There is a very interesting panegyric on Calliope (79–93), in which the eloquence
which she bestows on princes is specially brought out as a
great power in politics and lawsuits.   If there were any allusion
to the Muses as *three* (not as nine), I should be more ready to
agree with the German critics who regard these fragments of
Hymns as very old Bœotian poetry.

After this introduction the poet approaches the genealogies
of the gods, from primeval chaos downward till we come to
demigods and heroes.   The subject is very dry, and the crowds
of names make the poem spiritless and dull as a whole, but
there are frequent passages of strange power and beauty
scattered everywhere through it.   The famous passage describing the Styx shows the poet to have known and appreciated the wild scenery of the river Styx in Arcadia.[1]   The
description of Sleep and Death which immediately precedes
is likewise of great beauty.   The conflict of the gods and
Titans (655, sq.) has a splendid crash and thunder about it,
and is far superior in conception, though inferior in execution,
to the battle of the gods in the Iliad.   The same may be
said of the struggle between Zeus and Typhœus.   At the end
of the legend of Pandora a satirical description of the female
sex is foisted in, which differs widely in character from the subject of the poem, and is closely allied to the extant fragments
of Simonides of Amorgos, and his school.   This passage, if
genuine, would show how the poet ill concealed a shrewd and
bitter temper, in performing what may have been an ungrateful
task, and how the age of iambic satire, and of reflective elegy,
had already commenced.[2]   Some parts of the conclusion have
been tampered with, especially where Latinus and the Tyrrhe-
nians are mentioned, for though Strabo holds that Hesiod
knew Sicily, which supports the theory that he lived after the
settlement of that island by the Greeks about 700 B.C., it is

[1] vv. 775, sq.   This M. É. Burnouf, a most competent observer, testifies (*Lit. grecque*, i. p. 131).

[2] vv. 590, sq.   There are foretastes of this in the *Works*, vv. 701, sq.

absurd to foist upon him any statement about the descent of
Latinus from Ithacan parentage.

§ 84. Very little need here be said of the remaining poem
of 480 lines, attributed to Hesiod, the so-called *Shield of
Heracles*. It begins with an account of the birth of Heracles
and Iphitus, then passes to the conflict of Heracles and Iphitus
with Ares, and an elaborate description of the shield, from
which the poem takes its name. It will be observed that
the hero Heracles is not yet described as armed with a mere
club and lion's skin, but wears the same panoply as his
fellows. The poem was probably intended for recitation at a
contest, and seems to be one of the latest of the productions of
the epic age. Its genuineness was doubted by the Alexandrian
critics, especially Aristophanes, and by Longinus, and they
noted that the first fifty-six lines, which begin abruptly with
ἢ οἵη, were to be found in the fourth book of the *Eoiæ*, or
Catalogue of famous women (attributed to Hesiod), where they
would naturally appear in the history of Alcmena. But the
third preface or ὑπόθεσις, after stating these facts, adds that
Megacles (probably Megacleides), the Athenian, while censuring the merit of the poem, knew it to be genuine. It says that
Apollonius Rhodius supported it on internal evidence, as of
the same authorship with the *Catalogue*, and lastly that
Stesichorus ascribes it to Hesiod. This last authority would be
decisive, did we not suspect the writer of the preface of haste
or inaccuracy.[1]

It has been clearly shown by O. Müller, that-while the
shield of Achilles in Il. Σ is a mere fancy picture, the shield of
Heracles is described from actual observations of plastic productions, and even of favourite subjects which are still extant on
vases. While this must lower the date of the poem, it in-

---

[1] Göttling, who divides the poem into three distinct parts—the oldest,
taken from the *Catalogue of Women*, vv. 1-56; the second, also old, 57-
140 and 317-480; and, lastly, the far later description of the Shield,
141-317—thinks that Stesichorus may have quoted (in his *Cycnus*) from the
second part as a work of Hesiod's, and that some of it may really be such.
This would not establish the present poem to be genuine, but would admit
in it old fragments of the real Hesiod—a most reasonable hypothesis.

creases our sense of the inferiority of the imitator, who could not, with Homer and with actual plastic reliefs before him, imagine a more harmonious piece of work. Almost all the perfections of the grouping in the Iliad are lost, and the terrible and weird are substituted for the exciting and picturesque. in Homer. Had we lost the Iliad, we should doubtless admire many of its features in the copy, but fortunately we are not reduced to this extremity. One passage about the tettix, though not very apposite, has great merit.[1]

It should be added, as regards its ascription to Hesiod, that it resembles both the *Works* and *Theogony* in a great many expressions and phrases, which are collected by Steitz in the work above cited. It seems therefore, that with the hint concerning Stesichorus before us, we must concede to such conservative critics as choose to assert its authenticity, that their case is not hopeless.

§ 85. We turn for a moment to the extant fragments of other works attributed to Hesiod.

Of these Gaisford and Dindorf collected a great many, and by the labours of Marckscheffel, Göttling, Lehmann, and Hermann, the number has been raised to above 200, if we include mere allusions in scholia and commentators. As literature, they have to us no value, and will never be read, as the fragments of the tragic poets may be, for their own sake. Their general character is quite Hesiodic, that is to say, they treat of lists of gods and heroes in a partly genealogical, partly epical, way. They contain a perfect mine of mythological lore, and give the legends and stories of peoples far beyond the range of the ordinary Hellenic world, so that their composition, generally speaking, cannot fall before the epoch of extended Greek colonisation. Though it is false that Homer and Hesiod made the religion of the Greeks, in the sense of establishing

---

[1] vv. 393–9 :

ἦμος δὲ χλοερῷ κυανόπτερος ἠχέτα τέττιξ
ὄζῳ ἐφεζόμενος, θέρος ἀνθρώποισιν ἀείδειν
ἄρχεται, ᾧ τε πόσις καὶ βρῶσις θῆλυς ἐέρση,
καί τε πανημέριός τε καὶ ἠῷος χέει αὐδὴν
ἴδει ἐν αἰνοτάτῳ, ὁπότε χρόα Σείριος ἄζει.

gods and cults, or in altering any old local worships, it seems that Hesiod especially did give to the later *literary* Greeks a *Summa Theologiæ*, to which they referred for the origin and relationships of gods and heroes.

This is especially true of (1) the *Catalogue*, in three books, to which was joined the *Great Eoiai* (ἢ οἵη), or *Catalogue of Women*, in two more books, generally quoted as an independent work.[1] The *Catalogue* was a sort of Greek *Peerage*, and gave the family trees and relationships of the principal Greek heroes, so showing the parentage of the Æolic and Doric nobility. We have a fair idea of the fourth book from the fragment preserved at the opening of the *Shield of Heracles*. The date of the *Eoiai* cannot be determined more accurately than by the allusions quoted from it (a) to the nymph Cyrene, probably, therefore, after the founding of that colony; that of the *Catalogue* by allusions (β) to the Sicilian Ortygia, and (γ) to the fable of Io, which Kirchhoff thinks to have come into vogue about Ol. 30. But all these inferences are very uncertain. (2) The Αἰγίμιος attributed by most people to Hesiod, but by some to Cercops the Milesian, was a poem on the war of Ægimius, King of the Dorians, with Heracles as his ally, against the Lapithæ. It seems to have been mainly intended to bring the Doric conquerors of the Peloponnesus into relation with Heracles, through their chiefs, who boasted of their descent from him. (3) The Κήυκος γάμος was also a poem introducing Heracles as a leading character, and celebrating his exploits. (4) The Μελαμποδία was about Melampus, Teiresias, Calchas, and other famous prophet-priests, and may have contained some account of the history of prophecy.

§ 86. It was evidently owing to this poem that its supposed author, Hesiod, was considered the forerunner of the Orphic mystical school. Of his successors in this direction we have, besides Orpheus, Eumolpus, Musæus, and Epimenides, but to us these are mere names. In the genealogical and mythological direction, we have, similarly, the Laconian Kinæthon, Asius, Chersias of Orchomenus, the Corinthian Eumelus (Κορινθιακά),

---

[1] In Locris, the probable home of this poem, the importance of female ancestry (the primitive *Mutterrecht*) long survived. Cf. Bergk, *LG.* i. p. 1002.

the anonymous authors of the Ναυπάκτια ἔπη, Ἀργολικά, and the Φορωνίς, and others who were not apparently in any contact with the Ionic epic, but Hesiodic in character.

The Ἀριμάσπεια by Aristeas of Proconnesus was, on the contrary, a collection of fantastic fables about nations and countries beyond the knowledge, but within the rumour and the imagination, of the early Ionic adventurers into strange seas and coasts. There was, indeed, a supposed *journey round the world*, or γῆς περίοδος, ascribed to Hesiod, but probably of later origin.[1] A few lines are also preserved of the Χείρωνος ὑποθῆκαι, a set of moral instructions supposed to be given by Cheiron to Achilles, and which Quintilian says were thought Hesiod's till pronounced spurious by Aristophanes of Byzantium.[2]

§ 87. It remains to give a short sketch of the external history of the Hesiodic poems through antiquity, and down to our own day. It is very hard to say whether the strong family likeness in Archilochus to Hesiod arises from a similarity in tone and style, or from direct contact. The extant fragments are not sufficient to prove the latter, which would hardly place Hesiod at an earlier date than I am disposed to accord him. But if he were an earlier contemporary, and living in a parallel state of things, general similarities might be expected. Archilochus told beast fables like that in Hesiod. He unjustly reviles[3] the climate of Thasos and its barrenness, in contrast to the valley of the Siris, just as Hesiod censures the rich Bœotia, as compared with Kyme. Yet there is no proof of borrowing. The same may be said as regards Simonides of Amorgos, whom the critics place, doubtfully, in the middle of

---

[1] It is cited by Strabo, vii. p. 302, and there is also an *astronomy*, cited by Plutarch and Pliny.

[2] Of all these fragments there are several collections, of which those by Düntzer (Köln, 1840-41), by Marckscheffel (Lips. 1840, which also contains the fragments of the other authors above alluded to), by Göttling (appendix to his *Hesiod*, ed. 2, Gotha, 1843), and by F. S. Lehrs (in the Didot *Corpus Epicorum*, Paris, 1862), are all to be recommended, the last being, of course, the fullest and best. The old lists of the works ascribed to Hesiod are found in Pausanias, ix. 31, 5, and in Suidas, art. Ἡσίοδος ; they contain a few additional titles to those I have mentioned.

[3] Cf. above, p. 97, *note*.

the seventh century B.C., and contemporary with Archilochus. Here, again, there are strong family likenesses to the *Works;* but the only passage (in the *Theogony*) which could be supposed the direct model of Simonides' satire on women is decidedly an interpolation in Hesiod, and its use of the bee (in an opposed sense to that of Simonides) for the working men, with drones for the women, seems to me plainly a satiric correction of Simonides, and composed after his famous poem.

We know nothing whatever of Kerkops, who is mentioned as Hesiod's earliest follower and rival, nor is there any real evidence of Terpander having been such. In the extant lyric and elegiac fragments no certain trace appears till Alcæus, whose frag. 39 is a most distinct copy of Hesiod. So likewise the resemblances in Theognis are far more than general, and it seems undeniable that in the middle of the sixth century the poems of Hesiod—at least the *Works*—were well known and circulated.

Acusilaus is mentioned by Plato, Josephus, and a schol. on Apollonius Rhodius, as a commentator or prose paraphrast of the *Theogony.* Bernhardy supposes him to have been a Peloponnesian theologian, who collected genealogies and cosmogonies, and arranged them after the manner of Hesiod, but in prose. But we are left quite in the dark by our authorities concerning him.

Most critics refer to the same epoch an old poem on the *Contest and the Origin of Homer and Hesiod*, which is largely quoted in the extant tract of that title.[1] This poem seems, at any rate, to have originated in those days when the gnomic and sententious Bœotian school had obtained a greater popularity than its Ionic rival. The scene is laid at the contest of Chalcis, and the author aims at proving that, although Hesiod was declared victor, Homer was far the greater poet—a needless task. But, as we shall see presently, the very existence of such a poem is denied by the most recent critic, Nietzsche.

Shortly before and after the times of the Persian wars,

---

[1] Printed at the end of Göttling's and Lehrs' editions of Hesiod ; and more recently, with great critical care, in the *Acta Soc. Phil.* of Leipzig, vol. i. pp. 1, sq., by F. Nietzsche.

Xenophanes, and then Heracleitus, attack Hesiod—the first for his immoral teaching, along with Homer, about the doings of the gods (*Theogony* and *Catalogue*); the second for idle learning on the same profitless subject.

It seems that he was subjected to some critical revision, about this time, by the commission of Peisistratus, for Plutarch (*Theseus*, c. 20) mentions a verse which was then removed. Whether the poems had been hitherto preserved by a school of Hesiodic rhapsodists, is not sufficiently clear. It is certain, however, that they were recited at poetical contests, and in early days without musical accompaniment, for Pausanias[1] criticises a statue of Hesiod with a lyre on his knees as absurd, seeing that he sang with a bay branch in his hand. This was in contrast to the Ionic rhapsodising.[2] These opposed methods were not strictly adhered to in after times, and were even occasionally reversed.

But in Attic days Hesiod attained a widespread popularity as an author of moral instruction for the use of schoolmasters and parents. The Greeks, indeed, always regarded the *Works* as an ethical treatise, while the Romans laid more stress on its agricultural side. Plato constantly alludes to Hesiod, and quotes him, not very accurately, as an authority in morals and in theology. He is similarly cited by Xenophon. So thoroughly was this recognised that the comic writers brought him on the stage as the ideal of an old-fashioned schoolmaster, full of cut-and-dry moral advices. The philosophers who succeeded Plato, especially the Stoics Zeno and Chrysippus, made him the subject of criticism; and Epicurus is said to have got his first impulse towards philosophy from reading the *Theogony*. The same story is told of Manilius, the Roman poet.

---

[1] ix. 30, 2 : ἐπὶ ῥάβδου δάφνης ᾖδεν.

[2] Pausanias (x. 7, 3) tells us a story, that Hesiod was excluded from contending at the Pythian games, because he had not been taught to play the lyre along with his singing. But when he adds that Homer also was unsuccessful, because his training in the art could not be perfected owing to his want of sight, he seems to repeat the stories of the time when the richer and more elaborate lyric poetry came to look upon the old epic recitation as bald and poor.

Philologically, the works of Hesiod excited the same sort of interest as those of the Ionic epic poets, but in a lesser degree. We still have scanty traces of the critical notices of Zenodotus, Aristophanes, and Aristarchus; of Apollonius Rhodius, of Crates, and of Didymus; in fact, of almost all those whose names are found in the Homeric scholia. But Plutarch, as a Bœotian, wrote a special treatise in four books on Hesiod, which the remaining fragments show to have been both critical and explanatory, with discussions of an antiquarian and patriotic character, defending the poet against objectors. His work was the main source of the commentary of Proclus, who again was copied servilely by Tzetzes. The later commentary of Manuel Moschopulos is still extant, and completely printed in the Venice ed. of 1537.

§ 88. The prose tract, *The Contest of Homer and Hesiod*, is the work of some rhetor who mentions the Emperor Hadrian, but its date is not further fixed. It is very full on the legends and parentage of both Homer and Hesiod. The antiquity and authority of the legends told in this tract are worthy of a moment's discussion. The version in Plutarch's *Convivium* (cap. x.) professes to give Lesches as the authority for the contest, and apparently Lesches the cyclic poet. If this were so, the legend is old and of good authority, and as such is accepted by Göttling and other editors of the life of Hesiod. But the stray citation of Lesches in the middle of the Plutarchian narrative has offended modern critics, who have either emended the text, or considered it a marginal gloss indicating that the immediately following lines are to be found in Lesches' poem. Nietzsche goes further, and rejects the whole *Convivium* as spurious and not by Plutarch at all. This being so, there remains no older authority cited in the ἀγών than the rhetor Alkidamas, a well-known pupil of Gorgias, who will be considered hereafter. This man composed a treatise called τῆς φύσεως Μουσεῖον, *On mental culture*, in which he seems to have described the contest of Homer and Hesiod to show that Homer was the forerunner of Gorgias in rapid improvisation and extempore reply. Drawing his conclusions from slight and to me insufficient hints, Nietzsche infers that the opening part of Alkidamas' book contained a much fuller account of the contest of Homer and Hesiod, from which the author of our extant ἀγών abridged his narrative, particularly by cutting down the citations. When Nietzsche further asserts that Alkidamas invented the whole story of the *Contest*, and that to him we must refer all our legends of it, he goes, I think, a great deal too far. The passage in Hesiod's Works about the contest at Chalcis is probably older than Alkidamas, even if interpolated, and I can hardly believe that this alleged contest and rivalry between the two great epic bards was not thought of till the rhetor's time. But it is very likely that he worked up the old story into a smart rhetorical form, and made it popular. So far he may have been the chief source of the *Contest* as we have it.

The *Contest* also cites Eratosthenes the Alexandrian, who wrote a poem called 'Ησίοδος ἢ 'Αντερινύς on the story of the poet's death ; but whether he differed widely from Alkidamas, and used other legends, we cannot tell. So also Aristotle is said to have mentioned the tomb of Hesiod in his *Polity of the Orchomenians*, but here again we have only a stray citation.[1]

The γένος 'Ησιόδου, generally printed as a preface to his works, is probably a mere compilation of Joh. Tzetzes, from Proclus, but is very instructive, like the ἀγών, in indicating to us what materials were still at hand in that epoch.

§ 89. *Bibliographical.* Passing on to the MSS. left us, we find a very great number of copies of the *Works*, covered with scholia, and often with illustrations of the farming implements, but not critically valuable. The oldest seems to be the Medicean 5, of the eleventh century ; then the Medicean 3 (Plut. xxxii. 16); of the twelfth. The rest are all fourteenth and fifteenth century books, generally on paper, full of scholia and notes, and variously put together with the other Hesiodic works, and with Theocritus, Nonnus, the pseudo-Pythagorea, and other moral fragments. The MS. copies of the *Theogony* and *Shield* are not so frequent, and none, I believe, so old as the twelfth

---

[1] All these legends have been classified, with little positive result, by O. Friedel in Fleckeisen's *Jahrbücher* for 1879, pp. 235, sq. ; to which I refer the reader for elaborate details. There is also a paper on Hesiod's Life by G. H. Flach in *Hermes* for 1874, pp. 357, sq.

century.   The sort of collection generally found in the MSS. is
well reproduced in the beautiful Aldine ed. of 1495, which,
though the *Works* were brought out a year or two earlier at
Milan, is the first which gives the whole, and is the *Ed.
princeps* for the rest of Hesiod.   It contains a great many
other authors, and even stray collections of proverbs.   The
Juntine eds. of 1515 and 1540 are said to be mere copies of
the Aldine.   That of Trincavelli in 1537 gives the scholia in
full, and has independent merit.   Then come the great edition of Stephanus (1566), and a very complete one of D.
Heinsius.   Of later commentators the first place is due to
Gaisford, whose Oxford edition is admirable from its fulness of
research about both MSS. and scholia (*Poetæ minores Græci*,
1814–20).   Next may be mentioned Göttling's (2nd ed. Gotha,
1843), the most convenient for the ordinary student; and,
lastly, Mr. F. A. Paley's, which, with all its merits, is over-
loaded with very questionable notes about the Digamma,[1] and
the etymology of old Greek words.   The best complete text of
the poems and fragments is that of F. S. Lehrs in Didot's
series (2nd ed. 1862).   There are many special dissertations
cited in the new article *Hesiod*, in the *Encyclopædia Britannica*.
Mützell's book *De Emendatione Theogoniæ Hesiodeæ*, Lips.,
1833, is praised as very painstaking and complete.   An *Index
Hesiodeus* was published at Naples in 1791 by Ossorio di
Figueroa, but I have not seen it.   There is also an edition of
the *Theogony* by F. A. Wolf (1783).

The imitations in Virgil's *Georgics* are too well known
to require closer description.   There are translations into
German by Voss, and Uschner, and into French by Gin and.

---

[1] I have said nothing about the Digamma, because I do not believe its
presence or absence can be of the least use in determining the genuineness
or spuriousness of any line in Hesiod.   The careful researches of the Germans have shown that it is present or absent in the same word according
to the exigencies of the metre ; and there seems really evidence for the fact
that the Digamma was a letter which could be arbitrarily used or dispensed
with in epic poetry.   There is the most surprising variation, exactly of
the same kind, though without metrical reasons, in the inscriptions of the
same towns.   I will not deny that there may be a law of its use, but so far
this law does not seem likely to be discovered.

Bergier, in addition to the Latin hexameter translations of the Italians, N. Valla, and B. Zamagna, in the fifteenth century, and the early French one of Jacques le Gras in 1586.

As to English translations, I cannot find any mention of more than three. The first is of the *Works* only, the ' *Georgics* of Hesiod,' by George Chapman (1618). This, like all Chapman's work, is poetical and spirited, but often very obscure to modern readers, though it constantly cites the original in foot-notes. The book, which was very scarce, has been reprinted, with other of Chapman's translations, by J. R. Smith (London, 1858). Next we have the work of Cooke (1743), who seems unaware of Chapman's translation, and who gives us a pretentious and dull rendering of the *Works* and *Theogony* in heroic verse. The last and best, and the only complete translation, including the *Shield*, is that of Elton (2nd ed. 1815), who knew his predecessors well, and gives us scholarly renderings of the *Works* in heroic rimes, and of the other two poems in blank verse. Parnell's *Pandora, or the Rise of Woman*, is a free imitation of the corresponding pair of passages in Hesiod.

§ 90. There is no use in discussing the several busts and statues of Hesiod, which Pausanias saw and describes in his tour through Greece. It need hardly be stated that these, hke the portraits of Homer, were mere works of imagination, and have no historical claims. There are five epigrams or epitaphs upon him extant, two quoted at the end of Tzetzes' Greek preface to his works, and stated to be set over his tomb in the *agora* of Orchomenus—one of them ascribed to Pindar. Three others are in the Anthology, one of which, by Alcæus of Messene, has considerable merit.

_____

§ 91. There is sufficient evidence of the antagonism between the Homeric and Hesiodic rhapsodists in the legend of the contest of the poets, and we may even infer from the alleged victory of the inferior but more didactic poet, that as the audience became more reflective, and as they came to regard the poet as an educator, the more explicit moral purpose, and the plainer preaching of the Hesiodic school, came to be

regarded as superior to the mere stimulating of the sense of
honour through the imagination by the heroic poems.   But it
might have been easily foretold that the controversy would not
stop there, and that as philosophy arose, the whole system of
the chivalry of Homer and the Theogonic dogmatism of Hesiod
would find opponents from a totally different platform.   It
might perhaps even have been anticipated that these opponents
would choose the very form of the Ionic epos to embody their
criticisms.   The *Golden Verses*[1] ascribed to the school of Pythagoras, which contain the condensed morals of the older epics,
even were they genuine, are not so natural an outcome of the
clever restless Greek mind as the making of objections and
exceptions.

§ 92. These found their earliest spokesman in *Xenophanes*
of Colophon, who travelled through the Hellenic world during
most of the fifth century, but who seems to have formulated his
system in early life, and to have disseminated it in his wanderings
as a rhapsode, in opposition to those who were reciting the old
epics at every festival throughout Greece.   Xenophanes was
indeed a poet of various accomplishments, and we have admirable fragments of his elegiacs, which will be mentioned in
their place, as well as a few iambic lines.   But these, though they
show the independent and radical spirit of the man, were chiefly
social poems, and evidently did not contain his main philosophy.
This he published by going about as a rhapsode, and reciting
it in the same epic form as the poems of Homer and Hesiod.
We have sufficient remnants to show that he systematically
attacked the anthropomorphism of Greek religion, the plurality
and conflicting interests of the gods, and that he asserted the
unity and purity of the Deity.   But the allusions of such critics as
Aristotle prove that his polemic was not merely theological, and
that his negative criticism was associated with metaphysical
speculations on the unity, not only of the Deity, but of the
world.   It was from this point of view that he was the founder of
the Eleatic school, as he lived much of his later life in this
Italian city, and as his system was taken up and developed by
his great pupil Parmenides.

[1] Their remains are printed at the end of Göttling's *Hesiod*.

§ 93. If we could trust the chronological points in Plato's dialogues, *Parmenides* was sixty-five when Socrates was a 'very young man,' perhaps between fifteen and twenty ; but Plato cares for none of these things, and looks only to dramatic and not to historical propriety. It seems more likely that Parmenides came earlier, perhaps about the opening of the fifth century, and he still adhered in philosophy to the old didactic epic, which had been consecrated to serious teaching by Hesiod and his school. But it is evident that while prose composition, both in history and in philosophy, since Hecatæus and Heracleitus showed the way, made rapid progress among the Ionians of Asia Minor, the Greeks of Italy and Sicily adhered to the poetic form, as is the case with Empedocles, who wrote even a generation or two later. Thus the fact that Heracleitus had published his thoughts in prose at Ephesus is no proof that the hexameter poem of Parmenides may not have been later in date, though more primitive in form. We fortunately have the opening of the work preserved by Sextus Empiricus, and there is no doubt that it combined (like the poem of Empedocles copied by Lucretius) remarkable brilliancy of fancy with profundity of thought.[1]

[1] This introduction is preserved by Sextus Empiricus (*Adv. Math.* vii. 111) :

Ἵπποι ταί με φέρουσιν, ὅσον τ' ἐπὶ θυμὸς ἱκάνοι,
πέμπον, ἐπεί μ' ἐς ὁδὸν βῆσαν πολύφημον ἄγουσαι
Δαίμονος ἣ κατὰ πάντ' αὐτὴ φέρει εἰδότα φῶτα·
τῇ φερόμην, τῇ γάρ με πολύφραστοι φέρον ἵπποι
ἅρμα τιταίνουσαι· κοῦραι δ' ὁδὸν ἡγεμόνευον
Ἡλιάδες κοῦραι, προλιποῦσαι δώματα νυκτός,
εἰς φάος, ὠσάμεναι κρατῶν ἄπο χερσὶ καλύπτρας.
Ἄξων δ' ἐν χνοίῃσιν ἵει σύριγγος ἀϋτὴν
αἰθόμενος, δοιοῖς γὰρ ἐπείγετο δινωτοῖσι
κύκλοις ἀμφοτέρωθεν, ὅτε σπερχοίατο πέμπειν.
Ἔνθα πύλαι νυκτός τε καὶ ἤματός εἰσι κελεύθων,
καί σφας ὑπέρθυρον ἀμφὶς ἔχει καὶ λάϊνος οὐδός,
αὐταὶ δ' αἰθέρι κέκλεινται μεγάλοισι θυρέτροις
τῶν δὲ Δίκη πολύποινος ἔχει κληῖδας ἀμοιβούς.
τὴν δὲ παρφάμεναι κοῦραι μαλακοῖσι λόγοισι
πεῖσαν ἐπιφραδέως, ὥς σφιν βαλανωτὸν ὀχῆα
ἀπτερέως ὥσειε πυλέων ἄπο· ταὶ δὲ θυρέτρων

Other considerable extracts from Parmenides are quoted by Simplicius, in which we no longer find the theological tone of Xenophanes, but the purely metaphysical treatment of the doctrine known ever since as the Eleatic philosophy.   The eternal and incorruptible unity of Being, as opposed to the fleeting unreality of sense, is illustrated with much power and variety.   The celebrated dialogue of Plato, in which Parmenides is the chief speaker, as well as many allusions of Aristotle, give us full information concerning his philosophy.   But from a literary point of view, it is to be noted that though he wrote this hexameter poem *on Nature*, he was not a poet in the same sense as Xenophanes, who also composed both elegiacs and iambics, and was a professed reciter.   He even repeated his views, according to Plato (*Soph.* 237, A), in a prose form—the form exclusively adopted by his immediate followers, Zeno and Melissus. These therefore we must class under the head of early prose writers.

§ 94. It is indeed asserted in Aristotle's *Poetic*, that this sort of epic composition has nothing in common with Homer but the metre, wherefore, he adds, you call the one a poet, and the other rather a physiologer than a poet.   This remark specially applies to *Empedocles*, the third and greatest name on the list of our philosophic poets, and is but another example of the reckless judgments which the authority of Aristotle has disse-

χάσμ' ἀχανὲς ποίησαν ἀναπτάμεναι, πολυχάλκους
ἄξονας ἐν σύριγξιν ἀμοιβαδὸν εἰλίξασαι
γόμφοις καὶ περόνῃσιν ἀρηρότας· ᾗ ῥα δι' αὐτῶν
ἰθὺς ἔχον κοῦραι κατ' ἀμαξιτὸν ἅρμα καὶ ἵππους.
καί με θεὰ πρόφρων ὑπεδέξατο, χεῖρα δὲ χειρὶ
δεξιτερὴν ἕλεν, ὧδε δ' ἔπος φάτο καί με προσηύδα·
῏Ω κοῦρ' ἀθανάτοισι συνάορος ἡνιόχοισιν,
ἵππους ταί σε φέρουσιν ἱκάνων ἡμέτερον δῶ,
χαῖρ' ἐπεὶ οὔτι σε μοῖρα κακὴ προὔπεμπε νέεσθαι
τὴν δ' ὁδὸν (ᾗ γὰρ ἀπ' ἀνθρώπων ἐκτὸς πάτου ἐστίν),
ἀλλὰ θέμις τε δίκη τε. Χρεὼ δέ σε πάντα πύθεσθαι
ἠμὲν ἀληθείας εὐπειθέος ἀτρεκὲς ἦτορ,
ἠδὲ βροτῶν δόξας, ταῖς οὐκ ἔνι πίστις ἀληθής.
'Αλλ' ἔμπης καὶ ταῦτα μαθήσεαι ὡς τὰ δοκοῦντα
χρὴ δοκίμως γνῶναι διὰ παντὸς πάντα περῶντα.

minated by means of this corrupt treatise. For had the observation been applied to Parmenides, it might have been possibly
defended, though our scanty remains contain passages of lofty
imagination and true poetic fire. But applied to Empedocles,
the remark is simply ridiculous, and might have been contemp-
tuously rejected, even if there were not preserved to us by
Diogenes [1] the opinion of the true Aristotle, which happens in
express terms to contradict the criticisms of the *Poetic.* We
have furthermore the judgments of the careful Dionysius on
his 'austere harmony,' which he compares to that of Æschylus,
and the not inconsistent praise of Plutarch for his inspired enthusiasm. Mr. Symonds, in his essay on the poet, goes so far
as to call him the Greek Shelley, and gives some striking
grounds for this singular judgment.

As a poet, therefore, Empedocles must be ranked very high,
and Cicero expressly tells us that his verses were far superior
to those of Xenophanes and Parmenides, themselves no mean
artists on similar subjects. This is the more remarkable because he came late in the development of didactic poetry,
and in the age when prose had already been employed with
great success by Heracleitus for the purposes of philosophic exposition. But although Empedocles seems not to have been
born till about 490 B.C., and was about contemporary, both in
birth and death, with Herodotus, he was born, not in the home
of nascent prose, but at Agrigentum in Sicily, where he became
one of the forerunners of a literature widely different from that
of the Ionic race. For Gorgias is called his pupil, and though
he does not appear to have composed any treatise in prose, he
was considered by Aristotle the first founder of the art of rhetoric, which Gorgias made the occupation of his life.

Though of noble family—his grandfather Empedocles had
won with a four-horsed chariot at the 71st Olympiad, his
father Meton had been prominent in expelling the tyrant
Thrasydæus—he was firmly devoted to democratic principles,
and fought for the demos of his city against the aristocracy.

---

[1] viii. 3 : ἐν δὲ τῷ περὶ ποιητῶν φησιν ὅτι καὶ Ὁμηρικὸς ὁ Ἐμπεδοκλῆς
καὶ δεινὸς περὶ τὴν φράσιν γέγονε, μεταφορικός τ' ὢν καὶ τοῖς ἄλλοις τοῖς περὶ
ποιητικὴν ἐπιτεύγμασι χρώμενος.

But, like Herodotus and other patriots of that period, he found it unpleasant to live at home among hostile and jealous neighbours ; he accordingly left Agrigentum, and retired to the Peloponnese, where he seems to have died in obscurity. This we may infer from the many uncontradicted legends which became current through Greece upon the subject. Empedocles is one of the most curious and striking figures in Greek literature, for he combined the characters of soothsayer, magician and mystic with those of an earnest and positive speculator, who first attempted a mechanical explanation of nature. His account of the gradual growth and development of animated organisms even gives him the right to be called the oldest Greek forerunner of Darwin.

These physiological and physical speculations, which fascinated the mind of Lucretius, belong to the province of the historian of philosophy. But the literary form in which they were clothed causes much perplexity. For this poet-philosopher, this positivist-magician, would not clothe his metaphysic in any but allegorical dress. Thus the four elements [1] which he was the first to assert against Parmenides' single Being, and which lived in philosophy till yesterday, are clothed in the garb of the people's gods : and his attraction and repulsion, by which the world of experience was compounded out of the elements, were called Love and Hate ($\Phi\iota\lambda\acute{o}\tau\eta\varsigma$ and $N\epsilon\widehat{\iota}\kappa\upsilon\varsigma$), the former even Aphrodite. Along with these apparent concessions to the popular faith, he held Pythagorean doctrines as to the transmigration of souls, and the consequent crime of destroying animal life, though his politics separate him widely from the Pythagorean school. His metaphysic is an independent syncretism of Eleatic and Heracleitic doctrines, with a predominance of the latter, perhaps on account of the deeper poetry of Heracleitus' prose. But though the man's personality, his splendid dress, his numerous attendants, and his bold claims to supernatural power, made him a great figure in the Sicily of his day, his mystical and theological turn would not bear the light of positive science,

---

[1] $\tau\acute{e}\sigma\sigma\alpha\rho\alpha$ $\tau\widehat{\omega}\nu$ $\pi\acute{a}\nu\tau\omega\nu$ $\dot{\rho}\iota\zeta\acute{\omega}\mu\alpha\tau\alpha$ $\pi\rho\widehat{\omega}\tau\sigma\nu$ $\mathring{a}\kappa\sigma\upsilon\epsilon\cdot$
$Z\epsilon\grave{\upsilon}\varsigma$ [air] $\mathring{a}\rho\gamma\grave{\eta}\varsigma$ $"H\rho\eta$ [earth] $\tau\epsilon$ $\phi\epsilon\rho\acute{e}\sigma\beta\iota\sigma\varsigma$ $\mathring{\eta}\delta$' $'A\iota\delta\omega\nu\epsilon\grave{\upsilon}\varsigma$ [fire]
$N\widehat{\eta}\sigma\tau\acute{\iota}\varsigma$ [water] θ' $\mathring{\eta}$ $\delta\alpha\kappa\rho\acute{\upsilon}\sigma\iota\varsigma$ $\tau\acute{e}\gamma\gamma\epsilon\iota$ $\kappa\rho\sigma\acute{\upsilon}\nu\omega\mu\alpha$ $\beta\rho\acute{\sigma}\tau\epsilon\iota\sigma\nu.$

and he is therefore referred to with less respect by succeeding critics as a philosopher than as a lofty poet. The tragedies and political writings ascribed to him were spurious ; his φυσικά and καθαρμοί, the formal exposition of his metaphysic and of his theology, are the only works recognised by modern critics. It has been inferred from the fragments that these books were not very consistent, that the various purifications and rites recommended (in the καθαρμοί) were little in consonance with the mechanical and positive explanations of his φυσικά.

§ 95. They were, moreover, very alien to the dialectic of Gorgias and the succeeding sophists, who cared little for dogmatic theology, and consistently rejected the ritual of the old religion along with its dogmas. The sophists were still more marked in their rejection of epic verse as the vehicle for philosophic teaching, and in the uniform adoption of prose, which was even then introduced in the schools of Asia Minor. So strongly was this felt in the next generation, that there arises a formal opposition between philosophers and poets, the latter of whom were regarded as the mere exponents of the popular creed. Of course this would have been absurdly false in the days of Parmenides and Empedocles; but even the latter was almost behind his age, and from the middle of the fifth century B.C. onwards Greek philosophy consistently adopted prose instead of a poetical form. Anaxagoras was, no doubt, reflected in Euripides, and Epicurus in Menander ; but these speculative features in the drama were the mere natural reflex of the deepest thinking of the day upon its most thoughtful and serious poets. The philosophy of Euripides was a mere parergon of his tragedy. It is to this fixed purpose of philosophy to abandon poetry that we must attribute the defection of such imaginative minds as Hippocrates and Plato from the ranks of the Greek poets, among whom the latter (as an epigrammatist) even made his first essay. The history of philosophy since that day confirms the Greeks as to the literary propriety of this decision. Despite the splendid attempt of Lucretius to reproduce in the form of Empedocles the most prosaic and vulgar of systems, his poem had little influence upon his age, and is even spoken of by Cicero with some contempt. The Neoplatonists, however mystical and Eleatic in tone, never returned to the more ancient and indeed natural garb of their vague Pantheism. The Middle Ages were dominated by the prosaic Aristotle. Nor did any of the great heralding of modern thought, the rich imagery of Bacon, the mystic dawning of Boehme, the god-intoxicated cosmogony of Spinoza, proclaim itself to a world weary of the dry and arid light of prose logic in the form consecrated of old to the union of thought and fancy. In later days, though modern poetry is full, perhaps too full, of metaphysic and of anthropology, we have no greater attempt at writing systematic philosophy in verse than Pope's *Essay on Man*, or Mandeville's *Fable of the Bees*. Thus Empedocles is peculiarly interesting as the last thinker in European philosophy who brought out a new system in the form of a poem.

His fragments are preserved in Sextus Empiricus, Plutarch, and Simplicius, and are best collected by Müllach (in Didot's *Fragg. Philosoph.*). There are interesting monographs on him in all the histories of Greek philosophy, especially Zeller's, and in Mr. Symonds' first series on the Greek poets. The legend of his death in the crater of Etna has inspired poets down to our own day, like Mr. Arnold, and still lingers about the traditions of the mountain through changes of race and of language.

CHAPTER VIII.

THE HOMERIC HYMNS AND TRIFLES.

§ 96. THERE is yet another class of epic hexameter poetry extant, besides the proper Ionic epics, and the didactic poems of Hesiod and the philosophers.   There are transmitted to us, under the title of *Homeric Hymns,* a collection of five longer and twenty-nine shorter poems in epic dialect and metre, each inscribed to some particular god, and narrating some legend connected with him, but in no sense religious hymns, as were those of Pamphus or the hymns of the choral lyric poets.   The Homeric Hymns are essentially secular and not religious; they seem distinctly intended to be recited in competitions of rhapsodes, and in some cases even for direct pay ; [1] they are all in form preludes (προοίμια) to longer recitations,[2] apparently of epic poems,[3] though the longer five are expanded into substantially independent compositions.

[1] Hymn vi. *sub fin.* :

$$δὸς δ' ἐν ἀγῶνι$$
$$νίκην τῷδε φέρεσθαι, ἐμὴν δ' ἔντυνον ἀοιδήν.$$

And v. xxx. and xxxi. *sub fin.* :

$$πρόφρων δ' ἀντ' ᾠδῆς βίοτον θυμήρε' ὄπαζε.$$

[2] οἴμη, according to Bergk, meant any song, especially an epic poem. οἶμος is used with a genitive (ἐπέων, &c.) qualifying it.   Pausanias calls a hymn of Alcæus to Apollo a προοίμιον, probably because it was like in character to these Hymns.   The νόμοι were really devotional poems, and are as such contrasted by Pausanias with the secular hymns of the collection before us.

[3] Hymn xxxi. :

$$ἐκ σέο δ' ἀρξάμενος κλήσω μερόπων γένος ἀνδρῶν$$
$$ἡμιθέων, ὧν ἔργα Θεοὶ θνητοῖσιν ἔδειξαν.$$

§ 97. The *Hymn to the Delian Apollo,* apparently the third
in order in the archetype of our MSS., is by far the best known
and oftenest quoted of the collection. It owes this distinction
chiefly to the famous description near its close of the old
festival at Delos, whither all the Ionians came, with their wives
and children, to witness dancing, singing and boxing, and to
wonder at the ventriloquism which the Delian priestesses appear
to have studied to great perfection. Then follows a somewhat
boastful assertion of excellence on the part of the rhapsodist
—the blind man of Chios. The main body of the hymn narrates the adventures of Latona before the birth of Apollo, her
final reception by the personified island Delos, and the long-
delayed birth of the god. Artemis is not mentioned, and cannot therefore have been regarded as his twin-sister in the Delian
legend. The style of the poem is good and clear, and indicates a date when epic language and metre were perfectly
understood.

§ 98. Our MSS. combine this hymn (178 lines) and what
is now established to be quite a different work, the *Hymn
to the Pythian Apollo.* The allusions of Thucydides and of
Aristides [1] imply that they quote from the end of the former
hymn (v. 172), which is only the case if we separate the Pythian
hymn. Furthermore, the scholiast on Pindar [2] quotes some
lines as Hesiod's, in which he boasts of contending with Homer
at Delos in hymns to Apollo. This shows an old belief that a
second hymn to Apollo, by Hesiod, existed. The Pythian hymn
has quite this character ; it is altogether occupied with Bœotian
and Delphian legends, and celebrates the settlement of the god
at the rocky Pytho after his colloquy with the fountain-nymph
Delphusa, near Haliartus, and his slaying of the Python. Then
follows his adventure, in the form of a dolphin, with the Cretan
sailors, whom he brought round the Peloponnesus from their
course, and established as his priests at the oracle. Besides
the Bœotian character of its legends, the genealogical and
etymological tone of the poem betrays the didactic spirit of
the Hesiodic school ; and there seems little doubt that it was
composed by some Delphian or Bœotian poet in imitation of

---

[1] Cf. Bergk, *LG.* i. p. 753.　　　[2] *Nem.* ii. 1.

the former hymn, which it closely follows in its construction, and ofttimes in diction.

There are many disturbances in the text, and to these may be ascribed apparent blunders in the geography of Bœotia, which the author seems to have known accurately.   He is also fully acquainted with the coasts of the Peloponnesus.   There are several remarkable and evidently intentional omissions.   The site of Thebes is mentioned as being still forest, and therefore supposed to have been occupied after the settlement at Delphi. Delphi, again, is only known by the name of Pytho.   Kirrha, the seaport of Krissa, is never mentioned, but the latter is said to be near the harbour.   Though describing a curious augury with chariots at Onchestus (vv. 53, sq.), and therefore familiar with one form of horse-racing, the poet represents Delphusà as dissuading Apollo from settling near her fountain because the sound of horses and chariots would disturb him.   The Germans infer that this must have been written before the time when the Amphictyons, immediately after the sacred war (590 B.C.), established chariot races at the Pythian games.   This seems to me founded on a mistake, for these games were not carried on at Delphi, which is quite inaccessible to chariots, and where the stadium is far too small for such races, but at a special hippodrome in the plain below, which Pausanias specially mentions,[1] so that it may always have been held that the god chose his remote and Alpine retreat in order to avoid such disturbance.   The priests are told prophetically, at the close of the poem, that through their own fault they will become subject to a strange power, and this again is supposed to point to the events of the sacred war.   But there is no certainty in these conjectures.

Both this and the former poem seem to have been considerably interpolated, as for example with the episode [2] of the birth of Typhon, which is quite in the manner of the *Theogony* of Hesiod.   Other small inconsistencies may rather be ascribed to *naïveté* and want of critical spirit than to a diversity of poets. As the Delian hymn was intended for recitation at Delos, so the Pythian is clearly intended for some such purpose at Delphi,

---

[1] x. 37, 4.   [2] ii. vv. 127-77.

and seems not far removed in date from its forerunner. But as the Pythian contests were with the lyre, a Hesiodic poet could hardly have competed unless he abandoned his old custom of reciting without accompaniment; and indeed the complete silence of the hymn about the Pythian contests suggests some definite reason for not mentioning them.

§ 99. The *Hymns to Hermes* (iii.) and to *Aphrodite* (iv.) may be brought into comparison on account of their familiar handling of gods, though in other respects they are widely contrasted. The text of the former is the most corrupt of all the Hymns, so much so that G. Hermann and other destructive critics urge with great force their theory of its being a conglomerate of various short pieces by different authors. The opening lines are repeated almost verbatim in the lesser Hymn to Hermes, numbered xviii. in the collection; but it is clear from the critical discussion of the prefaces to Hesiod's poems, and from the many short procemia actually found in this collection, that these introductions were movable, and that the rejection of the preface entails no presumption against the unity of the main body of the poem. The Moscow MS. differs remarkably from the rest in its text of this poem; according to Hermann, because it followed another recension, according to Baumeister, with whom I agree, because the scribe copying the archetype was a learned man, and set himself to correct and emend what he thought corrupt.

The text of the *Hymn to Aphrodite* is, on the contrary, the purest and easiest of all, and it is only the perverse ingenuity of the Germans which has ventured to thrust upon us here their suspicions of interpolations. There appears to be also a considerable contrast between the two poems as to diction. While the Hymn to Aphrodite is in very pure Ionic—almost Homeric—Greek, and clearly composed in Asia Minor, the Hymn to Hermes abounds in phrases only to be found in Hesiod,[1] and shows evidence of Bœotian or Arcadian origin. Again, there is a good deal of humour, and of a low popular tone, about the latter, while this homely tone is not at all felt in the other. Nevertheless, these poems, as I have said, have

Cf. Mure, ii. p. 344, note

an all-important feature which makes it suitable to connect them together—I mean the bold and familiar handling of the foibles and passions of the gods. Their moral tone is perhaps lower than that of any other old Greek poem, if we except the episode called the lay of Demodocus, in the Odyssey—a poem which bears the most striking resemblance in tone and diction to the fourth hymn. The passion of the goddess is in both represented as a foible, but hardly as a fault, and her adventures in the hymn are represented as brought upon her by a sort of retaliation on the part of Zeus. The description of her progress through Mount Ida, her power over the lower animals (vv. 70, sq.), and her meeting with Anchises, are told with great beauty, but apparently without any feeling of reserve on the part of the poet. It was not till Praxiteles that sculpture dared to represent the undraped beauty of the goddess in marble. Poetry cast away such restrictions far earlier. There is also a fine description of the old age of Tithonus (vv. 237–46), and of the life of trees as bound up with that of the wood-nymphs. The main object of the poem seems the flattery of the family of Anchises and Æneas, whose alleged descendants (as is prophesied in the Iliad) were evidently important people in the poet's day. We have no evidence where they ruled, or whether the Dardanian princes encouraged Greek poetry.

The *Hymn to Hermes* does not describe such passion, and is an account of the birth and adventures of the god, setting forth his thieving and perjury with the most shameless effrontery. To the ordinary Greeks great ingenuity was enough at all times to palliate or even to justify dishonesty, and though Hesiod and the Delphic oracle raised their voices in favour of justice and truth, there can be no doubt that the nation was thoroughly depraved in this respect. The Hymn to Hermes goes through a variety of adventures of the god—his stealing of the oxen of Apollo immediately after his birth, his invention of the lyre, his trial and perjury before Zeus, and the amusement and good-nature of Apollo in being reconciled to him. The mention of the seven-stringed lyre has induced most critics to date the poem after Terpander's time, but, on the other side, it is declared

absurd that the poet should describe as an original invention of
the god a new improvement in the instrument made by a well-
known man at a well-known date. It is therefore argued that
the seven-stringed lyre was not unknown in ancient days in
some parts of Greece, though not generally adopted by literary
lyric poets till Terpander. This is indeed to be inferred from
Pausanias, who says that Amphion naturalised the Lydian
seven-stringed lyre in Greece. At all events, this improved
lyre must have been in common use when the poem was
composed, probably not before 600 B.C.

As to the literary merits of these hymns, authorities are
divided. Most of the Germans place the hymn to Hermes
very high, and think that but for its corruptions it would be
the most original and striking of the collection. Mure, on the
other hand, thinks the fourth to be the most beautiful of all
the hymns, and almost worthy of Homer himself. Both seem
to me to have great, but contrasted merits. The humour and
variety of the one are perhaps equalled by the luxurious richness
of the other. Both are precious relics of old Greek poetry,
and curious evidences of the rapid decay of the old Greek
religion. Shelley has left us a translation of the third as well as
of some of the shorter hymns. His version is of course very poetical, but accentuates the comic element perhaps too strongly.

§ 100. The *Hymn to Demeter* (v.), of nearly 500 lines, is of
a very different character, and is to be identified with some
Athenian worship, either the Panathenaic festival, if there was
any occasion at that festival for such a recitation, or some
religious ceremony at Eleusis. The hymn narrates the carrying off of Persephone, who wandered in search of flowers through
the Mysian plain, and was entranced with delight at the nar-
cissus, which is described with great enthusiasm as being an
important emblem in the Mysteries. The crying out of Persephone is heard by Hecate and Helios alone, from whom the
distracted mother finds out what has happened to her daughter.
But Demeter is still more wroth at hearing that it was done
with the connivance or approval of Zeus, and she deserts the
immortals to live among men. So she comes to Eleusis, where
she sits by the wayside and meets the daughters of Keleus going

to draw water.   They accost her with kindness, and she is installed as nurse of their infant brother Triptolemus.

It is not necessary to go at greater detail into the story, which is told in this hymn with singular clearness and beauty. Any difficulties which occur are due to the corruptions of our single MS., or to the covert allusions to the Mysteries which are evidently before the poet's mind all through the narration of the legend.   The critics generally do not speak with sufficient warmth of the beauty of this poem, which is, in my opinion, far the noblest of the hymns.   A good many Atticisms have been detected in it by the grammarians, but I am not aware of a single solid argument to prove its date, even approximately.[1] It was well known to the ancients, and is quoted four times by Pausanias, with considerable variations from our text, but these are probably due both to its corruption and to inaccuracy in Pausanias himself.   This author also quotes an ancient hymn of Pamphos on the same legend, which seems to have been very similar in argument.

§ 101. Of the lesser hymns the longest (vii.) is that to Dionysus, which describes his adventure with pirates, whom he astonished and overcame by miracles, when they had captured and bound him on their ship. The critics think that the portraiture of the god as a youth points to the age of Praxiteles, because older Greek plastic art had uniformly made him of severe aspect, and apparently middle age.[2]   I have shown above (p. 133) that in the case of Aphrodite poetry outran sculpture in its development, and I feel convinced that the change in the form of Dionysus also was adopted in poetry long before it was attempted, or perhaps could be attempted, in sculpture.   The hymn seems certainly to have been known to Euripides, who builds some of the plot of his *Cyclops* on it, and this subject, perhaps even this detail, was borrowed from the older Aris-

---

[1] Baumeister (*Comm. in Hymn.* p. 280) conjectures it to be of the time of the Peisistratidæ, when epic poetry experienced a considerable revival.

[2] This story is beautifully illustrated in the frieze of the graceful choragic monument of Lysicrates at Athens (erected 332 B.C.)—a monument which is now best studied, not on the spot, but in the drawings of Stuart and Revett, made a century ago, when the work of ruin had not advanced so far.

tias.[1]   The next hymn (viii.), to Ares, is quite of a later and
metaphysical turn.   It abounds in strings of epithets, and rather
celebrates the mental influences of the deity, than his personal
adventures.   This hymn is accordingly attributed by most critics
to the Orphic school.   The same may be said of Hymn xiv., *To
the Mother of the Gods;* nevertheless, all these Homeric hymns
differ widely from the Orphic hymns which still remain on the
same subjects.

I will only mention among the rest that to Pan (xix.),
which is supposed to have been composed after the time
when the worship of Pan was introduced at Athens (490 B.C.).
This little poem is remarkable as one of the few extant Greek
works which show a love and sympathy for the beauties of nature,
and which indulge the fancy in fairy pictures of bold cliffs and
leafy glens peopled by dancing nymphs, and resounding with
the echo of piping sweeter than the nightingale, and the voices
of sportive and merry gods.   It is common among English
critics to assert that only in Euripides and Aristophanes of
earlier poets can we find this peculiar and delightful form of
imagination.   The Hymn to Pan,[2] which reminds us strongly of

---

[1] Patin, *Études sur les tragiques grecs,* iv. 290.

[2]   Ἀμφί μοι Ἑρμείαο φίλον γόνον ἔννεπε, Μοῦσα,
        αἰγιπόδην, δικέρωτα, φιλόκροτον, ὅστ' ἀνὰ πίση
        δενδρήεντ' ἄμυδις φοιτᾷ χοροήθεσι Νύμφαις·
        αἵτε κατ' αἰγίλιπος πέτρης στείβουσι κάρηνα
        Πᾶν ἀνακεκλόμεναι, νόμιον θεόν, ἀγλαέθειρον,
        αὐχμήενθ', ὃς πάντα λόφον νιφόεντα λέλογχε,
        καὶ κορυφὰς ὀρέων καὶ πετρήεντα κέλευθα·
        φοιτᾷ δ' ἔνθα καὶ ἔνθα διὰ ῥωπήϊα πυκνά,
        ἄλλοτε μὲν ῥείθροισιν ἐφεζόμενος μαλακοῖσιν,
        ἄλλοτε δ' αὖ πέτρῃσιν ἐν ἠλιβάτοισι διοιχνεῖ,
        ἀκροτάτην κορυφὴν μηλόσκοπον εἰσαναβαίνων.
        πολλάκι δ' ἀργινόεντα διέδραμεν οὔρεα μακρά,
        πολλάκι δ' ἐν κνημοῖσι διήλασε, θῆρας ἐναίρων,
        ὀξέα δερκόμενος· τοτὲ δ' ἔσπερος ἔκλαγεν οἶος
        ἄγρης ἐξανιών, δονάκων ὕπο μοῦσαν ἀθύρων
        ἥδυμον· οὐκ ἂν τόνγε παραδράμοι ἐν μελέεσσιν
        ὄρνις, ἥτ' ἔαρος πολυανθέος ἐν πετάλοισιν
        θρῆνον ἐπιπροχέουσ' ἰάχει μελίγηρυν ἀοιδήν.
        σὺν δέ σφιν τότε Νύμφαι ὀρεστιάδες, λιγύμολποι,
        φοιτῶσαι πύκνα ποσσὶν ἐπὶ κρήνῃ μελανύδρῳ

Euripides' chorus (vv. 167 et seqq.) in the *Helena,* shows this limitation to be unfounded. The rest are short proems to various gods, very similar in character to the spurious opening lines of Hesiod's *Works;* one of them (xxv.) is even made up of lines from Hesiod's *Theogony.* The short Hymns (xiii. and xviii.), to Hermes and Demeter are mere selections from the greater poems in honour of the same gods.

It appears from this brief review that the so-called *Hymns* are a very various and motley collection of proems to the gods sung by rhapsodes on secular occasions. In some cases these preludes were expanded into independent poems. The older and Ionic pieces breathe a familiar and very secular handling of the adventures of the gods ; the Hesiodic pieces were more serious and intended to instruct the hearers in theology ; while the semi-Orphic pieces were still more reflective and solemn. But they all assume the tone and style of the Ionic epic school. It is not impossible, in spite of the later complexion of some few of them, that the collection was made by the commission of Peisistratus when they were editing or collecting the remains of both Homer and Hesiod.

§ 102. This kind of poetry was revived, as might be expected, at Alexandria, and we have still five hymns extant from the wreck of Alexandrian literature, by the celebrated Callimachus,[1] whose wonderful fertility was not destined to produce much permanent fruit. These hymns are to Zeus, Apollo, Artemis, Delos, and Demeter respectively. They are all of considerable length, those to Artemis and Delos being the longest, but none of them are interesting. They celebrate, like their Homeric prototypes, the birth and early fortunes of the god addressed ; but in the case of Delos, the wanderings and sufferings of Latona, who is, how- ever, encouraged by the consolations uttered by her unborn

μέλπονται· κορυφὴν δὲ περιστένει οὔρεος ἠχώ—
δαίμων δ' ἔνθα καὶ ἔνθα χορῶν, τοτὲ δ' ἐς μέσον ἕρπων,
πυκνὰ ποσὶν διέπει· λαῖφος δ' ἐπὶ νῶτα δαφοινὸν
λυγκὸς ἔχει, λιγυρῇσιν ἀγαλλόμενος φρένα μολπαῖς—
ἐν μαλακῷ λειμῶνι, τόθι κρόκος ἠδ' ὑάκινθος
εὐώδης θαλέθων καταμίσγεται ἄκριτα ποίῃ.

---

[1] Bergk thinks (*LG.* i. p. 749) that Callimachus imitated not the secular hymns, but the old religious *nomes*—on what evidence I know not.

child ! Perhaps the best of these over-learned and frigid poems is the Hymn to Demeter, which, unlike the rest, is in Doric dialect, and which describes with some humour the insatiable hunger of Erysichthon, with which Demeter visited him for cutting down a poplar in her sacred grove. The text has been lately edited, with more care than it deserves, by Meineke (Berlin, 1861); there is also an old metrical translation by Dodd (London, 1755). But modern scholars have long since decided that Callimachus, however famous among the Romans, is not to be regarded as a classical author, though he had the honour of being printed by Const. Lascaris, at Florence, in 1494, in capital letters, among the very earliest Greek texts.

§ 103. We have, in the collection of so-called Idylls ascribed to Theocritus, three poems which may properly be considered in connection with the Homeric Hymns. One of them (Idyll xxii.) is professedly a hymn to the Dioscuri, celebrating the victory of Pollux over Amycus, and of Castor over Lynceus. The work is both well conceived and executed, but Theocritus' mimic talent makes his dialogue between Pollux and Amycus rather more dramatic than was the fashion of the old hymns. There are also picturesque touches (vv. 37, sq.), which speak the poet of the pastoral Idylls. Of the two poems (xxiv. and xxv.) on Heracles, the first, which is called the *Infant Heracles*, and narrates his killing of the snakes in his cradle, is very like the Hymns, especially that to Demeter, though composed in the Doric dialect. It is not certain that we have the end of the poem preserved. The second poem is somewhat more epic in form, and is probably a fragment of a longer work, or composed with a larger plan. It narrates the visit of Heracles to Augeias of Elis, where he tells the king's son his adventure with the Nemean lion. There are bucolic expressions scattered all through this epic poem, which seem to vouch for its authorship. Many critics are disposed to view it as a mere fragment of the long epics on Heracles composed by Peisander and his school, and some refer it to Panyasis, or Rhianus. Nevertheless, as the poem stands, it detaches one or two adventures of a god, and tells them in epic form, so that it is fairly to be connected with the professed imitations of the Hymns in the other Theocritean poems just mentioned.   They all show not only a perfect handling of epic style and manner, but considerable force and beauty, and are quite worthy of the great name of their author.

§ 104. Of the Παίγνια, or sportive effusions attributed to Homer, I have already discussed the *Battle of the Frogs and Mice.* It is greatly to be regretted that a much more important poem, the *Margites*, has not been preserved, inasmuch as it was treated as the genuine work of Homer, even by Aristotle, who quotes it more than once, and sees in it (though falsely) the first germ of comedy.[1]   It was a humorous description of a foolish young man, dabbling in various knowledge, but ignorant of all practical matters, and making terrible blunders in the more delicate situations of life.   From the extract quoted in the good editions of Suidas,[2] it seems that the poem was not very decent in its wit.   There was a very remarkable feature about its form—a feature which has exercised modern critics greatly. Iambic lines were inserted at irregular intervals among the hexameters of which it mainly consisted.   As Suidas and Eudocia attribute the poem to Pigres,[3] it has been thought that he may have added or interlarded these lines.   This is the conclusion to which Bernhardy comes, without positively asserting Pigres to be the individual interpolator ; but the conclusion is not very safe, for in another of the παίγνια, the Εἰρεσιώνη, we have the same feature, and there is no reason to believe that iambics were invented by Archilochus ; they were rather an old popular form of verse adopted by him for literary purposes.[4] The *Margites* was held in high esteem by the ancients, and was quoted by Cratinus, possibly Aristophanes, Callimachus, and the stoic Zeno.   By Dio Chrysostom, apparently quoting from the latter, it was regarded as a juvenile work of Homer. In Suidas' day it seems to have been already lost.   The mere

[1] Arist. *Poet.* 4 ; *Nic. Eth.* vi. 7.

[2] *Sub voc.* Μαργίτης.

[3] *Sub voc.* Πίγρης, the brother of the famous Artemisia, who is said to have interpolated the Iliad with pentameters.

[4] The mixture of hexameters and iambics is to be seen in the 125th frag. (an epigram) of Simonides, ed. Bergk.

names of two other poems classed under this head are preserved, the Ἐπικιχλίδες and the Ἑπτάπεκτος αἴξ.

§ 105. In the pseudo-Herodotean Life of Homer there are preserved several other curious little poems, and fragments of poems, which were falsely ascribed to the great poet, but which are to us inestimable as showing a glimpse of the popular songs of early Greece. There is a beautiful epitaph on King Midas of Phrygia, who had taken a daughter of Agamemnon, despot of Kyme, to wife, and who died at the time of the Kimmerian invasion (*circ.* 680 B.C.). It is strictly an epigram on a bronze statue set over the tomb.[1] There is also an address to the poet's home, Smyrna, which he left ‚on account of the little appreciation of his art, which is probably (as Bergk well says) the earliest *échantillon* of lyric feeling, though clothed in epic verse. It is entitled *to the Kymæans*, which is thought a mistake, arising from the false reading Κύμης for Σμύρνης in the end of the poem. The poems numbered i. and ii. are fragments of similar personal addresses. Of the rest two deserve special notice—that entitled Κάμινος or Κεραμεῖς, a little address of a wandering minstrel to the potters as they are putting their work into the oven, praying success for them if they reward him, but calling upon a strange assembly of demons, Sabaktes and his comrades, Circe and the Centaurs, to spoil the work and crack the ware if they treat him with stinginess. The second, called Εἰρεσιώνη,[2] is a song of

> Χαλκέη παρθένος εἰμί, Μίδεω δ' ἐπὶ σήματι κεῖμαι·
> ἔστ' ἂν ὕδωρ τε ῥέῃ, καὶ δένδρεα μακρὰ τεθήλῃ,
> ἠέλιός τ' ἀνιὼν φαίνῃ, λαμπρή τε σελήνη,
> καὶ ποταμοὶ πλήθωσιν, ἀνακλύζῃ δὲ θάλασσα·
> αὐτοῦ τῇδε μένουσα πολυκλαύτῳ ἐπὶ τύμβῳ
> ἀγγέλεω παριοῦσι, Μίδης ὅτι τῇδε τέθαπται.

It was by some attributed to Cleobulus. It was known to Simonides, and is referred to by Plato (*Phædrus*, p. 264) as being a sort of poetical *Round,* in which the verses can be transposed without spoiling the sense.

[2]
> Δῶμα προστραπόμεσθ' ἀνδρὸς μέγα δυναμένοιο,
> ὃς μέγα μὲν δύναται, μέγα δὲ βρέμει ὄλβιος ἀεί.
> αὐταὶ ἀνακλίνεσθε θύραι· πλοῦτος γὰρ ἔσεισιν
> πολλὸς, σὺν πλούτῳ δὲ καὶ εὐφροσύνη τεθαλυῖα,
> εἰρήνη τ' ἀγαθὴ, ὅσα δ' ἄγγεα, μεστὰ μὲν εἴη,
> κυρβαίη δ' αἰεὶ κατὰ καρδόπου ἕρποι μάζα.

children going from house to house in autumn during Apollo's feast, and levying what they can get, just as poor children now go about on St. Stephen's or May-day. As already observed, this little piece ends with iambic trimeters. It was probably sung at Samos, but its age is unknown. These two poems, both in the practices they imply, and in the superstitions they mention, give us one of the few glimpses we have into the life of the lower classes in early times. They have nothing to do with Homer or with epic poetry, but as we have no class of poetry or of literature where they could find a natural place, they may still hold the place assigned to them by the ancients, as venerable fragments of what the common people sang, while the rhapsodists were reciting their refined epics at the courts of kings and nobles.

§ 106. It may be well finally to dispose in a few words of the external history of the collection. Our oldest testimony to the existence of these Hymns is a citation by Thucydides (iii. 104) from the first (to the Delian Apollo). His quotation is remarkable for differing considerably in expression, though not at all in sense, from our MSS., so that there appears to have been much liberty allowed the rhapsodists in the rendering of their texts. The historian goes on to cite the famous personal passage in which the poet describes himself as 'the blind old man of Chios' rocky isle'—a passage which Thucydides, and with him all the ancients, considered as clear proof of the blindness and of the Chian parentage of Homer. Accordingly, though seldom cited in antiquity, the hymns generally went under the name of Homer. There seems to be another allusion to the same hymn in Aristophanes' *Clouds,*

τοῦ παιδὸς δὲ γυνὴ κατὰ δίφραδα βήσεται ὕμμιν,
ἡμίονοι δ' ἄξουσι κραταίποδες ἐς τόδε δῶμα·
αὐτὴ δ' ἱστὸν ὑφαίνοι ἐπ' ἠλέκτρῳ βεβαυῖα.
νεῦμαί τοι, νεῦμαι ἐνιαύσιος, ὥστε χελιδὼν
ἕστηκ' ἐν προθύροις, ψιλὴ πόδας· ἀλλὰ φέρ' αἶψα
πέρσαι τῷδ' Ἀπόλλωνι γυιάτιδο
καί,
εἰ μέν τι δώσεις· εἰ δὲ μή, οὐχ ἑστήξομεν·
οὐ γὰρ συνοικήσοντες ἐνθάδ' ἤλθομεν.

and to the Pythian or second hymn in the *Knights* (v. 1015),
where he quotes (apparently) v. 265 [1] ; but after his day, the first
allusions, and those indirect, appear in a corresponding hymn
of Callimachus, and a note of Antigonus Carystius about lyre
strings.   Though five or six scholia, gathered from the Iliad,
Pindar, and Aristophanes, allude to them, we do not possess a
single remark upon them directly ascribed to the great Alexandrian critics.   Diodorus quotes the hymns generally as Homer's,
and so does Philodemus, in one of the recovered Herculanean
fragments.   Pausanias also speaks of Homer's hymns generally,
but specially cites that to the Delian Apollo, that to the Pythian,
and that to Demeter.   Athenæus cites the Hymn to Apollo,
but hesitates about its authorship.   The scholiast on Pindar
ascribes it to Kinæthon of Chios.   Suidas and the *Lives* of
Herodotus and Homer ascribe them without criticism to
Homer.

Thus we find almost no quotations from them in antiquity.
There is very seldom a reference to any other hymn but that
to the Delian Apollo.   Yet about the first century B.C. we find
the *Hymns of Homer* mentioned, and Pausanias seems specially
acquainted with that to Demeter.   The authors of good Greek
scholia cite them, and then we lose all trace of them till the
time of Suidas.

§ 107. *Bibliographical.* Our extant MSS. are late, none of
them earlier than the fourteenth century.   Of these the most remarkable is that found at Moscow by Matthiæ in 1780, and now
at Leyden, for it contains at the opening a fragment to Dionysus, and next the famous Hymn to Demeter, not elsewhere preserved.   Nevertheless, our best authority, Baumeister, prefers
the Laurentian codex (Plut. xxxii. 45), of about the same date,
for purity of text and general merit.   All the extant MSS. seem
taken from one older copy, now lost ; but the Moscow copy
was written by a more learned scribe than the rest, and therefore more seriously interpolated and emended.   The archetype
was already damaged, as is shown by the short fragment of the
Hymn to Dionysus, with which the Moscow codex opens.   But,

---

[1] v. 575, where Homer is said to have represented Iris winged ; cf.
the schol. on the line, who refers to the Hymns.

before it was again copied by the writers of our other codices, it had lost several more of the early pages, which contained the Hymn to Demeter.   From the mistakes made in our MSS. we can infer that even their archetype was not very old, and certainly not written in capitals.   They were first printed at Florence in 1488 in Demetrius' Chalcondylas' *editio princeps* of Homer.   Then follow H. Stephens, Joshua Barnes, and the Epistola critica of D. Ruhnken (1749).   After the discovery of the Moscow codex (now Leidensis), we have, among others, editions by F. A. Wolf (Halle, 1796), by Ilgen, a very complete book, by Matthiæ, Godf. Hermann, and Franke, almost all with the *Batrachomyomachia* and Trifles ; lastly, and most conveniently, the Hymns alone with commentary by A. Baumeister (Lips. 1860), who has also revised the text in the Teubner series.   Of translations I only know the old one of Chapman (reprinted 1858), of course without the hymn to Demeter ; but this latter has suggested to Mr. Swinburne one of his finest *Poems and Ballads.*

CHAPTER IX.

THE LATER HISTORY OF EPIC POETRY.[1]

§ 108. WITH the so-called cyclic poets, the natural course of epic poetry had reached the close of its development. Other species of poetry arose and satisfied the wants of a newer age. The historical sense of the Greeks, late in growth and slow in development, at last substituted prose narrative of real facts for the poetical treatment of myths. Nevertheless, the unsurpassed greatness of the old masterpieces perpetually tempted men of learning and refinement to try a new development on these models, which had shown a sustained grandeur that no succeeding form or metre could ever attain. But all these attempts were, nationally speaking, complete failures, though some of them which remain delight us by their beauty and the elegance of their execution.[2] They were in ancient days the study of the learned few, in later the arena for displaying grammatical accuracy and artificial culture. Even

---

[1] This chapter offers no interest to the general reader, and Apollonius is the only literary figure which it contains. But some information concerning the later epic poets may fairly be demanded by the special student, perhaps even because they are obscure.

[2] Chœrilus, in an extant fragment, probably from the opening of his *Perseis*, states the difficulties of the later epic poets with good sense and feeling :—

Ἆ μάκαρ, ὅστις ἔην κεῖνον χρόνον ἴδρις ἀοιδῆς,
Μουσάων θεράπων, ὅτ' ἀκήρατος ἦν ἔτι λειμών·
νῦν δ' ὅτε πάντα δέδασται, ἔχουσι δὲ πείρατα τέχναι,
ὕστατοι ὥστε δρόμου καταλειπόμεθ', οὐδέ πῃ ἔστι
πάντῃ παπταίνοντα νεοζυγὲς ἅρμα πελάσσαι.

in the last agonies of expiring heathenism, the school of Egypt
poured out its turbid utterance of mystery and magic in long
mythological epics, which are now unknown save to the curious
student of obscure books. All these epics are outside the
proper course of the national literature of Greece, which seems
always to have exhausted all the originality in each kind of
writing before it passed on to the next. Nor do they fall
properly within the scope of this book, which is concerned
with that literature which was in Greece national, and not the
heritage of the few. It seems well, therefore, to dispose of
them briefly here, in order to write the history of succeeding
kinds of literature without interruption. Those who desire
full and accurate information on this very dry and unprofitable
subject will do well to consult the elaborate and unwearied
work of Bernhardy, who has devoted 120 very long pages to a
thorough examination of these poems and fragments.[1]

§ 109. The earliest development of this kind seems to have
been in Asia Minor about a century after the chief cyclic poets,
and the favourite subject the adventures of Heracles. These
were specially treated in a poem called *Heracleia* by PISANDER of
Cameirus, a poet of early but unknown date, whose authority on
the labours of Heracles is often invoked, and who was the first
to arm him with the club and lion's skin. ASIUS of Samos
seems to have been an equally early genealogical poet, who is
quoted by Duris as describing the luxury of the Ionians at
Samos in terms not unlike Thucydides' account of the old
Athenians. Athenæus cites a few comic lines from an elegy of
the same poet, and Pausanias refers to him on obscure genealogical questions about local heroes. These two poets are
generally placed much earlier than those about to be mentioned,
and Dübner[2] believes there was a long sleep of epic poetry, till
the excitement of the Persian wars caused it to wake up again.
Herodorus of Heraclea, though a prose writer, was like them
in subjects and style.

PANYASIS, uncle of Herodotus, a man of political note

---

[1] *LG.* ii. 1, pp. 538–458.

[2] In his Preface to the Didot ed. of the Epic fragments, following
Suidas' ὃs σβεσθεῖσαν τὴν ποιητικὴν ἐπανήγαγε.

at Halicarnassus, where he fought for the freedom of the town against the tyrant Lygdamis, gained a good deal of temporary celebrity by another *Heracleia*, in fourteen books.   Considerable fragments of a social nature are quoted from it by Stobæus and Athenæus, which specially refer to the use and abuse of wine-drinking.   They are elegantly written, and remind us strongly of the elegiac fragments on the same subject by Xenophanes and Theognis.   He was also, according to Suidas, author of elegiac poems, in six books, called *Ionica*, on the antiquities of Athens, and especially on the Ionic migration.   This work was not without influence on his nephew Herodotus.

His younger contemporary, ANTIMACHUS of Colophon, lived up to the end of the Poloponnesian War as a very old man, and has been already mentioned (p. 31) as one of the learned critics who published a special edition of Homer, quoted in the Venetian scholia.   His great interest in Homer led him to attempt a learned and scholastic imitation (for original genius he had none) in a very long and tedious *Thebais*.   His *Lyde*, an elegiac poem, does not belong to the present chapter.   He is said by Plutarch, in a suspicious anecdote (*Vit. Lys.* 12), to have contended for a prize in a laudatory poem on Lysander, and, being defeated, to have destroyed the poem.   But Plato, he adds, being then young and a personal admirer of Antimachus, consoled him with animadverting on the blindness of his critics.   Plato is further said to have wished for a collection of his poems.   Hadrian preferred him to Homer, and introduced him to notice after he had long been forgotten. It was left for Mr. Paley to tell us that the little-noticed edition of Antimachus, the friend and contemporary of Plato, was perhaps the first publication of the Iliad and Odyssey in their present form !   The extant fragments of Antimachus with other epic poets are collected with care by Dübner at the end of the Hesiod in the Didot collection.   They have no literary interest, being chiefly citations to explain obscure words, which he affected, obscure myths, which he illustrated or narrated, or lastly, phrases either borrowed from Homer, or contrary to Homeric use.   The Alexandrian critics constantly quote him, and greatly admired him, and he may fairly be regarded the model or master of the Alexandrian epic poets. This did not save him from the criticism and ridicule of Callimachus. Quintilian[1] speaks of him as being indeed generally thought by the learned as second to Homer, but as second by an enormous interval. Plutarch, in his tract on Talkativeness, gives an amusing example of a babbler flooding the man who asks him a question with his answer, which comprises a whole history, 'especially if he have read Antimachus of Colophon.'

CHŒRILUS (of Samos also), a younger contemporary of Herodotus, and said by Plutarch to have been intimate with Lysander, is remarkable for having attempted a great novelty —to relate in the epic form the very subject with which Herodotus founded Greek history. His *Perseïs* sang the struggle of Hellenedom with Persia. Its style is said to have been less artificial than that of Antimachus, who was his rival in the estimation of the learned. Only three fragments of interest are left us from this poet, that above cited, then his description of the Jews in the army of Xerxes—an inaccurate picture, but very interesting from its early date—and lastly a striking sentence, supposed to be spoken by Xerxes after his defeat.[2] If a judgment upon such scanty evidence were allowable, I should be disposed to agree with the minority, who placed him above Antimachus.

§ 110. These three authors, together with the older Asius and Pisander, are the obscure representatives of the Greek epic poetry down to the Alexandrian period, when there was larger room for literary revivals, as the original genius of the nation was exhausted. Accordingly, the only later epic which has ever enjoyed any real celebrity is the *Argonautica* of the Alexandrian APOLLONIUS,[3] commonly called the Rhodian,

---

[1] x. I, § 53, Plutarch *de Garr.* cap. xxi.

[2]   χερσὶν δ' ὄλβον ἔχω, κύλικος τρύφος ἀμφὶς ἐαγός,
  ἀνδρῶν δαιτυμόνων ναυάγιον, οἶά τε πολλὰ
  πνεῦμα Διωνύσοιο πρὸς Ὕβριος ἔκβαλεν ἀκτάς.

[3] Rhianus, the editor of Homer, and contemporary of Eratosthenes, was the author of several voluminous epics, from one of which, the *Messeniaca*, Pausanias quotes the romantic legends concerning Aristomenes, the great Messenian hero.

from his long residence and citizenship there.   He was a pupil of the famous Callimachus, afterwards his bitterest opponent on æsthetic questions, and hence his personal enemy, on whom Callimachus wrote a bitter libel, the *Ibis*.[1]   Ultimately he succeeded Eratosthenes as librarian in Alexandria.   Apollonius, indeed, deserves more than a passing notice.   The aspect of criticism has veered constantly as regards him, nor can his position be yet considered finally determined.   For, on the one hand, we find a good many enthusiastic admirers, especially among older scholars, who see in him a man of genius, and in his poems not only a revival of an old and splendid style, but a revival with distinct and original features.   By them he is praised as one of the greatest lights in Greek literature.   On the other hand, the general neglect of later critics, backed by that of our classical public, consigns him to that oblivion in which all Alexandrian work, except that of Theocritus, has lain during the present century.[2]   This judgment is so completely based upon neglect, not upon critical censure, that we may well hesitate to endorse it, and may turn to a brief examination of a work once so famous, and so largely commented on in the days of the scholiasts, but which is now almost a novelty to the majority of our scholars.

The poem[3] opens with a catalogue of the heroes, and a very picturesque description of their departure, amid the tears and sympathy of their relations (i. 247, sq.).   It then proceeds to narrate their various adventures on the journey.   The writing is simple, and little ornamented, as if the poet's main object had been to record geographical and mythical lore, and not to fascinate the reader by his fancy.   There are few and short digressions throughout the work, too few, indeed, for an epic on the old model.   The more ornate passages in the first book are the descriptions of the song of Or-

[1] Cf. Mr. Ellis's learned article on this quarrel in the *Academy* for Aug. 30, 1879.

[2] The same variance of opinion existed of old; while Virgil must have greatly admired him, and Varro Atacinus translated him, Quintilian speaks of his poem as *non contemnendum opus æquali quadam mediocritate.*

[3] It is arranged in four books, but each of them so long as to equal two books of Homer.   The whole amounts to some 5,800 lines.

pheus, which is justly described as *Theogonic* in character, of the cloak of Jason, and lastly some similes which are not very apt (as the scholiasts note), except a very fine one comparing Heracles, when he hears of the loss of Hylas, to a bull maddened by a gadfly.[1] It may, indeed, be here remarked that the poet's similes are rather introduced for their prettiness than for their aptness, and that when he expands one taken from Homer (as in ii. 543, sq.) he does not improve it.

In the second book, which continues the adventures of the Argo, the description of the miseries of Phineus is very interesting, as is also the stirring account of the passage of the Symplegades. Various curious notices, such as that of the 'black country' of the Chalybes and the *couvade* of the Tibareni,[2] maintain our interest, which is, however, the same kind of interest as that excited by Xenophon's prose narrative on the same topics towards the close of his *Anabasis*.

In the third book we are introduced to the second great subject, which is combined with the adventures of the Argonauts—the passion of Medea. It is this intensely dramatic element which gives the poem its main value, and is an unique phenomenon in old Greek epic literature. This book is so vastly superior to all the rest, that we at once suspect the existence of some great model, from which Apollonius must have copied his great and burning scenes. But we look in vain through scholiasts and older poets for such a model. Sophocles' *Colchians*, which were on this subject, certainly did not make the psychological drawing of Medea prominent, or we must have heard it from the commentators either on Apollonius, or on Euripides' *Medea*. This latter picture is quite distinct from that of Apollonius, and he has not borrowed from it. There is, indeed, a sort of modernness, a minuteness of psychological analysis in Apollonius, which we seek in vain even in Euripides, the most advanced of the classical poets. The scene where Medea determines in her agony to commit suicide, but recoils with the reaction of a strong youthful nature from death, is the ancient parallel, if not the prototype, of the

---

[1] 496, sq., vv. 721–68, and vv. 1265, sq.

[2] 178, sq., and especially vv. 305–6, 551, sq., v. 1002.

splendid scene near the opening of Goethe's *Faust*, and is well worth reading.[1]

It is very strange that the third book of the *Argonautica* has not maintained a high place in public esteem. Adverse critics note that the character of Jason fades out before the stronger Medea, and that he is the prototype of Virgil's Æneas,[2]

[1]
> Ἦ καὶ φωριαμὸν μετεκίαθεν, ᾗ ἔνι πολλὰ
> φάρμακά οἱ τὰ μὲν ἐσθλὰ, τὰ δὲ ῥαιστήρι' ἔκειτο.
> ἐνθεμένη δ' ἐπὶ γούνατ' ὀδύρετο· δεῦε δὲ κόλπους
> ἄλληκτον δακρύοισι, τὰ δ' ἔρρεεν ἀσταγὲς αὔτως,
> αἴν' ὀλοφυρομένης τὸν ἑὸν μόρον. ἵετο δ' ἥ γε
> φάρμακα λέξασθαι θυμοφθόρα, τόφρα πάσαιτο.
> ἤδη καὶ δεσμοὺς ἀνελύετο φωριαμοῖο,
> ἐξελέειν μεμαυῖα δυσάμμορος —ἀλλά οἱ ἄφνω
> δεῖμ' ὀλοὸν στυγεροῖο κατὰ φρένας ἦλθ' Ἀΐδαο.
> ἔσχετο δ' ἀμφασίῃ δηρὸν χρόνον, ἀμφὶ δὲ πᾶσαι
> θυμηδεῖς βιότοιο μεληδόνες ἰνδάλλοντο.
> μνήσατο μὲν τερπνῶν, ὅσ' ἐνὶ ζωοῖσι πέλονται,
> μνήσαθ' ὁμηλικίης περιγηθέος, οἷά τε κούρῃ·
> καί τέ οἱ ἠέλιος γλυκίων γένετ' εἰσοράασθαι
> ἢ πάρος, εἰ ἐτεόν γε νόῳ ἐπεμαίεθ' ἕκαστα.
> καὶ τὴν μέν ῥα πάλιν σφετέρων ἀποκάτθετο γούνων,
> Ἥρης ἐννεσίῃσι μετάτροπος, οὐδ' ἔτι βουλὰς
> ἄλλῃ δοιάζεσκεν· ἐέλδετο δ' αἶψα φανῆναι.
> ἠῶ τελλομένην, ἵνα οἱ θελκτήρια δοίη
> φάρμακα συνθεσίῃσι καὶ ἀντήσειεν ἐς ὠπήν.
> πυκνὰ δ' ἀνὰ κληῖδας ἑῶν λύεσκε θυράων,
> αἴγλην σκεπτομένη· τῇ δ' ἀσπάσιον βάλε φέγγος
> Ἠριγενὴς, κίνυντο δ' ἀνὰ πτολίεθρον ἕκαστοι.

Other remarkable passages are vv. 615, sq., and 961_71.

> ἐκ δ' ἄρα οἱ κραδίη στηθέων πέσεν, ὄμματα δ' αὔτως
> ἤχλυσαν· θερμὸν δὲ παρηΐδας εἷλεν ἔρευθος.
> γούνατα δ' οὔτ' ὀπίσω οὔτε προπάροιθεν ἀεῖραι
> ἔσθενεν, ἀλλ' ὑπένερθε πάγη πόδας. αἱ δ' ἄρα τείως
> ἀμφίπολοι μάλα πᾶσαι ἀπὸ σφείων ἐλίασθεν.
> τὼ δ' ἄνεῳ καὶ ἄναυδοι ἐφέστασαν ἀλλήλοισιν,
> ἢ δρυσὶν ἢ μακρῇσιν ἐειδόμενοι ἐλάτῃσιν,
> αἵτε παράσσον ἔκηλοι ἐν οὔρεσιν ἐρρίζωνται
> νηνεμίῃ· μετὰ δ' αὖτις ὑπὸ ῥιπῆς ἀνέμοιο
> κινύμεναι ὁμάδησαν ἀπείριτον· ὣς ἄρα τώ γε
> μέλλον ἅλις φθέγξασθαι ὑπὸ πνοιῇσιν Ἔρωτος.

[2] Indeed Virgil's obligations to Apollonius may be traced on every page of the Æneid.

but this tradition was already established by Euripides in his *Medea*.

The fourth book returns to the fabulous adventures of the heroes, during which Medea only appears occasionally, and generally as supplicating their sympathy or reproaching them for their coldness in protecting her from the pursuit of her father. But the main interest to modern readers is gone. The poet often lets his own person appear, and even once apologises for telling an improbable myth.[1] Two picturesque scenes, the playing of Eros and Ganymede, and the description of the Hesperides with the wounded dragon,[2] are evidently drawn from celebrated pictures, or, as some think, from groups of statuary. The frequent breaking off with 'why should I pursue the subject further,' or some such excuse, also points to the modern condition of the poet, encumbered with an endless store of traditions. His slightly veiled scepticism produces a similar impression.

§ 111. *Bibliographical.* As to MSS., the principal one, which far exceeds all the rest in value, is in that most famous of all books, the Plut. xxxii. 9, of the Laurentian library at Florence, which contains a copy of the tenth century, along with the equally invaluable MSS. of Æschylus and Sophocles. There are twenty-five others known, at the Vatican, at Paris, and elsewhere. But all critical work must depend upon the Medicean codex. From it the *editio princeps* of Lascaris (in capital letters, Florence, 1496) was prepared, the Aldine (Venet. 1521) from the three Vatican MSS. Then comes the edition of Stephanus. There are, besides, editions by Brunck, Shaw (Oxon. 1777), and Schaefer. The newer are Wellauer's text, scholia and complete indices (Leipsig, 1828), Lehrs' (with Hesiod, &c. ed. Didot), Merkel's critical text (in Teubner's series, 1872), and Keil and Merkel's edition in 1854, with critical notes, and all the scholia—a fine book. In all these editions the Greek scholia form the most important element. Those of the Florentine MS. are very old and valuable, and are said at the end of the book to be selected from Lucillus Tarræus, Sophocles, and Theon. These men's notes are chiefly on mythological lore, but also give many valuable explanations,

---

[1] iv. 1379.   [2] iii. 114, sq., and iv. 1395, sq.

and, especially on the first book, cite the version of the poet's earlier edition which was then still extant. They criticise the speeches from a rhetorical aspect, and occasionally censure the similes, which they analyse with prosaic accuracy. Perhaps the most curious point in them is their frequent objecting to the poet's use of pronominal adjectives, which they roundly (and I think rightly) assert he did not understand.[1] The Paris MSS. contain a great many grammatical additions of later date. There are said to be three English translations, by Fawkes, Greene (1780), and Preston (1803), the last of which is a very scholarly work. They have fallen into such oblivion as to be now rare, even in large libraries.

§ 112. I know not whether it is worth wearying the reader with the later history of epic poetry. But as this obscure and feeble after-growth will give some idea of the sort of contrast which exists between classical and post-classical literature, I will for once inflict upon him a page of names and titles. These will serve me as a good apology for having avoided any fuller treatment of the Alexandrian epoch.

In the age of Apollonius, we have the epic studies among the poems of Theocritus, which have been already mentioned, but they seem to me more in the style of the Homeric Hymns than of the longer Homeric epics. They are careful and very perfect studies by the learned Alexandrian of the old epic style in short and complete episodes—in fact, idylls in the strictest sense of the term.

The *Europe* of Moschus (about 3rd cent. A.D.) seems to be an epic idyll of the same kind, of great elegance and finish, but with the erotic element more prominent than would have been natural to the real epic age. The description of the basket of Europe (vv. 37–63) is elaborated almost like that of the shields of Achilles and Heracles, and perhaps marks the contrast in the old and the new epic significantly enough. In the same category may be classed the *Megara*, or dialogue, of 125 lines, between Megara and Alcmene, concerning the absent Heracles, which is attributed to the same poet. This poem, like most of the short epic fragments of the Alexandrian epoch,

---

[1] Cf. schol. on ii. 544; iii. 186, 395, 600, 795 ; iv. 1327.

is not a whole in itself, but a sort of fragment, as it were, intended for a longer poem. This *Megara* ends with the dream related by Alcmene, which evidently portends the death of Heracles. These somewhat monotonous but elegant exercises will be most easily consulted in Ahrens' *Bucolici* (Teubner, 1875), where, however, too many of the Theocritean collection are called spurious, and printed at the end of the volume.

§ 113. From this period onward there is a long gap in our epic records, though we know that sophists and grammarians paid much attention to this style, and that the Indian adventures of Alexander gave rise to a taste for Indian and other Oriental fables, and especially descriptions of the Indian adventures of Bacchus. But we find no enduring result till the beginning of the fifth century, when an epic school was founded, principally in Upper Egypt, and of whom two representatives are well known—Nonnus and Musæus. There are several others mentioned in the fuller literature of the time. First, Quintus Smyrnæus (called *Calaber*, from the finding there of the MS.), who wrote a continuation of Homer in fourteen books, thus taking up the work of the cyclic poets, who were probably lost before his time. Then Tryphiodorus, who wrote an Odyssey and an extant *Capture of Troy*, in some 700 lines, and Collūthus, who wrote a *Rape of Helen*. These latter were Egyptians, and lived in the fifth or sixth century. They can be conveniently studied in the Didot collection, in which they are all printed after Hesiod.[1] But these works are not worth describing. Nonnus only, standing between the living and the dead, composing, on the one hand, his long epic on the adventures of Dionysus, and, on the other, his paraphrase of St. John's Gospel into Homeric hexameters, is a most interesting figure, though beyond the scope of the historian of Greek classical literature. Even the life of Christ

---

[1] Before the publication of this most useful volume (edited by F. S. Lehrs and Dübner), the later epics, and the fragments of the earlier, were very inaccessible, and only to be found in old uncritical or stray modern editions. Most unaccountably, the epic of Nonnus is excluded from this otherwise complete collection, which includes even Tzetzes.

was put together in Homeric hexameters, called *Centones Homerici*, which were attributed to the Empress Eudocia, and thought worthy of being printed by Aldus (1501) and Stephens (1568), but apparently as Christian literature.

The *Hero and Leander* of Musæus has, perhaps, maintained a higher place and greater popularity than any of the poems of this later age, and deserves it from the exceeding sweetness and pathos of both style and story.   But it is hard to find a reader who has ever seen the original, though it has been immortalised by Byron in his *Bride of Abydos,* and thus kept alive in modern memories.

CHAPTER X.

THE RISE OF PERSONAL POETRY AMONG THE GREEKS.

§ 114. THERE is a sort of general impression produced by the marked divisions of Greek Literature in our handbooks, that the newer kinds of poetry did not arise till the epic had decayed, and that this latter quickly disappeared before the splendour and variety of the new development. This is a great mistake. The most celebrated and popular of the cyclic poets were either contemporary with, or even subsequent to, the greatest iambic and elegiac poets, and the revival of epic poetry about the time of the Persian wars, and again at Alexandria, proves how deep and universal a hold it maintained upon the Greek mind. Nevertheless, after the opening of the seventh century B.C. it ceased to supply the spiritual wants of the Greeks of Asia Minor. No *original* successor of the poets of the Iliad and Odyssey had arisen, and the Greek public were not satisfied with the perpetual imitation of these old masterpieces. They were still less attracted by long mythical histories in epic verse, which pretended to be epic poems, but missed the tragic unity necessary to interest the hearer, and seemed rather designed to instruct the calm reader in mythical lore than to satisfy the longings of the heart, or feed its emotions. While, therefore, epic poetry was making no advance, the social and political development of the Asiatic Greeks was growing with giant strides. Contact with the old Empires of the East gave them material culture, while traffic with barbarians brought them wealth to carry out their ideas. Perpetual conflicts, and fusions of classes, and adventures of war and of travel—in the Odyssey still the appanage of kings—brought out the feeling of personality, of self-importance in the poorer classes, and this feeling could not but find its expression in popular poetry.

We cannot sever the poets of this age according to their metres, for they almost all used various metres indifferently; nor even according to their dialect, for this often varied with the metre : nor does Melic poetry stand in any real contrast (as to content) with elegiac and iambic. The division which I desire to follow is, first, subjective or personal poetry, including the early elegiac, iambic, trochaic, and such like verse, also those more strictly lyric poems which are called Æolic, and in which Alcæus or Sappho sang their personal joys and griefs; secondly, public or choral poetry—in this age always lyric, which consisted of those hymns to the gods, or processional odes, or songs of victory which were of public significance, and into which the poet only accidentally introduced his personality. These public poems were not at first composed by special bards, but as schools and tendencies became fixed and developed, poets like Stesichorus and Pindar came to devote themselves almost exclusively to this side.

§ 115. As I have already explained (p. 4), short lyrical effusions were never wanting among the Greeks, and irregular or varying metres were already common among the people, when the long pompous hexameter was constructed by educated men, and raised to the universal form of higher literature. Short halting rythms for fun and ridicule, bold anapæsts for war and for procession—these were no new inventions among the Greeks. Yet this in no way detracts from the capital merit of the great man who felt that epic poetry had exhausted its national history, and that he must seek among the people, and among the songs of the people, the inspiration for a renovation of poetry. The ancients are unanimous about the man, and fairly agreed as to his date, which they mark by the reign of Gyges, king of Lydia.[1]   Later researches have brought the date of Gyges con-

---

[1] It is, indeed, fixed by his frag. 25 (ed. Bergk, whose *Fragg. Poet. Lyr.* I quote throughout), quoted by a scholiast as the earliest use of the word τυραννίς :—

οὔ μοι τὰ Γύγεω τοῦ πολυχρύσου μέλει,
οὐδ' εἷλέ πώ με ζῆλος, οὐδ' ἀγαίομαι
θεῶν ἔργα, μεγάλης δ' οὐκ ἐρέω τυραννίδος·
ἀπόπροθεν γάρ ἐστιν ὀφθαλμῶν ἐμῶν.

siderably below 700 B.C.,[1] so that while Hesiod was in the poor and backward parts of central Greece modifying, with timid hand, the tone and style of epic poetry, without abandoning its form, ARCHILOCHUS, storm-tost amid wealth and poverty, amid commerce and war, amid love and hate, ever in exile and yet everywhere at home—Archilochus broke altogether with the traditions of literature, and colonised new territories with his genius.

The remaining fragments show us that he used all kinds of metre—elegiac, iambic, trochaic and irregular lyric. He is often said to have invented iambic and elegiac verse. But we know that older poems, such as the *Margites*, contained iambics, and this verse seems associated from the beginning with the feasts of Demeter,[2] who was specially worshipped at Paros, where Archilochus was born. And no doubt all the other metres he used, though improved and perfected by his genius, were known among the people.

One of them, however, deserves special mention, because even the ancients felt an interest about its origin—the so-called *elegiac.* The word ἔλεγος (ἐλεγεῖον) can hardly be originally a Greek word, and seems of Phrygian derivation.[3] It was applied in early times to a melody of plaintive character on the Phrygian flute, whether with or without a song is uncertain. The old shepherd's pipe (σύριγξ) seems to have been sup-

Archilochus further mentions the devastation of Magnesia by the Kimmerians. The evidence is summed up by Susemihl in a learned note to his translation of Aristotle's *Politics* (vol. ii. p. 185).

[1] Cf. Gelzer's curious paper *Das Zeitalter des Gyges*, who fixes his reign at 687-53 B.C. by references to him in Assyrian inscriptions.

[2] This is described in the legend as the cheering of the sad goddess by the maid Iambe and her coarse wit. Cf. *Hymn to Demeter*, v. 199, sq. :—

οὐδέ τιν' οὔτ' ἔπεϊ προσπτύσσετο οὔτε τι ἔργῳ
ἀλλ' ἀγέλαστος, ἄπαστος ἐδητύος ἠδὲ ποτῆτος,
ἧστο, πόθῳ μινύθουσα βαθυζώνοιο θυγατρός,
πρίν γ' ὅτε δὴ χλεύης μιν Ἰάμβη κέδν' εἰδυῖα
πολλὰ παρασκώπτουσ' ἐτρέψατο πότνιαν, ἀγνήν,
μειδῆσαι γελάσαι τε καὶ ἵλαον σχεῖν θυμόν·
ἣ δή οἱ καὶ ἔπειτα μεθύστερον εὔαδεν ὀργαῖς

[3] It is not older than the fifth century, ἔπη being at first applied even to elegiac verses. Cf. Theognis, v. 20.

planted by this better instrument (αὐλός),[1] made of reeds, which is alluded to in the marriage scene in Iliad Σ, and in the description of the Muses in the Hymn to Hermes. But the name elegy was gradually restricted to that peculiar modification of hexameters, by interposing the halting pentameter, which remained through the rest of Greek history a favourite mode of expression in personal poetry. We have all manner of subjects treated in this metre—morals, military and political exhortations, proverbial reflections, effusions of love and grief, epigrams of praise and epitaphs of sorrow—so much so that it is difficult to say what is its proper province. Perhaps there are three points, and three points only, which may be called permanent features in elegiac poetry. In the first place, it is *personal*, subjective as the Germans call it, and this feature comes out plainly enough even where the poet is discussing public topics, as in Solon's elegies, or narrating epic myths, as Antimachus in his *Lyde*. Even these were strictly personal poems. In the second place, it is almost always *secular*, religious poetry being either hexameter or strictly lyric in form. Thirdly, it is *Ionic*, and except in the case of epigrams or epitaphs, which are always of a local colour, is restricted to the dialect where it first arose.

We usually speak of the elegiac poets of Greece as if they were a distinct class, but there is hardly one of them at this epoch who did not use various metres, as appears even from the extant fragments. Thus Archilochus, so celebrated for his iambic satire, used the elegiac metre freely and with great elegance; Tyrtæus employed anapæsts, and Solon iambics. There is in fact hardly an early poet of whom we know much, except perhaps Mimnermus, who does not follow the example of Archilochus in the use of various metres. The previous use of elegiacs, of which the invention was attributed to Archilochus, may perhaps be established by the alleged quotations from CALLINUS, a poet of Ephesus about the fourteenth Olympiad (720 B.C.), who during the conflicts of Magnesia with his native town, and during the

---

[1] Mr. Chappell has shown (*Hist. of Music*, i. p. 276) that it was probably constructed on the clarinet principle, with a vibrating tongue of reed inside the mouthpiece.

dreadful invasions of the Kimmerians, wrote warlike exhortations in elegiac metre, of which a considerable fragment has been
preserved by Stobæus. There is, however, considerable doubt
whether this passage is not the work of Tyrtæus, or some other
early poet, and the shadowy figure of Callinus can hardly stand
for us at the head of this department of Greek poetry, though
Strabo distinctly asserts him to have been slightly anterior to
Archilochus.

§ 116. This latter poet is plainly the leading figure in the new
movement, and a strong and vigorous personality, who spoke
freely and fearlessly of all his own failings and misfortunes.[1] He
was born of a good family at Paros, but lived, owing to poverty,
a life of roving adventure, partly, it appears, as a mercenary
soldier,[2] partly as a colonist to Thasos ; nor do his wanderings
appear to have been confined to eastern Hellas, for he speaks
in praise of the rich plains about the Siris in Italy (frag. 21).
He was betrothed to Neobule, the youngest daughter of
Lycambes, his townsman ; but when she was refused him, probably on account of his poverty, he vented his rage and dis-
appointment in those famous satires, which first showed the
full power of the iambic metre, and were the wonder and the
delight of all antiquity. He ended his life by the death he doubtless desired, on the field of battle. In coarseness, terseness, and
bitterness he may justly be called the Swift of Greek Literature.
But even the scanty fragments of Archilochus show a range of
feeling and a wideness of sympathy far beyond the complete
works of Swift. He declares Mars and the Muse to be his

---

[1] 'Critias (says Ælian, *Var. Hist.* x. 13) blames Archilochus for reviling himself extremely, for had he not (says he) circulated this character of himself through the Greek world, we should not have learned that
he was the son of Enipo, a slave, or that, having left Paros on account
of poverty and distress, he came to Thasos, and there quarrelled with the
inhabitants ; or that he reviled alike friends and enemies ; nor should we
have known in addition, but for his own words, that he was an adulterer,
nor that he was licentious and insolent ; and, worst of all, that he threw
away his shield.'

[2] Mercenary soldiers, generally thought to belong to a later age, were
common at that time, for the Greeks were always ready to sell their services to the rich Asiatic kings. Cf. Archil. fragg. 24, 58.

enduring delights, but yet what can be more passionate than his love and his hate in all other human relations? He has noble passages of resignation too,[1] which sound like the voice of his later years, when his hardest taskmaster had lost his sway. But even these are as nothing compared to the real gush of feeling when he describes his youthful passions,[2] his love for Neobule, passing the Homeric love of women. Here he has anticipated Sappho and Alcæus, as in his warlike elegies he rivalled Tyrtæus, in his gnomic and reflective wisdom Solon and Theognis, in his jibes Cratinus and Aristophanes, in his fables Æsop.

Of his Hymns to Heracles and Dionysus we are not able to form any opinion. Moreover these belong to the choral lyric poetry of the Greeks, which we separate and regard under a different head. But it is clear that his Hymn to Heracles and Iolaus, also called an Epinikion of Heracles, after his labours, was so popular that it was regularly sung at Olympia by a friendly chorus in honour of the victors on the day or evening of the victory. This the scholiasts on Pindar's ninth Olympian ode tell us, and the custom must have lasted till the later lyric poets Simonides and Pindar were paid to write special odes for these occasions. It is remarkable that in this hymn, of which the scholiasts just mentioned have preserved two or three lines, the leader sang the refrain (in the absence of an instrument), while the chorus sang the body of the hymn.

---

[1] Frag. 66 : Θυμέ, θύμ' ἀμηχάνοισι κήδεσιν κυκώμενε,
[ἄνεχε] δυσμενῶν δ' ἀλέξευ προσβαλὼν ἐναντίον
στέρνον, ἐνδοκοῖσιν ἐχθρῶν πλησίον κατασταθεὶς
ἀσφαλέως· καὶ μήτε νικῶν ἀμφάδην ἀγάλλεο,
μήτε νικηθεὶς ἐν οἴκῳ καταπεσὼν ὀδύρεο·
ἀλλὰ χαρτοῖσίν τε χαῖρε καὶ κακοῖσιν ἀσχάλα
μὴ λίην· γίγνωσκε δ' οἷος ῥυσμὸς ἀνθρώπους ἔχει.

Cf. also fragg. 56, 74.

[2] Frag. 84 :   Δύστηνος ἔγκειμαι πόθῳ
ἄψυχος, χαλεπῆσι θεῶν ὀδύνῃσιν ἔκητι
πεπαρμένος δι' ὀστέων.

And frag. 103 : Τοῖος γὰρ φιλότητος ἔρως ὑπὸ καρδίην ἐλυσθεὶς
πολλὴν κατ' ἀχλὺν ὀμμάτων ἔχευεν.
κλέψας ἐκ στηθέων ἁπαλὰς φρένας.

Archilochus' poems, which were considered by competent critics inferior to none in Greek Literature, except in their subjects, were preserved and known down to the Byzantine age, when their outspoken coarseness caused them to be left uncopied, and even deliberately destroyed by the monks.

§ 117. The next poet of this period is SIMONIDES,[1] or, as some call him, Semonides, son of Krines, of Samos, who led a colony to the island of Amorgos, after which the poet is called, to distinguish him from the later Simonides of Keos. Here he dwelt in the town of Minoa. The chronologists place him about Ol. 29 or 30 (660 B.C.), and make him contemporary with, if not later than Archilochus. Though chiefly celebrated as one of the earliest iambic poets, he wrote the *Archæology of Samos*, in two books of elegiacs, of which no trace now remains. About forty fragments of his iambic verse are to be found in Bergk's collection, but only two of them are of any importance. One (25 lines) reflects on the restlessness and trouble of life, and recommends equanimity in a spirit of sad wisdom. The other (120 lines) is the famous satire on women, comparing them to sundry animals, owing to their having been created of these respective natures. Though sceptical critics have endeavoured to pull this fragment in pieces, and subdivide it into the work of various hands, we cannot but see in it the stamp of a peculiar mind, and a sufficient unity of purpose. The end only is feeble, and may possibly be by another hand, if feebleness be accepted as proof of spuriousness. The tone of the poem is severe and bitter, but with seriousness and strong moral convictions; the picture of the good woman at the close is drawn

---

[1] Bergk (*Fragg. Lyr.* pp. 515, 596, sq.) has shown considerable grounds for the existence of an early Euenus of Paros, who wrote erotic and sympotic elegies, of which fragments remain in the collection called by Theognis' name, and addressed to this Simonides as a contemporary. There was a later Euenus of Paros, with whom he may have been confused, and so forgotten. This is possible, but still so early an elegiast should have attracted sufficient notice to have escaped oblivion. I therefore hesitate to rehabilitate him, but think Bergk's arguments well worth indicating to the reader.

with warmth and feeling, and shows that the poet did not undervalue the sex.[1]

I have elsewhere [2] commented on the special features of the poem.   The general idea recurs in the fragments of Phokylides. One of the latter fragments (16) is notable as implying the ἑταίρα of later days to have been fullblown in the seaports of Ionia, even in the seventh century B.C., nor do I know of any other early mention so explicit.[3]

There is another early Iambic poet, Aristoxenus of Selinus, cited by Hephæstion on no less authority than Epicharmus'; but he quotes from him only one anapæstic line :

τίς ἀλαζονείαν πλείσταν παρέχει τῶν ἀνθρώπων; τοὶ μάντιες,

and we wonder at such scepticism in Ol. 29, the date attributed to the poet by Eusebius.   But we can say nothing more of him than to record the echo of his name.[4]

§ 118. We pass to a more famous and better preserved poet, TYRTÆUS, who does not hold a place among the ' Iambographi,' as his remains are either elegiac, or anapæstic—the metre suited for military marches.

When the famous Leonidas was asked what he thought of Tyrtæus, he answered that he was ἀγαθὸς νέων ψυχὰς αἰκάλλειν —good for stimulating the soul of youth—and the extant frag-

---

[1]

τὴν δ' ἐκ μελίσσης· τήν τις εὐτυχεῖ λαβὼν
κείνη γὰρ οἴη μῶμος οὐ προσιζάνει·
θάλλει δ' ὑπ' αὐτῆς κἀπαέξεται βίος·
φίλη δὲ σὺν φιλεῦντι γηράσκει πόσει,
τεκοῦσα καλὸν κοὐνομάκλυτον γένος·
κἀριπρεπὴς μὲν ἐν γυναιξὶ γίγνεται
πάσῃσι, θείη δ' ἀμφιδέδρομεν χάρις
οὐδ' ἐν γυναιξὶ ἥδεται καθημένη,
ὅκου λέγουσιν ἀφροδισίους λόγους·
τοίας γυναῖκας ἀνδράσιν χαρίζεται
Ζεὺς τὰς ἀρίστας καὶ πολυφραδεστάτας.

[2] *Social Greece*, 4th ed. p. 111.

[3] Archilochus' frag. 19 is not so characteristic.

[4] He is classed by O. Muller (ii. 55) as an actual forerunner of Epicharmus among the originators of comedy, which, if his date be truly ascertained, would be a grave anachronism.   The tone and spirit of all the early iambic poets was of course akin to comedy, yet we can hardly confuse them with a school so distant and so unlike.

ments confirm this judgment. We have several long exhortations to valour (about 120 lines), with pictures of the advantages of this virtue, and the disgrace and loss attending on cowardice. There are also slight remains of his ἐμβατήρια, or anapæstic marches, which were sung by or for the Spartans when going to battle, with a flute accompaniment. These warlike fragments differ little from the fragments of Callinus, so little that many critics attribute the chief fragment of the latter to Tyrtæus. He is also said by Pollux to have composed songs for three choirs—one of old men, one of middle-aged, and one of youths, and this is curiously illustrated by a fragment of such a composition preserved in Plutarch,[1] where each line is sung by a chorus of different age.

There are also some remains of a poem cited as εὐνομία, which was distinctly political in character, and intended to excite in the public mind of the Spartans an attachment to their constitution, and especially to Theopompus, the Spartan hero of the second Messenian war. This leads us to the circumstances of Tyrtæus' life. He tells us himself that he was contemporary with the second Messenian war, which was carried on by the grandsons of the combatants in the first. We are told that the hardships of this war to the Spartans were very great, that a large part of their territory adjoining Messene was left unculti-

---

[1] *Lycurgus*, 21 : Ἄμμες πόκ᾽ ἦμες ἄλκιμοι νεανίαι.

Ἄμμες δὲ γ᾽ εἰμές· αἰ δὲ λῇς, αὐγάσδεο.

Ἄμμες δὲ γ᾽ ἐσσόμεσθα πολλῷ κάρρονες.

Bernhardy (ii. p. 604) thinks that the tripartite νόμος mentioned by Plutarch (*On Music*, p. 1134 A), which Sakadas composed, with the first verse Doric, the second Phrygian, the third Lydian in scale, may have been similarly intended to convey the temper of various ages of human life, but the actual combination of Dorian and Æolian modes by Pindar seems rather to weaken the conjecture. The fragments of Tyrtæus are mere extracts quoted by Lycurgus, or Stobæus, or other authors, and have, therefore, no separate MS. authority. So also there are no separate editions, so far as I know, except that of W. Cleaver (anon. 1761), with an English metrical translation and notes, and the new Italian version, also with a text and notes by Felix Cavalotti (Milan, 1878). The most convenient text is that of Bergk in his *Lyrici*. The reader will find in his critical notes references to a number of special essays upon Tyrtæus by Osann.

vated; and Messenian elegies long preserved the tradition of
the hero Aristomenes chasing his enemies across hill and dale.
Under these trying circumstances chronic discontent, or what
the Greeks called στάσις, broke out, and the Spartans, by the
direction of the Delphic oracle, came to seek from Athens
an adviser.   Later panegyrists of Athens added that the
Athenians sent in derision the lame schoolmaster of Aphidnæ,
whose songs so inspirited the Spartans as to give them finally
the victory.   Other allusions, however, speak of him as a Lace-
dæmonian, others as an Ionian.   How much of these legends is
true it is very hard to say.   That the Spartans—a race very sus-
ceptible of excitement through poetry and music, but not productive in these arts—should have been advised to borrow a
famous poet of warlike elegies from some foreign city is not at
all incredible, nor is it more so that the style already popular
in the home of Callinus and Archilochus should have been
domesticated at Athens.   The consistent tradition as to
Tyrtæus' origin cannot be rejected by us, though he completely
identifies himself in his poems with his adopted country, and
writes as a Laconian.[1]

The story that he was summoned to Sparta on the authority
of the Delphic oracle is told of a number of other remarkable
poets about the same time, and shows, if true, that the priests
of the shrine had in their minds the fixed policy of improving
the culture and education of Sparta in the seventh century B.C.
It is not unlikely that they (and the Spartan kings) foresaw the
dangers arising from the one-sided Lycurgean training, which
was now in full force there, and sought to counteract them by
stimulating a love of poetry and music.   Thus a whole series
of poets is reported to have been invited to Sparta by the
behest of the Delphic oracle, and to have ordered and esta-

---

[1] It should be observed that he adheres to the traditional Ionic dialect
in his elegiacs, but writes his marching songs in the Spartan :—

Ἄγετ’, ὦ Σπάρτας εὐάνδρου
κοῦροι πατέρων πολιατᾶν,
λαιᾷ μὲν ἴτυν προβάλεσθε,
δόρυ δ’ εὐτόλμως βάλλετε
μὴ φειδόμενοι τᾶς ζωᾶς,
οὐ γὰρ πάτριον τᾷ Σπάρτᾳ·

blished not only the national songs of the Spartans, but public contests in music, poetry, and dancing.

§ 119. This brings us for the first time into contact with the true lyric poets of Greece, who, however, have been so constantly confounded with iambists and elegists (themselves also lyric poets) that it is necessary to call them by a technical name, and style them, as is always done in Germany, *Melic* poets. The distinctive feature of these poets, who were exceedingly numerous, but are exceedingly ill-preserved, and very various in character, was the necessary combination of music, and very frequently of rythmical movement, or *orchestic*, with their text. When this dancing came into use, as in the choral poetry of the early Dorian bards, and of the Attic dramatists, the metre of the words became so complex, and divided into subordinated rythmical periods, that Cicero tells us such poems appeared to him like prose, since the necessary music and figured dancing were indispensable to explain the metrical plan of the poet. I have no doubt many modern readers of Pindar will recognise the pertinence of this remark. It is therefore certain that the rise of melic poetry was intimately connected with the rise or development of music, and accordingly most historians of Greek literature devote a chapter in this place to that difficult subject. It is, however, so completely unintelligible to all but theorists in music, and there is even to them so much uncertainty about the facts, that I feel justified in passing it by with little more than a mere reference to the many special treatises on the subject.[1]

§ 120. It may, however, be well to enumerate briefly the various technical terms for the many different kinds of melic poetry. The simple song of the Æolic school was sung by one person, and was never complicated in structure, as it was merely intended to reveal personal and private emotion : the choral melic poetry of the Greeks was, on the contrary, grand,

---

[1] Cf. Westphal's *Griechische Musik* ; Fortlage's article in Ersch und Gruber's *Griechenland* ; Mr. Wm. Chappell's *Hist. of Music*, vol. i. ; and the chapter on the intelligible results of much abstruse investigation in my *Rambles and Studies in Greece.*

elaborate, and public in its tone. It was devoted to state interests and public affairs ; nor did the poet venture to obtrude himself except by passing allusions. In very old times, it seems that the *nome* (νόμος) addressed to the gods was sung before the altar, with the lyre, by one singer ; but this fashion early made way for choral performance, when it was called hymn (ὕμνος). Quite distinct was the προσόδιον, a processional song, accompanied by flutes, as the chorus marched to the temple. The *pæan* and *dithyramb* are hymns addressed to Apollo and Dionysus respectively. When the melic poem was accompanied with lively dancing it was called *hyporcheme* (ὑπόρχημα). All these poems were performed by men and boys, but there were special compositions for a chorus of maidens, called *parthenia* (παρθένια). These titles all indicate religious poetry, and no doubt this was the earliest field of melic verse ; but although secular matters had many other forms (such as the elegy and the Æolic song) suited to them, even the forms of religious song were adapted to them on great public occasions, and so we have in Pindar's day ἐγκώμια, songs of praise ; ἐπινίκια, songs of victory ; and θρῆνοι, laments for the dead—all secular applications of melic poetry. These technical details seem necessary to explain the constantly recurring terms, which the historian cannot avoid.

§ 121. As I have already mentioned, the poets of this early period, if we except the epic poets, were almost all composers in various metres, and, what is more important from the point of view of this work, they did not clearly separate their private feelings and public functions. The iambic metre, which in Archilochus was essentially personal and subjective, became, in the hands of the earlier Simonides and others, the vehicle for general sketches and for proverbial philosophy. The earlier elegy, which is essentially public and patriotic in character, down even to Solon's day, was, nevertheless, by Mimnermus brought back to its original scope—that of amorous complaint and tender grief, nor did subsequent ages and languages accept the tone of manly endurance and of political teaching as the natural voice of the elegy. When Tyrtæus and Alcman were friends or rival bards together at Sparta, the melic hymns of the Lydian were not recognised as more essentially public than the warlike elegies of the Athenian.   Thus even Theognis and Solon cloak their public advices under the form of personal exhortations to friends, or even to themselves, and Pindar carries on his private controversies under the cover of public hymns of victory and praise of the gods.   But according as the various styles were developed, certain precedents began to make themselves felt.   No severance, however, took place till after the rise of Doric choral poetry ; when this division of melic poetry appropriated all the public affairs of men.   On the other hand, the iambic, and more especially the elegiac, metres, which had been of universal application hitherto, began, with the Æolic songs, to affect a personal and private complexion. Hence, from this period onwards a division according to metres, though even now far from satisfactory, to some extent accords with that I have adopted above (p. 156).   I purpose treating first the personal poetry in the later iambic and elegiac poets, as well as in the Æolic melos, and then the public lyrists of the Doric type, including the sepulchral epitaphs, which were generally elegiac in form, but public in character.

§ 122. The student should carefully distinguish between κιθαρῳδική and (ψιλή) κιθάρισις, singing with a string accompaniment and mere harp playing, and similarly αὐλῳδική and αὐλητική. Thus Olympus was a mere αὐλητικός, to be expunged from the list of lyric poets, and Clonas of Tegea seems to be the first αὐλῳδικός, or composer of melic poetry with a flute accompaniment ; and this innovation was supported by the similar advance of Terpander.

For this remarkable man, who stands at the head of the melic poets, is called the first κιθαρῳδός, or composer of melic poems accompanied throughout by the lyre, in contrast, I suppose, to those epic recitations which began with an ἀναβολή or prelude on the instrument.   If this be true, it puts him in competition with his great contemporary Archilochus, who is said to have first composed independent accompaniments (ὑπὸ τὴν ᾠδήν), as previously the instrument had followed the voice note for note (πρόσχορδα κρούειν).

We know nothing of Terpander's youth, save that he was born in Lesbos, the real home of melic poetry, and came, or was called, to Sparta, where he established the musical contests at the Karnean festival about 670 B.C. (Ol. 26). He was said to have been victor at the Pythian contests for four consecutive eight-year feasts, which brings down his activity at least to the year 640 B.C. Thus we may imagine him the older contemporary of Tyrtæus. Not twenty lines of his hymns remain —solemn fragments in hexameters or heavy spondaic metres, which show that hymns to the gods (*nomes*) were his chief productions.[1] It is evident that epic poetry was still predominant when he wrote, and affected his style. One interesting personal fragment is quoted by Strabo to prove that he increased the strings of the lyre from four to seven.[2] Strabo seems sure about the sense, though not about the genuineness of the lines. But in spite of his authority, supported by that of Mr. Chappell,[3] and the curious statement of Plutarch,[4] that he deliberately gave up the use of many strings, and won his prizes by playing on *three*, I think Bergk has hit the truth where he interprets the passage not of the strings of the lyre, which according to the *Hymn to Hermes* had been originally seven, but to the divisions of his odes, which having been four, were, according to Pollux, increased by him to seven.[5]

§ 123. The names of Clonas of Tegea, of Sakadas of Argos, of Polymnestus of Colophon, of Echembrotus of Arcadia, are mentioned as successors to Terpander in the art of combining music and poetry, but have no place now in the history of Greek literature, as all their works have long perished. The same is the case with the more celebrated Thaletas of Crete,

---

[1] Here is one :

Ζεῦ πάντων ἀρχα, πάντων ἀγήτωρ,
Ζεῦ, σοὶ σπένδω ταύταν ὕμνον ἀρχάν.

On the metre cf. Bergk, *FLG.* p. 813. The lines are best scanned as molossi with a catalectic syllable.

[2] Σοὶ δ' ἡμεῖς τετράγηρυν ἀποστέρξαντες ἀοιδὰν
ἑπτατόνῳ φόρμιγγι νέους κελαδήσομεν ὕμνους.

[3] *Hist. of Music,* i. p. 30.   [4] *De Mus.* 18.

[5] Viz. ἐπαρχά, μεταρχά, κατατροπά, μετακατατροπά, ὀμφαλός, σφραγις, ἐπίλογος. Regarding the first two as equivalent to προοίμιον and ἀρχά, the third and fourth (transition members on either side of the ὀμφαλός), and the ἐπίλογος, were evidently the newer members.

summoned by the oracle (as Tyrtæus was) to heal pestilence and sedition, and attach the citizens more firmly to the Lycurgean constitution. He is reported to have organised afresh the *Gymnopædia* in Ol. 28 (664 B.C.), and to have composed, not only *nomes*, like Terpander, but *hyporchemes* and *pæans*, which were sung by a choir with rythmical movements. He is referred by Plutarch to the school of Olympus' nomes, played with the flute, and not to Terpander's.

§ 124. The first essentially lyric poet that lives for us is ALCMAN, who stands somewhat isolated at the head of the melic poets, and still belongs to that remarkable epoch of literary history when Sparta, during the seventh century, was gathering from all parts of Greece poets and musicians to educate her youth. Pausanias saw his tomb at Sparta, among those of celebrated and noble Spartans, and speaks of his odes as not deficient in sweetness, though composed in the unmusical Spartan dialect.[1] This is true, the fragments are of great merit ; but if the dialect does not impair their beauty, it certainly makes them to us, as it did to the old grammarians, very obscure. We learn from Alcman that he boasted his origin to be from no obscure or remote land—enumerating many countries which perplexed even the old commentators—but from the lofty Sardis.[2] It is to be presumed that he had, at least, an Ionian mother (if he was not brought as a slave to Greece in early youth) ; for no pure Lydian could have written as he did, not even in the Ionic dialect, but in that of his adopted country. But the whole history of the man, and the main features of his fragments, show us how completely the Sparta of the seventh

---

[1] ᾧ ποιήσαντι ᾄσματα οὐδὲν ἐς ἡδονὴν αὐτῶν ἐλυμήνατο τῶν Λακώνων ἡ γλῶσσα, ἥκιστα παρεχομένη τὸ εὔφωνον.

[2] Frag. 25:

οὐκ εἶς ἀνὴρ ἄγροικος οὐδὲ
σκαιὸς οὐδὲ παρὰ σοφοῖσιν
οὐδὲ Θεσσαλὸς γένος
οὐδ' Ἐρυσιχαῖος οὐδὲ ποιμήν,
ἀλλὰ Σαρδίων ἀπ' ἀκρᾶν.

And cf. frag. 118, quoted from Aristides, ii. 508 : Ἑτέρωθι τοίνυν καλλωπιζόμενος παρ' ὅσοις εὐδοκιμεῖ, τοσαῦτα καὶ τοιαῦτα ἔθνη καταλέγει ὥστ' ἔτι νῦν τοὺς ἀθλίους γραμματιστὰς ζητεῖν, οὗ γῆς ταῦτ' εἶναι.

century differed from the Sparta of the fifth, and how utterly
the Spartan gentleman who warred against Messene would
have despised the ignorant professional warrior who afterwards
contended against Athens. The very adoption of a Lydian at
Sparta (Suidas says a Lydian slave), and his proud enumeration of geographical names, imply a spirit the very reverse of
the later exclusiveness (ξενηλασία). So also the love of eating
and drinking which the poet confesses of himself, his account
of the various wines produced in the districts of Laconia, his
open allusions to his passion for Megalostrata, and the loose
character of his erotic poems generally,[1] are quite foreign to
the ordinary notions of Lycurgean discipline. I suppose that
the royal power, which endeavoured to assert itself in early
times, and was only reduced to subjection by the murder of
Polydorus, the submission of Theopompus, and the gradual
strengthening of the power of the ephors, attempted to carry out
a literary policy like that of the Greek despots. In the seventh
century, before the struggle was finally decided against them,
the kings, aided by the Delphic oracle, sought to emancipate
the subject races from political, the dominant from educational,
slavery; and so it came that poets like Alcman, who sing of
wine and love, who delight in feasting and eschew war, could be
tolerated and even popular at Sparta. But the first of the melic
appears also the last of the Spartan poets.

His six books contained all kinds of *melos*, hymns, pæans,
prosodia, parthenia, and erotic songs. His metres are easy and
various, and not like the complicated systems of later lyrists.
On the other hand, his proverbial wisdom, and the form of his
personal allusions, sometimes remind one of Pindar. But
the general character of the poet is that of an easy, simple,
pleasure-loving man. He boasts to have imitated the song of
birds (fr. 17, 67)—in other words, to have been a self-taught
and original poet. Nevertheless, he shows, as might be ex-

---

[1] Athenæus cites (through Chamæleon) Archytas to the effect that
Alcman γεγονέναι τῶν ἐρωτικῶν μελῶν ἡγεμόνα, καὶ ἐκδοῦναι πρῶτον μέλος
ἀκόλαστον ὄντα κ.τ.λ., and then quotes frag. 36. Of course Alcman had before him the example of his earlier contemporary Archilochus. The fragg.
35–9 are unfortunately inadequate specimens of this side of his genius.

pected, a knowledge and appreciation of Homer. Several fragments express a peculiar love and study of nature, somewhat exceptional for a Greek lyrist. Of these, the most remarkable is his description of night,[1] which is more like the picture we should expect from Apollonius Rhodius or Virgil than from an early Greek poet. The other is evidently written in advancing age, and with a presentiment of approaching death.[2]

But by far the longest and most interesting relic of Alcman was found in 1855, by M. Máriette, in a tomb near the second Pyramid—a papyrus fragment of three pages, containing a portion of his celebrated hymn to the Dioscuri. Two of the pages are wretchedly mutilated, and the sense of the whole composition is very obscure and difficult. This extraordinary discovery is not so precious in actual results as in the hope it gives us of rescuing in the same way other portions of the old Greek poets from their oblivion. It also gives us a very early specimen of Greek writing, and one of great value for the his-

---

[1] Frag. 60: εὕδουσιν δ᾽ ὀρέων κορυφαί τε καὶ φάραγγες,
   πρώονές τε καὶ χαράδραι,
   φύλλα θ᾽ ἑρπετά θ᾽ ὅσσα τρέφει μέλαινα γαῖα,
   θῆρες ὀρεσκῷοί τε καὶ γένος μελισσᾶν
   καὶ κνώδαλ᾽ ἐν βένθεσι πορφυρέας ἁλός·
   εὕδουσιν δ᾽ οἰωνῶν
   φῦλα τανυπτερύγων.

'A beautiful peculiarity,' says Mure (*Hist. Gk. Lit.* iii. 206), 'of this description is the vivid manner in which it shadows forth the scenery of the vale of Lacedæmon, with which the inspirations of the poet were so intimately associated ; from the snow-capped peaks of Taÿgetus down to the dark blue sea which washes the base of the mountain. The author would find it difficult to convey to the imagination of the reader the effect produced upon his own by the recurrence of the passage to his mind, during a walk among the ruins of Sparta, on a calm spring night, about an hour after a brilliant sunset.'

[2] Frag. 26: οὔ μ᾽ ἔτι, παρθενικαὶ μελιγάρυες ἱμερόφωνοι,
   γυῖα φέρειν δύναται· βάλε δὴ βάλε κηρύλος εἴην,
   ὅς τ᾽ ἐπὶ κύματος ἄνθος ἅμ᾽ ἀλκυόνεσσι ποτῆται
   νηλεγὲς ἦτορ ἔχων, ἁλιπόρφυρος εἴαρος ὄρνις.

The term κηρύλος was used for the male halcyon. On βάλε, the marginal note says the full word is ἀβάλε, σημαντικὸν εὐχῆς, and equal to ὄφελεν, εἴθε, εἴθε.

tory of palæography.   I append the more intelligible part in a note below.[1]

[1] Its restoration has been attempted (since its first publication by Egger in his *Mémoires d'histoire ancienne*) by Ten Brink and Bergk, with some success; lastly, by F. Blass in *Hermes*, vol. xiii. p. 27, from whose text I quote, as it differs considerably from earlier restorations. After celebrating the victory of the Dioscuri over the Hippocoontidæ, the poet proceeds to sing the praises of Agido and Agesichora.

COL. II.   Στρ. δ'.

2   Ἔστι τις σιῶν τίσις·   36
       ὅδ' ὄλβιος, ὅστις εὔφρων
       ἀμέραν διαπλέκει
5   ἄκλαυστος. ἐγὼν δ' ἀείδω
       Ἀγιδῶς τὸ φῶς· ὁρῶ   40
       ῥ' ὥτ' ἄλιον, ὅνπερ ἄμιν
       Ἀγιδὼ μαρτύρεται
       φαίνεν. ἐμὲ δ' οὔτ' ἐπαινὲν
10   οὔτε μωμέσθαι νιν ἁ κλεννὰ χοραγὸς
       οὐδαμῶς ἐῇ· δοκέει γὰρ ἤμεν αὖτα   45
       ἐκπρεπὴς τὼς ὥπερ αἴ τις
       ἐν βοτοῖς στάσειεν ἵππον
       παγὸν ἀεθλοφόρον καναχάποδα,
15   τῶν ὑποπετριδίων ὀνείρων.
                   Στρ. ε'.
       Ἦ οὐχ ὁρῇς ; ὁ μὲν κέλης   50
       Ἐνετικός· ἁ δὲ χαίτα
       τᾶς ἐμᾶς ἀνεψιᾶς
       Ἀγησιχόρας ἐπανθεῖ
20   χρυσὸς ὥτ' ἀκήρατος,
       τό τ' ἀργύριον πρόσωπον.   55
       διαφάδαν τί τοι λέγω ;
       Ἀγησιχόρα μὲν αὖτα·
       ἅδε δευτέρα πεδ' Ἀγιδὼν τὸ εἶδος
25   ἵππος εἰβηνῷ κόλαξ ἀὲς δραμεῖται.
       ταὶ Πελειάδες γὰρ ἄμιν   60
       Ὀρθίᾳ φάρος φεροίσαις
       νύκτα δι' ἀμβροσίαν ἀγεσήριον
       ἄστρον αὐειρομέναι μάχονται.
                   Στρ. ϛ'.
30   Οὔτε γάρ τι πορφύρας
       τόσσος κόρος ὥστ' ἀμύναι,   65
       οὔτε ποικίλος δράκων
       παγχρύσιος, οὐδὲ μίτρα
       Λυδία, νεανίδων

§ 125. Returning to the elegy, or personal poetry of the epoch, we come to a very distinctive and remarkable man, MIMNERMUS (called Liguastades, for his sweetness), the first composer of purely private and sentimental, as opposed to political, elegies. There are, indeed, in his fragments historical allusions, and he describes (fr. 14) with much fire, and in a spirit not unworthy of Tyrtæus, the valour of a hero ' who scattered the dense phalanxes of the Lydian horsemen through the plain of Hermus.' This he had heard from the elders who remembered the wars with Gyges, for the date of Mimnermus is given as Ol. 37, or the close of the seventh century, and he was an early contemporary of Solon. But his other fragments are those of the greatest interest, and are chiefly from his book or books, called *Nanno,* after a flute player whom he loved without success. He is himself called an αὐλῳδός, or singer with a flute accompaniment, and he probably revived the old plaintive

COL. III. τὰν οἶδα φαρῶν ἄγαλμα,
οὐδὲ ταὶ Ναννῶς κόμαι,   70
ἀλλ' οὐδ' Ἐράτα σιειδής,
οὐδὲ Συλακίς τε καὶ Κλεησισήρα,
5 οὐδ' ἐς Αἰνησιμβρότας ἐνθοῖσα φασεῖς
' Ἀσταφίς τέ μοι γένοιτο,
καὶ ποτιγλέποι Φίλυλλα,   75
Δαμαίπα τ' ἐρατά τε Ἰανθεμίς,'
ἀλλ' Ἀγησιχόρα με τηρεῖ
Στρ. ζ'.
10 Οὐ γὰρ ἀ καλλίσφυρος
Ἀγησιχόρα πάρ' αὐτεῖ;
Ἀγιδοῖ μέσφ' ἀρ μένει,   80
θωστήρια κἄμ' ἐπαινεῖ.
ἀλλὰ τᾶν[δ' ἀμ]ῶν, σιοί,
15 δέξασθ'· ἀπονητὶ ἄνα
καὶ τέλος· γραῦς τό τις
εἴποιμί κ' ' ἄπαν μὲν αὐτὰ   85
παρσένος μάταν ἀπὸ θράνω λέλακα
γλαύξ· ἐγὼν δὲ τᾷ μὲν Ἀώτι μάλιστα
20 ἀνδάνην ἐρῶ· πόνων γὰρ
ἄμιν ἰατωρ ἔγεντο·
ἐξ Ἀγησιχόρας δὲ νεάνιδες   90
ἦ ῥ' αἴνας ἐρατᾶς ἐπέβαν.'

elegy of the Phrygians, in close sympathy with the sorrowful laments of his sweet and tender muse.   To the later Alexandrians, and the Romans, whose reflective age peculiarly appreciated the sad world-weariness of this bard of Kolophon, the Nanno elegies of Mimnermus were a favourite model, and we may perhaps assign to him the position and title of the Petrarch of Greek literature.

It is remarkable that the contemporaries and immediate successors of Mimnermus were of a different opinion.   The poets who desired to sing of love and passion did not adopt his elegiac metre as their fittest vehicle.   It still remained the metre of political and philosophical expression, of wise advice, of proverb and of epigram.   To early Greek love, to the passion of Alcæus, Sappho, and Anacreon, no form could be more unutterably slow and cold than the deliberate hexameter. When bookworms at Alexandria and Roman dilettanti began to talk about love, it suited them well enough, and it was the subdued and resigned attitude of Mimnermus, his modernism, if I may so say, which made him to them, and to many of the moderns, so sweet and perfect a singer of love.

I do not think the famous fragment (12) on the perpetual labours of Helios so striking or characteristic as those which sing of the delights of love, and the miseries of old age [1]—γῆρας

ἡμεῖς δ' οἶά τε φύλλα φάει πολυανθέος ὥρη
ἔαρος, ὅτ' αἶψ' αὐγῆς αὔξεται ἠελίου,
τοῖς ἴκελοι πήχυιον ἐπὶ χρόνον ἄνθεσιν ἥβης
τερπόμεθα, πρὸς θεῶν εἰδότες οὔτε κακὸν
οὔτ' ἀγαθόν · κῆρες δὲ παρεστήκασι μέλαιναι,
ἡ μὲν ἔχουσα τέλος γήραος ἀργαλέου,
ἡ δ' ἑτέρη θανάτοιο· μίνυνθά δὲ γίγνεται ἥβης
καρπός, ὅσον δ' ἐπὶ γῆν κίδναται ἠέλιος·
αὐτὰρ ἐπὴν δὴ τοῦτο τέλος παραμείψεται ὥρης,
αὐτίκα τεθνάμεναι βέλτιον ἢ βίοτος ·
πολλὰ γὰρ ἐν θυμῷ κακὰ γίγνεται· ἄλλοτε οἶκος
τρυχοῦται, πενίης δ' ἔργ' ὀδυνηρὰ πέλει·
ἄλλος δ' αὖ παίδων ἐπιδεύεται, ὧντε μάλιστα
ἱμείρων κατὰ γῆς ἔρχεται εἰς Ἀΐδην·
ἄλλος νοῦσον ἔχει θυμοφθόρον· οὐδέ τις ἔστιν
ἀνθρώπων, ᾧ Ζεὺς μὴ κακὰ πολλὰ δίδοι.

ἀργαλέον, as he calls it, applying an epithet which he used with curious consistency of all manner of disagreeable necessities. In his hatred of old age, he struck a note which found response in many Greek hearts at all times, and Sophocles and Euripides repeat without improving the burden of his elegies.

Almost all the fragments (some 90 lines) express the same gloom and the same despair. We owe the preservation of most of them to Stobæus; Strabo has cited a few of geographical importance, Athenæus that on the sun's course. His ninth fragment tells how 'we left the lofty Neleïon of Pylos, and came in ships to the lovely Asia, and into fair Kolophon we settled with might of arms, being leaders of wild daring, and starting from thence by the counsel of the gods we took the Æolic Smyrna.' This is a very early and clear piece of evidence for what is called the Ionic migration, which has been doubted, or relegated to the region of myths by some sceptical historians.

§ 126. Mimnermus leads us over naturally to SOLON, who addressed him in a still extant fragment, in reply to his lines :—

αἰ γὰρ ἄτερ νούσων τε καὶ ἀργαλέων μελεδωνῶν
ἐξηκονταέτη μοῖρα κίχοι θανάτου.

Solon's answer was as follows :—

ἀλλ' εἴ μοι κἂν νῦν ἔτι πείσεαι, ἔξελε τοῦτο,
μηδὲ μέγαιρ' ὅτι σεῦ λῷον ἐπεφρασάμην,
καὶ μεταποίησον, Λιγυαστάδη, ὧδε δ' ἄειδε·
'Ογδωκονταέτη μοῖρα κίχοι θανάτου.

It appears then that these elegies were well known, and the poet yet alive, when Solon was a literary man. The events of Solon's great life form an important chapter in Greek history, and can be found there by the student. We are here only concerned with his literary side. He is remarkable in having written poetry not as a profession, nor as his main occupation, but as a relaxation from graver cares. He was first a merchant, then a general, then a lawgiver, and, at last, a philosophic traveller; and all these conditions of life, except the first, are reflected in his extant fragments. As usual

with the personal poets of that epoch, he employed various
metres, of which the elegiac was the chief, but the iambic
also prominent, and not for satire and invective, but for political and philosophic reflections.   Some lines, apparently from
early compositions, are cited to show his high appreciation of
sensual pleasures, and there are features in his laws which
prove that he made large allowance for this side of human nature in his philosophy.   Amid the various feelings which appear
in his personal confessions we miss the poetical despondency
of Mimnermus, and that peculiar beauty and sweetness of expression, which made him an unapproachable master of the
elegy in our modern sense.   Solon is a practical man, at times
a philosopher who speculates on Providence and the life of
man; again, a noble martyr for his country, who feels beset by
foes and jealous rivals, and complains bitterly that he stands
alone and unfriended in the state which he has saved.   But he
is always manly, and, perhaps, somewhat hard and plain in his
language, choosing poetry as the only known vehicle of expression in his day, but saying in verse what in after days would have
been said in prose.   Hence it is that the later orators found
him so suitable for quotation.   His political recollections, and
his advices to his friends, were in Athens handbooks of political education.

There remain but eight lines of his famous elegy called
Salamis, whereby he incited his people to persevere in wrest-
ing this island, the place of his birth, from Megara.   Of his
Meditations ('Υποθῆκαι εἰς 'Αθηναίους and εἰς ἑαυτὸν) several
long passages are quoted, one by Demosthenes,[1] to which the
student can easily refer; several by Plutarch and Diogenes
Laertius in their lives of Solon, another by Stobæus.   The
last, a passage of seventy lines, is of great interest as containing a summary of Solon's philosophy concerning human
life, but can hardly be fairly conveyed by quoting short extracts.
Many other snatches of proverbial wisdom, or gnomes, are
cited from these ὑποθῆκαι, and are among the sententious fragments which have made historians speak of the *Gnomic poets* of

---

[1] In his Παραπρεσβεία, p. 254.

Greece as a distinct class.[1] This was never the case, though there can be no doubt that the personal poets from this time onward adopted a philosophical tone which made them peculiarly fit for educational purposes. Many of his poems bore on their titles personal dedications, πρὸς Κριτίαν, πρὸς Φιλόκυπρον, πρὸς Φῶκον, thus preserving the personal character of the elegy, while treating public topics. The last cited was in tetrameters, and told of the temptations and solicitations to which the great lawgiver had been exposed.[2] He also composed melic poems for musical recitation at banquets. All these varied scraps, full of precious historical information, do not now amount to more than 250 lines. I will quote the elegy on the nine ages of man (though doubted by Porson), because it seems preserved entire in a somewhat inaccessible treatise of Philo, and because it develops an idea often since repeated in philosophical poetry. This poem is, indeed, constantly referred to by ancient authorities.[3]

[1] e.g.   πολλοὶ γὰρ πλουτεῦσι κακοί, ἀγαθοὶ δὲ πένονται
            ἀλλ᾽ ἡμεῖς αὐτοῖς οὐ διαμειψόμεθα
            τῆς ἀρετῆς τὸν πλοῦτον, ἐπεὶ τὸ μὲν ἔμπεδον αἰεί,
            χρήματα δ᾽ ἀνθρώπων ἄλλοτε ἄλλος ἔχει.

And   Πάντῃ δ᾽ ἀθανάτων ἀφανὴς νόος ἀνθρώποισιν,

a text admirably developed in his frag. 13, of *meditations* (ὑποθῆκαι εἰς ἑαυτόν).

[2] He was thought a fool by his friends not to seize and hold the tyranny of Athens when he had the power, for in their opinion it was worth being flayed alive to have once enjoyed such a position. Euripides gives an admirable expression of this Greek passion for holding a tyranny in the speech of Eteocles in his *Phœnissœ*, vv. 500, sq.—the solitary passage which may have come from Euripides through George Gascoigne into Shakespeare, as will be shown in a subsequent chapter.

[3]   παῖς μὲν ἄνηβος ἐὼν ἔτι νήπιος ἕρκος ὀδόντων
            φύσας ἐκβάλλει πρῶτον ἐν ἑπτ᾽ ἔτεσιν·
            τοὺς δ᾽ ἑτέρους ὅτε δὴ τελέσῃ θεὸς ἑπτ᾽ ἐνιαυτούς,
            ἥβης ἐκφαίνει σήματα γεινομένης·
            τῇ τριτάτῃ δὲ γένειον ἀεξομένων ἔτι γυίων
            λαχνοῦται, χροιῆς ἄνθος ἀμειβομένης
            τῇ δὲ τετάρτῃ πᾶς τις ἐν ἑβδομάδι μέγ᾽ ἄριστος
            ἰσχύν, ἥντ᾽ ἄνδρες σήματ᾽ ἔχουσ᾽ ἀρετῆς·
            πέμπτῃ δ᾽ ὥριον ἄνδρα γάμον μεμνημένον εἶναι

It is often maintained that Solon is the one great politician who holds a place in Greek literature, but this is only true for us, and would never have been asserted had the works of his contemporaries reached us. It seems, on the contrary, to have been the fashion at this period for every important political man to teach his fellow-citizens in elegies, and to write convivial songs, as we may see from the notices of Diogenes about Pittacus, and Periander, and Bias.[1] Hence the reputation of the so-called *Wise Men*, who, according to all the different lists of them, agree in combining poetical teaching with practical politics. Thus the wild confessions of Archilochus, which were followed up in Lesbos by no less passionate effusions, led the way to confessions of far different men, and to the development of the didactic side of elegiac and iambic poetry. The elegy assumes from this time onward this special character, and, if we except its public side, as epigram, and a few imitations of the older social tone, appears confined within limits unknown in the seventh century.

§ 127. Contemporary with the serious and philosophical poetry of Solon, we have that remarkable burst of genius in the island of Lesbos, which, though it lasted but a generation, has affected the lyrics of the world more than all the rest of Greek poetry. This school, though strictly melic, and always accompanied by music, differs fundamentally from the Doric

καὶ παίδων ζητεῖν εἰσοπίσω γενεήν ·
τῇ δ' ἕκτῃ περὶ πάντα καταρτύεται νόος ἀνδρός,
οὐδ' ἔρδειν ἔθ' ὁμῶς ἔργ' ἀπάλαμνα θέλει ·
ἑπτὰ δὲ νοῦν καὶ γλῶσσαν ἐν ἑβδομάσιν μέγ' ἄριστος
ὀκτώ τ'· ἀμφοτέρων τέσσαρα καὶ δέκ' ἔτη ·
τῇ δ' ἐνάτῃ ἔτι μὲν δύναται, μαλακώτερα δ' αὐτοῦ
πρὸς μεγάλην ἀρετὴν γλῶσσά τε καὶ σοφίη ·
τῇ δεκάτῃ δ' ὅτε δὴ τελέσῃ θεὸς ἕπτ' ἐνιαυτούς,
οὐκ ἂν ἄωρος ἐὼν μοῖραν ἔχοι θανάτου.

[1] By comparing Herodotus, i. 170, concerning Bias' political advice to the Ionians, with the verbally similar statement of Diogenes Laertius, i. 5, ἐποίησε δὲ περὶ Ἰωνίας, τίνα μάλιστα ἂν τρόπον εὐδαιμονοίη, εἰς ἔπη δισχίλια, I am persuaded that in Theognis, vv. 757–68, we have an actual fragment of Bias preserved, describing the blessings of the proposed Ionian settlement in Sardinia.

melos, in being personal, secular, and composed in a different and local dialect, the Æolic. I therefore prefer classing it with the personal poetry of the Greeks, and separating it from the public choral poetry, with which other historians have combined it. At the head of this famous Æolic poetry stand Alcæus and Sappho, contemporaries, and both of Lesbos, flourishing from the 40th Olympiad onward.

We know of ALCÆUS that he was an aristocrat of Mitylene, that he fought against the Athenians for the possession of Sigeum, but fled, and threw away his shield, which was hung up by his adversaries as a trophy. He was ever busy in the conflicts of the aristocrats against the rising power of the people, and against the tyrant who professed to represent them. About Ol. 45 he assisted, along with his brother Antimenidas, and with Pittacus, in the overthrow of the tyrant Melanchros; but when, after much trouble and the death of another tyrant, Myrsilus, the great body of the citizens chose Pittacus as their dictator (a power which he held 589–79 B.C., and then resigned), Alcæus and his party were exiled, and lived a roving and adventurous life. Alcæus went as far as Egypt, Antimenidas as a mercenary to fight under Nebuchadnezzar, King of Babylon, and distinguished himself by slaying an opposing Goliath. At some time during Pittacus' rule Alcæus' party attempted a forcible return, when he was taken prisoner, but at once liberated by the man whom he had reviled with the greatest bitterness and fury in his poetry. These few facts show us in Alcæus the perfect picture of an unprincipled, violent, lawless Greek aristocrat, who sacrificed all and everything to the demands of pleasure and power. These are the men, and this the type of aristocrat, which gave the tyrants all their opportunities.

§ 128. Of SAPPHO (in her own dialect Ψάπφα) we know that she was the daughter of Skamandronymus (or Skamon) and of Kleïs. She was small and dark, but, notwithstanding these defects, often called beautiful. The official position of her brother Zarichus, who was public cupbearer, and the adventures of her brother Charaxus, who was in the wine trade with Naucratis, and spent his substance on the fair Rhodopis, would imply that she too was of rich and aristocratic birth. She is said to have had a daughter Kleis, and to have stood in friendly relations to Alcæus.   She gathered about her a society of various maidens, who were inspired by her example to cultivate music and poetry.   Of these the most celebrated was Erinna, whose poem called Ἠλακάτη (*the Spindle*) was quoted and admired.

There is no hint of political writing in the remains of Sappho.   She seems to have devoted all her genius to the subject of love, and was decidedly the greatest erotic poet of antiquity.   The exceeding passion in her extant fragments, and the constant travesties of her in the middle and new comedy, to which her position as a literary woman made her peculiarly exposed, have produced a general impression against her moral character.   She sang of her unrequited love for Phaon, and a legend came to be believed that she had in despair cast herself from the Leucadian rock, at the remote end of the Greek world.   She is further accused of having felt an unnaturally violent passion for her girl friends, and her poetry has been called licentious and immoral.   There has been a warm controversy between Welcker, on the one hand, who with over-chivalry has vindicated the honour and purity of Sappho, and Mure, on the other, who has turned aside from his path [1] to undertake the unpleasant task of proving that her passion was no mere enthusiasm, and that she was no better than she ought to be.   Without entering upon this unsavoury discussion, I venture to suggest that both advocates are wrong in assuming that their own view excludes that of the other.   If I understand the aristocratic society of these times rightly, what we call purity and virtue, and what we call unchastity and vice, were as yet to a great extent fused in that larger and more human naturalism, which embraces impulses of both kinds in their turn, and which refuses to consider momentary passion a permanent stain upon honour or even purity.   The highest virtue of the Greek aristocrats did not exclude all manner of physical enjoyment.[2]

[1] *Hist. of Greek Lit.* iii. pp. 315, 496, sq.

[2] M. É. Burnouf (*Lit. grecque,* i. p. 194) points out with great good sense that most literary historians have falsely imagined the society and habits of

§ 129. Having thus summarised our scanty information concerning the lives of these great artists, we may approach at more leisure the more important question of their position and services in the development of Greek literature. The first point to be settled is their filiation, if any, or their utter independence from previous art, and their recurrence to the pure source of popular song. It seems to me that the direct heredity of Alcæus, at all events, from Archilochus has been very much overlooked.[1] No two poets in Greek literature are so like in temper. Not to speak of distinct copying, such as the confession of throwing away his shield in Alcæus, we can see in the abuse of Pittacus a political counterpart to the attacks on Lycambes, we can see the same employment of very various metres, the same enjoyment of love and wine, of rambling about the world, and of adventure. Neither poet uses the unvarnished dialect of his native town, but from experience of travel, and probably from purely artistic reasons, both write a literary form of their national speech. So far as the love poems of Archilochus are extant, they seem also the distinct forerunners of the poetry of Sappho; there is the same flow of passion, the same indescribable power of painting the

the Æolians at Lesbos to have been exceptionally free and even loose. They probably differed in no social or moral respect from their Ionic neighbours in Samos, Teos, and elsewhere. Both contrasted with the notions developed in course of time at both Sparta and Athens. 'A l'époque de Sapho et d'Alcée, les cités éoliennes et ioniennes avaient encore ces mœurs aristocratiques qui les font ressembler, à beaucoup d'égards, à la république de Venise du temps où le noble Marcello composait pour la haute société du Grand-Canal les psaumes qui ont rendu son nom célèbre : les relations sociales y étaient libres et faciles, quelquefois licencieuses, mais toujours empreintes d'élégance et de cette noblesse de manières qui appartienne aux aristocraties. Du reste le climat des îles et des rivages éoliens est d'une douceur qui tourne à la mollesse, et qui engendre aisément la volupté ; le canal de Lesbos est éclairé le soir d'une suave lumière et parcouru sans cesse par des brises tièdes, mais non énervantes, que parfument les arbustes odoriférants des montagnes. Les richesses et le luxe de l'Asie abondaient sur ces rivages et donnaient aux nobles Grecs de ces contrées ces habitudes de langueur et de poésie passionnée, dont nous retrouvons encore quelque chose dans leurs descendants italiens et asiatiques.'

[1] Horace (*Epist.* i. 19, v. 28) points out clearly the metrical filiation.

agony of desire.   In these features they both contrast with the gentler and more resigned complaints of Mimnermus, who naturally uses the calm elegiac metre, while the others felt the necessity of shorter and more hurried rythms.   The dialect of Sappho is more strictly the local language of Mitylene, and not so purified as that of Alcæus, but both were full of hard expressions, which are perpetually commented on by lexicographers.

On the whole, antiquity seems to have placed Sappho in the first rank, and despite the variety of subjects and of interests in Alcæus, preferred the pure voice of gentle and womanly feeling in her love poems.   But the Alexandrians thought differently, and while several of them edited critical texts of Alcæus, they seem to have paid no similar attention to Sappho.   Nevertheless, according to M. Burnouf, both poets survived till the eleventh century A.D., when they were burned at Constantinople and at Rome, in the year 1073, during the popedom of Gregory VII.   Thus these inestimable exponents of Greek feeling have only reached us in slight and scattered fragments, most of them by mere grammatical or lexicographical notes.

§ 130. Their lyrics, apart from the difficult dialect, are far more easy to comprehend than the more elaborate rythms of Pindar, Alcman, or Stesichorus.   For instead of long complicated systems, which required all the help of music, and even of dancing, to bring out the symmetry, and carry on the hearer to the antistrophe and the epode, the odes of Alcæus and Sappho were constructed in short simple stanzas, which were easily comprehended, and recitable even without their musical aecompaniment.   They were in fact the earliest specimens of what is called in modern days the *Song* or *Ballad*, in which the repetition of short rythms produces a certain pleasant monotony, easy to remember, and easy to understand.   It is this quality, in contrast with the elaborate systems of Pindar's metres, which makes Horace exclaim that Pindar is inimitable, and which led him to confine himself to the Æolic poets of Lesbos, and their simpler art. We know perhaps as much of Alcæus and Sappho through Horace as through their own fragments.   For though the genius of the Roman poet was totally different, though the political and erotic passions of the Greek aristocrat were not only strange to his nature, but the very reverse of his teaching, yet he adhered so closely to the idiom as well as the measures of his models, that much of the old Greek grace and some of the fire are ,felt through the colder medium of his translations.

But while Romans and moderns have proclaimed this side of the lyric poetry as the best and the most perfect, the verdict of the Greeks was quite different.   No one doubted the intense genius of both poets, or of their successor, Anacreon ; Sappho especially is praised through all Greek literature as a tenth Muse, as equal to Homer, as unapproachable in grace and sweetness. Yet the course and development of lyric poetry drifted away from them ; the simple song did not speak to the Greeks like the great choral systems of Stesichorus and Arion, and thus the last and most perfect development of this kind of poetry, of the melos of the Greeks, was no offshoot of the school of Lesbos. For the character of this Lesbian poetry was such as to dispense with *orchestic,* and this was to the Greeks so important an element in melic poetry, that the higher kinds were not to be appreciated without it.   All this will appear clearly when we come to treat of choral lyric poetry.

The poems of Alcæus were divided according to subjects— first *Hymns,* then *Stasiotica,* telling of adventures in politics and war, then *Skolia,* then *Erotica;* nor were the latter three very clearly distinguished.   Two books are cited from the editions of Aristophanes and Aristarchus.   Sappho's poems, on the contrary, were divided into at least nine books, and according to metres, but all called indiscriminately μέλη.   She wrote hymns, like Alcæus, but both poets composed in a free and secular spirit, nor did they take their place among the really religious poets of the Greeks.   Their metres are very various—some of them very difficult to analyse in our fragments, and there is no reason to think that what we know as the Alcaic and Sapphic metres were the most prominent in their works.   They are so fully described in the prefaces to Horace, that I need not detail them here.   Sappho was said to have first introduced the key known as Mixo-Lydian, and to have raised the epithalamium to a place in artistic poetry, though the form seems to have been fixed by Alcman or Stesichorus. Her two longer extant fragments have been preserved as specimens of excellence by Dionysius and Longinus.[1]

We have no fragment equally long from the works of Alcæus, though there are many beautiful thoughts still surviving, such as that cited by Plutarch, which makes Eros the child of Iris and the West wind—of the sunlit showers and soft breezes of spring. His fragment 40 is directly copied from a passage in Hesiod—if both do not repeat an older popular song. His metaphor of a storm-tossed ship for the agitated state became at once a commonplace in Greek literature.[2] The unusual forms of the Æolic dialect make the readings of all these fragments very uncertain and contested.

[1] Φαίνεταί μοι κῆνος ἴσος θεοῖσιν
ἔμμεν' ὤνηρ, ὅστις ἐναντίος τοι
ἰζάνει καὶ πλασίον ἇδυ φωνεύ-
σας ὑπακούει
καὶ γελαίσας ἱμερόεν. Τό μοι μὰν
καρδίαν ἐν στήθεσιν ἐπτόασεν,
ὡς γὰρ εὔιδον βροχέως σε, φωνᾶς
οὐδὲν ἔτ' εἴκει·
ἀλλὰ κὰμ μὲν γλῶσσα ἔαγε· λεπτὸν δ'
αὔτικα χρῷ πῦρ ὑποδεδρόμακεν·
ὀππάτεσσιν δ' οὐδὲν ὄρημ', ἐπιρρομ-
βεῦσι δ' ἄκουαι·
ἀ δέ μ' ἵδρως κακχέεται, τρόμος δὲ
πᾶσαν ἀγρεῖ, χλωροτέρα δὲ ποίας
ἔμμι· τεθνάκην δ' ὀλίγω 'πιδεύης
φαίνομαι ἄλλα.
ἀλλὰ πᾶν τολματόν—

[2] Ἀσυνέτημι τῶν ἀνέμων στάσιν·
τὸ μὲν γὰρ ἔνθεν κῦμα κυλίνδεται,
τὸ δ' ἔνθεν· ἄμμες δ' ἂν τὸ μέσσον
νᾶϊ φορήμεθα σὺν μελαίνᾳ,

χείμωνι μοχθεῦντες μεγάλῳ μάλα·
περ μὲν γὰρ ἄντλος ἱστόπεδαν ἔχει,
λαῖφος δὲ πᾶν ζάδηλον ἤδη
καὶ λακίδες μέγαλαι κατ' αὖτο·
χόλαισι δ' ἄγκυραι.

§ 131. This is the proper place, in accordance with the plan of my work, to notice the three imitations of the dialect, metre, and manner of the old Æolic poets by the Alexandrian Theocritus. They are the 28th, 29th, and 30th idylls in the collection ascribed to him (at least in the most recent editions, such as Ziegler's and Fritzsche's second editions), for the last of them was only recovered from a Milan MS. in the year 1864. The 28th is an elegant little address to an ivory spindle which the poet was sending as a present to the wife of his physician-friend, Nikias of Kos, and was probably composed on the model of a poem of Sappho. The other two are properly called παιδικὰ Αἰολικά, and are poems on the sort of love most prominent in the society of Alcæus. One of them has been even suspected to be the real work of Alcæus. To me that last in order, though in a most corrupt and hopeless state, as anyone may see in the transcript printed by Fritzsche before his emended version, seems poetically the best, and is full of grace and elegance. The dialect is believed to be an artificial Doric, to some extent coloured with the later local speech. The metres are either the *asclepiadics* common in Horace's Odes, which are imitated from the same source, or what are called Æolic dactylics. There is no trace of strophes in any of the three poems. Though Theocritus was probably one of the best imitators in any age, it cannot be said that this attempt to reproduce the love poetry of Alcæus has made much impression upon the world. It is, at all events, quite eclipsed by his bucolic side, in which his originals were far less known and less splendid, and his imitation fresher and full of genius.

CHAPTER XI.

THE PROGRESS OF PERSONAL POETRY.

§ 132. WE now come to the epoch of Greek ₊poetry which
was so brilliant and many sided, that it is not possible to treat it
in chronological order, nor to separate clearly the various threads,
which were becoming closely connected and interlaced. We
find Ol. 60 mentioned as the date of the flourishing of so many
poets, that we begin to wonder what circumstances favoured
literature at this juncture. Of the many which suggest themselves, three may be noted as of great breadth and importance.
First, the caste feeling of the Greek aristocracy was brought out
and intensified by the conflicts with tyrants and democracies; and
this stimulated the bitter hate, and the complaints of travel, of
exile, and of unfriendliness, which we find repeated in the remains of Theognis. Secondly, the rise of brilliant courts under
the tyrants, who reached perhaps their highest point about this
time—Samos, Syracuse, Athens, Corinth were now swayed
by them—had again created a lofty patronage for poets, and
high remuneration for their art, not to speak of the rivalry among
the cities of victors at the games to obtain their praises. Most
of the later lyric poets would have greatly disgusted Alcæus or
Solon. They had sunk back to the social position of depend-
ants on princes, like the old epic rhapsodes, when they did not
assert their liberty in turbulent exile by vehement and bitter
railing. Still the comforts and luxuries of being a well-paid
and well-honoured court poet favoured Anacreon, and Pindar,
and Simonides of Keos, and many others who lived in the great
art-centres of Greece.   ·

There remains yet a third widely different reason. While
education and consequently literature were being more and

more disseminated, prose had not yet been adopted as a vehicle of thought, and thus the whole intellectual outcome of the nation took the form of verse. Much of what remains is indeed prosaic in idea. Xenophanes followed the older wise men in attempting to clothe philosophy—and this time real philosophy—in a poetic form. The wisdom of Phokylides and of Theognis is not half so poetical as Plato's prose. But the Greeks awoke very slowly, as is well known, to the necessity of laying aside metre in writing for the public, and even when they did, we shall find their prose never shaking off a painful attention to rythm.

Thus the whole of the Hellenic world, now better informed, better read, better educated, had no other expression than poetry, and so this age, the end of the sixth century, became the greatest and most brilliant epoch in all the history of Greek poetry. Now for the first time, perhaps for the only time, the Greeks of Sicily, Italy, Hellas, Africa, the islands, and of Asia Minor were all contributing independently to the national literature. They did not all crowd to Sparta, as formerly, or to Athens, as afterwards. They were not all epic poets, as of old, or dramatic, as all the great ones of later days. They kept up elegiac, iambic, and hexameter verse ; they cultivated personal and choral lyrics with equal success ; nor was it till the close of this epoch that the latter form of lyrics asserted itself as having gained the suffrages of the entire Hellenic world. For this reason I have left the history of public choral poetry to the last, and will not take it up till I have sketched the varied developments of personal poetry in connection with the authors already discussed.

§ 133. Unfortunately, our most considerable remains from this epoch are those of elegiac poetry, which was perhaps the poorest and least characteristic species. Its day was gone, and with the exception of its survival in epigrams, it fell asleep till it was resuscitated by the Alexandrians, and became a favourite form of Roman poetry. Thus at this period, elegiacs and the lame iambics of Hipponax seem to have been the form adopted by less poetic minds, which would in a later century have spoken simple prose. We have a few pithy fragments of PHOKYLIDES of Miletus, giving his experiences in short proverbs with the formula *This too is Phokylides'* (καὶ τόδε Φωκυλίδεω), but we know nothing of his life.   He imitates Simonides in satirising women by comparing them to domestic animals, he speaks of Nineveh familiarly as a great city, he wishes to be of the middle class (μέσος ἐν πόλει), and even ridicules the advantages of high birth, so that he can in no wise be regarded as an instance of the common statement, that all the poets of the lyric age were aristocrats.   There are similar feelings scattered through the collection called that of Theognis, not to speak of Hipponax. But of Phokylides nothing more can be learned.[1]

§ 134. XENOPHANES is a clearer personality, whose life is not only in other respects very interesting,[2] but whose extant fragments are far the finest left us from this epoch of the elegy, if not altogether the finest we possess.   The first describes the conditions of a really pleasant feast,[3] the second is an attack on

[1] I purposely pass by in silence the spurious moral poem once attributed to him, consisting of some 250 hexameters (Bergk, pp. 455–75) neatly put together, and stating the Jewish moral code pretty completely.   There can be no doubt that it is the work of a late Alexandrian Jew.

[2] He seems to have written as much in epic hexameters (on which cf. above, p. 122) as in elegiac form.

[3]
Νῦν γὰρ δὴ ζάπεδον καθαρὸν καὶ χεῖρες ἁπάντων
   καὶ κύλικες· πλεκτοὺς δ' ἀμφιτιθεῖ στεφάνους,
ἄλλος δ' εὐῶδες μύρον ἐν φιάλῃ παρατείνει·
   κρητὴρ δ' ἕστηκεν μεστὸς ἐϋφροσύνης·
οἶνος δ' ἐστὶν ἕτοιμος, ὃς οὔποτέ φησι προδώσειν,
   μείλιχος ἐν κεράμοις ἄνθεος ὀσδόμενος·
ἐν δὲ μέσοις ἁγνὴν ὀδμὴν λιβανωτὸς ἵησιν,
   ψυχρὸν δ' ἔστιν ὕδωρ καὶ γλυκὺ καὶ καθαρόν·
πάρκεινται δ' ἄρτοι ξανθοὶ γεραρή τε τράπεζα
   τυροῦ καὶ μέλιτος πίονος ἀχθομένη·
βωμὸς δ' ἄνθεσιν ἂν τὸ μέσον πάντῃ πεπύκασται,
   μολπὴ δ' ἀμφὶς ἔχει δώματα καὶ θαλίη.
χρὴ δὴ πρῶτον μὲν θεὸν ὑμνεῖν εὔφρονας ἄνδρας
   εὐφήμοις μύθοις καὶ καθαροῖσι λόγοις.
σπείσαντας δὲ καὶ εὐξαμένους τὰ δίκαια δύνασθαι
   πρήσσειν· ταῦτα γὰρ ὦν ἐστι προαιρετέον,
οὐχ ὕβρεις πίνειν δ' ὁπόσον κεν ἔχων ἀφίκοιο
   οἴκαδ' ἄνευ προπόλου, μὴ πάνυ γηραλέος·
ἀνδρῶν δ' αἰνεῖν τοῦτον, ὃς ἐσθλὰ πιὼν ἀναφαίνῃ,
   ὡς οἱ μνημοσύνη καὶ νόος ἀμφ' ἀρετῆς·

the increasing mania for athletics and for physical training, which, keeping pace with the growing national importance of the public games, began to infest the Greece, very much as it has been infesting the England of later years. We know that Solon had protested against this evil a generation earlier, and had diminished the public rewards given to victors at the games. In the next century Euripides (whose scholiast quotes this fragment of Xenophanes) writes in the same spirit. In later days generals like Alexander and Philopœmen set their faces steadily against athletic training as unserviceable for military purposes. We hear from Xenophanes that he began to philosophize at the age of twenty-five, and had been spreading his thoughts through Greece for sixty-seven years, so that it is probable that his activity began while Solon was yet alive, at all events early in the sixth century.[1]

§ 135. The same may certainly be said of his contemporary THEOGNIS, under whose name we have a little volume of elegies (nearly 1,400 lines) of which the greater part, called the first book, contains all manner of political and social advices, while the rest is devoted to amorous complaints of the coldness or faithlessness of a favourite boy, whom the poet addressed throughout his works. From the allusions in these poems it appears that Theognis, who belonged to Megara in Greece, though he is also called a citizen of the Sicilian Megara, was one of the old aristocratic party, which had crushed and oppressed the lower classes, till after many internal feuds and troubles the dynasty of Kypselus in its turn defeated and exiled the oppressors, and gave liberty and property to the common people. After the fall of the Kypselids the party struggles

οὔτι μάχας διέπειν Τιτήνων οὐδὲ Γιγάντων,
οὐδὲ τὰ Κενταύρων, πλάσματα τῶν προτέρων,
ἢ στάσιας σφεδανάς· τοῖς οὐδὲν χρηστὸν ἔνεστιν·
θεῶν δὲ προμηθείην αἰὲν ἔχειν ἀγαθόν.

[1] Bergk places his appearance as a philosopher so far back as Ol. 46, 7, so that he would come quite close to Thales ; and this would account for his not departing from the poetical form of teaching, as Heracleitus did, whose work may be fifty years later. But this explanation is unnecessary, cf. above, p. 123.

recommenced, but with this difference, that the people had got possession of a considerable portion of the property of the better classes, and entered upon the conflict with some idea of their own rights and claims.   This was of course most galling to the aristocrats, who remembered their opponents ' wandering about in sheepskins and goatskins,' and glad to accept any benevolences in their despair.

The genuine elegies of Theognis appear to have been advices to a young aristocratic favourite, Kyrnus, also called by the patronymic Polypaïdes, on the importance of high breeding, on the essential vileness of the lower classes, on the decay of party spirit among the Megarian nobles, and the rising influence of wealth.   The nobles are called *the good*, as we call them the *better* classes, and the mere citizens (ἀστοί) are called the bad systematically, but by no means in such a way as to warrant the absurd inference that in the poet's mind *good* (ἀγαθός, ἐσθλός) and *bad* (κακός) had a purely political meaning.   There are ample evidences in the elegies of these words in their strictly moral sense, which indeed was established long before Theognis.

There are other allusions, such as to the threatened wars of the Medes, which might lead us to further inferences about the poet's life, if the elegies now collected under his name were the unalloyed expressions of one poet, and not a sort of politico-moral ' elegant extracts ' put together for educational purposes, long after the poet's death, and without any attempt to maintain his real teaching.   There is no Greek poet to whom the application of this Wolfian theory has been more eminently successful.   The allusions to the Lelantine war on the one hand, and to the Medes on the other, stretch far beyond the life of any one man, even were he to make such flagrantly inconsistent assertions about morals and politics as are found in the collection.   Moreover, lines elsewhere preserved as Solon's and as Tyrtæus' reappear as Theognis' ; and with this change, that in more than one case the opening and concluding lines (containing some general summary or reflection) are set down, omitting the body of the poem, as it appears in Stobæus, and as assigned to the older author.   This shows clearly the intentions of the compiler. He only wanted moral saws, and not personal poems. Bergk, who has worked all this out, shows furthermore that only the old elegiasts are excerpted, no notice being taken of such poets as Ion or Critias. The date of the compilation is limited by a passage of Isocrates, who wishes that such a collection were made, and again in the other direction by a passage in Plato's *Laws*, who says that some such plan was being adopted by practical educators. Our so-called Theognis therefore probably took its present form about the middle of the fourth century. I have already noticed how there is perhaps a fragment of Bias of Priene, among others, here preserved to us. Possibly Callinus and Mimnermus are also represented. Unfortunately the most valuable parts, both historically and æsthetically, have been omitted by the dry schoolmaster who made the selection. The poetical value of the collection is small, and the tone approaches the modesty and tameness of prose, as old critics observed. The convivial fragments are perhaps the best. It is to be remarked that the second book, which contains love-complaints almost exclusively, breathes a manly and vigorous tone, and reminds us of what the ancients have reported of the character of such attachments among the old Cretans and Eubœans. Fragments of the poems seem indeed to refer to Eubœa, others to Sparta, and the whole is composed in the educated Ionic dialect, which was far removed from the ordinary speech of the Megarians. This is accordingly the most striking instance of the close connection between a peculiar dialect and a peculiar form of poetry, to the exclusion of the ordinary language of the poet.

§ 136. *Bibliographical.* As to MSS. they are very numerous, at Paris and the Vatican especially, but also at Venice, Florence, and elsewhere. Bekker's collation has shown the paramount value of one (A) known as *Mutinensis* (which alone contains the second book), now in Paris (*Codd. Græc. Suppl.* 388), but he has not specified its age. Then one (K) of the Venetian (Marc. 522), and one (O) of the Vatican (Vatic. 915), which have been shown by Bergk to be of separate and considerable value. All the rest are far inferior and not independent. The *editio*

princeps is the Aldine of 1495 (together with Theocritus, Hesiod,
&c.) ; the most important subsequently are those of Camerarius
(1551), of Brunck and Gaisford (as *Poetæ Gnomici*).   The
critical editions are by Bekker (2nd ed., Berlin, 1827), Welcker
(1826), Orelli (1840), Ziegler (1868), and in Bergk's *Lyric Poets*.
There are four or five German translations, and a partial
English version in J. H. Frere's *Theognis Restitutus* (*Works*,
vol. iii.), which endeavours to construct the poet's life and
opinions from his poems ; but the whole attempt is vitiated
by the assumption of the unity of authorship of our text.   The
somewhat similar speculation of O. Müller in his *History
of Greek Literature* has been severely handled by Bergk
(*Neues Rhein. Mus.* vol. iii. pp. 227).

§ 137. We may here fitly sum up in a few words the later
history of the elegy, which for us may be said to close with
Theognis.   There were indeed many other elegiac poets, both
Ionic and Attic, of whom traces still remain, but to us they are
lost, nor have we reason to think that if extant they would occupy
a high place in Greek Literature.   The last important poem
of the species in older days was the *Lyde* of Antimachus,
whose learned epic was above mentioned (§ 109).   This lament
on the death of his beloved was a sort of *In Memoriam*, like the
great poem of our own day, passing from personal grief into
larger questions—but in Antimachus questions of mythical and
genealogical lore.   Though good critics always speak of the poet
as laboured and pedantic, there can be no doubt that his elegy,
as well as his learned epic, had great influence in moulding both
the epics and elegiacs of Alexandria, where these cold and
formal qualities were in high repute.   The few extant lines of
the *Lyde* give us no idea of the poem.[1]   There are other well-
known names handed down to us as having composed social
elegies, principally at Athens, such as Ion of Chios, Euenus of
Paros, and a certain Dionysius (nicknamed ' the Copper '),
from all of whom a few lines survive of grace and of elegant
workmanship.   In the next generation the notorious CRITIAS,
among his varied literary work, composed political elegies,
or descriptions of polities (πολιτεῖαι ἔμμετροι is their title),

[1] Bergk, *FLG.* p. 610.

in the style, though far removed from the temper, of Solon, and of these two considerable and interesting fragments survive.[1]

§ 138. An elegiac complaint in the *Andromache* of Euripides,[2] in Doric dialect, is a curiosity in dramatic literature. But while we have these few formal representatives of sustained composition in elegiac metre, it seems that with Simonides came in the fashion of composing short epigrams of a votive character on monuments, or epitaphs on tombs, for which this form was generally adopted. Those of Simonides were most famous, but in the later collections of the anthologies we have short elegiac inscriptions attributed to all manner of literary men, tragic poets like Æschylus and Euripides, lyric poets, even to prose writers like Thucydides and Plato. The genuineness of these little pieces is always a very difficult question; but that the general fashion prevailed, and that various literary men amused themselves in this way, apart from great competitions for public dedications, is certain. The reader

---

[1] Frag. 2 : Καὶ τόδ᾽ ἔθος Σπάρτῃ μελέτημά τε κείμενόν ἐστιν,
πίνειν τὴν αὐτὴν οἰνοφόρον κύλικα·
μηδ᾽ ἀποδωρεῖσθαι προπόσεις ὀνομαστὶ λέγοντα,
μηδ᾽ ἐπὶ δεξιτερὰν χεῖρα κυκλοῦν θιάσου
ἄγγεα   .   .   .   .   .
    . . . Λυδὴ χεὶρ εὗρ᾽ Ἀσιατογενής,
καὶ προπόσεις ὀρέγειν ἐπιδέξια, καὶ προκαλεῖσθαι
ἐξονομακλήδην, ᾧ προπιεῖν ἐθέλει·
εἶτ᾽ ἀπὸ τοιούτων πόσεων γλώσσας τε λύουσιν
εἰς αἰσχροὺς μύθους, σῶμά τ᾽ ἀμαυρότερον
τεύχουσιν· πρὸς δ᾽ ὄμματ᾽ ἀχλὺς ἀμβλωπὸς ἐφίζει·
λῆστις δ᾽ ἐκτήκει μνημοσύνην πραπίδων·
νοῦς δὲ παρέσφαλται· δμῶες δ᾽ ἀκόλαστον ἔχουσιν
ἦθος· ἐπεισπίπτει δ᾽ οἰκοτριβὴς δαπάνη.
οἱ Λακεδαιμονίων δὲ κόροι πίνουσι τοσοῦτον,
ὥστε φρέν᾽ εἰς ἱλαρὰν ἐλπίδα πάντ᾽ ἀπάγειν·
εἴς τε φιλοφροσύνην γλῶσσαν μέτριον τε γέλωτα.
τοιαύτη δὲ πόσις σώματί τ᾽ ὠφέλιμος
γνώμῃ τε κτήσει τε· καλῶς δ᾽ εἰς ἔργ᾽ Ἀφροδίτης,
πρός θ᾽ ὕπνον ἥρμοσται, τὸν καμάτων λιμένα,
πρὸς τὴν τερπνοτάτην τε θεῶν θνητοῖς Ὑγίειαν,
καὶ τὴν Εὐσεβίης γείτονα Σωφροσύνην, κ.τ.λ.

[2] vv. 104, sq.

will find in Bergk's *Lyrici* many such epigrams of great beauty under the authors to whom they were attributed.   To discuss them together is rather the task of the historian of post-classical literature.   For the Alexandrians not only revived the Ionic elegy in the hands of Callimachus, Philetas, Eratosthenes, Parthenius, and others, but exercised their wits in making subtle epigrams full of dainty conceits.   These are well worth reading in the anthology, where they are confused with many specimens of older and simpler work, and have been tastefully reviewed in a special chapter of Mr. Symonds' *Greek Poets.*   The erotic elegy of Callimachus, Philetas and their school is chiefly interesting as having been the model of the Roman elegy, which is one of the glories of Latin literature in the hands of Ovid, Catullus, Tibullus, and Propertius.   But the scanty remains of Callimachus,[1] and the almost total loss of the others, relieve me of the necessity of discussing them with the detail I have allowed to Apollonius.   Yet it is from the Alexandrian and Roman elegy that the whole modern notion of that kind of poem has been derived.   Thus the exceptional *Nanno* of Mimnermus was more lasting in idea than the far more ambitious and famous works of Solon and Theognis, of Xenophanes and Tyrtæus.

§ 139. While the elegy had taken its completed *pragmatical* form in Theognis, and while, as we shall see, Ibycus and Anacreon were each following up special forms of lyric poetry, the iambic metre, of which we hear hardly anything since the elder Simonides, revived with peculiar modifications under the hands of HIPPONAX of Ephesus, who is generally mentioned as the third iambic poet of the Greeks, along with Archilochus and Simonides.   He lived about the 60th Ol. at Clazomenæ, being exiled from his native town by the tyrants Athenagoras and Comas, and was chiefly noted for his scurrilous poems on Bupalus and Athenio, the celebrated sculptors, who had represented or exaggerated his personal deformity in a portrait statue.

---

[1] One elegy on the annual bathing of the statue of Athene at Argos in the Inachus, 140 lines in Doric dialect, and after the style of a Homeric hymn, on the adventures of Athene in Bœotia, and the blinding of Teiresias.   On Callimachus, cf. above, § 102.

He seems, however, also to have attacked a contemporary painter, and to have been a man of violent hates, and of an unhappy life. Ovid (in his *Ibis*) says that he died of hunger, but this may be a poetical inference from the complaints of cold and hunger in his extant fragments, which German critics take seriously, but which are more probably the comic outbursts of a somewhat low and pleasure-loving nature, as we may guess from the many allusions to cookery quoted from him. Though he used ordinary iambic trimeters, tetrameters, and also hexameters in epic parodies (which he perhaps invented), his distinctive feature was the use of choliambics, or iambics ending with a spondee, which, according to the Germans, gives the metre a halting low plebeian tone, only fit for vulgar and coarse subjects. Nevertheless, the refined Callimachus and Babrius came to use it for short fables of an innocent and even graceful description. There is no poetic beauty in the extant fragments, which are chiefly cited by grammarians either for peculiar customs, such as the sacrificing of φαρμακοί—the human sin offerings at the Thargelia, or for hard and obscene words, probably local or slang in character. Though well-known and oft quoted, Hipponax naturally formed no school, but there are fragments of a certain Ananius, who wrote in the same metre, and who seems to have lived about the same time. The constant invocations of Hermes in the fragments of Hipponax are remarkable, and point to some unexplained cause. This god may possibly have been the favourite deity of the lower classes in Ionic cities, and represented in the streets, as we know was the case at Athens. The names of the later choliambists are not worth enumerating.[1]

The spirit of personal satire was transmitted to Attic comedy, which is generally agreed to have started with an iambic vein, and in its political days, the attacks of the comic poets on leading men, or on notorious libertines at Athens were not less direct and angry than the verses of

---

[1] Cf. Bergk, *FLG.* pp. 788, sq. Herodas alone is still of interest, and his fragments worth reading. But his date is variously assigned from the age of Xenophon to that of Callimachus, and his history unknown.

Archilochus and Hipponax. The close alliance in spirit be-tween these two branches of Greek poetry is further illus-trated by the fact that Hermippus, one of the bitterest oppo-nents of Pericles among the old comic poets, was also the author of a book of iambic and trochaic poems, often quoted both by Athenæus and the scholiasts on Aristophanes.[1] These poems were personal attacks of the same kind as those in the parabasis of the earlier comedies, but here even in form imi-tated from the ancient masters of satire among the Greeks.[2]

§ 140. The most striking possible contrast to Hipponax was his contemporary ANACREON of Teos, who migrated with his townspeople to Abdera, when they were driven out by Harpagus. From thence he was called to grace the court of Polycrates of Samos, then the greatest man in the Greek world ; and after Polycrates's murder he is said to have passed his old age with the scarcely less splendid Hipparchus at Athens. Of his death nothing certain is known. Instead of the low virulence and bitter wants of Hipponax's life, we have here an accomplished courtier, a votary of love and wine, a man who enjoyed every human pleasure to the full, and felt no trouble save the touch of silver in his hair, and the scorn of stately youth or fair maiden for his advancing years. He concerned himself with no politics ; he gave no serious advice in morals ; he stands aloof from all the higher aims and aspirations of his age; he was essentially 'the idle singer of an empty day,' the minion in poetry of a luxurious and sensual court. The vigorous attack on Artemon (fr. 21) seems incited by erotic jealousy ; the hymns to Dionysus, who is with him as prominent as Hermes with Hipponax, were in no sense religious, but worldly compo-sitions. But this want of seriousness reached the very core of

---

[1] Cf. Meineke, *Hist. Com.* p. 96.

[2] When the Romans lay claim to the invention of *satire*, as their sole originality in poetry, it is to be remembered that this is only true in the peculiar Roman sense of *satira*, as a *poetical medley*, such as the satires of Horace and Persius ; and this we are not in a position to deny, as we have lost the mimes of Sophron. But we know that Sophron was the model of the latter, and therefore may have anticipated this phase of literature also. To say that satire, in the other and now received sense, was invented by the Romans is quite ridiculous.

his nature. His praise of love and of wine are not the passionate outbursts of Archilochus or Alcæus, but the elegant encomia
of an Aristippus, who lays hold of pleasure, but is not held by
it. The glow of passion and the pang of grief could not agitate
that worldly and selfish soul, even though he ventures to assert
'that Eros struck at him with a mighty axe, and plunged him
in a wintry torrent.' The great body of his fragments, and the
numerous copies of his poems, speak of love as an engrossing
amusement, of feasting as spoilt by earnest conversation, nay
even of old age with a sort of jovial regret, very different from
the dark laments of the earnest Mimnermus.[1] The poetry of
Anacreon is no longer the outburst of pent-up passion, but the
exercise of a graceful talent, the ornament of a luxurious
leisure. Had the court of Augustus not affected moral reforms
and national aims, we should have had in Horace a very similar poet. In both the very absence of intensity permitted a
peculiar polish and grace of form, so much so, that no Greek poet
excels Anacreon in the variety and elegance of his metres, or in
the purity of his diction.

It was for this very reason, because perfect form was
combined with trivial and shallow sentiment, that the poetasters of a worn-out culture chose him above all others as
their most suitable model. For a long time the Anacreontics
composed in the schools of the fourth century A.D., especially at Gaza, imposed their conceits upon the world as the
work of Anacreon—an imposture of which the brilliant translations of Thomas Moore are a happy result, but an imposture inconceivable had they attempted to copy the redhot
aristocrats, whose lyrics spoke their troubled and turbulent
life. I will not discuss these well-known love poems, which
were printed repeatedly with great elegance at Parma and at
Rome in the last century, so much so that they have become
of considerable value to lovers of beautiful books. The Roman
reproduction in plates and in type of the eleventh century
Palatine MS. (Spaletti, 1781) is particularly interesting. They

---

[1] They are elegantly characterised by Critias (in his 7th extant fragment,
Bergk, p. 605) as συμποσίων ἐρέθισμα, γυναικῶν ἠπερόπευμα, αὐλῶν ἀντίπαλον,
φιλοβάρβιτον, ἡδύν ἄλυπον.

are again edited with more care than they deserve by Val. Rose and by Bergk, though they are not without a certain elegance, and have produced innumerable translations and imitations. To us they are chiefly useful as evidences of the effect produced by the complete works of Anacreon upon the schools which studied him.

In form Anacreon belongs to the Æolic school of Sappho and Alcæus, and his poems were sung without chorus to the accompaniment of a lyre of twenty strings. His verses were monostrophic, like theirs, repeating simple but varied rythms, mixed iambics, choriambics, and tribrachs, after the manner of the verses of our modern songs. But he seems to have avoided the special metres called by us Alcaic and Sapphic, and to have preferred glyconics. In adopting this simple and personal form of the Æolic bards, he was led by a truer instinct than his contemporary Ibycus, who attempted to combine the erotic tone of the Lesbian school with the choral lyric form of the Dorians. But it will be better to class Ibycus with the latter and we shall accordingly return to him.

CHAPTER XII.

THE PUBLIC LYRIC POETRY OF THE GREEKS.

§ 141. WE have already recognised the first beginnings of this strictly Greek form of poetry in our notice of Alcman, though personal allusions are still frequent in his fragments, and his provincial character was noted in contrast to the broader features of his successors. The first of these who is sufficiently important for this brief history is ARION of Methymna, specially celebrated as having organised the dithyrambic[1] choruses in honour of Dionysus, whose worship, orgiastic and oriental in character, had hitherto been unsanctioned by either states or literary men, but was popular about the Isthmus. He arranged the chorus of fifty, so as to produce antistrophic effects, and brought into use dancing—the science of *orchestic*—as subsidiary to music and poetry. Historians of the drama have laid great stress on this improvement of the popular dithyramb. Arion was the first to introduce it into a Doric town, Corinth, and to give the chorus an artistic form, called cyclic, which was not changed till Thespis rearranged his tragic chorus to a square form. It seems, furthermore, that the dithyrambic choruses of Arion were not wildly joyous and licentious, like the original country dances which were his model, but honoured Dionysus as Zagreus, or god of the nether world, in a solemn Doric tone. Arion is even called the inventor of the tragic *tropos*, which corresponded to the ἐμμέλεια, or solemn dance of subsequent tragedy. It seems that his cyclic chorus did not wear masks,

---

[1] The derivation of the word *dithyrambos*, which appears to have been another name for Dionysus, is not yet satisfactorily explained. It was always used to designate those mimic combinations of music, poetry, and dancing which were performed in honour of the god.

but was a serious body of men, so that the dithyramb assumed in his hands something of the dignity of the choral worship of Apollo. The rude wild dithyramb of the country folks no doubt still subsisted, but Arion created a new literary form.

These important innovations are indirect inferences, in some cases not very certain, from the stray notes surviving about his literary position, which is little discussed by the ancients. Yet his personal fame was very great, as appears from the story of his being compelled by sailors, who coveted his amassed wealth, to jump into the sea on his return route from Italy, when a dolphin carried him to Tænarum. He re-appeared at the court of Periander, to the dismay of his would-be murderers. He seems, in fact, as intimate with Periander as Anacreon was with Polycrates. This fixes his date, and he is besides called a pupil of Alcman. As to the story of the dolphin, our evidence for it is curiously old and respectable. There is the charming narrative of Herodotus (i. 23), who mentions the figure of the poet on a dolphin, dedicated at Tænarum. This figure was well known, and was copied, or paralleled, by numerous coins of Methymna, Corinth, Tarentum, Brundusium, and other cities in Italy. Legends of Tarentum, however, connect both Taras and Phalanthus in a similar way with dolphins, so that we cannot be sure that all the coins represent Arion. But Ælian, in repeating the story, quotes a passage from Arion himself, distinctly alleging the facts. This elegant poem [1] has been, of course, declared spurious, because

---

[1]

Ὕψιστε θεῶν,
πόντιε χρυσοτρίαινα Πόσειδον,
γαιάοχ᾽, ἐγκύμον᾽ ἀν᾽ ἅλμαν·
βραγχίοις περὶ δὲ σὲ πλωτοὶ
θῆρες χορεύουσι κύκλῳ,
κούφοισι ποδῶν ῥίμμασιν
ἐλάφρ᾽ ἀναπαλλόμενοι, σιμοί,
φριξαύχενες, ὠκύδρομοι σκύλακες, φιλόμουσοι
δελφῖνες, ἔναλα θρέμματα
κουρᾶν Νηρεΐδων θεᾶν,
ἃς ἐγείνατ᾽ Ἀμφιτρίτα·
οἵ μ᾽ εἰς Πέλοπος γᾶν ἐπὶ Ταιναρίαν
ἀκτὰν ἐπορεύσατε πλαζόμενον Σικελῷ ἐνὶ πόντῳ,
κυρτοῖσι νώτοις ὀχεῦντες,

it asserts a miracle, or because it is unworthy of such a poet as Arion—that poet's works being otherwise unknown ! !—or because it is supposed to contain modernisms. All these are matters of opinion, and, on the whole, the absence of any mention of the poem by earlier authorities makes me doubt its genuineness, though I suspect it must be the ancient work of some immediate pupil, who passed it off as the poet's own.

It has not, I think, been suggested that the close connection between Arion and the cult of Dionysus may have suggested the dolphin legend, for we see from the Homeric hymn to Dionysus (above, p. 135) how that god was early identified with marine adventure, and more especially with dolphins, as a sort of sporting sea satyrs, whose gambollings might be thought analogous to a dancing chorus.

§ 142. There is yet another alleged composer of *tragic choruses* —like Arion's, whose work Herodotus notices in one of his precious literary digressions — *Epigenes* of Sicyon. Herodotus says that the Sicyonians honoured Adrastus in every possible way, and even celebrated his sufferings in tragic choruses, honouring not Dionysus, but Adrastus. Cleisthenes, for political reasons, restored the due honours to the god. But this early attempt to substitute a mortal hero's sufferings for those of Dionysus is a curious anticipation of the great stride to tragedy made in Attica at the close of the same century.

§ 143. Before passing on, a word may be said on the melic fragments quoted by Diogenes Laertius, as the most favourite of the songs composed by the seven wise men. He cites with this formula (τῶν δὲ ἀδομένων μάλιστα εὐδοκίμησεν αὐτοῦ τάδε) from Pittacus, Bias, Chilo, Thales, and Cleobulus. The metres are dactyls and trochees combined in logocedic manner. The diction seems antique. Yet I agree with the sceptical critics who deny their genuineness. Diogenes borrowed most of them from the book of the Argive Lobo, about whose age or authority we know nothing.

ἄλοκα Νηρείας πλακὸς
τέμνοντες, ἀστιβῆ πόρον, φῶτες δόλιοι
ὥς μ' ἀφ' ἀλιπλόου γλαφυρᾶς νεὼς
εἰς οἶδμ' ἀλιπόρφυρον λίμνας ἔριψαν.

§ 144. The inscription of *Echembrotus* the Arcadian, quoted by Pausanias from a tripod at Thebes, is genuine, and relates that this man contended at Delphi (evidently after the wide growth of the festival) and composed, *for the Hellenes, songs and elegies.* But his date is unknown. Another poet, *Xanthus,* is distinctly mentioned as older than Stesichorus, and his model in some things. But he too is a mere name, and only serves us to introduce his successor.

§ 145. STESICHORUS of Himera was a great figure in Greek literature, and evidently a man of the first importance, but his fragments, though numerous (above 50), do not afford us the materials for an independent judgment. His family was said to proceed from the Locrian colony Metaurus in Sicily, and, as we have seen (p. 105, note), the Locrian legends connect him with Hesiod. His original name is said by Suidas to have been Tisias. He lived about 630–550 B.C., and appears to have died at an advanced age in Catana, where a curious octagon monument, with eight pillars and eight steps, marked his tomb. As the oldest poet of Sicily, he was specially distinguished. More particularly he is praised for his Homeric tone, and only slightly censured by the later Roman rhetoricians for redundancy. His poems once comprised twenty-six books, of which a group of twelve poems with epic titles is specially noticed, such as *Eriphyla, the Fall of Troy, Helena, the Oresteia,* &c.; of these we shall speak again. There were also religious poems, of which we know very little; songs of revelry, sung in Athens at wine-parties; bucolic love poems about shepherds (particularly Daphnis), which are called by Ælian the forerunners of Theocritus' poetry, and lastly love stories in verse, which seem to have been unlike anything in Greek literature, except the Milesian tales, and their successors, the late Greek novels. Of these the *Kalyke,* much in fashion among women, told of that maiden being enamoured of a youth, and praying to Aphrodite that she might be joined to him in lawful wedlock; but when her desire could not be accomplished, she took away her own life. This sentimental poetic novel was remarkable for its moral tone, and indeed all Stesichorus' poetry produces the same impression.

§ 146. His position in the history of Greek religion is very important, for finding the taste for epic recitation decaying, he undertook to reproduce epic stories in lyric dress, and present the substance of the old epics in rich and varied metres, and with the measured movements of a trained chorus. This was a direct step to the drama, for when any one member of the chorus came to stand apart and address. the rest of the choir, we have already the essence of Greek tragedy before us. He added to the strophe and antistrophe the epode, and so gave choral lyric poetry the complete form, found in Pindar and the tragic choruses. But apart from these formal changes, he freely altered and modified the substance of the legends, or perhaps brought into notoriety old and little-known variations which from his day became popular, and passed into Attic tragedy. To judge from like variations in Pindar, some of these changes were suggested by moral reasons, but possibly most of them merely by a love of variety, and of refreshing the somewhat worn-out epic legends. On the siege of Troy especially he differed much from our Homer, and his famous palinodia about Helen gave rise to the most celebrated story about him.[1] He had, in the opening of a poem, spoken disparagingly of the heroine, who struck him with blindness. He then composed his re-cantation (the Ἑλένα), which asserted that not the real but a phantom Helen had gone to Troy (a legend recurring in Euripides' *Helena*), and he accordingly recovered his sight.[2]

The poet was apparently no politician, though his apologue of the horse who called in a rider to help him against the stag was reported to have been composed for the citizens of Agrigentum, to open their eyes to the danger of giving Phalaris the power

---

[1] From the authorities cited by Bergk (*FLG.* p. 981), it appears that Plato (*Phæd.* 243 A) is our earliest authority for the legend; then Isocrates (in his *Encom. Hel.* p. 64). But the fullest account is in Pausanias (iii. 19. 11). A host of other allusions is also cited. It is important to observe, that among them a scholion on Lycophron speaks of Hesiod as the first deviser of the story of an εἴδωλον of Helen.

[2] The first lines of this palinodia have survived :—

οὐκ ἔστ' ἔτυμος λόγος οὗτος,
οὐδ' ἔβας ἐν ναυσὶν εὐσέλμοις
οὐδ' ἵκεο Πέργαμα Τροίας.

which he afterwards so grievously misused. The language of Stesichorus, as befitted public choral poetry, was not a local idiom, and is seldom quoted as peculiar by the grammarians, but is epic in tone, and pure and classical in its diction. Unfortunately, his fragments, chiefly cited for new versions of legends, are more barren than usual for us; nor is there any poet of whom so much has remained who now presents so indefinite and vague a figure in Greek literature. But he has a certain family likeness to Pindar, whose 4th Pythian ode is probably similar in type to his poems on epic subjects.

§ 147. The remains of the poet IBYCUS are of a far more definite complexion. This poet, a native of Rhegium, flourished about Ol. 60, and has been variously regarded as a successor of Stesichorus, and as an offshoot of the Æolic school. There are strong reasons for both these views, but that which maintains the former is, in my opinion, the more correct. The poems of Ibycus were essentially choral poems, and intended for public performances. They have the complicated structure of Stesichorus' poems, and some fragments on epic subjects ascribed in turn to either poet, show how strong was the similarity between them. There are indeed a great many references in geographers and scholiasts to Ibycus as an authority on epic legends. But, on the other hand, the exceedingly glowing and beautiful confessions of love, and the fact that these were sometimes addressed to individual youths, seem to place the poet among the personal lyrists of the Æolic school, and suggest that he should be treated along with Sappho and Anacreon.

It has been surmised that these love poems were not really personal, that the Chalcidians had of old contests of beauty among boys, and openly legalised the love of them, and that Ibycus composed these passionate addresses as the public expression of the love of beauty among his fellow-citizens, so that we have here a literary effort even more artificial and self-conscious than the philosophic gaiety of Anacreon. But such excessive refinements are surely an ana-chronism in Ibycus' age, and we ought rather to regard his poetry as a very important attempt to combine the chief merits of the Æolic school with the richer and more popular forms of the Doric choral poetry. We know that many of his poems were of this strictly Stesichorean character, and it does not at all appear that he devoted himself wholly to love, like Sappho, or that he touched politics, like Alcæus. On the other hand, we find the feeling of love almost avoided by the public choral lyrics, so that these fragments stand out in peculiar relief. It is very remarkable that this noble attempt of Ibycus did not find imitators. Anacreon and Ibycus are the last Greek poets who touched these magic chords in human nature. The poetry of love disappears (except in *skolia*) during the period of the political greatness of Greece, and only revives as an artificial plant in the decay of its literature. It may have been felt that such personal and private feelings were unsuitable to public choirs, and the artistic sense of the Greeks may have forbidden such a combination. When this artistic sense was rapidly developing the rich antistrophic periods, and various metres, with orchestic to expound them to the eye as well as to the ear—it may have been felt that these complicated forms were greater and more national than the simple songs of Sappho and Anacreon, however pathetic and beautiful these latter might be. So it came that Ibycus, who is quoted with great enthusiasm by Athenæus, and other critics of late date, is not, so far as I can remember, commonly praised among the ancients, or placed at all on the level with Stesichorus. To us the extant fragments justify the reversing of this judgment, those of Ibycus being exceptionally beautiful.[1]

The legend of the cranes which exposed his murderers has been best told in a famous poem by Schiller, but does not rest on any very ancient authority.

[1] Frag. 2 : Ἔρος αὖτέ με κυανέοισιν ὑπὸ βλεφάροις τακέρ' ὄμμασι
          δερκόμενος
    κηλήμασι παντοδαποῖς ἐς ἄπειρα δίκτυα Κύπριδι βάλλει·
    ἦ μὰν τρομέω νιν ἐπερχόμενον,
    ὥστε φερέζυγος ἵππος ἀεθλοφόρος ποτὶ γήραι
    ἀέκων σὺν ὄχεσφι θοοῖς ἐς ἄμιλλαν ἔβα.

CHAPTER XIII.

§ 148. WE come at last to the two great masters of what the Germans call *universal melic,* Simonides and Pindar. Universal melic implies that these men rose above all local idioms and parochial interests, and were acknowledged as national poets[1] and composers of all sorts of lyric poetry. It must, however, be remembered, in limitation of these notions, that the love-songs of the Æolic school are not reproduced, that the personal experiences of the poet are no longer prominent, and that these men distinctly represent the triumph of the public lyrics over the personal lyrics of earlier schools. This change was either the cause or the effect, or both, of a changed social position in the poets themselves. Neither Simonides nor Pindar has anything in common with the turbulent aristocrats of earlier lyric days. The rise and prevalence of tyrants in Greece, and their desire of spreading culture about them, had created a demand, and a comfortable prospect, for professional court poets, of whom Anacreon has already been noticed as a specimen. Thus both Simonides and Pindar lived and composed at the courts of tyrants. But fortunately for them their epoch coincided with the outburst of democracy after the Persian wars, and the rise of free states which could rival the tyrants in patronising letters. Thus we find these distinguished men equal favourites with despots and with their bitterest enemies, and we can see how carefully they must have avoided politics. In the great national contest against Persia, Simonides took part by his numerous elegies

---

[1] This claim is, however, made by an earlier poet, Echembrotus, the Arcadian ; cf. above, p. 202.

and epigrams,[1] for which he seems to have revived the elegiac metre, which had fallen into disuse for philosophical and moral purposes.   But Pindar, whose city had taken the wrong side, and had Medized, was unable to glorify the Greek cause adequately at the expense of the Thebans, and hence Simonides maintained, among his contemporaries, a higher reputation.

SIMONIDES, son of Leoprepes, was born at Iulis, on the island of Keos—an island afterwards noted for good laws and for culture—and was consequently distinguished from his older namesake as ὁ Κεῖος.   As his life reached from 556 to 469 B.C., he may be said to have lived through the most glorious and certainly the most eventful period of Greek history.   Coming forward at a time when the tyrants had made poetry a matter of culture, and dissociated it from politics, we find him a professional artist, free from all party struggles, alike welcome at the courts of tyrants and among the citizens of free states ; he was respected throughout all the Greek world, and knew well how to suit himself, socially and artistically, to his patrons. The great national struggle with Persia gave him the opportunity of becoming the spokesman of the nation, in celebrating the glories of the victors, and the heroism of the fallen patriots. This exceptional opportunity made him quite the foremost poet of his day, and decidedly better known and more admired than Pindar, who has so completely eclipsed him in the attention of posterity.   In one department of poetry, in his elegies and epigrams, he indeed always held the foremost rank, but the sacerdotal and grandiloquent splendour of Pindar has long gained the day over the smoother and more worldly compositions of Simonides, which were more obvious and are believed to have been less profound.   He wrote concerning Lycurgus, and his influence on Sparta, probably in some choral piece intended for recitation there.   He was intimate with both Pausanias and Themistocles ; he was long the favourite leader of the cyclic choruses (in spite of his plain appearance) and composer of dithyrambic hymns at the Dionysiac festivals, which had become popular since the days of Peisistratus.   He was intimate with the Skopadæ, the hereditary grandees of Thessaly,

---

[1] Fragg. 90-110.

who may have been far behind Athenian culture, but were able to pay princely fees for the praise even of their dogs. He was also intimate with the great tyrants in Sicily, with Theron and Hieron, whose quarrels he allayed by his prudent advice. It seems that anyone could purchase his services, and this purely professional attitude appeared mean to most Greeks when compared with the red-hot passion of the old aristocratic lyrist, or the national importance of the Attic dramatist, whose aims were far above pecuniary rewards.

Most unfortunately we have no complete poem (save epigrams and epitaphs) now remaining from this great poet ; but the exquisite beauty, the pellucid clearness, and the deep but chastened pathos of his fragments make us wish to exchange a few of Pindar's more laboured odes for the masterpieces of his rival. Besides sepulchral inscriptions, we have remains of Epinikia, of Hymns, Dithyrambs, Parthenia, Hyporchemes, and Threni, or laments. Our finest fragments belong to the latter, and lead us to suppose that pathos was the peculiar gift in which he excelled. It was that calm and dignified grief which is so marked a feature in the monumental art of the Greeks, and of which the specimens in sculpture reach from the Attic tomb reliefs to the famous Laocoon.

Simonides was, moreover, famed for wise and witty sayings, and paid attention to the art of mnemonics. His modifications of the Greek alphabet point rather to his having brought additional letters, already known, into fashion in monumental inscriptions, than to his being the actual discoverer. He described poetry as *word-painting*, a remark with which Lessing opens his *Laocoon*, and styles Simonides ' the Greek Voltaire,' a very unhappy comparison. Of the great number of epigrams handed down to us in the *Anthology* under his name, many are doubtless spurious, nor is it easy to detect a clever imitator in such short and simple pieces, where a far inferior poet might often succeed in rivalling his master. Some of them however are attested by indubitable authority, such as that of Herodotus, or by respectable scholiasts. These are rather remarkable for extreme simplicity and for an avoidance of the conceits of later epigrammatists.[1] But in any case they are of inferior interest to the fragments of his greater poems, as, for example, the exquisite *lament of Danae.* [2]

Apart from his splendid expressions of nationality and of patriotism,[3] there is, apparently for the reasons above cited, an avoidance of politics in the remains of Simonides. On the other hand, we find a considerable advance in the critical and philosophical temper which pervades them. He dissects and censures the current saws of elder sages,[4] and sometimes

His high esteem for terse clear utterance, as a privilege of Greeks and of educated men, appears from the proverbs about his μακρὸς λόγος (cf. Bergk, frag. 189).

[2] Frag. 37 : Ὅτε λάρνακι ἐν δαιδαλέᾳ ἄνεμός τέ μιν
κινηθεῖσά τε λίμνα
δείματι ἤριπεν, οὐκ ἀδιάντοισι παρειαῖς
ἀμφί τε Περσεῖ βάλλε φίλαν χέρα
εἶπέ τε· ὦ τέκος, οἷον ἔχω πόνον·
σὺ δ' ἀωτεῖς γαλαθηνῷ τ' ἤθεϊ κνώσσεις ἐν ἀτερπεῖ
δώματι χαλκεογόμφῳ,
νυκτιλαμπεῖ κυανέῳ τε δνόφῳ τανυσθείς.
αὐαλέαν δ' ὕπερθε τεὰν κόμαν βαθεῖαν
παριόντος κύματος οὐκ ἀλέγεις,
οὐδ' ἀνέμου φθόγγων,
κείμενος ἐν πορφυρέᾳ χλανίδι, πρόσωπον καλόν.
Εἰ δὲ τοὶ δεινὸν τό γε δεινὸν ἦν,
καί κεν ἐμῶν ῥημάτων λεπτὸν ὑπεῖχες οὖας.
κέλομαι δ' εὗδε βρέφος, εὑδέτω δὲ πόντος,
εὑδέτω δ' ἄμετρον κακόν·
μεταιβολία δέ τις φανείη, Ζεῦ πάτερ,
ἐκ σέο· ὅττι δὲ θαρσαλέον ἔπος
εὔχομαι, τεκνόφι δίκαν σύγγνωθί μοι.

[3] Frag. 4 : Τῶν ἐν Θερμοπύλαις θανόντων
εὐκλεὴς μὲν ἁ τύχα, καλὸς δ' ὁ πότμος,
βωμὸς δ' ὁ τάφος, πρὸ γόων δὲ μνᾶστις, ὁ δ' οἶκτος ἔπαινος.
ἐντάφιον δὲ τοιοῦτον εὑρώς
οὔθ' ὁ πανδαμάτωρ ἀμαυρώσει χρόνος.
ἀνδρῶν δ' ἀγαθῶν ὅδε σακὸς οἰκέταν εὐδοξίαν
Ἑλλάδος εἵλετο· μαρτυρεῖ δὲ Λεωνίδας
ὁ Σπάρτας βασιλεύς, ἀρετᾶς μέγαν λελοιπὼς
κόσμον ἀέναόν τε κλεῖος.

[4] See also among his ἄτακτοι λόγοι, or 'wit and wisdom,' the advice (frag. 192) παίζειν ἐν τῷ βίῳ καὶ περὶ μηδὲν ἁπλῶς σπουδάζειν.

repeats them in a finer and richer form. Thus Hesiod's
famous lines on the 'narrow way that leadeth unto virtue'
are beautifully rendered.[1] But the leading feature in his philosophy seems a gentle and resigned fatalism, dwelling patiently
on the weakness and the ills of men, and the inscrutable
paths of Divine Providence.[2] The longer elegiac fragment
(85) bears quite the stamp of Mimnermus, and may, as Bergk
suggests, have strayed here (through Stobæus) from the older
Simonides. It seems a natural consequence of this fatalism,
which is curiously at variance with the splendid speculations
of Pindar on the future life of the blessed, that there should
be passages in Simonides asserting the paramount importance
of pleasure.[3] His other rival in cyclic choruses was *Lasus*
of Hermione, the teacher of Pindar, and one of the literary
men employed at the court of Peisistratus, of whose works
but a single fragment of three lines remains.

In concluding our account of these manifold fragments of

---

[1] Frag. 58 :

Ἔστι τις λόγος,
τὰν Ἀρετὰν ναίειν δυσαμβάτοις ἐπὶ πέτραις,
νῦν δέ μιν θοὰν χῶρον ἁγνὸν ἀμφέπειν.
οὐδὲ πάντων βλεφάροις θνατῶν ἔσοπτος,
ᾧ μὴ δακέθυμος ἱδρὼς
ἔνδοθεν μόλῃ, ἵκηταί τ' ἐς ἄκρον ἀνδρείας.

[2] Thus (fragg. 38, 39) :

Πάντα γὰρ μίαν ἱκνεῖται δασπλῆτα Χάρυβδιν,
αἱ μεγάλαι τ' ἀρεταὶ καὶ ὁ πλοῦτος.
Πολλὸς γὰρ ἄμμιν εἰς τὸ τεθνᾶναι χρόνος,
ζῶμεν δ' ἀριθμῷ παῦρα κακῶς ἔτεα.

And again :

Ἀνθρώπων ὀλίγον μὲν κάρτος, ἄπρακτοι δὲ μεληδόνες,
αἰῶνι δὲ παύρῳ πόνος ἀμφὶ πόνῳ ·
ὁ δ' ἄφυκτος ὁμῶς ἐπικρέμαται θάνατος ·
κείνου γὰρ ἴσον λάχον μέρος οἵ τ' ἀγαθοὶ
ὅστις τε κακός.

[3] As we have in fragg. 70 and 71. His rivalry with Pindar and
jealousy of him are said to have been expressed in the words of fragg. 75,
ἐξελέγχει ὁ νέος οἶνος, &c.

Greek poetry between Hesiod and Pindar, it may be well to mention that English versions of the most striking pieces will be found appended to Milman's *Agamemnon*, to Mr. Fitzgerald's *Hippolytus*, and in the chapters which Mr. Symonds has devoted to them in his *Greek Poets*.

§ 149. The Theban Pindar is the only Greek lyric poet of whose works any considerable or complete portion has been preserved, and it is fortunate that even this scanty dole should come from an artist of the highest name and fame. He was born at Cynoscephalæ, close to Thebes, the son of Daiphantus, in the spring of 521, or end of Ol. 64, 3.[1] His ancestors were known as flute-players, and apparently connected, through the Ægidæ, with Doric blood, as we may infer from his 5th Pythian ode. Lasus of Hermione was his master,[2] and indeed Thebes was generally celebrated at the time for flute-playing,[3] though an old proverb, which he twice quotes, spoke of his people as ' Bœotian swine.' Yet celebrated women, Myrtis and Corinna, contended against him and conquered him in his early youth in poetical contests, and from the latter he is said to have received advice and encouragement. .But he became known and esteemed at an early age, for we have one poem (*Pyth*. x.) apparently written when he was not above twenty. Two others (*Pyth*. vi. and xii.), which date from before the Persian wars, are simpler and less ambitious than his later poems, and may be regarded as showing the earliest phase of Pindar's

---

[1] He was certainly born at the very time of the 17th Pythian, but there is a grave doubt whether this may not correspond with Ol. 65, 3 (518 B.C.), for though the Pythian contest seems to have originated in the 48th Ol., the first contest was an ἀγὼν χρηματίτης, for money prizes, whereas in Ol. 49, 3 it was made στεφανίτης, and from this date the scholiasts on Pindar begin their reckoning. Boeckh, who counts from Ol. 48, 4, depends on Pausanias only, who seems hardly so good an authority as the excellent scholiasts on Pindar. Cf. on the question Bergk, *FLG*. p. 9, who says he probably lost his father early, and that his stepfather Scopelinus was a flute-player.

[2] Apollodorus and Agathocles are also mentioned, and it is more than probable that he received his instruction from all three masters at Athens.

[3] This fashion was not introduced at Athens till later, and is mentioned in connection with Alcibiades.

style. The great crisis of the Persian wars seems to have affected him as little as was possible, for being a Theban and opposed to the patriotic states of Greece, he could not offend his townsmen, and would not offend the greater states with whom his sympathy probably lay. From this time on he was employed writing occasional poems for the kings or citizens of various Hellenic cities, and it seems almost certain, from his allusions, that he visited Thessaly, Ægina, Argos, and, of course, Delphi and Olympia. He probably knew all the great cities ; but wrote very little for Athenians, and not at all (I believe) for Sparta. He went to visit Hieron at Syracuse in Ol. 76 or 77, and made friends in most of the Sicilian cities, but seems to have been annoyed at the rivalry and fame of Simonides and Bacchylides. Thus he may fairly be called a national lyric poet, and one who was honoured and rewarded by all manner of Hellenes alike. The end of his life was without incident ; he died in his eightieth year at the Bœotian Argos (441 B.C.).[1] There was a bronze statue erected to him at Athens, and he was specially paid by the Athenians for one of his poems. His house was spared by Alexander when destroying Thebes. He had the character of a pious reserved man, specially devoted to the worship of Apollo among the gods, and learned in the myths and ceremonies of local cults. He often gave proverbial advice like the older elegiasts, to whose tone and style his wisdom bears much resemblance. A closer estimate of his genius will occupy us presently.

His poems comprised Hymns, Pæans, Prosodia (of which two remain among our collection), Parthenia, Hyporchemes, Encomia, Skolia, Dithyrambs (of which one considerable fragment remains), Threni,[2] which seem to have been exceptionally

---

[1] Other authorities place his death in his sixty-sixth year (Ol. 82, 1). That the obscure Argos, mentioned as the birthplace of Acusilaus, is intended, seems likely from the other account, which speaks of him as dying in his own country. The various lives of Pindar from Suidas, the MSS. and elsewhere, were collected by Boeckh, and are copied from him into later editions. The fullest and best seems to be that in a Breslau MS. (Vratisl. A, which also contains the best scholia), which was first edited by Schneider.

[2] Suidas gives seventeen separate titles for the seventeen books, if we

fine, and the Epinikia, or hymns of victory, which form the chief part of the poems we possess. I do not believe the notice in Suidas that he wrote tragedies. For the theory that there existed lyrical tragedies, intermediate between the choral lyrics and the Attic tragedy, though sustained by Böckh and O. Müller, seems devoid of any better foundation than that grammarian's notice.

§ 150. The general features of all these varied poems may be gathered up under the following heads. In the first place, they were *non-political.* The poet seems to have carefully avoided identifying himself with any party or form of government. His patrons were sometimes free aristocrats, sometimes hereditary rulers, sometimes tyrants ; and the poet is willing for pay to praise the good points in all of them. Secondly, they are *religious*, and here a strong feature in the man shines through every line that he wrote. He was honestly attached to the national religion, and to its varieties in old local cults. He lived a somewhat sacerdotal life, labouring in honour of the gods, and seeking to spread a reverence for old traditional beliefs. He, moreover, shows an acquaintance with Orphic rites and Pythagorean mysteries, which led him to preach the doctrine of immortality, and of rewards and punishments in the life hereafter.[1] This striking feature was not generally adopted by later moral teachers, and shows that the religious teaching of Pindar had no lasting effect on the nation. Thirdly, the poems of Pindar are *learned*, and learned in this particular sense, that while he repudiates the newer philosophy, he lays great stress on mythical histories, on genealogies, and on ritual. He is indeed more affected by the advance of freethinking than he imagines ; he borrows from

omit the tragedies. The author of his life in some of the MSS. has only eight titles, giving two or more books under some of them. From the fact that Theophrastus, Aristoxenus, and other old authorities quote from the *skolia*, which do not appear in the second list, Bergk (*FLG.* pp. 280, sq.) infers that there was an old Attic collection in seventeen books, which Suidas' authority knew ; and that the more systematic list, reduced under fewer heads, was the Alexandrian recension, probably first edited by Aristophanes.

[1] The most explicit fragment (θρῆνοι, 3) is, however, not considered genuine by recent critics.

the neologians the habit of rationalising myths, and explaining away immoral acts and motives in the gods ; but these things are isolated attempts with him, and have no deep effect upon his general thinking.   Fourthly, they are *stately*, often grandiloquent, often obscure, but never smooth or witty, never playful with success, but striking from their splendid diction and strange imagery. The extant odes are exceedingly difficult, not as the choruses of Æschylus are difficult, from an inability to compass sublime thoughts with words, but from the involved constructions, the inverted order, and the imperfect logic of his long and complicated sentences.   Possibly the requirements of his elaborate metres may have further increased these difficulties.   And yet Eustathius tells us that these Epinikia were more popular than his other works.[1]   If this be so, what must the other poems have been ? for the extant odes teem with myths, often local and obscure, myths of little interest, and full of difficulty.

Nevertheless, it is certain that Pindar has kept his place as the very highest and noblest representative of Greek lyric poetry. He was honoured and courted all over Greece· One of his poems was inscribed on a stele in the temple of Jupiter Ammon at Thebes.[2]   The Athenians certainly set up a statue in his honour, and are said (in a letter of the pseudo-Æschines) to have paid him double the fine imposed upon him by the Thebans for calling Athens the mainstay of Greece,[3] as well as for calling Athens *the glorious* (λιπαραί). These silly stories represent both Athens and Thebes as infinitely more childish than we know them to have been. As for calling Athens λιπαραί, the epithet is applied in his extant remains to Marathon, Orchomenus, Naxos, Smyrna, Egypt, and Thebes ; nor do I think the story anything but

---

[1] διὰ τὸ ἀνθρωπικώτεροι εἶναι καὶ ὀλιγόμυθοι, καὶ μηδὲ πάνυ ἔχειν ἀσαφῶς κατά γε τὰ ἄλλα.

[2] Paus. ix. 16, 1.

[3] ἔρεισμα Ἑλλάδος. I ask the reader to observe the growth of the story. Isocrates (*Antidosis*, § 166) merely says that for the sake of the one phrase the Athenians made him a proxenus, with a present of 10,000 drachmæ ; the later letter embellishes the matter.

a scholiast's invention *à propos* of a well-known passage in Aristophanes.[1]   As for the Thebans fining a professional poet for praising his patrons, I cannot believe such an absurdity. Pindar was quite ready to praise tyrants, to praise democracies, to praise Dorians, with whom he felt special sympathies, to praise Ionians, and he did this professionally and for pay.[2]   He was a good friend of all parties, a religious and respectable man, and hated nobody except rival poets, at whom he is always sneering, and philosophers, who were becoming serious rivals to the poets generally, as teachers of morals and expounders of nascent science.   These two classes of people Pindar is constantly attacking ; he is constantly asserting his own powers and achievements against them in a rather undignified way—in fact, the personal allusions in Pindar's poems are not at all pleasant or in good taste.

But as my own judgment of Pindar is somewhat at variance with that of most classical scholars, I advise the reader to turn to the texts themselves, and decide for himself.   Apart from exceptional compositions, like that above alluded to as inscribed on stone, Pindar's works, being all occasional and special, soon passed out of note, and were forgotten by the masses.   He was not a patriotic poet, in the larger Hellenic sense.   He wrote little even for the greater Greek states, Sparta and Athens. Above all, he appeared at the close of the lyric epoch, and at the season when his contemporary Æschylus had found a newer and better way of touching public sympathy.   So Pindar came to be 'silenced by the want of taste in the public,' as an early comic poet says.   Yet Plato often quotes him with respect, and we may feel sure that he at no time wanted readers.

---

[1] *Acharn.* 636.

[2] He alludes feelingly to this lower condition of his muse, as compared with the older lyric poets, in *Isthm.* ii. 6, et sqq.

à Μοῖσα γὰρ οὐ φιλοκερδής πω τότ' ἦν οὐδ' ἐργάτις ·
οὐδ' ἐπερνάντο γλυκεῖαι μελιφθόγγου ποτὶ Τερψιχόρας
ἀργυρωθεῖσαι πρόσωπα μαλθακόφωνοι ἀοιδαί.
νῦν δ' ἐφίητι τὸ τὠργείου φυλάξαι
ῥῆμ' ἀλαθείας ὁδῶν ἄγχιστα βαῖνον,
χρήματα χρήματ' ἀνήρ, ὃς φᾶ κτεάνων θαμὰ λειφθεὶς
· καὶ φίλων.

§ 151. But when the learned men of Alexandria began studying old Greek poetry, and analysing and explaining myths, Pindar
was a welcome and much prized field for research. To such
poets as Apollonius Rhodius, who revelled in mythological
lore, Pindar's accounts of the local genealogies and legends
afforded endless material, and so we find full and excellent
scholia upon his works. We have ninety quotations from
him in Plutarch, who specially studied and prized him for
patriotic reasons, as he was the greatest of Bœotian poets, a
very small class in Greek literature. The Romans, who took
most of their opinions about Greek literature from the Alexandrians, esteemed Pindar very highly, and Horace speaks constantly of him in terms of the most extravagant praise. His
metres were, of course, impossible to reproduce for mere readers
like the Romans, and Horace saw well (what some obscurer
Romans failed to see) that any attempt at imitating the rich
and complicated systems of Pindar's verse would be ridiculous.
He therefore confined himself to the simpler forms of Æolic
poetry, while he often borrows a thought from Pindar. Cicero
(like ourselves) read the choral odes of the Greeks as if they
were prose ; he could not realise the effect of such verse. In fact,
without *orchestic*, without the rythmical motions of a chorus,
of which the figures corresponded to the strophes of the odes,
such vast and intricate structures are perfectly incomprehensible.
Anyone who questions this may study the whole subject in the
learned essays of Boeckh's edition, and in the discussions of
Von Leutsch, and of Westphal and Rossbach.

I pass it by in this history as unsuited to a handbook of
Greek literature.

§ 152. As to the structure of the odes of Pindar in the way
of *argument*, a curious revolution of opinion has taken place.
The Greek scholiasts seem, from various hints, to have thought
that the many sudden changes, the many covert allusions,
and interrupted digressions in the odes are due to some fixed
plan in the poet's mind. But the Romans and the general
public, from that day onward, rather looked upon him as an
intoxicated bard, whose poetic fervour carried him along
(as he himself often pretends) by a sort of inspiration alien

to the laws of sober argument. This opinion prevailed till the present century, when the Germans have revived the old theory with great exaggeration, and have endeavoured to show that each ode is based on one central idea, and that there is not a single clause without special reference to, and a logical nexus with, the leading idea of the poem. Boeckh, Hermann, Dissen, Rauchenstein, Schneidewin, and others, have ridden this theory to death, and nothing can be more unpoetical than their lumbering importation of beauties into Pindar. Westphal's Terpandrian theory is far the best. Nevertheless, it is certain that the circumstances of the victory, or of the victor, constantly suggested to Pindar casual and transient allusions, of which the point has now been lost. Thus, much of his apparent obscurity or irrelevancy has arisen from the *speciality* of his compositions. We must also remember that the introduction of local myths, to us wearisome, was another feature specially pleasing to the hearers of the poems.

An ingenious French critic, Havet, has shown great general resemblances between the stately lyrics of Pindar and the stately orations of Isocrates. The main object of both was *epideictical*, that is, both encomiastic in subject and elaborate in form. The complicated strophes of the poet may have even directly suggested the elaborate periods of the sophist. It is also to be noted that neither of them touches the heart, though they astonish the reason and fire the imagination ; both were too artificial for that deepest of all functions in great poetry and oratory. In both, again, we may admire the consummate skill with which they manage their transitions from one topic to another : Pindar, as I have explained already, with long-concealed art; Isocrates with ever-praised and admired invention. On the whole, we may say of Pindar that he is so intensely Greek as to have lost much of his beauty by transference from his native soil and society ; and, again, that his work was so strictly special and occasional that, of all the great poets left to us, he suffers most by being removed from his own time and circumstances. Taking all these things into account, and, moreover, that he worked for pay, his lasting and deserved reputation is perhaps the most wonderful tribute to Greek genius.

§ 153. The extant *Epinikia* of Pindar are divided into four books, determined (without strict accuracy) by the feasts at which the victories they celebrate were won, viz. Olympian, Pythian, Nemean, and Isthmian odes :[1] the three last Nemean, and 2nd Pythian, and perhaps others, are intended for other occasions. None of these poems has had its authenticity questioned except the 5th Olympian, for metrical reasons, as it approaches in structure to the Æolic school ; and it is remarkable that as soon as the critics doubted its genuineness they immediately discovered that it was feeble and unpoetical, and unworthy of Pindar's greatness. I have no doubt that many of Pindar's poems, were they taken from under the ægis of his name, would suffer the same injustice.

The rythms are divided into Dorian, Æolian, and Lydian ; and the researches of the commentators have pointed out that the Dorian are chiefly dactyls and trochaic dipodies, giving a slower and more solemn movement, with which the tenor of these odes corresponds. The Æolian and Lydian are lighter in character, and the latter specially used in plaintive subjects. Why the metres should vary with the quality of the scales employed is a matter for which we can now see no solid reason, and, indeed, we are told that Dorian melody might be set, and was set by Pindar, to an Æolian accompaniment. The odes are generally strophic and antistrophic, and meant for a marching or dancing chorus, which stood still when epodes were added. Some were performed at Olympia after the victory ; some at the victor's home, far away, and even a long time after the victory had been gained.

The general treatment of the subject shows that Pindar was expected to make the rejoicing a public one, reflecting on the whole clan and ancestry of the victor ; still more on his city, and on its tutelary heroes. Thus the poet conforms to the general law of Greek art, which ordained that it should be public, and not confined to private interests or private appreciation.[2]

---

[1] There were at this period innumerable athletic and musical contests throughout Greece, but these were the most celebrated, and national.

[2] In the Preface I have added an account of Westphal and Mezger's theory as to the Terpandrian structure of these odes.

He usually starts from the mythical splendours of the victor's family or city, selects such points in their history as have some practical lesson bearing upon the present circumstances of his hearers, and insists upon the importance of inborn qualities and high traditions. Such a line of argument was, of course, peculiarly meant for aristocrats. He then passes to the victor's family, enumerates any prizes gained by his relations, and ends with some sort of summary or moral reflection.

This general sketch is, however, so much varied, that it must be regarded only as the vaguest description of Pindar's odes. In some, such as the 4th Pythian, the longest and most important of those extant, an account of the adventures of the Argonauts, in relation to Thera and Cyrene, is developed at almost epical length; in others, such as the two odes addressed to Athenians,[1] the mythical narrative is left out. But the Athenians, being at this time poor, and doubtless devoted to higher objects than athletics, come in for little share of Pindar's praise. The wealthy mercantile Æginetans, on the contrary, and the luxurious Sicilians (especially the tyrants) occupy a very large place in his poetry. He must have been a peculiar favourite with both, for fifteen odes celebrate Sicilian, and eleven Æginetan victors. At Nemea especially, which was very close to them, the Æginetans contended with great success.

§ 154. If we proceed to consider the extant poems and fragments more specially, we find that the Olympian odes are, perhaps, the most splendid, not only as celebrating victories in the greatest Greek games, but as being composed for great personages, and probably most splendidly rewarded. The Pythian are more difficult, and replete with mythical lore, on account of Pindar's close connection with the worship of Apollo, and his probable intimacy with the colleges of priests at Delphi. About half the odes, in both cases, are for victors with chariots or mule-cars; both of which implied wealthy owners, such as the Sicilian or Cyrenæan tyrants. The narrative of the birth of Iamus,[2] the opening of the 12th, and the 14th Olympian odes, seem to me particularly fine.

---

[1] *Pyth.* vii., *Nem.* ii.　　　　[2] *Ol.* vi. 25, sq.

The last, being a short and very perfect specimen of Pindar's excellence, may here be quoted.[1]

Among the Pythian, the opening of the first is splendid.[2]

> [1] Καφισίων ὑδάτων λαχοῖ-
> σαι αἵ τε ναίετε καλλίπωλον ἕ-
> δραν, ὦ λιπαρᾶς ἀοίδιμοι βασίλειαι
> Χάριτες Ὀρχομενοῦ,
> παλαιγόνων Μινυᾶν ἐπίσκοποι,
> κλῦτ', ἐπεὶ εὔχομαι.
> σὺν γὰρ ὑμῖν τὰ τερπνὰ καὶ τὰ γλυκέα
> γίνεται πάντα βροτοῖς·
> εἰ σοφός, εἰ καλός, εἴ τις ἀγλαὸς
> ἀνήρ. οὔτε γὰρ θεοὶ
> σεμνᾶν Χαρίτων ἄτερ
> κοιρανέοντι χορούς,
> οὔτε δαῖτας· ἀλλὰ πάντων
> ταμίαι ἔργων ἐν οὐρανῷ,
> Χρυσότοξον θέμεναι
> παρὰ Πύθιον Ἀπόλλωνα θρόνους,
> ἀέναον σέβοντι πατρὸς
> Ὀλυμπίοιο τιμάν.
> Πότνι' Ἀγλαΐα, φιλησίμολπέ
> τ' Εὐφροσύνα, θεῶν κρατίστου παῖδες,
> ἐπάκοοι νῦν, Θαλία τε ἐ-
> ρασίμολπε, ἰδοῖσα τόνδε
> κῶμον ἐπ' εὐμενεῖ τύχᾳ
> κοῦφα βιβῶντα · Λυδῷ γὰρ
> Ἀσώπιχον ἐν τρόπῳ
> ἐν μελέταις τε ἀείδων
> μόλον· οὕνεκ' Ὀλυμπιόνικος ἁ Μινύεια
> σεῦ ἕκατι. Μελαντειχέα νῦν δόμον
> Φερσεφόνας ἴθι, Ἀχοῖ,
> πατρὶ κλυτὰν φέροισ' ἀγ-
> γελίαν, Κλεύδαμον ὄφρα ἰδοῖσ' υἱ-
> ὸν εἴπῃς ὅτι οἱ νέαν
> κόλποις παρ' εὐδόξου Πίσας
> ἐστεφάνωσε κυδίμων ἀέθλων
> πτεροῖσι χαίταν.

> [2] Χρυσέα φόρμιγξ, Ἀπόλλω-
> νος καὶ ἰοπλοκάμων
> σύνδικον Μοισᾶν κτέανον·
> τᾶς ἀκούει μὲν βάσις, ἀγλαΐας ἀρχά,
> πείθονται δ' ἀοιδοὶ σάμασιν,

There is a very picturesque narrative of the youth and adventures of the nymph Cyrene in the 9th.[1] The Nemean (with their appendix) and the Isthmian, though not less difficult, are, I think, less striking, both in general elevation and also in those peculiar beauties which I have pointed out in the Olympian and Pythian odes.

§ 155. The fragments left to us are very numerous (more than 300), and very various in form and style. Perhaps foremost in interest are the θρῆνοι, or *funeral laments*, in which he was wont to preach the purer doctrines either of the Pythagoreans, or of the Orphic and other mysteries. The first three fragments transmitted to us under this head support the famous passage in the 2nd Olympian ode,[2] in which this new hope, and this higher aspiration, is set forth with no faltering tongue. But it is not a little remarkable that in other poems—the 1st Olympian and 5th Pythian[3]—the older, or, perhaps, the more general view of the state of the dead is maintained, and we have here the doctrine of Æschylus preached, which is quite distinct from the more modern view. Accordingly the most explicit fragment in the new doctrine (fr. 100) is declared spurious by the best recent critics.[4] From his *Dithyrambs* we have a fine passage, written for one of the Dionysiac feasts at Athens, and preserved by Dionysius of Halicarnassus. The metre is remarkable for the frequent resolutions of long syllables, so

ἀγησιχόρων ὁπόταν τῶν φροιμίων
ἀμβολὰς τεύχῃς ἐλελιζομένα.
καὶ τὸν αἰχματὰν κεραυνὸν σβεννύεις
ἀενάου πυρός. εὕ-
δει δ᾽ ἀνὰ σκάπτῳ Διὸς αἰετός, ὠ-
κεῖαν πτέρυγ᾽ ἀμφοτέρω-
θεν χαλάξαις,
ἀρχὸς οἰωνῶν, κελαινώ-
πιν δ᾽ ἐπί οἱ νεφέλαν
ἀγκύλῳ κρατί, γλεφάρων
ἁδὺ κλαῖστρον, κατέχευας · ὁ δὲ κνώσσων
ὑγρὸν νῶτον αἰωρεῖ, τεαῖς
ῥιπαῖσι κατασχόμενος.

[1] vv. 14, sq.   [2] vv. 56, sq.   [3] vv. 85, sq.
[4] Zeller, *Phil. der Griechen*, i. p. 56, note.

giving a peculiarly rapid effect.   The same critic has preserved another poem of similar character, a hyporcheme composed for the Thebans, which treats of a recent eclipse of the
sun (probably April 30, 463 B.C.), and which in diction and
style reminds us strongly of some of the choral odes in the
tragedies, especially those of Sophocles.[1]

I will close these details with a word about Pindar's *skolia.*
His ponderous and splendid style was not suited to light or
frivolous subjects, and we can note, even in the scanty remains,
a great contrast to the more favourite *skolia* of other poets.   In
fact, Pindar's lighter effusions seem to differ only in subject,
not in style, from his solemn odes ; and the prominent subject
in the *skolia* seems to have been love.   The first was composed
for a chorus of 100 ἑταίραι, whom the Corinthian Xenophon
offered to bring to the temple of Aphrodite, to obtain the
goddess' favour for an Olympic competition.   The poet excuses the trade of these women on the ground of necessity,
but in another fragment apologises for appearing at Corinth in
connection with such company.   This poem, which was composed in his best style, shows how completely professional his

---

[1] 'Ακτὶς 'Αελίου, τί πολύσκοπε μηδομένα, μᾶτερ
      ὀμμάτων ;
   ἄστρον ὑπέρτατον ἐν ἀμέρᾳ κλεπτόμενον,
   ἔθηκας ἀμάχανον ἰσχὺν ποτανὸν
   ἀνδράσι καὶ σοφίας ὁδόν, ἐπίσκοτον
   ἀτραπὸν ἐσσυμένα
   ἐλαύνειν τι νεώτερον ἢ πάρος ;
   ἀλλά σε πρὸς Διὸς ἵπποις θοαῖς ἱκετεύω,
   ἀπήμον' ἐς ὄλβον τράποις Θήβαις,
   ὦ πότνια, πάγκοινον τέρας.
   πολέμου δ' εἰ σᾶμα φέρεις τινός, ἢ στάσιν
      οὐλομέναν,
   ἢ παγετὸν καρποῦ φθίσιν, ἢ νιφετοῦ σθένος
      ὑπέρφατον,
   ἢ πόντου κενέωσιν ἀνὰ πέδον
   χθονός, ἢ νότιον θέρος,
   ὕδατι ζακότῳ διερόν,
   εἰ γαῖαν κατακλύσαισα θήσεις
   ἀνδρῶν νέον ἐξ ἀρχᾶς γένος,
   ὀλοφύρομαι οὐδὲν ὅ τι πάντων μέτα πείσομαι.

work was, and how little his moral saws need be taken as evidences of a lofty character. The second *skolion* in the modern collections is addressed to Theoxenus of Tenedos, a boy whom the poet loved passionately in his old age. Indeed, this Greek form of the passion is prominent enough all through his works, as we should expect from a Theban poet ; and we find it in other scraps of his *skolia*.

I have already spoken of his philosophy. If in religion he shows great advance beyond earlier lyric and elegiac poets, this is probably to be attributed to the influences of the Delphic priesthood. In politics his opinions are not valuable, because they were accommodated to the views of his patrons. In morals he expresses the average feelings of the Greeks of his day ; while he is sometimes raised above them by his lofty conceptions of the unity and power of God, he often preaches the suspicion, the jealousy, and the selfishness which we find in Theognis. The resignation which he constantly inculcates is based on the same gentle fatalism which meets us in the consolations of Simonides.

§ 156. *Bibliographical.* I turn to the MSS., editions, and translations of note. We know that the greatest of the Alexandrians expended critical care on Pindar; and the notes of Zenodotus and Aristarchus, with others, were put together by the indefatigable Didymus into a commentary, from which our best sets of scholia are excerpts. Other Byzantine scholars added inferior work. The commentary of Eustathius is lost all but the preface.

As to our extant MSS., Tycho Mommsen has established several families, and has collated a vast number of copies under each. The oldest and best are the Ambrosian C, 122, of the 12th cent. (called by him A) ; the MS. of Ursini in the Vatican (No. 1312), called B ; and a Medicean of the thirteenth century—all furnished with scholia. These older MSS. are far better than the Thomani or Moschopulei. The earliest edition was the Aldine of 1513, followed by Calergi's (Rome) in 1515 ; then Stephanus (1560 and 1599) ; Erasmus Schmid (1616) ; an Oxford edition by West and Walsted in 1697. Modern studies began with Heyne's great book (1778, and reprinted); then A. Boeckh's monumental work (1811-22), supplemented by G. Hermann's notes, and Dissen and Schneidewin's elaborate commentary. The latest texts in Germany are Bergk's (in his *Lyrici*), and the exhaustive critical edition of Tycho Mommsen (Berlin, 1864), who first ordered and classified the legion of MSS. In England we have three good recent editions : Donaldson's (1841), a careful and scholarly work ; Cookesley's (Eton, 1852) ; and the newest by Mr. C. A. M. Fennell (Cambridge University Series, 1879), of which the Olympian and Pythian odes have just appeared. These, together with H. Bindseil's elaborate Concordance (Berlin, 1875), are quite adequate for the study of this difficult poet. We may now add Mezger's Commentary (Leipzig, 1880).

The translations of Pindar form a whole library, and are remarkable for having so many important prose versions among them. The earliest, in Latin verses, by Sudorius (in 1575), was followed in Germany by Damm (prose), 1771 ; then by Bothe, Thiersch, Hartung, Tycho Mommsen, W. Humboldt, and Donner, all weighty names. The Italians had a full text and Italian verse translation with notes, by G. Gautier, in four vols., a handsome work (Rome, 1762-8) ; and since, Borghi (1824). Our own Cowley, approaching the study of Pindar about 1650, speaks very severely of the extant translations, and, indeed, of the very attempt to render him into literal prose. 'If a man,' says he, 'would undertake to translate Pindar word for word, it would be thought that one madman had translated another, as may appear when he that understands not the original reads the verbal translations of him into Latin prose, than which nothing seems more raving; and sure rhyme, without the addition of wit and the spirit of poetry, would but make it ten times more distracted.' He proceeds to give specimens of loose versions of two 'Pindarique odes'[1]—so loose that all the Pindar vanishes, and only Cowley remains—the English Pindar, Virgil, and Horace, as he is called on his fulsome tombstone. Gilbert West made a version in 1749 ; there was an Oxford prose translation in 1824 ; then very beautiful paraphrases by Bishop Heber in

[1] *Ol.* ii. and *Nem.* i.

1840, and a highly praised version of A. Moore (with Turner's prose, Bohn, 1852). We have also Wheelwright (1830), Cary (1833), Tremenheere (1866), with a good preface, and omitting the mythical narratives, except in summary; also T. C. Baring (1875), into irregular rhymed verse; Frank D. Morice (1876, Ol. and Pyth. only); and an anonymous version (Winchester, 1876). Lastly, there are the new prose versions by Mr. Paley and Mr. Ernest Myers (1874), the latter of peculiar merit. Almost all these translations are enriched with dissertations on Pindar's genius, on the Olympic games, and on the difficulties of translating choral lyric odes into English. Their laudations of Pindar are, I think, indiscriminate; but I am bound to say that they show a general agreement against the view I have taken of the poet's position in his age.

§ 157. The other rival of Pindar's mature life was the nephew of Simonides, BACCHYLIDES of Keos, son of Meidon, or Meidylus. He lived with his uncle at the court of Hiero, and flourished about the 70th to 80th Olympiads. The scholiasts on Pindar tell us constantly[1] of the jealousy of Pindar, and even of the preference shown to Bacchylides. His art, and the subjects he treated, seem quite similar to those of Simonides and Pindar; but it has been the modern fashion, following the judgment of Longinus, and of Longinus only, to describe him as a man of no genius, who by careful study and great correctness attained a moderate position, and never rose to real fame. There is no doubt that he was not equal to either of his great contemporaries, but the extant fragments show that later criticism has underrated the man. Had they been attributed to the greater poets, many of the critics who now barely condescend to approve of them would have been full of enthusiasm about them. It should be noticed particularly that the ideas developed in the few extant fragments seem copied by the greatest writers of the next generation. Thus the second and third

Θνατοῖσι μὴ φῦναι φέριστον,
μηδ' ἀελίου προσιδεῖν φέγγος·
ὄλβιος δ' οὐδεὶς βροτῶν πάντα χρόνον.

---

[1] On *Ol.* ii. 154, *Pyth.* ii. 97, 161-7, *Nem.* iii. 143.

Παύροισι δὲ θνατῶν τὸν ἅπαντα χρόνον
δαίμων ἔδωκεν
πράσσοντας ἐν καιρῷ πολιοκρόταφον
γῆρας ἱκνεῖσθαι, πρὶν ἐγκύρσαι δύᾳ.

contain the substance and almost the words of the famous chorus in Sophocles' second Œdipus, and the no less splendid prose paraphrase in Herodotus.[1] The beautiful *pæan* on peace has more than one parallel in the choruses of Euripides :—

Τίκτει δέ τε θνατοῖσιν Εἰράνα μεγάλα
πλοῦτον καὶ μελιγλώσσων ἀοιδᾶν ἄνθεα,
δαιδαλέων τ' ἐπὶ βωμῶν θεοῖσιν αἴθεσθαι βοῶν
ξανθᾷ φλογὶ μῆρα τανυτρίχων τε μήλων,
γυμνασίων τε νέοις αὐλῶν τε καὶ κώμων μέλειν.
ἐν δὲ σιδαροδέτοις πόρπαξιν αἴθαι
ἀραχνᾶν ἱστοὶ πέλονται·
ἔγχεά τε λογχωτὰ ξίφεά τ' ἀμφάκεα δάμναται εὐρώς·
χαλκεᾶν δ' οὐκ ἔστι σαλπίγγων κτύπος·
οὐδὲ συλᾶται μελίφρων ὕπνος ἀπὸ γλεφάρων,
ἀμὸν ὃς θάλπει κέαρ.
συμποσίων δ' ἐρατῶν βρίθοντ' ἀγυιαὶ παιδικοί θ' ὕμνοι
φλέγονται.

It is surprising that great German critics should depreciate this beautiful fragment, and call it a mere correct school-exercise ; but as I have quoted it in full, the reader may judge the matter for himself. A good many lines of erotic *skolia* are also extant, which appear to approach much nearer to the Æolic metres and style than the *skolia* of Pindar. On the whole, then, Bacchylides seems hardly to have received justice, if the extant pieces are not far above his average performance.

Little is known of either Myrtis or Corinna, the Bœotian rivals of Pindar. Myrtis seems to have composed lyric love stories, like the *Calyce* of Stesichorus, and Corinna is chiefly cited by grammarians for her local dialect, of which some forty specimens are given. Two Dorian poetesses, Telesilla of Argos, and Praxilla of Sicyon, are cited as of the same age, and of the same character, the few lines we have of Praxilla indicating a somewhat erotic tone.

[1] *O. C.* v 1211, Herod. vii. 46.

§ 158. A more distinct and interesting personality is that of TIMOCREON the Rhodian. He was an athlete of renown, and an aristocrat of Ialysus, who was banished through suspicion of *medising;* he himself asserts that he bribed Themistocles to obtain his recall, and he reviles him for his refusal to interfere. He also quarrelled with Simonides, and the two poets gave vent to their anger in verses, of which those of Timocreon were the stronger, those of Simonides perhaps the keener. What is really interesting in Timocreon is his curious position as an aristocratic poet born out of due time. He wrote not for pay, but through passion, like Archilochus, like Alcæus, and the other stormy-lived bards of an earlier generation. Nevertheless, so firmly had the choral lyric form taken hold of the Greek mind, that this man's lampoons and satires are produced in the elaborate strophes of the Dorian hymns, and have puzzled the critics to assign them a title, which Bernhardy has made that of antistrophic skolion. This misfortune of a false form prevented Timocreon from pouring out his passion with the simple vigour of Archilochus; for the choral forms are not lyric in the modern sense, but epical and didactic, while real passion will not deck itself with such pomp and circumstance. We can imagine, too, how the paid poets of the early fifth century combined against this turbulent aristocrat, whose life was spent in war and travel, and who doubtless despised their mercenary muse. The ancient authorities concerning him are collected concisely by Bernhardy;[1] the chief of them is Plutarch, who quotes a famous passage.[2]

[1] ii. p. 744.

[2] *Themist.* 21: Ἀλλ' εἰ τύγε Πουσανίαν ἢ καὶ τύγε Ξάνθιππον αἰνέεις
ἢ τύγε Λευτυχίδαν, ἐγὼ δ' Ἀριστείδαν ἐπαινέω
ἄνδρ' ἱερᾶν ἀπ' Ἀθανᾶν ἐλθέμεν
λῷστον ἕν', ἐπεὶ Θεμιστοκλῆ' ἤχθαρε Λατώ,
ψεύσταν, ἄδικον, προδόταν, ὃς Τιμοκρέοντα
ξεῖνον ἐόντ', ἀργυρίοις σκυβαλικτοῖσι πεισθεὶς οὐ κατᾶγεν
ἐς πάτραν Ἰάλυσον,
λαβὼν δὲ τρί' ἀργυρίοι τάλαντ' ἔβα πλέων εἰς ὄλεθρον,
τοὺς μὲν κατάγων ἀδίκως, τοὺς δ' ἐκδιώκων, τοὺς δὲ καίνων,
ἀργυρίων ὑπόπλεως, Ἰσθμοῖ δὲ πανδόκευε γλοιῶς
ψυχρὰ κρέα παρέχων, οἱ δ' ἤσθιον,
κεύχοντο μὴ ὥραν Θεμιστοκλέος γενέσθαι.

The scholiast on Aristophanes [1] cites also a well-known skolion on *Wealth*, because it is parodied in the text with reference to a decree of Pericles.

§ 159. The student who examines Bergk's *Lyric Fragments* will perhaps wonder at the numerous poets in his list which are not mentioned in this chapter. It is due to him, and to myself, that I should explain that, in the first place, several of them, such as Aristotle, will be considered again under that species of literature which they cultivated with most success. Others are post-classical; and this objection is brought by the critics against many fragments attributed by Athenæus and Stobæus to classic names. Many others are known to us merely from a single citation, and neither their age nor their character can now be determined. Thus I have felt justified in avoiding here another list of barren names, such as we find at the close of the history of both epic and tragic poetry. Yet there are a few who are still interesting, and concerning whom I should gladly have said something in a more elaborate work. The fragments worth reading are those of Euenus, above mentioned; of the philosopher Crates; of Herodas, a writer of *Mimiambics* in the style of Hippònax; of Praxilla, a poetess who composed social lyrics; of Ariphron—a fine *Ode to Health;* of Timotheus, a celebrated musical composer at the end of the classical period; of Philoxenus, whose culinary ode, of which long fragments are extant, was in Aristotle's day very popular; and of Telestes. There are also many fine anonymous fragments, which seem to come from the greatest poets, such as Stesichorus or Pindar, and a few piquant popular songs, in addition to those already mentioned in this book. They indicate to us how small a fraction of Greek lyric poetry has survived, and how many great artists yet await a literary resurrection from the research of some fortunate explorer.

With the angry Timocreon I close the history of Greek lyric poetry, for though Pratinas and others were the contemporaries of the latter mentioned, they are closely connected with the dithyramb, and will be better discussed in the intro-

---

[1] *Acharn.* 532 (frag. 8).

duction to tragic than at the close of lyric poetry. The student should be reminded that in studying Greek Literature chronologically, he must now turn, before approaching the Attic Drama, to the history of prose writing, which was growing silently, and almost secretly, all through the sixth century B.C., though its bloom did not come till after the completion of Greek poetry by Æschylus and Sophocles. He will find this side of the subject treated in the opening chapters of my Second Volume.

CHAPTER XIV.

DRAMATIC TENDENCIES IN THE SIXTH CENTURY. THE RISE
OF TRAGEDY AND SATYRIC DRAMA. THE EXTERNAL AP-
PLIANCES OF GREEK PLAYS.

§ 160. THE first beginnings of the tragedy are enveloped in
mist. They did not become interesting till the details had been
forgotten, and we can now only patch together scanty shreds of
late tradition on this subject. A few facts, however, are indis-
putable. In the first place, it is certain that tragedy arose from
the choruses which danced and recited in honour of Dionysus.
These dithyrambs, as they were called, were the last form of
lyric poetry to assume a literary shape, and seem to have been
especially cultivated by the Dorians and Achæans near the
isthmus. I have already mentioned Arion and Epigenes in
connection with them (above, p. 200), but both of these appear
to represent only one side of the dithyramb—its serious side.
This phase was probably suggested by, or connected with,
the solemn mysteries which identified Dionysus with Zagreus,
with the decay and death of nature as a condition of its resurrection. The worship of this gloomy and mysterious Dionysus
was certainly in the mysteries performed by some sort of ceremony imitating his sufferings and death, and this must have
suggested in the dithyramb that serious vein which enabled
Epigenes to substitute the *sorrows* of Adrastus for those of the
god. This respectable and literary form of dithyramb was early
transplanted to Athens, where, under the hands of Lasus, it
assumed so elaborate a mimetic character, by means of the
higher development of music and dancing, that (like our
ballet) it almost became a drama, and has made many scholars

imagine the existence of a lyrical drama, alongside and independent of the real tragedy. All this development of the dithyramb seems to have been distinctly Dorian, as might be expected from its choral lyric character.

§ 161. There was also a rustic and jovial dithyramb common among the lower classes in the same districts, where the choruses imitated the sports and manners of satyrs in attendance on the god, and it is not improbable that these came more into fashion according as the serious dithyramb wandered from its original purpose, and was even applied to celebrate other personages than the god Dionysus. The proverb οὐδὲν πρὸς τὸν Διόνυσον ('there is no Dionysus in it') preserves the objections of old-fashioned people to such innovations, and these objections were permanently respected by the essentially satyric dithyramb, which was brought to Athens by PRATINAS[1] of Phlius, who with Chœrilus and other poets put it on the stage as a proper completion, and necessary adjunct to the nascent tragedy. This Pratinas was a brilliant poet, to judge from a fragment preserved by Athenæus, in which he complains of the increasing prominence of the instrumental accompaniments to the dithyrambs, possibly those of Lasus, and vindicates for his chorus their proper functions.[2] He is called the son of

---

[1] According to Fick (*Griech. Personennamen*, p. xxxv), this name, which is derived from the Doric form for πρῶτος, and is a collateral form for πρωτῖνος (= πρωτίονος), should be pronounced Πρατῖνας. I cannot find any direct authority in the classics for this quantity.

[2]   Τίς ὁ θόρυβος ὅδε; τί τάδε τὰ χορεύματα;
     τίς ὕβρις ἔμολεν ἐπὶ Διονυσιάδα πολυπάταγα θυμέλαν;
     ἐμὸς ἐμὸς ὁ Βρόμιος· ἐμὲ δεῖ κελαδεῖν, ἐμὲ δεῖ παταγεῖν
     ἀν' ὄρεα σύμενον μετὰ Ναϊάδων
     οἷα τε κύκνον ἄγοντα ποικιλόπτερον μέλος.
     τὰν ἀοιδὰν κατέστασε Πιερὶς βασίλειαν· ὁ δ' αὐλὸς
     ὕστερον χορευέτω· καὶ γάρ ἐσθ' ὑπηρέτας.
     κώμῳ μόνον θυραμάχοις τε πυγμαχίαισι νέων θέλει παροίνων
     ἔμμεναι στρατηλάτας.
     παῖε, παῖε τὸν Φρύγ' ἀοιδοῦ
     ποικίλου προαχέοντα·
     φλέγε τὸν ὀλεσισιαλοκάλαμον,
     λαλοβαρυόπα παραμελορυθμοβάταν θ

Pyrrhonides, and said to have composed thirty-two satyric dramas with fifty tragedies; he contested in Ol. 70 with Æschylus and *Chœrilus*, but was only once successful in carrying off the first prize. His son Aristias was equally celebrated as a satyric dramatist, and was second when Æschylus won with the *Seven against Thebes*, but apparently with a satyric drama of his father's. *Chœrilus* was active from 524 to 468 B.C. (if we believe Suidas), and is celebrated as one of the old tragedians, but still more for his satyric drama, which appears from the proverb, 'When Chœrilus was king among the Satyrs.'

§ 162. In fact all the early dramatists, not excluding Æschylus, laid great stress upon this peculiar style, which, however, passed out of fashion in the next century, especially when Euripides had devised the expedient of supplying its place with a melodrama, or tragedy with comic elements, like the *Alcestis*. The remarkable point about the satyric drama is its marked separation from comedy, and its close attachment to tragedy. It is called '*sportive tragedy*,' and was never composed by comic poets. We have only one extant specimen— the *Cyclops* of Euripides—in which we observe that the protagonist or hero (Odysseus) is not the least ridiculed or lowered in position ; in fact, we have no play in which he appears so respectable, but he is accompanied by a chorus of satyrs whose odes show no small traces of the old phallic songs in the rural dithyramb. The general character of the subjects left us in the titles of the satyric plays, and of the fragments (many of which, among the fragments of Æschylus and Sophocles, strike us by their open coarseness), lead us to compare the satyric drama of the Greeks to that peculiar species of drama among us which is comic, though quite distinct from comedy, and which treats some familiar legend or fairy tale with grotesque and conventional accessories. The reader will already have guessed that I refer to the *pantomimes* of the English stage, in which the earlier part is some adaptation of a well-known fairy tale,

ὑπαὶ τρυπάνῳ δέμας πεπλασμένον.
ἢν ἰδοὺ ἅδε σοι δεξιὰ
καὶ ποδὸς διαρρίφᾷ, θριαμβοδιθύραμβε·
κισσόχαιτ' ἄναξ ἄκουε τὰν ἐμὰν Δώριον χορείαν.

such as *Sinbad* or *Blue Beard*, in which there are horrible and tragic adventures, and generally a respectable chief character, coupled with grotesque accessories and conventional dancing. This curious parallel will illustrate to the English reader many of the difficulties in the position of the satyric drama at Athens.

It is remarkable that the old dithyrambs were spoken of as introductions to the more solemn cyclic choirs, whereas their dramatic outcome was always played after the tragedies. The critics are ready with æsthetical reasons for this, but we are left at a loss for historical facts. Though a flavour of humour was not foreign to the tragedy of Euripides, nor even to that of Æschylus, there seems no doubt that the early Greek drama did not afford scope for the violent contrasts so striking in Shakespeare, and preferred to relegate the low and the grotesque into a separate play associated with solemn tragedy. The extant *Cyclops* is a sort of farce without much extravagance, observing in its hero the decorum suited to a tragic writer, and giving to Silenus and to his attendant satyrs an evidently conventional character of laziness, drunkenness and license. The real contest was in that day among the tragedies, and this afterpiece was probably given while the public was discussing the previous plays. In later days the satyric drama seems to have been abandoned, and therefore all the other extant specimens were lost. It is a misfortune that we do not possess at least one from the hands of an acknowledged master in this department, or from the epoch when it had real importance. But the *Cyclops* explains to us the structure and style of these pieces. These few words may suffice to dispose of this byway of the Greek drama. I now return to the more important history of serious tragedy.

§ 163. All our authorities are agreed that despite the various approaches and hints at tragedy before *Thespis*—the Peloponnesians counted sixteen poets of Dorian tragedy before him— he was really the originator of that sort of poetry. We only know that he belonged to the deme or village of Icaria, on the borders of the Megarid, and doubtless in constant intercourse with these people, among whom the worship of Dionysus was said to be particularly at home. It is to be noticed that the neighbouring town of Eleusis, to which all Icarians must have constantly come, was apparently the chief place for the deeper worship of Dionysus Zagreus, and it is not unreasonable to suppose that this double experience of the local choruses to Dionysus at Icaria, and the solemn mimic rites of the mysteries, were the determining features of his great discovery.

For in what did this discovery consist? As was well known, tragic elements were present in Homer, and the characteristic dialogues in the old epics were far more dramatic than the early tragedies not only of Thespis, but of Æschylus. The misfortunes of heroes had already been sung by the dithyrambic choruses at Sicyon, and a mimetic character given to such performances by the expressive gestures of the choirs of Lasus. We have no reason to think that Thespis added a dialogue to the cyclic choruses, or lyrical element from which he started. From what is told us we merely infer that he to some extent separated the leader of the chorus from the rest, and made him introduce and interrupt the choral parts with some sort of epic recitation. What metre he used for this recitation we know not, nor the subjects he treated, for the titles transmitted by Suidas are of forgeries by Heracleides Ponticus, and Thespis probably left nothing written. Yet he certainly aimed at some illusion, by which he escaped from himself, and entered into the feelings of another person, when he undertook, as we are told, to perform the part of leader to his chorus. For he disguised himself, and so far imitated reality that Solon is said (by Plutarch) to have been greatly offended at the performance, and to have indignantly denounced the deliberate lying implied in his acting. Of course we must cast aside the nonsense, talked by Horace, of his being a strolling player, going about in a cart to fairs and markets. Not only did Horace confuse the origins of tragedy and of comedy, but the poetical requirements of the Athenian public trained by the enlightened policies of Solon and Peisistratus. In the Athens where Lasus, and Simonides, and Anacreon, and presently Pindar, found favour, no rude village song could find favour ; nay, we rather see an over-artificial taste prevailing in the lyric poetry of that date.

Thespis composed his dramas from about Ol. 61 for city

feasts and for an educated audience. The mere setting up of a stage, and donning of a mask, could not in such an atmosphere give to any poet the title of a great originator. Though the story just cited from Plutarch contradicts the inference, we would fain believe that an acquaintance with the mysteries, and deeper theology of the day, suggested to Thespis the representation of human sorrow for a moral purpose. There seems no trace of this idea in the earlier dithyrambs, which sang or acted the adventures of Dionysus merely as a cult, and not as a moral lesson. But it seems that with Thespis may have arisen the great conception which we see full-blown in Æschylus—the intention of the drama to purify human sympathy by exercising it on great and apparently disproportioned afflictions of heroic men, when the iron hand of a stern and unforgiving Providence chastises old transgressions, or represses the revolt of private judgment against established ordinance.

§ 164. It is quite plain that the portraiture of suffering was fully comprehended by the next among the old tragedians, *Phrynichus*, son of Polyphradmon, whom Aristophanes[1] often refers to as an old master of quaint sweetness, and in his day still a favourite with the last generation. There are several other persons of the name, one of them a comic poet,[2] so that we cannot be sure concerning the allusions to him. His son Polyphradmon, evidently called after the grandfather, seems to have contended with Æschylus. We have not sufficient fragments remaining to form a strict judgment, nor can we now decide how much of the development of tragedy was directly due to him. He is said to have been the first to introduce female characters, and to use the trochaic tetrameter in tragedy. It is also certain that he understood the use of dialogue, by separating the

---

[1] *Av.* 748 : ἔνθεν ὡσπερεὶ μέλιττα
Φρύνιχος ἀμβροσίων μελέων ἀπεβόσκετο καρπὸν
ἀεὶ φέρων γλυκεῖαν ᾠδάν.

Vesp. 219 : μινυρίζοντες μέλη
ἀρχαιομελεσιδωνιφρυνιχήρατα.

Cf. also v. 269. I quote uniformly from the 5th ed. of Dindorf's *Poetæ Scenici.*

[2] Cf. on these various persons the discussion of Meineke, *Hist. Com. Græc.* pp. 146, sq.

actor from the leader of the chorus, and making them respond
to each other.   Trimeters and Ionics *a minore* were metres not
unknown to him, but he was most esteemed among later Greeks
for his lyrical excellence, as the scholiasts on Aristophanes tell us.
Pausanias[1] alludes to his having first introduced the fatal brand
in the story of Meleager in Greek tragedy, not, however, as an
invention of his own, and quotes the lines in question.[2]   His
Phœnissæ was a particularly celebrated play; but we must
imagine chiefly a succession of lyrical choruses, with little or
no action, like the earlier tragedies of Æschylus.   It seems
that the play was brought out[3] by Themistocles as Choregus,
and with special reference to his own achievements, which were
growing old in the memories of the Athenians, in Ol. 75, 4;
and this is the earliest exact notice we have of a tragic competition such as was afterwards the rule at Athens.   It is said
that this play was the model on which Æschylus formed his
Persæ.   More celebrated is the story of the *Capture of Miletus*
(Μιλήτου ἅλωσις), brought out by the poet in Ol. 71, which
described lyrically the capture and destruction of the greatest
of Ionic cities.   The whole theatre, says Herodotus, burst into
tears, fined him 1,000 drachmas for having reminded them
of their domestic troubles, and directed that no one for the
future should use this drama.[4]   There has been a great deal
of æsthetic lucubration on this celebrated act of the Athenian
public—much talk of the ideal, and the desire to escape from
the woes of common life into an ideal atmosphere.   I feel
more confidence in the critics who suspect a political reason
for the play, and still more for the heavy fine.   Possibly
the poet belonged to a party who had urged active aid for
Miletus, and his drama was a bitter and telling reproof to
the timid or peace party, who may, nevertheless, have been
politically the leaders of the people, and able to inflict upon
him a fine for harrowing the public mind with his painful and

[1] x. 31, 4.
[2]
$$\kappa\rho\upsilon\epsilon\rho\grave{o}\nu \ \gamma\grave{a}\rho \ o\grave{\upsilon}\kappa$$
$$\mathring{\eta}\lambda\upsilon\xi\epsilon\nu \ \mu\acute{o}\rho o\nu, \ \mathring{\omega}\kappa\epsilon\hat{\imath}\alpha \ \delta\acute{\epsilon} \ \nu\iota\nu \ \phi\lambda\grave{o}\xi \ \kappa\alpha\tau\epsilon\delta\alpha\acute{\imath}\sigma\alpha\tau o,$$
$$\delta\alpha\lambda o\hat{\upsilon} \ \pi\epsilon\rho\theta o\mu\acute{\epsilon}\nu o\upsilon \ \mu\alpha\tau\rho\grave{o}\varsigma \ \mathring{\upsilon}\pi' \ \alpha\mathring{\imath}\nu\hat{a}\varsigma \ \kappa\alpha\kappa o\upsilon\eta\chi\acute{a}\nu o\upsilon.$$
[3] *Themist.* 5, as Plutarch tells us.
[4] vi. 21.   I suppose he means—use this story for a drama.

distressing play.   We see from the success of Æschylus' *Persæ* that they had no objection to being reminded of their domestic successes—certainly domestic in as real a sense as the events of Miletus—and I fancy covert allusions to present politics or other events were always well received by the Athenians; but they were certainly right to discourage the presenting of recent events upon the stage, for Greek tragedy was in no way suited for historical purposes.

There remain about seven titles of Phrynichus' plays, most of them the names of nations, which seems to imply the importance of his chorus.   All the older tragic poets were said to be dancing-masters, and to have taught anyone who wished to learn ; it is even said that the Athenians appointed Phrynichus to a military command, on account of his skill in performing the Pyrrhic war dance.

§ 165. Having now given a sufficient account of the forerunners of Æschylus, it may be well to say something of the materials at the disposal of the Greek tragic poets, of their theatres stage, actors, and general appointments.   When these things have been made as plain as our authorities permit, we can proceed to consider at our leisure the works of the three great dramatists which have survived.

It is necessary to give a brief description of the Greek theatres themselves, in order to help the reader better to imagine for himself the old tragic performances, and in order to obviate certain errors which were current on the subject, and have only been removed by recent researches.   The earliest stone theatre of which we know the date was the theatre of Dionysus at Athens, built (Ol. 70) against the south slope of the Acropolis. It was adorned and enlarged by the orator Lycurgus (about Ol. 112), when administering the finances.   We are told that before its building a wooden structure was used for plays, but that on the occasion of a contest between Æschylus and Pratinas it broke down, and then the Athenians determined to erect a permanent one for the purpose.   We are not told where the old wooden theatre was situated, but as the story implies that the *spectators* fell (for the stage always remained a wooden platform), it is unlikely that the old site could have coincided with the new, where the steep incline of the hill made all artificial scaffolding unnecessary. If the site *was* retained, we should imagine the audience of the primitive tragedies and, no doubt, of the older cyclic choruses, to have sat all round the performance, so that while at one side the hill served for tiers of seats, on the other a corresponding incline was constructed of wood. It would then have been this side only which could break down, and the new stone theatre may have been on the modified principle of enlarging one side of the primitive amphitheatre to hold all the spectators, and giving the actors a better stage with a rear and side entrances—a necessary change when the various illusions of varying dress and scenery were invented and came into use. While this conjecture would explain the occurrence of the accident on the present site of the theatre, it must be carefully noted that quite a different place at Athens also bore the name of *orchestra,* or dancing place, and may have had wooden seats applied in the same way. This orchestra was a small platform on the north slope of the Areopagus, just above the agora, on which the statues of Harmodius and Aristogeiton, and these only, were set up. Being above the throng of the agora, it seems to have been used in later days as a place for book-stalls. However this may be, the stone theatre of Dionysus became the model for similar buildings all over the Greek world, which everywhere (except at Mantinea) utilised the slope of a hill for the erection of stone seats in ascending tiers. These great buildings were also used by democracies for their public assemblies, and we cannot be sure that some of them did not precede in date the theatre of Dionysus. A great number of them still remain, though in no case, of course, has the wooden stage survived; but most of them have been modified by Roman work, especially in the form of permanent and lofty walls of masonry at the back of the stage. Happily in some cities the Roman theatre was built separately, and near the Greek, and this is the case at Athens and at Syracuse. The others which are most perfect, such as that of Aspendus in Pamphylia, and Taormina in Sicily, contain Greek and Roman work jumbled together. But there are remains throughout all Greek-speaking lands of these theatres, in which plays were performed as soon as Athens had shown the way. At Epidauros, Argos, Mantinea, Megalopolis, in the Peloponnesus alone, there are huge remains of Greek theatres. The smallest and steepest known to me is that of Chæronea in Bœotia.

The whole circuit of seats, generally semicircular (sometimes even a greater, but never a less segment of a circle), was called τὸ κοῖλον, and held the sitting room (ἐδώλιον) of the spectators, who were called *the theatre*, as we say *the house*, in old times. It was separated into concentric strips by one or more walks called διαζώματα. A radiating series of flights of steps (κατατομαί), ascending from below, divided these strips of seats into wedge-formed divisions (κερκίδες). In most cases, the spectators came in at the sides, between the stage and the seats, and ascended by these steps. The seats were broad and comfortable, but each person brought a cushion, or had it brought for him by a slave, who was not allowed to wait during the performance. In some later theatres there were outside staircases, which brought the spectators to the top of the theatre, where they entered the highest level through a colonnade. The audience had no covering over them, and were exposed to all extremes of weather. We do not know what was done in the case of rain, but it is probable that the stage had a penthouse projecting from the back wall, which protected the actors. The price of admission was fixed at two obols for the Athenian theatre, which went to the manager for its support, and which was paid from the public funds to the poorer citizens at Athens, in the days of the Athenian Empire, by way of affording all of them the opportunity of joint religious enjoyment which the feast of Dionysus offered. Women and boys were admitted to the tragedies, but the former were certainly excluded from the comedies in older days, and for obvious reasons. There were reserved seats in front, and the privilege of admission to them (προεδρία) was highly prized. It was given to magistrates and foreign ambassadors in early days, but on the marble armchairs of the front row in the theatre of Dionysus, as re-discovered in 1862, the names of religious dignitaries are inscribed, the priest of Dionysus Eleutherios possessing the central stall. This

arrangement does not, however, date before the days of He-
rodes Atticus. There is no evidence whatever that the Athenian
democracy allowed the front seats to be reserved for the richer
classes who could pay a higher entrance fee.[1]

The number of spectators must often have comprised the
whole male population of a large town and its suburbs, besides
sundry strangers, women and children. Some of the remaining
theatres would easily hold 10,000 people. It is consequently
evident that all could not have seen or heard delicate points
upon the stage. This, as will be seen, had no small effect upon
the way in which Greek tragedies were brought upon the stage.
Nevertheless, I will observe, that in the great theatre of Syracuse, I myself tested its acoustic properties, and found that a
friend talking in his ordinary tone could be heard perfectly at
the farthest seat—this, too, with the back of the stage open ;
whereas it was in the old performances closed by lofty scenes,
and an upper story from which gods were shown and oft
descended upon the stage.

§ 166. We pass from the circle of spectators to the part of the
building (ὀρχήστρα) corresponding to the pit of modern theatres.
The greater part of this was smoothed, empty, and strewed with
sand, hence called κονίστρα. In the centre was an altar to Dionysus (θυμέλη), the relic of the old times when nothing but
choral dances had been held in the area round the altar. But
in the part nearest the stage, which corresponds to our stage
boxes and orchestra, was a raised floor of wood, called, more
specially and scenically, orchestra, or dancing place of the
chorus, beginning at the altar, and communicating by steps
with the stage, which was somewhat higher. The chorus was a
sort of stage audience, at times addressing the actors, and
answering them through their leader, at times reflecting upon
them independently, especially in the choral songs, which
divided what we may call the acts of the play. The chorus was
not an ideal spectator, far from it, but rather represented the
average morality or courage of the public, as contrasted with

---

[1] This has been often asserted, owing to a misconception of the passage in Plato, *Apol. Socr.* § 26, which speaks of buying the work of Anaxagoras at the other orchestra above mentioned for a drachme.

the heroic character of the protagonist, or chief actor. Thus we find it frequently supporting the deuteragonist, or second actor, who was a foil for the principal personage. As M. Patin admirably remarks, *àpropos* of the chorus of the *Antigone* :[1] 'It has not been sufficiently observed what moral defects the Greek poets attach to the part which in these plays represents the interests of general morality. While assigning to the chorus those lofty ideas of order and of justice which dwell in every heart, and come naturally from the lips of all as the voice of conscience, they took care to add to this somewhat imaginary rôle, by way of realism, the vulgar features common to every multitude. The speech of the chorus was pure and noble ; its conduct cowardly, cautious, selfish, and marked by the weakness and egotism which are the vice of the common herd, and are only wanting in the exceptional few, both of tragedy and of real life.' But when it watched the progress of the play, the scenes must have been not unlike the play within the play in Hamlet, except that the great personages were in the Greek play the observed of the inferior observers. The entrances to the orchestra were the same as those of the audience, from the sides (πάροδοι), between the stage and the tiers of seats, and it is certain that there was no separate place for musicians, as the accompaniments to the choral songs, which were sung apparently in unison, were of the slightest kind—perhaps a single fluteplayer behind the scenes.

From the orchestra we mount by a few steps to the stage, and its appurtenances. It was technically called προσκήνιον, or the place in front of the σκηνή, which was originally the king's tent, or dwelling of the chief character, but, in ordinary Greek parlance, nothing more than the background of the stage. A particular place in the centre of the proscenium, or stage, appears to have been slightly raised, and specially used in great declamations: this was called the λογεῖον. The whole stage was very long and narrow, spanning all the way from one side of the huge circle of spectators to the other. As the chorus were brought forward to their place in the orchestra, the Greek theatre required no deep stage room, and had ample space for

---

[1] *Sophocle,* p. 260.

its very few characters within a narrow place.[1]   There was certainly one passage leading out from under the stage, and known
technically as Charon's stairs; but the old stages which I have
examined show such complicated substructures, so many separate
short walls and passages in their foundations, that I fancy there
must have been more to be done under the Greek stage than
most scholars imagine.   The front of the raised stage, which
was hidden by the scenic orchestra, was called ὑποσκήνιον.

§ 167. There was not much change of dress in the Greek
plays, but still some green room must have been required ; it is
never alluded to by our authorities, and was, I fancy, a wooden
structure at the side of the stage, which could be removed
with the other woodwork.   In the back wall of the stage, the
doors, three in number, indicated the position of the actor
who first entered through them.[2]   The middle door was for
the chief actor, the right for his foil or supporter (deuteragonist),
the left for his contrast or opponent (tritagonist).   These
parts were as much fixed as those of the soprano, tenor, and
barytone in modern operas, but of course for musical and æsthetical reasons the two principal voices are there co-ordinated,
whereas this was never done by the Greeks.   Messengers, who
played an important part in reciting stirring scenes, came in, if
from the home or city of the actors, by the right parodos ; if
from abroad, by the left side of the theatre, and went out by
the orchestra ; we find that in some theatres an additional door
at each end of the stage was provided for this purpose.   These
fixed arrangements served to a certain extent instead of play
bills, which the Greeks did not use.   The back scene was, as I
have said, lofty, and made of painted wooden panels and hang-

---

[1] With the decay of the chorus, the stage was made narrower, and the
ornamental front with marble figures, which we admire in the present remains of the theatre at Athens, was not built till the third century A.D.,
and was moved back eight or nine yards from the original limit of the
proscenium, in the days of elaborate choric dances, and of dialogues between the chorus and the actors.   The decoration of this surface seems to
imply that no scaffolding for an orchestra was then required in front of it.

[2] It is not to be imagined that this was an absolute rule.   The chief
personage was in most plays easily to be distinguished without any such for-
mality.   Cf. Bernhardy, ii. p. 93.

ings, for when the Romans came to build similar theatres, they built up this scene of masonry, which still remains in many places—most perfectly at the splendid theatre of Aspendus in Pamphylia. The upper story represented by this architectural front was called *episcenium*, and the wings, when they came forward and closed the ends of the stage, *parascenia*. When change of place was required, there existed scene shifting, in the sense of drawing back to the sides temporary structures. As there was seldom, if ever, more than one change of scene in a Greek tragedy, we can imagine the movable scenes used first, and drawn away, along with the revolution of the *periacti*, to make way for the view painted on the permanent back scene of the stage. For it is certain that at the parascenia were fixed two lofty triangular prisms, called revolvers (περίακτοι), on each face of which a different scene was painted, so that, according as the 'foreign parts' especially of the play changed, the right περίακτος μηχανή was turned (ἐκκυκλεῖν). These prisms must also have served to conceal such scenes as were drawn back, when not required. There was some complicated machinery in the upper story of the back scene, which enabled the gods to appear in the air, and address the actors from a place called the gods' stage (θεολογεῖον). This machinery seems to have been hidden by a large curtain (κατάβλημα) hung from above, but I suspect that this device did not exist in the early days of tragedy.

It is important to notice the lofty and permanent character of the wooden, and afterwards brick, structures at the back of the stage, as it destroys various sentimental notions of modern art critics about the lovely natural scenery selected by the Greeks to form the background of their stage. It is still believed by many that the Greeks desired to combine the beauties of a lovely view with the ideal splendour of mythical tragic heroes. Modern research has completely exploded the absurd idea. It is possible that, at the highest and worst back seats, some lofty mountain behind the stage might have been visible, but I am sure the intention of all the arrangements was to exclude such disturbance, and to fix the attention of the spectators on the play and its scenic surroundings. The sites of the Greek theatres were simply determined by the ground, and if almost every ascending slope near a city in Greece affords a fair prospect of sea and islands, and rugged outlines, we know that the Greeks of all civilised people thought least about landscapes as such, and neglected the picturesque.

§ 168. This reflection leads me naturally to say a few words about the scene-painting of the Greeks. When Æschylus arose, painting was in its infancy, and it was not till the empire of Athens was well established that the first great artist Polygnotus (about Ol. 78) rose into fame. But he was altogether a figure painter, and seems to have known nothing of perspective. Towards the end of Æschylus' life, Agatharchus first began to study the art of scene-painting, with the view of producing some illusion by means of perspective, and wrote a treatise on the subject. The optical questions involved were taken up by Anaxagoras and Democritus, and Apollodorus (about 400 B.C.) may be regarded as having brought to perfection this branch of art. Both he and Agatharchus are classed as skenographers, or skiographers (σκηνογράφοι, σκιογράφοι), these terms being used as synonymous, and showing that the painting of shadows was first attempted in order to produce effects of perspective in scene-painting. There can be no doubt, from an analysis of the scenes of our extant plays, that the great majority of these paintings was architectural, and the representation of Greek palaces and temples, with their many long straight lines, particularly required a knowledge of perspective. It is not certain that the old Greeks, in spite of their philosophic studies, were very perfect in this respect, for the architectural subjects in the Pompeian frescoes are very faulty, perhaps, however, because they were the work of ignorant persons, who never learnt the better traditions of the ancients. Some few plays were laid in camps, and wild deserts, such as the *Ajax* and *Philoctetes* of Sophocles; but by this time scene-painting had become an established art. To judge from the landscapes of Pompeii, these scenes had a very lofty blue sky painted above them, which was doubtless intended to exclude the natural background from the spectators. In the comedies, concerning which we have but little information in detail, familiar and everyday scenes in Attica must have been painted, and it would be most interesting to know what amount of reality satisfied the Athenian audience. In the tragedies, the scenes were either of remote palaces, or at least of palaces and cities in ancient and mythical times, so that no close approximation to the cities of the period would be required.

§ 169. Above all, we must insist upon the staid and conservative character of all the Attic tragedy. The *subjects* were almost as fixed as the scenery, being always, or almost always, subjects from the Trojan and Theban cycle, with occasional excursions into the myths about Heracles. But in treating the Trojan myths, we find a distinct avoidance of the Iliad and Odyssey, and a use of the cyclic poems instead. There are indeed a few titles from our Homer, but they are so constantly satyric dramas, that I suppose this was according to some rule, and that Homer, from his sanctity, or owing to the too great familiarity of the audience with him, was deliberately avoided.

The uniformity of subjects was moreover paralleled by the uniformity of the dress—the festal costume of Bacchus—and by the fixed masks for the characters, which allowed no play of feature. So also I fancy the older actors to have been monotonous and simple in their playing.. Later on we know that they became popular and were a much distinguished class, and then they began to take liberties with their texts, as we hear from many scholia. These liberties were repressed by a wholesome law of the orator Lycurgus, who enacted that official copies of the plays of the three great tragic masters should be made, and no new performance of them allowed without the applicant for the chorus and his company having their acting copies compared with the state MS.

As soon as tragic choruses and other dramatic performances became recognised by the state at Athens, they were not left to chance or to individual enterprise. The chorus was dressed and trained at the public expense, and the poet who desired to have his piece performed must go to the archon,[1] and ask to have a chorus assigned to him. The actors were said to have been distributed by lot, but in later days, we find particular actors so associated with poets that some more permanent

---

[1] The *eponymus* at the *Dionysia*, the king archon at the *Lenæa.*

connection must be assumed.   The archon granted choruses to the most promising applicants, so that young and unknown poets were fain to produce their piece under the name of an influential friend.   The poet, with the aid of a professional choir master, trained his chorus in the lyrical songs, and in early days took the chief acting part himself.

§ 170.   Unfortunately we know hardly anything of the way in which the competitions were managed, or how many plays were produced on the same day, and in succession.   We know certainly that they were composed (even by Euripides) in *tetralogies*, in groups of four, and their average length being moderate, I fancy a trilogy would not take up more time than the playing of *Hamlet*, followed by a short farce or satyric drama.   But how could the audience endure more than this at one time ; and yet we know that many of our extant plays obtained the third prize, showing that twelve plays must have been acted.   It is absolutely certain that such a competition must have lasted several days, and I believe that twelve plays was the limit ; for when I note the difficulty of 'obtaining a chorus,' and that even good poets were refused ; when I also observe that the third place was considered a disgrace, I infer that the number of competitors must have been limited, and that there were not lower places than the third to be assigned.   But when we hear that Sophocles contended, 'play against play,' by way of novelty, and that single plays from a group were called victorious, and yet that Euripides competed with groups, none of which has survived entire, we find ourselves in hopeless perplexities.

As to the adjudication of the prizes, it was made by judges selected from the audience by lot, and no doubt led by the public reception of the piece ; but their decision seems often to have been exceedingly bad.   As we have not the rival pieces of any competition for comparison, we may not dogmatise ; but still, when the scholiasts wonder at the *Œdipus Rex* being defeated, and when we find the *Medea* disgraced by obtaining the third place, we cannot help suspecting that the judgment of the day was utterly wrong.   Each victory was commemorated by a tripod, which was erected on an ornamental pillar or building like the choragic monument of Lysicrates, still extant at Athens, and from these inscribed monuments were drawn the valuable didascalia which Aristotle first collected, and from which Aristophanes (of Byzantium) afterwards compiled his invaluable prefaces to all the plays. Our extant prefaces seem to copy their chronological data—the year of the play, its competitors, and its place—whenever they vouchsafe us such information. Had Aristophanes' work been preserved, the whole history of the drama would be in a far different condition.

§ 171. There is still some hope of further light on this important point. Fragments of lists of dramatic authors, and their victories, are still being found about the acropolis and the theatre at Athens, and from the publications of them by Kumanudes in the *Athenaion*, Bergk has endeavoured to reconstruct the chronology of the drama.[1] His conclusions have been contested by Köhler,[2] and are as yet uncertain. But he has probably established this much, that while the tragic contests were carried on at the greater Dionysia in the city, and in spring time, and recorded since about Ol. 64, the winter feast of the Lenæa in the suburbs was originally devoted to comedy, which was not recognised by the state till about Ol. 79. In Ol. 84 new regulations were introduced, probably by Pericles, according to which tragic contests were established at the Lenæa, and comic admitted to the greater Dionysia. From this time both kinds of contests were carried on at both feasts, and in the great theatre.[3] But as the *Lenæa* was only a home feast, and not attended by strangers, a victory gained there was by no means of the same importance as a victory before the great concourse of citizens and visitors in the spring, and consequently they were separately catalogued. This accounts for variations in the number of prizes ascribed to the poets, some lists comprising all, others only the city prizes. No poet (except Sophocles) seems to have gained this latter distinction often, and many prolific authors obtained it only once or twice. But, as has been already remarked, the verdict of the judges is not to be taken as a conclusive estimate of real merit.

---

[1] Cf. *Rhein. Mus.* for 1879, pp. 292, sq.

[2] In the *Memoirs of the German Arch. Inst. of Athens*, vol. iii. pp. 104, sq.

[3] The *lesser* or *country Dionysia* were celebrated at a theatre in the Peiræus, which has just been discovered. Cf. Ἀθήναιον for August 1880.

CHAPTER XV.

ÆSCHYLUS.

§ 172. THE facts known to us about the life of Æschylus are few, and decked out with many fables. He was the son of Euphorion, born at Eleusis, the town of the Mysteries, in 525 B.C. He contended with Chœrilus and Pratinas, as well as Phrynichus, fiom about 500 B.C., and there is no doubt that he learned a great deal from the art of the latter. His first tragic victory was in Ol. 73, 4 (485), and from this time down to the middle of the century he worked with all the energy and patience of a great genius at his art. He fought in the battles of the great Persian war, and was wounded, it is said, at Marathon, at which his brother Kynægirus fell. He contended against Simonides with an elegy to be inscribed over the fallen, but was defeated. According to the most credible account he won thirteen tragic victories. He confessed it impossible to excel the Hymn to Zeus of the obscure Tynnichus, on account of its antique piety, which gave it the character of an inspiration.[1] And yet he is reported to have been exceedingly hurt at the success of Sophocles in tragedy, by whom he was defeated in 468 B.C. This may have induced him to leave Athens and go to Sicily, an island which he had already visited in Ol. 76 at the invitation of Hiero, for whom he had written a local piece called the *Ætnæans*, to celebrate the foundation of the city of Ætna on the site of the earlier (and later) Catana. He also brought out at Syracuse a new edition of his *Persians*. A better cause alleged for his second departure from Athens was the suspicion or accusation under which he lay of having divulged the Mysteries. He is even said to have been publicly

---

[1] Cf. Bergk, *FLG.*, p. IIII

attacked, and, though he pleaded that he was unaware of his crime, was saved with difficulty by the Areopagus. If this be so, we can understand his splendid advocacy of that ancient and venerable court, when attacked by Ephialtes, in his *Eumenides*, the third play of the extant trilogy with which he conquered in Ol. 80, 2 (458). He must have been at this moment one of the most important leaders of the conservative party, and have had far more weight through his plays than most men could attain by their eloquence on the bema. Nevertheless we hear of him dying at Gela in Sicily within three years of this great triumph. The people of Gela erected him a splendid tomb; the Athenians not only set up his statue in public, but rewarded and equipped any choregus in after days who would bring out again the works of so great and acknowledged a master.

Even this brief sketch can hardly be called certain as to its facts ; the many fables about his relationships, about his death, and about his professional jealousies have been here deliberately omitted. I only know of two personal recollections of him which still survive, beyond the remark on Tynnichus above mentioned. He was sitting beside Ion of Chios at the Isthmian games ; the audience cried out when one of the boxers got a severe blow, whereupon he nudged Ion, and said : 'See what training does, the man who is struck says nothing, while the spectators cry out.'[1] He is said to have described his tragedies as morsels (τεμάχη) gathered from the mighty feasts of Homer. This very humble claim and loyal feeling towards the old epics do not bespeak a jealous or self-asserting character. Of his plays there remain seventy-two titles, of which over sixty seem genuine, and a good many fragments, but only seven actual pieces : the *Supplices* (ἱκέτιδες), probably brought out in Ol. 71 or 72 ; the *Persæ*, 76, 4 ; the *Seven against Thebes*, 78, 1[2] ; the *Prometheus Vinctus*, not before 75, 2, in which the eruption of Ætna alluded to in the play

---

[1] This is reported by Plutarch, *De profect. in virt.* c. 8.

[2] The statement put into Æschylus' mouth in the *Frogs* (v. 1026, sq.) seems as if this usually received order were wrong, and the *Seven against Thebes* came earlier than the *Persæ*.

occurred, but probably as late as Ol. 79. Lastly, his greatest
and most perfect work, the Orestean trilogy, consisting of the
Agamemnon, *Choephori*, and *Eumenides*, in Ol. 80, 2, shortly
before his death.

§ 173. I take the *Supplices* first, because it is decidedly a
specimen of the early and simple tragedy developed by Æschylus; nor do I agree with some great critics who have thought it
composed as late as Ol. 79, on account of its complimentary
allusions to Argos. In the first place the chorus is the principal
actor in this play—the daughters of Danaus, who have come as
Suppliants to Argos, to escape the marriage of their cousins,
the sons of Ægyptus. In the next place, the number of the
chorus in the play seems to have been fifty, whereas in Æschylus' later days it was reduced to fifteen or twelve persons.
There is indeed a notice of Suidas that Sophocles raised
the old number twelve to fifteen, which would imply twelve
Suppliants only; but the fixed traditional number of the
Danaides, and the ample space on the orchestra, in a play
where there was no dancing, seem to make the full number not
impossible in this play. I have no doubt that it was the
requirements of this play which at all events made the critics
think of fifty choristers. The main body of the piece consists in
long choric songs complaining of the violence of the sons of
Ægyptus, the unholy character of the marriage they proposed,
and the anxieties of the fugitives. These odes are merely
interrupted by the actors—their father Danaus, Pelasgus, the
King of Argos, and the petulant Egyptian herald, who endeavours to hurry them off to the ship which has just arrived to
bring them back. The King of Argos is represented as a
respectable monarch, who, though absolute, will not decide
without appealing to the vote of his people, who generously
accept the risk of protecting the Suppliants. But the cautious
benevolence of Pelasgus, and the insolence of the Egyptian
herald, can hardly be called character-drawing, and the whole
drama, having hardly any plot, is a good specimen of that
simple structure with which Attic tragedy developed itself out
of a mere cyclic chorus. It is remarkable, however, that
though the individuals are so slightly sketched, there is the

most distinct characterising of nationalities throughout the
play. Not only is the very speech of the Danaides full of
strange-sounding words, as if to suggest their foreign origin,
but there is the strongest aversion conveyed by the poet for
the Egyptians, as a violent and barbarous people, whose better
few can only find protection in Argos. The Argives, again,
are described as an honourable, somewhat democratic people,
not perhaps very different from the stage Athenians under
Theseus. There is little known of the other plays in the
trilogy, or of the satyric piece which followed. The horror
of a marriage with cousins seems so absurd in the Egyptian
princesses that it must have been explained by the course
of a preceding play, and the critics are agreed that the so-
called *Danaides* followed, wherein the marriage and murder
of the sons of Ægyptus took place, and the trial of Hypermn-
estra, who alone disobeyed her father. She seems to have
been acquitted by the interference of Aphrodite herself, on the
ground of her own all-powerful influence on the human mind,
and from her speech Athenæus has preserved for us some fine
lines.[1]

Though this play is the least striking of those extant, and,
from the little attention paid to it, very corrupt, and often
hard to decipher, there are all the highest Æschylean features
in germ throughout it. Thus in the very first chorus, not to
speak of the elegant allusion to the nightingale, already celebrated in the Odyssey, there is a splendid passage on the
Divine Providence, which breathes all the lofty theology so
admirable in Æschylus.[2]

ἐρᾷ μὲν ἁγνὸς οὐρανὸς τρῶσαι χθόνα,
ἔρως δὲ γαῖαν λαμβάνει γάμου τυχεῖν·
ὄμβρος δ' ἀπ' εὐνάεντος οὐρανοῦ πεσὼν
ἔκυσε γαῖαν· ἡ δὲ τίκτεται βροτοῖς
μήλων τε βοσκὰς καὶ βίον Δημήτριον·
δενδρῶτις ὥρα δ' ἐκ νοτίζοντος γάμου
τέλειός ἐστι. τῶν δ' ἐγὼ παραίτιος.

2 vv. 86, sq. : Διὸς ἵμερος οὐκ εὐθήρατος ἐτύχθη,
πάντα τοι φλεγέθει
κἀν σκότῳ μελαίνᾳ ξὺν τύχᾳ
μερόπεσσι λαοῖς,

So also future punishments are threatened.[1] The concluding prayer of blessing on Argos, sung by the grateful Suppliants, is very fine, and there is all through the play an abundance of that mighty diction in which the epithets and figures come rolling in upon us like Atlantic waves. It is this feature in Æschylus which makes him so untranslateable.[2]

I will observe, in conclusion, that the description of Io's wanderings (in the ode, vv. 525, sq.) is a foretaste of the much fuller treatment of the same subject in the later *Prometheus*.

> πίπτει δ' ἀσφαλὲς οὐδ' ἐπὶ νώτῳ,
> κορυφᾷ Διὸς εἰ κρανθῇ πρᾶγμα τέλειον.
> δαυλοὶ γὰρ πραπίδων
> δάσκιοί τε τείνουσιν πόροι,
> κατιδεῖν ἄφραστοι.
> ἰάπτει δ' ἐλπίδων
> ἀφ' ὑψιπύργων πινώλεις βροτούς,
> βίαν δ' οὔτιν' ἐξοπλίζει,
> τὰν ἄποινον δαιμονίων· ἥμενον ἄνω φρόνημά πως
> αὐτόθεν ἐξέπραξεν ἔμπας, ἑδράνων ἐφ' ἁγνῶν.

And vv. 590, sq. :

> τίν' ἂν θεῶν ἐνδικωτέροισιν
> κεκλοίμαν εὐλόγως ἐπ' ἔργοις.
> πατὴρ φυτουργός, αὐτόχειρ ἄναξ
> γένους παλαιόφρων μέγας
> τέκτων, τὸ πᾶν μῆχαρ οὔριος Ζεύς.
> ὑπ' ἀρχᾶς δ' οὔτινος θοάζων
> τὸ μεῖον κρεισσόνων κρατύνειν
> οὔτινος ἄνωθεν ἡμένου σέβει κάτω.
> πάρεστι δ' ἔργον ὡς ἔπος
> στεῦσαί τι τῶν βούλιος φέρει φρήν.

[1] vv. 227-33, and v. 416.

[2] Thus we have (vv. 34, sq.) :

> ἔνθα δὲ λαίλαπι
> χειμωνοτύπῳ, βροντῇ στεροπῇ τ'
> ὀμβροφόροισίν τ' ἀνέμοις ἀγρίας
> ἁλὸς ἀντήσαντες ὄλοιντο.

Again, v. 350 :

> λυκοδίωκτον ὡς δάμαλιν ἂμ πέτραις
> ἠλιβάτοις, ἵν' ἀλκᾷ πίσυνος μέμυκε
> φράζουσα βοτῆρι μόχθους.

And

> ἄχορον ἀκίθαριν δακρυογόνον Ἄρη.

And the wonderful—

> λισσὰς αἰγίλιψ ἀπρόσδεικτος οἰόφρων κρεμὰς γυπιὰς πέτρα.

§ 174. The *Persæ* is profoundly interesting, apart from literary questions, for it is the first approach to a piece of contemporary history among the Greeks. Here we have the battle of Salamis described by an eyewitness, and the impressions made on the heroes of Marathon recorded with a poet's utterance.[1] The problem of making an ideal picture from materials of the present day was more imperative for a Greek than for any modern poet, and it is with no small acuteness that Racine (in the preface to his *Bajazet*) explains the artifice, and applies it in his own way. As M. Patin well puts it : 'il dépaysa, en quelque sorte, son, sujet, et lui donna cette perspective lointaine nécessaire à l'illusion tragique.'[2] Racine thought that to *his* audience the Turks were strange and mysterious enough for ideal purposes, just as Æschylus had devised the plan of laying his scene at the Persian court, where even living characters would not strike the audience as too close to themselves. By this means Æschylus avoids all the difficulties which beset him, and moreover was able to convey certain moral lessons to his audience by his picture of the despotic society in which Xerxes lived. It has been remarked that though the play teems with Persian names, not a single Athenian is mentioned ; nay, even the celebrated Ameinias, whom many commentators call the poet's brother, is anonymous, and his ship only noted as a 'Greek ship.'[3] Of course, the mention of any special name in the Attic theatre would have excited all manner of disturbing sympathies and antipathies.

The general features of the play being borrowed, as we are told, from the celebrated *Phœnissæ* of Phrynichus, it was of that archaic and simple structure which admitted almost no

---

[1] The differences between Æschylus and Herodotus, which are less than might be expected, have often been discussed by critics. Cf. Blakesley's *Herod.* vol. ii. p. 404. The introduction of modern subjects had already been attempted by Phrynichus (above, p. 236), not only in his *Capture of Miletus*, but in his *Phœnissæ*. It was again attempted in later days by Moschion and Philiscus in their *Themistocles*, and probably by others also. Cf. Meineke, *Hist. Com. Græc.* p 522.

[2] Cf. Patin, *Tragiques grecs.* i. p. 211.   [3] v. 409.

action, and very little play of various feeling. The chorus is here also of the first importance, and takes its place as an actor in the play. It is composed of elders left in charge of Xerxes' kingdom during his absence, who in the opening scene express their anxieties concerning the state of the Persian Empire. Atossa, the king's mother, next appears to tell her alarms, and then a breathless messenger narrates the defeat and destruction of the great host in a very splendid narrative. The chorus, in despair, are advised by Atossa to help her in calling up the spirit of Darius, who is represented as a great and just ruler, whose prophetic advice might still save his people. But he merely foretells, with calm dignity, the remaining defeat at Platæa, and gives no hope of returning fortune. After a choral song in praise of his great conquests, Xerxes appears in strong contrast, and the play ends with a long *commos* or ode of lamentation for him and the chorus—a common feature at the close of Greek tragedies, for which we moderns feel little sympathy.

The play is not very difficult, and the text in a much better condition than that of most of Æschylus' other plays. Its merits have been generally underrated, and it seems to have been left for M. Patin to discover, with the delicate sense of his nation, the finer points missed by other critics. The ghost of Darius in particular is to be noted as, perhaps, the only *character ghost* in the history of tragedy. He is brought up mainly to enable the poet to gather together the various triumphs of the Greeks, which could not be embraced in the limits of the action. But far beyond this particular requirement, Æschylus has endowed the vision of the great monarch with a certain splendid calm, a repose from the troubles of this mortal life, an indifference to all violent despair, which comes out strangely in his opening words to Atossa, and in his parting farewell.[1] The contrast with the erring, suffering, perturbed spirit of Hamlet's father will strike every reader. As for the other characters of the play, they merely exhibit various phases of grief, all modulated and varied according to the natural requirements of the persons. The grief of the messenger is patriotic, he thinks of the losses of Persia only; and yet there

[1] vv. 706–8, and 840–2.

is in him that fullness and explicitness of detail which mark the self-importance of a man of little dignity, when he becomes the bearer of weighty, even though lamentable, news. The grief of the queen is personal, she has her mind fixed on her son. That of the chorus is vehement and headstrong, almost seditious; that of Xerxes, gloomy and despairing; that of Darius, as we have said, is a calm and divine melancholy, which cannot disturb his eternal serenity. Thus a single theme is varied through all manner of tempers. Though the general merit of the piece is greater than that of the *Supplices*, there are not so many fine and striking passages. More especially the theology preached by Darius is by no means so lofty as that cited above from the earlier play. The lines in which Atossa describes the offerings of the dead are very beautiful, and very like in grace to the writing of Sophocles.[1]

The invocation of Darius also shows the use of the refrain, which is so effective in Æschylus, and is not common in the other tragedians. We are told in the didascaliæ that this trilogy —viz. the *Phineus, Persæ, Glaucus*, with the *Prometheus Pyrphoros* —gained the first prize. Of the other plays we know hardly anything, save that the Bœotian campaign, and the Carthaginian defeat in Sicily, were treated. There is a good edition by Teuffel.

§ 175. The *Seven against Thebes* brings us to a more advanced stage of the poet's development. Though the plot is still simple, it is not the chorus, but Eteocles who opens the play, and sustains the principal part. Moreover, the drawing of his character is very clear and sharp, and quite as striking as the warlike characters of the most developed tragedies. After his patriotic speech, a messenger details, with great

---

[1] vv. 610-18 :

νεκροῖσι μειλικτήρια,
βοός τ' ἀφ' ἁγνῆς λευκὸν εὔποτον γάλα,
τῆς τ' ἀνθεμουργοῦ στάγμα, παμφαὲς μέλι,
λιβάσιν ὑδρηλαῖς παοθένου πηγῆς μέτα
ἀκήρατόν τε μητρὸς ἀγρίας ἄπο
ποτὸν παλαιᾶς ἀμπέλου γανος τόδε ·
τῆς τ' αἰὲν ἐν φύλλοισι θαλλούσης ἴσον
ξανθῆς ἐλαίας καρπὸς εὐώδης πάρα,
ἄνθη τε πλεκτά, παμφόρου γαίας τέκνα.

beauty, the sacrifice and oath of the seven hostile chiefs, who swear to meet death rather than to turn back from Thebes.[1] The *parodos* of the chorus is composed with great skill, the precipitous hurried rythms and apparent disorder of the structure speaking clearly the agitation of the Theban maidens at the approach of the enemy. Eteocles breaks in upon them, and reproves them sharply for disturbing the town, and dispiriting the citizens with their lamentations, and prayers to the gods. After a long dialogue, he exhorts them to raise a pæan to the gods, and encourage the people. But the chorus, in an anxious and very beautiful strain, still harp upon their fears, upon the horrors of war, and upon the miseries of captured cities.[2]

---

[1] He adds a pathetic touch :

μνημεῖα θ' αὐτῶν τοῖς τεκοῦσιν ἐς δόμους
πρὸς ἄρμ' Ἀδράστου χερσὶν ἔστεφον, δάκρυ
λείβοντες· οἶκτος δ' οὐδεὶς ἦν διὰ στόμα.

[2] vv. 321–62 :

οἰκτρὸν γὰρ πόλιν ὧδ' ὠγυγίαν
Ἀΐδᾳ προϊάψαι, δορὸς ἄγραν,
δουλίαν ψαφαρᾷ σποδῷ
ὑπ' ἀνδρὸς Ἀχαιοῦ θεόθεν
περθομέναν ἀτίμως,
τὰς δὲ κεχειρωμένας ἄγεσθαι,
ἐή, νέας τε καὶ παλαιὰς
ἱππηδὸν πλοκάμων,
περιρρηγνυμένων φαρέων.
βοᾷ δ' ἐκκενουμένα πόλις,
λαΐδος ὀλλυμένας μιξοθρόου·
βαρείας τοι τύχας προταρβῶ.
κλαυτὸν δ' ἀρτιτρόποις ὠμοδρόπων
νομίμων προπάροιθεν διαμεῖψαι
δωμάτων στυγερὰν ὁδόν.
τί; τὸν φθίμενον γὰρ προλέγω
βέλτερα τῶνδε πράσσειν.
πολλὰ γάρ, εὖτε πτόλις δαμασθῇ,
ἐή, δυστυχῆ τε πράσσει.
ἄλλος δ' ἄλλον ἄγει,
φονεύει, τὰ δὲ καὶ πυρφορεῖ·
καπνῷ χραίνεται πόλισμ' ἅπαν.
μαινόμενος δ' ἐπιπνεῖ λαοδάμας

Then follows the celebrated scene in which the messenger describes the appearance of each chief, while Eteocles and the chorus answer. The length to which it is expanded has been criticised by Euripides. The picture of the sixth, the seer Amphiaraus,[1] is said by Plutarch to have 'brought down the house' by its plain allusion to Aristeides, then in the theatre. When Polynices is described, last of all, the rage of Eteocles bursts forth uncontrollably, and the awful curse resting upon the house of Laius urges him consciously to meet his brother in the field, in spite of the deprecating entreaties of the chorus. After an ode on the sorrows of Œdipus, the news of the Theban victory and the death of the brothers arrives. Presently the bodies are brought in, followed by Antigone and Ismene, who sing a *commos* over them, consisting of doleful reproaches and laments.

But in the last seventy lines the poet blocks out the whole subject of Sophocles' *Antigone.* The herald forbids the burial of Polynices, Antigone rebels, and by a curious device the chorus, dividing, take sides with both Antigone and Ismene, in upholding

μιαίνων εὐσέβειαν Ἄρης.
κορκορυγαὶ δ' ἀν' ἄστυ,
ποτὶ πτόλιν δ' ὁρκάνα πυργῶτις.
πρὸς ἀνδρὸς δ' ἀνὴρ στὰς δορὶ καίνεται·
βλαχαὶ δ' αἱματόεσσαι
τῶν ἐπιμαστιδίων
ἄρτι βρεφῶν βρέμονται.
ἁρπαγαὶ δὲ διαδρομᾶν ὁμαίμονες·
ξυμβολεῖ φέρων φέροντι,
καὶ κενὸς κενὸν καλεῖ,
ξύννομον θέλων ἔχειν,
οὔτε μεῖον οὔτ' ἴσον λελιμμένοι.
τίν' ἐκ τῶνδ' εἰκάσαι λόγος πάρα;
παντοδαπὸς δὲ καρπὸς
χαμάδις πεσὼν ἀλγύνει κυρήσας.
πικρὸν δ' ὄμμα ⁎ ⁎ θαλαμηπόλων·
πολλὰ δ' ἀκριτόφυρτος
γᾶς δόσις οὐτιδανοῖς
ἐν ῥοθίοις φορεῖται.

[1] vv. 592–4.

ard rejecting the decree of the city.[1]   M. Patin notes that the same device has been adopted by Schiller in his *Bride of Messina*, and that such a division was not at all unnatural in a Greek chorus.   Far from being an ideal spectator, 'les poètes grecs ne se piquaient pas de donner au chœur, réprésentant de la foule, des sentiments héroïques, et il me semble qu'Éschyle, dans cette peinture rapide, a fort ingénieusement caractérisé les commodes apologies de la poltronnerie politique.'

Aristophanes, in his *Frogs*, makes Æschylus quote this play specially for its warlike tone, and for the good effects it produced upon the spirit of the spectators.   It won the first prize with its trilogy, consisting of the *Laius*, the *Œdipus*, the *Septem*, and as a satyric afterpiece, the *Sphinx*.   This information having been copied from the Medicean didascaliæ discovered in 1828, it is interesting to study the earlier lucubrations of the Germans as to the place of the *Septem* in its trilogy.   Only one of their guesses was true, and that was shortly abandoned by its author, Hermann, for more elaborate hypotheses.   This collapse of the learned combinations about the grouping of Greek plays has decided me to pass them by in silence, merely giving the facts when preserved in the Greek prefaces, which are acknowledged trustworthy.

§ 176. The *Prometheus Vinctus* brings us to the perfection of Æschylus' art, and to a specimen, unique and unapproachable, of what that wonderful genius could do in *simple* tragedy, that is to say, in the old plotless, motionless, surpriseless drama, made up of speeches and nothing more.   There is certainly no other play of Æschylus which has produced a greater impression upon the world, and few remnants of Greek literature are to be compared with it in its eternal freshness and its eternal mystery.   We know nothing of the plays connected with it, save that it was followed by a *Prometheus Unbound*, with a chorus of Titans condoling with the god, who was delivered by Heracles from the vulture that gnawed his vitals, and was reconciled with Zeus.   Thus this group may

---

[1] So Aristophanes, in his *Acharnians* (vv. 520, sq.) divides his chorus, half of which is persuaded by Dicæopolis, while the other half remains obstinate and hostile.

have had a peaceful and happy termination, like the great extant trilogy; and we can fancy that the pious Æschylus, when he brought upon the stage conflicts among the gods, would not allow his plays to close in wrath and anguish, as he did the Œdipodean trilogy just discussed. The work before us shows clear marks of development above the earlier plays. Three actors appear in the first scene, the silent figure of Prometheus being evidently a lay figure, from behind which the actor afterwards spoke. The chorus is even more restricted than in the *Seven against Thebes*, and occupies a position not more prominent than in the average plays of Sophocles or Euripides. The dialogue is paramount, and possesses a terseness and power not exceeded by any of the poet's later work. As Eteocles, the heroic warrior, is in the *Seven* the central and the only developed character, so here Prometheus, the heroic sufferer, sustains the whole play. In the first scene he is riven, with taunt and insult, to the rocks by the cruel or timid servants of Zeus. Then he soliloquises. Then he discourses with the sympathetic chorus of ocean nymphs and their cautious father. Then he condoles with the frantic Io, and prophesies her future fates. Lastly, he bids defiance to Zeus, through his herald Hermes, and disappears amid whirlwind and thunder. Yet the interest and pathos of the play never flag.

With a very usual artifice of the poet, satirised by Aristophanes, the chief actor is kept upon the stage silent for some time, during which the expectation of the spectators must have been greatly excited, even though diverted by the exquisite pathos of Hephæstus' address to the suffering god. The outburst of Prometheus, as soon as the insolent ministers of Zeus have left him manacled, but have freed him from the far more galling shackles of proud reserve, is among the great things in the world's poetry. The approach of the ocean nymphs is picturesquely conceived; indeed the whole scenery, laid in the Scythian deserts beyond the Euxine, among gloomy cliffs and caverns, with no interests upon the scene save those of the gods and their colossal conflicts, is weird and wild beyond comparison. The choral odes are not so fine as in the earlier plays, but the dialogue and soliloquies more than compensate for them. The play is probably the easiest of the extant seven, and the text in a good condition, though the critics sus- pect a good many interpolations made by actors in their stage copies.

§ 177. But the external features of this splendid play are obscured, if possible, by the still greater interest attaching to its intention, and by the great difficulties of explaining the poet's attitude when he brought it upon the stage. For it represents a conflict among the immortal gods—a conflict carried out by violence and settled by force and fraud, not by justice. Zeus especially, his herald, and his subject gods, are represented as hard and fierce characters, maintaining a ruthless tyranny among the immortals; and the suffering Prometheus submits to centuries of torture from motives of pure benevolence to the wretched race of men, whom he had civilised and instructed against the will of Zeus. For this crime, and no other, is he punished by the Father of the Gods, thus set forth as the arch enemy of man.

How did the Athenian audience, who vehemently attacked the poet for divulging the Mysteries, tolerate such a drama? and still more, how did Æschylus, a pious and serious thinker, venture to bring such a subject on the stage with a moral purpose? As to the former question, we know that in all traditional religions, many old things survive which shock the moral sense of more developed ages, and which are yet tolerated even in public services, being hallowed by age and their better surroundings. So we can imagine that any tragic poet, who adhered to the facts of a received myth, would be allowed to draw his characters in accordance with it, especially as these characters were not regarded as fixed, but only held good for the single piece. In the Middle Ages much license was allowed in the mystery plays, but it was condoned and connived at because of the general religiousness of the practice, and because the main outlines of biblical story were the frame for these vagaries. Thus a very extreme distortion of their gods will not offend many who would feel outraged at any open denial of them. It is also to be remembered that despotic sovereignty was the Greek's ideal of happiness *for himself*, and that most nations have thought it not only reconcileable with, but conformable to, the dignity of the great Father who rules the world. No Athenian, however he sympathised with Prometheus, would think of blaming Zeus for asserting his power and crushing all resistance to his will. I do not therefore think it difficult to understand how the Athenians not only tolerated but appreciated the play.

The question of the poet's intention is far more difficult, and will probably never be satisfactorily answered. The number of interpretations put upon the myth by commentators is astonishing, and yet it is possible that the poet had none of them consciously before his mind's eye. They have been well summed up by Patin[1] under six heads. There are first the *historical* theories, such as that of Diodorus Siculus, a scholiast of Apollonius Rhodius, and others, that make Prometheus a ruler of Egypt or of Scythia, who suffered in his struggles to reclaim his country and its people. Secondly, the *philosophical*, which hold it to be the image of the struggles and trials of humanity against natural obstacles. This seems the view of Welcker, and is certainly that of M. Guignaut. Thirdly, the *moral*, which place the struggle within the breast of the individual, and against his passions, as was done by Bacon, by Calderon, and also by Schlegel, as well as by several older French critics. Fourthly, the *Christian*, much favoured by Catholic divines in France, supported by Jos. de Maistre, Edgar Quinet, Ch. Maquin, and others, who see in the story either the redemption of man, the fall of Satan, or the fall of man, dimly echoed by some tradition from the sacred Scriptures. Garbitius, a Basle editor of the *Prometheus* in 1559, seems to have led the way in this direction. But as Lord Lytton justly observes, ' whatever theological system it shadows forth was rather the gigantic conception of the poet himself than the imperfect revival of any forgotten creed, or the poetical disguise of any existing philosophy.' Yet there is certainly something of disbelief or defiance of the creed of the populace. Fifthly, the *scientific*, which regard it as a mere personification of astronomical facts, as is the fashion with comparative mythologies. Similar attempts seem to have been made of old by the alchemists. Sixthly, there is the *political* interpretation

---

[1] *Etudes*, i. p. 254. I have added Mr. Lloyd's, from his *Age of Pericles*.

of Mr. Watkiss Lloyd, who thinks the genius of Themistocles
and the ingratitude of Athens were the real object of the poet's
teaching, though disguised in a myth.[1]   There is lastly to be
noticed an unique theory, which may be called the *romantic*,
propounded by Desmaretz in 1648, when he published a
rationalistic imitation of Euemerus, entitled *La Vérité des
fables ou l'histoire des dieux de l'antiquité*.   He explains how
Prometheus betrays his sovereign, Jupiter, for the love of his
mistress Pandora, a lady as exacting as any princess of chivalry.   He retires in despair to the wastes of the Caucasus,
where remorse daily gnaws his heart, and he suffers agonies
more dreadful than if an eagle were continually devouring his
entrails.   Prometheus at the French court of the seventeenth
century was sure to cut a strange figure.

There can be no doubt that an acquaintance with the
Orphic and Eleusinian mysteries told upon Æschylus' theology,
and made him regard the conflicts and sufferings of gods as
part of their revelation to men, and we can imagine him
accepting even the harshest and most uncivilised myths as part
of the established faith, and therefore in some way to be
harmonised with the highest morals.   Yet it seems very strange
that he should represent Zeus as a tyrant, and Prometheus—a
god not by any means of importance in public worship—a
noble sufferer, punished for his humanity.   Still worse, Zeus is
represented as the enemy of men, and completely estranged
from any interest in their welfare.   I do not know how these
things are to be explained in such a man as Æschylus, and
cannot say which of the more reasonable theories is to be
preferred.   This seems certain, that the iron power of Destiny
was an extremely prominent idea in his mind, and that no
more wonderful illustration could be found than this story, in
which even the Ruler of the Gods was subject to it, and thus at
the mercy of his vanquished but prophetic foe.

§ 178. The history of opinion about the *Prometheus* is somewhat curious.   The great French critics of the seventeenth century could not comprehend it, and Voltaire, Fontenelle, and la
Harpe were agreed that it was simply a monstrous play, and the

[1] Cf. Bernhardy's Comm. on most of these theories, *LG.* iii. p. 272, sq.

work of an uncultivated boor with some sparks of genius. The colossal conceptions of the great Greek, and the gigantic words with which he strove to compass his thought, were essentially foreign to the rigid form and smooth polish of the French tragedians.   Of late years all this feeling has changed. Lemercier, Andrieux, and Edgar Quinet[1] have adopted the tone of Schlegel and Goethe, and everybody is now agreed as to the merit of the play.   I would they were equally persuaded of the impossibility of imitating it.   There are allusions to two translations or adaptations by the Romans, attributed to Attius, Varro, or Mæcenas.   Cicero seems to have been particularly attracted by it.   In. modern days Calderon's *Estatuta de Prometheo* is said to be a moral allegory on the conflicts in human nature.   Milton's Satan is full of recollections of Prometheus, and even the Samson Agonistes, though rather built on an Euripidean model, has many like traits.   Byron tells us that this was his great model for all the rebellious heroes who conflict with the course of Providence.   Shelley so loved to depict the struggle with a tyrannous deity that he reconstructed for us the *Prometheus Unbound* on his own model. But as Lord Lytton observes, Æschylus' power lies in concentration, whereas the quality of Shelley is diffuseness.   Keats' *Hyperion* shows the impress of the same original. Goethe attempted, but never finished a Prometheus.   Apart from the unworthy portraits in the *Pandora* of Voltaire and the *Prometheus* of Lefranc de Pompignan, E. Quinet has symbolised the fall of paganism and rise of Christianity in his drama (Paris, 1838), and several later French poets, MM. Lodin de Lalaire, V. de Laprade, and Senneville, have touched the subject—the latter in a tragedy on *Prometheus Delivered* (1844).   Thus we have before us in this play of Æschylus one of the greatest and most lasting creations in human art, a model to succeeding ages, and commanding their homage.   But no modern in-

---

[1] I am surprised to find in Villemain (*Litt. du xviiime siècle*, iii. 299) the expression : ' pièce monstrueuse, ou l'on voit arriver l'Océan qui vole, porté sur un animal ailé, et d'autres folies poétiques de l'imagination grecque.'   This is a curious sentence for so enlightened and elegant a critic.

terpreter has ever equalled the mighty original. As M. Patin says, it is owing to the unequal satisfaction provided for two very diverse requirements—a combination of great poetic clearness with a religious and philosophic twilight—that the work of Æschylus preserves its immortal freshness. There are German translations by Hartung and F. Jacobs. All earlier English versions may be forgotten in the presence of that of Mrs. Browning. There are editions by Wecklein and Schmidt.

§ 179. We now arrive at the *Oresteia*, the three plays on the fortunes of the house of Atreus, which were Æschylus' last and greatest work. These plays, the *Agamemnon, Choephori*, and *Eumenides*, are the only extant specimen of a trilogy, and are inestimable in showing us the way in which the older tragic poets combined three plays on a single subject. But unfortunately our single specimen is quite insufficient to afford us materials for an established theory.

The first of the series, the *Agamemnon*, is the longest and the greatest play left us by Æschylus, and, in my opinion, the greatest of the Greek tragedies we know. There is still no complication in the plot; the scenes follow one another in simple and natural order; but the splendid and consistent drawing of the characters, the deep philosophy of the choral songs, and the general grandeur and gloom which pervade the whole piece, raise it above all that his successors were able to achieve. The central point of interest is the matchless scene between Cassandra and the chorus—a scene which drew even from the writer of the dry didascaliæ an expression of the universal admiration it produced. The play opens with a night view of the palace at Argos, from the roof of which a watchman, in a most picturesque prologue of a homely type, details the long weariness of his watch, and betrays in vague hints the secret sores that fester within the house. But his soliloquy is broken by a shout at the sudden flashing out of the long-expected beacon-light that heralded the fall of Troy. Then follows a long and difficult chorus which reviews all the course of the Trojan war, the omen of the eagles, the prophecies of Calchas, and the sacrifice of Iphigeneia. The hymn marches on in its course, each member closing with the solemn refrain αἴλινον

αἴλινον εἰπέ, τὸ δ' εὖ νικάτω. The moral views of God and of his Providence are very pure and great, and remind us of the passages above quoted from the *Supplices*.[1]

It is not necessary to follow step by step the plot of a play so easily read in good translations. The character of Clytemnestra is boldly and finely drawn. She is evidently the master spirit of the palace, and seems stronger, not only than Ægisthus, but than Agamemnon, who does not awake in us much interest. Cassandra is of course a character of situation, but is remarkable as the pure creation of the poet, and not suggested by the old forms of the myth. Her prophetic frenzy, her attempts to speak plainly to the sympathetic chorus, her ultimate clearness, and noble despair as she casts away the fillets of the god and enters the house of her doom—all combine to form a scene without parallel in the Greek drama, and which has never been approached by the highest effort of either Sophocles or Euripides. But the play not only stands out alone for dramatic greatness; it abounds everywhere in picturesqueness—in picturesqueness of descrip-

[1] Ζεύς, ὅστις ποτ' ἐστίν, εἰ τόδ' αὐτῷ φίλον κεκλημένῳ,
τοῦτό νιν προσεννέπω.
οὐκ ἔχω προσεικάσαι,
πάντ' ἐπισταθμώμενος,
πλὴν Διός, εἰ τὸ μάταν ἀπὸ φροντίδος ἄχθος
χρὴ βαλεῖν ἐτητύμως.
οὐδ' ὅστις πάροιθεν ἦν μέγας,
παμμάχῳ θράσει βρύων,
οὐδὲν ἂν λέξαι πρὶν ὤν,
ὃς δ' ἔπειτ' ἔφυ, τρια-
κτῆρος οἴχεται τυχών.
Ζῆνα δέ τις προφρόνως ἐπινίκια κλάζων
τεύξεται φρενῶν τὸ πᾶν·
τὸν φρονεῖν βροτοὺς ὁδώ-
σαντα, τὸν πάθει μάθος
θέντα κυρίως ἔχειν.
στάζει δ' ἔν θ' ὕπνῳ πρὸ καρδίας
μνησιπήμων πόνος· καὶ παρ' ἀ-
κοντας ἦλθε σωφρονεῖν.
δαιμόνων δέ που χάρις,
βιαίως σέλμα σεμνὸν ἡμένων.

tion, as in the speeches of the watchman and the herald Talthybius; in picturesqueness of lyric utterance, as in the famous chorus on the flight of Helen, and the anguish of the deserted Menelaus.[1] Most striking also is the picture of the treacherous beauty under the image of a lion's whelp, brought up and petted in the house, and suddenly turning to its native fierceness.[2]

[1]
ἄγουσά τ' ἀντίφερνον Ἰλίῳ φθοράν,
βέβακεν ῥίμφα διὰ πυλᾶν,
ἄτλατα τλᾶσα· πολλὰ δ' ἔστενον
τόδ' ἐννέποντες δόμων προφῆται·
ἰὼ ἰὼ δῶμα δῶμα καὶ πρόμοι,
ἰὼ λέχος καὶ στίβοι φιλάνορες.
πάρεστι σιγᾶσ', ἄτιμος, ἀλοίδορος,
ἄδιστος ἀφεμένων ἰδεῖν.
πόθῳ δ' ὑπερποντίας
φάσμα δόξει δόμων ἀνάσσειν.
εὐμόρφων δὲ κολοσσῶν
ἔχθεται χάρις ἀνδρί.
ὀμμάτων δ' ἐν ἀχηνίαις ἔρρει πᾶσ' Ἀφροδίτα.
ὀνειρόφαντοι δὲ πενθήμονες
πάρεισιν δοκαὶ φέρουσαι χάριν ματαίαν.
μάταν γὰρ, εὖτ' ἂν ἐσθλά τις δοκῶν ὁρᾷ,
παραλλάξασα διὰ χερῶν
βέβακεν ὄψις οὐ μεθύστερον
πτεροῖς ὀπαδοῦσ' ὕπνου κελεύθοις.
τὰ μὲν κατ' οἴκους ἐφ' ἑστίας ἄχη
τάδ' ἐστὶ καὶ τῶνδ' ὑπερβατώτερα.
τὸ πᾶν δ' ἀφ' Ἑλλάδος αἴας συνορμένοις
πένθεια τλησικάρδιος
δόμων ἑκάστου πρέπει.
πολλὰ γοῦν θιγγάνει πρὸς ἧπαρ·
οὓς μὲν γάρ τις ἔπεμψεν
οἶδεν· ἀντὶ δὲ φωτῶν
τεύχη καὶ σποδὸς εἰς ἑκάστου δόμους ἀφικνεῖται.
ὁ χρυσαμοιβὸς δ' Ἄρης σωμάτων
καὶ ταλαντοῦχος ἐν μάχῃ δορὸς
πυρωθὲν ἐξ Ἰλίου
φίλοισι πέμπει βαρὺ
ψῆγμα δυσδάκρυτον ἀν-
τήνορος σποδοῦ γεμί-
ζων λέβητας εὐθέτους.

[2] vv. 735, sq.

There is one passage which has excited much criticism concerning the chorus. When the voice of Agamemnon is heard
within, crying that he is fatally wounded, there seems to be a
regular deliberation of the chorus, each member offering his
opinion, and summed up by the leader at the end of twenty-
five lines. This delay seems very absurd, except we have recourse to the natural solution, that the various members of the
chorus were made to speak *simultaneously,* so producing a confused sound of agitated voices, which is precisely what is most
dramatic at such a moment. It is well known to actors now
that this confused talking of a crowd is only to be produced
by making each person on the stage say something definite
at the same moment ; and I believe Æschylus to have here
used this expedient. Why has this natural explanation occurred to no critic? It is remarkable how the chorus, who
even after the murder treat Clytemnestra with respect, and
only bewail before her their lost king in bitter grief, start up
into ungovernable rage when the craven Ægisthus appears to
boast of his success. They will not endure from him one word
of direction ; and so the play ends with the entreaty of the over-
wrought queen to avoid further violence on this awful day.

The *Agamemnon* suggested the subject of plays to Sophocles
and to Ion among the Greeks, and gave rise to various imitations among the early Roman tragedians, as well as by Seneca.
In modern days, after a series of obscure attempts among the
French of the sixteenth and seventeenth centuries, it was imitated
(in 1738) by Thompson, in a play which was translated and
produced with success in France. It was also imitated by
Alfieri (1783), and then in 1796 by Lemercier in a somewhat
famous version. But all these modern Agamemnons differ
from that of Æschylus in introducing the two main innovations of modern tragedy—an interesting plot or intrigue, and a
careful and conscious painting of human passions. The great
original appeals to far loftier interests. Thus Alfieri altogether disregards and omits the splendid part of Cassandra,
both from his extreme love of simplicity, and in order that he may
find room for painting what Æschylus assumes as long since
determined—the struggle in Clytemnestra's mind between
passion, duty, vengeance, and honour. This development of the

mental conflicts in Clytemnestra is reproduced by Lemercier, who has, however, not made the error of omitting Cassandra. But the Clytemnestra of Æschylus has been for years tutored by her criminal passion. Her struggles with duty have long ceased, and her resolve is fixed. This is no mistake is psychology, no passive adherence (as M. Villemain thinks) to the received legend, but a well-known mental state in a degraded woman.

Among English translations I may specially notice the elegant but not accurate one of the late Dean Milman, in a volume already often cited on the lyric poets. Mr. Fitzgerald, the well-known translator of *Omar Khayyam*, has given us a fine, but free and modified version of the play in his ' Agamemnon, a tragedy taken from the Greek,' most of which, and the best parts of which, are literal translations. So have Conington, Professor Kennedy, Mr. Morshead, and Miss Swanwick; the last also published in a magnificent edition with Flaxman's illustrations. Lastly, Mr. Robert Browning has given us an over-faithful version from his matchless hand—matchless, I conceive, in conveying the deeper spirit of the Greek poets. But in this instance he has outdone his original in ruggedness, owing to his excess of conscience as a translator.

§ 180. The *Choephori*, so called from the chorus carrying vessels with formal offerings for Agamemnon, which follows, is unfortunately very corrupt, and even mutilated at its opening in our MSS. This, as well as the intrinsic sombreness and gloomy vagueness of the play, makes it probably the most difficult of our tragedies in its detail. But the main outline is very simple and massive. The scene discloses the royal portal, and close to it the tomb of Agamemnon. The proximity of the tomb to the palace seems merely determined by stage reasons, and does not rest in any sense upon a tradition that Agamemnon was buried in his citadel, as might be inferred from Dr. Schliemann's conjectures. Indeed, the whole tradition of Agamemnon's being buried at Mycenæ seems unknown to Æschylus, who ignores Diomede, and makes the seat of the great empire of the Atreidæ at Argos.

Orestes [1] in the opening scene declares his return to Argos to

[1] In a passage criticised for its redundant language by Aristophanes in the *Frogs.*

avenge the murder of his father, but he and Pylades stand aside
when the chorus of female domestics (probably Trojans) come
out in solemn procession to offer libations to the dead.   Here
Orestes sees and recognises Electra, who discusses with the
chorus how she is to perform the commands of Clytemnestra,
lately terrified by an ominous dream.   They then find the lock of
hair offered at the tomb by Orestes, and his foot-tracks, by which
Electra is at once convinced of his return.   It is evident that
Æschylus laid no stress on the recognition scene, and that any
marks sufficed for his purpose.   But he has naturally not
escaped the censure of Euripides, who ridicules this scene
in the parallel passage of his *Electra*.   When Orestes discovers
himself, there follows a splendid dialogue and chorus, I had
almost said duet and chorus, in which the children of Agamemnon and their friends pray for help and favour in their vengeance.
This scene occupies a large part of the play.   At its close
Orestes tells his plan of coming as a Phocian stranger and announcing his own death, so as to disarm suspicion, and thus
obtaining access to the palace.   Here we see the first dawning
of a *plot*, or of that complex tragedy which soon supplanted the
simpler form.   The chorus, who in this play are strictly not only
· the confidants but accomplices of the royal children, aid in the
deception, and when Orestes has been invited within by Clytemnestra, persuade the nurse, who is sent for Ægisthus, to disobey
her instructions, and desire him to come alone.   This character
(Kilissa), with her homely lament over Orestes, and her memories
of the vulgar troubles of the nursery, gives great relief to the
uniform gloom of the play, and, in her coarsely expressed
real grief, contrasts well with the stately but affected lamentation
of the queen.[1]   After Ægisthus has passed in, and his death-
cry has been heard, comes the magnificent scene in which Clytemnestra, suddenly acquainted with the disaster, calls for her
double-axe, but is instantly confronted by her son, and sees herself doomed to die.   There is here not an idle word, not a
touch of surprise or inquiry.   She sees and recognises all in a

---

[1] Sophocles seems to have produced a similar character in his *Niobe*,
cf. fr. 400 ; and this nurse was translated into marble in the famous Niobe
group, of which we see a Roman copy at Florence.

moment. An instant of weakness, the protest of Pylades, a short, hurried dialogue between mother and son, and she is brought in to be slain beside her paramour. The scene is then rolled back, and shows Orestes standing over the dead, but already stricken in conscience, and terrified at the dread Furies with which his mother had threatened him. With his flight the play concludes.

So great a subject could not but find imitators. Yet Sophocles and Euripides took quite a different course, as the very title of their plays indicates. Their *Electras* bring into the foreground the sorrows and hopes of the princess, who was doomed by her unnatural mother to long servitude and disgrace, and was sick at heart with hope deferred of her brother's return. Her despair at the announcement of his death, the ill-disguised mental relief of Clytemnestra, the sudden return of Electra's hope, the recognition of Orestes—these have afforded to Sophocles one of his most splendid, and to Euripides a very affecting tragedy. But a far more interesting analogy is suggested by the unconscious parallel of Shakspeare, whose *Hamlet,* dealing with the very same moral problem, gathers into one the parts of Electra and of Orestes, and represents not only the vengeance of the murdered king's son, but the long mental doubts and conflicts of the avenger, living in the palace, and within sight of his adulterous mother and her paramour. Shakespeare has made the queen-mother a weaker, and far less guilty character, and therefore has consistently recoiled from the dreadful crisis of matricide.[1] With him the uncertainty of evidence, in Hamlet, takes the place of the uncertainty of hope, in Electra, whether her brother would indeed return. Instead of the oracles that urge Orestes, and the ever-present tomb of Agamemnon, he employs the apparition of the king in person. These, and other kindred features, make *Hamlet* a very curious and instructive parallel to the *Chocphori,* the more curious because accidental. But, like all moderns (even including the later Greeks), Shakespeare has turned from the discussion of great world-problems to personal and psychological

[1] There is also, of course, the influence of Christianity in its repugnance to bloodshed, a repugnance which the Greek poet would not feel.

interests, and therefore his magnificent play wants the colossal
grandeur and the mystic gloom of the less developed, less
elaborated, but greater conception of Æschylus.

§ 181. The *Eumenides* forms a fitting conclusion to the
trilogy. It is a play remarkable for many curious features. First,
we may notice the quick changes of scene, which violate the
ordinary niceties of time and place. We have the rocky fane
at Delphi, and its surroundings, in the opening scene, then the
inside of the temple, with the sleeping Furies camped about the
suppliant; then again the Acropolis of Athens, and then,
apparently, the neighbouring Areopagus. The extraordinary
character of the chorus is also to be noted. They are not only
the chief actors in the play, but in hostility to the other players
and representing a separate principle. Their terrible appearance, their awful attributes, and the dread incantations
whereby they seek to charm their victim, so impressed the
ancients, that all manner of anecdotes are current as to the
effect they produced. The refrain of their song is very
striking.[1]

[1] ἐπὶ δὲ τῷ τεθυμένῳ
τόδε μέλος, παρακοπά,
παραφορὰ φρενοδαλής,
ὕμνος ἐξ Ἐρινύων,
δέσμιος φρενῶν, ἀφόρ-
μικτος, αὐονὰ βροτοῖς.

τοῦτο γὰρ λάχος διανταία
μοῖρ᾽ ἐπέκλωσεν ἐμπέδως ἔχειν,
θνατῶν τοῖσιν αὐτουργίαι ξυμπέσωσιν μάταιοι,
τοῖς ὁμαρτεῖν, ὄφρ᾽ ἂν γᾶν ὑπέλθῃ· θανὼν δ᾽
οὐκ ἄγαν ἐλεύθερος.

ἐπὶ δὲ τῷ τεθυμένῳ
τόδε μέλος, παρακοπά,
παραφορὰ φρενοδαλής,
ὕμνος ἐξ Ἐρινύων,
δέσμιος φρενῶν, ἀφόρ-
μικτος, αὐονὰ βροτοῖς.

γιγνομέναισι λάχη τάδ᾽ ἐφ᾽ ἁμὶν ἐκράνθη·
ἀθανάτων δ᾽ ἀπέχειν χέρας, οὐδέ τις ἐστὶ
συνδαίτωρ μετάκοινος.
παλλεύκων δὲ πέπλων

The whole play, though revolving round Orestes' deed, and though calling in at its close a jury of Athenian citizens, is, like the *Prometheus*, a conflict of gods and of great world principles, in which mortals seem hardly worthy to take part. Yet the play also gives us the first specimen of that love of trial scenes which runs through all the later drama. The Athenians were, as we know, peculiarly addicted to this duty, and became, indeed, a whole nation of jurymen. But in the present case Æschylus was promoting another object, and one which, in the hands of a lesser genius, might have spoilt his artistic work. He wished to show the august origin and solemn purpose of the Court of the Areopagus, which was at that very time being attacked by Ephialtes and Pericles. It should also be observed that this trilogy, unlike that on Œdipus, ends with a peaceful result, and with the solemn settlement of the Furies, under the title of *Eumenides*, in their sacred retreat beneath the rock of the Areopagus. The weary curse which had persecuted the house of Atreus thus becomes exhausted, and Orestes returns purified and justified to his ancestral kingdom.

Though it is deeply to be regretted that no other specimen of a trilogy has survived, it is more than probable that never again was such perfection attained, either in individual plays or in their artistic combination. We have the last and greatest outcome of Æschylus' genius, and Sophocles had already set the example of contending with separate plays. It is, I confess, somewhat shocking to think that a satyric drama, the *Proteus*, was performed after this complete and satisfying series. From the stray fragments of our poet's satyric muse which remain (especially from the ὀστολόγοι), we know that a good deal of coarse jesting was permitted and beast nature introduced in these merry afterludes ; and we cannot but fancy

> ἄμοιρος, ἄκληρος ἐτύχθην.
> δωμάτων γὰρ εἱλόμαν
> ἀνατροπάς, ὅταν Ἄρης
> τιθασὸς ὢν φίλον ἕλῃ.
> ἐπὶ τόν, ὦ, διόμεναι
> κρατερὸν ὄνθ᾽, ὁμοίως
> μαυροῦμεν ὑφ᾽ αἵματος νέου.

that the great effect of the trilogy must have been considerably effaced by such an appendix.

§ 182. The *fragments* of Æschylus, though many, are not interesting dramatically, as they seldom give us an insight into the structure of a lost piece, or even poetically, for he was not a poet who strewed his canvas with lyric flowers or sententious aphorisms, like his successors. He was essentially a tragedian, and every word in his play was meant for its purpose, and for its purpose only. He consequently afforded little scope for collectors of beautiful lines of general application. On mythical questions he is often quoted, and is a most important authority; likewise on geographical questions, for which he had a special fancy, as appears very plainly from his extant plays. He lived at the very time when the Milesian school of Hecatæus had stimulated a taste for these studies, and when the Greeks were beginning to interest themselves about foreign lands. The play which seems to me our greatest loss is the *Myrmidons*, in which the subject was the death of Patroclus, and therefore taken directly from the Iliad, but modernised in a remarkable way by the warmer colouring given to the affection subsisting between Achilles and his friend. It would indeed have been interesting to see more fully the treatment of such a subject by such a poet. The *Ransom of Hector* was also taken from the Iliad, but several other plays on the Trojan cycle were drawn from the events preceding and following the Anger of Achilles.

§ 183. The intelligent student, who has read for himself the extant plays of Æschylus, will form a better judgment of his genius than can be suggested by any general remarks in a sketch like the present. What I here offer by way of reflection is rather meant to guard against false theories and mistaken estimates, than to supply any substitute for the student's own knowledge of so capital a figure in Greek Literature. A comparison with Pindar and Simonides shows how great an advance he made, and how independently he approached the great moral problems which the Greek poets—the established clergy of the day—were obliged to expound. Æschylus was, indeed, essentially a theologian, meaning by that term not merely a man who is deeply interested in religious things, but a man who makes the difficulties and obscurities of morals and of creeds his intellectual study.   But, what is more honourable and exceptional, he was so candid and honest a theologian, that he did not approach men's difficulties for the purpose of refuting them, or showing them weak and groundless.   On the contrary, though an orthodox and pious man, though clearly convinced of the goodness of Providence and of the profound truth of the religion of his fathers, he was ever stating boldly the contradictions and anomalies in morals and in myths, and thus naturally incurring the odium and suspicion of the professional advocates of religion and their followers. He felt, perhaps instinctively, that a vivid dramatic statement of these problems in his tragedies was better moral education than vapid platitudes about our ignorance, and about our difficulties being only caused by the shortness of our sight.   He knew the strength of human will, the dignity of human liberty, the greatness of human self-sacrifice, and yet he will not abate aught from the omnipotence of Providence, the iron constraint of a gloomy fate, the bondage of ancestral guilt.   It is quite plain that the thought of his day was influenced by two dark undercurrents, both of which must have touched him—the Orphic mysteries, with their secret rites of sanctification, their dogmas of personal purity and future bliss; and, on the other hand, the Ionic philosophy, which in the hands of Heracleitus had not shunned obscurity and vagueness, but had shown enigmas in all the ordinary phenomena of human life.   These influences conspired with the strong unalterable genius of the poet, and produced results quite unique in the history of Literature.   For it is evidently absurd to attribute the massiveness and apparent uncouthness of Æschylus, as Schlegel does, to the conditions of nascent tragedy.   Phrynichus, his contemporary, was famed for opposite qualities, for gentle sweetness and lyric grace.   At no epoch could Æschylus have been softened down into a conventional artist.   Many critics speak of him as almost Oriental in some respects—in his bold metaphor, in his wild and irregular imaginings; and yet he is censured by Aristophanes for too much theatrical craft.   I suppose the former mean to compare him with the greatest of the Hebrew prophets; nor does the comparison seem unjust, if we confine it to this, that both found strange and striking images to rouse their hearers' imagination, and that neither felt bound by the logic of ordinary reasoning. In this matter Heracleitus and Æschylus are the masters of bold and suggestive inconsequence. But the obscurity of both was that of condensation—a pregnant obscurity, as contrasted with the redundant obscurity of some modern poets, or the artificial obscurity of the Attic epoch. His philosophy is in the spirit, and not in the diction of his works—in vast conceptions, not in laconic maxims. Both Sophocles (as he himself confesses) and Thucydides, the highest types of the Periclean epoch, are often obscure, but, as I said, are so artificially, not from endeavouring to suggest great half-grasped thoughts, but from a desire to play at hide-and-seek with the reader, and surprise him by cleverness of expression. We always feel that Æschylus thought more than he expressed, that his desperate compounds are never affected or unnecessary. Although, therefore, he violated the rules which bound weaker men, it is false to say that he was less an artist than they. His art was of a different kind, despising what they prized, and attempting what they did not dare, but not the less a conscious and thorough art. Though the drawing of character was not his main object, his characters are truer and deeper than those of poets who attempted nothing else. Though lyrical sweetness had little place in the gloom and terror of his Titanic stage, yet here too, when he chooses, he equals the masters of lyric song. So long as a single Homer was deemed the author of the Iliad and the Odyssey, we might well concede to him the first place, and say that Æschylus was the second poet of the Greeks. But by the light of nearer criticism, and with a closer insight into the structure of the epic poems, we must retract this judgment, and assert that no other poet among the Greeks, either in grandeur of conception, or splendour of execution, equals the untranslateable, unapproachable, inimitable Æschylus.[1]

§ 184. *Bibliographical.* Turning to the question of Æs-

---

[1] Aischulos' bronze-throat eagle-bark at blood
Has somehow spoilt my taste for twitterings !
R. BROWNING, *Arist. Ap.* p. 94.

T 2

chylean literature, we find the whole criticism of our texts to depend on one MS. of the tenth century, the celebrated *Plut.* xxxii. 9, of the Laurentian library at Florence, which contains, with Sophocles and Apollonius Rhodius, the seven plays written out in a beautifully neat hand with very slight, somewhat slanting characters ; it has numerous scholia, but is unfortunately mutilated through most of the *Agamemnon* and opening of the *Choephori.* From copies of the thirteenth and fourteenth centuries, at Florence, Venice, and Naples, these defects, and some gaps in the scholia, have been partially remedied. The scholia seem to be more Byzantine than Alexandrian, and it does not appear that, with the exception of the arguments prefixed by Aristophanes, much attention was paid to the poet by the great critics. Indeed, the same thing may be said of both Roman and French imitators. While they understood and copied Sophocles and Euripides, Æschylus was neglected as an uncouth and rude forerunner of the real drama. We must acknowledge this much merit in Schlegel, that he led dramatic criticism into a sounder and deeper course. The *Prometheus, Persæ,* and *Septem,* which stand first in the MSS., were very much more read than the rest, and are far better preserved. The *editio princeps* of the text was that of Aldus (1518); that of Robortellus (Venice, 1552) first gave the scholia. The whole *Agamemnon* appears in Victorius', and in the ed. Steph. 1557. Good early critics were Dorat, Canter, Stanley. Porson turned his critical acumen to bear upon the text in the Glasgow edition of 1794, and then followed the editions of Butler, of five plays by Blomfield, and of Peile. In the present day the editions best worth studying are those of God. Hermann, W. Dindorf, and H. Weil for criticism, Merkel's careful ed. of the Florentine MS., that of Mr. Davies on the *Agamemnon* and *Choephori,* and those of Kock, Gilbert (and Enger, 1874), Prof. Kennedy (1878), and Mr. Sidgwick (1881), on the *Agamemnon.* Mr. F. A. Paley has also supplied us with an excellent handy edition, the most serviceable for ordinary use. It is the result of long study spent on separate editions of the plays. Wellauer and Linwood have composed Æschylean lexicons which are useful, but even the latter (1848) now somewhat antiquated. The

German translations are endless.   Those of Voss, Droysen, and Donner may specially be named.[1]   The French have rather imitated than reproduced, if we except the versions of Du Theil and Brumoy.   In English we have the respectable version of Potter, the *Agamemnons* of Prof. Blackie (1850), Symmons, those already mentioned above (p. 268), Mr. J. F. Davies', and very spirited versions of select passages by Lord Lytton in his *Rise and Fall of Athens.*   I call special attention to the very able criticism accompanying these translations.   Mrs. Browning has given us an admirable *Prometheus*, and lastly, Mr. Browning has turned his genius for reproducing Greek plays upon this masterpiece, and has given a version which will probably not permit the rest to maintain their well-earned fame, though it is in itself so difficult that the Greek original is often required for translating his English.   I confess that even with this aid, which shows the extraordinary faithfulness of the work, I had preferred a more Anglicised version from his master hand.

The truest and deepest imitation of the spirit of Æschylus in modern times is not to be sought in the stiff formalism of Racine or Alfieri, but in the splendid *Atalanta in Calydon* of Mr. Swinburne, whose antitheism brings him to stand in an attitude between human freewill and effort on the one side, and ruthless tyranny of Providence on the other, not approached in poetry (so far as I know) from Æschylus' day down to our own.   Unfortunately, the very poetical odes of his chorus are diffuse, and written with all that luxuriance of rich sound which in Mr. Swinburne often dilutes or hides the depth and clearness of his thought.   The English reader must therefore by no means regard this part of the play as modelled upon Æschylus, nor as at all representing his poetry.   It is in the plot, and in the nervous compressed *stichomuthia*, or dialogue in alternate lines, and in the gloomy darkness which broods over the action, that the modern poet has caught the spirit of his great predecessor.   Since the *Samson Agonistes* of Milton, we have

---

[1] Full information on all the German versions of the *Oresteia*, from Von Halem (1785) to Donner (1854), will be found in an article by Eichhoff in the *Neue Jahrbücher für Philologie*, vol. cxv.

had no such reproduction of the Greek drama, and those who are not in sympathy with Mr. Swinburne's other poems should not fail to turn to this exceptional work, which he has never since equalled. The *Prometheus Unbound* of Shelley, as he himself tells us very plainly, is hardly intended as an imitation of Æschylus, but as an original and wholly independent work.

Before passing on, let me direct attention to the very ingenious and suggestive, but little cited *Prolegomena* to Æschylus by R. Westphal (Leipzig, 1869), a very high authority on the musical side of Greek poetry. He shows the strict adherence to fixed forms in the poet, and even considers the *Prometheus*, from its remarkable variations in this respect, to be a much interpolated and deformed piece. It was Æschylus' habit to construct his piece with *four* choric songs, and one *commos* or lament, replaced by a processional hymn, if the plot did not admit of the *threnos*. Westphal examines carefully the structure of these choral pieces, and starting from the taunt of Euripides in Aristoph. *Frogs*, 1281, shows that the old Terpandrian nome, expanding from a centre (ὀμφαλός) into pairs of parallel members, was the real model of the poet, so that the strophic form does not give us the key to the sense. Thus there is always an ἀρχά, ὀμφαλός, and σφραγίς; there may be two transition members (κατατροπά and μετακιτατροπά) joining them; there may be further a proem and epilogue. On this model Westphal analyses all the choral odes in the plays.

The commic or processional odes, with which the plays usually conclude, are framed upon a totally different model, that of the aulodic *Threnos*, which was always amœbean, and is divided between actors and chorus, or between sections of the chorus. The effect seems here to have been chiefly musical, as the text has little meaning, and consists in responsive utterances of woe, each side taking its clue from the other. In the *Septem* and *Persæ* this musical performance was not given to the chief actor. The whole theory is most ingenious, and his rearrangement of the amœbean strains convincing; but why did Æschylus preserve the *strophic* form, if the *nomic* form was the real basis of his choral odes? This difficulty still remains unanswered. The application of this theory to Pindar's odes is mentioned in my Preface.

CHAPTER XVI.

SOPHOCLES.

§ 185. THERE is even less told us about the life of Sophocles than about that of Æschylus, and, indeed, there seems to have been little that was eventful to be told. He was too young to take part in the great struggle of the Persian war, and his campaign to Samos, in middle life, was evidently no serious warfare. He refused, we are told, to leave Athens, which he loved, at the invitation of foreign cities and princes, and thus avoided the adventures of travelling which were fatal to both his rivals ; and though he took part in politics on the oligarchical side, as he was perhaps a *Probulus* when the four hundred were established, he seems never to have been a strong or leading politician. His gentleness, and beauty, and placid disposition seem to have saved him from most of the buffets and trials of the world ; and he is, perhaps, the only distinguished Athenian now known who lived and died without a single enemy.

He was born in the deme Colonus, within half an hour's walk of Athens, in the scenery which he describes in his famous chorus of the second Œdipus, and which has hardly altered up to the present day, amid all the sad changes which have seamed and scarred the fair features of Attica. I know not, indeed, why he calls it the *white* (ἀργῆτα) Colonus, for it was then, as now, hidden in deep and continuous green. The dark ivy and the golden crocus, the white poplar and the grey olive, are still there. The silvery Cephissus still feeds the pleasant rills, with which the husbandman waters his thickly wooded cornfields ; and in the deep shade the nightingales have not yet ceased their plaintive melody.

His father's name was Sophillus, and the scholiasts wrangle about the dignity of his position in life ; though he seems to have been no more than a man of middle rank, making his

income by practising or directing a trade.   Concerning his
mother and brethren there is absolute silence.   Born about
496–5 B.C., he was chosen, for his beauty and grace, to lead
the solemn dance in honour of the victory at Salamis.   He
was educated by Lampros, a rival of Pindar and of Pratinas,
as a scientific musician ; and this special training in *music*
enabled him, in spite of his weak speaking voice, to act with
great success the parts of Thamyras and of Nausicaa, in the
plays which he wrote concerning these personages.   In 468
he came forward as a tragic poet, and at the age of 28, with his
first piece, defeated the great Æschylus, who had been for a
generation the master of the tragic stage.   What made the
victory more remarkable was the selection of Kimon and his
victorious colleagues as judges, instead of the ordinary proce-
dure by lot.   From this date till his death, at the age of
90, the poet devoted all his energy to the production of those
famous works of art, which gave him such a hold over the
Athenian public, that he came to be considered the very ideal
of a tragic poet, and was worshipped after his death as a hero,
under the title *Dexion* (Δεξίων.)   He is said to have won
eighteen or twenty tragic victories, and though sometimes postponed to Philocles and others, was never placed third in all his
life.   The author of the *Poetic* and the Alexandrian critics
follow the judgment of the Attic public, and most modern critics
have agreed with them that the tragedies of Sophocles are the
most perfect that the world has ever seen.   It is, indeed, no
unusual practice to exhibit the defects of both Æschylus and
Euripides by comparison with their more successful rival.

The Athenian public were so delighted with his *Antigone*
that they appointed him one of the ten generals, along with
Pericles, for the subduing of Samos ; as regards which Pericles
is said to have told him that he knew how to compose well
enough, but not how to command.   It is conjectured that on
this expedition he met and knew Herodotus, by whom several
passages in his plays, and one in the fragments,[1] seem suggested.

---

[1] Fr. 380, about Palamedes' invention of games, like the Lydians' invention in Herod. i. 94.   This coincidence has not yet, I think, been
noticed.   So also the famous chorus in *O. C.* 1211, sq., seems copied

If the passage of the *Antigone* (which many critics declare spurious) be genuine, it was composed before the poet went to Samos ; and the conjecture here breaks down.   Yet I have personally no doubt that Herodotus, who lived much at Athens, suggested these passages ; and I am not disposed to admit that any of them is spurious, though they may belong to second editions of their respective plays.   He was (in 443 B.C.) one of the *Hellenotamiæ*, or administrators of the public treasury—a most responsible and important post.   He sided with the oligarchy in 411, if he be the *Probulus* then mentioned.   When Aristophanes brought out his *Frogs* in 405 B.C., the poet was but lately dead, and, amid the conflict of schools of poetry, is acknowledged the genial favourite of all ;[1] the comic Phrynichus, in his *Muses*, of the same date, spoke of him in very similar terms.   A splendid portrait statue of him, found a few years ago at Ostia, and now in the Lateran at Rome, is doubtless a copy of that set up in the theatre at Athens by Lycurgus, and represents him as worthy in dignity and beauty of all the praises bestowed upon him.   The various anecdotes which bear upon his character, and which seem to be partly, at least, drawn from the high authority of the memoirs of the contemporary Ion of Chios,[2] all speak in the same tone, and describe him as of easy temper, and much given to the pleasures of love.   He is even contrasted with Euripides in the more Greek complexion of his passion.   Most of his German panegyrists are unable to refute the jibe of Aristophanes,[3] that in his old days he turned miser, and worked for money like a second Simonides, but are indignant at the report that he became attached, late in life, to a courtesan named Theoris, of Sikyon.   He is, moreover, quoted in the first book of Plato's *Republic*, speaking of Eros as a fierce tyrant, from whose bonds he had escaped by advancing years. But this probably alludes to the passions formed in the palæstra, of which other dialogues of Plato tell us a great deal.   He is

from Artabanus' speech, Herod vii. 46.   The attack on Egyptian manners in the same play (vv. 337, sq.) is a still clearer case, perhaps also *O. T.* 981.   Lastly, we have *Antig.* vv. 909, sq.   Cf. vol. ii. p. 19.

[1]   εὔκυλος μὲν ἐνθάδ', εὔκυλος δ' ἐκεῖ.

[2] Cf. fr. 1 of *Ion* in Müller's *FHG.*   [3] *Pax*, 698.

said to have had a second family by this Theoris. All the Alexandrian authorities believed that his legitimate son was Iophon, son of his wife Nikostrate, but that of Theoris was born Ariston, who was father of the younger Sophocles. But·the testimony of inscriptions,[1] which speak of a Sophocles corresponding with the younger of that name, and even of an Iophon, son of (apparently this) Sophocles, makes it probable that the *Life* and scholiasts are wrong about the grandson. We have no more certain information about the more famous story of Iophon's attempt to take the old poet's property out of his hands by an action at law, and how he was defeated by the reading of the famous chorus in the *Œdipus at Colonus*, then just composed. Most critics now think that this play was not, like the *Philoctetes*, the product of Sophocles' old age, but of his mature life, though it seems not to have been brought out till after his death, probably by Iophon, with considerable interpolations. Aristophanes (in the *Frogs*) speaks of Iophon as a poet of uncertain promise, but still as the best of the *Epigoni*. Other stories, about the respect shown him by the besieging Spartans, when he died, and how his friends were allowed to bury him eleven stadia on the way to Dekelea, may be read in the *Life*. It seems odd he should not have been laid in his home at Colonus, which is quite close to Athens, but possibly, with this modification, the anecdote may be true. He was commonly called the Honey Bee, and was said, as almost every other great Greek poet, to have been peculiarly imbued with Homeric thoughts and style. This vague statement is not verified by his extant plays, though he is said in others to have adapted the Odyssey repeatedly. Indeed, we may suspect, with Mr. Paley, that the Homer alluded to by these old critics includes the Cyclic epics, from which he certainly borrowed almost all his plots.

But there are other and more definite things reported concerning his style, his method, and his influence on the history of the drama. These we shall best consider when we have given a sketch of the extant plays and fragments. Of the

---

[1] See Dindorf's *Poetæ Trag.* p. 12, note. The younger Iophon would be called after his grandfather.

elegies, the pæans, the prose essay on the chorus,[1] the seventy tragedies, the eighteen satyric dramas, which the poet (after making due deductions) seems fairly to be credited with, there remain only seven tragedies, and of the 1,000 fragments, but few are of any length or importance. A great many of them are indeed only quoted (chiefly by Hesychius) for the sake of curious and rare words which the poet had employed— a remarkable feature in these fragments. Of the seven tragedies now extant only two can be dated, even approximately—the *Antigone*, which was brought out just before the expedition of Pericles to Samos (440 B.C.), and the *Philoctetes*, which may possibly be the last play he wrote, and which appeared in 409. Both these plays won the first prize, and if we cannot expect immaturity in the one, we cannot find decay in the other. But considering these, as we are bound, first and last, we are at liberty to arrange the rest in whatever order is most convenient for critical purposes.

§ 186. The *Antigone* was said to be Sophocles' thirty-second work, and must, from its date, have at all events been the work of his mature and ripe genius. It is, therefore, in every respect suitable to show us the contrasts with the old masterpieces, and the supposed improvements which mark the epoch of the perfect Greek drama. The play formed no member of a trilogy, but stood upon its own basis, nor are we at all justified, with some loose critics, in supplementing the character of the heroine from the other plays on the Theban legend (the two *Œdipuses*), plays written in after years, and without any intention of being viewed in connection with the *Antigone*. It is never to be forgotten that as soon as the tragic poets abandoned connected plays, they assumed the liberty of handling the same personage quite differently at different times, nor do they feel in the least bound by an earlier conception. This apparent inconsistency, which contrasts so strongly with the practice of modern dramatists, is due to the fact, that while the moderns have an unlimited field for the choice of subjects, and therefore naturally choose a new title to embody a new type, the Greeks were very limited in the

[1] This, which rests upon Suidas alone, is very doubtful.

legends which they treated, and must therefore constantly re-produce the same heroes and heroines. But they avoided the consequent monotony by the poetic license of varying the character to suit the special play. We must therefore study the characters in each play by themselves, and without re-ference to their recurrence in other works of the same poet.

The first point to be remarked in the play is the subordination of everything else to the character of Antigone. In Æschylus' conception—the deepest conception—of a tragedy, the actors were, so to speak, subordinated to the progress of a great moral conflict, which involves them in its mysterious course. They act with apparent liberty and force of character, but are really the exponents of great opposing agents, which they cannot stay or control. In the tragedy of Sophocles, where character-draw-ing (ἠθοποιΐα, as it was called) was the first object, the power of human will is the predominant feature, and the real conflict of moral and social forces is thrown into the background.

Æschylus, as has been already noted (p. 257), had blocked out the whole plot briefly at the end of his Theban trilogy, and indicated where a tragic conflict might be found. But when Sophocles takes up the subject, the firm determination of Antigone to perform the sacred duties of fraternal love is op-posed to no principle of parallel importance, to no law which commands any respect, but simply to the timid submissiveness of her foil, Ismene, to the arbitrary decree of a vulgar and heart-less tyrant, and to the cold and self-interested apathy of a mean and cowardly chorus. Antigone is accordingly sustained from the beginning by a clear consciousness that she is ab-solutely right, the whole sympathy of the spectator must go with her, and all the course of the play is merely interesting as bringing out her character in strong and constant relief. But as she consciously faces death *for an idea,* she may rather be en-rolled among the noble army of martyrs, who suffer in the day-light of clear conviction, than among the more deeply tried who in doubt and darkness have striven to feel out a great mystery, and in their very failure have ' purified the terror and the pity ' of awe-struck humanity. A martyr for a great and recog-nised truth is not the best central figure of a tragedy in the highest and proper sense. The *Antigone* is therefore not a very great *tragedy*, though it is a mcst brilliant and beautiful dramatic poem. The very opening scene brings out the somewhat hard and determined character of the heroine, in contrast to her weaker sister. As the chorus hints,[1] she had inherited this fierce nature from her father. But the fatal effects of the ancestral curse on the house of Œdipus, though often alluded to, are no moving force in the drama. The chorus appears in the *parodos* unconscious of the plot, and sings a beautiful ode on the delivery of Thebes, relevant enough to the general subject, but not bearing on the real interest of the play; and this remark may be applied to all the following choral odes, which with much lyric beauty celebrate subjects akin to the action, but outside it. The decree against Polynices' burial is then formally announced by Creon, when one of the watchmen enters, a very striking and well-conceived character, whose vulgar selfishness and low cowardice seem meant as the opposite extreme in human nature to the heroine. The homely and somewhat comic vein in which he speaks may indeed be shocking to dignified French imitators of classic suffering, but affords an interesting parallel to the contrasts so affectingly introduced in the greatest English tragedies. The reader will not have forgotten the nurse Kilissa in Æschylus' *Choephori.* Then follows the brilliant narrative of the capture of Antigone, and her interrogation by Creon. She here shows no vestige of fear or of quailing, and even Ismene braves death, though harshly checked and even insulted by her more masculine sister. The chorus suggests that Creon's son was betrothed to the princess, yet does not press the point, but upon her sentence sings the woes of the Labdakidæ, and the horrors of an ancestral taint. The appearance of Hæmon is a point of deep interest, and has been treated by

---

v. 471 : δηλοῖ τὸ γέννημ᾽ ὠμὸν ἐξ ὠμοῦ πατρὸς
τῆς παιδός· εἴκειν δ᾽ οὐκ ἐπίσταται κακοῖς.

I quote these words to justify myself against the able criticism of Mr. Evelyn Abbott on the parallel argument concerning Antigone in my *Social Life in Greece.* I cannot but sympathise deeply with his enthusiastic reading of the character in the *Journal of Philology*, vol. viii. pp. 1, sq.

the poet in a very peculiar way.   The young prince argues the
policy of Creon to be a mistaken public policy, and cites the
general murmuring of discontent against it, all the while concealing his own strong personal interest in Antigone.   Creon
and the chorus both see through the young man's mind, the one
by repeatedly taunting him as Antigone's advocate, the other,
upon his angry exit, singing a famous ode on the powers of
Eros, which is not directly suggested by the preceding dialogue.[1]

It seems likely that to the Athenian public of that day
any pleading of Hæmon's on the ground of love would be
thought unseemly and undignified, until Euripides had taught
them that even on the stage art must not ignore nature.   Still
more remarkable is the absence of any allusion to Hæmon
in the long commos sung by Antigone and the chorus, as she
passes across the stage, on the way to her tomb.   For she
complains bitterly of the loss of bridal song and nuptial bliss,
as every dying Greek maiden did, thus exactly reversing the
notions of modern delicacy.   A modern maiden would have
lamented the separation from her lover, but certainly not the
loss of the dignity and the joys of the married state.   The
commos of Antigone has been criticised from another point
of view, as unworthy of the brave and dauntless character
of the heroine.   It is thought unnatural that she who had
deliberately chosen death for the sake of duty, should shrink
and wail at its approach.   But sound critics have justly

---

[1] Ἔρως ἀνίκατε μάχαν,
Ἔρως, ὃς ἐν τ᾽ ἀνδράσι πίπτεις
ὃς ἐν μαλακαῖς παρειαῖς
νεάνιδος ἐννυχεύεις,
φοιτᾷς δ᾽ ὑπερπόντιος ἔν τ᾽ ἀγρονόμοις αὐλαῖς·
καί σ᾽ οὔτ᾽ ἀθανάτων φύξιμος οὐδεὶς
οὔθ᾽ ἁμερίων ἐπ᾽ ἀνθρώπων, ὁ δ᾽ ἔχων μέμηνεν.
σὺ καὶ δικαίων ἀδίκους
φρένας παρασπᾷς ἐπὶ λώβᾳ·
σὺ καὶ τόδε νεῖκος ἀνδρῶν
ξύναιμον ἔχεις ταράξας·
νικᾷ δ᾽ ἐναργὴς βλεφάρων ἵμερος εὐλέκτρου
νύμφας, τῶν μεγάλων οὐχὶ πάρεδρος
θεσμῶν. ἄμαχος γὰρ ἐμπαίζει θεὸς Ἀφροδίτα.

vindicated this as a human feature, though a weakness, and therefore more interesting and affecting than its absence or contradiction. In my opinion there is even yet a lack of humanity in the character, and I should be sorry to see this very interesting passage condemned. But I confess that the counter revulsion from quailing and fear to a bold facing of death, such as Euripides has painted it in his Iphigenia, appears to me not only nobler but more natural. For it is impossible to escape the suggestion in the *Antigone* that her bold defiance of Creon was ostentatious, and that it breaks down in the face of the awful reality.[1] I would further call attention to the remarkably unsympathetic and cold attitude of the chorus, who far from being ' ideal spectators,' or even ' accomplices,' look on with respectful but heartless tears, and offer such cold comfort to Antigone, that her complete isolation affects the spectator with the deepest pity. Nowhere (I think) does the chorus declare for the laws of religion and humanity against the arbitrary voice of the tyrant. The entrance of Teiresias marks the commencement of the περιπέτεια, or catastrophe, and his character is conceived, as in the *Œdipus Rex*, to be that of a noble and gloomy prophet. But the poet does not fail to put sceptical sneers in the mouths of his opponents. As soon as Teiresias has passed off with his threatening prophecy, the chorus in alarm warn Creon of his danger, and the tyrant is made to change his mind and pass from obstinacy to craven cowardice, with a suddenness only to be excused because this character excites no interest, and must have wearied us had its changes been treated in detail. The catastrophe of the deaths of Antigone and Hæmon, which reminds us of the end of *Romeo and Juliet*, is followed by that of Eurydice, the wife of Creon. The lamentations of the tyrant, which the spectator views rather with satisfaction than with pity, conclude the play.

[1] Yet I am not sure—and this is a great heresy—that Sophocles thought of more than the immediate situation when he composed this commos. I will show other instances by and bye, where he seems to have sacrificed consistency of character distinctly for the sake of dwelling upon an affecting situation, and writing affecting poetry. This is a vice generally attributed to Euripides. I think we can show it to exist no less in Sophocles ; cf. below, pp. 291, 310.

This is the drama which has not only struck ancient critics as one of the greatest works of its great author,[1] but which has fascinated modern taste more than any other remnant of Greek tragedy. This latter effect is easily understood, for in the first place the conflicting interests are easily comprehended, and involve no mystery, and secondly, the whole play turns on strictly human interests and actions, and is absolutely devoid of any interference of the gods, which must be foreign to the modern stage. The conflict of liberty against despotism became in fact the dominant idea of the last century, and thus men turned with interest to the old Greek expression of the same conflict. But long before this, the subject was treated by Euripides in a lost tragedy, in which the love of Hæmon and Antigone was not handled with the coldness and reserve of the Periclean age.[2] Then came a celebrated paraphrase or imitation by the Roman Attius, which is said to have suggested some points even to Vergil. The treatment of the story in Seneca's *Thebais,* a tragedy of which most is preserved, and in Statius' epic poem of the same title, is quite independent of Sophocles. Polynices' wife, Argia, shares Antigone's heroism, and neither expresses the least fear of death shown by the greater and more natural Antigone of the Greek poet. These inferior works were unfortunately the models of most of the French imitators. There was, however, an old French translation by Baïf, in 1573. Garnier in 1580, Rotrou in 1638, and d'Assezan in 1686 brought out *Antigones* based upon Sophocles and all the Roman versions of the story, with features added not only from Euripides' *Phœnissæ,* but from the weak sentimentality of the French stage. No antique subject was more certain to attract Alfieri, with his monomaniac hate of tyranny and tyrants. But his Antigone (1783), though a bold attempt to reintroduce sim-

---

[1] Strangely enough, there was an opinion abroad in old times that it was spurious, being really the work of Iophon, and not of Sophocles. I can hardly fancy this opinion existing without some definite evidence. We only have it in a passage published in Cramer's *Anecdota,* and without reasons.

[2] Cf. Euripides, frag. 157 sq., and the remarks of Aristophanes (the grammarian) in his preface to Sophocles' *Antigone.*

plicity into his subject, is evidently based upon the French travesties of the play, and of course the relations of Hæmon and Antigone come into the foreground. His play is forcible, but monotonous, as he fails in all those delicate touches, and various contrasts of character, in which Sophocles, with all his simplicity, abounds. Marmontel's libretto for Zingarelli's opera (1790) seems to have excited little attention. A prose version of the legend by Ballanche (1814) is apparently very popular and highly esteemed in France.

The taste of the present century has fortunately reverted to the pure art of Sophocles, and in 1844 a peculiar attempt was made, with the aid of Mendelssohn's noble music, to reproduce the Greek *Antigone* in a form approaching the original perform· ance. But, in my opinion, this revival is a complete failure, not only from the character of the music, which would have been to a modern audience intolerable, had it been Greek, but on account of the modern playing of the parts, in which a quantity of action was introduced quite foreign to the antique stage. Of the English versions that of Mr. Plumptre is not only the most recent, but the best.

§ 187. A certain general resemblance leads us to consider the *Electra* next in order. The relation of the heroine to her sister Chrysothemis is very similar to that of Antigone and Ismene. There is also the same hardness in both heroines, a hardness amounting to positive heartlessness in Electra, who, when she hears her brother within murdering his and her mother, actually calls out to him to strike her again (v. 1415). This revolting exclamation, and, indeed, the easy way in which matricide is regarded all through the play, contrasts strongly with the far deeper, more human, and more religious conception of Æschylus' *Choephori*, and reduces the *Electra* as a tragedy to a far lower level. In fact, here as elsewhere, Sophocles has sacrificed the tragedy for the sake of developing a leading character. He desires to fix the sympathy of the spectator on Electra and Orestes. He therefore treats the command of Apollo as an absolute justification of the crime, and puts out of sight the dread Eumenides, with their avenging horrors. This is distinctly the old epic view of the matter, more than once suggested in the Odyssey, in contrast to the conception of Stesichorus, and perhaps other lyric poets, with whom the notion of blood-guiltiness, and the necessity of purification for sin, became of primary importance, and who served as a model for Æschylus. Thus here also Sophocles was truly Homeric, but may be held to have made a retrograde step in the deeper history of morals. There are, moreover, many Euripidean features in the play. The angry wranglings of his characters, which occur often in Sophocles, are by most critics forgotten, when they come to censure his successor. There is also not a little inconsistency in the effusiveness of the heroine on re-cognising her brother, an effusiveness which amounts to folly, and her stern repression of words when Ægisthus desires to plead for his life. This inconsistency was admitted, I venture to think, on account of the seductive lyrical opportunity offered by the scene of recognition. The same weakness is still more obvious when a pathetic lament is uttered by Electra over the unreal ashes of her brother, which the spectator, who is aware of the truth, admires but cannot hear with any real pity. But the speech was too affecting to be omitted.[1]

[1] vv. 1126-60 : ὦ φιλτάτου μνημεῖον ἀνθρώπων ἐμοὶ
ψυχῆς Ὀρέστου λοιπόν, ὥς σ' ἀπ' ἐλπίδων
οὐχ ὧνπερ ἐξέπεμπον εἰσεδεξάμην.
νῦν μὲν γὰρ οὐδὲν ὄντα βαστάζω χεροῖν,
δόμων δέ σ', ὦ παῖ, λαμπρὸν ἐξέπεμψ' ἐγώ
ὡς ὤφελον πάροιθεν ἐκλιπεῖν βίον,
πρὶν ἐς ξένην σε γαῖαν ἐκπέμψαι χεροῖν
κλέψασα ταῖνδε κἀνασώσασθαι φόνου,
ὅπως θανὼν ἔκεισο τῇ τόθ' ἡμέρᾳ,
τύμβου πατρῴου κοινὸν εἰληχὼς μέρος.
νῦν δ' ἐκτὸς οἴκων κἀπὶ γῆς ἄλλης φυγὰς
κακῶς ἀπώλου, σῆς κασιγνήτης δίχα·
κοὔτ' ἐν φίλαισι χερσὶν ἡ τάλαιν' ἐγὼ
λουτροῖς σ' ἐκόσμησ' οὔτε παμφλέκτου πυρὸς
ἀνειλόμην, ὡς εἰκός, ἄθλιον βάρος.
ἀλλ' ἐν ξέναισι χερσὶ κηδευθεὶς τάλας
σμικρὸς προσήκεις ὄγκος ἐν σμικρῷ κύτει.
οἴμοι τάλαινα τῆς ἐμῆς πάλαι τροφῆς
ἀνωφελήτου, τὴν ἐγὼ θάμ' ἀμφὶ σοὶ
πόνῳ γλυκεῖ παρέσχον. οὔτε γάρ ποτε

I cannot fancy Æschylus thus utilising an artificial situation. It is the victory of sentiment over greater and nobler interests, and in this Sophocles, and not Euripides, marks the rise of a new epoch—an epoch like that opened by Raffaelle and by Weber in other arts, where the master is still great, but is the author of a rapid and melancholy decay into sentimentalism. The attitude of the chorus differs notably from that of the *Antigone.* It is the confidant and helper of the king's children, and takes an active part in the progress of the play. But for this very reason, the choral odes, which are strictly to the point, are lyrically very inferior to the beautiful poems inserted in the *Antigone.* It is remarkable that while Æschylus never mentions Mycenæ, and lays the scene of his *Choephori* at Argos, Sophocles, more accurately, makes Mycenæ his scene, and in the opening even describes the relative positions of the two cities; but I am at a loss, though personally familiar with the country, to find the point of view from which the old pedagogue and Orestes approach it, and should not be surprised if this were one of the instances of geographical inaccuracy with which Strabo charges both Sophocles and Euripides.[1] I suppose the recent reassertion of Mycenæ, by the appearance of its citizens in the Persian war, must have made its name momentarily prominent in the youth of Sophocles,

μητρὸς σύ γ' ἦσθα μᾶλλον ἢ κἀμοῦ φίλος
οὔθ' οἱ κατ' οἶκον ἦσαν, ἀλλ' ἐγὼ τροφός ·
ἐγὼ δ' ἀδελφὴ σοὶ προσηυδώμην ἀεί.
νῦν δ' ἐκλέλοιπε ταῦτ' ἐν ἡμέρᾳ μιᾷ
θανόντι σὺν σοί. πάντα γὰρ συναρπάσας
θύελλ' ὅπως βέβηκας. οἴχεται πατήρ ·
τέθνηκ' ἐγώ σοι · φροῦδος αὐτὸς εἶ θανών
γελῶσι δ' ἐχθροί · μαίνεται δ' ὑφ' ἡδονῆς
μήτηρ ἀμήτωρ, ἧς ἐμοὶ σὺ πολλάκις
φήμας λάθρα προὔπεμπες ὡς φανούμενος
τιμωρὸς αὐτός. ἀλλὰ ταῦθ' ὁ δυστυχὴς
δαίμων ὁ σός τε κἀμὸς ἐξαφείλετο,
ὅς σ' ὧδέ μοι προὔπεμψεν ἀντὶ φιλτάτης
μορφῆς σποδόν τε καὶ σκιὰν ἀνωφελῆ.
οἴμοι μοι.

[1] Cf. on frag. 530.

and before Æschylus brought out his Orestean trilogy.[1] The scene of the drama must, therefore, have been determined by the local politics of the day, which would put forwardi Mycenæ, if Argos and Athens were at variance. But this is a mere conjecture. The critics have animadverted upon the anachronism of representing Orestes as killed at the Pythian games, but there is surely no sense in the objection. Almost all the games in Greece were ascribed to mythical, nay, even to divine founders, and to assign to any of them a late and historical origin would have offended Greek taste. About the beauty of the narrative there can be no question. It is remarkable that Sophocles reverses the order of the murders, and makes Clytemnestra suffer before Ægisthus, an arrangement which destroys the awful climax in the *Choephori*—indeed, when the mother has been sacrificed little interest remains about her paramour. The French critics are almost indignant at the idea of a king on the stage, who only comes in to die. But of course his death is necessary to the piece, and if Sophocles did not require him as a character, he shows true and great art in only introducing him when necessary. A perfect library has been written on the three *Electras* of the three Greek poets, generally with the object of detracting from Æschylus, and still more from Euripides, to extol Sophocles. The reader has already seen how false such an estimate is towards Æschylus. I shall not enter upon the *Electra* of Euripides till we have become acquainted with that poet in the course of the present history.

[1] All the critics follow Pausanias in assuming that Mycenæ remained independent up to 468 B.C., and that the συνοικισμός of this and other towns by Argos took place, through fear of Sparta, after the Persian wars. I cannot conceive this policy to have arisen so late, and believe the autonomy, and perhaps even the existence, of Mycenæ to have ceased at latest when Argos became great under Pheidon, about a century earlier. My views were published in the fifth number of *Hermathena*, and ultimately converted Dr. Schliemann, as I had predicted that no fifth century remains would be found in his excavations. He has translated my article in the French edition of his *Mycenæ*. The evidence he has produced points to a very old destruction of the city, perhaps even at the time of the Doric invasion.

Let us now pass to the imitations of the story, or the improvements attempted upon it, in subsequent times. There can be little doubt that there were several Roman versions. Cicero speaks of two, Suetonius alludes to them, and so evidently does Vergil, when using in a simile the ' Agamemnonius scenis agitatus Orestes.' But none of them have survived. The Orestes ridiculed by Juvenal may have been a mere fiction, but the choice of this title proves the popularity of the subject. In the 16th century, there was a translation by L. Baïf. But in 1708, Crebillon brought out his Electra, a play which introduced a series of love affairs between Orestes, Electra, and a son and daughter of Ægisthus, fabricated for the purpose. These novelties, together with storms and other adventures, so complicated and changed the play, that the author could fairly boast his own originality, and proclaim that he had taken nothing from Sophocles, whom he had never read. Passing by the now unknown work of Longepierre in 1719, we come to Voltaire's *Oreste* (1750), which is said to owe it a good many thoughts. Some of Crebillon's inventions are also adopted, but the main novelty is the excitement produced by the dangers which Orestes encounters in attaining his vengeance. For greater detail upon this and succeeding efforts, the reader should consult the history of French Literature in connection with the drama of Sophocles in M. Patin's admirable sketch.[1] He has forgotten to mention how closely the *Athalie* in Racine's celebrated play has been copied from Sophocles' Clytemnestra. The very device of a disturbing dream is employed to rouse Athalie's fears, and Joas stands to her in a similar relation to that of Orestes and Clytemnestra. The famous *Orestes* of Alfieri was of course based on Crebillon and Voltaire ; indeed, we know that the poet's very defective education did not then permit him to read a Greek play in the original. As was his habit, he simplifies the plot, and gets rid of all superfluous characters ; but the great strain he keeps up, and the monotony of his speakers, make it a tedious play to read. He is noted as having been the first to paint the quarrels and the remorse of the adulterous pair, and with his usual hatred of tyrants, he makes Ægisthus weep with terror

---

[1] *Sophocle,* pp. 366, sq.

when he finds he must die. There are several later versions, up to the *Orestie* of Alexandre Dumas.

§ 188. We may take up the *Trachiniæ* next, because its heroine—the only other extant heroine in Sophocles—stands in marked and pleasant contrast to those we have just discussed. As to the date of the play, it is agreed that it comes either very early or very late in the poet's career. The differences from the other plays, and supposed inferiority, are the grounds which have led to this opinion. Some have even declared it spurious, and the work of Iophon, or some other weaker hand. It is impossible to decide the dispute about its age, though its genuineness must certainly be asserted. On the whole, I rather incline to place it as the earliest extant work of Sophocles. There seems a certain hesitation in the author, who desires to make Deianira the protagonist, and yet chooses a myth of which Heracles is necessarily the central figure. Thus there are two distinct catastrophes—that of the heroine, which is first in interest, but is treated as a mere incident ; and that of the hero, who is absent during all the action, but whose death forms the solemn conclusion of the play. It almost seems to me as if the poet were feeling his way to making the character of a woman the prominent feature of the play, and yet afraid to do so without weaving in another catastrophe, afraid also to entitle his play (like his Antigone and Electra) *Deianira.* It is the only extant play of Sophocles which takes its name from the chorus, and when we reflect that at least one half of Æschylus' plays are so named, while less than one-third of Sophocles'—and mostly satirical plays—follow this rule, we may draw another slight argument in favour of its early date, before the poet had abandoned, perhaps, the Æschylean fashion of calling his plays after their most important feature—the chorus. Again, as the *Philoctetes*, which shows no sign of weakness or failure, appeared in 409, and the poet did not survive the year 405, it seems very strange that so rapid a decadence should take place in these years, in which no tradition mentions any play but the *Œdipus at Colonus.* Internal evidence from style has been freely employed by the advocates of both opinions, but is in any case, by itself, of little worth. The character of

Deianira can only be compared with that of Tecmessa, a second-rate character in the *Ajax*, and differs completely from the poet's so-called heroines.   But there is the deepest pathos in his drawing of a feeble, patient wife, ever widowed afresh for weary months, and now too exiled from her home and seeking in vain for tidings of her husband.   His enforced absence (to atone for a homicide), his careful disposition of his affairs before he departed, and the vague voice of old oracles, all conspire to fill her heart with sorrow and despondency. The aged nurse suggests the sending out of Hyllus to obtain news, and after a short dialogue, in which he repeats the vague reports of his father's return to Euboea, and his mother cites with fear the threatening oracles about this very place, the chorus of Trachinian maidens enters, and in a very beautiful ode to Helios, prays for tidings of the wandering hero.   Deianira's weariness of life saddens her first address to the chorus, whose virgin days of security she envies, while she reflects on the cares of married life.[1]

Then comes a self-appointed messenger, who has hurried in advance of Lichas, and tells her of Heracles' victory, and the momentary delay of the herald, who presently enters with the spoils and slaves from Œchalia, and gives his account to Deianira.   But she is chiefly struck by the beauty of a fair captive, concerning whose history and parentage she inquires, both from Lichas, who answers evasively, and from the girl herself, who preserves absolute silence.   Nothing can exceed the tenderness and grace of this passage.[2]   It contrasts strongly with

---

[1] vv. 140–50 : πεπυσμένη μέν, ὡς σάφ᾽ εἰκάσαι, πάρει
πάθημα τοὐμόν · ὡς δ᾽ ἐγὼ θυμοφθορῶ
μήτ᾽ ἐκμάθοις παθοῦσα, νῦν δ᾽ ἄπειρος εἶ.
τὸ γὰρ νεάζον ἐν τοιοῖσδε βόσκεται
χώροισιν αὐτοῦ, καί νιν οὐ θάλπος θεοῦ,
οὐδ᾽ ὄμβρος, οὐδὲ πνευμάτων οὐδὲν κλονεῖ,
ἀλλ᾽ ἡδοναῖς ἄμοχθον ἐξαίρει βίον
ἐς τοῦθ᾽, ἕως τις ἀντὶ παρθένου γυνὴ
κληθῇ, λάβῃ τ᾽ ἐν νυκτὶ φροντίδων μέρος.

This sentiment reappears in frag. 517 of the poet, and also in Euripides.

[2] vv. 294–334.

the imperious harshness of Clytemnestra to the captive Cassandra, and may possibly have been composed with this intention.   But the first messenger, who has heard the gossip of the town, and is eager to make himself important, comes forward again, as soon as Lichas has entered the palace, and with that love of telling bad news which infects the lower classes, informs the queen of the real truth about Iole.   The scene in which Deianira extracts the confirmation of the report from the unwilling Lichas, when he reappears, is one of the finest in the tragedy.   The largeness of heart with which the wife treats her husband's passion for another woman is far more splendid than the heroism of harder women on matters that cannot touch them so deeply.[1]   We must remember that we are reading of Greek heroic times and manners, when such license was freely accorded to princes, and when the attachment to Iole, though a great hardship to the wife, would never have been regarded as a breach of good morals.   When, therefore, some critics have sought the tragic justice of the play in Heracles' punishment for conjugal faithlessness, they have merely talked irrelevant nonsense.   There is no finer conclusion of a fine scene than the chorus which follows, and which describes the desperate conflict of Heracles for the possession of this very Deianira, who is now slighted and forgotten.   Then follows the hasty resolve of the wife to recover her husband by the potent charm of Nessus' garment, her fear and forebodings when she finds, after it is sent, that the wool with which she had laid on the unguent had been consumed when heated by the sun.   She anticipates the whole catastrophe, and is now as clear sighted as she was formerly dull of inference.   Then comes the terrible news by Hyllus, and his fierce accusation of his mother, who rushes in the silence of desperate resolve from the stage.   After an interrupting chorus, her death-scene is affectingly described, so affectingly as almost to rival the death of Alcestis in Euripides.

---

[1] Elle ne s'irrite ni contre sa rivale ni contre l'homme qui la trahit : sa douleur est celle d'une épouse, et non pas d'une amante, et cette nuance, qu'on a peine à exprimer, est indiquée par le poète avec une exquise délicatesse.—Patin, *Sophocle*, p. 73.

Here the main interest in the piece ends for moderns; and I may observe, before passing on, that it is hardly creditable to the critics that they have not better appreciated so noble and natural a character.   Deianira is a woman made to suffer and to endure, who submits to a hard fate with patience and sweetness, but whose love is strong, and will not waver with the rudest shocks.   When she sees a growing beauty brought into the home in which years and anxieties have caused her own charms to decay, she has recourse to a remedy ordinary in those days, and approved by the maidens who befriend her. And yet this device of the gentle, uncomplaining wife lets loose a terrific agency which robs all Greece of its greatest benefactor, and the human race of its proudest hero. The oracle must indeed be fulfilled; Heracles must die, but with what tragic irony!   The wretched worker of the catastrophe wanders for a while through the house, amazed, aimless, heartbroken, bursting into tears at every familiar face and object, then with sudden resolve she bares her side, and strikes the sword into her heart!

But among the ancients, the official catastrophe, the lyrical wailing of Heracles, his wrestling with agony, and final victory, his calm review of his life—all this was far more celebrated and striking.   Such lyrical dialogues, when the excited actor spoke in turn with the chorus, were highly prized on the Greek stage, and were a leading feature in most tragedies.   Cicero[1] gives us a version of the agony of Heracles, and there are many modern French versions.   Seneca and Ovid have reproduced the story, but have altogether missed the delicacies of Sophocles' treatment.   Among French imitators by far the best was Fénelon, who has given a very elegant prose version in his *Télémaque.*   All the rest, for want I suppose of both taste and knowledge of Greek, followed Seneca's travesty.

§ 189. The *Œdipus Tyrannus*, which serves as a sort of canon in the *Poetic* of Aristotle, has been placed by the scholiasts, and by most modern critics, at the very summit of Greek tragic art, and certainly dates from the best period of Sophocles' literary life.   But when some exercise their ingenuity in suggesting

---

[1] *Tusc.* ii. 8-9.

that the opening scene was painted from the horrors of the plague at Athens, and that by Œdipus the poet means to convey the failure of Pericles, and his melancholy death, they seem to have actually found the one impossible date for the play. The Lacedæmonians, in opening the war, had demanded from Athens the exile of Pericles, as blood-guilty through his ancestors in the massacre of the Kylonians, and had affected to make the refusal their *casus belli.* To bring out the *Œdipus,* when this demand, and the plague which shortly after ensued, were still fresh in men's minds, would not only have been a profound disloyalty to the Athenian cause, and a justification of Sparta, but a direct personal attack on the memory of Pericles. We know that Sophocles, of all Athenians, was most free from personal animosities, and we have also reason to think he was a friend of Pericles. This period, therefore, of the poet's life is the only one at which the *Œdipus* cannot have been brought out.

It may perhaps rather be referred to an earlier period, when sceptical opinions, and especially a contempt of oracles, came into fashion with the rising generation during the supremacy of Athens. The moral lesson conveyed is distinctly the importance of oracles and prophecies, which interpret to men the secret and inexplicable ways of Providence, and the awful, nay, to us disproportionate, vengeance which ensues upon their neglect. This apparent injustice is even vindicated as being the necessary course of the world appointed by its ruler, Zeus —in fact, by an appeal to religious, as distinguished from moral, laws.

The progress of the play is so well known that I will only notice its perfections and defects from a critical point of view. Nothing can be nobler and more natural than the opening dialogue of Œdipus and the priest, and in this, and the short scene when Creon appears with the answer of the oracle, the character of Œdipus, as an able, benevolent, but somewhat self-conscious man, is laid clearly before us. The old objection, why the murder of Laius had never been before investigated, may be coupled with another, why the plague had been so long delayed, seeing that the cause of it existed since Œdipus had come to Thebes. These difficulties are, however, not objections to the play, but to the supposed antecedents of the play, though they are real objections. Sophocles would probably have answered them by saying that he sought a dramatic situation in which to develop the character of his hero, and that he despised such inquiries into antecedent probabilities. But unnatural assumptions cannot enter a work of art with impunity, and nature will avenge herself upon the artist, however great, as we shall see in the sequel of this very play. The choral hymn to Apollo, as the healer, which follows, is among the finest of Sophocles' choral odes. Indeed, if we except the second *Œdipus*, the choruses of this play are much grander than is usual with Sophocles; and this is attributable to the character of the chorus, which here, if anywhere, is the ideal spectator, though not without some touches of vulgar complaisance.[1] But the principal character maintains an importance so much higher than in Sophocles' other plays, that the chorus assumes the purer function of observing the action, rather than that of encouraging or deprecating the hero's sentiments.

Passing by the imprecation scene, which has greatly benefited by Ribbeck's transposition of a few lines,[2] we come to the unwilling appearance of Teiresias, the impatience of Œdipus, and a consequent angry wrangle, in which the outspokenness of the prophet seems to me a great flaw in a play so much admired for the gradual development of the plot. Teiresias tells him so explicitly that he is the murderer of Laius, and is the husband of his mother, that a man who knew his Corinthian parentage was doubtful, that an oracle had predicted to him these very crimes, and that he had committed a homicide, could not but hit upon the truth. In fact he does so presently at a far less obvious suggestion of Iocasta's. The excuse for this defect is, I suppose, that Œdipus was in a rage when Teiresias discloses the facts, and that his rage makes him perfectly blind. But this seems quite too artificial an answer to the objection, though it has been urged as a subtle psychological point, that the same man who cannot perceive the plainest indications in the heat of dispute,

---

[1] Cf. Patin, *Sophocle*, p. 183.

[2] vv. 252-72 before v. 246; cf. Bernhardy, *LG.* iii. p. 355.

when he calms down, fastens on a trivial detail in friendly conversation, and starting from it, unravels for himself the whole
mystery. The spectator is hurried on by the angry violence
of Œdipus, who turns accuser instead of defendant, and
roundly charges both Teiresias and Creon with being the real
murderers of Laius, and accomplices in seeking to oust
from the kingdom its rightful lord. But surely here the
antecedent improbabilities assert themselves with irrefragable
force. If the murder of Laius and the present events were indeed twenty years apart, the charge of Œdipus becomes
ridiculous. The ambitious claimants for the throne murder
Laius, and then rest silent for twenty years, when they vamp up
a charge of the murder against his long-established successor !
The matter will not bear the light of common sense, unless we
conceive the murder followed closely by the accession of Œdipus,
the plague, and the threatening oracle. But here the legend
which gives time for the birth of four children seems to interpose
an impassable barrier. The important tragic point to be noted
in this dispute is that the violence of Œdipus, and especially
his sneers at the venerable and respected soothsayer, are meant
to palliate our sense of horror at the extremity of his punishment.
The same may be said of Iocasta, whose feeble and shallow
scepticism is with great skill represented by the poet as failing
in the hour of terror and of need. Her account of the death
of Laius, intended to soothe Œdipus, is so framed as to stir up
his deepest mind with agitation, and that, too, by means of an
apparently trifling detail. Even though the plain speaking of
Teiresias had more than prepared us, this passage is of the
greatest dramatic beauty. Indeed, these double confidences of
the husband and wife form a scene which has perhaps not been
equalled of its kind. The result is now plain before Œdipus'
mind, yet he and Iocasta cling to the faint hopes arising
from false details of the murder. It is very remarkable that
the chorus, here rising above the special situation, sings a
solemn ode [1] upon the insolence and folly of scepticism,
and the decay of belief in the old tenets of religion. At its
close Iocasta appears, bearing suppliant offerings to the god

[1] vv. 860-910.

whose oracles she has just despised, but to whom she turns in dismay at the mental agony of her husband, for which she can find no remedy.

The appearance of the messenger announcing the death of Polybus comes too late in the play, and the sudden return of Œdipus to confidence on this point is strange. He had long ago doubted his alleged origin, and the previous course of the play had so confirmed these doubts, that his easy acceptance of the solution is not natural, and is a flaw in the work. At an earlier period, and just after the warnings of Teiresias, we may fancy such a delay in the catastrophe better placed. But the intention of the poet is here to approach the second crime of Œdipus, his incestuous marriage, and he approaches it with the somewhat ridiculous fears of Œdipus that he may unwittingly marry the aged Merope, whom he knows perfectly well. This leads to the final explanation of his birth, and presently of the details of his father's murder, which the Corinthian messenger, the aged shepherd, and the king discover in a dialogue of awful and breathless interest. I will only notice from the end of the play that the character of Creon is that of a calm and just ruler, far different from his figure in the *Antigone*, and also that in his lamentations Œdipus lays great and natural stress on the indelible stain which adheres to his daughters, and which will make their marriage impossible—a consideration never mentioned, I think, in the *Antigone*. This proves, if it be necessary to prove it, the complete independence of these plays, which critics are always citing in connection, when they discuss the characters of Sophocles, and wish to explain the unresolved harshness of his morality. The concluding scene with his infant daughters is very affecting, but thoroughly Euripidean, and may be intended to introduce the softer element of pity where terror too much predominates.

Indeed, the whole play is a terrible exhibition of the iron course of Fate, which ensnares even great and good men in its adamantine chains, and ruins the highest human prosperity with calm omnipotence. There can be no crime urged against Œdipus and his parents but the neglect of oracles, or an attempt to evade them, and it is evidently this scepticism or carelessness which brings upon them consequences too horrible to bear.   I do not think that the haughtiness of Œdipus—a feature which the Greeks did not consider inconsistent with an ideal character—has any direct relation to the catastrophe, and the homicide was evidently regarded not as an act of violence, but of fair retaliation, until the person of the victim throws a horrible complexion over the act, and makes it a hideous crime.   After all, Œdipus is a noble man mocked by an awful destiny; he suffers without adequate evil desert; and the lesson of the play is not that of confidence in the final result of a great moral struggle, but rather of awe and despair at the possible cruelties of an arbitrary and irresponsible Fate.

It may have been this grave objection, it may have been its orthodoxy, or it may have been the defects of plot above noticed, which caused its defeat by a play of Philocles, or brought out by Philocles, the nephew of Æschylus, at the same time.   Subsequent criticism has reversed this decision.   Not only is the very name of Philocles' play forgotten, but the scholiasts and other critics express their wonder at the bad taste of the Athenian public, and exhaust themselves in praise of the *Œdipus Tyrannus.*   Seneca spoilt it in a rhetorical version.   Among the moderns, both Corneille (1659) and Voltaire composed plays on this subject, not to speak of inferior attempts.   Corneille added amorous and poetical intrigues, and borrowed rather from Seneca than from Sophocles. Voltaire degraded it into a formal attack on the justice and wisdom of the gods—in fact, a vehicle for the scepticism which he preached.   Many faults of economy in his play, which dissatisfied him as an early and crude production, have been noticed by his own *Lettres.*   The *Œdipus* of Dryden and Lee, given in 1679, is one of the few adaptations of the Greek drama upon the English stage; Lacroix's translation (1858) has just been reproduced in Paris.   Dryden's play does not avoid any of the faults of the French stage—pompousness, needless complication, irrelevant love affairs, false rhetoric—and is, moreover, said to have added some of those to be found in his own country.

§ 190. A very different picture is presented to us by the

Œdipus at Colonus, wherein the poet, probably in later years, seems to have softened and purified the figure of the deeply injured hero by a noble and dignified end. We know that the play was not exhibited till four years after Sophocles' death, and tradition speaks of it as the last composed by the old man ; but later critics seem more disposed to place its composition in the best period of his life.[1] I hardly think their arguments, based on its purity of metre and strength of diction, will weigh against the current tradition, backed up by the strong feeling of every reader from Cicero to our day, that its mildness and sadness, nay even its weariness of life, speak the long experience and sober resignation of an old man near the grave. The choral odes are, however, far more brilliant and prominent than those of the *Philoctetes*, whose late date is un-doubted, and indeed the chorus holds a sort of Æschylean position in the play. The lyrical writing, especially in the choral odes on Colonus, and on the miseries of human life, may safely be pronounced the most perfect we possess of the poet's remains. Nevertheless, the moral attitude of the chorus in the action is low and selfish. Their attempt to break faith with Œdipus, their vulgar obtrusiveness about his past history, and the rapid change in their estimate of him, when they find he will be useful to them—all these features mark the vulgar public which ordinarily appears in the Greek tragic chorus. The play may be composed with some reference to the earlier *Œdipus*, at least with the intention of soften-ing the cruel treatment of Œdipus, which is there portrayed. Though worn out with age and suffering, there is a splendid dignity about him, a consciousness of innocence, an oft-ex-pressed conviction that he did all his so-called crimes un-wittingly, and without moral guilt, and that he is justified by the important mission assigned him by the gods—that of pro-

---

[1] There have been endless discussions as to the date, and efforts to deduce it from the political temper of the play, and its very friendly allu-sions to Thebes. But according as this or that line is declared spurious, or this or that passage interpolated, the theories vary, and the doctors differ. The main result of the controversy is to show that no result is attainable.

tecting for ever the land which affords him a hallowed resting-place. He even approaches with a surance and without fear the dread Eumenides, whom others will scarcely name, and whose grove men hurry by with averted face.   This spiritual greatness separates the dying Œdipus widely from King Lear, with whom he is often compared.   But in his violent and painful execration of his ungrateful but repentant son—a jarring chord in the sweet harmony of the play—he reminds us of the angry old man in Shakespeare, though still more of his vehement and haughty self in the *Œdipus Tyrannus.*   But Creon is here changed, and represented in his low and insolent type, as in the *Antigone.*   This heroine, also, is not consistently drawn, and does not here manifest the strong features which Sophocles had given her in his early play.   These points show how little the Athenian public cared to compare the plays of different years, and how little they attached a fixed type of character to mythic names.   It was possibly on account of these liberties that the tragic poets avoided as a rule the Iliad and Odyssey, for in a play derived from them any marked deviation might, perhaps, have offended a public really familiar with their texts.

The episode of Polynices, though it delays the main action of the play, is singularly striking from the contrast it affords to the position of Œdipus.   Both father and son are approaching their fate, but the father, an innocent offender, and purified by long suffering, shines out in the majesty of a glorious sunset after a stormy day ; while the son, who violated his filial duties through selfishness and hardness of heart, is promptly punished by exile ; but even when apparently repentant, and seeking forgiveness for his offence, the leaven of ambition and revenge has so poisoned his heart, that when stricken by his father's awful curse, he rushes upon his doom, partly in despair, partly in contumacy, partly from vanity and a fear of ridicule :

> ' His honour rooted in dishonour stood,
> And faith unfaithful kept him falsely true.'

It is this combined insincerity and desperation in Polynices which alone can justify the violence of Œdipus' curse, and even so it is a painful prelude to his solemn translation to the nether world.

Nothing at first sight can appear to modern notions more monotonous than the way in which Œdipus fixes himself to the single spot which he will not leave, while all the other characters pass in succession before him. But nothing could be more pathetic or striking to the Greek mind than these divers efforts to subdue or persuade the inflexible old man, whom the divine curse has hardened in his wrath. The changing scenes give endless variety to the monotony of the situation, or rather of the main figure, whose very monotony is his greatness, because it expresses the endurance of his misfortunes and of his hate.[1] In the finest and truest English reproduction of Greek tragedy—the *Samson Agonistes* of Milton—Samson, who has great points of resemblance with Œdipus, occupies a similar fixed position, while the various actors pass before him. The episode of Dalila takes the place of the scene with Polynices, and brings out the angry element in Samson. There are, however, many other Greek plays, and many Æschylean and Euripidean features, imitated in the *Samson*, though all these materials are fused into harmony with a great poet's highest art. The *commos* of the sisters after his departure is the essentially Greek feature of the play, which a modern writer would omit, but which is formed closely upon the model of the end of Æschylus' *Seven against Thebes*. But on the whole, for vigour, for variety, and for poetic beauty, no play of Sophocles exceeds this *Œdipus*, and I am even disposed to agree with those who rank it the first of his dramas. As, however, each new critic makes this assertion about a different play, it is idle to attempt a decision.

The essentially antique nature of the tragedy, its special glorification of Theseus, of Athens, of Colonus, made it less fit than others, as M. Patin observes, for modern imitation. Nevertheless, in 1778, long after the other *chefs d'œuvre* of the Greek drama had been imitated or travestied on the French stage, Ducis brought out his *Œdipe chez Admète*, a sort of com-

---

[1] Cf. Villemain, *Litt. du xviiime siècle*, iii. p. 312.

bination of the *Œdipus Coloneus* with Euripides' *Alcestis*, which
seems as much imitated from *King Lear* as from *Œdipus*, and
misses the perfections of both. An abridged and altered version
appeared in 1797 under the exact title of the Greek play.
There was, moreover, an opera on the same subject, with
music by Sacchini, brought out in 1787. An imitation by
Chenier, which is not much praised by the critics, and one by
the Italian Niccolini, who translated some of Æschylus' plays,
are the most important modern attempts in this special field.
In all the French imitations the Christianity of the writers was
so shocked by the relentless cursing of Polynices by Œdipus,
that they reject this feature, and introduce a scene of forgiveness, which the gods, however, will not ratify. The worship of
old Greek poetry in the eighteenth century was as inaccurate as
the worship of Greek architecture. In both the results were attempted without any real knowledge of the principles involved,
or of the spirit which produced every detail in strict harmony
with the original design, and for some definite purpose beyond
mere ornament.

§ 191. In variety and richness the play just considered contrasts strongly with the *Ajax*, which stands perhaps more remote than any of Sophocles' works from modern notions.[1] If
a modern dramatist were told to compose a play upon such a
subject—the madness of a hero from disappointed ambition,
the carnage of flocks of sheep in mistake for his rivals and
judges, his return to sanity, remorse and suicide, and a quarrel
about his funeral—he would, I suppose, despair of the materials ;
and yet Sophocles has composed one of his greatest character
plays upon it. There is no finer psychological picture than the
awakening of Ajax from his rage, his deep despair, his firm
resolve to endure life no longer, his harsh treatment of
Tecmessa, and yet his deep love for her and his child. Even
his suicide is most exceptionally put upon the stage, for the
purpose, I think, of the most splendid monologue which
Greek tragedy affords us. He is for one day, we are told,
under the anger of Athene, and if he can escape it, he will be

---

[1] The interesting parallel of the *Hercules Furens* of Euripides will
come under discussion in the chapter on that poet.

safe, and this inspires the spectator with a peculiar tragic pity, when he sees a great life lost, which might so easily have been saved. But the action of Athene is not otherwise of importance in the play. She appears not at the end (as usual), but only at the opening, and in those hard and cruel features which are familiar to us in Homer.[1] Thus in this play also, religion and morals are dissociated, no doubt unconsciously, by the tragic poet, who sought to be a moral teacher of his people. This momentary introduction of gods at the opening and close of tragedies shows plainly the process of humanization which was completed by Euripides, and which made the gods a mere piece of stage machinery, tolerated by tradition, but only to be called in when the web of human passion required prompt and clear explication. But in old Greek plays they furthermore performed the important tragic service of justifying the cruel side, the iron destiny, of the drama. They were the main agents *in purifying the terror of the spectator*, which had else been akin to despair at the miseries entailed by necessity upon the human race.

As regards the haughty, unyielding character of Ajax, I cannot agree with the critics that the poet meant to regard his pride as justly punished, and meant to show that brute force must succumb to a heroism tempered by wisdom and forethought. This would be to assume that the Ajax of the play was the hero of the Iliad, which is not the case. Sophocles' Ajax is not the least wanting in refinement, or in sensitiveness, nay, his appeal to all the calm beauty of nature around him, in contrast to his own misery, his undisguised lamentations and despair, show a mind which steels itself with effort to a high resolve, and which does not possess the brute courage of insensibility. Moreover, he consistently considers himself unjustly treated, and would never acquiesce in the fairness either of the decision of the Atridæ or of the persecution of Athene. And in this conviction he draws even the modern spectator with him, far more the Greek public, which did not

---

[1] I am bound to say that M. Patin, an excellent critic, speaks of Athene's language as 'grave and sublime,' and regards her as a lofty exponent of moral laws. Let the reader of the play judge between us.

reprove self-assertion except as dangerous on account of the jealousy of the gods. The inferiority of Odysseus in perso-nal courage is brought out pointedly in the very first scene, but at the same time his prudence and his favour with the gods. His appearance at the end of the play is calm and dignified, but having obtained a complete victory over his rival, we feel that his generosity, though just what it ought to be, is cheap, and consists merely in the absence of vindictiveness. The whole of the wrangling scene between the Atridæ and Teucer concerning the burial of Ajax, is very inferior to the earlier part of the play, is called 'rather comic' by the scholiast, and is certainly open to all the criticism brought against the wrangling scenes in Euripides. Some critics even think it the addition of an inferior hand to an unfinished play of Sophocles. But this is mere random effort to save the uniform greatness of a poet, who was known by the ancients to be unequal, and often to sink to an ordinary level. The Atridæ are drawn as vulgar tyrants, and without any redeeming feature. It was of course fashionable, in democratic Athens, to make every ab-solute ruler a villain, so much so that respectable actors would not play such ungrateful parts. The Tecmessa of the play is a patient, loving woman, almost as tragic as Andromache, who attracts the reader from the outset, and seems to me far more interesting, and more natural, than the poet's fierce and wran-gling heroines. The choral odes are not very striking, if we except a beautiful hyporcheme to Pan.[1] The chorus is throughout the confidant of Tecmessa, and by their conversa-tions the action is artfully disclosed ; they are also the affec-tionate followers of Ajax, though they do not forget that their personal safety depends upon him. The praise of Salamis, and the glory of a hero from whom the proudest Athenians claimed descent, were collateral features likely to recommend the play to an Athenian audience.

The story of the suicide of Ajax, though alluded to in the Odyssey, when Odysseus encounters the shade of the hero in the nether world,[2] was borrowed by Sophocles from the *Little Iliad* of Lesches. It had already afforded Æs-

---

[1] vv. 692, sq.   [2] λ, 541-64.

chylus the subject of a trilogy, in which the middle piece
described the suicide in very different terms, laying special
stress on the supposed invulnerability except in a single spot,
which his evil fate discloses to him. Sophoclès, too, composed a *Teukros* and an *Eurysakes*, but, as was his custom,
without mutual connection. No subject was more attractive
to the Greeks than this dispute of Ajax and Odysseus.
Besides the tragedies, there were celebrated pictures of it by
Timanthes and Parrhasius, and rhetorical versions of it, such
as that alluded to in the tragedy of the rhetor Theodectes,
in Aristotle's *Rhetoric*, and the countless imitations of Greek
and Roman followers. Ennius, Pacuvius, and Attius appear
to have *contaminated* Æschylus with Sophocles in their versions. A fine fragment of Pacuvius' play is cited by Cicero.
Even the Emperor Augustus attempted an *Ajax*, but told a
courtly inquirer ' that his Ajax has fallen upon the sponge.' In
Ovid's *Metamorphoses* [2] there is an elegant version, and both
Horace and Juvenal allude to it as the best known of subjects, both for moral and scholastic purposes.[3] There was a
parody of the rhetorical exercises in the *Menippea* of Varro.
We may judge from these incomplete details, that of all the
subjects handled upon the Attic stage, none was more widely
popular among the Romans. The modern version of Sivry
(1762) is so ridiculous as to excite the amusement of even
French critics. The reader will find a sketch of it at the close
of M. Patin's admirable chapter, which I have here mainly
followed.

§ 192. We close our list with the *Philoctetes*, in which German critics, since the ascertainment of its date (409 B.C.), have
found marks of decaying power, which were formerly unknown,
and which would doubtless be again ignored if our information
were found incorrect. The *Philoctetes* is, like the *Ajax* and the
Antigone, essentially a drama of character; the interest of the
plot is nothing as compared to the study of the characters of
Philoctetes and Neoptolemus. The whole piece is Euripidean
in construction. There is indeed no proper prologue, but the

---

[1] *De Orat.* ii. 46.   [2] Lib. xii.
[3] Cf. *Sat.* ii. 3, 187, sq. ; *Od.* i. 7, 21 ; ii. 4. Juvenal, *Sat.* xiv. 283.

dialogue of Odysseus and Neoptolemus, in which the former explains the object of their mission, answers the purpose. He tells how the Greeks on their way to Troy had been obliged, at his advice, to leave on this island of Lemnos, where the scene is laid, the hero Philoctetes, who had been bitten by a viper in the foot on the neighbouring isle of Chrysa, and whose cries and execrations, as well as the disgusting nature of his wound, made him intolerable to his friends. But now the seer Helenus has foretold that Troy cannot fall without him and his famous arrows of Heracles, and so Odysseus has undertaken to bring him back. For this purpose he associates with him the youthful Neoptolemus, who had no share in the abandonment of Philoctetes, and to whom he suggests a fictitious account of a quarrel with the Atreidæ about Achilles' arms, which had sent him home to Scyros in disgust, as a suitable means of entrapping Philoctetes on board, and carrying him back to Troy. Neoptolemus protests strongly against lying, but is easily—I think too easily—seduced by the prospect of the glorious consequences of his deceit. Accordingly, he undertakes his part, and, upon Odysseus retiring, is presently hailed with delight by Philoctetes, whose den or cave he had at the opening of the play already found, with manifest tokens of the hero's misery and his loathsome disease. A long series of mutual confidences between the heroes takes place, Neoptolemus in particular telling his father's friend all the doleful tidings of the great heroes who had fallen before Troy. But at last he bids him farewell, and is about to leave for his vessel, when Philoctetes addresses him with a very touching appeal not to leave him on this desolate and desert island, but to take him away to his home.

This celebrated speech, in Sophocles' best style, is one of the great beauties of the play, but is not, I think, naturally introduced. It was no part of Neoptolemus' scheme to seem hard-hearted, or to treat Philoctetes as anything but an old guest-friend, nor can we see how his assumed heartlessness, which is with difficulty overcome by the chorus, is in any way calculated to increase the confidence of his victim. As they are delaying their departure, a pretended merchant comes to tell Neoptolemus that the Greeks have sent Phœnix and the Tyndaridæ to fetch him back, and then throws in by accident that, according to the oracle, Diomede and Odysseus were also coming for Philoctetes. This urges the latter to depart; but while returning to his den to gather some leaves which he used as anodynes, he is overtaken by a paroxysm of his disease, which rends him with such anguish that he surrenders his bow and arrows to Neoptolemus, saying that *of him* he will take no oath for their safe keeping, and sinks into deep sleep. This episode seems to have been imitated from the *Philoctetes* of Æschylus. The chorus at once suggest that they should decamp with the weapons. To this Neoptolemus will hardly deign a reply, and presently Philoctetes revives refreshed, and again master of himself. Then Neoptolemus breaks to him the news that he must go to Troy, and refuses to give him back his bow. But he is so shaken by the powerful appeal of Philoctetes that he is about to yield, when he is stopped by the opportune advent of Odysseus, who immediately assumes a tone of command, insists on carrying off Philoctetes by force, or if not, threatens to carry his arms to Troy, and wield them himself, or place them in the hands of Teucer. The prayers, the lamentations, the execrations of Philoctetes are passionate beyond the utterance of any other Greek hero; but he is not for one moment to be shaken in his resolve, that neither by force nor persuasion will he return to Troy. At last the others leave him, the chorus being ordered to wait for a few moments, as the lonely man supplicates to have human company, and despairs at another return to solitude. Then follows the great scene where Neoptolemus comes back, followed anxiously by Odysseus, who exhausts arguments and threats to dissuade him from his resolve. He has been conquered by Philoctetes' iron constancy, and determines to give him back his arms. He then beseeches him, on the ground of gratitude, to change his purpose, and come to Troy; but Philoctetes, though far more sorely tried by kindness than by fraud or force, is still absolutely firm. Thus he finally conquers Neoptolemus, all the policy of Odysseus is set at naught, and the miserable suppliant in rags and tears, whose lamentations have occupied the stage for many scenes, is actually leaving the island victorious, and on the way to his home, when this conclusion, which would violate all mythic history, is reversed by the divine interposition of Heracles, who directs him to return to Troy, and aid in the destruction of the city.

A more manifest *character* play cannot be conceived. The hero is in rags and in misery, his lamentations have offended ancient philosophers, as teaching unmanliness, and occupied modern critics, as requiring justification on æsthetic grounds. But the constancy and inflexible sternness of an unimpressionable, blunt nature is no interesting psychological fact, nor do we come to admire Philoctetes' heroism, till we are made fully to feel the horror of his condition, and the despair which filled his mind. The character of Neoptolemus has been greatly and perhaps unduly praised. His spasmodic chivalry is after all that of a youthful enthusiast, who spoils a great policy, and endangers the life of a far greater hero. For it seems to me that Odysseus is clearly intended to be the great man in the play. An Athenian audience did not censure his duplicity as we do, but thought it more than justified by the important ends he had in view. No doubt many of them regarded Neoptolemus as an obstinate young fool, whose misplaced generosity would have foiled a great national cause, had the gods not miraculously interfered. I will only repeat that this play contains most of the features objected to by the critics in Euripides, who even speak as if the latter had invented the knave-Odysseus, a conception probably dating from the comedies of Epicharmus, and perhaps as old as the Cyclic poems.

The story of Philoctetes is alluded to by Homer in the Catalogue of the Iliad and by Pindar in his first Pythian ode, but was taken, like many other tragedies, from the *Little Iliad* by Sophocles, who seems however to have added the all-important part of Neoptolemus. The subject had already been handled both by Æschylus and by Euripides, the *Philoctetes* even of the latter preceding that of Sophocles by more than twenty years, for it is ridiculed in the *Acharnians* of Aristophanes. But both these poets had represented the island of

Lemnos as inhabited, and the chorus was composed of the natives, whereas Sophocles, far more poetically, though unhistorically, makes it a savage desert. Both, again, seem to have represented the hero vanquished by having his arms purloined, whereas Sophocles makes him superior even to this fierce compulsion. In Æschylus Odysseus was so aged as not to be recognised by Philoctetes; in Euripides, Athene had disguised him. These and other details are given by Dion Chrysostom, who not only compares the three works, but gives an abstract of the opening scenes of Euripides' play.[1] It appears manifest that in this case, at all events, Sophocles had far surpassed both his rivals. There were also versions by Philocles, Antiphon, and Theodectes, and a play of Attius, founded apparently on that of Æschylus, and of which a good many fragments remain. Cicero cites it, and Ovid touches the story in his *Metamorphoses*. Quintus Calaber not only gives us a full account of Philoctetes at Lemnos, probably according to the version of Euripides, but brings him to Troy, and thus to the period handled in another play of Sophocles. In modern days, Fénelon has an elegant prose paraphrase in his *Télémaque*, remarkable for its simplicity and faithfulness, when we consider the ridiculous travesty of Chateaubriand (1754), who attempts endless improvements on Sophocles.[2] He gives Philoctetes a daughter Sophia, with a governess, in order that Neoptolemus may fall in love with Sophia ! The version of La Harpe (1783) is less ridiculous, but not more faithful. The Greek play itself has been more than once performed in French seminaries, owing to the interest excited by Fénelon's paraphrase.

§ 193. We need not delay in this history over the *Fragments*, which are only of interest to the very special student of Sophocles.[3] In no case can we reconstruct the plan of any lost drama from them, even with the help of the fragments of Attius and Pacuvius, who imitated him, though loosely. The myths he used, and the possible conjectures as to their treatment, have been classified and expanded, with endless learn-

---

[1] These interesting passages from Dion's orations are cited in full in Dindorf's edition of the fragments of Euripides' play.

[2] See Patin, p. 146. [3] Cf. Prof. Campbell's *Sophocles*, ch. xv.

ing, by Welcker,[1] in whose great work the curious student may see how small is the result of all his combinations. As I remarked above (p. 283), a great many of the fragments are mere citations of γλῶσσαι, or curious words, which the poet used, and which form a strange and exceptional vocabulary. A few passages have been preserved, for their beauty and philosophic depth, by Stobæus; others are cited by the scholiast on Euripides as parallel passages. The finest is probably the following :

᾽Ω παῖδες, ἤ τοι Κύπρις οὐ Κύπρις μόνον,
ἀλλ᾽ ἐστὶ πολλῶν ὀνομάτων ἐπώνυμος.
ἔστιν μὲν Ἅιδης, ἔστι δ᾽ ἄφθιτος βία,
ἔστιν δὲ λύσσα μαινάς, ἔστι δ᾽ ἵμερος
ἄκρατος, ἔστ᾽ οἰμωγμός. ἐν κείνῃ τὸ πᾶν,
σπουδαῖον, ἡσυχαῖον, ἐς βίαν ἄγον.
ἐντήκεται γὰρ πνευμόνων, ὅσοις ἔνι
ψυχή. τίς οὐχὶ τῆσδε τῆς θεοῦ βορά;
εἰσέρχεται μὲν ἰχθύων πλωτῷ γένει,
ἔνεστι δ᾽ ἐν χέρσου τετρασκελεῖ γονῇ·
νωμᾷ δ᾽ ἐν οἰωνοῖσι τοὐκείνης πτερόν,
ἐν θηρσὶν, ἐν βροτοῖσιν, ἐν θεοῖς ἄνω.
τίν᾽ οὐ παλαίουσ᾽ ἐς τρὶς ἐκβάλλει θεῶν;
εἴ μοι θέμις, θέμις δὲ τἀληθῆ λέγειν,
Διὸς τυραννεῖ πνευμόνων· ἄνευ δορός,
ἄνευ σιδήρου πάντα τοι συντέμνεται
Κύπρις τὰ θνητῶν καὶ θεῶν βουλεύματα.

But there are fine thoughts and rich poetic expressions to be found scattered everywhere through them.

§ 194. The technical improvements made by Sophocles in his tragedies were not many or important. He reduced the chorus, it is said, from fifteen to twelve. He added a third actor, and in the *Œdipus at Colonus* a fourth may possibly have been employed. Above all, he abandoned the practice of connecting his dramas in tetralogies, and introduced the competing in single tragedies with his rivals. As they, however, continued to write in tetralogies, it is a riddle which none of our authorities

---

[1] We are accordingly not surprised to hear (Schol. in *Elect.* 87, on γῆς ἰσόμοιρ᾽ ἀήρ) that he was parodied by the comic poet Pherecrates. This is, perhaps, the only hint we have of any criticism upon the Attic darling in his own day.

have thought fit to solve for·us, how a fair competition could be arranged on such terms.[1] He is also said to have added *scenography*, or artistic decoration of the stage, with some attempt at landscape painting—an improvement sure to come with the lapse of time, and marked accidentally as to date by Sophocles. But these outward changes, in themselves slight, are the mark of far deeper innovations in the tone and temper of Greek tragedy. Sophocles is not the last of an old school ; he is not the pupil of Æschylus : he is the head of a new school ; he is the master of Euripides. We still possess his own judgments as regards both these poets, and his relation to them. Plutarch reports him to have said[2] : ' that having passed without serious effort through the grandiloquence of Æschylus, and then through the harshness and artificiality of his own (earlier) style, he had at last adopted his third kind of style, which was most suited to painting character, and (therefore) the best.' Whatever reading we adopt, the sense as regards Sophocles seems certainly to be that in early years, and before he had seriously settled down to write, he had got rid of any dominant influence from Æschylus. We have indeed no traces of Æschylean style or of Æschylean thinking in any of the plays or fragments ; but there is ground for separating the second *Œdipus* and the *Philoctetes* from the rest, and regarding them as the representatives of the milder and smoother tone of his ripest years. But who can deny that this

---

[1] We should be disposed to question the truth of the statement, which rests upon Suidas alone, and refer it merely to the disconnecting of plays in subject, which were yet performed successively, were not all the didascaliæ silent concerning any trilogy or tetralogy of Sophocles, while they frequently mention them in Euripides, and speak of the practice as still subsisting. The satyric dramas of Sophocles, which can hardly have been acted by themselves, seem, however, to prove that Sophocles brought out several plays together, though he is always reported to have conquered with *one*. We have not sufficient evidence to solve this puzzle.

[2] Here is the text of this much disputed passage : ὥσπερ γὰρ ὁ Σ. ἔλεγε, τὸν Αἰσχύλου διαπεπαιχὼς ὄγκον, εἶτα τὸ πικρὸν καὶ κατάτεχνον τῆς αὑτοῦ κατασκευῆς, τρίτον ἤδη τὸ τῆς λέξεως μεταβάλλειν [μεταλαβεῖν] εἶδος, ὅπερ ἐστὶν ἠθικώτατον καὶ βέλτιστον. The word διαπεπαιχώς troubles the critics, who suggest διαπεπλακώς, διαπεπλιχώς, and διαπεφευγώς.

change of style was most probably caused by the rivalry of
Euripides? For there is in the earlier plays a great deal of
that affected ingenuity of diction, which Thucydides describes
(in the mouth of Cleon) as the fashion of those days at Athens.
Prose writing had sprung up, political speeches were becoming
frequent, and the historian paints with curious felicity the respective efforts of the speakers and the audience in that too
highly tempered generation—the one to astonish by some new
and unexpected point; the other to outrun the speaker, and
anticipate the surprise. Thus Sophocles, like the speakers in
Thucydides, displays his subtlety to his hearers, and often
when his expression seems at first sight easy, a further reflection
discloses unobserved difficulties and new depths of meaning.
In this I would compare him to his greatest Roman imitator,
Vergil, who, under an apparent smoothness of style, hides great
difficulties, and often new and unsuspected meanings.[1] But
the easy and transparent writing of Euripides must have impressed his generous rival, and hence we may reckon this to be
one of the points in which Sophocles improved by contact with
his great successor in art. Nor was the influence limited to
mere style. The scholiast at the close of the *Orestes*, in commenting on the melodramatic[2] endings of the *Alcestis* and
Orestes, notes that the Tyro of Sophocles ended with a happy
recognition scene.

§ 195. The contrast between the poets is said (in Aristotle's
Poetic) to have been expressed by Sophocles in the famous words,
'that he had painted men as they ought to be, Euripides as they
were.' After many years' study of both poets, and after a careful
reading of all the expositions of this passage, and proofs of it,
offered by the critics, I am unable to change my deliberate
opinion that, if Sophocles intended to say this, it is not true.
There is no kind of heroism in Sophocles to which we

---

[1] This is the description of Vergil's style which I have often heard from
the lips of the late Dr. James Henry, who knew more than all the rest of
'the world put together about Vergil. He used to say that the obvious
meaning was very frequently the wrong meaning in Vergil, and could be
proved so.

[2] He calls them *comic*, by which he of course means like the *new*
comedy.

cannot find adequate parallels in Euripides ; there are no human weaknesses or meannesses in Euripides which we cannot fairly parallel in the scanty remains of Sophocles, and which would not, in all probability, be amply paralleled had we larger means of comparison. The chorus, which in Æschylus was a stirring actor in the progress of the play, was not by Euripides, but by Sophocles first degraded to be a mere spectator of the action—sometimes an accomplice, sometimes a mere selfish, sometimes an irrelevant, observer. Rags and lamentations are not monopolised by Euripides, neither are dishonesty and meanness the apanage of his stage. The wrangling of heroes and heroines is as common in the model poet as in his debased successor. Thus we can hardly defend the statement even if we interpret it, as Welcker does, to mean this : that Sophocles represented men *as a tragic poet ought* to represent them, Euripides as they were. It is a far more probable and modest translation, yet even here we are not borne out by the facts. But there is in any case one point of real importance in the remark. It implies the essential truth that Sophocles, like Euripides, made the characters and passions of *men* his object, and did not dwell upon the Divine or supernatural element in the moral order of the world. As Socrates brought down philosophy, so Sophocles brought down tragic poetry from heaven to dwell upon earth. The gods are thrown into the background, and are there merely to account for moral difficulties, and justify cruelties which human reason cannot but resent. In his latest play (the *Philoctetes*), the *Deus ex machina* actually comes in to reverse the result, and undo all that has been so laboriously worked out by human passion and human resolve. There is here already a great gulf separating us from Æschylus—a difference in kind ; we can pass over to Euripides easily, and by an ill-defined boundary.

§ 196. Nevertheless, ancient and modern critics have agreed to place Sophocles first among the Attic tragedians. Though an inferior poet to Æschylus, and an inferior philosopher to either, Sophocles may be regarded a more perfect artist. It is for this reason that he was so perpetually imitated by the

Romans and the French, while among our deeper poets both
Æschylus and Euripides have maintained a greater influence.
For as an artist, as a perfect exponent of that intensely Attic
development which in architecture tempered Doric strength
with Ionic sweetness, which in sculpture passed from archaic
stiffness to majestic action, which in all the arts found the
mean between antique repose and modern vividness, as the
poet of Athens, in the heyday of Athens, Sophocles stands
without an equal. His plots are more ethical than those of
Euripides, his scepticism is more reverent or reticent, his
religion more orthodox. He does not disturb his hearers with
suggestions of modern doubts and difficulties. He is essentially
εὔκολος, as Aristophanes calls him, without angles or contradictions. And thus he is wisely set aside by the comic critic
in the great controversy between the old and the new, for he
belonged to the new, and yet had not broken with the old. I
will only add that his greatness has been enhanced by the preservation of only a few, and those his greatest, works. Had we
eight or ten additional plays, of the quality of the *Trachiniæ*—
for the poet was known to be unequal in power—the comparisons with Euripides, who has survived in his weakness as well
as his strength, might possibly have been more just and a little
less foolish.

§ 197. *Bibliographical.* The recension of the text of our extant plays depends altogether on the Medicean codex, already
mentioned in connection with Æschylus. Venetian MSS. supplied the *Editio princeps* of Aldus (Venice, 1502), a beautiful
little book, and not uncommon in good libraries. Three of the
plays, the *Ajax, Electra,* and *Œdipus Tyrannus,* were much
more studied than the rest, and exist in many MSS., which are,
however, not so pure, and have been corrupted in the Byzantine
age. From this inferior text came all the editions from Turne-
bus (1533) to Brunck (1786), who first recognised the superior
value of the Parisinus A, but the Medicean L is preferred since
Elmsley's day. In the present century the three editions of
G. Hermann (1817–48), those of Wunder, of G. Dindorf, of
Schneidewin and Nauck, of Bergk, are best known. Wecklein's
school editions are the newest. We have besides English
editions by Linwood, Blaydes, Campbell, and of some plays

in the *Catena Classicorum* published at Cambridge. On the whole, the text is not so corrupt as that of the other dramatists, although, apart from the Byzantine corruptions, the German critics have noted many lines which they suppose due to early stage traditions, nay even some of them to the family of Sophocles. It is obvious that when we throw back interpolations to such an age, their discovery depends altogether on subjective taste, and need not detain us here. The reader will find these suspected lines printed at the foot of Dindorf's text in his *Poetæ scenici* and elsewhere.

There is a good deal of sound ancient learning preserved to us in the prefaces and scholia, first published by Lascaris at Rome (1518) without the text, then by Junta at Florence in 1544, and then several times before the edition of Stephanus in 1568. The best of the notes came from what are called the ὑπομνηματισταί, who certainly as early as the Alexandrian period wrote on the text, and collected the *Didascaliæ* as to the performances. Aristophanes is known to have paid attention to Sophocles. Aristarchus is also named, but Didymus seems the chief source of the extant scholia. Those on the *Œdipus at Colonus* are particularly good. There is a good edition of the scholia by Elmsley and Gaisford in 1826, and several special *lexicons* of Sophocles' language, of which the best are those of F. Ellendt, and of G. Dindorf : the latter was prosecuted by Ellendt's representatives, and the edition suppressed, so that copies of this most valuable book are now scarce. Of complete translations the most celebrated among the many German is that of Donner; other scholars, like Schöll and Böckh, have done single plays. The French, besides the imitations above cited under the separate plays, have the *Théâtre* of Brusmoy, and Villemain mentions with praise a literal version of Sophocles by Malézieux. In English we have Potter (1788), and in our own day Dale, whose book is now very rarely to be found ; also Mr. Plumptre's version—a meritorious work, and several plays ably done by Prof. L. Campbell. Special studies on Sophocles, both generally and on particular plays, are endless in Germany. Welcker's is of course the most exhaustive ; Klein's, inaccurate and capricious, but very suggestive; Bernhardy's, simply laudatory and full of empty wordiness in criticism, together with deep and accurate learning as to facts. Our great living poets, who are accomplished Grecians, have, so far as I know, said nothing of consequence on Sophocles.[1]

---

[1] Professor Campbell's monograph now supplies the English reader with a detailed and most enthusiastic estimate of the poet's genius and of his extant plays. It will be observed that none of the points in which I have suggested imperfections are adopted by Mr. Campbell, and that the poet is everywhere vindicated from any attempt (I will not say at adverse, but even) at depreciative criticism. Though I deeply respect this large-hearted enthusiasm, it does not appear to me the only way of stimulating the study of any writer ; and hence I do not regret that the views set forth in the previous chapter were written and printed before I had the advantage of being influenced by the elaborate analysis of so competent a scholar. I will not attempt to criticise his work, which differs from mine mainly in this contrast of spirit, and no doubt in the greater elegance of its language, but will only add that there are many facts in the history of the poet and his works which may be learned from the present chapter even after the perusal of his more detailed work.

CHAPTER XVII.

EURIPIDES.

§ 198. EURIPIDES was born in the year of the battle of Salamis
(480 B.C.)—nay, according to the legends, on the very day of
the battle (20th of Boedromion)—and apparently on the island,
whither his parents had fled, with other Athenians, for refuge.
He is said to have afterwards had a fancy for this island, and to
have composed his tragedies there in a retired spot, within view
of the sea, from which he borrows so many striking metaphors.
His father, Mnesarchus or Mnesarchides, is said to have formerly lived in Bœotia, but most probably as a foreigner, and
afterwards in the Attic deme of Phlyïa, according to Suidas.
Some of the *Lives* say he was a petty trader, but this is inconsistent with his son's apparent wealth and literary leisure, and
would hardly have been passed over in silence by Aristophanes. The mother's name was Kleito, and she was perpetually ridiculed by the comic poets as an herb-seller. The
story is most probably false, and rests upon some accidental coincidence of name, or some anecdote which gave
contemporaries a sufficient handle for their joke, though it
is lost to us. The youthful poet is said to have been trained
with some success for athletic contests by his father, and
perhaps to this we may ascribe the strong contempt and
aversion with which he speaks of that profession. There
were, moreover, pictures shown at Megara, which were ascribed
to him, so that he evidently had the reputation of a man of
varied culture. But he abandoned his earlier pursuits, whatever
they may have been, for the study of philosophy under Anaxagoras, probably also Protagoras, and possibly Prodicus, and in
mature life seems to have stood in close contact to Socrates.
He was essentially a student, and such a collector of books
that his library was famous, but he took no part in public

affairs.[1] But he began at the age of twenty-five to compete in tragedy (with his *Peliades*), and continued all his life a prolific and popular, though not a successful poet. He was known to have won the first prize only five times,[2] though he may have written ninety tragedies, and, even if we hold him always to have contended with tetralogies (or trilogies followed by a satyric or melodrama), must have contended over twenty times. He was twice married, and unfortunately: first to Chœrile, who was mother of his three sons, Mnesarchides, a merchant; Mnesilochus, an actor; and the younger Euripides, who wrote dramas, and brought out some of his father's posthumous works, such as the *Iphigenia in Aulis*, and *Bacchæ*. The comic poets do not scruple to reflect upon the unfaithfulness of his wives, and deduce from it his alleged hatred of women. Late in life he removed to the court of Archelaus of Macedon, where he was received with great honour, and wrote some plays (especially the *Archelaus* and *Bacchæ*) on the local legends. He appears to have died there at the age of seventy-four, having been attacked and torn by sporting-dogs, which were set upon him maliciously. He was honoured with a pompous tomb in Macedonia, and a cenotaph at Athens, on which the historian Thucydides is said to have inscribed an epitaph.[3]

[1] His moral portrait cannot be better expressed than in the words in which he may possibly have meant to describe his own aspirations :—

> ὄλβιος ὅστις τῆς ἱστορίας
> ἔσχε μάθησιν
> μήτε πολιτῶν ἐπὶ πημοσύνην
> μήτ' εἰς ἀδίκους πράξεις ὁρμῶν,
> ἀλλ' ἀθανάτου καθορῶν φύσεως
> κόσμον ἀγήρων, πῇ τε συνέστη
> καὶ ὅπη καὶ ὅπως.
> τοῖς δὲ τοιούτοις οὐδέποτ' αἰσχρῶν
> ἔργων μελέτημα προσίζει (fr. 902).

[2] Cf. the learned and interesting note in Meineke's *Comic Fragments*, II. p. 904, on the small number of victories gained by the greatest poets, and the frequent preferment of obscure names. It was not unfrequent, as he notes in the text, for great poets to be even refused a chorus by the archon, a slight of which both Sophocles and Cratinus had to complain.

[3]
> μνῆμα μὲν Ἑλλὰς ἅπασ' Εὐριπίδου, ὀστέα δ' ἴσχει
> γῆ Μακεδών · τῇ γὰρ δέξατο τέρμα βίου.
> πατρὶς δ' Ἑλλάδος Ἑλλάς, 'Αθῆναι. πλεῖστα δὲ Μούσας
> τέρψας ἐκ πολλῶν καὶ τὸν ἔπαινον ἔχει.

The aged Sophocles is said to have shown deep sorrow at the death of his rival, in this contrasting strongly with Aristophanes, who chose the next performance for his bitterest and most unsparing onslaught upon him (in the *Frogs*). The poet is described, upon not the highest authority, to have been of gloomy and morose temper, hating conviviality and laughter. There is no Greek author whose portrait is so distinctive and familiar in museums of ancient art. The sitting statue in the Louvre, and two busts at Naples, probably copied from the statue set up by Lycurgus in the theatre at Athens, are the most striking. The face is that of an elderly and very thoughtful man, with noble features, and of great beauty, but not without an expression of patience and of sorrow such as beseems him who has been well called *der Prophet des Weltschmerzes.* As we should expect, the face is not essentially Greek, but of a type to be found among thoughtful men of our own day. His social position and comfortable means are proved not only by his possession of a valuable library, but by his holding one or two priestly offices, which were probably rich sinecures, and would in no case have been intrusted to a man of mean origin or low consideration.

As regards the possible ninety-two dramas written by the poet, the ancients seem to have known seventy-five, of which the names, now partly erased, were engraved on the pedestal of the extant sitting statue. We possess about one fifth of the number, viz. seventeen tragedies and one satyric drama, excluding the *Rhesus*, as of very doubtful authorship. This large legacy of time, if we compare the scanty remains of Æschylus and Sophocles, does not seem to comprehend any choice selection of his *chefs d'œuvre*, but a mere average collection, of which our estimate is probably lower than that we should have formed, had fewer plays, and the best, survived. The dates of some of them are fixed by the didascaliæ, and of others (partly at least) by the allusions in Aristophanes' plays. The usual *à priori* argument, which infers from laxity of metre or style either crudity or decadence of genius, fails signally in the case of Euripides, for his latest plays which are known are far stricter in form than others preserved from preceding years, such as the *Helena.*

§ 199. Innumerable attempts have been made to gather from his writings an estimate of his politics, of his social views, and of his religion.   But although the ancients have led the way in this course, and have everywhere assumed that the philosophic utterances of the poet's characters were meant to convey his own sentiments, such an inference must be very dangerous in the case of a thoroughly dramatic poet, and especially a dramatic poet who paints upon his stage the violence of human passion.   There is indeed an anecdote of little authority, but of great aptness, preserved, in which we are told that the audience cried out against the immorality of the praise of wealth above virtue, but that the poet himself came forward and bid them wait to see the punishment of the character who uttered it.[1] Thus, again, had the famous line, 'my tongue has sworn, but my heart is free,' which Cicero and others quote with reprobation from the *Hippolytus,* been preserved as a mere fragment, we could not have known that this very speaker actually loses his life rather than break his oath.   It is therefore an inquiry of great interest, but of greater uncertainty, to reconstruct this poet's mind from the words of his characters, and with this caution I refer the reader to the special tracts of Lübker, Haupt, Goebel, and others, as well as to the fuller work of Hartung.   A great many more books are also indicated in the exhaustive discussion of Bernhardy.[2]   As a general rule, I should be disposed to lay down this axiom, that the poet's own views are likely to be found either (α) in the soliloquies of his characters, where they may be imagined turning to the audience, or (β) in the *first* strophe and antistrophe of his choruses, which usually express general sentiments, before passing into the special subject of the play in the second strophe.   I have elsewhere[3] remarked on this feature in Euripides.   But of course the actors may have had some conventional sign for expressing elsewhere the poet's thoughts, which made them clear to the audience, but which we have now irreparably lost.

As to his works I will here follow, with a few exceptions, the order critically determined by W. Dindorf, noting its uncer-

---

[1] Cf. Plutarch, cited on the passage of the *Ixion.*
[2] Vol. iii. § 119.   [3] *Social Greece,* p. 197.

tainties as we proceed. The vexed question not merely of the poet's merits, but of his own views of his mission, and the consequent intention of his writing, will be discussed when our survey has been completed.

§ 200. The *Alcestis* is the earliest play which has survived, if it was performed as the last play, along with the Κρῆσσαι, Ἀλκμαίων ὁ διὰ Ψωφῖδος, and Τήλεφος, in Ol. 85, 2 (438 B.C.). But as the same prefatory note calls it his sixteenth work, there may be something wrong in the figures, for he probably composed more tragedies before that date. The poet obtained the second prize, Sophocles being placed first. The *Telephus* seems to have struck the fancy of the age, for its ragged hero, who suffered from an incurable and agonising wound, like Sophocles' *Philoctetes*, is often ridiculed by Aristophanes. But to us the *Alcestis* is a curious and almost unique example of a great novelty attempted by Euripides[1]—a novelty which Shakspeare has sanctioned by his genius—I mean the mixture of comic and vulgar elements with real tragic pathos, by way of contrast. The play before us is not indeed strictly a tragedy, but a melodrama, with a happy conclusion, and was noted as such by the old critics, who called the play *rather comic,* that is to say, like the *new* comedies in this respect. The intention of the poet seems to have been to calm the minds of the audience agitated by great sorrows, and to tone them by an afterpiece of a higher and more refined character than the satyric dramas, which were coarse and generally obscene. But while no great world-conflict is represented, while no mighty moral problem is held in solution, there are a series of deep and practical moral lessons conveyed by the exquisite character-painting of the play. The first scene is between Apollo, who is peculiarly attached to the house of Admetus, and Death, who has arrived to take away the mistress of the house, for she alone has consented to die for her husband. There is something comic in the very prologue, which describes how Admetus, ' having tested and gone through all his friends,

---

[1] There are slight touches of low humour in the watchman and the nurse of Æschylus, but only in special scenes, which afford but a momentary relief in the saddest and severest of tragedies.

his aged father and the mother who bore him,' can find no one else to volunteer to die for the mere purpose of saving his life. The short dialogue between Apollo and Death is, however, very striking and justly admired. Then enter the chorus in suspense, and expecting hourly the death of Alcestis, but they are more minutely informed in the matchless narrative of a waiting maid, who describes how Alcestis bade farewell to all her happiness, her home, her children, her servants, and calmly, though not without poignant regrets, faced death from pure self-denial for the sake of her husband. She is presently led in by him, and in a most affecting dialogue gives him her parting directions, prays him not to replace her in his affections by a second wife, and apparently dies upon the stage—a most exceptional thing in Greek drama—amid the tearful outcries of her infant son and her husband. There is no female character in either Æschylus or Sophocles which is so great and noble, and at the same time so purely tender and womanly.

The effect is heightened by the contrast of Admetus, whose selfishness would be quite grotesque were it not Greek. After going the round of all his friends in search of a substitute, he deeply resents the gross selfishness of his parents, whose advanced age made it ridiculous, in his opinion, that they should not sacrifice themselves for his comfort. He complains bitterly of his dreadful lot in losing so excellent a wife, but here again evidently on selfish grounds, and vows eternal hatred to and separation from his father, who comes with gifts for the dead, and defends himself against his son's attack by protesting his own equal love of life, and that it was no Greek fashion to sacrifice the parent for his child. This is the only feature of the play which modern critics have been able to reprehend, and they have done so with some unanimity, whether they regard the play as one of the worst of Euripides, like Schöll, or as one of the best, like Klein and Patin. It seems to me that they have totally missed Euripides' point, and the most profound in the play, by this criticism. The poet does not conceive the sacrifice of Alcestis, as the speaker in Plato's *Symposium* (179 B) does, to be a sacrifice of one lover for another—an aspect sure to predominate in all the modern versions. It is not for the love of

Admetus that she dies. She represents that peculiar female heroism, which makes affection the highest duty, but obeys the demands of affection in the form of family ties, as the dictates of the highest moral law. We see these, the heroines of common life, around us in all classes of society. But I venture to assert that in no case does this heroic devotion of self-sacrifice come out into such really splendid relief, as when it is made for selfish and worthless people. It is therefore a profound psychological point to represent Admetus a weak and selfish man, blessed, as worthless men often are, by special favours of fortune in wealth and domestic happiness, and very ready to perform the ordinary duties of good fellowship, such as hospitality, but wholly unequal to any real sacrifice. It is for such an one that Alcestis dies—in fact, she dies not for Admetus, but *for her husband* and children's sake, and would have done so had she been given in marriage to any other like person. This is the true meaning of those disagreeable but profoundly natural scenes, which shocked those advocates of rhodomontade in tragedy who make Admetus vie with his wife in heroism. If M. Patin holds that such sentiments, though natural, are concealed within the breast, and never confessed, he forgets that Euripides wrote in a vastly more outspoken society than ours.

This curious and very comic dialogue is, however, interrupted by the entrance of Heracles, who comes on his journey to visit his guest friend, and is received with the truest hospitality by Admetus, who conceals his misfortune, in order to make his friend at home. As M. Patin observes, the height of pathos already attained would be impossible to sustain, and therefore the tone of the play is most skilfully changed.[1] The rollicking and convivial turn of Heracles is in sharp discord with the

[1] The contrast of grief and of mirth, brought out by this scene, which greatly disgusted Voltaire, and is totally opposed to French notions of tragic dignity, has been by later French critics compared with the musicians' scene near the end of *Romeo and Juliet*. It is remarkable that Milton's preface to the *Samson Agonistes*, which adopts the tone of the French drama (I suppose quite independently), specially censures the introduction of low comic characters in tragedy, and sets up the great Greek tragedies as the proper models, apparently in opposition to Shakspeare's school.

profound grief of the household, and no one is more pained by it than the worthy hero himself, who with true practical energy sets about at once to rescue Alcestis from death, and so requite his friend for his kindness. The character of Heracles is not inferior in drawing to any of the rest, and every fair critic will be justly astonished at this profound and curious antici- pation of many strong points in the modern drama. The chorus is throughout a sympathetic spectator of the action, and the choral odes are not only highly poetical and elegantly con- structed, but all strictly to the point. Thus even in the ode which is supposed to express the poet's mind,[1] the learning alluded to by the chorus is that Thracian learning which was naturally accessible to Thessalians. The usual attacks on Euri- pides' lyrics have therefore no place here.

§ 201. There is a strange external resemblance between the concluding scene and that of the *Winter's Tale*, which has not escaped the commentators. No subject has proved more attrac- tive than this beautiful legend, and yet no one has ever ap- proached in excellence its treatment by Euripides. There is an old Indian parallel in the Mahâbhârata, where Sâvitri, like Alcestis, rescues from the power of Yama, the Lord of the nether world, her husband's life. Euripides' play was parodied by Anti- phanes in a comedy brought out in the 106th Olympiad. There were two Latin versions, one by Attius, and another of doubtful authorship. Buchanan produced a Latin translation in 1543, which was acted by the pupils of the Collège de Bordeaux. It is not worth while specifying the series of travesties or modifica- tions which occupied the French stage from 1600 to the end of the last century. Racine, it may be observed, turns aside in the Preface to his *Iphigénie* to defend it against the shallow criticism of his day. Gluck's famous music has perpetuated through Europe a very poor Italian libretto by Calzabigi in 1776. But in 1798 Alfieri, who had abandoned writing, was so struck with the play, which he then learnt to know in the original, that he not only translated it, but wrote an *Alcestis* of his own, which was published after his death. As usual, he has

---

[1] vv. 962, sq. :   ἐγὼ διὰ Μούσας
καὶ μετάρσιος ᾖξα κ.τ.λ.

made all the characters great stage heroes at the sacrifice
not only of nature but of all real interest. Like the French
imitators, he makes Admetus, and even Pheres, heroes, and
creates a romantic ground of natural love and respect for the
sacrifice of Alcestis, and for a competition between husband and
wife, which completely spoils Euripides' deep and subtle plan.
Translations and moderately faithful imitations were produced
on the Paris stage in 1844 and 1847 ; others have been since
published in France. Among English poets Milton has alluded
to the legend in his 23rd sonnet,

> Methought I saw my late espoused saint
> Brought to me, like Alcestis, from the grave ;

and recently Mr. Wm. Morris has given a beautiful and original
version, not at all Euripidean, in the first volume of his *Earthly
Paradise*. There is a good translation by Banks (1849). By far
the best translation is Mr. Browning's, in his *Balaustion's Adventure*, but it is much to be regretted that he did not render the
choral odes into lyric verse. No one has more thoroughly
appreciated the mean features of Admetus and Pheres, and
their dramatic propriety. A tolerably faithful transcript, adapted
for the lyrical stage by Frank Murray (from Potter's version),
was set to music by Henry Gadsby, on the model of Mendelssohn's *Antigone*, which seems likely to inspire a good many
imitations. There are excellent special editions by Monk and
G. Hermann, as well as a recension by G. Dindorf.

§ 202. The *Medea* came out in 431 B.C. along with the
poet's *Philoctetes, Dictys*, and the satyric *Reapers* (the last was
early lost). It was based upon a play of Neophron's, and only
obtained the third prize, Euphorion being first, and Sophocles
second. It may accordingly be regarded as a failure in its
day—an opinion apparently confirmed by the faults (viz. Ægeus
and the winged chariot) selected from it as specimens in Aristotle's *Poetic*. There is considerable evidence of there being a
second edition of the play, and many of the variants, or so-
called interpolations, seem to arise from both versions being
preserved and confused. Nevertheless there was no play of
Euripides more praised and imitated by both Romans and

moderns.   It is too well known to demand any close analysis
here.   The whole interest turns upon the delineation of the
furious passion of Medea, and her devices to punish those who
have offended her.   The other characters, with the exception
of the two aged and faithful servants, who admirably introduce
the action, are either mean or colourless.   Iason is a sort of
Æneas, who endeavours to justify his desertion of his wife by
specious falsehoods, and is not even, like the hero of Virgil, incited by the voice of the gods.   His grief for his children is
considered by some critics to atone for these grave defects.
The rest are not worth mentioning, if we except the chorus of
Corinthian women, which in this play justifies the censure of the
critics, inasmuch as it coolly admits the confidences of Medea
and hears fearful plots against the king and the princess of the
land, without offering any resistance.   It remonstrates but feebly
even with her proposed murder of her children.   The most
celebrated chorus, which is a beautiful eulogy upon Athens,
is merely suggested by the accident that Ægeus, its king,
is about to harbour a sorceress and a wholesale murderess,
even of her own family.   Yet the passage, though quite irrelevant, is very famous.[1]   The whole episode of Ægeus, who is
introduced in order that the omnipotent sorceress, with her
winged chariot, may not be cast out without a refuge, has been
justly censured in the *Poetic* and elsewhere as a means not
required, and as an otiose excrescence to the play, not without
offensive details.[2]   Nevertheless the vehement and commanding figure of the heroine has fascinated the great majority of
critics, who, like every public, seem to miss finer points, and
appreciate only the strong lines, and the prominent features of
violent and unnatural passion.

M. Patin[3] draws a most interesting comparison with the *Tra-*

---

[1] vv. 824-45.

[2] If Medea, as some critics suppose, and as the chorus appears to
assume (v. 1385), really offers herself in marriage to the childless Ægeus
in this scene, I can hardly conceive Aristophanes passing over such a
feature.   According to the legend, she did live with him, and bore him a
son called Medus.   She seems to have appeared as his wife in Euripides'
tragedy of Ægeus, in which she endeavours to poison Theseus.

[3] *Euripide,* i. p. 118.

chiniæ of Sophocles, which certainly bears some relation of conscious contrast to the *Medea*, but unfortunately we do not know which of the two plays was the earlier, and therefore which of the poets meant to criticise or improve upon the other. I venture to suppose that Sophocles desired to paint a far more natural and womanly picture of the sufferings of a deserted wife, who, without the power and wickedness of Medea, still destroys her deceiver, and brings ruin on herself, in spite of her patience and long-suffering. The coincidence of the two plays, the foreign residence of both heroines, the poisoned robe, the pretended contentment of both to attain their ends, is very striking. But the *Trachiniæ*, in my opinion the finer play, has made no mark in the world compared to the *Medea*, whose fierce fury has always been strangely admired.

The Greek critics even went so far as to censure what we should call the only great and affecting feature of the play—the irresolution and tears of the murderess,[1] when she has resolved to sacrifice her innocent children for the mere purpose of torturing her faithless husband. This criticism is apparently quoted in the Greek argument as the opinion of Dicæarchus and of Aristotle. Surely it may be affirmed, that if this feature caused the failure of the piece, we may indeed thank Euripides for having violated his audience's notions of consistency. The scene of irresolution and of alternation between jealous fury and human pity must always have been, as it now is, a capital occasion for a great display of genius in the actor or actress of the part, and this is doubtless the real cause of the permanent hold the piece has taken upon the world. I may also call attention to the great speech of Medea to Iason,[2] which argues indeed the very strongest case, but is nevertheless, especially at its conclusion, an admirable piece of rhetoric.

§ 203. We actually hear of six Greek *Medeas*, besides the early play of Neophron,[3] not to speak of the comic parodies. Ennius

---

[1] vv. 1021, sq. [2] vv. 465, sq.

[3] The text of the ὑπόθεσις to our *Medea*, which mentions this play, being corrupt, some critics have thought that the play of Neophron, from which Stobæus cites the monologue of Medea, was an imitation by a poet of the date of Alexander. I do not think the author of the argument can possibly have meant this, however the words are taken.

imitated the play of Euripides,[1] and both Cicero and Brutus are said to have been reading it or citing it in their last moments—no mean distinction for any tragedy. The opening lines are very often cited in an elegant version by Phædrus. Horace too alludes to it, and Ovid's earliest work was a *Medea*, which was acted on the Roman stage with applause, when the author, years after, was in exile. It is praised by Tacitus and Quintilian, and does not seem to have been a mere translation from Euripides. There remains to us, unfortunately, a Medea among the works of Seneca, who could not refrain from handling a subject so congenial to Roman tastes. But in this play the magic powers of the sorceress are the great feature, the age having turned from an effete polytheism to the gloomy horrors of magic and witchcraft. The fury of the murderess is exaggerated even beyond the picture of Euripides, and the whole play glitters with the false tinsel of artificial rhetoric. Buchanan gave a Latin version of the play, and Dolce an Italian, but Pérouse followed Seneca in his French play (1553), as did Corneille (1635), and Longepierre (1694). These poor imitations dilated on the amours of Iason, and represented Creon and his daughter in a sort of *auto da fé* on the stage ; but Voltaire, in criticising them and Seneca's *Medea*, thinks fit to include the Greek play, which, as M. Patin observes, he seems not to have read. There was an English version by Glover in 1761, which humanises and christianises both Iason and Medea, and makes her crime the result of a delirious moment. Grillparzer's trilogy (the *Golden Fleece*) in its last play likewise softens the terrible sorceress, and drives her to the crime by the heartlessness of her children, who will not return to her from the amiable Creusa, when the latter desires to surrender them. The same features mark the *Medeas* of Niccolini, of Lucas, brought out in Paris in 1855, and of Ernest Legouvé,

---

[1] Cicero speaks of it as a literal translation from the Greek, but this is not verified by the fragments, which both in this and the other Ennian imitations cannot be found in our Greek originals. This variation from the models is too persistent to be accounted for by first editions, or by emended copies of the Greek plays used by Ennius, and must be taken as conclusive evidence that his versions were free renderings, paraphrasing the sense, and changing the metres, as we can show from extant fragments.

which in its Italian dress has afforded Mde. Ristori one of her greatest tragic triumphs, and which is still performed in Paris. But the play is no longer the savage and painful play of Euripides, and is, I confess, to me not inferior. The opera offers us Hoffmann's elegant version, set to music by Cherubini, and I might add the *Norma* of Bellini, where the main situation is copied from the Medea, though compassion prevails. The best editions are Kirchhoff's (1852) and Prinz' (1879) for criticism, those of Wecklein (1879) and A. W. Verrall (1881) for exegesis also, the last excellent.

Klinger's modern reproduction is praised by the Germans. The beautiful epic version of Mr. Morris, in the last book of his *Life and Death of Iason*, handles the myth (as is his wont) very freely, and dwells chiefly on the gradual estrangement of Iason through the love of Glauce, and the gradual relapse of Medea from the peaceful and happy wife to the furious sorceress.

§ 204. The *Hippolytus* (στεφανίας, or crowned, to distinguish it from the earlier καλυπτόμενος, veiled, of which the explanation is now lost) appeared three years after the *Medea*, in 428 B.C., and is our earliest example of a *romantic* subject in the Greek drama.[1] We are told that it obtained the first place against Iophon and Ion's competition, but we are not told whether or what other plays accompanied it, nor of the plays it defeated. The earlier version of the play was not only read and admired, but possibly copied in the play of Seneca; yet it failed at Athens, chiefly, it is thought, because of the boldness with which Phædra told her love in person to her stepson, and then in person maligned him to his father. In Seneca she uses incantations to the moon, and justifies her guilt by Theseus' infidelities. It is only upon his death that she confesses her guilt and dies. This may have been the plan remodelled in the play before us, and it is a literary fact of no small interest to know that Euripides certainly confessed his earlier failure and strove to improve upon it, with success, while at the same time he allowed the earlier form to be circulated. For it implies both a real desire to please the Athenian audience, and also a certain contempt for their censure, in which the smaller reading public of the day probably supported him.

---

[1] We have lost Æschylus' *Myrmidons*, perhaps an earlier example.

The delineation of the passion of Phædra is the great feature of the play, and it is indeed drawn with a master hand. But in one point[1] the modern reader feels shocked or dissatisfied, in her sudden determination, not adequately motived in the play, of involving Hippolytus in her ruin by a bare falsehood, and it is peculiarly Greek that this odious crime should not be held to prevent her dying with honour and good fame (εὐκλέης). In our day we should be more disposed to pardon unchastity than this deliberate and irremediable lying, nor would any modern poet paint it in a woman of Phædra's otherwise good and noble character.

All the advances to Hippolytus, and the inducements to crime, which Phædra at first honestly and nobly resists, are suggested by her nurse, a feeble and immoral old woman, who perhaps talks too well, but plays a very natural part. The character of Hippolytus, which is admirably sustained through the play, is cold and harsh, and what we might call offensively holy. It was a character with which no Greek public could feel much sympathy, as asceticism was disliked, and even censured on principle. There is indeed no commonplace more insisted upon all through the tragedies than that the delights of moderate love (as compared with the agonies of extreme passion) are to be enjoyed as the best and most real pleasure in this mortal life. It is, therefore, from this point of view that the poet, while he rewards Hippolytus' virtue with heroic honours after death, makes him a capital failure in life. The hatred of Aphrodite, who is drawn in the worst and most repulsive colours, seems to express the revenge of nature upon those who violate her decrees. Probably the spite of Aphrodite, as well as the weakness of Artemis, the patron goddess of the hero, is also intended to lower the conception of these deities in the public mind. It is a *reductio ad absurdum* of Divine Providence, when the most awful misfortunes of men are ascribed to the malice of hostile and the impotence of friendly deities. Some good critics have indeed defended Artemis, and called her a noble character in this play ; but what shall we say of a deity who, when impotent to save her favourite, threatens[2]

---

[1] *Aristoph. Apology*, p. 26.   [2] v. 1420.

that she will be avenged by slaying with her arrows some favourite of Aphrodite? This is verily to make mankind the sport of malignant gods. Euripides cannot have given them these miserable parts, without intending to satirise the popular creed, and so to open the way for higher and purer religious conceptions. The chorus is a weak, and sometimes irrelevant spectator of the action, a necessary consequence, indeed, of its being present during the whole of the action, and, therefore, not fairly to be censured. One very elegant chorus on the power of Eros [1] may be compared with the parallel ode in Sophocles' *Antigone.* There is a chorus of attendants (what was called a παραχορήγημα) which accompanies Hippolytus at the opening, and which is distinct from the proper chorus—a rare device in Greek tragedy. Nothing will show more clearly the sort of criticism to which Euripides has been subjected, in ancient and modern times, than the general outcry against a celebrated line uttered by Hippolytus: ' My tongue has sworn, but my mind has taken no oath ' (ἡ γλῶσσ' ὀμώμοχ', ἡ δὲ φρὴν ἀνώμοτος). He exclaims this in his fury, when the old nurse adjures him by his oath not to betray her wretched mistress. It seems indeed hard that a dramatic poet should be judged by the excited utterances of his characters, but it is worse than hard, it is shamefully unjust, that the critics should not have read on fifty lines, where the same character Hippolytus, on calmer consideration, [2] declares that, *were he not bound by the sanctity of his oath,* he would certainly inform Theseus. And he dies simply because he will not violate this very oath, stolen from him when off his guard. I doubt whether any criticism, ancient or modern, contains among its myriad injustices, whether of negligence, ignorance, or deliberate malice, a more flagrantly absurd accusation. And yet Aristophanes, who leads the way in this sort of falsehood, is still extolled by some as the greatest and deepest exponent of the faults of Euripides.

Æschylus and Sophocles, as might be expected, did not touch this subject, but Agathon appears to have treated it. [3]

[1] vv. 525-64; translated for me by Mr. Browning in my monograph on Euripides, p. 116.

[2] v. 657.   [3] Aristoph. *Thesmoph.* 153.

There was an *Hippolytus* by Lycophron, and though the older Roman tragedians have left us no trace of a version, the allusions of Virgil in the *Æneid*,[1] and the perpetual recurrence of the subject in Ovid,[2] show how well it was known in the golden age of Roman literature.

The *Hippolytus* of Seneca, from which the scene of Phædra's personal declaration to Hippolytus was adopted by Racine in his famous play, is still praised by French critics. It was highly esteemed, and even preferred to the Greek play, in the Renaissance. It was acted in Latin at Rome in 1483, and freely rehandled by Garnier, in a French version, in 1573. The next celebrated French version was that of Gilbert, Queen Christina's French minister in 1646. But his very title, *Hippolyte ou le Garçon insensible*, sounds strange, and the play is said nevertheless to have admitted a great deal of gallantry in the hero. In 1677 Racine produced his famous *Phèdre*, of which the absolute and comparative merits have been discussed in a library of criticism. A hostile clique got up an opposition version by Pradon, and for a moment defeated and disgusted the poet, but the very pains taken by Schlegel, and even by French critics, to sustain Euripides against him, shows the real importance of the piece. For a long time, in the days of Voltaire and La Harpe, and of the revolt against antiquity, Euripides was utterly scouted in comparison. But now-a-days, when the wigs and the powder, the etiquette and the artifice, of the French court of the seventeenth century can hardly be tolerated as the decoration for a Greek tragedy, it is rare to find the real merits of Racine admitted, in the face of such tasteless and vulgar anachronism. Yet for all that, Racine's *Phèdre* is a great play, and it is well worth while to read the poet's short and most interesting preface, in which he gives the reasons for his deviations. He grounds the whole merit of his tragedy, as Aristophanes makes Æschylus and Euripides argue, not on its poetical features, but on its moral lessons. He has spoilt Hippolytus by giving him a passion for the princess *Aricie*, whom Theseus, for state reasons, had forbidden to marry. But this

---

[1] vii. 761.
[2] *Fasti*, iii. 266, vi. 733 ; *Metam.* xv. 492 ; *Epist. Her.* iv.

additional cause of Hippolytus' rejection of Phædra's suit adds
the fury of jealousy to her madness, and is the main cause of
her false charge against him, thus giving a motive where there
is hardly a sufficient one in Euripides. The passage in which
she shrinks from the death she is seeking, at the thought ot
appearing before her father Minos, the judge of the dead, is
very finely conceived ; on the whole, however, she exhibits too
much of her passion in personal pleading on the stage, and so
falls far behind Euripides' Phædra in delicacy.

There was an English Phædra by Edmund Smith in 1707,
based on both Racine's and Pradon's, and like them full of court
intrigues, captains of the household, prime ministers, and the
like.   There were operas on it attempted by Rameau (1733),
and by Lemoine (1786), neither of which is now known.   The
Greek play was put on the German stage faithfully in 1851, but
was found inferior to Racine's for such a performance.   There
are special editions by Musgrave, Valckenaer, Monk, and lastly
by Berthold.[1]   We know from the fragments of lost plays, and
from the criticisms of Aristophanes, that Euripides chose the
painful subject of a great criminal passion for several plays, the
Phrixus, Sthenobœa (Bellerophon), and certainly the *Phœnix*,
built upon the narrative of the aged hero in the ninth book of the
Iliad.   If we could trust Aristophanes, we might suppose that
he was the first to venture on such a subject, but the allusions
of the critics to Neophron's *Medea*, and the traces of similar
subjects in the fragments of Sophocles, make it uncertain
whether he was the originator, as he certainly was the greatest
master, in this very modern department of tragedy.

§ 205. The *Andromache* need not occupy us long, being
one of the worst constructed, and least interesting, plays of
Euripides. The date is uncertain, as it was not brought
out at Athens, perhaps not till after the poet's death, and is
only to be fixed doubtfully by the bitter allusions to Sparta,
with which it teems.   It has indeed quite the air of a
political pamphlet under the guise of a tragedy.   It must,

[1] I can recommend a very faithful poetical version by Mr. M. P. Fitzgerald (London, 1867), in a volume before cited, and entitled *The Crowned
Hippolytus*.   Another by Miss Robinson has since appeared.

therefore, have been composed during the Peloponnesian war,
possibly about 419 B.C.[1]   The character of Andromache (now
the slave and concubine of Neoptolemus), who opens the play
as a suppliant telling her tale and mourning her woes *in elegiacs*
(a metre never used elsewhere in our extant tragedies), is well
conceived, and the scene in which her child, whom she had
hidden, is brought before her by Menelaus, and threatened with
instant death if she will not leave the altar, is full of true Euripidean pathos.   The laments of mother and child, as they are
led away to execution, are in the same strain, but are interrupted by the *surprise* of Peleus appearing just in time—a rare
expedient in Greek tragedy.   On the other hand, the characters
of the jealous wife Hermione, and her father Menelaus, are
violent, mean, and treacherous beyond endurance.   They
represent the vulgarest tyrants, and are rather fit for Alfieri's
stage.   All this is intended as a direct censure on Sparta,
a feeling in which the poet hardly varied, as Bergk justly observes, though it is seldom so unpleasantly obtruded upon us as
in this play.[2]   When Andromache and her child are saved, after
a long and angry altercation between Peleus and Menelaus, the
play is properly concluded, but is awkwardly expanded by a
sort of afterpiece, in which Hermione rushes in, beside herself
with fear at what she has dared in the absence of her husband.
This emotional and absurd panic opens the way for the appearance of Orestes, with whom she at once arranges a *mariage de
convenance* of the most prosaic kind, and flies.   Then follows the
elaborate narrative of the murder of her former husband Neoptolemus at Delphi, owing to the plots of Orestes.   The lamen-

---

[1] The choral metres, which are chiefly dactylico-trochaic, instead of the
glyconics afterwards in favour, and which Dindorf considers a surer internal
mark than general anti-Spartan allusions, point to an earlier date, and
agree with the schol. on v. 445, which conjectures the play to have been
composed at the opening of the Peloponnesian War.   On the other hand,
the allusion to this play at the end of the *Orestes* (vv. 1653, sq.) seems as
if its memory were yet fresh, and suggests a later date.

[2] The *Helena* is an exception (below, p 353).   When Menelaus asserts
(vv. 374 and 585) that he will kill Neoptolemus' slaves, because friends
should have all their property in common, this seems like a parody on the
habits, or supposed habits, of the club life led by the Spartans at home.

tations of Peleus, and the divine interposition, and settlement of the future, by Thetis, conclude the play.   Though justly called a second-rate play by the scholiasts, it was well enough known to be quoted by Clitus [1] on the undue share of glory obtained by the generals of soldiers who bore the heat and burden of the day, and thus it cost him his life at the hands of the infuriated Alexander. The *Andromache* of Ennius, of which we have a considerable fragment, seems to embrace the time of the capture of Troy, and not the period of this play ; but the 5th book of Vergil's Æneid is evidently composed with a clear recollection of it.[2]   The famous *Andromaque* of Racine only borrows the main facts from the story as found in Euripides and Vergil, and expands it by introducing a motive which does not exist in the Greek play, that of the passion of love.   He moreover felt bound to soften and alter what Euripides had frankly put forward, not only as the usage of heroic times, but even of his own day—the enforced concubinage of female captives, however noble, and the very slight social stain which such a misfortune entailed. On this I have elsewhere commented.[3]   The ode on the advantages of noble birth [4] strikes me as peculiarly Pindaric in tone and diction—more so than any other of Euripides' choral songs.   The tirade [5] against the dangers of admitting gossiping female visitors to one's house seems just like what Aristophanes would recommend, and may be a serious advice intended by the poet.

§ 206.   The *Heracleidæ*, a play less studied than it deserves, owes some of this neglect to its bad preservation.   It dates somewhere in Ol. 88–90, and celebrates the honourable conduct of Athens in protecting the suppliant children of Heracles, and her victory over the insolent Argive king Eurystheus, who invades Attica to recover the fugitives.   The play was obviously intended as a political document, directed against the Argive party in Athens during the Peloponnesian War.   It is certain that at this agitated time the tragic stage, which should

---

[1] vv. 693, sq.

[2] The contrasts between the conception of Vergil and that of Euripides have been admirably pointed out by Patin, *Euripide*, i. p. 291.

[3] *Social Greece*, p. 119.   [4] vv. 764, sq.   [5] vv. 930, sq.

have been devoted to joys and griefs above mean earthly
things, was degraded, as its modern analogue the pulpit has
often been, to be a political platform, but a platform on which
one side only can have its say.   But together with this main
idea, Euripides gives us a great many beautiful and affecting
situations, and it may be said that for tragic interest none of his
plays exceed the first part, ending, unfortunately, with a huge
gap after the 629th line.   Many critics have censured it in
ignorance of this capital fact, and also of some lesser mutila-
tions at the end, which is now, as we have it, clearly unfinished,
and therefore unsatisfactory.[1]

The play opens with the altercation between the violent
and brutal Argive herald, Kopreus, who is very like the herald
in Æschylus' *Supplices*, and the faithful Iolaos, who in extreme
age and decrepitude endeavours to guard the children of his old
comrade in arms.   It is remarkable how Greek tragedians seem
consistently to ascribe this impudence and bullying to heralds,
so unlike those of Homer.   The chorus interferes, and presently
Demophon appears, and dismisses the insolent herald, not without being seriously tempted to do him violence.   The poet
evidently had before him the other version of the legend, that
this herald was killed by the Athenians.   But when the Athenian king has undertaken the risk of protecting the fugitives,
the prophets tell him that a noble virgin must be sacrificed to
ensure his victory.   This news gives rise to a pathetic scene of
despair in Iolaos, who has been driven from city to city, and
sees no end to the persecution.   But the old man's idle offer
of his own life is interrupted by the entrance of Macaria, one
of the Heracleidæ, who when she hears of the oracle, calmly
offers herself, despising even the chance of the lot among her
sisters.   Nothing can be finer than the drawing of this noble girl,
one of Euripides' greatest heroines.   But unfortunately the
play breaks off before the narrative of her sacrifice, and there
is doubtless also lost a *kommos* over her by Alcmena and the

---

[1] These lacunæ are obvious from the fact that more than one ancient
citation from the play is not in our texts.   Kirchhoff was (I believe) the
first to lay stress on this, and to seek the exact places where the gaps
occur.   The name Macaria does not occur in the text.

chorus. The interest of the spectator is then transferred to the approaching battle, and the warlike fire of the decrepid Iolaos, who insists on going into the ranks ; and as the putting on of armour would, I suppose, have been impossible to an actor on the Greek stage, the messenger, a servant of Hyllus, discreetly offers to carry it till he has reached the field. The manifestly comic drawing of Iolaos in this scene appears to me a satire on some effete Athenian general, who, like our Crimean generals, undertook active service when no longer fit for it. But by a miracle, which is presently narrated, he recovers his youth, and, with Hyllus, defeats and captures Eurystheus. The mutilated concluding scene is again a discussion of a matter of present interest—the fate of prisoners taken in battle. Alcmena, with the ferocity which Euripides generally depicts in old women, demands his instant death. The chorus insist that by the laws of Hellenic warfare an adversary not killed in battle cannot be afterwards slain without impiety. Eurystheus seems to facilitate his own death by prophesying that his grave will serve Athens ; in this, very like the later Œdipus at Colonus of Sophocles—a play with which the present has many features in common. The chorus appears to yield ; the real settlement of the dispute is lost.

The imitations of this play are few. Dauchet's (1720) and Marmontel's (1752) are said to contain all the vices of the French tragedy in no ordinary degree. The only special edition quoted is that of Elmsley. To many ordinary students of Greek literature the very name of Macaria is unknown.

§ 207. I take up the *Supplices* next, of which the date, also uncertain (most probably 420 B.C., shortly after the battle of Delium), is not far removed from that of the *Heracleidæ*, and of which the plan is very similar, though the politics are quite different. For as in the former play hostility to Argos, and its wanton invasion of Attica, were prominent, so here alliance and eternal friendship with Argos are most solemnly inculcated. If it be true, as all critics agree, that these plays were brought on the stage within three or four years of one another, during the shifting interests and alliances of the Peloponnesian War, it will prove how completely Euripides regarded them as temporary political advices, varying with the situation, and in which the inconsistencies were not of more importance than would be the inconsistencies in a volume of political speeches. I think, moreover, that we may clearly perceive in the discussions on monarchy, democracy, and general statecraft, which lead away the characters from their proper business, a growing tendency in tragedy to become a written record, and to appeal to a reading public, instead of the listening crowd in the theatre. Euripides, in the long and interesting debate between the Theban herald and Theseus, is so conscious of this, that he makes Theseus comment on the volubility of the herald in matters not concerning him, and wonder at his own patience in replying to him. It is thus quite plain that what are called rhetorical redundancies in this and other Euripidean plays are deliberately admitted by the poet as subservient to an important purpose—that of the political education of the people from his point of view.

The author of the argument, of which only a fragment remains, regards the play as an encomium of Athens. But this direct or indirect laudation of Athens occurs so perpetually all through Greek tragedy, that it seems a mistake to make *that* the main object of the play in which it differs only in degree from so many others. I think the wearisome recurrence of this feature, and the favour with which we know it was received, bespeak a very vulgar vanity on the part of the Attic public, and a great deficiency in that elegance and chastity of taste which they and their modern critics perpetually arrogate as their private property.

This play is among the best of Euripides. After a short prologue from Æthra—which is really an indirect prayer to Demeter at Eleusis—the chorus enters with a truly Æschylean parodos, as indeed, all through the play, the chorus takes a prominent part in the action. It consists of the seven mothers of the slain chiefs before Thebes, together with their seven attendants. At the end of the play there is, besides, a chorus of the orphans. The long dialogue between Theseus and Adrastus, who accompanies the suppliants, is full of beauty, and also of proverbial wisdom, on which account it has been also considerably interpolated. Theseus is, as usual, represented as a constitutional monarch, who practically directs a democracy —probably on the model afforded by Pericles. But when he determines to help the suppliants and to send a herald to demand the burying of the slain, he is anticipated by the Theban herald, who comes to threaten Theseus and to warn him not to take these steps. The long discussion between them, ending, as usual, in an agitated *stretto* of stichomuthia,[1] is the most interesting exponent of the poet's political views in all his extant works. The two divisions of seven in the chorus sing an amœbean strain of anxious suspense, till in a few moments a messenger comes in, and (in violation of the unity of time) narrates at length Theseus' victory. Then come in the bodies of the slain chiefs with Theseus, and there follows a great lamentation scene, in which Adrastus speaks the *éloge* of each. Presently Evadne, the wife of Capaneus, and sister of Hippomedon, followed upon the stage by her father Iphis, from whom she has escaped in the madness of her grief, enters upon a high cliff over the stage, and casts herself into the pyre. The laments of Iphis are written with peculiar grace. The continued wailing of the two choruses, children and parents of the seven chiefs, are interrupted by Adrastus' promise of eternal gratitude. Lastly, Athene comes in *ex machina* in a perfectly otiose and superfluous manner, to enforce the details of the treaty between Athens and Argos.

The subject had been already treated in Æschylus's *Eleusinians*. The celebrity of the present play may be inferred from the dream of Thrasyllus, on the night before Arginusæ, that he and his six colleagues were victorious in playing the *Phœnissæ* against the hostile leader's *Supplices*, in the theatre of Athens, but that all his colleagues were dead. Elmsley's and G. Hermann's are the best editions, Elmsley's completing Markland's labours.

§ 208. The *Hecuba* was brought out before the *Clouds* of Aristophanes, where it is alluded to (in Ol. 89, 1). From a

---

[1] M. Patin (ii. p. 195) notices this just representation of nature by the Greek tragic poets, for discussions, at first cool, are apt to become violent, and compares it to the parallel feature in the modern opera.

further allusion in the play itself to the Deliac festival, restored in Ol. 88, 3. it seems tolerably certain that it must have appeared in Ol. 88, 4 (425 B.C.), and may therefore have been earlier than the plays last mentioned. But it belongs to the same period of the poet's style, and differs considerably in this respect from the *Troades*, which treats almost the same subject, but was brought out eight or nine years later. I will therefore not discuss them in conjunction, as some critics have done, but follow in preference the order of time. The *Hecuba* has always been a favourite play, and has not only been frequently imitated, but edited ever since Erasmus' time for school use. It is by no means so replete with political allusions as the *Supplices*, and is on the whole a better tragedy, though not so interesting to read. It treats of the climax of Hecuba's misfortunes, the sacrifice of Polyxena at the grave of Achilles,[1] and the murder of Polydorus, her youngest son, by his Thracian host, Polymestor. The chorus of Trojan captives sings odes of great beauty, especially that on the fall of Ilium,[2] but does not enter into the action of the play. The pleading of Hecuba with Odysseus, who comes to take Polyxena, is full of pathos ; and so is the noble conduct of the maiden, who is a heroine of the same type as Macaria, but varied with that peculiar art of Euripides which never condescends to repeat itself. Macaria has the highest motive for her sacrifice—the salvation of her brothers and sisters. Polyxena is sacrificed to an enemy, and by enemies, and is therefore obliged to face death without any reward save the escape from the miseries and disgrace of slavery. Yet though she dwells upon these very strongly, she seems to regret nothing so much as the griefs of her wretched and despairing mother.

The narrative of her death (which in Macaria's case is unfortunately lost) forms a beautiful conclusion to the former half of the play, which is divided, like many of Euripides', between two interests more or less loosely connected. In the present play

---

[1] It is to be noted that the scene being laid in Thrace, and the tomb of Achilles being in the Troad, the so-called unity of place is here violated, as often elsewhere in Greek tragedy.

[2] vv. 905, sq. :   σὺ μέν, ὦ πατρὶς Ἰλιάς, κ.τ.λ.

the nexus, though merely accidental, is most artfully devised, for the fellow slave, who goes to fetch water for Polyxena's funeral rites, finds the body of Polydorus tossing on the shore. This brings out the fierce element in the heart-broken mother. She debates, in an aside not common on the Greek stage,[1] whether she will plead her case of vengeance to Agamemnon, and then she does so with great art, if not with dignity. Upon his acquiescence, she carries out her plot vigorously, murders Polymestor's children, and blinds the king himself, whose wild lamentations, with Hecuba's justification by Agamemnon, and the Thracian's gloomy prophecies, conclude the play. The change of the heart-broken Hecuba, when there is nothing more to plead for, from despair to savage fury, is finely conceived, and agrees with the cruelty which Euripides is apt to attribute to old women in other plays. M. Patin compares her to the Margaret in Shakspeare's *Richard III.* Nevertheless Hecuba's lamentation for her children is conceived in quite a different spirit from that of the barbarous Thracian, who is like a wild beast robbed of its whelps, as the poet more than once reminds us.

It may fairly be doubted whether Sophocles' Polyxena was superior, or even equal to Euripides' heroine. Ennius selected the *Hecuba* for a translation, which was admired by Cicero and Horace. Vergil and Ovid recur to the same original in some of their finest writing. The earliest modern versions were by Erasmus into Latin, Lazare Baïf into French, and Dolce into Italian. In *Hamlet* the sorrows of Hecuba are alluded to as proverbial, but probably in reference to Seneca's play, which will be considered when we come to the *Troades.* *Contaminations* of the two plays were common in France all through the seventeenth and eighteenth centuries. M. Patin selects for special censure those of Pradon (1679), and Chateaubrun (1755). Porson and G. Hermann have spent critical labour on the recension and illustration of this play ; the scholia upon it are unusually full. There was an anonymous English version called ' Hecuba, a tragedy,' catalogued as by Rich. West, Lord Chancellor of Ire-

---

[1] This feature recurs in the famous dialogue between Ion and Creusa (*Ion*, 424, sq.), and elsewhere in that play, and may belong to the later style of Euripides.

land, published in London in 1726.[1]   Though the author, who
does not name himself, says nothing about his handling of
the play, and speaks of it as a translation, he has made
notable changes ; in fact, it is rather a French than a Greek
tragedy.   The chorus and second messenger's speech are
omitted, and both Polymestor and Hecuba have attendants,
with whom they converse.   The plot is considerably changed.
I have never seen any copy of this rare print, except that in
the Bodleian Library.

§ 209. The *Raging Heracles* ('Ηρακλῆς μαινόμενος), which
is among the plays preserved to us by the Florentine MS.
called C, is one of the most precious remains of Euripides, and
is full of the deepest tragic pathos.   It seems to have been
brought out about Ol. 90, a year or two later than the *Hecuba*,
and is counted one of his best plays in metre and diction by
the critics.   Here, again, as in the *Hecuba*, two apparently
distinct actions are brought together really by an unity of interest, but technically by a new prologue of Iris, who explains
the sequel of the drama.   Nothing can be more suited to
excite our pity and terror than the plot, unconventional as it is.
The prior part of the play, which is constructed very like that
of the *Andromache* and the *Heracleidæ*, turns upon the persecution of the father, wife, and children of the absent Heracles,
by Lycos, tyrant of Thebes.   With a brutal frankness then often
appearing in Athenian politics, but which it was fashionable to
ascribe to tyrants, he insolently insists upon their death, and
proposes to drive them from their asylum in the temple of Zeus
by surrounding them with fire.   The aged Amphitryon is for
excuses and delays, in the hope of some chance relief, and
shows far more desire for life than the youthful Megara, who
faces the prospect of death with that boldness and simplicity
often found in Euripides' heroines.   Her character is drawn
with great beauty, as is also the attitude of the chorus of old
men, who fire up in great indignation at Lycos, but feel unable
to resist him.   When the woeful procession of the family of

---

[1] It was brought out at Drury Lane Theatre ; but, as the author complains in his preface, 'a rout of young Vandals in the galleries intimidated
the young actresses, disturbed the audience, and prevented all attention.'

Heracles, who have obtained the single favour of attiring themselves within for their death, reappears on the stage, and Megara has taken sad farewell of her sons, Heracles suddenly appears ; and there follows a splendid scene of explanation, and then of vengeance, the tyrant being slain within, in the hearing of the chorus, just as in the parallel scene of the *Agamemnon.*   The chorus sing a hymn of thanksgiving ; and so this part of the drama concludes.

But at the end of the ode they break out into horror at the sight of the terrible image of Lytta, or Madness, whom Iris brings down upon the palace, and explains that now Heracles is no longer protected by Fate, as his labours are over, and that he is therefore open to Here's vengeance.[1]   There is no adequate motive alleged for this hatred, but before a Greek audience it was so well admitted as to be reasonably assumed by the poet.   The dreadful catastrophe follows, and takes place during an agitated and broken strain of the chorus, who see the palace shaking, and hear the noise, but learn the details from a messenger in a most thrilling speech.   The devoted wife and affectionate children, whom Heracles has just saved from instant death, have been massacred by the hero himself in his frenzy ; and he was on the point of slaying his father, when Athena appeared in armour, and struck him down into a swoon.   The awakening of Heracles, the scene of explanation between him and Amphitryon which follows, the despair of the hero, who is scarcely saved from suicide by the sympathy of Theseus, and who at last departs with him for Athens—all this is worked out in the poet's greatest and most pathetic style.   M. Patin specially notices the profound pyschology in painting the method of Heracles' madness, so unlike the vague rambling often put upon the stage, and compares with this scene the parallel one in the *Orestes.*   The awakening of the hero may be intended to rival the corresponding scene in Sophocles' *Ajax,* to which the play shows many striking resemblances.   Indeed, the resolve of Heracles to face life, after his pathetic review of his ever-

---

[1] The student should notice the trochaic tetrameters here, which become more frequent in Euripides' *late* plays, so affording an iuternal test where there is no date.

increasing troubles, is far nobler and more profoundly tragic than Ajax' resolve to fly from disgrace by a voluntary death.

The choral odes are of great, though not of equal, merit, especially the famous complaint against age, and praise of youth,[1] so like Shakspeare's *Crabbed Age and Youth;* indeed, the whole play is well worthy of greater study than it usually receives. The sceptical outbreaks against Zeus and other gods are here particularly bold, but are tempered by the poet's splendid utterance, that all their crimes are but 'the inventions of idle singers.' The praise of archery[2] seems to imply a feeling that light-armed troops were coming into fashion, and that their usefulness was now recognised. We know that Plutarch was fond of this play, and Cicero refers to the ode on old age in his tract *De Senectute.* We have a *Hercules Furens* among the plays of Seneca, exhibiting all the faithless and inartistic copying of great models which we find in the other Latin tragedies of this school. Wecklein's ed. of Klotz (1877) is the most useful. We can now recommend the admirable translation in Mr. Browning's *Aristophanes' Apology*, as giving English readers a thoroughly faithful idea of this splendid play. The choral odes are, moreover, done justice to, and translated into adequate metre—in this an improvement on the *Alcestis,* to which I have already referred.

§ 210. The *Ion* seems to date from the same period. The mention of the obscure promontory of Rhion, where a great Athenian victory was gained in 429, and the stress laid on the architectural wonders at Delphi, where the Athenians, according to Pausanias, built a *stoa* in honour of the victory, seem to fix it not earlier than 425. But the prominence of monodies in the play rather points to a more recent date, when Euripides was about to pass into his later style. The play is no tragedy, but a melodrama with an ingenious plot full of surprises, and was certainly one of the earliest examples of the kind of plan adopted by the genteel (or new) comedy of the next century. Were there not great religious and patriotic interests at stake, which make the play serious throughout, it might more fairly be called a comedy than the *Alcestis* or *Orestes.* Even the most violent detractors of Euripides are obliged to acknowledge the perfec-

---

[1] vv. 637, sq.   [2] vv. 190, sq.

tion of this play, which is frequently called the best he has left us. But surely excellence of plot in a Greek play is not so high a quality as great depth of passion and sentiment. The *Ion*, however, is not failing in these, the peculiar province of the older tragedy, which has but little plot.

Passing by Hermes' prologue, which is tedious and dull, and is in my opinion altogether spurious, though defended by good critics, we come to the proper opening scene, one of the most beautiful of the Greek stage, in which Ion, the minister of Apollo's temple at Delphi, performs his morning duties about the temple, and drives away the birds which are hovering round the holy precincts.[1] There is no character in all Greek tragedy like this Ion, who reminds one strongly of the charming boys drawn by Plato in such dialogues as *Charmides* and *Lysis*. In purity and freshness he has been compared to Giotto's choristers, and has afforded Racine his masterpiece of imitation in the Joas of the *Athalie*. But I would liken him still more to the child Samuel, whose ministrations are painted with so exquisite a grace in the Old Testament. For Euripides represents him to us at the moment when his childlike innocence, and absence of all care, are to be rudely dissipated by sudden contact with the stormy passions and sorrows of the world. The chorus (of Creusa's retinue) come in to wonder at the temple and its sculptures ; and presently Creusa herself enters to inquire of the god, cloaking her case under the guise of a friend's distress. Then follows a scene of mutual confidences between the unwitting son and mother, which is full of tragic interest.

I will not pursue further the various steps by which Ion is declared first a son of Xuthus, then hated of Creusa as a stepchild, then her attempt to murder him, and at last her recognition of him by the clothes and ornaments with which she had exposed him. The agitated monologue of Creusa, when confessing her early shame, is in fine contrast to the innocent freshness of the

---

[1] In support of my belief in the spuriousness of the prologue, which, if admitted, makes the whole splendid dialogue of Ion and Creusa idle repetition, I may mention that the *Andromeda* and *Iphigenia in Aulis,* both without prologues, open with the actor's attention fixed on the heavens, as in the monody of Ion.

monologue of Ion. The refusal of the boy to follow his new father to Athens is in thorough keeping with his character, but expressed with such political insight as shows the poet plainly speaking through the character. As I noted two prologues in the *Heracles*, so here there are two resolutions of the plot—as it were, two *dii ex machina*—one by the Delphic priestess, the other by Athena, who appears at the end to remove all doubt. With very good taste Apollo, who could hardly appear with dignity, and Xuthus, who has been deceived, are kept out of sight. But in spite of much sceptical questioning and complaint, the chorus insists at the end that the gods' ways are not our ways, and that their seeming injustices are made good in due time. This and the glorifying of the mythic ancestors of the Athenians are the lessons conveyed in the spirit of the play. We can hardly call Creusa one of Euripides' heroines, for she is altogether a victim of circumstances, but still she powerfully attracts our sympathy in spite of her weak and sudden outburst of vindictiveness. The situation of a distracted mother seeking her son's death unwittingly was again used by Euripides, apparently with great success, in the *Cresphontes*, from which one beautiful choral fragment remains.

The chorus in this play is more than elsewhere the accomplice, and even the guilty accomplice, of the chief actress, and its other action is merely that of curious observers, if we except one most appropriate ode,[1] in which Euripides draws a fairy picture of Pan playing to the goddesses, who dance on the grassy top of the Acropolis, while he sits in his grotto beneath. The grotto is there still,[2] and so are the ruined temples, but no imagination can restore the grace and the holiness of the scene, now a wreck of stones and dust, of pollution and neglect.

There have been fewer imitations of this play than might be expected. It was translated into German by Wieland, and about the same time (1803) brought on the stage at Weimar by A. W.

---

[1] vv. 452, sq.

[2] This play decides a question which has divided archæologists, whether the grottoes of Apollo and of Pan, on the northern slope of the Acropolis, were identical or not. A comparison of vv. 502-4 with v. 938 shows that they were the same.

Schlegel, but unfortunately in a very vulgar and degraded version, which gave Xuthus a principal part and produced Apollo on the stage, and which so displeased the Weimar students, that old Goethe, in imitation of whose *Iphigenia* the play was written, and who had taken great pains about its representation, was obliged to stand up and command silence in the pit. There was an English imitation by W. Whitehead in 1754. The *Ion* of Talfourd has only the general conception of Ion in common with the Greek play, from which it is in no sense imitated. As to commentaries, after Hermann's recension (1827) we have three most scholarly editions by C. Badham (1851, 1853, and 1861), of which the second is the fullest and best, but in all the critical powers of the author and the unmistakeable influence of Cobet are apparent.

§ 211. The *Troades* came out in 415 B.C. as the third play with the *Alexander* and *Pulamedes:* it was followed by the *Sisyphus* as the satyrical piece. It was defeated by a tetralogy of Xenokles—the *Œdipus, Lycaon, Bacchæ,* and *Athamas.* Treating of the same subject as the *Hecuba,* it somewhat varies the incidents and the characters, the death of Astyanax supplanting that of Polyxena, and both Cassandra and Andromache appearing. There is, however, far less plot than in the *Hecuba,* and we miss even the satisfaction of revenge. It is indeed more absolutely devoid of interest than any play of Euripides, for it is simply 'a voice in Ramah, and lamentation—Rachel weeping for her children, and would not be comforted, because they were not.' It is the prophet's roll 'which was written within and without with mourning and lamentation and woe.' Nevertheless the wild and poetic fervour of Cassandra reminds us of the great passage in the *Agamemnon.* The litigious scene in which Hecuba and Helen argue before Menelaus, and the constant appearances of Talthybius, are not agreeable diversions. Above all, the ruthless murder of the infant Astyanax is too brutal to be fairly tolerable in any tragedy. As regards the loose connection of the scenes, Patin very properly[1] shows how, in what may be called Euripides' *episodic* pieces, he reverts to the trilogistic idea of Æschylus, but crowds together the loosely connected plays

[1] i. 333.

of the trilogy into the loosely connected scenes of a single play. This sort of tragedy, which is in effect very like the old lyrical pieces, such as the *Supplices* and *Persæ*, was put on the stage in contrast to the tragedies of intrigue, the one being intended to affect the heart, the other to excite the imagination of the spectator. The main sign of Euripides' later style is the prevalence of monodies, in which he excels, in spite of all Aristophanes' ridicule, and which are the most splendid features in both the *Ion* and in this play.

The many imitations have so naturally *contaminated* the *Troades* with the *Hecuba*, that it is not easy to treat them separately. Several passages in Vergil's Æneid, such as the appeal of Juno to Æolus, and the awful picture of the fall of Troy, are plainly adopted from the *Troades*. The *Troades* of Seneca is considered by good critics as the finest of that collection of Latin plays, and, in spite of its faults of tinsel, of false rhetoric, and of overdone sentiment, has real dramatic merit. The deaths of Polyxena and of Astyanax are both wrought in, thus copying features from each of Euripides' tragedies. But there is a very splendid tragic scene added on the attempts of Andromache to deceive Ulysses, and hide her child. Her violent fury and her threats are, however, foreign to the conception of both Homer, Vergil, and Euripides. Thus again, Seneca's Talthybius is led into sceptical doubts at the sight of the Trojan misfortunes, and a whole chorus is devoted to the denial of any future life—a grave and inartistic anachronism. There is a French *Troades* by Garnier (1578), built as much on Seneca as on Euripides, one by Sallebray (1640), and numerous obscure plays towards the end of the last century. I cannot but think that the epics of Homer and Vergil have been the real reason of the great popularity of these subjects upon the stage. I do not suppose that either of Euripides' plays would have sufficed to lead the fashion.

§ 212. The *Helena*, which comes to us, like some other plays, through the Florentine codex C alone, and in a very corrupt and much corrected state, has been placed very low among the plays of Euripides. It seems to have come out with the *Andromeda*, in 412 B.C. (Ol. 91, 4). and was certainly ridiculed with it by Aristophanes in his *Thesmophoriazusæ,* not without reason.   The play is a very curious one, and to be placed on a par with the *Electra* (which distinctly[1] alludes to it) on account of its very free handling of the celebrated legend of the rape of Helen.   The version which kept the heroine in Egypt, and denied that she had ever been in Troy, was first given by Stesichorus, and was repeated by the Egyptian priests to Herodotus, whose history did not appear till about this time.   Stesichorus, moreover, invented or found the notion of a phantom Helen at Troy.   The palinode of Stesichorus (cf. above, p. 203) was very celebrated, and is repeatedly alluded to by Plato.   Nevertheless, it seems very bold to transfer to the stage the fancy of a few literary men, or in any case to contradict the greatest and the best established of all the popular myths.   It is evident that this innovation did not prosper.   Isocrates, in his *Encomium,* takes no notice of it, and no modern has attempted to reproduce it except the German Wieland.   Apart from this novelty, there is throughout a friendly and even respectful handling of Sparta and the Spartans, which contradicts the general tone of the poet's mind, and stands, I think, alone among his extant plays.   Again, though there is much scepticism expressed, especially of prophecies, as was his wont at this period, the noblest character is a prophetess, who possesses an unerring knowledge of the future.   Menelaus, too, who is elsewhere a cowardly and mean bully, is here a ragged and distressed, but yet bold and adventurous hero, with no trace of his usual stage attributes.   And, lastly, Helen is a faithful and persecuted wife, though in the *Troades,* which shortly preceded, and the *Orestes,* which followed, this play, she appears in the most odious colours, and in accordance with the received myth.   All these anomalies make the *Helena* a problem hard to understand, and still harder when we compare it with the masterly *Iphigenia in Tauris,* which is laid on exactly the same plan, and is yet so infinitely greater, and better executed.   The choral odes are quite in the poet's later style, full of those repetitions of words which Aristophanes derides.[2]   The ode on the sorrows of

---

[1] v. 1271.

[2] Mr. Browning has not failed to reproduce this Euripidean feature with

Demeter is absolutely irrelevant, though gracefully composed.

Nevertheless, there is at least one scene, that of the recognition of Menelaus and the real Helen, witnessed by an old and faithful servant, which is of the highest merit in beauty and pathos, and we wonder how the poet should have chosen that mythical couple, whose conjugal relations in all his other tragedies were most painful, to exemplify the purest and most enduring domestic affection. This recognition scene should take its place in Greek literature with the matchless scene in the Odyssey, for the love of husband and wife was rarely idealised by the Greeks, and these grand exceptions are worthy of especial note. I suppose that by this bold contradiction not only of the current view of Helen, but of his own treatment of her and Menelaus in other plays, the poet meant to teach that the myths were only convenient vehicles for depicting human character and passion, and had no other value. Since Hermann's recension, the most important special edition is that of Badham,[1] who has done much for the text.

§ 213. We may choose next in order the *Iphigenia among the Tauri*, a play of unknown date, but evidently a late production of the poet's, to judge from the metres, the prevalence of monodies, and the irrelevant choruses. It is very like in plot to the *Helena*. In fact, the main elements are the same in both plays. Iphigenia, like Helen, is carried off by a special interposition of the gods to a barbarous land, where she is held in honour, but pines to return to her home. Both plays turn on the mutual recognition of the heroines and their deliverers, the husband and the brother, and then upon the dangers of the escape, the deceiving of the barbarian king in attaining it, and the superior seamanship and courage of the Greek sailors. But in this second play, Euripides has not contradicted any received myth, or distorted any well-known mythical type, and has, moreover, woven in the mutual friendship of Orestes and Pylades, and

great art and admirable effect in his version of the *Heracles*. We might adduce examples from a totally different school, the lyrics of Uhland and Platen, and how beautiful they are !

[1] Along with the *Iph. Taur.* in 1851.

made Iphigenia a heroine not only of situation, but of character. In both plays, though he has not scrupled to make barbarians talk good Greek, he has avoided the objections to a barbarian chorus, by giving the heroine a following of Greek attendants, who are naturally her accomplices. They even interfere actively in the *Helena* by literally laying hold of the enraged king, and striving to turn away his vengeance from his priestess sister; in the *Iphigenia*, by the more questionable expedient (unique, I think, in the extant tragedies) of telling the anxious messenger a deliberate falsehood to delay the king's knowledge of the prisoners' and the priestess' escape.[1]

The prologue, spoken by Iphigenia herself, explains how she had been snatched from under the knife of Calchas and carried by Artemis to the Tauric Chersonese, where, as her priestess, she was obliged to *prepare* for sacrifice (Euripides has here artistically softened the fierce legend) such luckless strangers as were cast upon the coast. Doubtless early Greek discoverers and adventurous merchantmen often met this fate at the hands of the wild Scythians, and it added to the excitement which enveloped the commerce of the early Greeks—'cette race,' says Dumas, 'qui a fait du commerce une poésie.' The first ode of the chorus[2] embodies this feeling with great spirit. But Iphigenia has been agitated by a dream, which portends to her the death of Orestes, upon whom she had long fixed her vague and undefined hopes of restoration to her home. The dream is admirably conceived, but it seems to me that the absolute certainty which it breeds in her mind, and her consequent sacrifice of libations, is somewhat of a flaw in the action of the play. At no epoch have men been forthwith persuaded by mere dreams without any other evidence. In the next scene Orestes and Pylades appear, who have been directed by Apollo, in spite of the acquittal before the Areopagus, to complete the recovery of Orestes by carrying off the image of the Tauric goddess to Attica—a detail which gives the story a local interest to

---

[1] It is remarkable that Iphigenia addresses them individually (vv. 1067, sq.)—a device not elsewhere used in Greek tragedy, so far as I can remember. Cf. Patin, iv. 109, on the point.

[2] vv. 392, sq.

the audience. The long responsive monodies of Iphigenia and the chorus over their funeral libations are interrupted by the fine narrative of a shepherd, who tells of the discovery of the friends, the madness of Orestes, the devotion of Pylades, and the difficult capture of the heroic young men. The soliloquy of Iphigenia when she hears the news is peculiarly beautiful.[1] After the above-mentioned most appropriate chorus, they are led in bound, and there ensues between Iphigenia and Orestes the finest dialogue left us by any Greek tragic poet. At its close she proposes to save Orestes and send him with a letter to Argos, but she is stayed by his devotion, for he will not escape at the cost of his friend's life. The contest between Orestes and Pylades, as to which should sacrifice himself for the other, has afforded all the imitators great scope for a dramatic scene, but was evidently not prominent to Euripides, who treats it with some reserve and coldness. The recognition by means of the letter of which Iphigenia tells the contents has been praised ever since Aristotle, and the ensuing scene may be compared with the rejoicings of brother and sister in Sophocles' *Electra,* which it closely resembles. The devices to overreach king Thoas, the attempted flight and danger of the three friends, and the inter-position of Athene conclude a play second to none of Euripides' in depth of feeling and ingenuity of construction. The last ode on the establishment of Apollo's worship at Delphi is perfectly irrelevant, but very Pindaric in style and feeling, and is, like all the odes of the play, full of lyric beauty.

Aristotle mentions a play on the same subject by Polyidos, in which Orestes was actually led to the altar, and recognised by his passionate comparison of his own and his sister's fate.

[1] vv 344–53 : ὦ καρδία τάλαινα, πρὶν μὲν ἐς ξένους
γαληνὸς ἦσθα καὶ φιλοικτίρμων ἀεί,
ἐς θοὐμόφυλον ἀναμετρουμένη δάκρυ,
Ἕλληνας ἄνδρας ἡνίκ' ἐς χέρας λάβοις.
νῦν δ' ἐξ ὀνείρων οἷσιν ἠγριώμεθα,
δοκοῦσ' Ὀρέστην μηκέθ' ἥλιον βλέπειν,
δύσνουν με λήψεσθ', οἵτινές ποθ' ἥκετε.
καὶ τοῦτ' ἄρ' ἦν ἀληθές, ᾐσθόμην, φίλαι,
οἱ δυστυχεῖς γὰρ τοῖσιν εὐτυχεστέροις
αὐτοὶ καλῶς πράξαντες οὐ φρονοῦσιν εὖ.

Sophocles had composed an *Aletes*, and an *Erigone*, both based on the adventures of the characters upon their return to Greece. Euripides was imitated perhaps by Ennius, certainly by Pacuvius in his famous *Dulorestes*, in which, according to Cicero, the mutual contest of the friends to encounter death for each other excited storms of applause. One of the earliest Italian dramatists, Ruccellai, composed a Tauric Iphigenia about 1520. There was another by Martello, about two centuries later. The French dramatists insisted, as usual, on improving on Euripides, especially by introducing a love affair. The Scythian king filled the gap, and appeared on the stage, as the French say, *en soupirant*. Even in Racine's sketch, which is preserved, and which gives a short abstract of the matter for the scenes of a first act, the king's son is enamoured of the heroine, and would evidently have been made the means of saving Orestes and Pylades from their impending death. This element was exaggerated, and the splendours of a French court and of foreign diplomacy added to the *Oreste* of Le Clerc and Boyer, and to the *Oreste et Pylade* of Lagrange-Chancel, the supposed successor of Racine. Guimond de la Touche's play (1757) is said to be more simple, and pleased everybody at the time except— Voltaire, Grimm, and Diderot ! But with the aid of Gluck's music, the opera of 1778 laid permanent hold of public taste.[1]

There yet remains the very famous *Iphigenia* of Goethe for our consideration. This excellent play has been extolled far beyond its merits by the contemporaries of its great author, but is now generally allowed, even in Germany, to be a somewhat unfortunate mixture of Greek scenery and characters with modern romantic sentiment. It therefore gives no idea whatever of a Greek play, and of this its unwary reader should be carefully reminded. Apart from the absence of chorus, and the introduction of a sort of confidant of the king, Arkas, who does nothing but give stupid and unheeded advice, the character of Thoas is drawn as no barbarian king should have been drawn— a leading character, and so noble that Iphigenia cannot bring herself to deceive him, a scruple which an Athenian audience

---

[1] Gluck brought out both the *Iph. Aul.* and *Taur.* Cf. Patin, iii. p. 6, and iv. p. 127, who gives 1774 and 1778 as the years of their appearance.

would have derided.   Equally would they have derided Orestes' proposal, of which Thoas approves, to prove his identity by single combat, and still more the argument which Iphigenia prefers to all outward marks—the strong yearning of her heart to the stranger.   The whole diction and tone of the play is, moreover, full of idealistic dreaming, and conscious analysis of motive, which the Greeks, who painted the results more accurately, never paraded upon the stage.   The celebrity of this so-called imitation will afford an excuse for so much criticism.

§ 214.   The *Electra* must have appeared during the closing years of the Peloponnesian War, and was fresh in men's memory when, as Plutarch tells us,[1] during the deliberations about the fate of conquered Athens, a Phocian actor sung the opening monody of Electra, and moved all to pity by the picture of a whilome princess reduced to rags and to misery.   The incident is said to have had a distinct influence in saving the city from destruction.   This testimony to the merit of at least one scene in the play is hardly admitted by the majority of critics, who have made the *Electra* a source of perpetual censure and perpetual amusement, and have generally set it down as the weakest extant production of Euripides, and a wretched attempt to treat with originality a subject exhausted by his greater predecessors.   I need not go into detail as regards these objections, which have been set forth with great assurance and with an air of high superiority by A. W. Schlegel, who nevertheless, as I have already stated (above, p. 351), himself signally failed in his endeavours to improve upon the *Ion* of the despised Euripides.

Turning to the play itself, the first remark to be made is that it was clearly meant as a critique on certain defects in the earlier *Electras*.   Apart from its intention as a drama, it is a *feuilleton spirituel*, as M. Patin calls it, and so far takes its place with the literary criticism common in the Middle Comedy.   Euripides attacks[2] the three various signs of recognition which satisfied the simpler Electra of Æschylus, viz. a likeness of colour and texture in the hair, an identity in the size of the foot, shown by deep footprints, and the design

---

[1] *Lys.* c. 15.   [2] vv. 524, sq.

of a garment which must have been long since worn out. The new Electra ridicules all these tokens, and passing by without comment the family ring used by Sophocles, is content with a scar on the forehead of the unknown brother, which has not escaped similar criticism, but which, we must remind the triumphant objectors, is not discovered by the young princess, but by an aged servitor, who had known Orestes as a child, and was merely directed by this mark to tax his memory of the face. As soon as the recognition is completed, the poet plainly criticises the long and dramatically absurd scene of Electra's rejoicing in Sophocles, by cutting short these ebullitions and proceeding at once to the plot against the royal murderers. He implies a censure of both his predecessors' economy by setting aside as impossible and hopeless what they had admitted without hesitation—an attack on the reigning tyrants in their own palace—and makes the success of the attempt turn on the absence of both from their fortress and their guards. This alters the plan of his play ; he represents Ægisthus as slain at a sacrifice to which he had invited the strangers, and Clytemnestra as enticed to visit Electra's peasant home under pretence of a family sacrifice. But these are only external points.

The really important ethical criticism of his predecessors is his approval of Æschylus, and condemnation of Sophocles, in painting the hesitation of Orestes when he sees his mother approaching, and the outburst of dread and of remorse in both brother and sister when the deed is done—a pointed contrast to the happy piety of the pair in Sophocles (above, p. 289), where the voice of Apollo's oracle sets at rest every scruple of filial duty or of natural conscience. In other respects Euripides' Electra is nearer to the conception of Sophocles : she is harder and fiercer than her brother, and is brought in acting at the matricide, instead of being more delicately removed from the action, as in the play of Æschylus. But he seems to me to have intended it as a further, and a sound, criticism on the improbabilities of the earlier stage, when he represents Ægisthus as unable to bear with this sharp-tongued and furious Irreconcileable in his palace, and the mother as a sort of weak defender of her child, submitting to the ignoble compromise of marrying her to a peasant. He has moreover attributed a certain gentle contrition to Clytemnestra,[1] which makes her an amiable contrast to Electra, and excites some sympathy in spite of her crimes, so that we come to look upon her as we do upon the queen in *Hamlet*, erring and even defending her errors with criminal sophistry, but not reprobate. This point gives peculiar bitterness to the remorse of the murderers, at least in the spectator's mind.

If we continue our study of the play, and observe its general temper, it strikes us as of all the extant tragedies the most openly democratic in tone. In many other of his plays, Euripides has represented trusty slaves of noble character and self-devotion, and reiterated the sentiment that slavery is an accident, and that there is nobility in men of low degree. But these instances are almost all in the retinue of princes. In the present play Euripides not only puts peasants on the tragic stage, but makes them the noblest and most intelligent of his characters. Electra's husband is the moral hero of the play, as Orestes testifies in a remarkable aside;[2] the aged farmer from the Spartan frontier is the moving spirit in the devising of the plot. Not only are these excellent people in every respect equal to their tragic parts, but the obscurity of their life secures them from the misfortunes and miseries to which great houses are almost hereditarily exposed. Orestes and Electra are the playthings of oracles and family curses, and of an ambitious position, which forces them into exile and into crime. When the catastrophe is over, the poor people who have helped them return to their simple and uneventful life, only altered by the gratitude of their princes. If Euripides was indeed ever influenced by what the Germans call the Ochlocracy, it was in this drama, where he vindicates the dignity of the lower classes, and exhibits the dangers and responsibilities of greatness. The grace and nature of the bucolic scenes at the opening show a remarkable idyllic power in the poet, unlike anything we possess before Theocritus, and we may well wonder at the curious want of taste in the critics who have ridiculed this part of the play—

---

[1] vv. 1102-10.   [2] vv. 367, sq.

Triumphant play, wherein our poet first
Dared bring the grandeur of the Tragic Two
Down to the level of our common life,
Close to the beating of our common heart.[1]

The choral odes are slight and unimportant ; the fawning flattery shown to Clytemnestra, whose danger they know, and have prepared, exhibits a degradation very unusual in any but the later plays of Sophocles or Euripides, when the chorus was waning rapidly in importance. I cannot but think that this play was rather intended for a reading public than for the stage. Hence, though it never made its mark as a tragedy, it is among the most characteristic and instructive pieces left us in early criticism.

§ 215. The *Orestes*, brought out in 409 B.C. (in the archonship of Diokles, Ol. 92, 4), is agreed on all hands to exhibit most strongly both the merits and defects of the author. In the looseness and carelessness of the metre, in the crowding of incidents at the end of the play, in the low tone of its morality—they are all base, says the scholiast, except Pylades, and yet even he advises a cold-blooded murder for revenge's sake—there is no play of Euripides so disagreeable. On the other hand, for dramatic effect, as the same scholiast observes, there is none more striking ; but this applies only to the opening scenes. The subject is the same as that of Æschylus' *Eumenides*, but instead of visible Furies in visible pursuit, the consequences of remorse, the horrors of a distraught imagination, and the suffering of disease, are put upon the stage, and the purely human affection of a sister seeks to relieve the woes which the gods can hardly heal in Æschylus. Yet all through the play there are satirical and even comic elements, which have led to the reasonable conjecture that it was meant, like the *Alcestis*, to supply the place of a satyric drama.

Thus, after Electra's prologue, of which Socrates is said to have peculiarly admired the first three lines, Helen, who has just arrived from sea, proposes to her to bring funeral offerings to the tomb of Clytemnestra, under pretence of her own unpopularity and Hermione's youth. This ab-

---

[1] R. Browning, *Aristoph. Apol.* p. 357.

surdly tactless and evidently selfish request is politely but
venomously declined by Electra, who comments upon the
niggard offering of Helen's hair.[1] The arrival of the chorus,
whom Electra strives with intense anxiety to quiet, for
fear of disturbing Orestes, leads to his awakening, and to
the famous scene, which has excited the wonder of all
its readers, and which I will not profane by a dry abridg-
ment.[2] The arrival of Menelaus leads to a dialogue which
shows him both cowardly and selfish ; but in the speech of old
Tyndareus, who comes in to urge the death of Orestes, and to
dissuade Menelaus from interfering, there are most wise and
politic reflections on the majesty of the law, and the necessity
of submitting men's passions to its calm decrees.   Granting,
he argues, that Clytemnestra did murder his father—a most
shocking crime, which he will not palliate—Orestes should
have brought an action against her, and ejected her for-
mally from his palace,[3] but not have propagated bloody
violence from generation to generation.[4] This very enlightened argument, one which was familiar to the Athenian
democracy of the day, but has not since asserted itself until
now, and even now only partially through Europe, is surely
the most advanced and modern feature in the literature of the
Periclean age.   The character of Pylades, who supports
the tottering Orestes to the public assembly, where his fate
is to be decided, their touching affection, and the sarcas-
tic description of the meeting and of the speakers, in which
critics have found portraits of the demagogue Cleophon and of

---

[1] vv. 126-31: ὦ φύσις, ἐν ἀνθρώποισιν ὡς μέγ' εἶ κακόν,
      σωτήριόν τε τοῖς καλῶς κεκτημένοις.
      εἴδετε παρ' ἄκρας ὡς ἀπέθρισεν τρίχας,
      σώζουσα κάλλος ; ἔστι δ' ἡ πάλαι γυνή.
      θεοί σε μισήσειαν, ὥς μ' ἀπώλεσας
      καὶ τόνδε πᾶσάν θ' Ἑλλάδ'. ὦ τάλαιν' ἐγώ.

[2] vv. 211-313.   [3] vv. 496-502.

[4] 523-25 :   ἀμυνῶ δ', ὅσονπερ δυνατός εἰμι, τῷ νόμῳ,
      τὸ θηριῶδες τοῦτο καὶ μιαιφόνον
      παίων, ὃ καὶ γῆν καὶ πόλεις ὄλλυσ' ἀεί

Socrates[1]—all this is still on a high level, and worthy of its
great author. But when Orestes and Electra turn, at the
advice of Pylades, from pathetic laments to revenge, and
invoke the aid of Agamemnon to murder Helen and Electra,
our sympathies are estranged, and no interest remains except
in the very comic appearance of the Phrygian slave, and his
remarkable monody. The reconciliation and betrothal of
the deadly enemies at the end is plainly a parody on such
dénouements. There are, as usual, many sceptical allusions
throughout the play, and one remarkable assertion of physical
philosophy.[2]

Though the quotations and indirect imitations of the
Orestes, as well as translations from the great scene, have
been frequent in all ages, the defects of the whole as a play have
naturally prevented any direct reproduction on the modern
stage. The famous lines upon the blessed comfort of sleep
to the anxious and the distressed, may be paralleled in many
conscious imitations, yet in none of them more closely than
in two passages of Shakspeare.

The ravings of Orestes have suggested to Goethe his wild
wanderings at the moment when his sister declares herself;
but anyone who will compare the elaborate and far-fetched
images of Goethe's, with the infinite verity and nature of Euripides' scene, will see how far the great imitator here falls behind his model. Above all, Goethe misses the truth of making the moment of waking a moment of calm and sanity, and
cures Orestes suddenly, upon the prayer of his sister and a
manly personal appeal from Pylades. So much nearer were
the Greeks to nature!

The actors have tampered a good deal with the text, as may
be seen from the many lines rejected by later critics, but our
text is exceptionally noted in the MSS. as corrected by a collation of divers copies. The second *argument*, which discusses
why Electra should sit at Orestes' feet, and not his head, is a
curious specimen of Alexandrian or rather Byzantine pedantry.
There are special recensions by Hermann and Porson.

§ 216. The *Phœnissæ* seem to have appeared, according to a

---

[1] vv. 866–959.   [2] vv. 982, sq.

very corrupt and doubtfully emended prefatory note in a Venetian MS., along with the *Œnomaus* and *Chrysippus*,[1] of which
a few fragments remain. It gained the second prize in the
archonship of an unknown Nausicrates,[2] probably during Ol.
93. It is really a tragedy on the woes of the house of Labdacus,
but is called after its chorus, which is composed of Phœnician
maidens on their way to Delphi, and stopped on their passage
through Thebes by the invasion of the Seven Chiefs under
Adrastus. There would indeed be some difficulty in naming
the play otherwise, for it is an *episodic* one, consisting of a series
of pictures, all connected with Œdipus' family, but without one
central figure among the nine characters—an unusual number
—who successively appear. The name Thebaïs, given to it by
modern imitators, suggests an epos and not a drama. Perhaps
Iocasta is the most prominent figure, but yet her death is, so
to speak, only subsidiary to the sacrifice of Menœkeus, and
the mutual slaughter of the brothers. All the scenes of
the play, though loosely connected, are full of pathos and
beauty, and hence no piece of Euripides has been more frequently copied and quoted. The conception of the two
brothers is very interesting. Polynices, the exile and assail-
ant, is the softer character, and relents in his hate at the
moment of his death. Eteocles, on the contrary, is made, with
real art, to die in silence ; for he is a hard and cruel tyrant,
and defends his case by a mere appeal to possession of the
throne, and the determination to hold by force so great a
prize. Antigone is introduced near the opening only for the
sake of the celebrated scene on the wall, when her old nursery slave[3] tells her the various chiefs, as in the scene

---

[1] According to Meineke (*Com. Frag.* ii. 904, note) the schol. on
Ran. 44 would imply that it came out as the middle play with the *Hyp-
sipyle* and *Antiope*, and won the first prize. But the scholiast may be referring to these plays as separate specimens of Euripides' excellence, and he
only calls them καλά, which implies general approbation, but not necessarily the first place.

[2] Dindorf suggests that he was a suffectus, or *locum tenens*, the proper
archon having died or resigned.

[3] παιδαγωγός. Schiller, in his version of the passage, is seduced by
French influences, I suppose, into calling him the *Hofmeister.*

between Helen and Priam in the Iliad.[1] She again appears at the close, with the features given her by Sophocles
in his *Antigone* and *Œdipus Coloneus* combined. Perhaps
the most brilliant part of the play is the dialogue between
the brothers, and Iocasta's efforts to reconcile them, followed by the narrative of their death-struggle. The speech
of Eteocles,[2] asserting that as he holds the tyranny he will keep
it by force in spite of all opposition, is a peculiarly characteristic passage, and may be compared with the advice given to
Solon by his friends (above, p. 177). If the choruses, which are
very elegant, do not help the action of the play, and are rather
calm contemplations of the mythical history of Thebes, Euripides might defend himself by pleading that he had accordingly
assigned them to a body of foreign maidens, who could feel but
a general interest in the action. It is not unlikely that the
crowding of incident was intended as a direct contrast to
Æschylus' *Seven against Thebes*, which, with all its unity of purpose and martial fire, is very barren in action. The long description of the Seven Chiefs in that play is distinctly criticised
as undramatic by Euripides.[3] There are, indeed, all through
the play, reminiscences of both Æschylus and Sophocles.

There were parodies of the play, called *Phœnissæ*, by Aristophanes and Strattis. There was also a tragedy of Attius, and
an Atellan farce of Novius, known under the same title, the
former a free translation of Euripides. Apart from Statius'
Thebais, there is a *Thebaid* by Seneca, and then all manner of old French versions, uniting the supposed perfections of both these, which they could read, with those of
Euripides, whom they only knew and appreciated imperfectly.
Exceptionally enough, there is an English version almost
as old as any of them, the *Iocasta* of George Gascoigne and
Francis Kinwelmersh (1566), a motley and incongruous piece,
built on the basis of the *Phœnissæ*. It professes to be an
independent translation of Euripides, but I was surprised to

---

[1] This idea has been borrowed from Homer very frequently indeed.
M. Patin cites parallel passages from Statius, from Tasso, from Walter
Scott (in *Ivanhoe*), and from Firdusi.

[2] vv. 500, sq.   [3] vv. 751-2.

find it really to be a literal translation of Dolce's Italian version, without any trace of an appeal to the original. Thus the παιδαγωγός is called the *Bailo*, a regular Venetian title. Its chief literary interest lies in the loose paraphrase of Eteocles' speech, above noticed, which appears to have suggested directly to Shakspeare the speech of Hotspur in the first part of *Henry IV.* (i. 3):

> By heaven, methinks it were an easy leap
> To pluck bright Honour from the pale-faced moon,
> Or dive into the bottom of the deep
> Where fathom-line could never touch the ground,
> And pluck up drowned Honour by the locks ;
> So he, that doth redeem her hence, might wear
> Without corival all her dignities.[1]

There is the translation of Dolce (Italian) called *Iocasta*, and *Antigones* of Garnier (1580) and Rotrou (1638). Then comes the early play of Racine, for which he apologises, the *Thebaide, ou les Frères ennemis*. He rather adds to than alters incidents in Euripides. But as to characters, he makes Eteocles the favourite with the people, he misses the finer points of Polynices, and makes Creon a wily villain promoting the strife for his own ends. The love of Hæmon and Antigone is of course brought in ; but at the end, upon the death of Hæmon, old Creon suddenly comes out with a passionate proposal to Antigone, and on her suicide slays himself. He is in fact the successful villain of the piece, whose golden fruit turns to ashes at the moment of victory. Alfieri in 1783 rehàndled the well-worn subject in his *Polinice*, to whom he restored the interest lent him by Euripides, but made Eteocles the horrible and hypocritical villain of the piece. The almost successful reconciliation is broken off by Eteocles' attempt (at

---

[1] So far as I know, this is the only direct contact with, or rather direct obligation to, the Greek tragedy in Shakespeare. Here are the lines which correspond in Euripides—the likeness is but slight, yet it is real :

> ἄστρων ἂν ἔλθοιμ' αἰθέρος πρὸς ἀντολὰς
> καὶ γῆς ἔνερθε, δυνατὸς ὢν δρᾶσαι τάδε,
> τὴν θεῶν μεγίστην ὥστ' ἔχειν τυραννίδα κ.τ.λ.

the instigation of Creon) to poison Polynices, whom he afterwards treacherously stabs, when coming to seek pardon for
having defeated and mortally wounded him. This version was
done into French by Ernest Legouvé in 1799. Schiller has not
only given an excellent and literal version of part of the play,
but has taken a great deal from its incidents in his *Braut von
Messina;* there is a translation in Halevy's *Grèce tragique.*
Its popularity gave rise to many interpolations by actors, and
the general reputation of the play has produced a large body
of scholia. The best special editions are by Valckenaer, Porson, Hermann, Wecklein (1881, re-ed. of Klotz), and Geel
(Leiden, 1846), with a critical appendix by Cobet.

§ 217. After Euripides' death, the younger Euripides brought
out at Athens from his father's literary remains a tetralogy containing the *Iphigenia in Aulis*, *Alcmæon* (ὁ διὰ Κορίνθου), *Bacchæ,*[1] and a forgotten satirical play. With this tetralogy he gained
the first prize—a clear proof how little effect upon the Athenian
audience had been produced by Aristophanes' *Frogs*, which chose
the moment of the great master's death to insult and ridicule
him. It is not impossible that a recoil in the public from such un-
generous enmity may have contributed to the success of the posthumous dramas. But we might well indeed wonder if the two
plays which are extant had failed to obtain the highest honours.
Unfortunately, the *Iphigenia* was left incomplete by the master,
and required a good deal of vamping and arranging for stage
purposes. Hence critics have in the first instance attributed some of its unevennesses to the subsequent hand. But
other larger interpolations followed, some by old and well-
practised poets, who understood Attic diction, others by mere
poetasters, who have defaced this great monument of the
poet's genius with otiose choral odes and trivial dialogue. Such
seems to be the history of the text, which has afforded insol-
uble problems to higher criticism. I suspect that, as usual,
the German critics have been too trenchant, and that on the
evidence of their subjective taste they have rejected, as early
interpolation, a good deal that comes, perhaps unrevised, from
the real Euripides. But allowing all their objections, and

---

[1] We learn this from the schol. on Aristophanes' *Ran.* v. 67.

even discounting all that W. Dindorf, for example, has enclosed in brackets, there remains a complete series of scenes, finished in composition, exquisite in pathos, sustained in power, which not only show us clearly the conception of the master, but his execution, and compel us to place this tragedy among the greatest of all his plays.   It is evident that, like Sophocles, whose *Philoctetes* was produced in advanced age, Euripides preserved his powers to the last, and was even then perfecting his art, so that his violent death, at the age of seventy-four, may literally be deplored as an untimely end.

The prologue, at least in substance, of the play, comes in, not at the opening, but after a very beautiful and dramatic scene between the agitated Agamemnon and an old retainer, who through the night has watched the king writing missives, destroying them again, and evidently racked by perplexity or despair.   With a passing touch the poet describes the stillness of the calm night and the starlit sky; and though his approximation of Sirius to the Pleiades may be astronomically untenable, he seems to have caught with great truth the character of a long spell of east wind, which is wont to blow in southern Europe, as with us, at the opening of the shipping season, and, having lasted all day, to lull into a calm. Hence the objection brought against this scene, that the fleet at Aulis was detained by contrary *winds*, loses its point.   For calm nights were of no service to early Greek mariners, who always landed in the evening, and might thus be wind-bound in a spell of east wind with the stillest night.

This dialogue in anapæsts is to us a far more dramatic opening than the prologue, and even when it comes, as an explanation from Agamemnon, it interrupts the action tamely enough.   But here already there are marks of interpolation, and it seems as if a prologue, which Euripides had perhaps exceptionally abandoned for dramatic effect, but had left in outline, was clumsily adapted to fill up a gap in the dialogue.[1]

---

[1] This plan of blending the prologue with the opening dialogue appears in the *Knights* and *Wasps* of Aristophanes, but not elsewhere in tragedy. But in the frags. of the *Andromeda*, preserved in the scholia on Aristophanes' *Thesmophoriazusæ* (v. 1038), we have the opening lines—a lyric

With anxious detail the old man is at last despatched by Agamemnon to countermand the arrival of Clytemnestra, and of Iphigenia, who had been sent for under the pretence of a proposed marriage of the princess with Achilles, but really to be sacrificed to Artemis, and obtain favourable weather for the fleet.   This deceit is discovered by the old man, when he asks in wonder how Achilles will tolerate the postponement of his marriage, which had been announced in the camp.   On his departure, the chorus of maidens from Aulis begin an ode descriptive of the splendours of the Greek fleet and army, which seems considerably interpolated, though the main idea is doubtless that intended by Euripides.   The next scene opens with an angry altercation between Menelaus and the old man, who has been intercepted by the former, and his missive opened and read.   The old man protests against such dishonourable conduct, and upon Agamemnon coming out, the dispute passes into the hands of the two brothers.   Menelaus upbraids Agamemnon's weakness, and his breaking of his word ; Agamemnon retorts with pressing his claims as a father and a king.   The dispute descends, as always with Euripides, into wrangling, and the imputing of low motives ; in the midst of it Agamemnon is terror-stricken by the news that his wife and daughter with the little Orestes have reached the camp, and have been received with acclamation by the army.   His despair melts the ambitious heart of Menelaus, who gives way, and beseeches his brother not to sacrifice Iphigenia.   But now Agamemnon in his turn remains firm, chiefly, however, from cowardice, and a feeling that as his daughter has really arrived, her fate is now beyond his control.[1]

The chorus, in an ode of which the genuine part is very beautiful, deprecate violent and unlawful love, with its dread consequences.   Then follows the greeting of Agamemnon by

monody of the heroine, and a night scene.   This proves those critics to be wrong who insist upon Euripides having always opened his plays with a prologue.   I believe the *Ion* to be another example, where the dialogue of Ion and Creusa replaced the prologue—the existing one being wholly spurious.

[1] Cf. the parallel of Polynices in Sophocles, above, p. 304.

his innocent daughter, and his ill-concealed despair—a scene which none of the imitators has dared to modify; and Clytemnestra begins asking motherly practical questions about her future son-in-law. But when Agamemnon proposes that she shall return home, and leave him to arrange the wedding, she stoutly refuses, and asserts her right to the control of domestic affairs. This adds to the perplexity of the wretched king, who leaves the stage defeated in his schemes of petty deceit. Presently Achilles enters, and is hailed by Clytemnestra, to his great surprise, as her future son-in-law. This somewhat comic situation is redeemed by the perfect manners, and the graceful courtesy of Achilles, whose character in this play approaches nearest of all the Greek tragic characters to that of a modern gentleman. But the scene becomes tragic enough when the old retainer stops Achilles, who is leaving to seek Agamemnon, and discloses to him and to Clytemnestra the horrible design. Achilles responds calmly and nobly to Clytemnestra's appeal for help, and promises to protect her daughter with the sword, should she be unable to persuade her husband to relent. He deprecrates with great courtesy Clytemnestra's proposal to bring Iphigenia in person from the tents to join her in personal supplications. After a choral ode on the marriage of Peleus and Thetis, Agamemnon returns, and is met by Clytemnestra, who has left her daughter in wild tears and lamentation[1] on hearing of her proposed fate, and compels him to confess his whole policy. She then attacks him in a bitter and powerful speech, which is meant to contrast strongly with that of Iphigenia. This innocent and simple pleading of an affectionate child for life at the hands of her father, with her despair at the approach of death, and her appeal to her infant brother to join in her tears, is the finest passage in Euripides, and of its kind perhaps the finest passage in all Greek tragedy. Upon Agamemnon's craven flight, she bursts out into a lyrical monody, which is interrupted by an approaching crowd and tumult, and the actual entrance of Achilles in arms, who tells

---

[1] v. 1101 : πολλὰς ἱεῖσα μεταβολὰς ὀδυρμάτων.

Clytemnestra that the whole camp are in arms against him, that his own soldiers have deserted him and are led on by Odysseus, but that he will do battle for her to the death. This rapid dialogue in trochaic metre is followed by the second great speech of Iphigenia (in the same metre) in which, with sudden resolve, she declares that her death is for the public good, and that her clinging to life will but entail misery upon her friends ; she therefore devotes herself to the deity, and resignedly braves the fate from which she had but lately shrunk in terror. Achilles is struck with admiration, and speaks out his regrets that the pretended marriage was no reality, but he bows to her decision, perhaps because it would have been impious to defraud the gods of a voluntary victim ; yet he proposes to bring his arms to the altar, in case she should change her mind at the last. The affecting adieus of the princess to her mother and her little brother, and her enthusiastic hymn as she leaves them for her sacrifice, conclude the genuine part of the play. A messenger's narrative of her death was doubtless intended by the poet, but he did not live to complete the work. It appears from two verses cited by Ælian, in which Artemis announces that she will substitute a horned hind for Iphigenia, that the piece really ended with this consolation, from the goddess *ex machina.* But to modern readers the epilogue is no greater loss than the prologue, if such there was. The real drama is complete, and requires not the dull interpolations with which our MSS. conclude.

There were *Iphigenias* by both Æschylus and Sophocles, which were soon obscured by the present play. Both Nævius and Ennius composed well-known tragedies upon its model. Erasmus translated it into Latin in 1524 ; T. Sibillet into French in 1549. Dolce gave an Italian version in 1560. There are obscure French versions by Rotrou (1640), and by Leclerc and Coras (1675), the latter in opposition to the great imitation of Racine in 1674. Racine's remarkable play, written by a man who combined a real knowledge of Euripides with poetic talent of his own, is a curious specimen of the effects of French court manners in spoiling the simplicity of a great masterpiece. In order to prevent the sacrifice of so virtuous a person as Iphigenia, Racine takes from an obscure tradition an illegitimate daughter of Helen (by Theseus), whom he makes the rival of Iphigenia in the love of Achilles, and a main actor in the play. He substitutes Ulysses for Menelaus, and inserts many features from the first book of the Iliad into the disputes between Agamemnon and the angry lover. As Racine himself honestly confesses, the passages directly borrowed from Homer and Euripides were those which struck even his Paris audience. The character of Agamemnon is, however, spoilt by giving him that absolute control over his family and subjects, which only priestcraft could endanger, and the French Iphigenia, with her court manners, and her studied politeness, is a sorry copy of the equally pure and noble, but infinitely more natural Greek maiden. A comparison of her speech to her father, when pleading for her life, in both plays, will be a perfect index to the contrast.[1]

An English version of Racine's play, called ' Achilles, or Iph. in Aulis,' was brought out at Drury Lane in 1700, and the author in his preface to the print boasts that it was well received, though another Iphigenia failed at Lincoln's Inn Fields about the same time. This rare play is bound up with West's *Hecuba* in the Bodleian. The famous opera of Gluck (1774) is based on Racine, and there was another operatic revival of the play in Dublin in the year 1846, when Miss Helen Faucit appeared as the heroine. The version (by J. W. Calcraft) was based on Potter's translation, and the choruses were set to music, after the model of Mendelssohn, by R. M. Levey. I fancy this revival was limited to Dublin. Schiller translated Euripides'

---

[1] Qui ne sent la différence des deux morceaux? C'est, chez Racine, une princesse qui détourne d'elle-même sa douleur, et la reporte sur les objets de son affection [sc. sa mère et son amant] ; qui, soigneuse de sa dignité, demande la vie sans paraître craindre la mort. C'est, chez Euripide, une jeune fille, surprise tout à coup, au milieu de l'heureuse sécurité de son âge, par un terrible arrêt, qui repousse avec désespoir le glaive levé sur sa tête, qui caresse, qui supplie, qui cherche et poursuit la nature jusqu'au fond des entrailles d'un père, &c. (Patin, *Études*, iii. p. 35.) But I quite differ with him when he thinks that the elegant verses of Racine are in any degree approaching in excellence to the passionate prayer in Euripides.

play (1790), and there is an English poetical version by Cart-
wright, about 1867 (with the *Medea* and *Iph. Taur.*).

The translation of Schiller, which ends with the departure of Iphigenia, is very good indeed. It is divided into
acts and scenes, and might be played with the omission of
the choruses. He has appended not only notes, comparing
his own version of certain passages with that of Brumoy,
but a general estimate of the play, in which he has been too
severe in discovering defects, though he highly appreciates
the salient beauties of the piece. Thus he thinks the weak
and vacillating Agamemnon a failure, whereas this seems to
me one of the most striking and natural, as well as Homeric,
of personages. He also protests against the dark threat of
Clytemnestra, which may not be very noble or appropriate to
the fond mother of the stage, but is certainly very Greek and
very human.

The special editions of note are Monk's, Markland's (with
additions of Elmsley's, Leipzig, 1822), then G. Hermann's, and
Vater's (1845). A great number of critical monographs are
cited by Bernhardy, of which those of Vitz (Torgau, 1862–3) and
H. Hennig (Berlin, 1870) are the latest, and discuss fully the
many difficulties of the play.

§ 218. The *Bacchæ*, which was composed for the court of
Archelaus, is a brilliant piece of a totally different character, and
shows that the old connection of plays in trilogies had been
completely abandoned. Instead of dealing with the deeper
phases of ordinary human nature, the poet passes into the
field of the marvellous and the supernatural, and builds his
drama on the introduction of a new faith, and the awful punishment of the sceptical Pentheus, who, with his family, jeers at
the worship of Dionysus, and endeavours to put it down by
force. His mother Agave, and her sisters, are driven mad
into the mountains, where they celebrate the wild orgies of
Bacchus with many attendant miracles. Pentheus, who at first
attempts to imprison the god, and then to put down the Bac-
chanals by force of arms, is deprived of his senses, is made
ridiculous by being dressed in female costume, and led out by
the god to the wilds of Cithæron, where he is torn in pieces by

Agave and the other princesses. The lament of Agave, when she comes in with the bleeding head, and is taught by old Cadmus of her fearful delusion, has been lost ; but we know its general tenor from the rhetor Apsines and from an imitation in the religious drama called *Christus Patiens* (ascribed to Gregory Nazianzen). While the wild acts of the new Mænads, whom the god has compelled to rush from Thebes into the mountains, are told in two splendid narratives of messengers, the chorus, consisting of Asiatic attendants on the god, show by contrast in their splendid hymns what joys and hopes a faithful submission will ensure. These lyric pieces are very prominent in the play, which, though sometimes called *Pentheus*, is more rightly called after its most important chorus, and is among the best left us by Euripides. It is of course undramatic that Pentheus, who proceeds so violently against all the other Mænads, should leave this chorus to sing its dithyrambs in peace, but ordinary probabilities must often be violated for such a personage as the chorus of a Greek tragedy.

The general tenor of the play, which may contain the maturest reflections of the poet on human life, is that of acquiescence in the received faith, and of warning against sceptical doubts and questionings. And yet it is remarkable that the struggle is about a new and strange faith, and that the old men in the play, Cadmus and Teiresias, are the only Thebans ready to embrace the novel and violent worship, which ill suits their decrepitude. We may imagine that among the half-educated Macedonian youth, with whom literature was coming into fashion, the poet met a good deal of that insolent secondhand scepticism, which is so offensive to a deep and serious thinker, and he may have desired to show that he was not, as they doubtless hailed him, an apostle of this random arrogance. It is also remarkable how nearly this play, at the very end of the development of Greek tragedy, approaches those lyrical *cantatas* with which Æschylus began. The chorus is here reinstated in its full dignity. The subject of Bacchic worship naturally occupied a prominent place in the theatre consecrated to that very worship, and it seems that every Greek dramatist, from Thespis and Phrynichus down to the ignoble herd of later tragedians known to us through Suidas, wrote plays upon the subject. Sophocles alone may be an exception.

But the play of Euripides always stood prominent among all its rivals. It was being recited at the Parthian court when the head of Crassus was brought in, and carried by the Agave on the stage. It was imitated by Theocritus in Doric hexameters,[1] apparently as part of a hymn to Dionysus. It was produced upon the Roman stage by Attius. It is quoted by every rhetorician, by every Latin poet of note.[2] It has even suggested, with its incarnate god, his persecution, and his vengeance, a Christian imitation. But in modern days, its fate was different. The marvels and miracles with which it abounds, and the prominent vindictiveness of its deity, made it unfit for the modern stage. In the last century A. W. Schlegel and Goethe alone, so far as I know, appreciated it. In our own time, the play has again taken the high place it held in classical days, and is reckoned one of the best of its author. There are special recensions by Elmsley and G. Hermann, and commentaries by Schöne, Weil, Tyrrell, Sandys, and Wecklein, besides school editions, and special tracts in Germany. The text of one of the two remaining MSS., the Florentine C, breaks off at v. 752, so that for the rest we depend altogether on the Palatine (287) in the Vatican. There are blank pages left in the codex C by the scribe, who went on to other plays and never finished the transcription.

§ 219. I have kept for the last of the tragedies the *Rhesus*, which, were it accepted as Euripides', should have come first, as all those, since Crates, who defend it as genuine make it an early work of the youthful poet, and place its date about the time when the ambitious designs of Athens were directed towards Thrace, and resulted in the founding of Amphipolis. This would place the drama about 440 B.C. But though so great a critic as Lachmann thought it even the work of an earlier contemporary of Æschylus, and though some of the Alexandrian critics recognised in it the traces of Sophocles' hand, the weight of modern opinion, since Valckenaer's discussion, leans to its being a later production, written at the close of the Attic period, and about the time of Menander. For there is

---

[1] Idyll xxvi.   [2] Cf. for a list, Patin, iv. 239.

undoubtedly a waste and ineptness of economy—the introduction of two almost idle characters, Æneas and Paris, the
appearance of Athena *ex machina* in the middle of the play,
and the still stranger *threnos* of the mother of Rhesus, also
ex machina—there are also scholasticisms of various kinds,
both in thought and diction, which seem to indicate the work
of a weaker poet copying better models. On the other hand,
the Alexandrian critics received it as genuine, and have left us
very full and valuable comments on the earlier part, as well as
extracts (in one of their prefaces) of two prologues, one of
which was ascribed to the actors, but neither of which appears
in our text. It is moreover, certain that Euripides wrote a
Rhesus, but if, as one of the prefaces tells us, it was called
γνήσιος, this must have been meant to distinguish it from
another as νόθος (as in the case of the Αἰτναῖαι γνήσιοι, and
νόθαι, in the catalogue of Æschylus' remains) ; and it is more
than probable that the play we possess is the spurious one, and
not from the hand of Euripides. For, besides the faults above
mentioned, and the many peculiarities of a diction which seems
rather eclectic than original, it wants the two most prominent
features of his extant plays, pathos and sententious wisdom.

Nevertheless, its merits have been by many unduly depreciated. It is a bold and striking picture of war and camp life,
producing an impression not unlike Schiller's *Wallenstein's
Lager.* Choral odes are dispensed with as inappropriate to
a night-watch, and there is at least one exquisite epic passage
on the approach of Dawn.[1] The bragging of both Hector

[1] vv. 527–36:

> τίνος ἁ φυλακά ; τίς ἀμείβει
> τὰν ἐμάν ; πρῶτα
> δύεται σημεῖα καὶ ἑπτάποροι
> Πλειάδες αἰθέριαι · μέσα δ' αἰετὸς οὐρανοῦ ποτᾶται.
> ἔγρεσθε, τί μέλλετε ; κοιτᾶν
> ἔγρετε πρὸς φυλακάν.
> οὐ λεύσσετε μηνάδος αἴγλαν ;
> ἀὼς δὴ πέλας ἀὼς
> γίγνεται, καί τις προδρόμων ὅδε γ' ἐστὶν ἀστήρ.

vv. 546–55 :   καὶ μὴν ἀΐω, Σιμόεντος
> ἡμένα κοίτας

and Rhesus estranges the reader's sympathy, so that the death of the latter excites but little pity ; the whole interest lies in the changing scenes and fortunes of an anxious night amid ' excursions and alarums.' The scholia to this play were first fully published in the Glasgow edition of 1821 (with the *Troades*), and then with critical and explanatory notes in the edition of Vater (1837). There are numerous monographs upon its age, style, and authorship, in which the large divergence of opinion on the same facts affords an admirable specimen of the complete subjectivity of most of the so-called higher criticism.

§ 220. There remains, however, another genuine play of Euripides—the *Cyclops*—which must be separated from the tragedies, as being the only extant specimen of a *satyric drama*. I have above (p. 233) discussed the general features of this sort of play, which is carefully distinguished by the critics from all species of comedy, even from parody, of which I think there are distinct traces in the *Cyclops*. As Plato saw clearly,[1] the talents for the pathetic and for the humorous are closely allied, and we should wonder how it was that no tragic poet among the Greeks ever wrote comedy, did we not find that scope for comic powers was provided in this ' sportive tragedy.' It is indeed strange how the sombre and staid genius of Euripides condescends to gross license in this field ; and no doubt if we had a specimen from Æschylus or Pratinas— the acknowledged masters of it—we should find that here, as elsewhere, the Greeks preserved their supremacy in literature. There is great grace and even beauty in the extant play, though we can hardly imagine Euripides' taste as lying in that direction. Silenus (who speaks the prologue) and his

φοινίας ὑμνεῖ πολυχορδοτάτᾳ
γήρυϊ παιδολέτωρ μελοποιὸν ἀηδονὶς μέριμναν ·
ἤδη δὲ νέμουσι κατ᾽ Ἰδαν
ποίμνια · νυκτιβρόμου
σύριγγος ἰὰν κατακούω ·
θέλγει δ᾽ ὄμματος ἕδραν
ὕπνος · ἄδιστος γὰρ ἔβα βλεφάροις πρὸς ἀοῦς.

[1] *Symposium*, sub fin.

satyrs are in search for Dionysus, who (according to the Homeric hymn) has been carried into the western seas by pirates. But they are thrown on the coast of Sicily, and made slaves by Polyphemus, who for dramatic reasons cannot devour them as he does other visitors. The opening chorus is very graceful and pastoral, reminding us strongly of scenes in Theocritus. As it is little read I shall quote it.[1] Odysseus then

---

[1] vv. 41-81 :   πᾶ δή μοι γενναίων μὲν πατέρων,

γενναίων δ' ἐκ τοκάδων,

πᾶ δή μοι νίσσει σκοπέλους ;

οὐ τᾷδ' ὑπήνεμος αὔρα

καὶ ποιηρὰ βοτάνα,

δινᾶέν θ' ὕδωρ ποταμῶν.

ἐν πίστραις κεῖται πέλας ἄν-

τρων, οὗ σοι βλαχαὶ τεκέων.

ψύττ', οὐ τάδ' οὖν οὐ τάδε νεμεῖ,

οὐδ' αὖ κλιτὺν δροσεράν ;

ὠή, ῥίψω πέτρον τάχα σου,

ὕπαγ' ὦ ὕπαγ' ὦ κεράστα

μηλοβότα στασίωρον

Κύκλωπος ἀγροβότα.

σπαργῶντάς μοι τοὺς μαστοὺς χάλασον ·

δέξαι θηλαῖσι σποράς,

ἃς λείπεις ἀρνῶν θαλάμοις.

ποθοῦσί σ' ἀμερόκοιτοι

βλαχαὶ σμικρῶν τεκέων.

εἰς αὐλάν ποτ', ἀμφιθαλεῖς

ποιηροὺς λιποῦσα νομάς,

Αἰτναίων εἴσει σκοπέλων ;

οὐ τάδε Βρόμιος, οὐ τάδε χοροὶ

Βάκχαι τε θυρσοφόροι,

οὐ τυμπάνων ἀλαλαγμοὶ

κρήναισι παρ' ὑδροχύτοις,

οὐκ οἴνου χλωραὶ σταγόνες,

οὐ Νύσα μετὰ Νυμφᾶν.

Ἴακχον Ἴακχον ᾠδὰν

μέλπω πρὸς τὰν Ἀφροδίταν

ἃν θηρεύων πετόμαν

Βάκχαις σὺν λευκόποσιν.

ὦ φίλος ὦ φίλε Βακχεῖε,

ποῖ οἰοπολεῖς

ξανθὰν χαίταν σείων ;

appears, and his adventure with the Cyclops occupies the rest of the plot, in which the Odyssey is adhered to as closely as was possible, consistent with the addition of a chorus of satyrs, and the necessity for Odysseus' free egress from the cave to narrate the cannibal feast of the Cyclops. The satyrs are represented as a most sympathetic but cowardly chorus, desirous to help Odysseus and escape with him, but far more desirous to drink his wine than to incur any danger in aiding him to blind the Cyclops. The scene in which Silenus acts as cupbearer to Polyphemus, and keeps helping himself, is really comic, and the frank cynicism of Polyphemus' brutal philosophy [1] is expressed in an admirable speech. Odysseus' impassioned exclamation, when he hears it, is in the highest tragic vein, nor does the hero anywhere condescend to respond to the wicked jokes of the satyrs. The whole work is a light and pleasant afterpiece, but seems to me to have required much more acting than the tragedies ; and I suppose the costume worn by Odysseus to have been far less pompous, and his figure less stuffed out than in tragedy ; so that this would be possible. With this condition, it must have been an effective piece, and was possibly preserved as being better than the seven others known from the same author. There are few editions, and no imitations of this play. A recension by Hermann, a German version by Schöll, and a few good monographs, such as the chapter in Patin's *Études*, are all that can be cited as of special import. Shelley has fortunately left us a translation (with a few omissions), which is invaluable for such English readers as cannot compass the somewhat difficult original. The play takes its place, of course, in the complete editions and translations, with the tragedies.

§ 221. A full review of the 1,100 extant *Fragments* would be

ἐγὼ δ' ὁ σὸς πρόσπολος
θητεύω Κύκλωπι
τῷ μονοδέρκτᾳ,
δοῦλος ἀλαίνων σὺν τᾷδε
τράγου χλαίνᾳ μελέᾳ
σᾶς χωρὶς φιλίας.

[1] vv. 316, sq.

here impossible. Some of them are sufficient to give us an idea of the plot of famous plays now lost, but most of them are only selected for philosophic depth or beauty of expression. I have referred above (p. 312) to the analysis of the *Philoctetes* given by Dion Chrysostom. There are also a good many titles cited by the Aristophanic scholia in explanation of the parodies of Euripides, with which the comedies abounded. It may safely be asserted, that had we no other evidence of the poet's work than these fragments, we should probably have reversed the judgment of the old critics, and placed him first among the tragedians. For in grace of style and justice of proverbial philosophy he has no rival but Menander, with whom indeed, as with the new comedy generally, his points of contact are many. But in simplicity and purity of diction he far exceeds Æschylus and Sophocles. Thus there is hardly a single curious or out-of-the-way word quoted by the lexicographers from his poetry; but rather innumerable moral sayings and pathetic reflections on human life (in Stobæus), many deep physical speculations in the Christian Apologists[1] and their adversaries; many striking points by the rhetoricians. Apart from the spurious *Danae*, of which the opening is preserved in the Palatine MS., there is a large fragment of the *Phaethon*, from which one of the choruses is very beautiful.[2] Goethe attempted a restoration of the play from the fragments. A new fragment of fourty-four lines has been found in Egypt, and printed in many periodicals.

The *Erechtheus* is now remarkable for having given Mr. Swinburne not only the plot of his like-named tragedy, but one of the finest of the speeches—that of Praxithea—to which he has acknowledged his obligations. It seems that this play brought out prominently not the self-sacrifice of the daughter, but the patriotic devotion of the mother. The daughter is not even specially named in our fragments. Mr. Swinburne has made her a second heroine in his version, but somewhat cold and statuesque, neither acting on her own responsibility, and as the eldest of the house, like Macaria, nor, on the other hand, showing the simple innocence and instinctive horror of death

---

[1] Cf. frags. 596, 639, 836, 935.

[2] vv. 25-36.

which we find in Iphigenia. His choruses are, moreover, far too long and exuberant for a really Greek play, however splendid they may be in themselves. I note these points not by way of criticism, which I should not venture, but to indicate to any English reader, that he must look to actual translations to obtain an accurate notion of the course of a Greek play. There are, besides the great speech of Praxithea, two important fragments from Euripides' play—one the farewell advice of a father to his son, very similar to that of Polonius to Laertes in *Hamlet;* the other an ode which longs for peace, and which is paralleled by the famous strophe from the *Cresphontes*, which has been so well rendered by Mr. Browning (*Aristophanes' Apology*, p. 179). It is to be noticed that most of the philosophical fragments are quoted as the poet's own sentiments, and this is specially mentioned by rhetoricians and scholiasts,[1] some of whom even call his choruses *parabases*, or open addresses to the audience, and others, such as Dionysius of Halicarnassus, insist that the person of the poet and that of his characters are throughout blended and confused.[2] The letters attributed to Euripides, and first published by Aldus in his collection (ed. 1499), were apparently composed by some Roman sophist, and have no value, even in preserving facts then current about the poet's life, which might since have been lost. They have been critically sifted by Bentley.

§ 222. The external changes introduced into tragedy by Euripides were not very great. He seems to have adhered to Sophocles' example in contending with separate plays, though he represented tetralogies together—that is to say, we have no clear evidence that there was any connection in subject between the plays which were produced together, as, for example, the *Bacchæ* and *Iphigenia in Aulis*. But he adopted a distinct method, which Sophocles imitated in his *Ajax* and *Philoctetes*— of curtailing the opening and close of his plays, in order to expand more fully the affecting or striking scenes in the body of the play. This was attained, first by the *prologue*, often spoken

---

[1] Cf. the frags. of the *Danae.*

[2] Cf. the passage cited on the *Melanippe* (ἡ σοφή) in Dindorf's frags.

by a god, or other personage not prominent in the real play, who set forth the general scope and plot of the piece, and told the audience what they might expect—a matter of great necessity in such a play as the *Helena,* or *Iphigenia in Tauris,* where either the legend, or the handling of the legend, was strange, and not familiar to the public. Secondly, the *deus ex machina,* who appeared at the end, loosed the knot, or reconciled the conflict of the actors. There is evidence that the prologues were much tampered with by the actors, and some are even altogether spurious. In written copies of the plays these pro- logues may have originally served as *arguments,* but for stage purposes, their recital by some indifferent actor was (I fancy) intended to fill up the time while the Athenian audience were bustling in and taking their seats. The appearance of a god at the end was likewise a sign that the play was over, for it was always plain what he would say, and the last words of the chorus were even the same in several of the plays, being evidently not heard in the noise of the general rising of the crowd.

It was the fashion of the scholiasts to follow Aristophanes in censuring the poet for introducing certain novelties in music and in metres. But we cannot now appreciate even the points urged as to the latter, nor do I think that the modern critics who follow the same line of censure have at all proved their case by argument. I would rather point to at least one very interesting metrical novelty whereby the poet admirably ex- pressed the contrast of calmness and excitement in a dialogue. This was the interchange of iambics with resolved dochmiacs, which we find in several fine scenes, such as that of Admetus with his wife (*Alc.* 243, sq.), of Phædra with the chorus (*Hipp.* 571, sq.), and of Amphitryon with Theseus (*Herc. Fur.* 1178, sq.). The modern reader can here easily feel the appropriate- ness of a remarkable innovation.

§ 223. As to the general complexion of his plays, the critics note that the chorus declines in importance, that it does not interfere in the action of the play, except as a con- fidant or accomplice, and that its odes are often irrelevant or personal expressions of the poet's feelings. These statements are to be qualified in two directions : in the first place, we find the decay of importance and occasional irrelevance of the chorus manifestly in Sophocles, so that he must either have begun, or countenanced by his practice, the change. Secondly, it is false that Euripides did not introduce an active chorus, and one of great importance, in his plays, for we have before us the *Supplices*, the *Troades*, and the *Bacchæ*, rightly called after the most important rôle. It ' is furthermore asserted that he invented the tragedies of intrigue or of plot, where curiosity as regards the result replaces strong emotions as regards the characters and sentiments expressed. This again is only true with limitations. For there are three different interests which may predominate in a tragedy, and accordingly we may classify them as tragedies of *character*, like the *Medea*, as tragedies of *plot*, like the *Ion*, and as tragedies of *situation*, like the *Troades*, in which there is a mere series of affecting tableaux, or episodes.   But evidently all elements. must co-exist, and the fact that Euripides does complicate his plot, and excite an intellectual interest in the solving of it, does not prevent these very plays from being most thoroughly plays of character also.   There is no finer character-drawing than that of Ion and the Tauric Iphigenia, and yet these characters take part in subtle and interesting plots.   It is therefore distinctly to be understood that the prominence of plot in some of Euripides' plays does not exclude either character-drawing, or the dwelling upon affecting situations—this latter a very usual feature in the poet, and one in which he may be said to have reverted to the simple successions of scenes in. the earliest tragedy.

§ 224. But there is this important point in Euripides' character-drawing, that except in the *Medea*, he does not concentrate the whole interest on a single person, but divides it, so that many of his strongest and most beautiful creations appear only during part of a play.   Thus Hippolytus and Phædra are each splendidly drawn, but of equal importance in their play; so are Alcestis and Heracles, Ion and Creusa, Iphigenia, Agamemnon and Achilles.   This subdivision of interest makes his plays far more attractive and various, but naturally fails in impressing upon the world great single figures, such as Ajax, Antigone, or, in our present poet, Medea. Again, it is very remarkable that Euripides seems to have disliked, or to have been unable, to draw strong or splendid male characters. Almost all his kings and heroes are either colourless, or weak and vacillating, or positively mean and wicked. This may be the misfortune of our extant selection of plays, for the Odysseus of his *Philoctetes* seems to have been an ideal Periclean Athenian. But in the plays we have, the most attractive men are Ion and Hippolytus, in both of whom the characteristics of virgin youth, freshness, and purity are the leading features—a type not elsewhere met in extant tragedies, but very prominent in the dialogues of Plato. On the other hand, no other poet has treated female passion, and female self-sacrifice, with such remarkable power and variety.[1] We have remaining two types of passion in Phædra and in Medea—one of the passion of Love, the other of the passion of Revenge, and we know that in other plays he made erring women his leading characters. But when these characters are assumed mischievously by Aristophanes, stupidly by the old scholiasts, servilely by modern critics, to afford evidence that the poet hated women, and loved to traduce them upon his stage, we wonder how all his splendid heroines have been forgotten, and his declarations of the blessings of home, of the comforts of a good wife, of the surpassing love of a mother, passed by in silence. His fragments abound with these things, just as they do with railings against women, both doubtless spoken in character. But it is indeed strange criticism to adopt the one as evidence of the poet's mind, and to reject the other.

[1] Mr. Hutton, in his delightful *Life of Scott*, contrasts (p. 107) the genius of Scott, who failed in drawing heroines, with that of Goethe, who was unsuccessful with his men, but unmatched in his drawing of female character. Some such natural contrast seems to have existed between Sophocles and Euripides, and is indeed implied in the scandalous anecdotes about them, which intimate that Sophocles was too purely an Athenian to share Euripides' love of women. Sophocles had an opportunity of drawing the purity and freshness of youth, which was so interesting to the Greeks, in his Neoptolemus (*Philoctetes*). Yet this character appears to me very inferior to either Ion or Hippolytus.

There are, moreover, in the extant plays, four heroines who face death with splendid calmness and courage—Alcestis, Macaria, Iphigenia, Polyxena—and all with subtle differences of situation, which show how deeply he studied this phase of human greatness. Alcestis is a happy wife and mother, in the heyday of prosperity, and she gives up her life from a sense of duty for an amiable but worthless husband. Macaria, in exile and in affliction, seizes the offer to resign her life, and scorns even the chance of the lot, to secure for her helpless brothers and sisters the happiness which she has been denied. And so of the rest, but I pass them by rather than treat them with unjust brevity.[1] Enough has been here said to show that, instead of being a bitter libeller of the sex, he was rather a philosophic promoter of the rights of woman, a painter of her power both for good and evil, and that he strove along with Socrates, and probably the advanced party at Athens, to raise both the importance and the social condition of the despised sex.

§ 225. He seems to have similarly advocated the virtues and the merit of slaves, who act important parts in his plays, and speak not only with dignity, but at times with philosophic depth. Yet while he thus endeavoured to raise the neglected elements of society, he may fairly be accused of having lowered the gods and heroes, both in character and diction, to the level of ordinary men. He evidently did not believe in the traditional splendour of these people ; he ascribed to them the weakness and the meanness of ordinary human nature ; he even made them speak with the litigious rhetoric of Attic society. When in grief and misery, they fill the theatre with long monodies of wail and lamentation, not louder or more intense than those of the Philoctetes of Sophocles, but without the man's iron resolve. Again, in calmer moments he makes them reflect with the weariness of world-sickness, often in the tone of advanced scepticism, sometimes in that of resignation ; he also makes his chorus turn aside from the immediate subject to speculate on the system of the world, and the hopes and dis-

---

[1] I must refer the reader to the chapter of my monograph on Euripides for a fuller discussion of this interesting question.

appointments of mankind. When we note these large and deep features in his tragedies, when we see the physical philosophy of Anaxagoras, the metaphysic of Heracleitus, the scepticism of Protagoras produced upon his stage, when we see him abandoning strictness of plot, and even propriety of character, to insist upon these meditations of the study, we fancy him a philosopher like Plato, who desired to teach the current views, and the current conflicts of thought, under the guise of dramatic dialogue, and who accordingly fears not to preach all the inconsistencies of human opinion in the mouths of opposing characters. A picture of every sort of speculation, of every sort of generalization from experience, can be gathered from his plays, and we obtain from them a wonderful image of that great seething chaos of hope and despair, of faith and doubt, of duty and passion, of impatience and of resignation, which is the philosophy of every active and thoughtful society. We can imagine the silent and solitary recluse despising his public, writing not for the many of his own day, but for the many of future generations, and careless how often the critics might censure him for violating dramatic dignity, and the judges postpone him to inferior rivals. And he may well have smiled at his five victories as the reward for his great and earnest work.

§ 226. But this natural estimate is contradicted by the perpetual notes of the scholiasts, who assert that Euripides was altogether a stage poet, and sacrificed everything to momentary effect. They speak of his plays as immoral, as ill-constructed, but as of great dramatic brilliancy. I confess I am slow to attach any weight to the critics who censure the tears of Medea and Iphigenia as blunders in character-drawing.[1] But there are independent signs that what they say has a real foundation, and that Euripides was too thoroughly the child of his age to soar above the opinions of a public which he may often, and in deeper moments, have despised. Thus we hear of his re-casting his *Hippolytus*, so as to meet objections ; we find him indulging in long monodies which can hardly have been intended for more than an immediate musical effect ; above all, we find

---

[1] Cf. the argument to the *Medea*, and Aristotle's *Poetic*, cap. xv.

him writing patriotic plays, with extreme travesties of the enemy of the day, and with fulsome praises of Athens, which are far below the level of the 'philosopher of the stage.' We find him also adopting a combination of two *successive* plots, so as to gather into one the pathetic scenes of separate stories, at the expense of dramatic unity. These things show that if he really adopted the stage as a means of conveying the newer light, it became to him an end, which he strove to perfect in his own way, and without surrendering his philosophy.

He felt himself, as Aristophanes tells us, in direct opposition to Æschylus, whom he criticises more than once. There are not wanting cases where he seeks to correct Sophocles also, but nothing is more remarkable than the small number of allusions or collisions between rivals on the same stage, and often in the same subjects. Yet they could not but profit by the conflict. It seems to me, however, that as Euripides was the poet of the younger generation, and of the changing state, he acted more strongly on Sophocles than Sophocles did in return, and though we may see in the *Bacchæ* much of the religious resignation of Sophocles, we see in the *Philoctetes* a great deal of the economy and of the stage practice of Euripides.

The next generation, while leaving the older poet all his glories, declared decidedly for Euripides; the poets of society embraced him as their forerunner and their model; philosophers, orators, moralists—all united in extolling him to the skies. Thus the poet who was charged with writing for the vulgar, with pandering to the lowest tastes of the day, with abandoning the ideal and the eternal for the passions and interests of the moment—this is the very man who became essentially the poet, not of his own, but of later ages. He was doubtless, as I have already said, an inferior artist to Sophocles; he was certainly a greater genius, and a far more suggestive thinker.[1]

§ 227. The old critics paid much attention to this author, but are unfortunately not often cited. Dicæarchus is the earliest

---

[1] An immense number of monographs on special points in the poet's diction, economy, style, and temper are enumerated by Bernhardy and by Nicolai, *LG.* I. i. pp. 201–2.

mentioned, especially in the *Arguments*, then Aristophanes of
Byzantium, and his pupil Callistratus, as well as other Alexandrians, and Crates, but Aristarchus is only mentioned once in
a note on the *Rhesus*. Didymus is the most important, and
most cited, and a commentary by Dionysius, added to his notes.
The present collection of scholia, though it must have then
existed, was unknown to Suidas. They were first edited on
the seven popular plays, by Arsenius (Venice, 1534), and often
since. Those on the *Rhesus* and *Troades* were first given from
the Vatican MS. (909), in the Glasgow edition of 1821. This
copy also supplies fuller notes on other plays, all of which have
been carefully edited by W. Dindorf in his *Scholia Græca in
Eurip.* (Oxon. 1863), with a good preface. There are only
full notes on nine plays, viz. *Hecuba, Orestes, Phœnissæ, Medea,
Hippolytus, Alcestis, Andromache, Troades,* and *Rhesus*. On the
rest there is hardly anything, about a dozen notes each on the
Ion, Helena, Hercules Furens and *Electra ;* on the others even
less. The history of the influence of his plays on the Roman
and modern drama is very curious, but I must refer the reader
for this and other details to my larger monograph on the poet.[1]

§ 228. *Bibliographical.* I proceed to notice the principal
MSS. and editions. The extant MSS. have been carefully
classified by Elmsley (Pref. to *Medea* and *Bacch.*), by Dindorf,
and by Kirchhoff in the preface to his *Medea*. None of them
contains all the plays. The older selection contains the nine
plays of the Vatican MS. just mentioned, but of these the first
five are in a Venice MS., which is the oldest and best, and
six in a Paris MS. (A, 2712). We accordingly have these plays
better preserved, and with scholia. The rest are extant in
two fourteenth century MSS., the Laurentian C (plut. 32, 2,
at Florence), which contains all the plays but the *Troades* and
a portion of the *Bacchæ*, and the Palatine (287), at the Vatican
Library, which contains seven of the latter section, except the
end of *Heracleidæ.* Thus there are three plays, the *Hercules
Furens*, the *Helena*, and the *Electra*, which depend upon the
Florentine C alone, which has only been of late collated once

---

[1] *Euripides*, in Mr. Green's series of classical writers. (Macmillan,
1879.)

(by de Furia) for the edition of Matthiæ. An examination of this codex on the *Helena* and *Hercules Furens* proved to me that a good deal of help might still be derived from another and more careful collation. The same result appears from the recent collation of the *Electra* by Heyse.[1] More recent copies need not here be mentioned. Most critics are now agreed that all these texts are full of interpolations, arising from repetitions, school reading, and from additions to the choral odes by grammarians. As to editions, four plays (*Medea, Hippolytus, Alcestis, Andromache*) were first edited by J. Lascaris, in capitals, at Florence, about 1496—a rare and undated book. The proper *princeps* edition is that of Aldus (1503), containing eighteen plays, the *Electra* not appearing till 1545 (Victorius, Rome). This edition is based upon good MSS., and its value is much greater than those which succeeded it, and which I therefore pass over till the studies of Valckenaer, whose *Diatribe* on the fragments marks an epoch. I have already noted all the good special editions of each play under its heading. Of late critical editions we may mention that of Matthiæ (1829–39), of Fix, in Didot's series (1843), of A. Kirchhoff (1868), of Nauck (Teubner), of H. Weil (sept tragédies, Paris, 1868), and of Mr. Paley, who has given us a text and commentary in three volumes (1860). Besides the versions of single plays already mentioned, there are translations of the whole works into German by Bothe, Donner, Hartung, Fritze, and Kock, into French by Prévost and Brumoy, into Italian by Carmelli (Padua, 1743), into English by Potter (reproduced in Valpy's classics, 1821), and by Woodhull (1782, four volumes). Carmelli and Woodhull not only give all the plays, with many good notes, but all the fragments then collected by Barnes and Musgrave, with an index of names and even of moral sentiments. There is also an edition of four select tragedies produced anonymously in 1780. There are unfinished lexicons to Euripides by Faehse and Matthiæ, and a full index in Beck's Ed.

[1] Cf. *Hermes*, vii. 252, sq.

CHAPTER XVIII.

THE LESSER AND THE LATER TRAGIC POETS.

§ 229. NOTHING is more remarkable than the deep shade thrown over all the other Greek tragic poets by the splendour of the great Triad which has so long occupied us. It may perhaps not excite wonder that their contemporaries should be forgotten, but we are surprised that of their successors none should have stood the test of time, or reached us even through the medium of criticism. Nevertheless, of the vast herd of latter tragedians two only, and two of the earliest—Ion and Agathon—can be called living figures in a history of Greek literature. And these, as it happens, encountered the living splendour of Sophocles and Euripides. Moreover, our scanty information seems to have omitted some of the most popular of the later playwrights, for of the 700 tragedies which are attributed to them in the notes of Suidas and elsewhere, we can only find fifteen victorious pieces. Who then won the prizes? or was the taste of the Athenian ochlocracy so conservative, that they persisted in reserving all the honours for reproductions of the old masterpieces? If this were so, how comes it that the writing of new and unsuccessful tragedies became so dominant a fashion? And yet even the *Poetic* of Aristotle, which treats mainly of the laws of tragic poetry, hardly mentions any of them, and then almost always by way of censure. This much is therefore certain, that while comedy was making new developments, and affording a field for real genius and for real art, tragedy, though for a time maintaining its importance and even its popularity, had attained its zenith, and its later annals are but a history of decay. Of the older poets, who were contemporary with Sophocles and Euripides, we

hear in Suidas of *Aristarchus of Tegea*, the author of 100 plays,
and only twice a victor, from whom Ennius seems to have
borrowed his *Achilles;* also of *Achæus of Eretria*, who contended with Euripides in Ol. 83, who only won once, though
the author of forty-four. The scholia to the *Medea* of Euripides
cite *Neophron* or Neophon as the author of the poet's model,
and quote from him two good fragments, which, when supplemented by the soliloquy of his Priam from Stobæus, seem to
indicate some talent. But these scanty hints, and the notice
of Suidas that he first brought on the stage tutor-slaves and
the torturing of domestics—whatever that may mean—are all
that remains to us of his 120 dramas.

§ 230. But we hear a great deal more of *Ion of Chios*, who
was in many respects a remarkable figure. As he told of his
having when a youth met Kimon in society at Athens, his
birth must fall about Ol. 74; his death is alluded to by
Aristophanes [1] as recent, I suppose, and therefore shortly
before Ol. 89, 3. Though in character as well as in birth
a pure Ionian, he seems to have lived much at Athens, and
from a drinking song quoted in Athenæus appears also well
acquainted with Spartan traditions and cults. But these could
have been learned from Kimon's aristocratical society at
Athens, as they always affected Spartan style, in the same manner that foreign nobles of sundry nations mimic Englishmen.
Ion seems to have met Æschylus, and possibly Sophocles, at
the opening of his career, and to have been a much-travelled
and social person, of large experience, agreeable manners, and
ample fortune. Perhaps he is the earliest example of a literary
dilettante, who employed his leisure in essays of various sorts
of writing. He composed elegies,[2] melic poems, both dithyrambs
and hymns, especially a *hymn to Opportunity* (ὕμνος Καιροῦ), epigrams, tragedies, and prose works in Ionic dialect—the latter
either on the antiquities of Chios, or in the form of *memoirs*
(called also ἐπιδημίαι and συνεκδημητικοί). These latter, which
must have been a novel form in literature, are often cited by

---

[1] *Pax*, 835, with a good scholion.
[2] Cf. above, p. 192.

Plutarch and Athenæus as valuable historical sources, and were discussed in a special work on Ion by Baton of Sinope. We are here, however, concerned with his tragedies, of which the number is variously stated from twelve to forty. Perhaps the lesser number refers to trilogies. He first contended in Ol. 82, was unsuccessful against Euripides in 87, 4, but when afterwards victorious, sent the Athenians a present of Chian wine. We have ten titles, some of them very curious, e.g. the *Great Drama* (Μέγα δρᾶμα). His satyrical play, the *Omphale*, was very popular. None of the fragments are sufficient to give an idea of the plot, but their style is good, and the expression easy and elegant.

Achæus of Eretria flourished between Ol. 74 and 83, but only gained a single prize out of forty-four dramas. He is once praised as second only to Æschylus in satyrical drama. Athenæus speaks of him as smooth in style, but at times dark and enigmatical. His scanty fragments afford us no means of correcting this judgment.

§ 231. We may pass next to a poet whose figure comes before us with peculiar clearness in the pictures of Plato and Aristophanes. Whether their portraits are faithful is not easy to say, but it is not likely that they were far from the truth, especially as they are not inconsistent, though very dissimilar in many respects.

In the opening of the *Thesmophoriazusæ* AGATHON (son of Tisamenus) is appealed to as an effeminate and luxurious man whose soft and sensuous poetry was the natural outcome of his nature. A specimen—of course a parody—is given of an alternate hymn between the poet and his chorus, which is not without grace and beauty. But this satirical picture is much modified by the hearty friendliness of the allusion in the *Frogs*, where Dionysus, in reply to Heracles, who asks about Agathon next after Sophocles, says 'he is gone and has left me, a good poet and a deep regret to his friends. *H.* Whither has the poor fellow gone? *D.* To the feast of the blessed.' The hospitable and social side of the man is not less prominent in Plato's *Symposium*, the scene of which is laid in his house, where he acts the part of a most gentlemanly and aristocratic host,

and makes a remarkable speech on the nature of ˉLove, which
may possibly be drawn from his writings, but of this no evidence
remains to us. There is indeed a corrupt passage in Dionysius, which makes him, with Likymnius, a pupil of Gorgias,
and this hint has prompted Blass [1] to analyse with care his
speech in the *Symposium,* and his language in the parody
of Aristophanes, to detect Gorgian features. There seems to
be strong evidence in the speech, which is evidently a dramatic
imitation of a peculiar style, that Agathon did borrow its
complexion from his friend Gorgias. There is the same attention to a fixed and obvious scheme, the same love of playing
upon words, and seeking alliterations. As these features recur
in the odes ascribed to him by Aristophanes, it is probable
that his style was really formed from the oratory of the great
Sicilian.

Though he is proved by these and many other allusions
and anecdotes to have been a prominent figure in Attic society, we have very few facts transmitted about his life. Born
about Ol. 83, he first gained a prize in Ol. 90, 4, and is mentioned as having praised Antiphon's great defence of himself to the orator, who felt consoled in his condemnation by
the approval of one competent judge among the ignorant
public. He left Athens before the end of the 93rd Ol. for the
Macedonian court, where the good living and absence of sharp
criticism probably suited his easy-going and perhaps indolent
genius ; and there he died in the prime of life, before 405 B.C.
There remain to us the titles of only seven of his tragedies,
Thyestes, the *Destruction of Ilium*—in which alone, says the
Poetic of Aristotle, he failed—*Alcmæon, Aerope, Thyestes,* and
lastly *the Flower* (ἄνθος), so strange a title that some critics
consider it a false reading for some proper name. But as we
are told [2] that both the characters and the plot were in this
play invented, the curious title is not improbable ; and we
have here an original attempt at a tragedy departing from the
received myths, consequently from all religious basis, and a
notable advance in the history of the drama. We learn from
the *Poetic* also, to me a suspicious source, that he was the ori-

---

[1] *Attische Beredtsamkeit,* i. 76.   [2] *Poet.* 9.

ginator of the habit of composing choral odes loosely or not at all connected with a plot—an innovation commonly attributed to Euripides. The few extant fragments, as well as the speech in Plato, point to great neatness of style, and an epigrammatic turn, which the Attic writers called κομψότης or rhetorical finish. This quality makes him a favourite source of quotation with Aristotle. We find, therefore, in Agathon an independent and talented artist,·working on the same lines, and in the same direction, as Euripides, but without his industry or philosophic seriousness.

§ 232. The case of CRITIAS is more difficult to decide. One play, the *Sisyphus,* often ascribed to Euripides, seems to have been composed by Critias, but the frank atheism expressed in the extant fragment makes us think he did not mean it for public performance. Another, the *Peirithous,* is doubtfully ascribed to him by Athenæus, but elsewhere called Euripidean. Thus the tragedy of Critias seems to have been distinctly intended to convey sceptical views in theology and in natural philosophy, outdoing the more artistic and reticent character of Euripides's teaching.[1]

During the same period the families of the great tragic poets were either reproducing, or composing, with some success. Two sons of Æschylus were tragic poets, one of whom, Euphorion, succeeded four times with unpublished plays of his father, and defeated Euripides in Ol. 87, 4. He also composed original plays. Iophon, son of Sophocles, is spoken of as gaining victories, and also as a bad poet. But the grandson, the younger Sophocles, who produced the *Œdipus Coloneus,* was of more repute, and often declared victor. The younger Euripides, nephew of the great poet, is not prominent. There appear also among the descendants of Æschylus his nephew Philocles, an ugly and mean-looking man, who defeated Sophocles' *Œdipus Rex;* and then a series of grandsons and nephews—Morsimus, Melanthius, Astydamas, and a younger Philocles. These men are chiefly known by the ridicule of the comic poets, which has immortalised a host of obscurities.

---

[1] His prose works will be noticed hereafter.

The famous passage in the *Frogs*[1] gives us Aristophanes' judgment on this herd of tragic poetasters, whose names are not worth enumeration here.   I will only observe that the German critics have adopted far too literally the scorn and ridicule of Aristophanes, who was often an unfair critic, and probably gave rein to private spite and party feeling in many of his judgments. If we had only his ridicule of Agathon in the *Thesmophoriazusæ* preserved, and had lost the *Frogs* and Plato's *Symposium*, I have no doubt Agathon would occupy a very different place in the judgment of learned philologists. Of the lesser poets Meletus has gained notoriety by his attack on Socrates ; Critias by his political activity, and his elegies, of which no mean fragments have been preserved ; there was also Dionysius of Syracuse, whose vanity and anxiety to succeed in literature were of old much ridiculed.   His poems were recited with great pomp at Olympia (98, 1), and received with jeering and laughter.   He really studied, and had his works revised and criticised by Philoxenus and the tragic poet Antiphon ; it is probably an Attic joke that he died of joy at a victory gained in the Athenian Lenæa (Ol. 103, 1).

[1] vv. 89, sq. : HP. οὔκουν ἕτερ᾽ ἔστ᾽ ἐνταῦθα μειρακύλλια
τραγῳδίας ποιοῦντα πλεῖν ἢ μύριας,
Εὐριπίδου πλεῖν ἢ σταδίῳ λαλίστερα ;
ΔΙ. ἐπιφυλλίδες ταῦτ᾽ ἐστὶ καὶ στωμύλματα,
χελιδόνων μουσεῖα, λωβηταὶ τέχνης,
ἃ φροῦδα θᾶττον, ἢν μόνον χορὸν λάβῃ,
ἅπαξ προσουρήσαντα τῇ τραγῳδίᾳ.
γόνιμον δὲ ποιητὴν ἂν οὐχ εὕροις ἔτι
ζητῶν ἄν, ὅστις ῥῆμα γενναῖον λάκοι.
HP. πῶς γόνιμον;
ΔΙ.   ὡδὶ γόνιμον, ὅστις φθέγξεται
τοιουτονί τι παρακεκινδυνευμένον,
αἰθέρα Διὸς δωμάτιον, ἢ χρόνου πόδα,
ἢ φρένα μὲν οὐκ ἐθέλουσαν ὀμόσαι καθ᾽ ἱερῶν,
γλῶτταν δ᾽ ἐπιορκήσασαν ἰδίᾳ τῆς φρενός.
HP. σὲ δὲ ταῦτ᾽ ἀρέσκει; ΔΙ. μᾶλλα πλεῖν ἢ μαίνομαι.
HP. ἦ μὴν κόβαλά γ᾽ ἐστίν, ὡς καὶ σοὶ δοκεῖ.
ΔΙ. μὴ τὸν ἐμὸν οἴκει νοῦν · ἔχεις γὰρ οἰκίαν.
HP. καὶ μὴν ἀτεχνῶς γε παμπόνηρα φαίνεται.
ΔΙ. δειπνεῖν με δίδασκε.

The later notices of tragedy are not clear enough for any short survey.   I must refer the reader to the careful discussion in Welcker's third volume, and the long summary in Bernhardy. The school of Isocrates produced one man, Theodectes, rather a rhetorician than a tragic poet, who was honoured with the friendship of Alexander and Aristotle.   Then follows the head of the ἀναγνωστικοί, Chæremon, who wrote for a reading public, and altogether in that rhetorical style which infected all later tragedy in Greece, in Rome, and in the French renaissance. The Alexandrian tragedians, the best seven of whom were called the Pleias, and who were thought in their day very wonderful people, do not concern us in a survey of Greek classical literature.

CHAPTER XIX.

THE ORIGIN OF COMEDY—THE DORIC SCHOOL, EPICHARMUS, SOPHRON—THEOCRITUS AND HIS SCHOOL.

§ 233. 'COMEDY did not attract attention from the beginning, because it was not a serious pursuit. Thus the archon did not assign a chorus to the comic poets till late, for they were (at first) volunteers (ἐθελονταί, apparently a technical term). But it was not until it had attained some fixity of form that its poets are recorded as such. It is forgotten who fixed its characters (masks) or style, or number of actors, or such other details.' This is the statement in Aristotle's *Poetic*, from which all historians of ancient comedy now start. While tragedy, being distinctly associated with religion, soon came under state protection, comedy, which was indeed a part of the Dionysiac feast, but a mere relaxation of revelry, was allowed to take care of itself, and to develop as best it could. But in most cases it was found that the political and social license of democracy was favourable to its claims, and its political capabilities raised it to great glory in the old Attic school of Aristophanes. This side of comedy gave rise to part of the claim justly made by the Dorians, that they had originated both tragedy and comedy —a claim the more reasonable, as it is clear that the Dorians were the originators, and the Ionians the perfecters, of many forms of literature. 'Wherefore (says Aristotle) the Dorians lay claim to both tragedy and comedy, to comedy the people of Megara, both those of this (Nisæan) Megara because of their democracy, and those of Sicily (on account of Epicharmus). And they cite the terms used as evidence. For the outlying villages which the Athenians call δῆμοι they call κῶμαι, as comedians were so called not from joining in the κῶμος (procession of revellers), but on account of their wandering through the villages, because they were held in no repute in the city.' This derivation of κωμῳδία is probably the right one, and does not conflict with the term τρυγῳδία, the song of the lees, or of the vintage feast, at which time such diversions have been common with all southern nations. Another passage in the *Poetic* which speaks of comedy being originally impromptu, and being derived from the phallic processions, still common in most Greek towns, is not so accurate, and only means that these phallic processions were carried on both at the season, and in the frame of mind which suited the old rude comedy. The phallic feasts of the Egyptians, described by Herodotus,[1] show this combination of the worship of nature, and of satirical and comic personalities. But there is no evidence that these processions, even when they gave rise to special hymns, of which we have traces, ever advanced to any dramatic form. Of course this account of the origin of comedy, which is evidently historical, disposes of the remark in the *Poetic*, that what is called Homer's *Margites* was the first model of comedy, as the Iliad was of tragedy. This poem was probably the earliest attempt at drawing a genuine character from a ridiculous point of view; but I am not sure that the Thersites of the Iliad could not have served the purpose just as well.

It results from the obscure origin of comedy among village people, that it should develop itself variously, according as the same seed fell upon various ground, both as to circumstances and as to the special genius of the men who raised it into literature. But there is one great division which we may separate at once, and relegate to after discussion—I mean the Attic comedy, which, though apparently imported from Megara, and long dormant, in due time developed into a great and fruitful branch of Greek poetry, with a definite progress and a well-determined history. The other branch, to which we now turn, is rightly called the Doric, because we find it among no other Greeks than Dorians, and almost everywhere among them, but differing so widely in form, tone and temper, accord-

[1] ii. 58.

ing to its age and home, that there is perhaps no name of wider and more various acceptation. But, in the first instance, the reader should be warned against taking the Spartans of history as representatives of the Dorian type. Whatever they may have been before the Ephors reduced them to a camp of ignorant and narrow-minded soldiers, under what is called the Lycurgean discipline—this much is certain, that all other Dorians—Megarians, Argives, Italiots, Sikeliots, Rhodians— differed widely from the Spartan type. We might as well take the Roman type as representative of those lively volatile Italic people, out of which they rose by a peculiar history, and peculiar social and political conditions.

§ 234. (*a*) The Spartans had a sort of comedy, in which players, who were called δεικηλικταί, acted in pantomime certain comic parts, apparently of both special adventures (such as those of a thief) and of characters (such as that of a foreign physician). Δείκηλον is said to be synonymous with μίμημα. Apparently those who represented women were called βρυαλ- λικταί. These actors were, as might be expected, held in contempt by the Spartans, and were always either periœci or helots. Thus a reply of Agesilaus, given by Plutarch, ex- presses the contempt which grave persons of the Periclean type would feel for a 'play-actor.' (*b*) The efforts of the Megarians are more important,[1] though hardly less obscure, inasmuch as through Susarion they led the way to Attic, and through their Sicilian colony to the highest Sicilian, comedy. The violent political conflicts in which the citizens were engaged seem to have excited their natural taste for lampoon and libel, and in the democratic period which followed the expulsion of Theagenes (about 600 B.C.) they developed a rude and abusive comedy, which is only known to us through the contemptuous allusions of the old Attic comedians. It was probably never written down, so that on'y stray verses survived.[2] *Susarion* wandered into Attica

---

[1] The phallic pomps celebrated at Sikyon and the neighbouring Doric towns of Achaia can hardly be identified with even the widest acceptation of Doric comedy.

[2] Strangely enough, the extravagance of their stage appliances (purple

about Ol. 50, and was said to have performed in Attic villages. The lines against women cited as his are not genuine. *Tolynus* is called the inventor of the metrical forms, but is probably, as Meineke has suggested,[1] confused with the celebrated Tellen, an early flute-player, whose epitaph in the Anthology says he was πρῶτον γνόντα γελοιομελεῖν. Of *Myllus* we know only the proverb 'Myllus hears everything,' which seems as if he had represented the daily failings of his townsmen upon the stage. *Mæson* was the most celebrated, but was perhaps a Sicilian Megarian, and was popular at the court of the Peisistratidæ. Character masks were called *Mæsons*, and on one of the Hermæ at Athens was inscribed his gnome, ἀντ᾽ εὐεργεσίης Ἀγαμέμνονα δῆσαν Ἀχαιοί.

§ 235. (*c*) We pass to the more important Sicilian branch of Doric comedy. The earliest of whom we hear anything is *Aristoxenus* of Selinus, placed by Eusebius about Ol. 29, who is spoken of as 'the originator of those who recited iambics according to the ancient fashion.'[2] The word ἰαμβίζειν was early used (like γεφυρίζειν) for lampooning, and we may be certain that among the rich and prosperous Sicilians there was ample time and occasion to encourage this sort of amusement. Cicero and Quintilian speak of the Sicilians as particularly quick and lively people, always ready with a witty answer even in untoward circumstances, much as the Irish would be described by an English stranger now-a-days. But I think the Germans are wrong in inferring that this Roman description applies to the Sicilians as compared with other Greeks, and not merely to the contrast Cicero felt to the stupid Roman boors, who, like the English rustic, combined political sense with social ignorance and dullness. But the Sicilian smartness at repartee, and their love of gossip and amusement, arose not merely from the lively Greek temperament, but from this combined with material wealth and political education.

hangings) is cited by Aristotle (*Nic. Eth.* iv. 2, § 20) as an example of wastefulness. But this was in the fourth century B.C.

[1] *Hist. Com.* p. 38.

[2] Hephæstion adds a specimen of his anapæsts, which has been already quoted above (§ 117).

The splendour of the Syracusan court under Gelon and Hieron developed, among other literary forms, that of a distinct and real comedy, in which three masters distinguished themselves —all in the earlier part of the fifth century B.C. These were Epicharmus, Phormos and Deinolochos. Concerning the pre-parations for this comedy, the obscure forerunners of these men, and concerning the details of their performances, we are totally in the dark.

Of the latter two we only know that *Phormos* (perhaps a local form for Phormis [1]) was contemporary with Epichar-mus, and came from the district of Mænalon in Arcadia; that he was intimate in Gelon's palace and the instructor of his children; that he was, moreover, so renowned in war under Gelon and Hieron as to justify his dedicating certain offerings at Olympia, which Pausanias describes; and that he was the author of six comedies on mythological subjects—*Admetus*, *Alkinoos*, the *Fall of Ilion*, *Perseus*, &c., of which not a single fragment has survived. He also improved the stage dresses and hangings.

Deinolochos, who is placed in the seventy-third Ol. and called a pupil or rival of Epicharmus, composed fourteen dramas in the Doric dialect, which are only cited about a dozen times by grammarians for peculiar forms. The titles known are the *Amazons*, *Telephus*, *Medea*, *Althea*, and the *Comic Tragedy*. So far as we can see, these two men developed that peculiar form of comedy for which Epicharmus also was famous, that of the travesty of gods and heroes. This mythological farce of the Sicilians is thought by the Germans to have differed from the satyrical dramas of the Attic tragedians in that the gods and heroes were here themselves ridiculed, whereas in our extant satyrical drama, the *Cyclops*, the hero Odysseus retains his dig-nity, but is brought into the society of Silenus and his lazy and wanton followers. It seems to me, however, that there is evi-

---

[1] This is Lobeck's notion. But the curious variation in the name and the single mention of Phormis, the general or warrior, by Pausanias, have led Lorenz, I think justly, to doubt the identity of the warrior with the comedian, and assume the latter to have been Phormos. Cf. his *Epi-charmos*, p. 85, note.

dence of a close relation between the two branches, as will presently appear.

§ 236. EPICHARMUS was a much greater man, and accordingly somewhat more of his work and influence has survived. On his life we have only a short and dry article by Diogenes Laertius, who classes him among the philosophers, without mentioning his comedies, and a jumbled notice in Suidas, which seems altogether untrustworthy when it contradicts the statements of Diogenes. According to this latter, Epicharmus was the son of Elithales of Kos, and came, when three months old, with his father to the Sicilian Megara. If he was a follower of Pythagoras during his life, he must have visited Magna Græcia. But he afterwards removed to Syracuse, which claims the chief honour in being the scene of his works. Diogenes' account of his writings is very curious and unsatisfactory. ' He left memoirs (ὑπομνήματα), in which he φυσιολογεῖ, γνωμολογεῖ, ἰατρολογεῖ—discusses nature, utters moral gnomes, and gives medical receipts.' This implies that the compiler had access only to a selection of notable passages from his works, and did not know his comedies.· He adds that he marked them as his own by anagrams, which looks as if the writings were spurious, and we know that false Epicharmian writings were extant ; also that he died aged ninety years. Yet the main substance of this notice seems to be true. The poet was born about Ol. 60, and must have visited Magna Græcia before the break-up of the Pythagoreans in Ol. 68. Whether he really entered the Pythagorean order we do not know. On his return to Sicilian Megara, he set himself to giving a more literary form to the rüde farces which already existed among the Megarians. About Ol. 73 he appears of great fame at the court of Gelon, and more especially of Hieron in Syracuse, where he met the greatest literary men of the day, and died at a great age.

§ 237. The notice that he added letters to the alphabet arises either from some later letters being first adopted in his works, or from his intimacy with Simonides at Syracuse. It is not impossible, as Simonides did adopt some additions, that he persuaded Epicharmus to spread their use in copies of his very popular plays.   There are two or three anecdotes preserved of his intercourse with Hieron.   The best epigram upon him is not that quoted by Diogenes, but one remaining to us among the poems of Theocritus, which seems genuine.   We must imagine the court of Hieron, notwithstanding his occasional cruelty and suspicion, as the most brilliant and cultivated centre in the Hellenic world.   It is likely that Epicharmus here met not only Simonides, but also Bacchylides, Pindar, and Æschylus.[1] We must add to this list an acquaintance with Theognis, who resided at the Sicilian Megara during the poet's earlier years Being thus in contact with the greatest literary men of the age, he was not less familiar with early Greek philosophy.   Pythagoras we have already mentioned.   There are remaining distinct allusions, perhaps polemical, to the opinions of both Xenophanes and Heracleitus.   Nay more, so profound were the speculative allusions in his comedies, that they seem to have been gathered, and to have obtained great importance at an early date, so much so that his latest biographer holds him to have composed a didactic poem περὶ φύσιως, on nature.   This notion is, however, in itself improbable.   The obscure notices of his medical, and even veterinary, treatises rest on equally untrustworthy grounds.   But his comedies were very widely known and quoted ; and in them he was said to put forth his views in dramatic form, perhaps for safety's sake, as may have been the case with Euripides. Plato knew them well, and cites them as Heraclitic in tone, and the work of the chief of comic writers.[2]   The younger Dionysius wrote about them.   The most important work upon him was the critical essay of Apollodorus, in ten books.   Ennius compiled a poem called *Epicharmus* from his philosophical utterances, of which a few lines on physical speculations survive, which were perhaps put into the poet's mouth.[3]

---

[1] He is even said to have ridiculed the latter (Schol. Æsch. *Eumen.* 626) for his constant use of the word τιμαλφούμενος.

[2] *Theæt.* 152 D.

[3] The statement of Horace, (Dicitur) Plautus ad exemplar Siculi properare Epicharmi (*Epp.* ii. 1, 58), has given rise to great discussion.   He mentions this as only the theory of the critics who liked old Latin poetry, and compared it with great Greek models.   But ' properare ' is a curious word, and seems only to apply to the easy flow of the dialogue.   There

§ 238. We have still the names and some fragments of the thirty-five comedies acknowledged as genuine.[1] Our fragments do not tell us much about the plots of these plays; but it is more than probable that there was not much plot, as is the case even with the old Attic comedy, and that the whole interest lay in a clever dialogue, and the working out of single comic scenes, in which either celebrated myths were travestied, or philosophical notions aired and parodied. There is also reason to think that rhetorical subtleties, such as antitheses, and other devices which led to the system of Korax and Tisias, were also ridiculed, and that accordingly the first beginnings of Greek eloquence are here to be detected.[2] Lorenz, in his monograph, compares with a good deal of point the simpler pieces of Molière, such as the *Mariage forcé*.[3] The love of eating and drinking, so prominent in Sicily, suggested to him his travesty called the *Marriage of Hebe* (with Heracles), in which the feast seems to have occupied most of the play, and in which the gluttony of the gods was portrayed.[4] On account of the numerous dishes cited, we have it quoted, some forty times, by Athenæus, in its two editions. Athenæus has also preserved to

is no evidence of any plot of Plautus being borrowed from Epicharmus. The prologue of the *Menæchmi* only asserts Sicilian scenery and manners in the play, and is, moreover, probably spurious. The Romans copied the new Attic comedy in these plays, their Atellanæ or farces were taken from Italic or Sikelic sources.

[1] They may be divided into three classes—mythological travesties, such as the Ἄμυκος, Βούσιρις, Ἄβας γάμος, brought out afterwards in a new edition as Μοῦσαι, Ὀδυσσεὺς αὐτόμολος, Ὀδυσσεὺς ναυαγός, &c. ; character plays, such as Ἐλπὶς ἢ πλοῦτος, Θεαροί, Ἐπινίκιος ; and lastly, dialectical plays, based on the love of dispute and argument among Sicilians, which seems to have been quite as remarkable as it was at Athens. This class is represented by his Γᾶ καὶ θάλασσα, the contest of sea and land (as to advantage), and the λόγος καὶ λογίνα.

[2] Cf. Blass, *Att. Ber.* i. p. 17.
[3] Lorenz, p. 226.
[4] Here is the picture of Heracles at his dinner (Lorenz, p. 223) :—

πρᾶτον μὲν αἴ κ' ἔσθοντ' ἴδοις νιν, ἀποθάνοις.
βρέμει μὲν ὁ φάρυγξ ἔνδοθ', ἀραβεῖ δ' ἁ γνάθος,
ψοφεῖ δ' ὁ γόμφιος, τέτριγε δ' ὁ κυνόδων,
σίζει δὲ ταῖς ῥίνεσσι, κινεῖ δ' οὔατα.

us his picture of the *parasite*, a character first invented for the stage by him, from the Ἐλπίς, a character comedy.[1] A great many of the other fragments are likewise upon dishes and eating.

By far the most important philosophical passages remaining to us are, however, preserved from another curious and accidental source. Diogenes, who says nothing of Epicharmus' comedies in his short official notice of the poet, quotes in his life of Plato a Sicilian rhetor, Alkimos, who wrote a book to show that all Plato's doctrines were borrowed from Epicharmus. In support of this theory, which owes its existence to the Pythagorean and Eleatic elements in Plato's teaching, which the Sicilian poet brought on his stage, several dialectical, metaphysical, and rhetorical arguments are quoted.[2] The discussion of their deeper import, however, belongs rather to the history of philosophy than of literature. The narrative form, which seems predominant in his plays, has misled Lorenz and others to ascribe these passages to a poem περὶ φύσεως.

§ 239. As there never was but one Greek theatre at Syracuse —that of which the magnificent remains still strike the traveller of to-day—we must conceive these comedies performed in it, probably with a chorus like that of modern plays, and not a

Συνδειπνέω τῷ λῶντι, καλέσαι δεῖ μόνον,
καὶ τῷ γα μηδὲ λῶντι κωὐδὲν δεῖ καλεῖν.
τηνεῖ δὲ χαρίεις τ᾽ εἰμὶ καὶ ποιέω πολύν
γέλωτα καὶ τὸν ἱστιῶντ᾽ ἐπαινέω.
καί κά τις ἀντίον τι λῇ τήνῳ λέγειν,
τήνῳ κυδάζομαί τε καπ᾽ ὧν ἠχθόμαν.
κἤπειτα πολλὰ καταφαγών, πόλλ᾽ ἐμπιών,
ἄπειμι. λύχνον δ᾽ οὐχ ὁ παῖς μοι συμφέρει·
ἕρπω δ᾽ ὀλισθράζων τε καὶ κατὰ σκότος
ἐρῆμος· ὅκκα δ᾽ ἐντύχω τοῖς περιπόλοις,
τοῦθ᾽ οἷον ἀγαθὸν ἐπιλέγω τοῖς θεοῖς, ὅτι
οὐ λῶντι πλεῖον ἀλλὰ μαστιγῶν τί με.
ἐπεὶ δέ χ᾽ εἴκω οἰκάδις καταφθαρείς,
ἄστρωτος εὕδω καὶ τὰ μὲν πρῶτ᾽ οὐ κοῶ,
ᾶς κά μ᾽ ἄκρατος οἶνος ἀμφέπῃ φρενάς.

[2] Diog. L. iii. 12, 9. sq.

constant element as in tragedy.   The dialect of the fragments
is a refined and literary Doric;[1] the metres, of which the
trochaic tetrameter was called the Epicharmian metre from
his frequent use of it, are simple and correct.   We still have
anapæsts and iambics combined with the trochees.   There were
many lines so celebrated as to be quoted all through Greek
literature.[2]

If we consider the great celebrity of Epicharmus' plays
which were brought out at the most brilliant centre of Greek
literature, at the town which took up the literary splendour
ruined at Miletus, and only dawning at Athens, we need not
be surprised that he exercised a strong influence on the Attic
drama.   But this is not felt in Attic comedy so much as in
the Attic satyric drama, where the titles of the plays constantly
suggest Epicharmian models, and even in the later tragedy,
where we find many heroes endowed with low qualities, and
perpetually appearing on the stage in a sorry garb and still
sorrier character.   Thus the serio-comic features in the Heracles
of Euripides' *Alcestis,* and especially his voracity ; the meanness of Menelaus, and knavery of Odysseus in many other plays,
appear to me to have been suggested by the great popularity of
the travesties of the Sicilian comedian.   It is not impossible
that the introduction of philosophy upon the stage may also
have been borrowed from him by Euripides, who seems to me
to have more points of contact with Epicharmus than have yet
been observed.[3]

§ 240. We pass to the Syracusan SOPHRON, son of Agathocles and Damnasyllis, who lived about the middle of the

---

[1] Yet both Epicharmus and Sophron are cited by the scholiasts as
writing in the old and harsh Doric dialect, in contrast to Theocritus, who
writes the softer and more elegant new Doric.

[2] As, for example :

Νόος ὁρῇ καὶ νόος ἀκούει · τἆλλα κωφὰ καὶ τυφλά,

and

Νᾶφε καὶ μέμνασ' ἀπιστεῖν · ἄρθρα ταῦτα τᾶν φρενῶν.

[3] The best monographs on Epicharmus are by Grysar (*de Dor. Comœd.*
sub fin.), Welcker (*Kl. Schrift.* i.), Bernhardy (in *Ersch und Gruber's
Encyclop.*), Holm, *Gesch. Sic.* i. 231, sq., and lastly, A. O. F. Lorenz's *Epi-
charmos,* which has a complete collection of the fragments in the appendix.

fifth century B.C., and composed *Mimes*, or mimic dialogues, probably in rythmical prose, both with male and female characters. His son *Xenarchus* followed his example in the time of the elder Dionysius, who employed him to lampoon the people of Rhegium. The dialect was a somewhat broader and more vernacular Doric than Epicharmus', but the dramatic force and truth of Sophron's writing made him justly celebrated. Not only did Plato study him carefully in order to give life to his dialogues, but two of the best of Theocritus' poems, the second and fifteenth idylls, are stated to have been directly copied from the 'Ακέστριαι and 'Ισθμιάζουσαι—the former clumsily (ἀπειροκαλῶς) copied, says the scholiast, in spite of its acknowledged excellence.[1] Botzon argues that the title of the Isthmian mime was Ταὶ θάμεναι τὰ Ἴσθμια, and, what is more important, points out that, to judge from Theocritus' imitation, it was probably an account of the ceremonies of the Lament for Melicertes, which were closely analogous to the Adonis cult and were a more natural scene for women's conversation than the Isthmian games, to which married women were not admitted. As to the *Akestriæ*, he prefers to translate it *the Stitchers*, and imagines it to have been a dialogue among girls, corresponding to the French grisettes, in which their love affairs were discussed. From Theocritus' imitation, I think this view wrong, and that it means the *Curing Women*, those old half quacks half witches, who are common in every superstitious society. But the scantiness of our fragments leaves room for nothing but conjectures.

As to the controversy whether the mimes were in prose or in verse, I fancy them like Walt Whitman's so-called poems,[2] which, if they survive, may yet give rise to a similar discussion. The mimes of Sophron were evidently very coarse also—another parallel—and were full of proverbs, and full of humour, often using *patois*, which is very rare in Greek literature. But Sophron's neglect of form did not imply a revolu-

---

[1] In his careful program (Lyck, 1856).

[2] Botzon quotes a scholiast on a Hymn of Gregory Naz., which was imitated, as to style, from Sophron: οὗτος γὰρ μόνος τῶν ποιητῶν δυθμοῖς τισι καὶ κώλοις ἐχρήσατο ποιητικῆς ἀναλογίας καταφρονήσας.

tionary creed, it was rather a carefully concealed submission to the laws of art. We have no hint whatever as to the performance of these mimes, but their early date and style seem foreign to a reading public, and we may imagine them brought out in private society after the manner of the Syracusan juggler's performance at the end of Xenophon's *Symposium*, where the marriage of Dionysus and Ariadne was pantomimed in a very suggestive way. Plutarch's mention of an attempt at Rome to perform Plato's dialogues dramatically seems to point in the same direction. We hear that the Latin satirist Persius also copied Sophron, apparently with little success in elegance or dramatic power. There can, however, be no doubt of the remarkable genius of the man, who was only in part a successor to Epicharmus—in his proverbial features, and in the portraiture of ordinary life. But Epicharmus' philosophic earnestness found no Syracusan successor.

The extant titles of these mimes suggest the life and pursuits of the lower classes ; viz. The Tunny Fishes, the Νυμφοπόνος or Bride-dresser, παιδικὰ ποιφύξεις, Ὁλιεὺς τὰν ἀγροιώταν, the Fisher and the Husbandman (in what relation the loss of the verb leaves us in doubt) ; The Women who say they draw down the Goddess (moon ?). Also a *Prometheus* and a *Nuntius* are named. The few remaining fragments are collected by Bloomfield, *Classical Journal*, vol. iv., and by Botzon in a Program (separately printed as a tract, Marienburg, 1867).[1]

§ 241. The comedy of the Italiots, which found its chief seat in the luxurious and laughter-loving Tarentum, does not come within the range of classical Greek literature : its chief representative, Rhinthon, belongs to the Ptolemaïc age, and his work only survives in the imitation of his *Amphitryo*, a comic tragedy, or parody of tragedy, by Plautus. The whole subject of the varied comic performances, which were of old popular in Magna Græcia, and gave rise to various subdivisions, *Hilarodia*,

[1]   Botzon's collection comprises some 150 words and phrases, almost all cited for their dialect by Athenæus, or by grammarians and lexicographers. They give us no idea of Sophron's literary skill, but show his local colour, and his strongly proverbial tone.

a parody of tragedy, *Magodia,* a parody of comedy, *Autalogia* and *Kinadologia,* moralising and indecent satires, *Phlyakographia, Hilarotragœdia,* and the rest, together with lists of names of authors and pieces—all these belong to the curiosities of Greek literature, and still more to the prolegomena of Roman comedy and satire, and have accordingly been fully handled by O. Jahn in the introduction to his Persius. It is said that many painted vases of Magna Græcia represent scenes from their various farces. This whole class of indecent, scurrilous, or merely amusing comic performances naturally came into favour at the courts of Alexander and his successors, also among the later tyrants, whose intellectual calibre may be estimated by their recreations. The gastronomical turn of this and other Greek comedy was developed by Hegemon of Thasos, who was popular at Athens by his parody of epical grandeur well delivered on this homely subject. This line was adopted by Archestratus of Gela, whose ἡδυπάθεια Ennius translated. Crates and Matron are mentioned later. But the most remarkable and serious of all the parodists seems to have been Timon of Phlius, a serious and bitter sceptic of the school of Pyrrho, who lived about 280 B.C. Of his various works the most celebrated were the Σίλλοι, in three books, one narrative, the rest in dialogue, in which he introduced Xenophanes, and ridiculed the dogmatists in epic fashion. This man's fragments are given by Mullach (*FPG.* i. 82), and discussed in a Latin monograph by Curt Wachsmuth. The indecencies of Sotades, and other later parodists, were in the Ionic dialect, and therefore do not come under the head of Doric comedy ; they are, in any case, not worth discussing.

§ 242. But from another side, the mimic poetry of the Sicilians made a great mark in Greek literature. There can be no doubt that the *bucolic* vein was early and strongly developed among Sicilian shepherds. The use of the shepherd's pipe and of responsive song was early developed in the country, and from the oldest time in some peculiar relation to the shepherd life in the mountains of Arcadia—worshipping the same god, Pan, honouring the same traditions, and pursuing the same habits. It even appears to me that in the great days of Gelon and Hieron there was a considerable emigration from Arcadia to Sicily—the Alpheus flowing into Arethusa—for we know that their mercenary armies were recruited from Arcadia, and doubtless the veterans were better rewarded with upland pastures in rich Sicily than by returning to their harsh and wintry home. But the Arcadian music found itself already at home in a country where the legends of the shepherd Daphnis were older than Stesichorus, and had been raised by him into classical literature. According to various authorities, Daphnis was the son of Hermes and a nymph, and brought up in a grove of laurels. Being an accomplished singer, and taught by Pan to play on the pipe, he became the companion of Artemis in her hunting, and delighted her with his music. His tragic end, which is connected with his love for a nymph, and his faithlessness, was variously told, and these versions were the favourite subject of pastoral lays, which were attached to the worship of Artemis throughout Sicily, and celebrated in musical contests at her feasts in Syracuse, where shepherds, called βουκολιασταί, sang alternately in what was called Priapean verse, of which the scholiasts have preserved a specimen.[1] Other shepherds, such as the Komatas and Menalkas of Theocritus, and the Diomus of Epicharmus, were also similarly celebrated. Indeed, there are slight but distinct traces that the pastoral element was not absent from the comedies of Epi-

[1]
Δέξαι τὰν ἀγαθὰν τύχαν
Δέξαι τὰν ὑγίειαν
Ἃν φέρομεν παρὰ τᾶς θεοῦ
Ἃν ἐκαλέσσατο τήνα.

There are the most interesting modern parallels in Sicily quoted in Holm's chapter (*Geschichte Sicilien's*, vol. ii. pp. 306-7) on this subject. Contests in improvisation, carried on in question and answer, or in statement and counter statement, preserving the metre, are still common in Sicily, where the competitors are obliged to lay aside their knives when they commence, so great is their excitement. Both the satiric and the erotic tone in the old bucolics survives, as we might expect ; but it is indeed surprising to learn that the religious side—of old the worship of Artemis, and the laments for Daphnis, her favourite—is still there, and trustworthy observers were present in churches during the Feasts of St. John Baptist, the *inventio crucis* (May 3), and of other saints, when the day was spent in alternate impro- vising on the lives of the saints and on the sufferings of our Lord.

charmus.[1] The satyric drama of Athens, as we ˜know from the only extant specimen, the *Cyclops*, was very pastoral in its scenes, and there is nothing more *Theocritean*, as people would say, than the first chorus of satyrs in that play. What is even more important, the comic poet Eupolis, who may have borrowed more than is suspected from Epicharmus, brought out an Αἶγες, of which the scanty fragments indicate the same pastoral tone. We may be certain that Sophron did not omit this side of common life in his Mimes, though it can hardly have been prominent, as the scholiasts do not cite examples in the arguments to Theocritus' poems.[2]

§ 243. But it seems to me highly improbable that THEO-CRITUS, a poet of so strictly imitative an age, and of so very imitative a genius, should have developed a remarkable originality in this single direction, and I therefore do not hesitate to class him as an imitator of the Sicilian mimic poetry. Two direct imitations of Sophron (not strictly bucolic poems) have just been noticed, and I have already spoken of Theocritus' epic and lyric efforts in connection with the Homeric Hymns, the later epics, and the poems of Alcæus and Sappho.

But his real fame rests upon his pastoral poems, in which he introduced shepherds, herdsmen, and fishermen in familiar discourse, and in the dialect of Sicily, but refined by the highest literary skill. These bucolic poems have throughout a mimic or *dramatic* character, as the scholiasts observe; the poet's person is concealed under those of his speakers, or he is himself (as in the 7th Id.) merely one speaker among several. They have also a common feature in the *pastoral* scenery in which they are laid. It is well known that earlier Greek poetry was a poetry of cities and of men, and very seldom approached what we call the picturesque. In the rare exceptions

---

[1] He was figuratively called the son of Χίμαρος and Σηκίς, and we even have a fragment in which he says ποιμενικόν τι μέλος αὐλεῖσθαι. Lorenz, fragg. B 130.

[2] Unfortunately, our scholia on Theocritus are such poor stuff, in spite of their fullness, that we cannot depend upon this argument, and Sophron may have treated many of Theocritus' subjects without being mentioned by these late authorities.

(such as the Homeric Hymn to Pan, and some of Euripides' lyrics) we find the sounds of nature more prominent than the sights, and this feature survives in all the pictures of Theocritus. But the growth of large cities on such sites as that of Alexandria, and the consequent wear and weariness of modern city life, gave a peculiar charm to the *loca pastorum deserta, atque otia dia.* Hence the growth of a literary taste for the pursuits and pleasures of the country. Thirdly, the great majority of bucolic poems have an *erotic* vein. It seems hard indeed to know what other subjects could engross the mind of Sicilian shepherds, whose day was idled away in attending on grazing herds and flocks. But a good deal of harmless banter, and some satirical touches, relieve the generally sad tone of the Sicilian muse, which loves to dwell on the misfortunes and griefs of love.

§ 244. We know but little of Theocritus' life. He is called the son of Praxagoras and Philinna, and also (owing to his apparently calling himself Simichidas) the son of Simichus, concerning whom the learned have much puzzled themselves. Whether his native land was Kos or Syracuse is uncertain. He lived much in Sicily, but was also educated by Askle piades of Samos and Philetas, apparently at Kos, and was very intimate with the physician Nikias of Miletus, and the poet Aratus of Soli. He spent, moreover, some time at Alexandria, and at the court of Ptolemy Philadelphus, where he wrote his fourteenth, fifteenth, and seventeenth idylls, about the year 259 B.C. His poem in praise of Hieron II. seems to date earlier, when he lived in Syracuse, about 265 B.C. We may therefore consider the poet to have flourished about 270–50 B.C., and accordingly he belonged to that learned epoch, when Alexandria led Greek literature, and when the greatest men of the day spent their lives in imitating or in criticising the older masters. Only two of the poets of that age have attained to a permanent fame. Callimachus, Philetas, and others highly prized in their day decayed with Roman culture. Apollonius Rhodius and Theocritus have survived, and are now the two Alexandrian poets of importance. But Apollonius' models were so great that his talents are necessarily eclipsed by them; Theocritus, among the various styles he attempted, struck upon a fresh vein, which had not before attained to world-wide fame. His models being either early lost or altogether obscure, he is to us of like importance with those earlier masters, who enriched the worn-out ways of literature by a new form, sought in the true source of all living song—the voice of the people. Hence it is to this part of his work, his bucolic and mimic poems, that he owes all his reputation. His imitations of epic hymns and Æolic love-songs, though excellent in their way, are only, like the poem of Apollonius, the copies of greater originals.

§ 245. It is, I think, the most reasonable among the many conflicting views as to the date of the various poems, to assume that the epic attempts of Theocritus were his earliest, and were written before he had found out the true bent of his genius. The brilliant Alexandrian school of literature was only in its infancy ; many poets were each contributing what they could to give a new impulse to Greek literature ; and there can be no doubt that the tendency of the day was towards reviving the epic form. But epic poetry and epic hymns without faith in the myths of the heroic age were not likely to prosper. Thus in the elegant Hymn to the Dioscuri which Theocritus has left us, the concluding adventure describes the Twins as engaged in a most unjust dispute, and slaying Lynceus, who represents the cause of fairness and honesty. Not even Pindar would have done this, not to say the tragic poets, who had trained the Greek public to a moral handling of the old legends: But all such deeper views were foreign to Theocritus. He found the facts of the myth before him, and he tells them with the simplicity not of faith, but of moral indifference. After attempting another epic piece on Heracles and the Nemean lion in Ionic dialect, he adopted the Doric style more natural to him, in which he composed the *Infant Heracles*, and the short fragment on Pentheus, which properly belongs to a hymn to Dionysus, and is modelled on Euripides' *Bacchæ*. The 13th Idyll on the rape of Hylas may be connected with the same epoch of the poet's work, but shows very distinctly the erotic vein prominent all through his later life. We may regard it, therefore, a transition to such poems as the 12th Idyll, and perhaps even to the 19th and 30th, though these latter may belong to a later and maturer time. It is fairly conjectured that while Theocritus was making these various essays in poetry, many of which, such as the Προιτίδαι, ’Ελπίδες, Ἡρωίναι, ἴαμβοι, &c., mentioned by Suidas, are now lost, he was hoping to attain the favour of Ptolemy, but the competition was too great, and he apparently returned to Syracuse, where he addressed Hieron about the year 269 in a bold petition for the favour and support he had elsewhere sought in vain. The tone of this Idyll (16), as well as of the 17th, composed a few years after, when he returned with new renown to Alexandria, is somewhat low and servile. The bidding for royal favour, which we can hardly excuse in Pindar and Simonides, is still more unpleasant in a later and more conscious age. But there is an impatient and self-asserting tone in the earlier poem which makes way for downright adulation in the later. The object of both was the same—an introduction to favour at court, but the former from an unsuccessful, the latter from an accepted suitor.

We may fairly assume that he turned his attention at Syracuse to the mimes of Sophron, and the bucolic poetry of the people, and returned to Alexandria the discoverer of a new style, which at once distinguished him from his rivals, and brought him his well-deserved rewards. His bucolic poems were composed in mature life, and probably at Alexandria, where their pastoral tone was very delightful to the inhabitants of a crowded capital situate in the midst of bleak and scorching sandhills. One of these, the 7th, may be regarded as in some sense introductory to the rest. It celebrates a pleasant day spent with friends at a harvest feast, and a bucolic contest carried on by the way. It is remarkable that, though the scene is a real scene in Kos, which can still be indentified, most of the names are fictitious shepherd names; the poet himself being called Simichidas, his friend Asklepiades Lykidas, another Sikelidas. These men, who were men of learning and culture, are presented under the guise of shepherds, living their life and attired in their garb. So completely artificial is this poem that we are tempted to believe in a club or society of poets at Kos, like the Italian Arcadia of the seventeenth century, and that bucolic poetry had already found a literary development when Theocritus in his youth sojourned at Kos. The speakers make hardly any effort to conceal their real character under the pastoral mask, and Theocritus mentions with reverence his masters Philetas and Sikelidas, though he by and bye professes to have learnt from the Muses as he fed his flocks upon the mountains.

The other bucolic poems are simpler in structure, and more dramatic in form—the poet concealing himself behind his characters. They comprise amœbean strains, or contests of shepherds before an umpire, and monologues of unhappy lovers, such as Polyphemus. The names Daphnis, Thyrsis, Komatas, &c., are used as stock names, nor are the critics at all justified in rejecting as spurious poems where the Daphnis does not agree with previous types. The metre generally used is the bucolic hexameter, which is a mere literary form of the Priapean verses already quoted, thus :—

ἁδὺ μὲν ἁ μόσχος γαρύεται, ἁδὺ δὲ χἀ βῶς
ἁδὺ δὲ χἀ σύριγξ, χὠ βούκολος, ἁδὺ δὲ κἠγών.

The cæsura after the fourth foot, and the beginning again with the same word immediately after it, show how closely Theocritus followed the popular taste. In the refrains, too, which are constant and prominent in his poems, we find a feature which, though as old as Æschylus and Euripides, was particularly frequent in the Sicilian folk songs. The poetic contest of the eighth poem is (exceptionally) in elegiacs.

§ 246. There are, properly speaking, but ten bucolic poems in the collection, in which I include the *Reaper's Dialogue* and the *Lament of Polyphemus.* These appear to have been edited by Artemidorus shortly after the poet's death, before 200 B.C., and contained the first eleven poems of our collection (omitting the second), the ninth being placed last, as is evident from a sort of postscript to that poem, appended by the editor of the collection. The very striking mimic poems (ii. and xv.), which were imitated from Sophron, and the erotic poems, were afterwards added. Finally, his youthful efforts in the epic style, and several spurious pieces,[1] were appended to the collection as his fame became assured. The fifteenth is a scene from common life in Alexandria, which describes two women and their maids going to the laying out of Adonis, in which their dialogue is of the greatest vivacity and dramatic power. Some flattery of Ptolemy and his queen. however adroitly brought in, rather jars upon us in so excellent a mimic piece. The second, which represents a maiden preparing magic charms, and confessing to the moon the story of her love and her desertion, is a splendid painting of passion, which has attracted critics of all ages. Racine thought he had found nothing greater in Greek literature.

§ 247. These and the bucolic poems, with their homeliness, their picturesqueness, and their outspoken realism, are the masterpieces of the collection. The shepherds of Theocritus are not pure and innocent beings, living in a garden of Eden, or an imaginary Arcadia, free from sin and care. They are men of like passions as we are, gross and mean enough for ordinary life. But though artificially painted by a literary townsman, they are real shepherds, living in a real country, varying in culture and refinement—the Italiot characters are the ruder —but all speaking human sentiments without philosophy and artifice. Nay, even the strong contrast of town and country life, which must have been ever present to the poet, is never

---

[1] The question of the genuineness of each individual poem in our collection is exceedingly difficult, seeing that Theocritus certainly composed in various styles, and that in an artificial and learned age any great unity or harmony of thought is not to be assumed in the works of such an author. I therefore incline to the side of the conservative critics, who reject only a few of the later idylls, and some of the epigrams. But the decision in almost all cases is one of subjective fancy, and therefore in no way conclusive. Thus the *Fishermen* (xviii.) is commonly rejected because it contains a moral lesson at the end, and because love plays no part in it (cf. Fritzsche, *in loc.*), as if the brilliant 15th did not contradict such a notion. For my part, seeing that Sophron wrote a θυννοθήρας, and another mime concerning a fisherman and a cowherd, I accept it as one of the most certainly genuine of the collection. There is, so far as I know, no objection to the language or to the allusions. The playing of the fish, which greatly puzzles the Germans, is described with great truth, and shows the poet to have had practical knowledge of the Sicilian tunny fishing.

expressed in words, but with truly artistic feeling left to be inferred by the educated reader. There is neither allegory nor apologue intruded ; the political or moral eclogue of Vergil and his school is a false imitation of these pictures, which from their simplicity, their variety, and their novelty, soon came to be designated by a special name—little pictures, or *idylls.* The term was probably unknown to Theocritus himself, and we are not accurately informed of the circumstances of its choice. But under it both erotic poems concerning beautiful youths— some of them in lyric metre—occasional poems, such as the *Spindle* and the *Epithalamium* of [1] Helen, epic pieces, and bucolic mimes, are now included. They are the latest original production in Greek poetry, though, as I have already observed, their originality may have been overrated, owing to the careless- ness of older, and the ignorance of later critics. Still it were unjust, upon these problematical grounds, to deny Theocritus the noble position he deserves among the great and matchless masters of Greek poetry, though to him the Muse came last, ' as to one born out of due season.' [2]

[1] This nuptial song is peculiarly interesting, as perhaps containing the only direct allusion to Hebrew literature which is to be found in classical Greek poetry. The comparison of Helen (v. 30) to a Thessalian horse in a chariot, the mention of 4 times 60 maidens, whom she excels, and the immediately following verses, in which she is compared to the Dawn, pos- sibly to the moon (the text is corrupt, and variously restored), and to the spring (vv. 23-8), have too striking a resemblance to the *Song of Solomon* (i. 9 ; vi. 8-10) to escape the myriad commentators on Theocritus. It is therefore suggested that he became acquainted with at least part of the LXX version at Alexandria. The strained and Oriental features in these comparisons are best explained by this hypothesis, which is fairly borne out by the facts, and is of great interest in literary history. If adopted, it should be made an argument against Meineke's emendation of the passage, which gets rid of the night and the moon altogether.

[2] For the benefit of younger students I here quote a characteristic passage. Idyll xi. vv. 19-29 :

’Ω λευκὰ Γαλάτεια, τί τὸν φιλέοντ’ ἀποβάλλῃ ;
λευκοτέρα πακτᾶς ποτιδῆν, ἀπαλωτέρα ἀρνός,
μόσχω γαυροτέρα, φιαρωτέρα ὄμφακος ὠμᾶς.
φοιτῇς δ’ αὖθ’ οὕτως, ὅκκα γλυκὺς ὕπνος ἔχῃ με,
οἴχῃ δ’ εὐθὺς ἰοῖσα, ὅκα γλυκὺς ὕπνος ἀνῇ με.
φεύγεις δ’ ὥσπερ ὄϊς πολιὸν λύκον ἀθρήσασα.

The critics in his own and the next generation paid little attention to a new master, and not even a master of epic learning, like Apollonius Rhodius. Hence we only hear of ὑπομνήματα by Asklepiades, Nikanor, Amaranthus, and Theon ; later came Munatus and Eratosthenes. But none of them, as Bernhardy remarks, seems to have been a formal commentator, and this accounts for the poverty of our knowledge as to special allusions, and as to the models used by the poet. In Byzantine days Moschopoulos and Triclinius made the additional collation of scholia which was not edited by Calliergi in his *princeps* of the scholia (Rome, 1516), but by Warton and by Adert (Zurich, 1843). Then come the fuller editions of Gaisford (Ox. 1820, *Poetæ Minores*, &c.) and of Dübner (Paris, 1849). The best and fullest is now acknowledged to be Ahrens', in the second volume of his *Bucolici Græci* (Leipzig, 1859). They are very inferior to most of our scholia, especially to those on Apollonius, though Theocritus comes from the same age and of the same school.

§ 248. *Bibliographical.* There is a perfect host of MSS., of which the oldest and best are the Ambros. 222 at Milan, and the Vatican 912, both of the thirteenth century. The earliest edition is of the first eighteen idylls, probably at Milan, about 1481 ; then comes that of twenty-four idylls (with Hesiod, Theognis &c.) by Aldus (1495), of which there are corrected copies, with some faulty sheets cancelled. The first complete edition with scholia was Calliergi's. Since that time the poet (either singly, or more often with the *Bucolici Græci*) has been constantly and ably edited. I mention as the most remarkable editors Stephens (an Oxford edition in 1676), Heinsius (1604), Reiske, Warton, Gaisford, Jacobs (1824), Wüstemann (1830), Meineke (1856), an excellent critical edition ; Briggs (Camb. 1821), Wordsworth (iterum ed. 1877), Ameis (Didot, 1846), Ahrens (1855-9), Ziegler (ed. iii. 1877), with an independent collation of Italian MSS., and the two editions of Fritzsche

ἠράσθην μὲν ἔγωγα τεοῦς, κόρα, ἀνίκα πρᾶτον
ἦνθες ἐμᾷ σὺν ματρί, θέλοισ' ὑακίνθινα φύλλα
ἐξ ὄρεος δρέψασθαι · ἐγὼ δ' ὁδὸν ἀγεμόνευον.
παύσασθαι δ' ἐσιδὼν τὺ καὶ ὕστερον οὐδ' ἔτι πῶ νῦν
ἐκ τήνω δύναμαι· τὶν δ' οὐ μέλει, οὐ μὰ Δί', οὐδέν.

(with German notes, Leipzig, 1857, and more full and critical, 1865-9, in two vols., with a third on MSS. scholia, &c., promised, but not yet published). For English readers there is, in addition to Bishop Wordsworth's Latin Commentary, a handy but too brief edition by Mr. Paley, and Mr. Kynaston's. Young scholars want help in the dialect, which is at first very puzzling, and for this I recommend Fritzsche's earlier edition, which has a good glossary of forms, and also excellent botanical notes on the very prominent *Flora* of the bucolics—neither of which is repeated, but only referred to, in his larger edition. This latter is, moreover, weighed down with ponderous learning, and on many hard passages revokes the reading or rendering of his former edition. Nevertheless, for the bibliography of Theocritus, and for summaries of various opinions, it is the most recent and the fullest. I specially refer to it, as monographs, or partial editions, are too numerous and special for mention here. Rumpel's *Lexicon Theocriteum* (1879) is the newest and best analysis of the vocabulary of the poet. There are French translations by Didot, German by Voss (1808), Hartung (with notes, 1858), and especially by the poet Rückert (1867). In English we have first Thos. Creech (Oxon, 1684), a rimed version in the style of that day; then Banks' prose version (Bohn, 1853).[1] In our own day J. H. Chapman (London, 1866) has produced a good and careful translation of all Theocritus, with Bion and Moschus, with many good notes on the imitations of early English poets. But this scholarly work is not equal to C. S. Calverly's (Cambridge, 1869), which is one of the best English versions of any Greek author. If Mr. Calverly had not made his book a drawing-room volume, it would doubtless have been a far closer version of the original. The *Eclogues* of Vergil, and the pastorals of Sannazaro and his school, of the German Gesner, and of the Spaniards, prove the lasting effect of Theocritus on the literature of the world, nor is there any classical poet to whom our Laureate owes so much.

§ 249. A word may be here added concerning *Bion* and *Moschus*, whose remains are preserved with the MSS. of Theocritus, and printed after his idylls in most of our editions. These

---

[1] Mr. A. Lang's prose version is also excellent.

poets are somewhat later than Theocritus in age ; Bion was born
near Smyrna, but lived in Sicily, and died of poison before
Moschus, whose longest poem is an exaggerated lament over his
friend and perhaps master ; Moschus himself is set down in
Suidas as an acquaintance of Aristarchus. More we cannot determine. We find the term βούκολος and βουκολιασδῆν used by
Moschus technically for poets and poetry, in a sense far removed
from their original simplicity in Theocritus. The remains of
both poets are, perhaps, best in their epic vein, and concerning
this side I have spoken above. The *Lament on Adonis* of Bion,
and the *Lament on Bion* of Moschus, are both elaborate, and
with refrains in bucolic form, but artificial and exaggerated.
Their erotic fragments remind one of the false anacreontic
fragments, which Thos. Moore has made so familiar to us.
The urchin Eros with his rosy wings, his mischievous temper,
and his waywardness, is manifestly the Alexandrian, not the old
Greek god. Hermann and Ziegler have critically edited the fragmentary and corrupt remains of these poets, and there have not
been wanting modern imitations, such as the well-known—

> Suns that set, and moons that wane,
> Rise and are restored again ;
> Stars that orient day subdues,
> Night at her return renews, &c.[1]

The history of the rise in modern literature of an ideal
Arcadia—the home of piping shepherds and coy shepherdesses,
where rustic simplicity and plenty satisfied the ambition of
untutored hearts, and where ambition and its crimes were
unknown—is a very curious one, and has, I think, been first
traced in the chapter on Arcadia in my *Rambles and Studies in
Greece*. Neither Theocritus nor his early imitators laid the
scene of their poems in Arcadia ; this imaginary frame was
first adopted by Sannazaro.

---

[1] Here is the original : —

> Αἰαῖ ταὶ μαλάχαι μὲν ἐπὰν κατὰ κᾶπον ὕλωνται,
> ἠδὲ τὰ χλωρὰ σέλινα τὸ τ᾽ εὐθαλὲς οὖλον ἄνηθον,
> ὕστερον αὖ ζώοντι καὶ εἰς ἔτος ἄλλο φύοντι ·
> ἄμμες δ᾽ οἱ μεγάλοι καὶ καρτεροί, οἱ σοφοὶ ἄνδρες,
> ὁππότε πρᾶτα θάνωμες, ἀνάκοοι ἐν χθονὶ κοίλᾳ
> εὕδομες εὖ μάλα μακρὸν ἀτέρμονα νήγρετον ὕπνον.

CHAPTER XX.

THE OLD ATTIC COMEDY UP TO ARISTOPHANES.

§ 250. WE have now disposed of the older Doric comedy, with its later Siciliot and Italiot offshoots. It was certainly more primitive than its Attic sister ; it was also spread over a greater surface and a longer period of the Hellenic world, but perhaps for this very reason was loose and varying in form, and did not attain to any fixed type, or any splendid tradition. The very opposite was the case with Attic comedy. Starting from an equally obscure origin, it attained in democratic Athens such a strict and formal development, it answered such great political and artistic purposes, that no remnant of Greek litera-ture has attained a more lasting and universal fame.

All the old grammarians and writers about comedy associ-ate it directly with the Athenian democracy, which alone, they think, would tolerate its outspoken and personal character. This, indeed, is so distinctive a feature, that it comes out in the traditions of its first origin. We constantly find the story repeated that the country people in Attica, when injured by their town neighbours, used to come in at night, and sing per-sonal lampoons at the doors of their aggressors, so as to bring the crime home to them, and excite public censure against them—that this practice was found so useful that it was for-mally legalised, and that the accusers disguised themselves with wine lees for fear of consequences to themselves. These accounts prove at least how indissolubly personal censure was associated with old Attic comedy. It is a further confirmation of this remark, that though Susarion was said to have intro-duced comedy from Megara very early, it was not tolerated under the personal government of the Pisistratidæ, and only

revived when democracy had made its outspokenness—its
παρρησία—secure. Other obscure names, such as Euetes and
Euexenides, are alluded to as of the same date, and altogether
it seems likely that as the old Attic comedy faded out with the
greatness of the Athenian democracy at the end of the fourth
century, so it originated with its origin just before the Persian
Wars. But until the climax under the direction of Pericles,
it seems barely to have existed, and as an obscure appendage
of the Dionysiac revelry. There were no written texts, no
fixed plots, no artistic finish. Licentious jokes and personal
jibes were its only features, so that the first great organiser
(Cratinus) is said to have abandoned its ἰαμβικὴ ἰδέα, or likeness to the satire of Archilochus both in form and style, and
its extant master (Aristophanes) boasts that he has risen above
the vulgar obscenities of the old Megarian farce. Still both
elements are manifest enough in the comedies of Aristophanes,
though ennobled by political censure and social grace ; so that
we may fairly hold the whole type to be adequately represented
in the eleven extant plays.

But the numerous fragments give us no definite idea of either
plot or literary execution. This is, indeed, a most remarkable
feature in the old Attic comedy. Were we reduced to judge
Aristophanes from the fragments of his lost plays, we should
have no notion whatever of his greatness, and for this reason
critics are to be blamed, who have extolled him at the expense
of his rivals, who are known to us only in this utterly inadequate
way. It is nevertheless probable, from the evidence of the
ancients who had all the documents complete, that he was
indeed the greatest of Attic comedians. We will therefore
discuss the general scope and character of old Attic comedy in
connection with this typical genius, as soon as we have given a
rapid sketch of his lesser known predecessors and rivals.

§ 251. We are told that at first the comedians were distinctly
licensed by the law to make personal attacks—a statement repeated by Cicero [1] and Themistius, but which may have arisen
from the supposition that there must be a law to permit, as well
as a law to restrain, libel of individuals. For this latter law was

---

[1] *De Rep.* iv. 10.

certainly enacted under the Archonship of Morychides (85, 1),
and lasted three years, when it was repealed. A similar re-
straint seems to have been imposed again in Ol. 91, 1,[1] and
there can be little doubt that the oligarchs of 411 B.C. silenced
political comedy, if not by law, at least by terror. It flashed
up again at the close of the Peloponnesian War, as we know
from Aristophanes' *Frogs*, to succumb finally to the thirty
tyrants, and the impoverished and timid times which followed,
when the Athenians had no wealth to adorn, or spirits to enjoy,
the comic chorus—the real pith and backbone of the old political comedy. Thus the period of its greatness is confined to
an ordinary human life, some sixty years, reaching from Ol. 80
to Ol. 96. Towards the close of this epoch constant attempts
were made, by such men as the dithyrambist Kinesias, and the
demagogue Agyrrhios, to curtail the public outlay upon comedy,
and hence impair its dignity. These facts as to the history of
the relation of the state to comedy are chiefly attested by the
excellent scholia on Aristophanes, from which they have been
gathered and illustrated with infinite learning by Meineke.
We may infer the relative expenses of bringing out a tragedy
and a comedy by the fact that in the year 410 B.C. a tragic
chorus cost 3,000 drachmæ, whereas in 402 B.C. a comic chorus
cost only 1,600. This latter was, however, in the poorest days
of Athens, and after many attacks had been made on the outlay
for what had become a mere idle amusement; so that these
facts (quoted by Klein from Boeckh) are not so conclusive as
might appear.

§ 252. Passing by Myllus, who has been already mentioned
(p. 400), and who is probably not a member of the Attic branch,
we come to CHIONIDES (Χιωνίδης is the form preferred by Meineke to Χιονίδης), whose date is placed too early in Suidas, and
who probably composed his plays about Ol. 80. Three titles,
the *Heroes*, the *Persians* or *Assyrians*, and the spurious *Beggars*

---

[1] This second decree (of Syracosius) is justly inferred by Droysen to
have had special reference to those then charged with profanation of the mysteries, and to have restrained comic satire, as likely to prejudice the courts
against them. As the old comedy always treated the events of the day, such
a provision would deprive it of its main interest. Cf. Meineke, *FCG.* ii.
p. 949.

(πτωχοί), are námed.   Aristotle speaks of him, along with
Magnes, as much later than Epicharmus.   We know nothing
of him save a very few fragments, which tell us only the
fact that he was acknowledged the earliest of the proper Attic
comedians.   The name of MAGNES, which comes next in the
list, is more important, and he is mentioned in the celebrated
parabasis of Aristophanes' *Knights*[1] as having once been very
popular, but in his old age failing to please, and neglected
by a once friendly public.   He was therefore dead, and had
died in old age, when this play was brought out, Ol. 88, 4:
We may consequently place his activity about Ol. 80.   He
came from the Icarian deme, like Thespis, and won many
victories.   The nine titles of his plays which survive are suspected, and perhaps retouched or modified by other hands.
We hear of a *Birds* and a *Frogs* among them, and it appears
from Aristophanes' allusion that the chorus (as in Aristophanes
himself) imitated the sounds of both.   There is also a Γαλεο-
μυομαχία cited as his, which seems a strange title for an Attic
comedy, but not stranger than Cratinus' parody of the
Odyssey.

There is hardly so much known ot ECPHANTIDES, nicknamed Καπνίας by his rivals, by way of comic contrast to his
real name.   We hear that he had a definite chorus assigned to
him, and that he attacked a certain Androcles, also attacked by
Cratinus.   These facts show us that his age was about that of
Magnes.   We hear of only one title of his plays, the *Satyrs*, a
subject treated by other comic poets, but we have unfortunately no data for a comparison with the standing scenery of
the properly satyric dramas, which seem so near and yet so
separate from comedy.

§ 253.   We now come to CRATINUS, the real originator—
the Æschylus—of political comedy.   This was the opinion
of the sensible grammarian quoted in Meineke.[2]   'Those,'
he says, 'who first in Attica devised the general idea of
comedy (Susarion and his school) brought in their characters
without method (ἀτάκτως), and placed no object before them
but to excite laughter.   But when Cratinus took it up, he first

---

[1] vv. 520, sq.   [2] i. p. 540.

established a limit of three in the characters of comedy,
thus correcting the irregularity ; and, moreover, he added a
serious moral object to the mere amusement in comedy, by
reviling evil doers, and chastising them with his comedy,
as it were with a public scourge.   Nevertheless, even he
shows traces of earliness, and even slightly of want of
method.' This invaluable notice is supported both by the
fragments of Cratinus, and by the observations upon him
in various scholia.   He is called the son of Callimedes, and
if he was really 'taxiarch of the tribe Œneis,'[1] must have
been a man of some means.   This is corroborated by his
policy, which was distinctly conservative and aristocratic, and
opposed to that of Pericles.   As he is said to have lived ninety-
seven years, and brought out his last play in Ol. 89, 1, his
birth may be placed about 520 B.C. ; but there is some evidence that his genius was late in development, for we do
not know that he won any victory earlier than his *Archilochi*
in Ol. 82, 4 (452 B.C.), if not later.   Aristophanes says [2] he
died of grief at the loss of a jar of wine, when the Lacedæmo-
dians invaded Attica.   But both fact and date are invented,
for we know of no invasion which will harmonize with our
other information.   When Aristophanes had ridiculed him
in the *Knights* [3] as a broken-down old man, who had once been
the popular poet, so that every society rang with songs from
his plays, the aged Cratinus is said to have given a practical
reply by composing his famous *Wineflask* (Πυτίνη), which gained
the victory over his detractor's *Clouds*, as well as over an
obscurer play of Ameipsias, the *Connos*, which took the second
prize.   Shortly after this he died.   He composed but little,
as only twenty-one plays are attributed to him, nine of which
won the first prize; but the impetuous flow of his verse, and
the alleged looseness of his plots towards their close, rather

---

[1] In an excellent note on the total absence of humour, or the appreciation of it, in many German authors, Grote (viii. 456) observes that this
statement, preserved by Suidas (*sub. voc.* 'Επειοῦ δειλότερος), is plainly a
joke à *propos* of the poet's over-fondness for wine.   Nevertheless he was
probably a taxiarch, or the joke was tame, as Dr. Kock suggests to me.

[2] *Pax*, v. 700.   [3] v. 528.

point to idleness and over-conviviality (as he admitted in the
Πυτίνη) than to slowness of production, as the cause of so scanty
a record of his life's work. Furthermore, it has long since
been observed that the writers of the old comedy were far less
prolific than their tragic contemporaries, who doubtless wrote
a trilogy of their somewhat conventional plays on well-known
plots in less time than the comic poets took to elaborate their
more imaginative dramas. The titles of all Cratinus' plays
survive, and some 270 fragments are quoted from 17 of them,
besides 180 citations of uncertain place in his works. Yet it
is melancholy how little all this material, on which Meineke
gives us 200 pages, tells us of his genius. The plot of only one,
the Πυτίνη, is even approximately known, in which the aged
poet represented himself as lawfully wedded to *Comedy*, but
given to neglecting her for her rival *Inebriety*, so that Comedy
brings an action for desertion against him, and discusses with his
friends her sad case.

The attacks on Pericles (in the Θρᾷτται and Χείρωνες), and
the praise of Kimon (in the 'Αρχίλοχοι), are very prominent,
and so are scurrilous attacks on various poets and rivals,
among whom he twits Aristophanes with over-subtlety and
pedantry. It is also to be noticed that he at times treated of
mythical subjects and of literary criticism, as in his Νέμεσις
(birth of Helen), Σερίφιοι, and in his 'Αρχίλοχοι, in which
Homer and Hesiod, as well as later poets, were brought in;
his 'Οδυσσῆς was a travesty of the Odyssey, which is noted as not
having even a parabasis or choric songs, though fr. 15 shows his
chorus to have been of Ithacan sailors. Many of his fragments
also paint the happiness of a long past golden age, either mythi-
cally under Cronos, or ideally in the old Attic times—a subject
on which Athenæus has collected many interesting quotations.[1]

The general impression produced by the rags and tatters of
this great poet is very similar to that which we form on fuller
grounds of Aristophanes. There is the same terse rigour, the
same unsparing virulence, the same Attic grace and purity, nor
need we at all wonder that he was held worthy by the Athenians of a higher place than his great rival on more than one

[1] vi. p. 267.

occasion. But we may reserve any remarks upon the moral and political intent of his plays, until we come to discuss the deep and serious aim attributed to the old comedy by grammarians and modern critics.

§ 254. CRATES was a younger contemporary of Cratinus, and is said to have been at first his actor. He is noticed by Aristotle (in the *Poetic*) as having adopted the style of Epicharmus and Phormis, and abstained from personal satire, while confining himself to the portraiture of types. He composed between Ol. 82, 4 and 88, 4. Aristophanes notices his career in the passage from the *Knights*, already so often quoted. Fourteen titles of his plays are cited, of which only eight are thought certain by Meineke. The fragments of the Θηρία, in which the golden age was painted with animated and docile furniture instead of slaves, and without animal food (the chorus of beasts protested against it), are interesting. The stray lines quoted by Stobæus have a curiously gentle and moderate tone about them.

PHERECRATES comes next, and of his life we know nothing but that he too had been an actor, and was victorious as a comic poet in Ol. 85, 3. Of the plays ascribed to him, thirteen titles seem genuine. He also, though his extant fragments contain personal attacks on Alcibiades, Melanthius the tragic poet, and others, is said by an anonymous author on comedy to have imitated Crates in avoiding personal abuse, and to have been remarkable for the invention of new plots ; in fact, to have been of the Middle Comedy, as it is called. More than 200 fragments remain, some of those quoted by Athenæus being very elegant, and showing the refined Atticism of the poet. He spoke much of social vices, of gluttony and drunkenness, and of luxury, and named more than one play after a *hetæra.* The *Cheiron*, if it be his, and other plays, contained great complaints about innovations in music, on which a remarkable fragment remains. The *Wild-men* (ἄγριοι), brought out in Ol. 89, 4, painted, according to Kock, the desire of certain Athenians to escape from their city, like the two men in the *Birds*, and settle among savage men. He also originated the idea of a play with scenes in Hades (Κραπάταλοι),

in which Æschylus appeared—an idea so splendidly appropriated in Aristophanes' *Frogs.* His Κοριαννώ (on manners of
hetæræ), Κραπάταλοι, and Μεταλλῆς afford us many characteristic and humorous fragments.

TELECLEIDES and HERMIPPUS are both cited by Plutarch for
their attacks on Pericles, the former (*fr. incert.* 4) complains of
the absolute favour shown him by the Athenians ; the latter
charges him with lust and cowardice. They painted, like all their
compeers, pictures of the golden age, but chiefly from a gour-
mand point of view, the lines from Teleclides' *Amphictyons*
being particularly good. He praises Nikias, and mentions Mnesilochus and Socrates as helping Euripides in his plays ; Hermippus alludes to Cleon, so that both poets must have lived
to see the so-called ochlocracy. The iambics of Hermippus have been noticed above (p. 196). Even in him there
are traces of mythological plays, and in his Φορμοφόροι remarkable hexameter passages which smack of parody—one of
them on the various produce of the Mediterranean coasts
(fr. 1), the other on the comparative merit of various wines
(fr. 2).

§ 255. There are many other contemporaries of Aristophanes,
who were even at times successful against him, but who need not
be here fully enumerated. *Philonides,* who undertook the performances of Aristophanes' *Daitaleis* and *Frogs,* was himself the
author of a play called Κόθορνοι, the buskins, in which he lampooned Theramenes. *Ameipsias* defeated Aristophanes' *Clouds*
and *Birds* with his *Connos* and *Revellers.* Nine of his comedies are named. *Archippus* was the author of an Ἰχθῦς or
Fishmarket comedy, and of an *Amphitryo,* which Plautus may
have imitated. *Phrynichus,* the son of Eunomides, is often confounded with the son of Polyphradmon, the tragic writer, also
with a certain military man, and perhaps with a dancer—the
name being apparently very common. This comic poet enjoyed a high reputation. Of the ten tragedies attributed to him
the *Revellers* contained allusions to the affair of the Hermæ,
his *Monotropos* (Ol. 91, 2) was on a misanthrope, of the type
of Timon ; his *Muses* stood second to Aristophanes' *Frogs*
(Ol. 93, 2) and contained a celebrated eulogium on Sophocles.

I will here add *Plato*, the latest poet who seems to be truly of the old comedy, though often classed with the middle on account of his date,[1] for he flourished from Ol. 88 to Ol. 97 at least, when the political aspects of comedy had disappeared. Nevertheless no poet is more prominent in his attacks upon all the demagogues, beginning with Cleon, and writing distinct plays upon Cleophon and Hyperbolus. He is said to have attacked even Peisander and Antiphon, the leaders of the aristocratic reaction in 411 B.C., but this seems to me more than doubtful. He was, for a comic writer, rather prolific, twenty-eight plays being ascribed to him. The reader who desires to know all that can be said about them may wade through the laborious volumes of Meineke, and there are doubtless many hints concerning the politics, the literature and the social life of the period to be drawn from the scanty remnants left to us. But as literature, these scraps are only valuable in showing us the development of that pure Attic diction, which reached its perfection about this time.

§ 256. But before we proceed to discuss the general points concerning the position of comedy, as Aristophanes found it, we must expand this dry enumeration by adding yet one name, but a name of greater importance than any which we have yet mentioned in this field—I mean that of Aristophanes' fellow poet and rival, EUPOLIS. This man, the son of Sosipolis, was born at Athens Ol. 83, 3 (449 B.C.), and wrote his first play at the age of seventeen, a most unusual precociousness, of which Antiphanes and Menander are also examples. A scholiast on Aristophanes[2] says there was a law against any poet bringing out a comedy before the age of thirty, but this I suppose means that the state would not undergo the expense of a chorus for a young and untried candidate, and hence the comic poets generally brought out their early plays under other people's names, and also began as actors for elder poets. Eupolis is said to have been drowned in one

---

[1] The fact that some of his plays, like the *Phaon*, had the character of the middle comedy, is an argument of no value, as there is hardly a single poet of the old comedy of whom such a statement would not be true.

[2] *Nub.* 526.

of the battles in the Hellespont,[1] probably Kynossema (410
B.C.), and with the connivance or assistance of Alcibiades,
who hated him for his political satire. This fact has even been
expanded into a story that Alcibiades when sailing to Sicily had
him drowned,[2] with a joke retorting the term ($\beta\acute{a}\pi\tau\alpha\iota$) under
which the poet had ridiculed some profligate young aristocrats
of his set. Of his life we know nothing more except some anecdotes about his faithful dog, and his faithless slave, Ephialtes,
who was charged with stealing his comedies. The attempts of
Platonius and others to characterise Eupolis as a poet are
hopelessly vague, either from the confusion of the writers or the
corruption of the texts. They compare and contrast him with
Cratinus and Aristophanes, but not in accordance with either
the extant fragments or any intelligible theory. That he was
brilliant in his wit, and refined in his style, is plain from the fact
that he co-operated with Aristophanes in his *Knights*, of which
the last parabasis, beginning from v. 1290, is recorded by the
scholiast to have been his composition. He afterwards may
have quarrelled with Aristophanes, for they satirised one another freely. In style and in genius he stood nearest to his
great rival, and his comedies seem to have possessed most, if
not all, of the features which make the Aristophanic comedy
so peculiar in literature. He was witty, coarse, unsparing, in-
ventive both in diction and in scenic effects, and appears to
have pursued the same relentless opposition policy against the
democratic party and their aristocratic leaders.

At least fourteen of the titles ascribed to him appear to be
genuine. His *Goats* had a chorus of goats, and does not seem
to have been so political as his other plays. The fragments have
a rustic and bucolic complexion. The *Autolycus* was a satire on
a youth of great beauty and accomplishments, the favourite of
the rich Callias, and also known to us from Xenophon's
Symposium. This play came out in Ol. 89, 4, under the
management of Demostratus. Callias himself and his Sophist
friends were treated in the *Flatterers* (Ol. 89, 3), in which he

---

[1] It is said that in consequence the Athenians made a law that poets
should be exempt from military service.

[2] Cf. Cicero *Ad Att.* vi. 1 in refutation of the story.

figured like the *Timon* of Shakspeare, at the opening of the play. The Βάπται ridiculed the worship of Cotytto for its ribaldry and obscenity, probably in Ol. 91, 1, before the Sicilian expedition. There is no clear evidence that Alcibiades was lampooned in this play, as is usually asserted. We must deeply regret the loss of the Δῆμοι (about Ol. 91, 4), in which Nikias and Myronides were represented as questioning the great old politicians, who had come back from the dead, and lamenting the condition of the state. Solon, Miltiades, Aristeides, Kimon, and others appeared, and so did Pericles,[1] who asked many questions concerning his son and the prospects of Athens. The youth and inexperience of the newer generals were especially censured. A parallel play was the Πόλεις, in which the personified tributary cities formed the chorus. His Μαρικᾶς (Ol. 89, 4) attacked Hyperbolus, and the play was charged by Aristophanes [2] with plagiarism from his *Knights*. The Προσπάλτιοι seems to have attacked the litigiousness of the people of that deme. In the *Taxiarchs* the celebrated admiral Phormio played a leading part, and seems to have undertaken the military training of Dionysus, who objects greatly to any hardships. In the *Golden Age* he exhibited, and may have ridiculed, pictures of a return to a primitive state of innocence and peace.[3]

[1] The description of Pericles' eloquence is happily preserved to us.

    α. Κράτιστος οὗτος ἐγένετ' ἀνθρώπων λέγειν,
    ὁπότε παρέλθοι δ', ὥσπερ ἀγαθοὶ δρομῆς
    ἐκ δέκα ποδῶν ᾕρει λέγων τοὺς ῥήτορας.
    β. Ταχὺν λέγεις μέν, πρὸς δέ γ' αὐτοῦ τῷ τάχει
    πειθώ τις ἐπεκάθιζεν ἐπὶ τοῖς χείλεσιν·
    οὕτως ἐκήλει, καὶ μόνος τῶν ῥητόρων
    τὸ κέντρον ἐγκατέλειπε τοῖς ἀκροωμένοις.

[2] *Nub.* vv. 553-5.

[3] The other titles are Ἀστράτευτοι, Νουμηνίαι, Φίλοι. I add a remarkable fragment :

    Ἀλλ' ἀκούετ', ὦ θεαταί, πολλὰ καὶ ξυνίετε
    ῥήματ'· εὐθὺ γὰρ πρὸς ὑμᾶς πρῶτον ἀπολογήσομαι,
    ὅ τι μαθόντες τοὺς ξένους μὲν λέγετε ποιητὰς σοφούς,
    ἢν δέ τις τῶν ἐνθάδ' αὐτοῦ μηδὲ ἓν χεῖρον φρονῶν,
    ἐπιτιθῆται τῇ ποιήσει, πάνυ δοκεῖ κακῶς φρονεῖν,
    μαίνεταί τε καὶ παραρρεῖ τῶν φρενῶν τῷ σῷ λόγῳ,
    Ἀλλ' ἐμοὶ πείθεσθε πάντως μεταβαλόντες τοὺς τρόπους
    μὴ φθονεῖθ', ὅταν τις ἡμῶν μουσικῇ χαίρῃ νέων.

§ 257. A few words of summary may here be useful on the general condition to which comedy had attained when Aristophanes arose. The long, or rather crowded, series of poets up to Eupolis had brought it out of the rude and extemporaneous amusement of amateurs on a holiday into the stricter form of a drama imitated in its general outline from the externals of tragedy. There was the same sort of application to the archon for a chorus, which was carefully trained, and had indeed a more arduous task than the tragic chorus. For its larger number (twenty-four) enabled the poet to use sections of it for different purposes, so that some of them took part in the play itself, while the rest remained more or less interested spectators, as in tragedy. The plots, if such they can be called, were also far looser and admitted of all manner of changes, according to the exuberance of the poet's fancy. Nevertheless the actors seem to have been limited to three (as in tragedy), and the licenses, as in all true art, were controlled by imperceptible yet strict laws. The dialect was gradually determined between the stilted grandeur of the tragic stage and the common language of Attic society, so as to become, in the hands of Aristophanes and his contemporaries, the most perfect diction in all Greek literature. For there is no Greek which can compare for vigour, for grace, and for fullness with the language of the old Attic comedy.

It will be seen in the foregoing list that the comic writers were not at all so prolific as their tragic brethren, and Antiphanes, in an extant fragment, shows us ample reasons for it. In tragedy the plots were given beforehand by the myths, and allowed a very moderate amount of originality in the poet, whose whole attention was directed to the sentiments and diction of given characters. The title and the prologue told the whole plot.

But in comedy—that is to say, in the purely old Attic comedy—everything was due to the invention of the poet.

Indeed, as we have already seen, even in the Sicilian plays of Epicharmus, mythological travesty and parody were jocular variations upon a given theme.

It is, however, a great mistake to think that the non-political forms did not exist in the fourth century at Athens. All the notable comic playwrights composed plays in this style, so much so that I believe the origin of the Epicharmian and the Attic comedy not to have been very different, and that what is called the *Old Comedy* was really an accidental and temporary outburst of political writing in the feverish climax of the Athenian democracy. As soon as these special conditions passed away or even halted for a moment, comedy returned to its older and tamer function of criticising general types in society, literary work, and crude superstitions. Thus the Middle Comedy was no new development, but a survival of the older and more general type, which came again into the foreground when no longer obscured by a brilliant innovation. The so-called Old Comedy was then really nothing but the political period of Attic comedy, which was indicated not only in the plots, which were political burlesques, but in the famous interludes (*parabases*), in which the chorus turned and came forward to address the house in the person of the poet, with personal advice, complaint, sarcasm, or solemn warning. It is not unusual for one of the characters to lay aside his part, and assume the poet's voice, thus occupying the place of the parabasis. This was said to have been a fashion in Euripides' plays also, in which, for example, Melanippe was supposed to be a mouthpiece of his views. The nearest approach we have to a parabasis nowadays is the *topical song* in our pantomimes, which is always composed on current events, and has verses added from week to week, according as new points of public interest crop up. The analogy between this digression and the Aristophanic parabasis is striking enough.

This so-called *parabasis*, and the choral songs, are the really distinctive feature of the earlier Attic plays, and whenever one was composed without it, or on a mythological instead of a political subject, we are told by the critics that it *approaches the character of the Middle Comedy*—in reality it merely conforms to the general type. By most modern authorities the *parabasis* is held to be the original nucleus from which the Attic comedy developed. If the above remarks be well grounded, this view is incorrect, and the older, now abandoned, theory is true, that

originally the volunteer actors assembled for the performance of some rude masque or farce, and that they gradually
came to abuse this disguise for the purpose of making personal
attacks with impunity. The very title *parabasis* seems to me a
strong argument for this account of the matter. The analogy
of tragedy has been pushed too far by modern critics. There
the chorus was indeed the nucleus, and the actors, at first one,
then two, then three, were added slowly and sparingly. The
origin of comedy was different. Apparently any member of the
twenty-four persons performing might come forward as an actor;
they did so irregularly, and what Cratinus did was not to increase, but to limit the number to three, and give them the
acting parts all through, reserving his chorus for the parabasis
and choral odes. The separate odes require little notice here,
as they were not frequent ; they generally consist of hymns to
the gods or hymenæal songs based upon the tragic models as
to metre and diction. But the parabasis, which interrupted
the course of the play with a most interesting intermezzo, was
far more characteristic. In its complete form, as we find it in
Aristophanes' *Birds*, it opens with an introductory κομμάτιον,
then the proper *parabasis* or address to the audience by the
coryphæus; generally in anapæstic tetrameters, and called ἀνά-
παιστοι ; and then the πνῖγος, or μακρόν, from its demands upon
the voice. Then comes a short lyrical hymn (in the *Birds*, sixteen lines), followed by an appendix to the parabasis called *epirrhema*, with an antistrophe and an *antepirrhema*. But in most
plays this elaborate form is not observed, and there are addresses
from the actors, and scattered odes which supply its place.[1]

§ 258. There are some other facts disclosed by the notices
on earlier playwrights, as well as on Aristophanes, which are of
the highest interest, as showing the natural analogies between
the growth of the drama in this and in other ages and nations.
We hear in numerous cases that the authors began as players

---

[1] I note here the divisions in the *parabasis* of the *Birds* : κομμάτιον,
vv. 677-84 ; parabasis, 685-736 ; melic ode, 737-52 ; epirrhema, 753-68 ;
antistrophe of ode, 769-84 ; antepirrhema, 785-800. There are besides
three short personal songs of satirical character for the chorus—viz. 1101,
sq., 1470, sq., and 1553, sq. The *Wasps* has also a complete parabasis.

for older poets, and gradually advanced to independent efforts. There is a passage in Aristophanes (*Knights*, 541, sq.) which possibly points to a similar progress in his case. The parallels of Molière and of Shakspeare will at once occur to the reader. It was on the stage itself that these writers learned what suited their public, and what effects were practically attainable. So also the early Attic acting-authors, whose great object was to provide the public every year with an entertainment bearing on the events of the day, must have worked very fast, and one of them speaks of it as something extraordinary, that he had spent two years at one of his plays. We find that Aristophanes, when he started in his career, produced a play every year, and we know from the number assigned to him, and from the didascaliæ, that he must sometimes have composed even faster. It was probably owing to this pressure that we hear so often of comic poets bringing out altered editions not only of their own, but of other poets' plays—a practice common in Shakspeare's day.[1] We also hear constantly of two poets producing a play together, and this is especially attested in the case of Aristophanes' *Knights*, of which Eupolis wrote a part. This joint authorship often led to mutual recriminations, and after-charges of plagiarism, and doubtless often to disputed authorship. The latter difficulty was increased by another Elizabethan habit—that of consigning a play (doubtless for some pecuniary consideration) to another person, who applied in his own name for the chorus, discharged the duties of the performance, and was proclaimed the victor, if the play was successful. There must necessarily have been some money value for this substitution, as it was adopted not only by young and timid, but by experienced authors, who nevertheless, in the very play thus disowned, referred to their own acknowledged works in such a way as to disclose their present secret. Accordingly the nominal author must merely (I fancy) have been paid, in such cases, for the labour of training the chorus and actors. Of course in many other cases real help

---

[1] Cf. Prof. Dowden's excellent *Primer on Shakspere*, pp. 10–13, for a summary of points to which I am here giving the old Greek parallels.

was given privately by one poet to another, and to this we also have allusions.[1]

§ 259. It remains for us to say a word on the political and moral aspects of comedy at this epoch. The Alexandrian monarchists, followed by the mediæval and modern antidemocrats, have been loud in the praises of the Attic comedy as a censor of morals, as a scourge of political dishonesty, as in fact fulfilling an office similar to that of the public press of our day in pamphlets and leading articles. The comic poets themselves boast their serious intention amid laughter and buffoonery; they claim to be public advisers and benefactors. But their evidence is surely no better than that of a daily journal which professes to attack on purely moral grounds, and for the public good, whereas all its complaints are strictly limited to the opposite party in politics. It is very remarkable, and shows some closer bond among the comic poets than has been suspected by the moderns (in spite of its frequent assertion in the Greek tracts on these writers), that not a single comedy, so far as we know, took the radical side, and ridiculed old-fashioned ignorance, or stupid toryism. On the contrary, the whole body of the comic writers knew no higher ideal than to return to the golden age of Miltiades, if not of Saturn. They knew no higher happiness in this age than the absence of new ideas and the presence of material comforts. They revile every radical leader, especially if of low birth, and do not spare the aristocrats, like Alcibiades and Callias, who adopted either radical opinions or courted novelties in education and in philosophy. I will not say that there were not ribald jokes about Kimon, when he was long dead, or occasional praise of Pericles, in comparison with low orators of his party. But the main fact is certain ; the whole political aim of the old Attic comedy was to support conservatism against radicalism, and not even the transcendent genius and noble personality of Pericles could save him from the most ribald

---

[1] e.g. the parabasis of the *Knights*, where Aristophanes speaks of himself as ἐπικουρῶν κρύβδην ἑτέροις ποιηταῖς, cannot refer to Philonides and Callistratus, but to this sort of partial and really secret assistance given to well-known dramatists, perhaps on account of the sudden and hurried requirements of political comedy.

attacks, and the grossest libels, at the hands of these so-called guardians of morals and censors of vice. It was so with all the noblest advocates of reform in all directions—with Protagoras, with Socrates, with Euripides. They were all equally the butt of comic scorn and the victims of comic falsehoods. Probably the comic poets were persuaded of the mischievousness of these men and their ideas ; but they were persuaded as party men, not as calm judges of right and wrong ; and I have no doubt they were as easily persuaded of the innocence of the greatest miscreants in their own party. If these things be so, there will obviously be great caution required in using them as historical evidence. They are, in fact, never to be believed without independent corroboration.

But though their political merits have been greatly overrated, they stand pre-eminent in another, and that the original object of comedy. The volunteer chorus had originally met for the purpose of amusement, for the interchange of wit and the promotion of laughter, and in this the perfected Attic comedy seems still unapproachable. We have indeed only stray flashes from the lost poets, but it is evident from the attribution of Aristophanes' plays to Archippus, from the frequent success of other poets over him, from his anxious and jealous rivalry, that we have in him a playwright not ' primus longo intervallo,' but ' primus inter pares,' and that the lost comedies sparkled all over with gems of wit like his inimitable farces. So necessary an element was this moving of laughter, that none of them were ashamed to make use of obscenity, provided it was ridiculous, and we must suppose that this element was as much looked forward to and relished by the audience as the inuendos of the modern French drama. Literary satire and parody were only beginning to be popular, because the busy Athenian public were only now beginning to be a reading public—all their time having been hitherto spent in active politics or commerce. But the spread of books was beginning ; literary discussion was made popular by the sophists, and the field of literary travesty lay open whenever politics became too serious to tolerate the satire of public men, or became too trivial to keep up the interest in such censure.

Such seems to have been the general condition of Attic comedy when Aristophanes arose.[1]

[1] The reader will find the various documents on which our knowledge of the history depends—extracts from Platonius, from various anonymous scholiasts, from Tzetzes—in the appendices to vols. i. and ii. of Meineke's *Fragmenta Comicorum*, and summaries of the modern tracts on the subject in Bernhardy's and Nicolai's histories. I still quote from Meineke throughout the following chapters, as Th. Kock's newer and more complete collection is only in progress. Here and there I have made corrections according to his excellent suggestions, as well as some criticisms, which he has kindly communicated to me.

CHAPTER XXI.

ARISTOPHANES.

§ 260. THE dates neither of the birth nor the death of Aristophanes are accurately known, but as he was a young man when
his first play came out, we may conjecture him to have been
born 450–46 B.C. He is explicitly called τὸν δῆμον Κυδαθηναιεὺς
Πανδιονίδος φυλῆς, but his father, Philippus, had property in
Ægina, to which the poet alludes when he speaks (in the *Acharnians*) of this island being claimed in order to secure him ;
and the fact that he was persecuted by Cleon on a γραφὴ ξενίας,
for being a foreigner assuming civic rights, has thrown some
doubt even on the origin of his father, who is said by some to
have been a Rhodian or a Greek of Naucratis in Egypt. We
know nothing of the poet's private life or education. If Plato's
fancy picture in the *Symposium* could be trusted, he was a man
of aristocratic breeding and culture, living in the best society
at Athens. But the fact that Agathon his host, and Socrates
the chief speaker on the occasion, were the constant butt of
the poet's severest satire makes one doubt that this wonderful
Symposium has even historical verisimilitude. We know
from an allusion of Eupolis that he was bald before his time,
and that he had once been a joint worker with that poet.
He also speaks himself of secretly helping other poets, and
of his reluctance to demand a chorus in his own name. We
know that the last play he composed was the *Plutus*, in 388
B.C., and the biographers tell us he died soon after, leaving
three sons, Philip, Nicostratus, and Araros, the last of whom
he commended to the public by letting him bring out this
play. Araros came out as an original poet about 375 B.C., but
this affords no certain evidence that his father was then dead.

Our authorities on the life of Aristophanes are two Greek *Lives*
—one by Thomas Magister, the other fuller one anonymous.
and besides the notice by Suidas.   These are supplemented by
the poet's own confessions in the parabases of the *Acharnians*,
Knights, and *Wasps*. We have the titles of forty-three plays,
and thirty are said to have been read by John Chrysostom, but
Suidas only knows the. eleven we have now remaining. Aristophanes' life is so closely bound up with his works, that it will
be necessary to enter at once upon his remains, and treat them
as far as possible chronologically.

§ 261. His first play, the *Epulones* (Δαιταλῆς), came out in
Ol. 88, 1 (427 B.C.), and was not only well received, but obtained
lasting reputation. He seems in this play to have opened his
career by a politico-social criticism, by contrasting the old
simple conservative education with that of the sophist teachers,
which was then becoming fashionable.   In the following year
appeared his *Babylonians*, in which he turned his satire against
the magistracies, both those elected by ballot and by vote, as
well as also against Cleon—and this at the great Dionysia,
when crowds of embassies which had come with tribute from
the subject cities were in the theatre. .For this he was accused
and prosecuted by Cleon, and he alludes to it in his next
year's play, the *Acharnians*,[1] the first of those now extant, which
was produced (Ol. 88, 3) at the *Lenæa*, or country Dionysia,
where no strangers were present.

§ 262. The play attained the first prize, but was brought
out under the name of Callistratus, who had been the producer
of both the earlier plays.   In the *Acharnians* the poet already
stands before us in his full strength, his graceful and refined
diction, his coarse and pungent wit, his contempt of plots, his
mastery of character and of dialogue.   It is a bold attempt
to support the aristocratical peace party against the intrigues
and intimidations of the democratic war party, who according
to the poet concealed selfish ends and personal aggrandise-
ment under the cloak of patriotism.   The leading character,
Dicæopolis, around whom all the scenes are grouped, is the
honest country farmer, who is weary of serving in discomfort on

[1] vv. 377, 502, 630, sq.

garrison duty, and paying high for the fare afforded him without stint by his farm. He comes to the agora determined to howl down anyone who proposes any subject for debate save that of peace. The idleness and delays of the assembly, the humbug of embassies to the great king, and of strange ambassadors, are paraded on the stage, and at last Dicæopolis in disgust determines to make a private peace with the Lacedæmonians. The solemn and yet licentious celebration of peace with his family is then performed. But the chorus of Acharnians, the violent war party, whose lands have been laid waste, and who will not hear of peace, attacks him, and it is only by securing one of their coal-baskets as hostage that he escapes their rage. He then proposes to defend his cause, and the cause of his peace, with his head upon the block, and for this purpose goes to beseech Euripides to lend him a miserable and suppliant garb from some of his tragedies, wherewith to move the pity of his audience. The scene in which he appeals to the student poet, and gradually reviews all the heroes of misery in his tragedies, is one of great power, full of wit and parody, and intended as a vigorous satire of the new school rhetoric, with which the plays abound. When he has succeeded in partly persuading his judges, the malcontent section go off for Lamachus, the swashbuckler-general, who lives by wars and expeditions, and there is a good deal of hard hitting in exposing the intrigues of place-hunters and the neglect of honest citizens. Then follow the proceedings at Dicæopolis' free market, in his country-seat, whither a starving Megarian brings his daughters for sale—a scene of no little pathos, mingled with some obscenity. There comes a Bœotian with various luxuries, which Dicæopolis receives in exchange for a troublesome sycophant, who turns up to protest against any market with enemies. The play concludes with a humorous responsive dialogue between Lamachus, who laments the hardships of campaigning, and is presently led in wounded, and Dicæopolis, who celebrates the pleasures and plenty of peace, and is led in mellow with wine, and exuberant with license.

This famous piece, which is an excellent specimen of the poet's work, and even touches on the principal subjects which occupy all his life, is in no sense a comedy with a plot, or an attempt to portray nature or society. It is rather an extravagant political farce, in which the poet gives rein to his imagination, strings together loosely connected scenes, and introduces the impossible and the imaginary wherever it suits his purpose. Nevertheless, there is always a political or social object kept in view, nor are the faults and failings of any class spared. We are not surprised that it was placed first even against the competition of Cratinus and Eupolis. The text is pure and not difficult, and the Greek scholia are particularly good. It has been specially edited, among others, by Elmsley, Mitchell, Blaydes, W. C. Green, and W. Ribbeck (Leipzig, 1864). I will speak of translations separately.

§ 263. The *Knights* ('Ιππῆς) appeared the very next year (424). We know in fact seven plays produced by the poet in seven successive years, the last four of which are extant, and each of them may fairly be called a masterpiece. But this extraordinary rate of production, which in a poorer epoch would have been well-nigh impossible, was not by any means a very rapid rate of composing for an Attic poet, who seems to have thrown off piece after piece with the same rapidity that Molière produced his immortal plays. Nor were the comic poets at all so prolific as their tragic brethren, who could produce four plays every year. Possibly the assistance of Callistratus in working up the stage representation aided the poet materially, by leaving him free for composition. The *Knights* were produced in the poet's own name, but he was assisted by Eupolis, to whom the scholiasts attribute part of the second parabasis.[1] The play is more serious and bitter than the *Acharnians*, and critical scholars think they perceive in it greater finish of style and richness of diction. Nevertheless, even the greater strictness of plot, which must be admitted, does not atone for the monotony of the dialogue in which Cleon is out-Cleoned by his rival the sausage-seller. The play personifies the Athenian demos as an easy-going, dull-witted old man, with Nikias, Demosthenes, and Cleon among his slaves, among whom the latter has attained a tyrannical ascendancy by alternate bullying

---

[1] vv. 1290, sq. ; cf. above, p. 430.

his fellows and flattering his master. By the advice of oracles, which play a great part all through the play, and which imply an earnest faith in religion among the Athenian people of that day, the former two persuade a low sausage-seller (Agoracritus) to undertake the task of supplanting Cleon. He is assisted by the chorus of Knights, who are determined enemies of Cleon, and who come in to defend their friends, and attack the demagogue, in their famous parabasis. The greater part of the remainder is occupied with the brazen attempts of both demagogues to out-bully one another, and to devise bribes and promises to gain Demos' favour. At last Agoracritus prevails and retires with Demos, whom he presently reproduces, apparently by *eccyclema*, sitting crowned, and in his right mind, heartily ashamed of his former follies. Agoracritus, who in this scene appears as changed in character as his master, advises him most sincerely concerning his politics and his duties to the subjects. The ideal of Aristophanes is the usual one of bigoted conservatives—a return to the good old days at Athens, to those of Marathon, and to the policy of Aristeides. Such dreams are hardly less foolish than those of socialists and communists as to the future of human society. The parabasis of the *Knights* is the most precious document we have on the history of the comic drama, and I therefore quote it without apology.[1]

---

[1] vv. 507–550 :

εἰ μέν τις ἀνὴρ τῶν ἀρχαίων κωμῳδοδιδάσκαλος ἡμᾶς
ἠνάγκαζεν λέξοντας ἔπη πρὸς τὸ θέατρον παραβῆναι,
οὐκ ἂν φαύλως ἔτυχεν τούτου· νῦν δ' ἄξιός ἐσθ' ὁ ποιητὴς
ὅτι τοὺς αὐτοὺς ἡμῖν μισεῖ, τολμᾷ τε λέγειν τὰ δίκαια,
καὶ γενναίως πρὸς τὸν Τυφῶ χωρεῖ καὶ τὴν ἐριώλην·
ἃ δὲ θαυμάζειν ὑμῶν φησιν πολλοὺς αὐτῷ προσιόντας,
καὶ βασανίζειν, ὡς οὐχὶ πάλαι χορὸν αἰτοίη καθ' ἑαυτόν,
ἡμᾶς ὑμῖν ἐκέλευε φράσαι περὶ τούτου· φησὶ γὰρ ἀνὴρ
οὐχ ὑπ' ἀνοίας τοῦτο πεπονθὼς διατρίβειν, ἀλλὰ νομίζων
κωμῳδοδιδασκαλίαν εἶναι χαλεπώτατον ἔργον ἁπάντων·
πολλῶν γὰρ δὴ πειρασάντων αὐτὴν ὀλίγοις χαρίσασθαι·
ὑμᾶς τε πάλαι διαγιγνώσκων ἐπετείους τὴν φύσιν ὄντας,
καὶ τοὺς προτέρους τῶν ποιητῶν ἅμα τῷ γήρᾳ προδιδόντας·
τοῦτο μὲν εἰδὼς ἄπαθε Μάγνης ἅμα ταῖς πολιαῖς κατιούσαις,
ὃς πλεῖστα χορῶν τῶν ἀντιπάλων νίκης ἔστησε τροπαῖα·

The newest special editions are by Velsen (1869); Born, with a German version; W. Ribbeck (1867); Th. Kock (in Haupt and Sauppe's series); and by Mr. Green in the Cambridge *Catena*. § 264. In the very next year (Ol. 89, 1, or 423 B.C.) Philonides brought out for the now famous poet his *Clouds*—an arrangement, as I have already suggested, merely intended to save him the labour of the stage practising. The play is certainly far superior to the *Knights*, yet nevertheless was defeated not only by the brilliant *Wine-flask* of old Cratinus, but by the *Connus* of Ameipsias, a little known poet. The extant play is a second edition, modified, we know not how much, from the unsuccessful original. One of the Greek arguments (No. vi.) mentions as altered the parabasis, in which the poet lectures

πάσας δ' ὑμῖν φωνὰς ἱεὶς καὶ ψάλλων καὶ πτερυγίζων
καὶ λυδίζων καὶ ψηνίζων καὶ βαπτόμενος βατραχείοις
οὐκ ἐξήρκεσεν, ἀλλὰ τελευτῶν ἐπὶ γήρως, οὐ γὰρ ἐφ' ἥβης,
ἐξεβλήθη πρεσβύτης ὤν, ὅτι τοῦ σκώπτειν ἀπελείφθη.
εἶτα Κρατίνου μεμνημένος, ὃς πολλῷ ῥεύσας ποτ' ἐπαίνῳ
διὰ τῶν ἀφελῶν πεδίων ἔρρει, καὶ τῆς στάσεως παρασύρων
ἐφόρει τὰς δρῦς καὶ τὰς πλατάνους καὶ τοὺς ἐχθροὺς προθελύμνους·
ᾆσαι δ' οὐκ ἦν ἐν ξυμποσίῳ πλὴν Δωροῖ συκοπέδιλε,
καί, τέκτονες εὐπαλάμων ὕμνων· οὕτως ἤνθησεν ἐκεῖνος.
νυνὶ δ' ὑμεῖς αὐτὸν ὁρῶντες παραληροῦντ' οὐκ ἐλεεῖτε,
ἐκπιπτουσῶν τῶν ἠλέκτρων, καὶ τοῦ τόνου οὐκ ἔτ' ἐνόντος,
τῶν θ' ἁρμονιῶν διαχασκουσῶν· ἀλλὰ γέρων ὢν περιέρρει,
ὥσπερ Κοννᾶς, στέφανον μὲν ἔχων αὖον· δίψῃ δ' ἀπολωλώς,
ὃν χρῆν διὰ τὰς προτέρας νίκας πίνειν ἐν τῷ πρυτανείῳ,
καὶ μὴ ληρεῖν, ἀλλὰ θεᾶσθαι λιπαρὸν παρὰ τῷ Διονύσῳ.
οἵας δὲ Κράτης ὀργὰς ὑμῶν ἠνέσχετο καὶ στυφελιγμούς·
ὃς ἀπὸ σμικρᾶς δαπάνης ὑμᾶς ἀριστίζων ἀπέπεμπεν,
ἀπὸ κραμβοτάτου στόματος μάττων ἀστειοτάτας ἐπινοίας·
χοὖτος μέντοι μόνος ἀντήρκει, τοτὲ μὲν πίπτων, τοτὲ δ' οὐχί.
ταῦτ' ὀρρωδῶν διέτριβεν ἀεί, καὶ πρὸς τούτοισιν ἔφασκεν
ἐρέτην χρῆναι πρῶτα γενέσθαι, πρὶν πηδαλίοις ἐπιχειρεῖν,
κᾆτ' ἐντεῦθεν πρῳρατεῦσαι καὶ τοὺς ἀνέμους διαθρῆσαι,
κᾆτα κυβερνᾶν αὐτὸν ἑαυτῷ. τούτων οὖν οὕνεκα πάντων,
ὅτι σωφρονικῶς κοὐκ ἀνοήτως ἐσπηδήσας ἐφλυάρει,
αἴρεσθ' αὐτῷ πολὺ τὸ ῥόθιον, παραπέμψατ' ἐφ' ἕνδεκα κώπαις
θόρυβον χρηστὸν ληναίτην,
ἵν' ὁ ποιητὴς ἀπίῃ χαίρων,
κατὰ νοῦν πράξας,
φαιδρὸς λάμποντι μετώπῳ·

the audience on their want of taste in refusing him- the prize, the dialogue of the two λόγοι, and the conclusion of the piece. But the work, as we have it, seems imperfectly recast, and was not again brought on the stage by the poet. If so, it is a curious evidence for the existence of a reading public apart from the theatrical audience at Athens.

The play opens with a night-scene, in which the principal actor, Strepsiades (Turn-coat), tells of his miseries, his expensive Alcmæonid wife, and his spendthrift son Pheidippides, whose very name is a compromise between country saving and city luxury. Even the slaves have become insolent in these war times, and the old gentleman cannot sleep with thinking of his debts and his son's extravagant habits. The only safety he can devise is to send his son to the Phrontistery (Thinking-shop) of Socrates, who assumes the character in this play of the vulgar sophist, and will train any young man to win his cause, however unjust, by subtle rhetoric. But when the fashionable horsy young man refuses, the old gentleman presents himself instead at the door of the Phrontistery, and finds the sage swinging in a basket aloft observing the sun and æther. A solemn disciple informs the astonished Strepsiades of various wonders in the school, and groups of pale students are seen wrapped in mysterious meditations. Socrates, who poses as a physical philosopher and a freethinker, promises to transform Strepsiades into an accomplished sophist. He calls down his new divinities, the *Clouds*, who rule the world under *Vortex* (Δῖνος, Mr. Browning's *Whirligig*), the supplanter of Zeus. The choral odes of these Clouds are extremely beautiful, and reveal a lyric power in Aristophanes which is not found in the earlier plays. But with the license of comedy they not only pass into the poet's person in the parabasis, they even at the end assume the character of the ' lying spirits ' in the Old Testament, and declare that they are meant to mislead into condign punishment such as profanely disbelieve in the national faith.

Accordingly on their entrance they join Socrates in emancipating Strepsiades from the religion of his fathers. But in other respects he is found an inept and stupid pupil. The parabasis is again of the utmost independent value, owing to its personal character, and the sketch which Aristophanes gives of his aims in writing comedy.[1] It is delivered while Socrates and his pupil are within at their lessons. When they return to the stage, Strepsiades is put through a long exercise in grammatical points, but breaks down through want of memory and quickness, and is advised by the Clouds to bring his son to the Phrontistery instead. The son objects, but is ultimately persuaded, though reluctantly, to enter the school. Here a choral ode is missing, after which follows the famous dialogue of the Just and Unjust arguments, in which the poet paints with enthusiasm the old education, and the splendour of old Attic life in purity and in beauty.[2] But the unjust advocate of the new, immoral, intellectual education wins the battle, and obtains the control of the pupil in consequence. Strepsiades at once assumes airs of great impertinence to his creditors, trusting to his son's future subtleties; but the first result is a quarrel between father and son as to an after-dinner song, when the son beats his father and threatens his mother with his newly acquired sophistry. This suddenly opens the old Turncoat's eyes; he deplores his folly, and is severely reprimanded by the now serious and orthodox Clouds for his blindness and immorality. He ends the play by taking vengeance on Socrates, and setting the Phrontistery on fire. Such is the general outline of this remarkable piece. But it is also full of minor traits of great interest, and these are the special features which make both the dialogue and the odes as interesting as anything now extant of Greek comedy.

§ 265. Some of the questions raised about the *Clouds* are not easily answered. But I think the scholiasts, as well as their modern followers, have expressed far too much surprise at its failure. We do not know how far the original piece was inferior to the extant recension, and must merely note this possibility as an element in the problem. But if we consider that Aristophanes had been declared victor for at least two preceding years, we can in the first place imagine a widespread jealousy of the new favourite, and an idea that Attic comedy

---

[1] Cf. especially vv. 518-62.   [2] Cf. vv. 961, sq., 1000, sq., &c.

would suffer if all the first prizes were adjudged to one poet. Added to this feeling, and to the love of variety common to every public, and very prominent in the Athenians, there was this remarkable coincidence, that old Cratinus, the greatest master of his day, who had retired into private life, suddenly flashed out in his old vigour this year with the famous *Wine-flask*, a play not only of great general excellence, but full of personal confessions, and perhaps regrets, which must have keenly excited the sympathy of a somewhat capricious, but easily repentant public. It is likely that the enthusiasm excited by the Πυτίνη would have given it the victory over any play opposed to it. It is more difficult to say why the *Connus* of Ameipsias was also preferred, as we know very little of either the poet or the piece ; but one fact is very significant. Socrates and a chorus of Thinkers (φροντισταί) appeared in it, and there is a fragment extant which describes the sage as dressed in poor and ragged dress, but nevertheless above condescending to meanness and flattery.[1] If, then, Socrates was a leading character in the play, which was called after a celebrated *Citharœdus*, who was his master, Aristophanes was defeated on his own subject by Ameipsias. This makes it less likely that any injustice was done by the judges. For while granting all the formal excellence of the play, there can be no doubt that the drawing of Socrates in the *Clouds* is completely unhistorical. The caricature is, indeed, so broad that we must acquit the poet of any hostile intention, and assume that he merely chose this well-known name to hang upon it all the eccentricities and immoralities which he desired to reprehend in the new school of rhetoric and of education. Plato's *Symposium*, which introduces the philosopher and the poet as boon companions, corroborates this view. The physical speculations of Socrates were an early and unimportant part of his thinking; he was no mountebank, no swindler, no rhetorician in the sense of the other sophists. Yet all these qualities are ascribed to him in the *Clouds*. It is, indeed, true that the poet saw with deeper insight than his public that the Socratic teaching was in real substance negative and sceptical, and might easily be

[1] Meineke, ii. p. 703.

distorted into vicious word-splitting and idle chicanery. But the Athenian public, on the other hand, felt rightly that the personality of the man was honest and noble, and it is not impossible that his bravery at the battle of Delium, not a year earlier, helped to disgust them with the caricature, and reject the clever but deeply unjust caricature of Aristophanes. It is also likely that a very large part of the audience took no interest in the physical speculations of Anaxagoras and Euripides, and were somewhat bored by the prominence given to barren subtleties. To such people the ridicule of Cleon and his dishonesty would come home at once, for every Athenian was more or less a politician; accordingly the *Knights* would command far more public interest than the *Clouds* at Athens, as the *Happy Land*, which ridiculed Mr. Gladstone's Cabinet, would command it in England, far more than any unjust caricature of Mr. Darwin and his philosophy. There are many special editions and translations of this play. I may specify those of F. A. Wolf (1811), Welcker (1810), Teuffel (ed. 3, Leipzig, 1868), Bothe, and Green. The best is that of Th. Kock (2nd ed. in Haupt and Sauppe's series). It is discussed in all the histories of Greek *Sophistic*, in connection with Socrates.

§ 266. We pass to the comedy of the following year, the *Wasps* (*Hornets?*). There is some confusion in the Greek argument of the play, which states that it was brought out by Philonides, and obtained second prize, but that the first prize was obtained by the *Rehearsal* (πρυάγων), also brought out by Philonides, and also written by Aristophanes.[1] This producing

---

[1] Mr. Rogers, in his careful and shrewd preface to his edition, proposes to emend the corrupt scholium differently, and reads it to this effect : that the play came out in the second year of the 89th Ol., under Aristophanes' own name, and was first. The πρυάγων (which ridiculed Euripides) was brought out by Philonides, and was second, Leucon with the *Ambassadors* third. This correction seems to me more probable than the others proposed. Mr. Rogers' refutation of the usual view of the play, as a satire upon the Athenian jury system, is also perfectly sound. He shows some inconsistencies in the plot, which point to haste or change of mind in the composition. Thus the chorus on entering speak of their comrade as suddenly and unexpectedly absent, whereas the opening scene represents him as long confined and prohibited from attending the courts.

of two plays by the same author in the same year seems very strange, in the face of the competition of many poets to obtain a chorus, and it is likely that the passage has been so corrupted that the real sense is lost. The play is not so brilliant as the *Clouds,* and is intended to ridicule the simplicity of the body of poorer Athenian citizens, who spent their life sitting in judgment upon all the affairs of the empire, and receiving their three obols daily by way of support. They imagined themselves the rulers of the empire, whereas they were really the tools of demagogues and of rhetoricians who pocketed the real profits. Though the principal characters are called Philo-cleon and Bdely-cleon, no living personage is introduced, and the play is remarkable as the earliest we have which deals wholly in imaginary characters. The old dicast, who has gone mad with love of sitting on juries, is confined by his sensible son with the aid of slaves ; and here we find, perhaps, the only case in which Aristophanes represents the younger generation as having more sense than the old. But he probably merely intends to intimate a very general Greek feeling, that old age, instead of being venerable and excessively wise, is really feeble and prejudiced. The Homeric attempt of the old man to escape, like Odysseus from the cave, is very comic. His friends, the chorus of Wasps, come to his aid, but are driven off by Bdelycleon, and compelled to listen passively to an argument between father and son, in which the former boasts all the nominal grandeur of the sovereign Athenian people sitting in judgment, while the latter shows the hollowness and vanity of their pretensions. Ultimately the old man is appeased by a mock trial of a dog for stealing cheese, which is got up for him at home. The attempt at humanising the old dicast, and bringing him back into the ways of society, is, however, too sudden. Though he shows much quickness of political repartee in the *skolia* which his son proposes, he is rude and unmannerly, and his behaviour to his associates shows the license of a sudden emancipation from the trammels of self-imposed political duties. The latter part of the play gives us much insight into the nature of social intercourse at Athens. The subject was imitated by Racine in his solitary comedy, *Les Plaideurs,* which is a melancholy contrast to its original as to freshness and humour. There are excellent editions by Mitchell, Hirschig (with special collations first by Bekker, then Cobet, Leiden, 1847), Julius Richter, with Latin notes (Berlin, 1858), and by Mr. Rogers, with a metrical translation. Many of the political allusions have been fully discussed by Müller-Strübing in his *Aristophanes und die historische Kritik.*

§ 267. In the following year (Ol. 89, 3) Aristophanes brought out the first edition of the *Peace*, when Eupolis gained the first prize with his *Flatterers*, and Leucon the third with his *Clansmen.* The *Peace* seems to have been rehandled by the poet, but there are not in our text (though there are in the scholia) signs of a recension. The object of the play is to recommend the then expected peace of Nikias, as both Brasidas and Cleon had lately been killed, and thus the war party at both Athens and Sparta was sensibly weakened. It was acted at the great spring festival, when the deputies of the allies with their tribute were present, as appears from many allusions. The scene is partly laid in heaven, evidently on the upper story above the stage, whither Trygæos (the Vintager), an elderly citizen, flies up on a dung-beetle to bring down the goddess Peace, who has been immured by War, while the gods in disgust have gone away, leaving War to do as he chose. Hermes, an insolent but servile doorkeeper, is the only god who appears. Two slaves who are fattening Trygæos' beetle open the piece with a dialogue which passes into the prologue, as was often the case in Aristophanes' plays. When Peace is brought down again to earth, and upon the stage, the preparations for her marriage with Trygæos occupy the rest of the play, of which the action halts after the first 800 lines, but the dialogue is all through very witty and full of clever parodies. On the whole the play is more brilliant and imaginative than the *Wasps*, but too much flavoured with that obscenity, which, however comical, disfigures several of the poet's later works, and which he himself deprecates in earlier plays. Some passages in the Parabasis and elsewhere are copied from older productions, and yet we cannot but wonder at the fertility of the poet's treatment of the same subject which he had handled

in the *Acharnians*, with such completely different scenery and
arrangement. It seems as if the phantastic element had become
much more prominent in him about this period of his life.
The best special editions of this, as of the last play, are by
Julius Richter (Berlin, 1860) and Mr. Rogers.

§ 268. There is now, in our extant remains, a gap of seven
years before the date of the next play, the *Birds*. This accident
suggests to critics a distinction between the poet's earlier and
later style, which is hardly warranted by the plays themselves.
The *Peace* seems to me to possess all his later characteristics in
full development, and is nevertheless brought out in close connection with his older, more serious, and more political plays.
The temperate allusion to Cleon shortly after his death[1] is a
curious contrast to the attack on Euripides in the *Frogs* under
the same circumstances. Here there is a sort of *de-mortuis-
nil-nisi-bonum* feeling implied. The *Birds* came out in the
spring of 414 B.C., in the year following the sending out of the
Sicilian expedition, the panic about the Hermæ, and the recall
and banishment of Alcibiades. The law of Syracosius limiting
the freedom of lampooning in comedy was doubtless connected
with the public excitement of the time, when the jibe of a
comedian might bring upon any man suspicion, prosecution,
and exile. It is doubtless to these circumstances that we may
ascribe the political vagueness of this piece, which is a general
satire upon the vain hopes and wild expectations of young
Athens, and ridicules their ideal empire in the western Mediterranean, which contrasted so strongly with the poet's conservative notions about old Attic purity, dignity, and simplicity.
We may now declare that this retrograde ideal of the old party
was not less impossible than the *Cloudcuckootown* of the advanced thinkers, and even in the Middle Comedy there were not
wanting parodies of the ancient heroic simplicity analogous to
this in the *Birds*. Nevertheless, to us the comedy is profoundly
interesting as a piece of brilliant imagination, with less political
rancour, and less obscenity than most of the author's work, and
justly accounted one of the best, if not the best, of his extant
plays.

---

[1] vv. 646, sq.

The play was brought out by Callistratus, and obtained second prize, Ameipsias being first with his *Revellers*, Phrynicush third with his *Monotropos.* It opens with a dialogue between two Athenian typical characters, *Persuader* (Πειθέταιρος) and *Hopeful* (Εὐελπίδης), who are disgusted with litigious Athens, and are wandering, conducted by a crow and jackdaw, and attended by two slaves, in search of the *avified* Tereus, now a hoopoe, who will show them a quiet city where they may live without law. This is told us, as usual, by one of the characters in the first dialogue. It is remarkable that these, like almost all Aristophanes' leading characters, are not young, but elderly men. They find the hoopoe, who calls out his wife, the nightingale,[1] and these summon all the birds to council. No sooner has Persuader asked a few questions about the life of the birds, than he conceives and propounds a scheme to the hoopoe of settling all the birds into a great polity, and shutting off by means of it the ways from earth to heaven, so that the gods, being starved out by want of offerings, shall come to terms, and resign the sovereignty of the world to the birds. This scheme is accordingly carried out, the city is established and there are very comic scenes, when all sorts of worthless sycophants, mountebank priests, and windy poets

---

[1] The beautiful invocation to the nightingale is worth quoting (vv. 209-24):

ἄγε σύννομέ μοι, παῦσαι μὲν ὕπνου,
λῦσον δὲ νόμους ἱερῶν ὕμνων,
οὓς διὰ θείου στόματος θρηνεῖς
τὸν ἐμὸν καὶ σὸν πολύδακρυν Ἴτυν
ἐλελιζομένη διεροῖς μέλεσιν
γένυος ξουθῆς·
καθαρὰ χωρεῖ διὰ φυλλοκόμου
μίλακος ἠχὼ πρὸς Διὸς ἕδρας,
ἵν' ὁ χρυσοκόμας Φοῖβος ἀκούων
τοῖς σοῖς ἐλέγοις ἀντιψάλλων
ἐλεφαντόδετον φόρμιγγα, θεῶν
ἵστησι χορούς·
διὰ δ' ἀθανάτων στομάτων χωρεῖ
ξύμφωνος ὁμοῦ
θεία μακάρων ὀλολυγή.

come to Persuader to get wings and live among the birds. Iris is caught flying through the city on an errand from Zeus to order men to sacrifice, as the gods are starving. She is sent back, and meanwhile a herald comes up from the earth to say that the mortals have consented to submit to the Birds' sovereignty. Presently Poseidon, Heracles, and Triballus—a barbarian god, who does not know how to put on his cloak— come as an embassy from the gods. But Heracles, who is very gluttonous, and moreover hungry, is ready to accept any terms, when he finds Persuader cooking a rich meal to which he hopes to be invited. Triballus is unintelligible, but sides with Heracles, and so Poseidon is forced to comply with the disgraceful terms of submitting to the Birds, and allowing Basileia (Sovereignty) to be brought down and married to Persuader. The play ends, as the *Peace* does, with the Hymeneal song.

It is full of the richest imagination and the brightest wit, but it is idle to discuss the endeavours of modern critics to pierce the disguise under which the poet may have ridiculed definite persons. As a general satire on young Athens it is full of point, and a real work of genius. I have already pointed out (above, p. 434) the careful and complete structure of the parabasis. It is surprising how few special editions of this play have been published in recent times. The earlier part has been reproduced for the stage, with sundry modifications, by Goethe in 1780, and the whole play has been translated by the poet Rückert. There is a handy school edition by Th. Kock (Haupt and Sauppe's series).

§ 269. The *Lysistrata* appeared in 411 B.C., after the Sicilian disaster, when ten *Probouloi* had been appointed to manage the city, and when its democracy was just being overthrown by the oligarchs under Peisander and Antiphon. We may take for granted that comic license was forbidden. The Peisander mentioned in the play was probably therefore not the politician, and there is no allusion to Antiphon. Nevertheless, under the mask of obscene ribaldry there is no play of Aristophanes more seriously in earnest about the affairs of the state. His usual policy is enforced by representing the women of all Greece determined to refuse conjugal rights to their husbands until peace is proclaimed, and at the same time seizing the Acropolis in order to secure the treasure of the Parthenon from being applied to war purposes. A chorus of old men who come to attack the Propylæa with fire, and a chorus of the elder women who defend it with water, replace with their responsive odes and comic abuse the usual single chorus. There is no parabasis. The Spartan woman, Lampito, who is remarkable not only for her splendid physique, but for her character and self-control, speaks throughout in her own dialect, as do the Spartan ambassadors at the close of the play, and they thus afford us an excellent specimen of that remarkable Doric which is hardly represented in any extant branch of Greek literature. The political advice comes not from the chorus, but from the leading character, whose typical name, Lysistrata, indicates hei policy. She recommends forgetfulness of past offences, in fact amnesty and a coalition of interests with the allies, who had been hitherto treated as mere subjects. There is no vain picturing of past happiness or future glory, but rather a homely, anxious review of the situation, with a determination to do the best in a frightful crisis.[1] The spectacle of an Athenian public

---

[1] I call particular attention to the following passage, as the most distinctly *pathetic* which we have in Aristophanes.

vv. 588, sq. :

ΠΡΟ. οὔκουν δεινὸν ταυτὶ ταύτας ῥαβδίζειν καὶ τολυπεύειν
     αἷs οὐδὲ μετῆν πάνυ τοῦ πολέμου ;

ΛΥ.   καὶ μήν, ὦ παγκατάρατε,
     πλεῖν ἢὲ διπλοῦν αὐτὸν φέρομεν. πρώτιστον μέν γε
     τεκοῦσαι
     κἀκπέμψασαι παῖδας ὁπλίτας.

ΠΡΟ.   σίγα, μὴ μνησικακήσῃς.

ΛΥ. εἶθ᾽ ἡνίκ᾽ ἐχρῆν εὐφρανθῆναι καὶ τῆς ἥβης ἀπολαῦσαι,
     μονοκοιτοῦμεν διὰ τὰς στρατιάς. καὶ θἠμέτερον μὲν
     ἐᾶτε,
     περὶ τῶν δὲ κορῶν ἐν τοῖς θαλάμοις γηρασκουσῶν
     ἀνιῶμαι.

ΠΡΟ. οὔκουν χἄνδρες γηράσκουσιν ;

ΛΥ.   μὰ Δί᾽, ἀλλ᾽ οὐκ εἶπας ὅμοιον.
     ὁ μὲν ἥβῶν γάρ᾽ κἂν ᾖ πολιός, ταχὺ παῖδα κόρην
     γεγάμηκεν·
     τῆς δὲ γυναικὸς σμικρὸς ὁ καιρός, κἂν τούτου μὴ
     ᾽πιλάβηται,
     οὐδεὶς ἐθέλει γῆμαι ταύτην, ὀττευομένη δὲ κάθηται

coming together in their direst misfortune, to hear a play of which the very argument could not be explicitly stated in modern society, and of which the details fully develop the main idea, shows us a great gulf between Attic and modern culture.   I will only observe in explanation of so painful a phenomenon that many ceremonies of the Greek religion— nay even the spiritual mysteries of Demeter—admitted obscene emblems and obscene jokes as a necessary part of the festival, and this element was as prominent in the feasts of women as in those where men only were engaged.   Thus the naturalism of Greek polytheism, as contrasted with the asceticism of Christianity, engendered a state of feeling, even in the most refined, which would be accounted among us shocking gross- ness.   The indulgence, therefore, of Athenians in such amuse- ments as the *Lysistrata,* though under all circumstances ob- jectionable, is not by any means to be regarded as parallel to a similar performance in modern times.

The scene being laid at the Propylæa of the Acropolis is full of local allusions to the surrounding features, which have been missed by most commentators owing to their want of familiarity with the place.   Of course the play from its very nature has been little commented on in special editions.   There is a text with scholia and full commentary by Mr. Blydes (Halle, 1880). Mr. Rogers has done all that can be done to bring it within the range of modern readers in his excellent version, and his commentary on selections from the text.

§ 270. From the following year (Ol. 92, 2) we have the *Thesmophoriazusæ,* or celebrators of the Thesmophoria, in which the poet again makes the female sex prominent, but is less in earnest about politics, which had in the meantime taken a definite turn, and permitted no interference.   This play is perhaps the most comical which we have, and might be called a 'screaming farce,' but for the determined attack on the morality of the Athenian women, which is laid by Aristophanes wittily, and by the commentators stupidly, on the shoulders of Euripides.   This poet appears with his father-in-law Mnesilo- chus in search of Agathon, whose effeminate appearance and style will enable him to attend the Thesmophoria, and defend

Euripides from the conspiracy made by the women against him, on account of his misoguny and his pictures of female passion. Agathon is cleverly parodied, with coarse asides from Mnesilochus, who is the stock Athenian of the poet. But Agathon refuses the dangerous mission among the women, and Euripides persuades Mnesilochus, with the aid of shaving and of Agathon's borrowed dress, to make the attempt. At a very comic assembly speeches are made against Euripides, but Mnesilochus ruins his case by arguing that Euripides had far understated the vices of women. This leads to altercation, and then the news brought by the effeminate Cleisthenes, that a man had entered the women's exclusive gathering, leads to the discovery and apprehension of Mnesilochus. By a device akin to that of Dicæopolis in the *Acharnians*, he threatens in his peril to slay a child, which turns out to be a wine skin, and he is at last put under the charge of a Scythian policeman. The devices of Euripides, who approaches under the guise of various characters from his plays, especially from the recent *Helena* and the *Andromeda*, and is answered by Mnesilochus, afford scope for much brilliant parody. At length, under the garb and by the devices of a procuress, Euripides entices away the Scythian, and extricates his friend.

The chorus, though prominent, sings no proper parabasis, nor is there any serious address to the audience. All the play is full of fun, and parody, and ribaldry. The attack on women is a fiercer one than all the plays of Euripides condensed could furnish. As to the travesties of Agathon and of Euripides, they are all comic, and show, I think, no personal hatred, though many hard hits are dealt. Plato makes Aristophanes a personal friend of Agathon, and the allusion to him, after his death, in the *Frogs* corroborates this. But the *Frogs* are far more severe on Euripides than this play, for here his cleverness only is ridiculed, and his plays quoted as the most popular, while his attacks on the weaker sex are more than justified. The insinuations of effeminacy against Agathon are quite as foul as those in the end of the play against Euripides for dealing in immorality. There are editions by Thiersch, F. V. Fritzsche, and Enger. Some fragments remain of a second

Thcsmophoriazusæ, which continued the plot of this play, and inveighed chiefly, according to our fragments, against female luxury. Mr. Blaydes' full edition has since appeared (Halle, 1880), and Velsen's recension (1880).

§ 271. Passing by the *Plutus,* as our version of it was produced later (it was first played in Ol. 92, 4), we come to the *Frogs,* certainly the most interesting, if not the best constructed of all Aristophanes' extant plays. It came out in 405 B.C., just before the battle of Ægospotami, when Athens was approaching the crisis of her history. Phrynichus and Theramenes are still the leading men of the state ; people are longing for Alcibiades, but afraid to recall him. It is at such a moment that this wonderful play occupied the public with its buffoonery, and its profound literary criticism. It obtained first prize under Philonides' direction, and defeated (the comic) Phrynichus' *Muses* and Plato's *Cleophon.* Its repetition is said to have been ordered owing to the prudent and moderate parabasis, which recommends amnesty for past offences, especially in the affair of the Four Hundred, and unity among all the citizens to avert the ruin of the state.[1] This political advice is very similar in tone to that in the *Lysistrata.* The plot is separated into two parts : first, the adventures of Dionysus on his journey to Hades in search of a good poet, Sophocles and Euripides being lately dead; and secondly, the poetical contest of Æschylus and Euripides, and the final victory of Æschylus. These subjects are logically though loosely connected together, but remind us strongly of the dramatic economy of the very poet whom Aristophanes is here attacking so vehemently. No analysis can reproduce the real brilliancy of the piece, which consists in all manner of comic situations, repartees, parodies, and unexpected blunders.

The attack on Euripides, and parallel defence of Æschylus, carried on by the poets themselves, is of course profoundly interesting as a piece of contemporary literary criticism by so great a poet ; but great poets are not always good critics. Moreover, whether from dramatic propriety, or from serious conviction, the points urged on both sides are all shallow and unimportant, and only of weight before an idiotic judge, such as Dionysus. How this character can have been intended to

[1] vv. 352, sq.

represent the Athenian public without insulting them is hard to understand. For if this be the poet's meaning, the æsthetic judgment of the Athenian public, and their art criticism, is ridiculed far more bitterly than the fashionable tragedian. The attacks of the poets on one another are partly grammatical, partly rythmical, partly ethical, but hardly at all æsthetic, if we except the objection to the peculiar stage effect which Æschylus so often used, of introducing his leading character upon the stage in silence, and keeping the audience in long suspense before he spoke. The grammatical points are minute and trifling, and as to the rythmical argument against Euripides' prologues,[1] most good iambic trimeters can be concluded with ληκύθιον ἀπώλεσεν, so that there is no point in it at all. The melic ramblings of Euripides may be open to the charge of disconnection and of effeminate softness, but assuredly the obscurity of Æschylus is an equally important defect in poetry addressed to a listening public.

By far the most important part of the controversy is that concerning the moral effects of tragedy, for it is assumed as an axiom by all parties,[2] that the poets (whether dramatic or not) are moral teachers—in fact, the established clergy of the age— and perform the same office for men which schoolmasters do for children. Assuming this standpoint, Euripides can only defend himself by urging that the legends he represented were as he found them, and that he encouraged practical good sense and homely shrewdness among the citizens—in fact, educated them in good sense.[3]

The reply which we should make to Æschylus would rather insist that he himself was not a great poet because he had a moral object, but because in prosecuting that object he stated great world problems, great conflicts of Destiny and Freedom, of Law and of Feeling, and set them forth with extraordinary power and beauty. Euripides may have made the mere changes of human character, and the scourge of passion, his conscious objects, but in portraying these things well he was no less a great teacher of humanity, and a lofty moralist in his own way. It is as if we should contrast Sir

[1] vv. 1200, sq.   [2] vv. 1056, sq.   [3] vv. 948, sq.

W. Scott's romances, their chivalry, their ideality, and their obvious rewarding of vice and virtue, with the subtler and deeper teaching of George Eliot, who makes the tangled web of human life her object, and does not accommodate her catastrophes to traditional morality. Sir W. Scott wrote great novels, not because he wrote with an earnest moral purpose, but because he drew periods of history, and varieties of human character, with boldness and with poetic truth. These are the eternal features of dramatic art, but they are often most deeply felt by great artists who cannot consciously express them.

As to special editions, we have those of Welcker (1812); Pernice, with notes and version (1856), and Fritzsche (1863); also Th. Kock's (in Haupt and Sauppe's series), a good schoolbook.

§ 272. There is a great descent in literary merit to the *Eccleziazusæ*, or *parliament of women*, which came out about 393 B.C., when Athens was striving along with Thebes and Argos to check the power and encroachments of Sparta. If the success at Knidos and the recovery of the maritime supremacy had taken place, still more if the long walls were being rebuilt, it is indeed strange that such a poet as Aristophanes should have made no allusion to these great successes and the hopes they inspired. But the political allusions of the play contain no solemn warning, no hearty advice ; they are merely a bitter satire on the faults and weaknesses of the revived democracy, its unstableness and vacillation, the selfishness and greed of both poor and rich, the postponing of all public interests to private advantage. All the faults reproved by Demosthenes and Phocion are already prominent ; we have before us no longer the Periclean, but the Demosthenic Athenian. The poet of a greater and better time has no heart to advise, but only to ridicule such people.[1] His main interest turns from

---

[1] It is chiefly from this evidence that the Germans draw their pictures of the debased ochlocracy, and no doubt they draw it according to the notions of Aristophanes and his aristocratic friends. But whether Athens was really thus debased is quite another question, and those who have studied Grote's history, and the affairs of the restored democracy, will come to a very different conclusion. There was no doubt a great decadence in energy, but not in social and intellectual qualities.

political to social questions, from practical to theoretical reforms, and he occupies himself with the schemes of socialism and communism which were floating in the air of the schools, and which may even then have had some countenance in Plato's oral lectures. These theories he satirises by making the women meet in the assembly, dressed in their husbands' clothes, and decide that they must in future assume the management of the state, with full community of goods, of husbands—in fact. of everything. There is of course a great deal of humour in all the discussions, especially in the home conversation between Praxagora, the leading character (like the Lysistrata of a former play), and her husband, in which he is fully persuaded by gross material prospects to acquiesce in the scheme. The dialogue between the honest citizen, who in obedience to the decree brings out all his goods into the street for the common fund, and the dishonest neighbour, who keeps back what he has, and waits to see how things will turn out, is the best in the play, and is an epitome of the conduct of Athens from that day onward, when patriotism was required of her. The scenes which follow are apparently written for obscenity's sake, and are too absurd to be a genuine satire upon Athenian women. These features, and the concluding appeal of the coryphæus (vv. 1155, sq.), to remember the jokes, and not to deny the author his prize because his play came first in the competition, indicate how much both poet and audience had fallen. The chorus assumes a leading part in the play, but sings no parabasis, unless indeed a choral ode which is lost may have replaced it. But the whole complexion of the piece resembles what is called the Middle Comedy, in which the chorus disappears.

The play is difficult, and has not been sufficiently commented upon, doubtless on account of the features which it has in common with the far superior and more earnest *Lysistrata*. The commentators on Plato's *Republic* have much occupied themselves with the question, what system or theory of socialism the poet had before him, as Plato's immortal dialogue was not published till many years later. We can find no more specific answer than to say that such a work had probably many predecessors, and that such speculations must have been long in the air before they assumed the definite form in which Plato has transmitted them to us. For the history of Socialism and of the theory of woman's rights the play is an early and valuable document.

§ 273. Last in our list comes the *Plutus*, which, as we have it, was produced Ol. 97, 4 or 388 B.C., in the poet's old age. But we are informed that this was the second edition, and that it was first played in 408 B.C., before the *Frogs*. To this latter play it is remarkably inferior in every respect, but chiefly perhaps because it is of the tamer type known as that of the Middle Comedy. The characters are all general, and there is no chorus beyond a collection of neighbours, who do not interfere in the action, and sing no lyrical odes, or parabasis. The prominence of the slave is another feature which allies it to both Middle and New Comedy. Politics disappear altogether, and the whole object of the work is a dramatic satire upon the irregularities and injustices of society, and upon the apparently false distribution of wealth by the gods. The worthy Chremylus, having by the help of the oracle discovered Plutus, whom as an old blind man he does not recognise, but who at length reveals himself, undertakes to have the god's sight restored, and so to enable him to choose his residence amongst honest men. Poverty, a gaunt female figure, protests against this proceeding, and explains the advantages which she bestows on men. There are several indications of a chorus at the conclusion of each act, or pause in the plot, but these were either never written, or omitted (as I suspect) in the revised edition which we possess, or lost by the carelessness of transcribers. This last theory seems very improbable. The slave in a long messenger's speech, only interrupted by exclamations from Chremylus' wife, recounts the cure of Plutus in the temple of Æsculapius—a very interesting comic picture of the religious quackery of the age. The rest of the play is occupied with the appearance of a sycophant priest and other characters who come to visit Chremylus on hearing of his good fortune. The general structure of the play seems imitated from the earlier *Peace*. The god of riches corresponds to the goddess of peace. The opposing figures of War and Poverty are closely analogous.

The good Hermes in both plays acts the mean part of a sort of understrapper, and not a faithful one, among the gods.   Both plays end their plot early, and fill up the remainder with dialogues arising out of the successful conclusion of the enterprise. But the *Peace* is far livelier and more spirited than the *Plutus.* The tame and sober character, and the absence of special political allusions in this work, have made it an easy and suitable play for younger students, and there have accordingly been a good many scholia upon it, and a good many editions in Byzantine days ; but there is no recent German edition except Marback's (Leipzig, 1844), and now Velsen's (critical, 1881).

§ 274. The *Fragments* of Aristophanes (about 750) are neither long nor interesting.   Were our knowledge of the poet confined to them, we should be perfectly incapable of forming any notion of his true character and transcendent merits, and this fact should make critics more cautious than they have been in estimating other comic poets, only known by the light of this delusive evidence and thus compared with the extant master.   The *Amphiaraus* seems to have ridiculed superstitious treatment of diseases, like the scene of the *Plutus* just mentioned, and may therefore have been of that type.   So was the *Æolosikon,* a parody on Euripides' Æolus, a play which was written without chorus, later than the *Plutus,* and committed to the care of the poet's son Araros.   The *Kokalos,* also committed to Araros, was even considered a forerunner, in its love intrigue and recognition, of the New Comedy of Menander ; so that this type too was probably inherent in Greek comedy, and only rose to greater prominence owing to social causes.   All that can be known about the plots of the lost plays, and many conjectures besides, may be found in the collection of the fragments at the end of Meineke's second volume.   There is an equally good collection in Dindorf's *Poetæ Scenici,* and many monographs about them are cited by Nicolai.[1]

§ 275. If we take a general view of the dramatic resources shown by this great poet, we shall be somewhat surprised at the poorness of his plots and the fixed lines of his invention. As is well known, old Attic comedy cared little about plots ;

[1] *LG.* i. p. 231.

any extravagant adventure was sufficient to give it scope for the development of character, and for comic dialogue which sparkled by means of witty repartee and satirical allusion. Like the plays of Euripides, which pause in the middle, and then start with a new interest, it is common for the Aristophanic plays to work out at once the project of the principal actor, and then occupy the rest of the play in comic situations produced by the introduction of any stray visitor. Examples of this design will be found in the *Acharnians, Peace, Plutus, Wasps*, and *Birds*. The *Frogs* is a more artistic instance, as the poetical conflict which ensues upon Dionysus' visit to Hades is strictly to the point. But here too the adventures of Dionysus in search of a tragic poet are a separate play (so to speak) from the scenes in Hades after his reception by Pluto. The *Knights* and *Clouds* have more plot than the rest, though the action in the *Knights* is too much delayed by the coarse Billingsgate of the rival demagogues.

A good deal of sameness may further be observed in this, that the economy of the opening scenes preserves a certain uniformity. Either the principal character begins with a soliloquy, which explains the whole plot, as in the *Acharnians* and *Clouds*, or the first scene is a dialogue, in which one of the speakers presently turns to the audience, and explains the situation by what may be called a delayed prologue. These speakers are either two slaves under orders (*Wasps, Knights, Peace*), or the leading character with his slave or confidant (*Frogs, Plutus, Birds, Thesmophoriazusæ*). The *Lysistrata* and *Ecclesiazusæ* open with a combination of both devices. The leading character comes on, but in expectation of others, as in the *Acharnians*, and the plot is presently expounded in a conversation with the new characters. These considerations show that, with all the wildness and license of the poet's imagination, he kept not only his diction, which was a model of the strictest Attic, but even his plots, under close regulations.[1]

Turning to his characters, we find the same regularity in their conception. They are almost all elderly, both men and

---

[1] Westphal (*Proleg. zu Æschyl.* pp. 30, sq,) has shown that Aristophanes' *form* of play resembled Æschylus, and not later tragedy.

women, and even when father and son are brought on the stage together, as in the *Wasps*, the son impresses us as already mature in age and good sense. This arises from the aristocratic temper of the poet, who only satirised and ridiculed the middle and lower classes, among whom the young are seldom prominent, especially in war times, when they were employed in field and garrison duty. The Athenian democracy is always imaged by the poet under the guise of an elderly man, and all the leading characters which are intended to be representative are very uniform in type—shrewd, somewhat coarse, and not very educated. This is likely to have been specially true of the Attic countryman, whom he contrasts sharply with the city folk. Pheidippides in the *Clouds* is the only portrait he ventures to draw of a young aristocrat, and he is very slightly sketched, until he appears transformed into a Socratic sophist. The chorus of *Knights* is purely political and impersonal, and reveals to us no social or individual features. Were we therefore reduced for our knowledge of the Athenian aristocracy to the comedies of Aristophanes, we must be content with a single passage in the opening of the *Clouds*, and we should be completely ignorant of any of their failings but that of an overfondness for horses. Yet surely the young aristocrats were fully as open to satire and comic travesty on the stage as the old dicasts.

These remarks show the error of the assertion usual in Aristophanes' German critics, that he lashed *all* the vices and defects of Athenian society in his day. They ignore that the poet was an aristocrat, who ridiculed radicalism and the advanced democracy, but spared the vices of his associates and his party. What a subject Alcibiades would have afforded ! Yet in spite of his democratic leanings, his high birth and connections saved him from any but stray shafts on the stage.[1] It is in the orators that we find him painted in his dark

---

[1] According to various late authorities, of whom a scholiast on Juvenal is the best, the Βάπται of Eupolis were expressly directed against Alcibiades. But it must have been indirectly, and without naming him personally, for the twenty-two extant fragments do not contain a single mention or even allusion to Alcibiades.

colours. I have already noticed the constant retrospects, and longing for the good old times, which characterised all the comic poets of this period. I will only add that in his late plays Aristophanes seems to have laid aside these aspirations as hopeless, and applied himself to the practical teaching of union and forgiveness among the rival parties in the agony of the last years of the war.

As to his position in matters of religion, he is a great defender of orthodoxy against the new physical school, and is never weary of attacking Socrates and Euripides for their breaking up of the old faith. But all this seems rather from policy than from real devoutness, for he does not hesitate to travesty the gods after the manner of Epicharmus, and to present the religion of the people under a ridiculous form. Though he permits himself to indulge in orthodox profanity and ridicule about the gods, he feels a profound difference in the serious attacks of the sceptical school upon the received faith. In this he was doubtless quite correct, but it throws a doubtful light upon his seriousness as a religious thinker.

§ 276. His parody of the tragedies is to us more interesting. Though commonly aimed at Euripides, there is frequent parodying of both Sophocles and Æschylus, and of the less known tragic poets, probably much oftener than even the scholiasts detected. Of course his ridicule of Euripides was most unsparing, and most unjust, but the latter was no mere innovator in tragedy, he was also an opponent on social and political questions. There is no greater proof of the real greatness of Euripides, than that his popularity combated and overcame the most splendid comic genius set in array against it during the period of its development. The loose and irrelevant choral odes of his later plays are doubtless open to the parody of the *Frogs*, but the very same change of taste as to the importance of the choral interludes made Aristophanes himself diminish and abandon his choruses, and even replace them with a musical or orchestic performance. For this seems the meaning of the word χορού inserted in the pauses of the later plays, especially the *Plutus*. Hence in this, as in most other points, the same tendencies which modified Euripides' tragedies had their effect upon the plays of his censor. Among the features of detail, nothing is more cleverly ridiculed than those repetitions of the same word which occur in the pathetic lyrical passages of Euripides. Yet this has been felt by great hearts of various ages, and by the still greater heart of popular song, to be a natural and poetical enhancement to the expression of deep feeling. The modern poet who best understands Euripides has followed his example in this point.[1] The German lyrist von Platen, in his beautiful and artistic imitations of folk-song, has reproduced the same effect—an effect still more clearly and universally exemplified in music, where the repetition of even a single note often conveys intense feeling.

§ 277. Turning from points of detail to the general scope of Aristophanes' plays, we come upon a controversy as to the true aim of comedy, and as to the conception which the poet formed of his art. The passage on the nature of comedy in the *Poetic* of Aristotle is unfortunately lost, but if we can trust stray hints on the subject, his definition of comedy (which applied mainly to Menander) ran parallel to that of tragedy, and described the art as a purification of certain affections of our nature, not by terror and pity, but by laughter and ridicule. This deep moral object has been strongly advocated by Klein, who exalts Aristophanes to a pinnacle attained by no other Greek poet. On the other hand, Hegel, who without any special knowledge has theorised on the matter in his *Æsthetic*, speaks of comedy as the outlet of a great uncontrolled subjectivity, which feels that it is so superior to all ordinary human affairs, that it can afford to laugh them down and treat them

> Dances, dances, and banqueting
> To Thebes, the sacred city through,
> Are a care ! for, change and change
> Of tears and laughter, old to new,
> Our lays, glad birth, they bring, they bring !

—*Aristoph. Apol.*, p. 266. There are many more instances in this version of the *Hercules Furens*. This allusion to Mr. Browning suggests the remark that he has treated the controversy between Euripides and Aristophanes with more learning and ability than all other critics, in his *Aristophanes' Apology*, which is, by the way, an *Euripides' Apology* also, if such be required in the present day.

with ridicule. Probably both theories have their truth as regards Aristophanes. His early plays seem written with high political aspirations, and with a strong conviction that he was the adviser of the people for good, and could lead them from sophistry and chicanery to a sounder and nobler condition. This feeling transpires in his personal addresses to the audience, in his professed contempt for obscenity and buffoonery, and in the serious tone of his political advices. As the war went on, and the people became gradually impoverished and degraded, when the oligarchs broke down in their attempt to abolish the democracy, and the power of Athens was ruined by Lysander, we see the poet, not without stray touches of sadness, adopt a lower tone, abandon serious subjects, and turn almost wholly to obscenity, buffoonery, and mere literary and social satire. At this stage he may have been indulging his 'infinite subjec- tivity,' as Hegel chooses to call it, and may have felt that serious advice, and efforts at political and social reform, were mere idle dreams, and not worth treating except as stuff for travesty. This is indeed a melancholy contrast to the life of the extant tragic poets, all of whom seem to have risen and ripened with age, and to have left us in their latest pieces the noblest and most perfect monuments of their genius.

§ 278. A word in conclusion should be said concerning the lyric side of Aristophanes, which the old scholiasts so neglected, that they note his graceful ode to the nightingale (in the *Birds*) as a parody on Euripides. Modern writers, on the contrary, have advanced to the absurd statement, that his real greatness was not dramatic, but lyric. There can, indeed, be no doubt that the lyrical pieces in the comedies are of the highest merit ; nevertheless, it would be as absurd to say that the real genius of Sophocles was lyric because he wrote beautiful lyric odes. Lyric poetry and the drama were so combined in Periclean days, that although a lyric poet might be no dramatist, every dramatist must be a lyric poet. And we have reason to think that the occasional lyric pieces of the great dramatists in that day were far finer than the works of professed lyric poets after the age of Simonides. Nevertheless, the true greatness of Aristophanes ever has been, and will be, dramatic greatness.

But it is rather in extraordinary fertility and brilliancy of dialogue, than in ingenuity of plot, that he excels.

We cannot tell whether the statement of Plato at the end of the *Symposium* was seriously meant, that the composer of comedy must have the same sort of genius as the composer of tragedy, and that the same poet should compose both. If it was, we can hardly avoid the inference that it was meant to apply to Aristophanes, who plays a leading part in the dialogue, and whom Plato evidently esteemed at his real worth. The combination of which he speaks was not attempted in classical days, though there are not wanting signs that Aristophanes could have composed with pathos and seriousness, and might perhaps have been more dangerous to Euripides as a rival than as a professed opponent.

§ 279. The later Greeks, who became accustomed to the strict form and the social polish of the New Comedy, could not bear the wildness and license of the great political comedian. Aristotle completely ignores him, and the Old Comedy generally, in his dramatic theories, and evidently regards him as nothing compared with his successors in later days and in the tamer style. Plutarch, in a special comparison of Old and New Comedy, is both severe and depreciating in his remarks upon him.[1] These tamer and more orderly people look upon the wayward exuberance of the Old Comedy with much the same temper as the French school of tragedy look upon the license and irregularity of Shakspeare. Fortunately, the Alexandrian critics did not share these prejudices, and seem to have directed more attention to this poet than to any other except Homer.[2] Callimachus collected the literary and chronological notices ; Eratosthenes, Aristophanes, Aristarchus and Crates

---

[1] His little tract on Aristophanes and Menander is still worth reading, in order to show how completely formal excellence and polish of style outweighed the greater merits of old comic poetry in the opinion of his age. Aristophanes is blamed for violations of the later rhetorical artifices, for excessive assonances, and for such matters as he would have scorned to observe, in his writing ; moreover, for allowing inconsistency in characters, which were with him only a vehicle for political satire.

[2] The following information on the Alexandrian studies is compressed from the fuller account of Bernhardy, *LG.* ii. 670.

followed (with others) in explaining and commenting upon hard passages. There seem to have been collections of these commentaries, first by Didymus, and finally by Symmachus, who added Heliodorus' theatrical studies. These form the older basis of the *Scholia*, enlarged and diluted by later Byzantine work, but, on the whole, the best Greek commentary we have on any Greek author, and of inestimable value in understanding the difficult allusions of the text. The text of these scholia was first printed (with nine plays) by Aldus in 1498. There are excellent monographs of J. Schneider, Ritschl and Keil upon them, and they have been lately critically edited by Dindorf, and by Dübner (Paris, 1868).

§ 280. *Bibliographical.* Far the best MS. of both text and scholia is the *Ravennas* of the eleventh century, a large vellum quarto of 192 pages, of which the margin is here and there badly stained with damp, so that the scholia are often almost illegible. This is one of the best and most trustworthy of our Greek MSS. It contains the extant plays, not in their chronological order, but according to their popularity, the first three being much more read and commented than the rest, viz. *Plutus, Clouds, Frogs, Birds, Knights, Peace, Lysistrata, Acharnians, Wasps, Thesmophoriazusæ, Ecclesiazusæ.*

Owing to the difficulty of reaching Ravenna formerly, few scholars have seen or collated this MS., which is preserved in the public library, and now readily shown to visitors.[1] There is a later MS. at Milan in the Ambrosian Library which seems to correspond with it very closely, but which is not mentioned by the principal critics.[2] There is besides the *Venetus* 471, the Θ of the Laurentian at Florence, and a Parisinus A, which are valued by the editors. Of the three popular plays there are endless later copies.

As to editions there is the *princeps* of nine plays by Aldus (1498), a handsome folio, followed by the Juntine in 1515, which added the two missing plays (*Thesmophoriazusæ* and *Lysistrata*) as an appendix in 1516. Bentley, Dobree, Dawes, and

---

[1] There is an interesting article on its history by W. G. Clark, in the third volume of the Cambridge *Journal of Philology*.

[2] This was shown to me by M. Ceriani, the learned librarian at Milan.

Porson, all worked at this poet, and wrote critical notes upon
the text, and in this direction Cobet (in the Leiden *Mnemosyne*)
has contributed more than anyone else to the purifying of this
purest of Attic writers. The best complete editions in modern
days are Bekker's, Dübner's (Didot), Bergk's (Teubner),
Dindorf's (*Poetæ Scenici*), and Meineke's. Holden has also published a critical text (Cambridge, 1868), with the fragments and
an index to them, but unfortunately expurgated and therefore
not useful for scholars. In addition to the Greek scholia there
is a general commentary of moderate merit by Bothe, an index
by Caravella, edited at Oxford (1822), and a poor Lexicon by
Sanxay (Oxford, 1811). The principal plays must be studied
in the separate editions I have noticed under each, and the
complete editions are chiefly valuable for embracing the pieces·
which have not tempted special editors. There are German
translations by Voss, Droysen, Donner, and others ; French by
Brumoy and by Poinsinet de Sivry (*Acharnians* and *Knights*) ;
and English, a good modern prose version, by Mitchell, in
addition to the splendid version of five plays by J. H. Frere,[1]
and the *Wasps, Peace*, and *Lysistrata* of J. B. Rogers. There
are good school editions of some of the plays in the Cambridge
Catena Classicorum. Julius Richter has even composed a Greek
comedy in our own day on the model of Aristophanes, in which
he handles contemporary questions. This learned and clever
piece is curious and worthy of perusal.

[1] Frere's version, like Mitchell's *Sophocles*, was at first privately published and inaccessible ; it is now to be found in his collected works. The
proper preface to it is his critique of Mitchell (*Works*, ii. p. 178, sq.).

CHAPTER XXII.

THE HISTORY OF COMEDY FROM ARISTOPHANES TO MENANDER.

§ 281. THERE is no branch of Greek literature which seems to have been more prolific than comedy; and yet, of the many hundreds of pieces cited, there is not a single complete specimen surviving. We saw above how Aristophanes, towards the close of his life, produced works of a complexion approaching what is called by the grammarians the *Middle* and *New Comedy*. They have laid it down that the former sort of comedy was produced from about the period of the Restoration to that of the battle of Chæronea (390–38 B.C.). The period following is called that of the *New Comedy*.

These grammarians, and the modern historians who follow them, have sought to enumerate special points in which each period of comedy was distinguished from the rest. But, as I have already remarked (p. 433), they have drawn their lines of distinction too sharply. They assert that the Middle Comedy was rather a character-comedy than a personal and political critique on passing events. Hence there appear in the very titles the names of courtesans, of parasites, of philosophers, and of literary men—the latter generally of past generations. We find that parody of old mythology was frequent, and there are many plays devoted to the *birth of gods*, such as Διὸς γοναί, which ridiculed mimetic dithyrambs, and other scenic representations of these events. In this parody of mythology, and this ridicule of general types of character, we know that Epicharmus in Sicily, and Crates, Hermippus, and Cratinus in the Old Comedy, had shown the way; and we have from Hermippus the title of a play ('Αθηνᾶς γοναί), which, from his known antagonism to Pericles and his friends, I take to have been somehow connected with Pheidias' famous pediment on the Parthenon, representing the birth of the goddess. So also in the constant ridicule of Plato and his school we find Alexis and his fellows only following in the track of Aristophanes' attack upon Socrates.

Nevertheless, it is their general tendency to draw general pictures of life, and to abstain from the subjects of the moment, which makes Aristotle include them under comedy, which is general; while he appears to have classed the more violent and personal Old Comedy under the head of personal satire ($\iota\alpha\mu\beta o$-$\pi o\iota\iota a$). The days for political satire had indeed passed away. We hear of no attempts after the Restoration to bridle the license of personal libels on the stage, until the days when adulation of great men replaced nobler feelings. But the desire of economy made both the state and individuals unwilling to submit to the expense of a chorus, and the poets indicated the close of their acts by the mere word *Chorus* and a gap, which was afterwards filled up by a musical *intermezzo*.

Another leading feature in Middle Comedy was said to be the fancy for discussing riddles ($\gamma\rho\tilde{\iota}\phi o\iota$) on the stage, and many such appear in the fragments. But, as Meineke notes, here too Cratinus had showed the way in his *Cleobulinæ*. I do not suppose that any of their frequent literary criticisms on poets—Athenæus quotes a special work on the subject—equalled in force and pungency Aristophanes' *Frogs*. But instead of ridiculing sophists and rhetoricians, we find that Platonists and Pythagoreans, the luxurious and the mendicant philosophies, were their constant topics. There is, however, clear evidence in the fragments that only the outside of these philosophies, the dress and manners of the school, were criticised. There was no attempt at any metaphysical argument, or any serious discussion of moral tendencies. The same shallow ethics, or want of ethics, is shown in their far severer and more earnest satirising of courtesans. They never attack the real vices of society, but warn against the folly of carrying them on imprudently.

§ 282. Thus I have shown that in every leading feature

ascribed to the Middle Comedy, we have parallels in the older masters. What had they then peculiar to themselves? Nothing I fancy in *subjects* except the neglect of present politics, the decay of moral earnestness, and the increased prominence of a particular kind of street and market scenes—I mean those relating to feasts and good cheer. There was also an increased prominence of courtesan life. In fact, Antiphanes, the greatest master of this comedy, is said to have told Alexander the Great, who took no interest in such things, that he must have been used to drinking with these people, and brawling about them, to appreciate comedy. Verily a noble education!

If in subject there were only these negative or ignoble peculiarities, there was an equal decay both in the power of their diction, and the variety and richness of their metres.[1] Of course this decay was gradual. The chorus with its expensive training went out of fashion, and was gradually disused. The aspiration of the poets was not to guide and ennoble their public. Hence they studied clearness and simplicity without any rigid adherence to purity of dialect or poetic choice of words. Moreover, the enormous number of dramas they produced must have made careful composition impossible. Athenæus asserts that he had read and copied from more than eight hundred plays of the Middle Comedy, but though we hear of fifty-seven poets, many of them only left a couple of plays. On the contrary, the pieces of the acknowledged masters, Antiphanes and Alexis, were counted by hundreds. No doubt they were not all intended for stage representation, but were a sort of substitute for our modern novels and magazine articles, circulated among the reading public of Athens. It is, however, possible that the great increase of theatres throughout Greece may have created a large demand for new pieces.

§ 283. It would lead us far beyond our limits to attempt

---

[1] It is observed that the shortening of vowels before $\beta\lambda$ and $\gamma\lambda$, which is never allowed in Aristophanes, occurs in the Middle Comedy ; so also the shortening of the accusative of nouns in $\epsilon\upsilon\varsigma$. As to metres, they often used dactylic hexameters ; once in Antiphanes an elegiac distich occurs (Meineke, iii. 82, frag. of the *Milanion*). Glyconics were rare, but we often find combinations of dactyls and trochees, at least one specimen of Eupolidean verse, and one lyric system (cf. Meineke, i. 300-2).

any enumeration of these poets (thirty-nine of whom are still
known by name), nor have their remains much literary interest.   In no case are the fragments sufficient to reconstruct
the plots of their plays; and, most unfortunately, the great
majority of the extant quotations are those made by Athenæus, with special reference to marketing, cooking, and the
pleasures of the table.   This gives a tedious uniformity to the
laborious volume in which Meineke has collected their remains,[1] an uniformity not agreeably relieved by notes of im-
pure diction from the *Antiatticista.*   Here and there comes a
moral reflection from the collection of Stobæus, and it is only
such passages which show us the neatness of point and smartness of expression which made them so popular in their day.
In this respect they regarded Euripides as their great model.
His secret, which Aristotle notices, of saying things elegantly
in common words, was the perpetual riddle which all the comic
poets, down to Menander, tried to solve.   But this last and
greatest of the *Epigoni* in Comedy was the only successful
stylist.

A few words on some of the most celebrated of these poets
will suffice for such readers as do not wish to make their fragments a special study.[2]

§ 284. First and probably greatest among them was *Antiphanes,* who is commonly regarded as the head of the Middle
Comedy.   Of course the boundary line, as I have already
explained, is very vague, and a glance into Meineke's account
of the later poets of the Old Comedy, such as Plato, will show
how difficult it is to sever the Middle from the Old.   In fact,
we are obliged generally to acquiesce in the decision of Suidas
on the subject.   Antiphanes was probably the son of Stephanus,
and, according to the sensible *Anon. scholiast on Comedy,* born
at Athens, though Suidas records various other opinions.   He
lived from Ol. 93 to Ol. 112, and died at the age of seventy-four

---

[1] *FCG.* vol. iii. ; the general history in vol. i. pp. 271–435.

[2] To such Meineke's work affords all the materials ; the social side
of their plays has been illustrated in my *Social Greece,* in G. Guizot's
Ménandre et la Comédie grecque, and in Klein's *History of the Drama,* ii.
206, sq., from which I have taken many suggestions.

in Chios. His son Stephanus brought out some of his plays. He began to write at the age of twenty, and is credited with the enormous number of 260 comedies, of which about 230 titles are still known. Though Meineke[1] has collected a good many examples of debased diction in his fragments, he was celebrated as a clear and elegant writer. Among various criticisms on tragic language, we have a good fragment from his *Poetry* on the contrasts of tragedy and comedy, which I quote below.[2] The *Proverbs* (Παροιμίαι) were cited by the Isocratic opponents of Aristotle as the comic counterpart of his collection of proverbs. It may even have been a satire on the philosopher. The titles of Antiphanes' plays are very various, including many mythological names, many historical personages and courtesans, as well as names of trades or professions, and of provinces and cities. But probably owing to the ostentation of Athenæus, who desired to quote as many various plays as possible, we seldom have more than one fragment, and never

---

[1] iii. 309.
[2] Meineke, iii. 105 :

  . . . . Μακάριόν ἐστιν ἡ τραγῳδία
ποίημα κατὰ πάντ', εἴ γε πρῶτον οἱ λόγοι
ὑπὸ τῶν θεατῶν εἰσιν ἐγνωρισμένοι,
πρὶν καί τιν' εἰπεῖν, ὥσθ' ὑπομνῆσαι μόνον
δεῖ τὸν ποιητήν. Οἰδίπουν γὰρ ἂν γε φῶ,
καὶ τἄλλα πάντ' ἴσασιν · ὁ πατὴρ Λάϊος,
μήτηρ Ἰοκάστη, θυγατέρες, παῖδες τίνες,
τί πείσεθ' οὗτος, τί πεποίηκεν; ἂν πάλιν
εἴπῃ τις Ἀλκμαίωνα, καὶ τὰ παιδία
πάντ' εὐθὺς εἴρηχ', ὅτι μανεὶς ἀπέκτονεν
τὴν μητέρ', ἀγανακτῶν δ' Ἄδραστος εὐθέως
ἥξει, πάλιν τ' ἄπεισι . . . .
ἔπειθ', ὅταν μηδέν (γε) δύνωντ' εἰπεῖν ἔτι,
κομιδῇ δ' ἀπειρήκωσιν ἐν τοῖς δράμασιν,
αἴρουσιν, ὥσπερ δάκτυλον, τὴν μηχανήν,
καὶ τοῖς θεωμένοισιν ἀποχρώντως ἔχει.
Ἡμῖν δὲ ταῦτ' οὐκ ἔστιν, ἀλλ' ἅπαντα δεῖ
εὑρεῖν, ὀνόματα καινά, τὰ διῳκημένα
πρότερον, τὰ νῦν παρόντα, τὴν καταστροφήν,
τὴν εἰσβολήν · ἂν ἕν τι τούτων παραλίπῃ,
Χρέμης τις, ἢ Φείδων τις, ἐκσυρίττεται ·
Πηλεῖ δὲ ταῦτ' ἔξεστι καὶ Τεύκρῳ ποιεῖν.

more than three, from any single piece, among the 900 lines which remain. Thus all possibility of judging his dramatic power is precluded.

§ 285. Three sons of Aristophanes are mentioned, *Araros*, *Philippus*, and *Nicostratos*, the first of whom contended in Ol. 101 with a play of his own, having already brought out his father's *Kokalos* and *Æolosikon* in earlier years (circ. Ol. 98). About the parentage of the others, scholars seem doubtful; the fragments of Nicostratos, which are confused strangely with those attributed to Philetærus, are the best. Passing by *Ephippus* and *Epigenes*, we come to *Eubulos*, the author of 104 pieces, and regarded as occupying a transition place between the Old and Middle Comedy, about the earlier half of the fourth century B.C. His subjects were chiefly satires of mythic fables and of tragic poets. His diction is very pure, and his verses seem to have been often plagiarised by other comic poets.

Anaxandrides of Camirus produced plays from Ol. 101, onward (Suidas' favourite epoch for these poets). He was reputed a man of rich and splendid life, as well as of a contemptuous and haughty temper, who destroyed his works when they were not successful. He was the author of sixty-five pieces. Aristotle frequently quotes him, and he is said to have first introduced the παρθένων φθοραί, so common in New Comedy. This invention is, however, also ascribed to Aristophanes. Anaxandrides is also said to have composed dithyrambs.

§ 286. *Alexis* was born at Thurii just before its destruction by the Lucanians, circ. B.C. 390, and came probably with his parents to Athens, where he was made a citizen. He was said to have lived 106 years, and to have been productive up to his death. In a fragment he mentions the marriage of Ptolemy Philadelphus (288 B.C.), and thus confirms this tradition. Though writing in the style of the Middle Comedy, he lived far into the period of the new, and is said to have been the uncle and master of Menander. We have no clearer picture of his mind and work than we have of Antiphanes, though fragments amounting to 1,000 lines of his 245 plays remain. He is called by some the inventor of the stage *parasite*, owing to the importance of this character in his plays; but the picture of one has been above quoted from a fragment of Epicharmus, and seems to have been again drawn in the Old Comedy of Eupolis. The name may be due to Alexis, for Araros' play, in which it occurred, may be posterior to Alexis' early works. Attacks on the school of Plato are frequent in his fragments,[1] but we have more remarkable passages on the hetæræ.[2]

None of them are so clever as the fragments of *Epicrates* on Plato's school, and his picture of Lais in advancing years.[3] This poet was an Ambrakiot, and lived early in

[1] Meineke, iii. 421.

[2] Cf. frag. of the *Isostasion*, Meineke, iii. 422; also pp. 382, 451, 455, 468.

[3] *Ibid.* p. 365:

Τὰς μὲν ἄλλας ἔστιν αὐλούσας ἰδεῖν
αὐλητρίδας πάσας 'Απόλλωνος νόμον,
  · · · · Διὸς νόμον ·
αὗται δὲ μόνον αὐλοῦσιν 'Ιέρακος νόμον.

  · · · · · ·

Αὕτη δὲ Λαῒς ἀργός ἐστι καὶ πότις,
τὸ καθ' ἡμέραν ὁρῶσα πίνειν κἀσθίειν
μόνον · πεπονθέναι δὲ ταὐτά μοι δυκεῖ
τοῖς ἀετοῖς · οὗτοι γὰρ ὅταν ὦσιν νέοι,
ἐκ τῶν ὀρῶν πρόβατ' ἐσθίουσι καὶ λαγάς,
μετέωρ' ἀναρπάζοντες ὑπὸ τῆς ἰσχύος ·
ὅταν δὲ γηράσκωσιν ἤδη τότε ...
ἐπὶ τοὺς νεὼς ἵζουσι πεινῶντες κακῶς·
κἄπειτα τοῦτ' εἶναι νομίζεται τέρας.
καὶ Λαῒς ὀρθῶς γοῦν νομίζοιτ' ἂν τέρας ·
αὕτη γὰρ ὁπότ' ἦν μὲν νεοττὸς καὶ νέα,
ὑπὸ τῶν στατήρων ἦν ἀπηγριωμένη,
εἶδες δ' ἂν αὐτῆς Φαρνάβαζον θᾶττον ἄν.
ἐπεὶ δὲ δόλιχον τοῖς ἔτεσιν ἤδη τρέχει,
τὰς ἁρμονίας τε διαχαλᾷ τοῦ σώματος,
ἰδεῖν μὲν αὐτὴν ῥᾷόν ἐστι καὶ πτύσαι ·
ἐξέρχεταί τε πανταχόσ' ἤδη πιομένη,
δέχεται δὲ καὶ στατῆρα καὶ τριώβολον,
προσίεται δὲ καὶ γέροντα καὶ νέον ·
οὕτω δὲ τιθασὸς γέγονεν, ὥστ', ὦ φίλταται,
τἀργύριον ἐκ τῆς χειρὸς ἤδη λαμβάνει.

p. 370:   *A.* Τί Πλάτων
καὶ Σπεύσιππος καὶ Μενέδημος,
πρὸς τίσι νυνὶ διατρίβουσιν;

the period before us.   It were tedious to repeat the same remarks on *Anaxilas*, and *Aristophon*, and *Cratinus* junior, and *Amphis:* all these are but names.   Perhaps *Timocles*, the satirist of Demosthenes, deserves mention, as apparently the purest Attic writer, and the most pungent in style, of all the list. He is the only one of them whose scanty remains excite a strong regret that time has not spared us more of his poetry.

ποία φροντίς, ποῖος δὲ λόγος
διερευνᾶται παρὰ τοῖσιν ;
τάδε μοι πινυτῶς, εἴ τι κατειδὼς
ἥκεις, λέξον, πρὸς γᾶς · · ·
Β. ἀλλ᾽ οἶδα λέγειν περὶ τῶνδε σαφῶς ·
Παναθηναίοις γὰρ ἰδὼν ἀγέλην
μειρακίων
ἐν γυμνασίοις ᾿Ακαδημίας
ἤκουσα λόγων ἀφάτων ἀτόπων ·
περὶ γὰρ φύσεως ἀφοριζόμενοι
διεχώριζον ζῴων τε βίον
δένδρων τε φύσιν λαχάνων τε γένη.
κᾆτ᾽ ἐν τούτοις τὴν κολοκύντην
ἐξήταζον τίνος ἐστὶ γένους.
Α. καὶ τί ποτ᾽ ἄρ᾽ ὡρίσαντο καὶ τίνος γένους
εἶναι τὸ φυτόν ; δήλωσον, εἰ κάτοισθά τι.
Β. πρώτιστα μὲν οὖν πάντες ἀναυδεῖς
τότ᾽ ἐπέστησαν, καὶ κύψαντες
χρόνον οὐκ ὀλίγον διεφρόντιζον.
κᾆτ᾽ ἐξαίφνης ἔτι κυπτόντων
καὶ ζητούντων τῶν μειρακίων
λάχανόν τις ἔφη στρογγύλον εἶναι,
ποίαν δ᾽ ἄλλος, δένδρον δ᾽ ἕτερος.
ταῦτα δ᾽ ἀκούων ἰατρός τις
Σικελᾶς ἀπὸ γᾶς καπέπαρδ᾽ αὐτῶν
ὡς ληρούντων.
Α. ἦ που δεινῶς ὠργίσθησαν
χλευάζεσθαί τ᾽ ἐβόησαν ·
τὸ γὰρ ἐν λέσχαις ταῖσδε τοιαυτί
ποιεῖν ἀπρεπές.
Β. οὐδ᾽ ἐμέλησεν τοῖς μειρακίοις ·
ὁ Πλάτων δὲ παρὼν καὶ μάλα πρᾴως,
οὐδὲν ὀρινθείς, ἐπέταξ᾽ αὐτοῖς
πάλιν . . .
ἀφορίζεσθαι τίνος ἐστὶ γένους ·
οἱ δὲ διῄρουν.

His picture of Autocleides sitting like Orestes at the altar, surrounded by notorious courtesans, because he had despised
their charms, suggests a brilliant and effective parody.[1]

As I said before, the enormous fertility of these poets
compared with the small number of their victories—even Antiphanes and Alexis each won only about fifteen times—makes
it probable that they intended their plays to be read, and fulfilled the office of the critical press in our days. This very
condition would explain the slight permanent effect they produced in Greek literature. Like our newspapers, these plays
were only intended for momentary purposes, and in the next
generation their importance had passed away for all except
historians and antiquaries. This, too, would account for their
want of seriousness. They had retired from the agora of
politics ; they had not yet unclosed the secrets of domestic life,
with which their successors charmed and impressed society.
So they wandered in the streets and markets without certain
aim, and drew from the outside mean and trivial phases of
human character.

§ 287. We pass to the *New Comedy*, to which the grammarians assign the period from the extinction of Greek liberty by
Philip to the rise of the Alexandrian school.[2] Indeed, the
latest poets of this epoch composed their plays at Alexandria,
as, for example, Machon, who is said to have instructed the
grammarian Aristophanes in the history and nature of comedy.[3]
Sixty-four of these writers were known, and many hundred
plays, but we now possess only a volume of fragments,[4] which
give us no better information than that afforded concerning the
Middle Comedy. From the considerable body of Menander's
fragments no vestige of a plot could be recovered, had not
later critics given us some slight sketches, and had not the
Roman comedians honestly told us how they had borrowed
from him both plot and language. But even here the unfortu-

---

[1] Meineke, i. 432.   [2] *Circ.* 340-270 B.C.
[3] This Machon was also the author of a collection of anecdotes in elegant trimeter iambics, called χρεῖαι, and often cited by Athenæus.
[4] Meineke, vol. iv.

nate habit of filling up the incidents of the plot with scenes from a second Greek original has obscured our best source.

As in the case of the Middle Comedy, I shall not attempt an enumeration of the extant titles and fragments—a dry and fruitless task, and one in which the dull uniformity of moral platitudes, commonplace complaints of human troubles, and details of cookery, weary the modern student. But this uniformity is not altogether to be regarded as the vice of the New Comedy, but rather as the consequence of our fragments being either derived from Athenæus, who searched all this literature for the archæology of cooks and cookery, or from Stobæus', and other collections of moral sayings—a most unfortunate and worthless kind of citation, which never reproduced the dramatic or really characteristic points of a play, but selected those generalities which were suitable for random quotation.

§ 288. The general features of the New Comedy as compared with its forerunners, have been carefully described by many critics. The collection of facts will be found in Meineke, who is always instructive, even when his inferences are wrong. He rightly, however, points out the mistake of believing that these poets confined themselves to domestic life in their plots. Athenæus' quotations show that in Diphilus, for example, the cook and parasite—leading features in the Middle Comedy— were still prominent figures. The philosophers of the day, Epicurus, Zeno, and the rest, were still the constant butt of the dramatists. Mythological parody, and ridicule of the tragic poets, were not extinct; and, what is still stranger, and very much overlooked, political attacks on living personages, not excepting Alexander the Great, were freely and boldly made, as can be shown from the extant fragments. Thus all the permanent features of the Old Comedy were inherited through the Middle by the New ; indeed, I am not sure that the political boldness of Philippides, who flourished about Ol. 120, in the days of Lysimachus, can be paralleled anywhere save in the Old Comedy.

§ 289. Yet these things are forgotten on account of the increased importance of a certain kind of play, which had obtained little prominence in older days—the drama of domestic life, in which, as in the modern novel, love affairs were the almost universal subject. The Attic family, as may well be imagined, afforded little scope for variety of incidents, or for that large psychological study which makes the modern novel so important a branch of literature. We are told that Aristophanes, in one of his latest dramas, the *Kokalos,* had anticipated the staple device of his successors—the mishap of a respectable maiden, and her rehabilitation by marriage at the end of the piece. As seduction was well-nigh impossible, owing to the secluded habits of Greek maidens,[1] the poets had recourse to violence done in consequence of intoxication, and thus they made room for the *recognition* which would otherwise have been absurd. But we may well ask whether this sort of violence was at all more probable, and whether the basis of these plots was not only an offensive, but an impossible occurrence in ordinary Attic life. In the complications which follow we have certain general types repeated without much variety, and represented by fixed marks. There were two kinds of old men, the harsh, and the indulgent, father; two kinds of sons, the scapegrace and the sedate; two kinds of women, the injured maiden, who seldom appears, and the designing courtesan. The braggart captain, the time-serving parasite, and the knowing slave, who serves his young master or mistress, and outwits the elders—these make up the remainder of the characters.[2]

This is the sort of play which is known to us as a *New Comedy,* and which has made its impress on the world through the imitation of the Romans. When we hear it repeated that all these poets went back to Euripides as a model, and that he was the real founder of this drama of intrigue, and thus of genteel comedy—such a piece of criticism conveys to me no meaning.

---

[1] The seduction of a married woman is also unheard of in the New Comedy, and this should be insisted on, as some German historians have spoken of *Verfuhrer* as occurring (Nicolai, i. 235). Thus the Attic public would not tolerate what the courtiers of Charles II. enjoyed and modern Frenchmen witness without revulsion.

[2] Apuleius mentions the Roman technical names : *leno perjurus, amator fervidus, servulus callidus, amica illudens, sodalis opitulator, miles prœliator* (gloriosus), *parasitus edax, meretrix procax.*

˙ The *style* of Euripides, in which Aristotle praises the peculiar
secret of saying things clearly and elegantly with the plainest
and commonest words, was certainly the model of the New
Comedy.   Hence Diphilus said that he would willingly hang
himself if he could be certain of meeting Euripides.   For to
poets with little variety of plot, excellence of style was of the
last importance, and made the difference of success or failure.
But, so far as I can see, Euripides was no more a model for
Menander than he was for Antiphanes or Alexis.[1]   In style he
was acknowledged a model not to them only, but to Aristophanes, their master.

§ 290. I will notice a few of the more important names
among the sixty-four poets of this period, reserving Menander
for the last.

Philemon of Soli appeared as a writer about Ol. 112, and
died at a very advanced age, in Ol. 129, 3.   Fragments of
fifty-six from his ninety plays are extant.   He is not easily dis-
tinguishable from his son, the younger Philemon, to whom
fifty-four were attributed.   His Ὑποβολιμαῖος was said to be
directly suggested by, and to have criticised, Aristophanes'
Kokalos.   The majority of Philemon's fragments, being preserved by Stobæus, are elegant, but not profound, reflections
on the 'changes and chances of this mortal life.'   In his
Philosophus he ridiculed the Stoic sect,[2] which was not at
all to the taste of the play-going Attic public.   His plays
were used as models by Plautus.[3]   He was constantly pitted

---

[1] The importance of the prologue in comedy can hardly be ascribed to
his example, seeing that it was the natural resource for expounding the
opening situation, and as such had been used by Æschylus. Moreover, in the
absence of a *parabasis*, the poet could find no other means of communicating directly with his audience, as we see in Terence. The long rhetorical
debates between plaintiff and defendant, which Euripides draws out upon
his stage, were not only strange, but positively distasteful to the later comic
poets.

[2] Cf. Meineke, iv. 29 :

φιλοσοφίαν καινὴν γὰρ οὗτος φιλοσοφεῖ,
πεινῆν διδάσκει καὶ μαθητὰς λαμβάνει.
εἶς ἄρτος, ὄψον ἰσχάς, ἐπιπιεῖν ὕδωρ.

[3] Particularly his Θησαυρός for the *Trinummus,* and his Ἔμπορος for the
Mercator.

against his younger contemporary Menander, and often defeated him, so that there was much jealousy between them, as
sundry anecdotes testify. *Diphilus* of Sinope was a contemporary of Menander, and younger than Philemon. His intimacy
with celebrated courtesans, and his frequent representation
of them on the stage, remind us of Antiphanes and Alexis.
As most of the extant fragments come from Athenæus, they
are full of cookery, and these, together with the occurrence of
some mythological titles, make his fragments appear quite
similar in character to those of the Middle Comedy. Though
the *Antiatticista* complains of sundry late words used by him,
his style is pure and bright. His Κληρούμενοι was the model of
Plautus' *Casina*, as we learn from the prologue. So also the
lost *Commorientes* of Plautus was copied from the like play of
Diphilus, and then by Terence in his *Adelphi*. The *Rudens*
of Plautus was likewise due to a play of Diphilus. Our longest
fragment (forty-one lines) is from the *Painter*, and describes a
cook telling what sort of banquets he prepares for his various
clients.

From *Hipparchus*, *Lynceus*, and *Archedicus* we have similar
notes on cookery.

§ 291. More important was *Apollodorus* of Carystos (there
were other poets of the name), from whom we have a long fragment on the philosophy of pleasure, which Epicurus was then
advocating at Athens.[1] He is remarkable as having afforded
Terence the models of two plays, the *Hecyra* and *Phormio*.[2]
We may perhaps venture to offer a judgment on Apollodorus
from the evidence afforded by these two plays. The *Phormio*
is a very ingeniously constructed comedy with a double intrigue, which seems not due to any *contaminatio* by Terence.
It is full of interesting passages of great merit as stage
scenes, though we perceive no regard whatever towards morals,
and it is only the success or failure of knavery which deter-

---

[1] Cf. the similar long extract from the σύντροφοι of *Damoxenus* (seventy
lines) in Meineke, iv. 530, and another more dramatic scene between an
angry father and a slave in *Baton's* Συνεξαπατῶν, *Ibid.* p. 502.

[2] The Greek title of the latter was 'Επιδικαζομένη, according to Donatus'
correction of Terence's Prologue. Cf. Meineke, i. p. 464.

mines approval or censure. The *Hecyra,* which found great difficulty in obtaining a hearing, is very inferior in power, the *soupirant* being a tearful and colourless youth, and his slave confidant stupid and tiresome. The really curious feature in the play is the honest courtesan, who sets herself to restore peace and harmony in the disturbed family, and reconcile her former lover with his new wife. This Bacchis is the *Dame aux Camélias* of ancient comedy, without the tragic points. She is appealed to by her lover's father to help him. She thinks more of the young man's future than of her own selfish ends. It marks, I think, a real novelty in the New, as compared to the Middle, Comedy, that a harlot should be thus glorified. For all through the Middle Comedy, and generally in the New, they were brought upon the stage with a full display of their moral ugliness.

Of *Philippides'* forty-four plays fifteen titles remain. There is nothing to add to what I have observed concerning him already, except that a *psephism* honouring his patriotism was found in the theatre at Athens in the excavations of 1862. Our principal interest in *Posidippus,* who came immediately after Menander, is the splendid sitting portrait statue of him, now in the Vatican at Rome, which represents him as a careworn, thoughtful philosopher, not without traces of humour between the lines.[1] *Demophilus* is only known by the record of Plautus, who took his *Wild Ass* for a model in his *Asinaria.*

§ 292. I will now close this barren enumeration, merely remarking that, owing to the likeness of subject and treatment, the same titles were as frequently used by different comic poets as we formerly noted common titles used in tragedy. We have *Adelphi, Epidicazomeni,* and *Synephebi,* and *Philadelphi,* and *Anargyri,* and a host of other such names. The same rule

---

[1] There is an interesting protest against the tyranny of the Attic purists in his *frag. incert.* 2 :

Ἑλλὰς μέν ἐστι μία, πόλεις δὲ πλείονες
σὺ μὲν ἀττικίζεις, ἡνίκ' ἂν φωνὴν λέγῃς
αὑτοῦ τίν', οἱ δ' Ἕλληνες ἑλληνίζομεν
τί προσδιατρίβων συλλαβαῖς καὶ γράμμασιν
τὴν εὐτραπελίαν εἰς ἀηδίαν ἄγεις ;

applied to characters in the plays. It is one of the remarkable negligences of the New Comedy, that it did not seek to fix a peculiar and successful picture of character by giving it a fixed name, and so handing it down, as it were, with its trade-mark to posterity. The names of characters, *Simo, Chremes, Pamphilus, Davus, Syrus, Sostrata,* &c. were so indifferently applied, that the Roman imitators changed them without any care. They were like the ordinary names set to the figures in the social comedies which Mr. Du Maurier draws in *Punch.* These little sketches have indeed a great deal in common with the New Comedy. In both it is not the character, but the situation, not the person who speaks, but the thing said, which is the matter of importance. Hence, though the ordinary characters of society constantly reappear, and so produce uniformity of colour, they are not distinct individuals belonging to each class, and therefore not worth being noted by a special and exclusive name.[1]

§ 293. We may fitly close our chapter on Comedy with a notice of MENANDER, the acknowledged master and representative of the period. He was an Athenian by birth, the child of Hegesistrata and of Diopeithes, the general whom Demosthenes defended in his speech *On the Chersonese.* In the very year of this speech, 342 B.C., Menander was born. He was fortunate in obtaining the friendship of Epicurus, and probably of Theophrastus, in whose school psychological studies of character were prosecuted with much care. Critics who accept the extant *Characters* as Theophrastus' work, have compared its appearance in the days of Menander with the like association between the *Caractères* of La Bruyère and the comedies of Molière. The philosophic intercourse of his friends alternated, in Menander's case, with indulgence in all the pleasures of sense. He was exceedingly luxurious and devoted to women, so much so that his connection with Glycera is not less renowned than his intimacy with Epicurus. It is indeed the

---

[1] This is the case even in Menander's famous play of the *Superstitious Man* (Δεισιδαίμων). We happen to know that the leading character was called Pheidias; nevertheless, in none of the references to this play, and to its excellence as a psychological drawing, do we hear of 'the Pheidias of Menander.'

weakest point in Epicurus' system, that during his life, and while he was there to correct it, the lowest and most sensual interpretation was given to his doctrine of *Utility.* He called it Pleasure (ἡδονή), and his contemporaries took him at his word.

Menander brought out his first comedy the year of Demosthenes' and Hypereides' death (322 B.C.), and so a new genius in poetry arose to survive the last great masters in prose. But it was no new kind of poetry ; it was only a perfection of the already fashionable form. Doubtless the friend of Theophrastus studied the tracts of Aristotle on poetry, and we know that Menander's drama was the very kind of play which corresponded to Aristotle's theory. The poet won his first prize in 321 B.C. with the 'Οργή, and from that time brought out in rapid succession 108 plays. He enjoyed the favour, and suffered from the suspicion, of the autocrats who then ruled Athens, but doubtless found means to conciliate those in power, as he was essentially a courtier, and fond of the splendour of high society. He was drowned while bathing in the Peiræus at the age of fifty-two. The Athenians erected him a tomb near the cenotaph of Euripides, the older poet whom he most loved and imitated.

Our information on the plots of Menander is scanty, but sufficient for a general estimate. I am not aware that Plautus ever distinctly mentions him as his model, and perhaps to the older and ruder Roman master the plays of Philemon offered greater facilities for transference to a foreign stage.[1] On the other hand, Terence, living in a more polished circle, was evidently anxious to produce the acknowledged master of style, Menander, in Roman dress, but found the amount of incident so insufficient, that he ordinarily worked up two plots, or scenes from two plays of Menander, in each of his comedies. We know this to be the case even in the *Eunuchus,*[2] and in the *Self-*

---

[1] The *Stichus* and *Bacchides* are, however, said to be derived from the *Philadelphi* and *Double Deceiver* (δὶς ἐξαπατῶν) of Menander.

[2] Cf. the Prologue, v. 30, on his obligations to the κόλαξ. We learn from an old note on Persius, *Sat.* v. 161, sq., where a passage is adapted from Menander's *Eunuchus,* that Terence also changed all the names of the characters.

Tormentor (ἑαυτὸν τιμωρούμενος), which are professedly based
on the like-named plays of Menander. The grammarian Ælius
Donatus, however (in his notes on Terence), and Aulus Gellius[1]
have saved for us sketches (with extracts) of three arguments :
the *Treasure*, the *Apparition*,[2] and the πλόκιον.[3] The last
story was treated by other dramatists, and much resembles that
of the *Hecyra*.

These plots, such as we have them, offer so few distinctive
features, they are so homogeneous with the plots borrowed
from Philemon, Diphilus, and Apollodorus, that we may safely
assert Menander's superiority did not consist in ingenuity of
invention. The secret of his success was in his more elegant
handling of the materials and devices common to other poets.
He must have stood to them in the same sort of relation that
Terence did to other Roman dramatists. A critic tells us that
Philemon worked up his dialogue with such care as to be
superior for reading purposes, and that on the stage only could
Menander be fully appreciated. This remark does not agree
with the fact that Menander was in after days chosen for the
reading lessons of growing boys and girls. But there is so
much of a calm gentlemanly morality about his fragments ;
he is so excellent a teacher of the ordinary world-wisdom—
resignation, good temper, moderation, friendliness—that we can
well understand this popularity. He reflected, if not the best,
at least the most polite and refined life of the age ; and he
reflected it so accurately as to draw from an admirer the
exclamation, ' O life, O Menander, which of you has imitated
the other ? '

We have no means of judging more closely the poet's
economy. We know that he reproduced the prologue of
Euripides so accurately, that he even used the various personages—from protagonists to allegorical figures—to which the

---

[1] *Noct. Att.* ii. 23.

[2] The φάσμα of Menander had been produced at Rome by Luscius
Lavinius, to which Terence alludes in the prologue of his *Eunuchus*. In
a note Donatus gives a brief sketch of the story.

[3] Whether a proper name, or the *necklace* by which the maiden
Pamphila is recognised, remains uncertain.

tragic prologues had been entrusted.   The very numerous fragments which are still incompletely collected, even by Meineke,
are partly from Stobæus and Athenæus, partly from scholiasts
or other Greek authors, partly from the notes of Donatus on
Terence.   Thus the notes on the prologue of the Latin *Andria*
tell us of the openings of that play and the *Perinthia*, from which
Terence patched together his comedy, and in some dozen other
passages Donatus gives the Greek original for a Latin phrase.
The Γεωργός, the Φάσμα, the Θησαυρός, the Μισούμενος, the Πε-
ρικειρομένη, the Μισογύνης are all noted as celebrated plays.   So
was the *Superstitious Man* (δεισιδαίμων), from which Plutarch is
supposed to have borrowed in his tract of the subject.[1]   To
this the *Priestess* afforded the female parallel.   Perhaps the
most brilliant was the *Thais*, in which the manners and character of that personage were painted with thorough experience
as well as genius.   The opening words of the prologue are
preserved.[2]   There is a good specimen of his gentle pessimism
in the *Thesphorumena*.[3]   I quote below a few more fragments.[4]

---

[1] Meineke, iv. p. 100.
[2]   Ἐμοὶ μὲν οὖν ἄειδε τοιαύτην, θεά,
                 θρασεῖαν, ὡραίαν τε καὶ πιθανὴν ἅμα,
                 ἀδικοῦσαν, ἀποκλείουσαν, αἰτοῦσαν πυκνά,
                 οὐδενὸς ἐρῶσαν, προσποιουμένην δ' ἀεί.
[3] Mein. p. 134.
[4] *Ibid.* vol. iv. p. 149 :

                 Ὤιμην ἐγὼ τοὺς πλουσίους, ὦ Φανία,
                 οἷς μὴ τὸ δανείζεσθαι πρόσεστιν,\οὐ στένειν
                 τὰς νύκτας, οὐδὲ στρεφομένους ἄνω κάτω
                 οἴμοι λέγειν, ἡδὺν δὲ καὶ πρᾶόν τινα
                 ὕπνον καθεύδειν· ἀλλὰ τῶν πτωχῶν τινα.
                 νυνὶ δὲ καὶ τοὺς μακαρίους καλουμένους
                 ὑμᾶς ὁρῶ πονοῦντας ἡμῖν ἐμφερῆ.
                 ἆρ' ἐστὶ συγγενές τι λύπη καὶ βίος ;
                 τρυφερῷ βίῳ σύνεστιν, ἐνδόξῳ βίῳ
                 πάρεστιν, ἀπόρῳ συγκαταγηράσκει βίῳ.

Ibid. p. 211 :
                 Τοῦτον εὐτυχέστατον λέγω,
                 ὅστις θεωρήσας ἀλύπως, Παρμένων,
                 τὰ σεμνὰ ταῦτ' ἀπῆλθεν, ὅθεν ἦλθεν, ταχύ,
                 τὸν ἥλιον τὸν κοινόν, ἄστρ', ὕδωρ, νέφη,
                 πῦρ· ταῦτα. κἂν ἑκατὸν ἔτη βιῷς ἀεὶ

Attacks on marriage, assertions of the supremacy of Fortune, advices on good manners—these, expressed with the greatest neatness and clearness, and in the new Attic dialect of the better classes of his day, made Menander the delight of succeeding generations. The purists indeed attacked him for deviations from the strict laws of Attic speech ; but more sympathetic critics extolled his style as far superior even to that of Demosthenes. The contrast to the latter was indeed remarkable, and brings out one leading feature in the diction of the New Comedy—its utter avoidance of rhetoric. To ears wearied with the periods of Isocrates, Demosthenes, and all the herd of their inferior followers, the ease and natural grace of Menander must have been truly fascinating. Even Aristotle's uncouthness must have been a pleasant relief.

§ 294. Accordingly Menander was widely studied. Aristo-phanes of Byzantium commented specially upon him, echoed by Didymus. The rhetor Alciphron, in the second century A.D., composed an elegant correspondence between the poet and his mistress Glycera, in which he utilised the plays. Plutarch drew out a comparison of Aristophanes and Menander, in which he depreciates the wild exuberance of the older poet and extols the elegance, the terseness, and the literary finish of his later rival. Moral gnomes, expressed in single verses, are still extant in collections amounting to 750 lines, many of them no doubt spurious. These, and the first score of the fragments of uncertain plays (in Meineke's collection), are the most characteristic of Menander's philosophy.

We are told that his plays were known in Byzantine days,

ὄψει παρόντα, κἂν ἐνιαυτοὺς σφόδρ' ὀλίγους,
σεμνότερα τούτων ἕτερα δ' οὐκ ὄψει ποτέ.
Πανήγυριν νόμισόν τιν' εἶναι τὸν χρόνον,
ὃν φημι, τοῦτον ἢ 'πιδημίαν, ἐν ᾧ
ὄχλος, ἀγορά, κλέπται, κυβεῖαι, διατριβαί ·
ἂν πρῶτον ἀπίῃς καταλύσεις, βελτίονα
ἐφόδι' ἔχων ἀπῆλθες ἐχθρὸς οὐδενί ·
ὁ προσδιατρίβων δ' ἐκοπίασεν ἀπολέσας,
κακῶς τε γηρῶν ἐνδεής του γίγνεται,
ῥεμβόμενος ἐχθροὺς εὗρ', ἐπεβουλεύθη ποθέν,
οὐκ εὐθανάτως ἀπῆλθεν ἐλθὼν εἰς χρόνον.

and they were certainly used by Eustathius when composing his commentary on Homer (circ. 1160 A.D.). Leone Allacci even speaks of twenty-four comedies being extant at Constantinople in the seventeenth century. And this is not inconsistent with the account of Demetrios Chalkondylas, who says that the MSS. of Menander and Philemon, together with the erotic poems of the old lyric poets, were destroyed by Byzantine emperors at the instigation of zealot monks, who desired to replace them with the effusions of Gregory Nazianzen. A stray copy might easily survive such a persecution. But as yet all search for the plays of Menander in Greek convents has been unavailing.[1]

I confess to greater regret for the splendid old lyrists, Alcæus, Sappho, Mimnermus, than for this later model of exquisite style. His plays would have been excellent for school reading ; they would have inspired endless imitations among the moderns ; they would have shown us what was the best and purest literature which the Attic decadence was able to produce. But no modern critic would have ventured to endorse the judgment of Plutarch, and rank him anywhere on a par with, not to say above, Aristophanes. Both poets were *primi inter pares*, standing out among contemporaries not recognised as inferior till the verdict of posterity was added to the doubtful judgment of their own age. But the men of Aristophanes' day were indeed giants ; those of Menander's only showed

---

[1] A fragment copied years ago by Tischendorf from a very old MS. in the East, has been lately published by Cobet in the *Mnemosyne*, and is discussed in the eleventh volume of *Hermes* by Gomperz, and by Wilamowitz-Mollendorf. It turns out to be an additional scrap of the Δεισιδαίμων, and Wilamowitz endeavours to patch it up with the remaining fragments into a scene. But this combination is doubtful, and we still have no remnant of Menander's *dramatic* art, though we know so much about his style and about his philosophy.

The fragment of Euripides alluded to above (p. 380) has since been published by H. Weil for the *Société pour l'encouragement des études grecques*, and is an interesting speech of forty-four lines, possibly from the *Temenidœ*. There are lesser fragments in Æschylean style on the same papyrus.· Blass also prints (*Rhein. Mus.* xxxv. p. 291) a new fragment of forty-five lines from the *Melanippe* (ἡ δεσμῶτις).

how strong and thorough was the culture which in art and literature outlived the decadence of the nation.

§ 294. With Menander closes the classical age of poetry in Greece. Shortly after his death, the national centre of gravity, as regards learning, shifted to Alexandria, and there the latest poets of the New Comedy brought out their plays. Nor do we hear of any regrets at the transference. The poetry of the Alexandrian age was not without flashes of genius, but on the whole it has not maintained the standard of Attic culture. Whenever a particular poet, such as Apollonius or Theocritus, seemed worthy to be ranked among the mightier dead, I have exceeded my plan, and have spoken of him briefly in connection with the corresponding form of classical poetry. The criticism of Alexandrian grammarians has constantly occupied us in connection with Homer and the other poets whom they emended and expounded. But to write a history of Alexandrian literature is a task of a different kind from that which I have undertaken, and I therefore remand it to some future day, or to some abler hand than mine. The social life of the Greeks under Alexander and the Diadochi yet remains to be written, and for that purpose the voluminous remains of the epoch afford the most interesting materials ; but this too is a huge subject which deters the serious student by its vastness and its intricacy.

But in a companion volume I have traced the history of Greek prose literature within the same classical limits.

APPENDIX A.[1]

ON THE LANGUAGE OF THE GREEK EPIC POETS, AND MORE
ESPECIALLY OF THE ILIAD AND ODYSSEY.

IN determining the age and character of the Iliad and Odyssey,
the most certain and important evidence to which we can
appeal is the language of the poems. Here there can be no
room for the individual taste or fancy of the critic ; the conjectures and probabilities of the 'higher criticism,' as the Germans
call it, have to make way for solid facts. If we know the age
and locality of a particular word or grammatical form, we know
also the limit of time to be assigned to the passage in which it

[1] Mr. D. B. Monro has criticised certain statements and conclusions of
this Appendix, in the *Journal of Philology*, x. 18 (1881). My reply will be
found in the same periodical, x. 19, pp. 110–120 (1881). Since then, in
a very able article in Bezzenberger's *Beiträge*, vii. 2 (1882), August Fick
has pursued the same line of argument as myself, and with the help of the
Æolisms embedded in our present Homeric text, endeavoured to restore
the Æolic original of the first 427 lines of the Iliad. His facts are mainly
derived from Harder's Dissertation, 'De alpha vocali apud Homerum
producta' (1876), and more especially the admirable treatise of Hinrichs,
'De homericæ elocutionis vestigiis Æolicis' (1875), to which I take this
opportunity of recording my own obligations. Fick, writing as a comparative philologist, aptly calls the Homeric dialect 'a marvellous hodge-
podge,' and holds that the digamma had been lost in Ionic before 700 B.C.,
when he supposes the old Æolic poems to have been handed on to the
rhapsodists of Ionia. Much of what other scholars regard as Old Ionic, he
would term Æolic. Like myself, he endorses Merzdorf's summing-up of
an elaborate examination of the Ionic dialect (Curtius' *Studien zur g. und
l. Gramm.* 1876, p. 214), to the effect that the Ionic of Homer and the
Ionic of Herodotos are in the same stage of development.
As I find that what I have said about Middle Ionic has been misunder-

occurs, as well as the geographical horizon of the author. A form like ἄκων,[1] instead of the older ἀϜέκων, could not have come into existence until all recollection of the digamma had disappeared, while the Æolisms, which, as we shall see, occur here and there in Homer, point to an early connection of epic poetry with the Æolic towns of Asia Minor.

stood, it is as well to explain here that the *philological* periods through which a dialect passes are of course not the same as *chronological* periods, all intermediate forms not being necessarily contemporaneous, any more than the use of stone or bronze tools in all parts of the world. In one important point, it will be seen from my reply to Mr. Monro, I have changed my opinion since this Appendix was written, as I now feel convinced that Prof. Paley is right in considering our present Homeric text not older than the age of Periklês. This, however, only supplements, and in no way corrects, the conclusions already arrived at in the Appendix, which is accordingly left unchanged. I also now feel doubtful whether the lengthening of a short vowel before μέγας is due to false analogy; at all events, as I have pointed out in the *Journal of Hellenic Studies*, i. 1, p. 258 (1880), the initial of the word is aspirated in Pamphylian, being written μ H, and may have been so in Cyprian, a dialect of which traces can be detected in Homer. I have only to add that the Appendix offers nothing more than a summary of linguistic criticism on the text of Homer. Most of the facts adduced have already been published by former scholars.

I have to thank Mr. George MacMillan for verifying and correcting the references.

Additional note.—I have suggested another explanation of ἀ(ν)δροτῆτα than that given above, in the *Journal of Hellenic Studies*, i. p. 258 (1880). As ὅπου is found in the New Ionic inscription of Halikarnassos published by Newton (*Essays on Art and Archæology*, pp. 427, &c.), which seems to belong to the age of Herodotus, it is possible that the Homeric ὅπως, &c. should be ascribed to one of the New Ionic dialects. But in this case the form (derived from the old Epic ὅππως) would be a very late one. In the *American Journal of Philology*, Mr. Packard has impugned some of the statements made in the text. His corrections, however, are usually wrong, e.g., ἄν κεν occurs only once in the Iliad, not twice ; ἀριθμός and εὐχή are *not* found in the Iliad ; for the purposes of the argument it does not matter whether φύλακος is a common noun or a fictitious proper name ; I have naturally not said that θύω and τίω do not occur in Homer, as my argument is that old and new are mixed together in the Epic dialect ; 'Attic poets' are not necessarily the tragic poets ; Sappho's dialect is certainly an 'artificial' one.

[1] *Il.* E 366 ; *Od.* γ 484.

Thanks to Comparative Philology and the discovery and accurate study of numerous inscriptions during the last quarter of a century, the history of the Greek language and its dialects is now fairly well known. We can tell with certainty what sounds and grammatical forms are later than others, what are the dialects to which each must be referred, what words must be regarded, not as the creations of a living speech, but as the artificial products of a learned language. Thus a word like ἐπιάλμενος,[1] which preserves a lingering trace of the original sibilant we find in the cognate Latin *salio*, is plainly of older date than the contracted ἐπάλμενος,[2] in which all such trace has vanished. Thus, again, the form ἐννοσίγαιος, which is found twenty-one times in the Iliad and fifteen times in the Odyssey, and in which the initial digamma of its second component element (Greek Ϝωθέω, Sanskrit *vâdh*) has been assimilated to the preceding nasal, belongs to the Æolic dialect; while the form εἰνοσίφυλλος, which is found twice in the Iliad [3] and once in the Odyssey,[4] declares itself to be Ionic by its initial diphthong. And thus, finally, a form like ἐείσατο,[5] from εἶμι, the Latin *ire*, has evidently been coined for merely metrical reasons after the analogy of words like ἔειπον and ἐείσατο (from *vid*, 'to wit'), where the hiatus really represents a lost digamma.

A close examination of the language of Homer shows that it is a mosaic in which words belonging to different ages and three different dialects—Æolic, Ionic, and Attic—are mixed together in such a way as to prove it to be an artificial dialect, never really spoken by the people, but slowly elaborated by successive generations of poets for the needs of epic composition. In its present form it cannot be earlier than the seventh century before the Christian era—the age, in fact, to which Euphorion and Theopompus assigned Homer. Let us review as shortly as we can the evidence on which these assertions are based.

In the first place, then, the staple of the Homeric dialect is

[1] *Il.* H 15 ; *Od.* ω 320.   [2] *Il.* H 260, Λ 421, M 404 ; *Od.* ξ 220.
[3] *Il.* B 632, 757.   [4] *Od.* ι 22.
[5] *Il.* O 415, 544 ; *Od.* χ 89.

Ionic, but Ionic of three different periods, which may be conveniently termed Old Ionic, Middle Ionic, and New Ionic. By
New Ionic is meant the language of Ionia as it existed in the
time of Herodotus, and of the greater part of the Ionic inscriptions we possess ; and it may be considered to date back as far
as the beginning of the sixth century B.C., to which two or three
inscriptions belong. For both Old and Middle Ionic we have
only the Homeric poems themselves, the older grammatical
forms of which can be determined by a comparison with Sanskrit, Latin, and the other allied languages. The New Ionic
genitive singular in -ου, for example, presupposes an older uncontracted genitive in -οο, and this again must be connected with the
Sanskrit -*asya*, which, after the usual Greek change of *y* into a
vowel and loss of the sibilant, would have taken the form of
-οιο. Now in Homer, besides the New Ionic genitive in -ου, we
also find the older form in -οιο, as well as in a few instances the
intermediate form in -οο. Examples of the latter will be seen
in such phrases as Ἰλίοο προπάροιθεν,[1] Ἀιόλοο κλυτά,[2] and ' ὅο
κράτος,[3] where the ignorance of copyists has introduced into
the text the impossible forms Ἰλίου and ὅου, and by reading
Ἀιόλου has ruined the metre of the passage in the tenth book
of the Odyssey.[4] The discovery of these Middle Ionic genitives and the consequent restoration of Homeric grammar and
metre are due to Comparative Philology.

It would be both tedious and useless to multiply instances
of this juxtaposition in Homer of forms which belong to different
stages in the growth of the Ionic dialect. Thus we have the
older genitive plural νυμφάων, where the sibilant, which appears
as *r* in the Latin *nympharum* for *nymphasum*, has been dropped
between the two vowels in accordance with Greek custom, and
by the side of νυμφάων we have also the later νυμφέων with a
shortened vowel, and the still later contracted νυμφῶν.[5] Thus,

---

[1] *Il.* O 66.   [2] *Od.* κ 60.   [3] *Od.* α 70.

[4] See also *Il.* B 518, Γ 340, I 137, 279, Λ 130, 715 ; *Od.* ο 334, π 313,
396, φ 124, 149. Ahrens was the first to discover this form (*Rhein. Mus.* ii.
161).

[5] The old genitive in -άων, like most archaic forms in Homer, always
occupies a fixed place (except in *Il.* Σ 364 and Ω 615, and in the case

too, along with the Old Ionic νηος, where the initial vowel represents the long vowel and digamma of the Sanskrit *nāv-as* and Latin *nāv-is*, we meet the shortened New Ionic νεύς ; and the datives ἥρωι and γήραϊ [1] stand by the side of the abbreviated ἥρῳ and γήρᾳ.[2] When we find the late contracted ἥλιος [3] with the erroneous Attic aspiration, we may feel sure that we are dealing with a passage of much more modern date than the phrases and formulæ which contain the older ἠέλιος (for ἠσέλιος, the Old Latin *Aurelius* or *Auselios*, from the root *ush*, ‘ to burn ’). So, too, the short quantity of the first syllable of θύω, λύω, φύω, and τίω (for θυίω, λυίω, φυίω, and τίγω) reminds us that Homer is in all these cases adopting the usage of the New Ionic dialect, and is thus less primitive than the Attic poets who preserve the original length of the syllable in question.[4] Still more instructive is the varying employment of certain words, sometimes with a double *s*, sometimes with a single one, the choice of the form being frequently determined by metrical reasons alone. Comparative Philology teaches us that in almost every instance the form with double *s* was the original one, the form with single *s* being the result of that phonetic decay which made Old Ionic pass successively into Middle and New Ionic. A large number of stems both of nouns and verbs ended in a sibilant, which was naturally doubled when a suffix which began with another sibilant was attached to them. From the stem μελες, for example, we

---

of the pronoun τάων). This place is either (1) the end of the line, or (2) the thesis of the first or second foot (in the *Il.* only in disyllabic stems, contrary to the use of the Odyssey, see *Od.* α 334, γ 307, ν 126, π 416, σ 210, φ 65), or (3) the fourth foot (in the arsis when preceded by a short syllable, in the thesis when preceded by a long one).

[1] *Il.* Γ 150, E 153, K 79, Σ 434 ; *Od.* β 16, ο 357.

[2] *Il.* H 453 ; *Od.* θ 483, λ 136, ψ 283. Similarly we find ἕρῳ (*Od.* σ 212), γελῳ (*Od.* σ 100), ἵδρῳ (*Il.* P 385, 745).

[3] *Od.* θ 271.

[4] However, we find ἄτιτος in *Il.* Ξ 484, though ἄτιτος occurs in the preceding book (N 414). Similarly we meet with πρίν sometimes with the vowel long (as in *Il.* B 348, E 288, Z 81, H 390, Θ 474), sometimes with the vowel short (as in *Il.* B 344, 354, 413, Γ 132, Δ 114, E 127, 472, Z 125, I 403).

ought to get μέλεσ-σι by adding the suffix of the dative plural, and from the stem τελεσ the verbal forms τελέσ-σω and ἐτέλεσ-σα by adding the suffixes of the sigmatic future and aorist.   In the same way from a stem like ποδ we should have the dative plural πόδ-σι, and then by assimilation πόσσι. The shortened forms could have come only gradually into use in the actual language of the Ionians, and their existence in the epic dialect side by side with the fuller and older forms reveals unmistakeably its real nature.   We may gain some idea of the relative antiquity of the Iliad and Odyssey from the fact that whereas there are fifty-eight aorists with double *s* as against forty-two with single *s* in the first poem, the proportion in the second poem is fifty-four to fifty-three.

The use of the digamma, however, affords the clearest illustration of the mode in which the Homeric dialect was formed.   This letter, which corresponded in sound to our *w*, tended to disappear at an early date in the Ionic dialect, much as *w* tends to disappear in certain English dialects, which say *'ooman* for *woman*, or as it has universally disappeared in the pronunciation of proper names like *Woolwich* and *Harwich.* The other Greek dialects retained it up to a considerably later date, though it was eventually lost in all of them.   The Eleian inscriptions found at Olympia show that the digamma was there in common use, official documents from Bœotia write it in cer-tain words up to the third century B.C., and the Æolic dialect of Cyprus, as revealed to us by the decipherment of the so-called Cypriote syllabary, preserved it in everyday speech at least as late as the fourth century before the Christian era.

We may approximately refer the disappearance ot the digamma in Ionia to the beginning of the seventh century B.C.   No example of it happens to occur in the inscriptions scratched by the Ionic mercenaries of the Egyptian king Psammetichus on the colossi at Abu-Simbel, B.C. 620 (or, as is perhaps more probable, B.C. 590)—inscriptions which show how widely spread a knowledge of writing must have been at the time in Ionia.   A short inscription, however, assigned to about B.C. 500, has been discovered in Naxos, on which we read the word AFYTO (=αὐτοῦ), though unfortunately the genuineness of this inscription is disputed. But no doubt hangs over certain Chalcidian inscriptions of Magna Græcia, which contain examples of the digamma ; and since the Chalcidian colonies were sent out about 700–660 B.C., the digamma could not have been lost in the Ionic dialect until a subsequent period. Accordingly the Old Ionic of Homer in which the digamma is preserved must have been still spoken in Euboea at the beginning of the seventh century B.C.

But besides digammated words we find in Homer a number of undigammated ones. These fall into two classes. The first class consists of words like οὐρανός, ὄχος, ὦνος, which we know from the cognate languages once possessed a digamma, but which show no trace of it in Homer, that is, which have lost the sound in question in the earliest form of Old Ionic with which we are acquainted. The second class contains words which appear in the poems sometimes with, sometimes without, a digamma, the pronunciation bieng frequently determined by metrical reasons alone. Of such words there are at least thirty-five. Examples of them are given in the foot-note.[1]

---

[1] Οἶκος always with digamma except in *Il.* Ω 572 ; *Od.* μ 135, ν 42, ξ 223, 318, ο 21, π 70, 303, σ 419, ω 208 ; οἶνος always with digamma except in *Il.* B 641, E 706, 813, I 224, K 497, Σ 545 ; *Od.* γ 40, 46, 51, ζ 77, λ 61, ο 334, 507, τ 122, υ 260, φ 142 ; οἶδα always with digamma except in *Il.* Σ 185, and *Od.* ρ 573 ; ὄψ always with digamma except in *Il.* Λ 137, Φ 98 ; *Od.* ε 61 ; Ὀδυσσεύς without digamma except in *Il.* Λ 140 ; *Od.* α 21, ν 126, ξ 152, ρ 157, υ 239, φ 197, 204, 244, χ 45, ω, 328; οἴσειν without digamma (*Il.* A 89, B 229, E 257, Θ 400, K 337, N 820, Ξ 308, X 425, Ψ 663, 858; *Od.* γ 429, π 438, τ 24, υ 154, χ 101) except in *Il.* Ψ 441 ; οὖρος without digamma (*Il.* A 479, Ξ 19 ; *Od.* γ 176, δ 360, 585, ε 167, 176, λ 640, μ 167) except in *Od.* δ 520 ; οἴχομαι without digamma except in *Od.* π 142 ; ὅπλον without digamma except in *Od.* β 430, φ 390; οἰωνός without digamma except in *Il.* Z 76. So, again, Ἶρος has digamma in *Od.* σ 73, 75, 333, 334, 393, but wants it in σ 233 ; and ἠχή, which has the digamma in four passages of Hesiod (*Scut.* 279, 348, 438 ; *Opp.* 582), wants it in Homer. Οἰγέτης in *Il.* B 765 preserves the initial digamma of ἔτος (Sanskrit *vatsas*), which is elsewhere lost, as in the compound ἐπετήσιος of *Od.* η 118. Cauer has drawn up the following table of the cases in which the pronoun of the third person, which was the last to retain traces of its consonantal beginning, (1) must be pronounced with digamma, (2) may or may not be so pronounced, (3) cannot be so pronounced :—

K K 2

From these examples it is clear that three conclusions must be drawn : (1) Portions of the Homeric poems consisting of certain phrases and formulæ belong to the Old Ionic dialect in which the sound of the digamma was still heard. (2) Other portions belong to a later stage of the dialect, when the digamma had ceased to be pronounced, and even such traces of it as a hiatus or a lengthened vowel had passed away. (3) A time arrived when the existence of the digamma had so far faded from the memory of the rhapsodists that they came to regard the hiatus representing the lost digamma in certain traditional verses and expressions as due to 'metrical necessity,' and consequently to be admitted or excluded according to the requirements of the verse.

The last conclusion is confirmed by the occurrence of the hiatus in the case of words in which no consonant had ever been lost. Thus, as has already been noticed, we find ἐείσατο from εἶμι, the Latin *ire*, a form which owes its origin to the mistaken analogy of words like ἔειπον (for ἐϝέϝεπον, root ϝεπ). Another instance will be νεοαρδής in Il. Φ 346, where the second part of the compound represents the Sanskrit *ârdras*, 'wet,' unless we adopt the variant reading νεοαλέ'. In fact, the use of the digamma shows that a large part of the Iliad and Odyssey is composed in quite as artificial a language as the epics of Apollonius Rhodius or Quintus Smyrnæus. The digamma is frequently observed in appearance only, a hiatus being allowed by the poets, not because they remembered that it took the place of an original consonant, but because they found what seemed to them a hiatus in the poetical 'tags' and formulæ which had been handed down to them. In this way alone can we explain the disproportionate preponderance of the hiatus in a few words like ὅς, οἷ, and οἶδα—the very words which also show a hiatus in other epic and elegiac poetry—or the fact

	Digamma necessary	Not necessary	Neglected
εἷο, ἕο, εὖ	14 times	7 times	1 time
ἕθεν	7 ,,	11 ,,	—
οἷ	643 ,,	over 180 ,,	23 times
ἕ	64 ,,	15 ,,	1 time
ὅς	45	176	31

pointed out by Hoffmann, that although in the Iliad a short final syllable remains short before οἶ, the latter word never causes the elision of a preceding vowel or the shortening of a preceding long syllable.[1]

If we enquire into the use of the digamma in Hesiod, the Homeric Hymns, the fragments of the Cyclic poets, and in Empedocles, Tyrtæus, and the Elegiac and Iambic writers generally, we shall find some reason for the old Greek tradition which assigned all epic heroic literature, along with the Hymns, the *Margites*, and the *Batrachomyomachia*, to the author of the Iliad and Odyssey. In the earliest of these productions remains of the Old Ionic dialect are embedded much as in the Homeric poems, while in the rest the hiatus that distinguishes originally digammated words is due to the mere repetition or imitation of ancient epic formulæ. Thus in the *Theogony* the proportion of cases in which the digamma is observed to those in which it is not is as 3 or 4 to 1, a larger proportion than that presented by the Odyssey; in the *Works and Days* the proportion is as 3 to 1, as also in the Hymn to Aphrodite; whereas in the Hymn to Demeter the proportion is exactly equal, in the Hymn to Hermes as 1 to 1⅓, and in the cyclic fragments (excluding the *Kypria*) and the *Batrachomyomachia* as 1 to 6. On the other hand, the proportion in Empedocles is as 1 to 3, though how little Empedocles was acquainted with the true origin of the epic hiatus is shown by his incorrect introduction of it in such analogic coinages as ἐέδμεναι (root *ad*) and ἄασπετος. The Elegiac and Iambic poets preserve the digamma, or rather the hiatus which had taken its place, in a good number of the words in which it occurs in Homer, and Theognis has it even in ἴον, 'a violet,' and ἴδιος, where it has been lost in the language of our Iliad and Odyssey (except ε 72, δ 314). In his use of these two words, however, Theognis was probably imitating some portion of the old epic literature.

But the digamma is not the only lost letter of which traces survive here and there in Homer. Another sound which disappeared at a yet earlier time than the digamma was the *yod*

[1] Hoffmann, *Quæstiones Homericæ*, p. 56.

or *y*. The conservative dialect of Cyprus was the only one in Greece which preserved the *yod* into the days of writing ; here it regularly occurs along with the digamma in inscriptions written in the characters of the Cypriote syllabary as late as the fourth century B.C. It is commonly supposed that ὅς, ὧς, and ὅτι primitively began with this letter, and answered to the Sanscrit *yas* and *yâvat;* in this case the *yod* would have to be restored to these words in such phrases as θεὸς ὧς, where the lengthening of the final syllable of the first word implies an initial consonant in the second.[1] The Locrian inscriptions of the fifth century B.C., however, write Ϝότι with digamma and not *yod;* and it is therefore better to connect ὅς and its derivatives with the Latin *qui, quis*, and Sanskrit *chit*, and to regard its lost letter as a digamma. A more certain instance of the presence of the *yod* is ἵεσθαι (from the root *yâ*), which has a consonantal beginning in twenty-two passages.

A tendency to drop a *sigma* seems to have set in at an even earlier period than a tendency to drop the *yod*. Words like ἱδρώς (English *sweat*), which originally began with two consonants (*sw*), must have lost the first at quite a remote date ; indeed, in this particular word and its derivatives even the digamma is only once preserved (in Il. Δ 27). Sometimes, however, the digamma became φ, as has happened in the case of the reflexive pronoun σφε, though even this change did not always preserve the sibilant.[2] When the second consonant was λ, μ, or ν, the initial sibilant was generally retained in Æolic (as σμικρος) and probably also in the Old Ionic of Homer, or else was assimilated to the sound that followed. Thus we have ἄ-λληκτος for ἀ-σληκτος (our *slack*), or φιλο-μμειδής for φιλο-σμειδής from the root *smi*, ' to *smile.*' Wherever such compounds occur in the poems, or wherever the lengthening of a short syllable indicates the preservation of the sibilant at the commencement of the following word, we may be sure that we are in the presence of an old formation. It is quite other-

---

[1] When the final syllable remains short, as in βόες ὣs (*Od.* χ 299) we may feel sure that we are dealing with the product of a later age.

[2] Bugge. for instance, has argued that φι-λός has the same root as σφε, and originally meant ' one's own.'

wise, however, when the word before which the short syllable
is lengthened or a letter doubled can be proved by comparison
with the allied languages to have never possessed more than
one initial consonant. When, for example, we find such compounds as ἐπιλίγδην, 'grazing,'[1] ἐπιτέλλω,[2] or such expressions
as αἴθωνα μεγάθυμον,[3] Αἴαντα μεγαλήτορα,[4] κατὰ μοῖραν,[5] we
are transported to a wholly new era, an era when the poets had
forgotten the real origin of the doubled letter and the lengthened syllable, and imagined that they too might double a
letter or lengthen a syllable at will should the metre so require.
Such cases of false analogy belong to an artificial dialect which
is separated by many generations from the Old Ionic of the
earliest parts of Homer. The origin, for instance, of ἔλλαβε
(root *labh*) and ἔμμαθε (root *manth*) is the same as that of
ἔλλιπε in Apollonius Rhodius—the misleading analogy of mis-
understood archaisms.

We must here turn aside for a moment to point out the
cases in which the hiatus or the lengthening of a naturally short
syllable may be assumed to imply a lost consonant. It is well
known that other causes may be called in to account for both.
Sometimes such violations of Greek metrical usage are due to
the cæsura, sometimes to the misconceptions of the later poets.
A careful examination of Homeric literature, however, would
seem to show that licenses of this kind were not originally
permissible, and only crept in through the progress of phonetic
decay in the Ionic dialect which occasioned the shortening of
syllables and the loss of letters, and the consequent belief that
the earlier poets had allowed themselves licenses 'for the sake
of the metre.' Thus the final α of neuters plural and the final
-ι of datives singular were once long, and Hartel has shown
that passages exist in Homer in which the primitive quantity of
these terminations is preserved. So, again, the frequent hiatus
after the particle ἦ arises from the fact that the word was
originally ἦϜε, and consequently the apparent hiatus is no hiatus at all except in the verses of later imitators. Elsewhere
the hiatus is found after -ι and -υ, the explanation being that the

[1] *Il.* P 599.   [2] *Od.* ψ 361.   [3] *Il.* Π 488.
[4] *Il.* P 626.   [5] *Il.* Π 367.

semi-vowels *y* and *v* were sounded after these letters in Old Ionic when another vowel followed, so that formations like ἀμφ-ουδίς [1] or ἀμφ-ήκης [2] must be assigned to the New Ionic period. Similarly, we find prepositions which, like ἐκ and ἐν, begin with a vowel admitting the hiatus because of the genitives and datives in -ου and -ῳ or -ι with which they were used (e.g. ἐϋπλέκτῳ ἐνὶ δίφρῳ). Wherever another vowel precedes, there can be little doubt that we have to do with the product of false analogy and of a later age. In other cases the hiatus is explained by its coming after stems which originally ended with a consonant, such as βοϝ or ταναϝ. Its occurrence after πρό (as in προερέσσω or προιάλλω) may be accounted for by the original form of the preposition πρωϝι. The contracted forms προὔτυψαν,[3] προὔθηκεν,[4] and προὔχων [5] betray their more recent date. Apart from certain composite or polysyllabic words, all other examples of the hiatus or the lengthening of a short syllable in the older parts of Homer must be taken to indicate a lost consonant.

If we assign the transition of Old Ionic into Middle Ionic to the beginning of the seventh century B.C., we shall not be far from the truth. New Ionic may be said to commence with the inscriptions of Abu-Simbel, referred to above, and to continue to the age of Hippocrates, when it becomes considerably tainted by Atticisms. It is best illustrated by the dialect of Herodotus and contemporaneous inscriptions, a dialect, be it observed, which is substantially identical with that of the New Ionic portions of Homer. The proof of this it would take too long to give here, but the fact can easily be tested by comparing a dictionary of Herodotus with a dictionary of Homer.[6]

[1] *Od.* ρ 237. [2] *Il.* Κ 256; *Od.* π 80. [3] *Il.* Ο 306.
[4] *Il.* Ω 409. [5] *Il.* Χ 97; *Od.* ζ 138.
[6] Thus Herodotus and Homer have τιθεῖσι, ἱεῖσι, διδοῦσι, ῥηγνῦσι instead of the Attic τιθέασι, &c.; Herodotus and Homer alone have the later εἰμέν for ἔσμεν; Herodotus usually omits the temporal augment, especially before double consonants (e.g. ἀρρώδεον, ἔρδον, ἀπαλλάσσοντο) and diphthongs (e.g. εἵκαζε, αἵρεε), and drops it in χρῆν and the iterative and pluperfect; and Homer uses the New Ionic εἰς of Herodotus as well as the old Ionic ἐσσι. The analogic διδώσομεν (*Od.* ν 358, ω 314) reminds us of λάμψομαι in Herodotus, and the latter's μεμετιμένος can be

In two or three respects, indeed, the forms of Herodotus are more archaic than those of the Iliad and Odyssey. Thus the MSS. of Herodotus still offer ἑάνδανε (for ἐϝάνδανε),[1] whereas we have the Ionicised form ἑήνδανε in Il. Ω 25, and Od. γ 143, and the later contracted from ἥνδανε in Il. Α 24, 378, Σ 510, &c.[2] The Attic contraction of ἀείρω, again, which ' occurs in Il. Ν 63, is not found in Herodotus, and while Herodotus has the more original κορέσω, Homer has the later (Atticising) κορέει and κορέεις.[3]

What is much more remarkable, however, is that the MSS. of Homer contain numerous examples of two forms which do not appear in New Ionic inscriptions before the beginning of the fourth century B.C., and are probably due to Attic influence. These forms are those of the genitives in -εν and -ευς, instead of the older -εο and -εος. Thus we have ἐμεῦ, γένευς, θέρευς.

No doubt it is possible that the diphthong in question is a scribe's error, introduced where the double syllable εο was pronounced by 'synizesis' as one. But this does not alter the really important fact of the case. Whether we call it synizesis or anything else, εο is in very many instances pronounced as a single syllable in the Homeric poems, that is, has become a diphthong. It is quite immaterial whether this diphthong was

paralleled in Homer by similar products of false analogy. The hysterogen σταίησαν for σταῖεν occurs in the Iliad (P 733) as well as in Herodotus and Thucydides ; the plural terminations -οίατο, -ήατο, and -έατο, which alone are found in Homer, are Herodotean, as is also ἔωθα (Il. Θ 408), instead of the older εἴωθα ; and Homer and Herodotus alike have the forms ἦια, ἦιε, ἦισαν (Il. Α 47, Η 213, Κ 197, Ν 305). Homer also offers us the Herodotean φύλακος (Il. Ζ 35, Ω 566 ; Od. ο 231), and μάρτυροι (Il. Α 338, Β 302, Γ 280, Ξ 274, Χ 255 ; Od. α 273, ξ 394). Other New Ionicisms will be ἱστίη for ἑστία, μίν, Πάριος (Il. Γ 325) by the side of Πάριδος, and the lost aspirate in μετάλμενος (Il. Ε 336), ἐπάλμενος (Il. Η 260), ἐπίστιον (Od. ζ 265), and αὐτόδιον (Od. θ 449). About ninety iteratives in -σκον are met with in Homer, as against only ten in Hesiod. Pindar has three, and the Attic tragedians four, which are plainly adopted from Homer, and none are found in Attic prose. Many, however, occur in Herodotus, though it must be added that the iteratives of the sigmatic aorist (like ἐλάσασκε) all belong to Homer.

[1] Herod. ix. 5, 19.   [2] Similarly ἐπιήνδανε (Od. ν 16, &c.).
[3] Il. Θ 379, Ν 831.

sounded exactly in the same way as ευ or not. The inscriptions show that before the fourth century B.C. εο had *not* become a diphthong in New Ionic, and that when it did become a diphthong it was represented as ευ. It is hard to believe that an artificial dialect like the Epic, which aimed at being archaic, would have anticipated the innovating pronunciation of the spoken language.

But there are some other philological peculiarities in the language of Homer which seem to imply that the poems were revised and additions made to them here and there as late even as the New Attic period. Thus we find words known to us by Alexandrine use like βλώσκω,[1] στιχεῖν,[2] σκάζω, κροαίνω[3] and στυγεῖν,[4] ἔχραισμον and παιφάσσω,[5] which are common to Homer and Apollonius Rhodius, and ἐρυκανάω, which elsewhere occurs only in Quintus Smyrnæus. From the post-Homeric κηκίς we get the verbal ἀνε-κήκιε, and the weak passive future μιγήσεσθαι[6] has been formed after the false analogy of forms like βήσομαι.

We must now pass on to the second point we have to prove, the existence of other dialects than Ionic in the language of the Iliad and Odyssey. These dialects are the Æolic and the Attic. Of the Doric dialect there is no trace. The forms which have been quoted as Doric are really archaisms which belonged to Old Ionic and were preserved among the conservative Dorians after their disappearance among the Ionians. In ἐσσεῖται, for instance, we have the old formative of the future *ya* which existed in Sanskrit as well as in ancient Greek ; the dative τείν for τεφι(ν) is an archaic form which belonged to Old Ionic as much as to Doric ; and infinitives like χολώσεμεν are equally survivals from an early period of the Ionic dialect itself. The pronoun τύνη, which occurs six times in the poems, similarly preserves the nasal which makes its appearance in the Æolic τούν and the Sanskrit *twam*, and has been counted as Doric only because that most conservative of the Greek dialects preserved a word which in later times elsewhere disappeared.

---

[1] *Od.* π 466, τ 25, φ 239, 385.   [2] *Il.* Π 258.   [3] *Il.* Z 507, O 264.
[4] *Od.* κ 113.   [5] *Il.* B 450.   [6] *Il.* K 365.

The Ionic poets would have nothing to do with that de-
tested Dorian race which drove their forefathers from their old
homes in Greece, and the only passage in which Dorians
are named is Od. τ 177, where a list is given of the various
tribes inhabiting Krete. The elegiac poets whose dialect was
based on that of epic literature show the same aversion to
anything Dorian. It is only his *Embateria* that Tyrtæus
composes in Doric, and even Theognis but once uses the preposition ποτί, which is found eighty-nine times in Homer and,
though originally common to all the Greek dialects, had come
to be preserved in Doric alone.[1]

The avoidance of the Doric dialect on the part of Homer
is brought out into greater relief by the usage of the Hesiodic poems in which we find such decided Dorisms as the
shortened final syllable of προπᾰς,[2] two genitives in -ᾱν instead
of the Ionic -ῶν,[3] the pronoun ἲν for οἷ,[4] and the Doric ἦν for
ἦσαν.[5] Ahrens believes that the Dorisms of Hesiod are specifically Delphian; however that may be, the contrast between
the two classes of epic poetry, the heroic and the didactic, in
this respect confirms in a striking way the Asiatic origin of
Homer. It is difficult to believe that a dialect which had
grown up on the soil of either the Peloponnesus or Northern
Greece could have remained so thoroughly untainted by Doric
forms and words.

It is quite different when we turn to the remains of the Æolic
dialect which have been detected in the poems. Æolisms are embedded in Homer like flies in amber ; they are scattered up and
down both in the Iliad and Odyssey, though almost always in
fixed places in the verse. Thus we find ζάθεος with the Æolic
ζα for διά as an epithet of the Æolic towns Killa,[6] Nisa,[7] Krisa,[8]
and Pheræ,[9] the Ionic form of which was Theræ, but always at
the beginning of the thesis of the second foot ; once, and once

---

[1] Πρός is found two hundred times in Homer, and the older προτί sixty
times. The word has no connection, except in meaning, with ποτί and the
contracted πός.

[2] So, too, κούρᾰς (*Th.* 60), δήσᾰς (*Th.* 521).   [3] *Opp.* 144, *Th.* 41.
[4] *Frag.* 134.   [5] *Th.* 321, 825.   [6] *Il.* A 38, 452.
[7] *Il.* B 508.   [8] *Il.* B 520.   [9] *Il.* I 151, 293.

only,[1] do we meet the word in a different formula and in a different place, the end of the line. Here, however, it is an epithet of the Doric Kythera, and belongs plainly to an imitator of a later age who found the old stock epithet convenient for terminating his verse. Other Æolic epithets of the same kind are ζαής,[2] ζατρεφής,[3] and ζαχρηής.[4] Indeed, as might have been expected, it is especially in the case of epithets that remains of the Æolic dialect have been handed down. Ἀμύμων, for instance, where the Æolic υ takes the place of the Ionic ω, has become so trite and meaningless an epithet as to be applied to Ægisthus.[5] Ταλαύρινος and καλαύροψ, again, are Æolisms, as also ἀγανός, as well as the numerous compounds of which ἐρι-, instead of the Ionic ἀρι-, forms the first part. Since the use of ε in place of α before ρ characterised Æolic, the form of the name Θερσίτης is an evident proof that Thersites belonged to the older portions of the Homeric poems, and figured in the legends that circulated in Æolis. The same may also be said of Halitherses,[6] Thersilokhus,[7] and Polytherseides.[8] If Herodian is right, the varying declension of the name Sarpêdon as Σαρπήδοντος and Σαρπηδόνος is due to the fact that the first is an Æolism; but this statement is extremely doubtful, since the vocalisation of the word is Ionic, and the hero himself was a Lycian, and belongs therefore to Ionic and not Æolic legend, while the preservation of the initial sibilant merely shows that the name has come down unchanged in its Old Ionic dress.[9] Similarly it is probable that the form σμικρός is old Ionic and

[1] *Il.* O 432.   [2] *Od.* ε 368, μ 313.
[3] *Il.* H 223; *Od.* ξ 19, δ 451.   [4] *Il.* E 525, M 347, 360.
[5] *Od.* α 29.   [6] *Od.* β 157, 253, ρ 68, ω 451.
[7] *Il.* P 216, Φ 209.   [8] *Od.* χ 287.
[9] The root is that of ἕρπειν, *serpere*, Sanskrit *sarp*. In bringing him from Lycia the legends made the usual confusion between the terrestrial Lycia and the celestial Lycia ('the land of light,' Latin *lux*), though no doubt the struggles between the Ionic emigrants to Asia Minor and the Lycian natives occasioned the localisation of the myth in that particular spot. It is possible, however, that the name Lycia was of Greek origin, given to a mountainous country where the inhabitants of the coast saw the sun rise in the morning, since the Lycians called themselves Termilæ (Tramelê in the native inscriptions).

not Æolic, which, as in Σμύρνα, kept the original *s* before *m*, although σμυγερός, σμυγερῶς are certainly Æolisms. Solitary Æolisms have been preserved by the metre in πίσυρες,[1] κεκλήγοντες,[2] and the vocative νύμφα,[3] and in φήρ.[4] To the metre, again, we must ascribe the preservation of the Æolic forms of the personal pronouns.[5] Other Æolisms, no doubt, once existed here and there in the text of which no trace now remains, since in two passages, φλίψεται for the received θλίψεται,[6] and πόρδαλις for the Aristarchean πάρδαλις,[7] were read by Zenodotus and the Venetian Codex. A fortunate chance has preserved for us the specifically Æolic title αἰσυμνήτης in Od. θ 258. Several other Æolisms may further be detected in the poems;[8] among these κέν, by the side of the Ionic ἄν, is the most noticeable. In the Iliad κὲν occurs 121 times before vowels, 78 times before consonants; κὲ occurs 145 times, κ' 76 times, χ' 4 times, εἰσόκεν 7 times, εἰσόκε 18 times, εἰσόκ' 3 times, ὥς κεν and ὥς κε 11 times. On the other hand, ἄν is found 137 times, and the compound ἄν κεν once.[9] Such a compound could only have been formed when all sense of the original meaning of κεν had passed away. Perhaps, however, the best-known Æolism is the nominative of masculine nouns of the first declension, like νεφεληγερέτα. We find it almost always in certain stock phrases and set positions. In αἰχμητά[10] the form has been half Ionised after the model of αἰχμητής, which thrice occurs[11] in imitation of the older usage.

---

[1] *Il.* O 680; *Od.* ε 70.

[2] *Il.* Γ 130; *Od.* δ 743.

[3] *Od.* μ 256, ξ 30.

[4] *Il.* A 268, B 743.

[5] Namely, ἄμμες (*Il.* Φ 432; *Od.* ι 303, 321, χ 55); ἄμμι(ν) twenty-one times; ἄμμε (*Il.* A 59, H 292, 378, 397, K 346, Ξ 62, Σ 268, X 219, Ω 355; *Od.* ι 404, κ 209, μ 221, χ 73); ὔμμες (*Il.* A 274, 335, Ξ 481, Ψ 469, Ω 242; *Od.* φ 231); ὔμμι(ν) seventeen times; ὔμμε (*Il.* Ψ 412; *Od.* ν 357, σ 407, ω 109).

[6] *Od.* ρ 221.

[7] *Il.* N 103, P 20, Φ 573.

[8] Ἀλκί (*Od.* ζ 130), ἄλλυδις (*Od.* ε 71, 369), ἄμυδις, ὕπαιθα (five times in the Iliad alone), ἐπασσύτεροι (always after the first trochee, *Il.* A 383; *Od.* π 366, &c.), ἀχεύων, ἀπουράς, δεύω (by the side of the Ionic δέω), ἔμμεναι (instead of the Ionic εἴμεναι, forty times in *Il.*, twenty-one times in *Od.*), ἐγρήγορθαι, ἐκίχημεν.

[9] *Il.* N 127.

[10] *Il.* E 197.

[11] *Il.* Γ 179, P 588; *Od.* β 19.

This has also been the case in ἠπύτα for ἀπύτα.[1] The later Ionic poets, forgetting the origin of the form, identified its termination with that of the accusative in -α, and hence we find εὐρύοπα used as an accusative in Il. A 498, Θ 206, Ξ 265, Ο 152, Ω 98, 331. The grammarians of Alexandria carried the misconception still further, and Priscian and the Scholiasts lay down that such words are indeclinable and may be used in any case whatever.

The inferences to be drawn from these facts are irresistible. Æolic lays form the background of those Ionic poems which we call Homer. It was among the cities of Æolis, in that very Trojan land in which the scene of the Iliad is laid, that the Greek Epic first grew up. From the hands of Æolic bards it passed into those of their Ionic neighbours, but carrying with it memorials and evidences of its origin. Epithets and phrases that had become part of the rhapsodist's stock-in-trade were interwoven into the Ionic versions of the old lays ; the proper names and the legends attached to them were handed on to the new schools of Homeridæ ; and here and there an Æolic word or form was retained where it suited the metre better than its Ionic equivalent. Philology thus confirms the tradition which made Smyrna the birthplace of Homer and the earliest seat of Homeric poetry, and is confirmed in its turn by the subject-matter of the Iliad which localises the ' tale divine ' of ancient Aryan mythology in the Troad. It was there that the Æolic fugitives from the Dorians had to wrest a new home for themselves from the hands of its Asiatic possessors.

But Æolisms are not the only alien elements that we find in Homer. There is an Attic colouring in the poems as well. So strong, indeed, is the latter that Aristarchus held Homer to have been an Athenian, and Cobet considers the poems to have been partially Atticised.

We must, of course, be on our guard against assuming too hastily that a form is Attic because it occurs in Attic writers and not in the Ionic of Herodotus. Attic is an offshoot of the Ionic dialect ; Old Attic may be regarded as a sister of Old Ionic ; and it would only be natural to find

---

[1] *Il.* H 384.

many archaic forms in New Attic which have been lost even in Old Ionic. It does not follow that they did not exist in Old Ionic. The form ἀνέωγε, for example, is not an Atticism, but an Old Ionicism. Only those forms and words must be accounted Atticisms which can be shown by Comparative Philology to have grown up subsequently to the separation of the Attic from the remaining Ionic dialects. Forms originating in phonetic decay or false analogy which are not found in New Ionic are Attic peculiarities, the growth and creation of Attic soil; but no others. Genuine Atticisms, however, exist in abundance in both Iliad and Odyssey. Thus we have the accusatives Τυδῆ,[1] Μηκιστῆ,[2] Ὀδυσῆ,[3] like ἱερῆ in Euripides ;[4] θεά used about 200 times in place of the older θεός ; νώ occurring twice, σφώ once, σφῶν once,[5] and σφίσι fifty-five times ; contracted futures like κτενεῖ, τελεῖ and κομιῶ, ἀγλαϊεῖσθαι ;[6] heterogen aorists like ἔπεσον ; and optatives like ἐπισχοίης with ο instead of ε, and the termination dropped in the third person singular [7] (ὑπέρσχοι for ὑπερσχοίη[τ]).[8] Were we to listen to Professor Paley, the list of Atticisms might not only be largely extended, but also be referred to the language of the Periklean age. Among the Atticisms he quotes we find such phrases as ὅτε μεν—ὅτε δέ ; οἱ ἀμφὶ Πρίαμον,[9] παραβάλλεσθαι ψυχήν,[10] ποιεῖσθαι παῖδα in the sense of 'adopting,'[11] ἐπὶ δώρων, 'while gifts last,'[12] like μάχης ἐπί,[13] περιδόσθαι τινος, 'to wager,'[14] δειπνεῖν ἐν ὥρῃ, 'to take an early dinner,'[15] ἐκεῖνοι, in the sense of 'the enemy,'[16] μὴ ὤφελλε γενέσθαι,[17] ὁ αὐτός,[18] a phrase which

[1] *Il.* Δ 384.   [2] *Il.* Ο 339.   [3] *Od.* τ 136.
[4] *Alk.* 25. Compare Aristoph. *Acharn.* 1150.   [5] *Od.* δ 62.
[6] *Il.* Ο 65, Τ 104 ; Δ 161, *Od.* ψ 284 ; *Il.* Β 389, Υ 140, Κ 331, Α 232, Ι 132, 274, Φ 373, *Od.* μ 230, υ 229 ; *Il.* Κ 331, Λ 454, Σ 133 ; *Od.* ο 546. The contracted futures in -ιῶ, -ιοῦμαι, however, occur eleven times in Herodotus.

[7] See *Il.* Ι 284, 142, Ξ 241; *Il.* Λ 838. Herodotus, however, has ἐνέοι (vii. 6).

[8] *Od.* ξ 184 ; *Il.* Ξ 107 ; *Od.* ρ 317.
[9] *Il.* Γ 146.   [10] *Il.* Ι 322.   [11] *Il.* Ι 495.
[12] *Il.* Ι 602.   [13] *Il.* Π 368.   [14] *Il.* Ψ 485 ; *Od.* ψ 78.
[15] *Od.* ρ 176.   [16] *Il.* Σ 188.   [17] *Il.* Ρ 686.
[18] *Il.* Ζ 391 ; *Od.* η 55, 326, &c.

certainly has a very modern ring about it. Equally striking are some of his instances of single words, as, for example, κατα-δημοβορῆσαι, where κατὰ has its peculiarly Attic sense,[1] ἐπέδωκε in the sense given to it by Attic law,[2] ἀνάξασθαι with the meaning of 'reckoning,'[3] ἐθελοντῆρες,[4] ξύνετο,[5] ἀήρ in the sense of 'air,' not, as in Old Ionic, of 'mist,'[6] ἄλλοτε for ἐνίοτε, σπουδῇ for μόλις, αἰκῶς for ἀεικῶς,[7] ἐπίτηδες, ἀμόθεν, ἄσσα,[8] δῆσεν for ἐδέησεν,[9] γενναῖος in the sense of 'legitimate,'[10] ἀλλοῖος, ὅσακις, σκότιος 'illegitimate,'[11] ἐπιδοῦναι,[12] and ἐπάλξεσι.[13] The use of the old demonstrative pronoun as an article also points to a comparatively late date,[14] and the same conclusion may be drawn from verbal forms in -άζειν and -ίζειν, like παππάζειν, μετοκλάζειν, οἰνοποτάζειν, νευστάζειν and δικάζειν (which reminds us of the Athenian law-courts), or ἐρατίζειν, ἀτίζειν, κελητίζειν, ἀλεγίζειν, μεγαλίζεσθαι.[15] Perhaps Mr. Paley goes too far when he claims a philosophic origin for such Homeric verbs as ἀφραίνειν, δειλαίνειν, μωραίνειν, χαλεπαίνειν, μαργαίνειν, ὁρμαίνειν, θαυμαίνειν, μενεαίνειν, κυδαίνειν, though we should have expected to meet with them in Theophrastus, rather than in Old Ionic poems addressed to a popular audience.

It is not difficult to account for this Attic colouring. Some of the Atticisms are probably due to the belief of Aristarchus in the Attic birth of Homer ; indeed, we know that in certain passages where he adopted an Attic form the readings of Zeno-. dotus were different. Others, again, may be explained by early errors on the part of copyists. But the greater number admits of but one interpretation. The Homeric poems, as we have them, must have passed through Attic hands, and undergone an Attic recension. Nor is this at variance with what we know of their history. The pseudo-Platonic *Hipparchus* ascribes to Hipparchus an edition or redaction of Homer which later writers, Cicero, Josephus and Pausanias, ascribe to Peisistra-

[1] *Il.* Σ 301.
[2] *Il.* I 148.
[3] *Od.* γ 245.
[4] *Od.* β 292.
[5] *Od.* δ 76.
[6] *Il.* Ξ 288.
[7] *Il.* X 336.
[8] *Il.* K 208, &c.
[9] *Il.* Σ 100.
[10] *Il.* E 253.
[11] *Il.* Z 24.
[12] *Il.* Ψ 559.
[13] *Il.* X, 3.
[14] As in *Il.* Γ 55, Z 201, K 11, Σ 10, Υ 320, Φ 526, X 59, Ψ 295.
[15] [The old verb μηδίζειν disproves this.—M.]

tus. We cannot suppose that the public library. Peisistratus founded was without copies of Homer, or that when one of his editors was convicted of altering and interpolating documents so sacred as the Oracles of Musæus,[1] the old epic literature would have been treated more reverently. Solon is accused of inserting certain passages in Homer in order to glorify the Athenians, and this accusation of itself implies a consciousness of the Attic origin of some parts of the poems. It is not impossible that Mr. Paley may be right in referring some of the Atticisms he has enumerated to so late a period as the Periklean age, since it is hard to see in Od. η 81 an allusion to any other building than the Erechtheum, which was erected about the year 432 B.C. At any rate there is plain proof that the Homeric poems underwent a process of manipulation in Attica; at how late or early a time this process terminated must remain undecided.

It must now be quite clear that the language of the poems is an artificial one, a sort of curious mosaic in which archaisms and modernisms, fragments of Æolic, Attic and Ionic are embedded side by side. It testifies to slow growth among guilds of professional poets who received from their predecessors a series of stock subjects, a stock mode of treating them, and a body of traditional words and phrases. This fact is confirmed —though further confirmation is not needful—by the occurrence in Homer of words and forms which are the product of false analogy, and owe their existence to the misinterpretation of the older part of the Homeric language.

Reference has been already made to some of these, and, indeed, so numerous are the examples of such erroneous formations in Homer, that it is easy to find illustrations of them. In some cases we can actually see the process of creation, as it were, going on. Thus in Od. η 95 we read : ἐν δὲ θρόνοι περὶ τοῖχον ἐρηρέδατ’ ἔνθα καὶ ἔνθα. Here ἐρήρεδατο is a perfectly normal Ionic formation from the root of ἐρείδω ; the dental belongs to the root, and accordingly appears in all the other tenses of the verb. But a few lines before (86) we have another verse, which is evidently formed on the model of the

---

[1] See Hdt. vii. 6.

one just quoted, and only differs from the latter half of it in substituting ἐληλέδατο for ἐρηρέδατυ. Ἐληλέδατο, however, is etymologically and grammatically an impossible form; the present tense is ἐλαύνω and the root is *lav*, with no trace of either a dental or a vowel ε. The word, in fact, is due to the false analogy of ἐρηρέδατο and the misunderstanding of the archaic pluperfect form. In the Odyssey,[1] again, we find a verse which can only be explained as the creation of false analogy. The translation, 'seals, the offspring of the sea-foam,' gives a radically wrong sense to both νέποδες and ἀλοσύδνη. The last word is a compound of ἅλς and συδνή, an old Ionic feminine, answering to a Sanskrit *sun-ya* (from the root *su*, 'to beget'), and signifying 'daughter' or 'offspring.' The Sanskrit *sun-ya* (by the side of the masculine *sunus*, 'son') would have been represented in Old Ionic by συνγη, but the *yod* after first developing a dental, as is so frequently the case in Greek, disappeared, leaving συνδη, and by metathesis συδνή. Some early 'Homeric' verse, now lost, must have once existed in which the seals were called νέποδες ἀλόσυδναι, 'footless off-spring of the sea,' νέποδες (or rather νήποδες)[2] being a compound of πούς and the same negative that we meet with in νηκερδὴς or the Latin *nefas*. The second part of the epithet, however, came to be misinterpreted; ἀλοσύδνη was divided into the genitive ἅλος, and the non-existent νδνη, which the rhapsodists connected with ὕδωρ and ὑδαρής, and the change of meaning was complete. It only remained to explain νέποδες, which, now that its substantive had been turned into a genitive, necessarily signified 'offspring,' and this was easily done by referring it to ἀνέψιος. The superfluous dental did not trouble the etymological consciences of the Homeric poets. It is probable that this passage of the Odyssey was not the only place in Homeric literature in which the mistaken use of νέποδες occurred, since we find both Kallimachus[3] and Theokritus[4] employing the word in the same sense.

---

[1] δ 404 : ἀμφὶ δέ μιν φῶκαι νέποδες καλῆς ἀλοσύδνης.

[2] The shortened form would belong to the New Ionic period.

[3] ὁ Κεῖος Ὑλλίχου νέπους.

[4] xvii. 25 : ἀθάνατοι δὲ καλεῦντα ἑοὶ νέποδες

Two other instances of false analogy may be quoted, which will show even more clearly the artificial character of the Homeric dialect. In Il. Z 289 the loss of the digamma caused some rhapsodist or scribe to alter the original phrase πέπλοι, παμποίκιλα ϝέργα γυναικῶν into πέπλοι παμποίκιλοι, ἔργα γυναικῶν, and this corrupt reading has been imitated by the author of Od. ο 105, where we have πέπλοι παμποίκιλοι, οὓς κάμεν αὐτή. A similar blunder occurs in Il. Ω 6, a verse, it is fair to state, which was rejected by Aristophanes and Aristarchus themselves. Here the impossible form ἀνδροτῆτα originates in the corrupt reading of Il. Π 857 and X 363, where Clemm has restored ὁροτῆτα (for νὁροτῆτα as ὁρῶψ for νὁρῶψ).

Perhaps one of the oddest of these new creations of the Homeric poets is the adjective ἴος, 'one,' in Il. Z 422.[1] From the root σεμ, the Greeks had formed a numeral 'one,' which was declined in the nominative σεμς, σεμια, σεμ. By the ordinary phonetic laws of the language these finally became εἷς, μία (for σμία), ἕν, and in epic μία sometimes lost its initial consonant like some other words (e.g. λείβω, γαῖα). Then came the misconception of later composers. The feminine ἴα was supposed to be an adjective declined like τίμιος, and hence the monstrous ἰῷ instead of ἑνί.

The intensive ὄχα has arisen in much the same way. The root of ἔχω could never of itself have passed into the meaning given to ὄχα ; it was only in combination with ἐξ (as in ἐξέχω) that it was able to acquire an intensive or superlative sense. But there must have been some passage or passages in which the rhapsodists divided the compound ἔξοχα in an incorrect way, assigning ἐξ to the verb of the sentence by supposing that in the obsolete dialect of early Ionia ὄχα alone meant 'very.' Hence the numerous passages in which it is used in this sense. If Mr. Paley is right, ὑπέρμορα[2] has had a similar origin, being formed after the analogy of such Attic compounds as παράλογος or ἀνάλογον.

The same scholar has pointed out a passage[3] in which the

---

[1] οἱ μὲν πάντες ἰῷ κίον ἤματι ῎Αϊδος εἴσω.   [2] *Il.* B 155.

[3] *Il.* K 466 : δέελον δ' ἐπὶ σῆμα τ' ἔθηκεν.

adjective δέελον (=δῆλον) is used as if it were a substantive with the meaning of 'mark.' This mistake could only have been made after the contraction of the original δεϜελος through δέϜλος into the New Ionic δῆλος and a forgetfulness that the two words were really the same.[1] Another example of the same kind is the use of ἀγγελίης, the genitive of ἀγγελίη, as a masculine nominative meaning 'messenger.'[2] A passage must have occurred in the traditionary lays in which the form of the sentence rendered the blunder possible, and since the primitive *alpha* of the termination had already become *êta*, the passage in question would have been of later date than the separation of the Attic dialect from the Ionic stock.[3] Other instances of similar blundering that may be quoted are the confusion of χέρηα, the accusative of the substantive χέρης, with the comparative χερείονα,[4] and the use of πλέες, 'full,' as πλείονες,[5] 'more.'

Of a somewhat different character are the false presents εἴκω, πεφεύγω, ἀνώγω, πέφράδω, &c. from the perfects εἶκα (=ἔοικα), πέφευγα, ἄνωγα, πέφραδα, which had come to be employed in a present sense, or the false futures χραισμήσω, πεπιθήσω, ἐνισπήσω (like ἰδήσω in Theoc. 3, 37) from the aorist infinitives χραισμεῖν, πεπιθεῖν, ἐνισπεῖν, &c., which were confounded with the present infinitives of contracted verbs in -έω. The contraction they imply indicates the late date at which they were coined, and they point to a belief that the forms of the Epic dialect were so far removed from those of the dialect of everyday life as to admit among them almost any new coinage which suited the metre and had an archaic ring.

---

[1] Δέελον is the same word as the second part of the compound epithet εὐ-δείελος, where we ought certainly to read εὐ-δήελος. In the latter, however, the first syllable remains long by way of compensating for the loss of the digamma, whereas in δέελον it has been shortened in accordance with the usual habit of New Ionic.

[2] *Il.* Γ 206, N 252, O 640.

[3] Since the Attic dialect retains the original *alpha*.

[4] *Il.* Δ 400.

[5] *Il.* B 129, Λ 395 : τόσσον ἐγώ φημι πλέας ἔμμεναι υἶας Ἀχαιῶν Τρώων · οἰωνοὶ δὲ περὶ πλέες ἠὲ γυναῖκες.

To the same belief must be ascribed many of the other products of false analogy in Homer. Thus nineteen aorist infinitives in -εειν which stand for -εγειν are found in the poems [1] which are erroneously formed after the model of the uncontracted present infinitives of verbs in -εω. Curtius has shown from a comparison of the forms of the infinitive in Ionic, Doric, and Æolic that φέρειν represents an original φερε-ϝεν, which in Ionic became successively φερεεν and φέρειν (for φερεῖν), so that the first ε of the Homeric forms in -εειν is historically false. [2] Thus, again, the futures ἀνύω from ἀνύτω, [3] ἐρύω, [4] and ἐντανύω, [5] are modelled upon the Atticising futures of verbal stems in -s, which primitively had a double sigma in this tense, afterwards in New Ionic dropped one of them, and finally lost both. Thus, too, the form διδυῖσθα, [6] from the root *da*, is a mere imitation of οἶσθα for οἶδ-θα from the root *vid*, the sibilant being erroneously imagined to be part of the second person ending in the archaic Epic dialect; [7] the compounds ἰθαιγενής, [8] γυναιμανής, [9] are due to the analogy of Θηβαιγενής, where alone the locative Θήβαι is right; and the so-called diectasis or resolution of vowels, which is so frequently resorted to for help-ing out the metre, has been proved by Mangold and Wacker-nagel's researches to be an affected archaism. Ἐλόωσι, for example, in *Il.* N 315, *Od.* η 319, is a false resolution of the contracted ἐλῶσι of Herodotus, κρεμόω, in *Il.* H 83, of the κρεμῶμεν which we find in the *Plutus* [10] of Aristophanes. Forms like γανόωσαι, ἡβώοντες, ὁρόῳτε, γοόωντα, αἰτιόωντο, ἀλόω, πρώ-ονες and θόωκος are grammatically and phonetically impos-sible. According to the phonetic laws of the Ionic dialect, the middle stage between ὁράω and ὁρῶ is ὁρέω, not ὁρόω, and the theory of an assimilation of the vowels is set aside by the in-variable usage of Ionic authors and of the Epic dialect itself,

[1] Ex. gr. *Il.* Δ 263, Σ 511, T 15, Ψ 467, Ω 608; *Od.* α 59, ε 349, ι 137, λ 232, μ 446, τ 477, χ 437.

[2] The infinitive in -εειν is found thrice in Hesiod's *Shield*; never in the *Works and Days*, or in the elegiac writers.

[3] *Il.* Δ 56, Λ 365.

[4] *Il.* Λ 454, O 351, X 67.

[5] *Od.* φ 97, 127, 174.

[6] *Il.* T 270.

[7] Similarly we find ἔχεισθα and φίλεισθα in Sappho, which made the grammarians fancy the form to be an Æolic one.

[8] *Od.* ξ 203.

[9] *Il.* Γ 39.

[10] v. 312

except in the limited number of cases under consideration. Moreover, ου and η could not become ω, much less could ο do so. The whole set of forms is the creation of rhapsodists and scribes endeavouring to restore the metre of lines which the contraction of two short syllables, the loss of the digamma, or the decay of some other peculiarity of early pronunciation, had violated, and who looked for the means of effecting this to the supposed analogy of other old words.

If further proof is wanted of the artificial nature of the Homeric dialect, it would be found in two facts. The first of these is that the parallel forms of various date and origin which coexist in the poems are generally of different metrical quantity, and accordingly highly convenient for the verse-maker's purposes. Thus the Æolic ἔμμεναι serves as a dactyl, ἔμεναι as an anapæst, ἔμμεν as a trochee, ἔμεν as a pyrrhic, and εἶναι as a spondee, and it is plainly metrical necessities that have preserved the Æolic forms of the personal pronouns. The second fact is that short syllables are lengthened where too many come together to allow the word in which they occur to be otherwise used in the hexameter. Hence it is that the first syllable of ἀθάνατος is always long, that ὑψηρεφέος is the genitive of ὑψερεφής, that ἄορ has ᾰ in dissyllabic forms and ᾱ in trisyllabic ones, and that we find indifferently ἀπειρέσιος and ἀπερείσιος, μέλανι and μειλανι.[1] Hence, too, we find κύανος, κυανόπρωρος, and κυανῶπις, but κυάνεος, κυανόπεζα, κυανόπεπλος, and κυανοχαίτης.[2]

The long vowels and diphthongs by which the lengthened quantity of these naturally short syllables is pointed out in writing are due to the scribes, and are probably of late date. How modern the manuscripts were which Aristarchus had before him is shown, as Giese has remarked, by his uncertainty regarding the insertion of the aspirate except where it was indicated by an elision. The alterations made in the text by the scribes both of the Alexandrine and of an earlier period were numerous and sometimes revolutionary. No doubt of this can

---

[1] *Il.* Ω 79.

[2] So, also, σύβοσια (*Od.* ξ 101), ἀπονέεσθαι, ἠπερο-πεύω (Sanskrit ᾱpᾱrᾱ), ἠνεμόεις, διηνεκής, εἰλάτινος, θεμείλια (*Il.* Ψ 255), εἰανός (*Il.* Π 9), ἀγνοίῃσι (*Od.* ω 218), εἰαρινός, εἰρεσίη, ἀκάματος, &c.

remain after the labours of Nauck, Cobet, and Wackernagel. The hiatus caused by the loss of the digamma was mended in various ways. Sometimes ρ' is inserted,[1] sometimes τ',[2] sometimes τε,[3] sometimes δ',[4] sometimes γ' or γε,[5] sometimes κ'.[6] At other times the plural takes the place of the dual (as Il. Υ 371, 372, for χεῖρε Γέροικε), or the vocative the place of the nominative used vocatively, as in Il. Γ 277.[7] New forms, again, are substituted for older ones, as in Il. N 107, where Zenodotus and Aristophanes preserve the older reading νῦν δὲ ἕκας πόλιος corrupted into νῦν δ' ἕκαθεν πόλιος in the MSS. of Aristarchus, and the words of a verse may even be transposed or changed, as when[8] στῆ δὲ πάροιθ' ἵππων δηδισκόμενος is turned into στῆ δ' ἵππων προπάροιθε· δεδισκόμενος or τοίονδε Γίδον into τοιοῦτον ἴδον.[9] A frequent source of error has been the contraction of short syllables during the age of Attic influence, resulting in various corruptions of the text in order to restore the violated metre. Equally frequent has been the misreading of the older MSS. in which E represented both η and ει as well as ε, and O ω and ου as well as ο. But it must be remembered that it is often far from easy to distinguish false forms which have arisen from the mistakes of the later copyists and critics from those which belonged to the older period of oral recitation. In many cases we shall never be able to determine with accuracy whether we are dealing with a corruption of the written text or with a product of the age before the poems were first written down.

About one point, however, there need be no hesitation. Throughout the whole of Homer words which in Doric have κ from an original *kw* (Latin *qu*) appear with π, never κ. Thus we find ὅπως, πῶς, κοῦ, ποῖ, &c. Yet we know both from inscriptions and the MSS. of Kallinos, Mimnermus, and He-

---

[1] *Il.* B 342, Δ 467. [2] *Il.* E 467, Ξ 348; *Od.* φ 401.

[3] *Il.* I 379, M 162; *Od.* α 41, ο 507.

[4] *Il.* Δ 509, Λ 792, M 412, O 403; *Od.* β 332, γ 216, δ 556.

[5] *Il.* A 548; *Od.* σ 233. [6] *Il.* A 64, Υ 250.

[7] An instance is quoted by Hoffmann from *Il.* B 8, where for οὖλε ὄνειρε we should read οὖλος.

[8] *Od.* ο 150. [9] *Od.* ζ 160.

...t the New Ionic still preserved the older κ up to ...ı century B.C. It is difficult to ascribe the change of ...ıg to the Atticising influence discussed above, since the ...er would not well explain the thoroughness with which the change has been carried out. The change is rather the work of the copyists of a later day, influenced, no doubt, by the theory that Homer was of Attic birth. Quite parallel is the appearance of an aspirated letter in many words which retained the simple *tenuis* in the Ionic of Herodotus and the inscriptions. An instance of this is δέχομαι in the place of δέκομαι.

The conclusions to be derived from a close examination of the language of the Iliad and the Odyssey make it almost superfluous to refer to the question whether these two works were the production of one author or of two. Since, however, the question is even now keenly debated, it is as well to see what light can be thrown upon it by the language of the poems. Though this has shown us that the national Epic of ancient Greece, like the national Epics of all other peoples—the Mahâbhârata of India, the Edda of Scandinavia, the Nibelungen Lied of Germany, the Kalevala of the Finns—grew up slowly and gradually, passing through the mouths of numberless generations and schools of poets and reciters, and assuming new forms among each ; nevertheless there must have been definite individuals to whom the arrangement and grouping of this traditional matter was due, to whom, in fact, the Iliad and the Odyssey, the *Thebais* and the *Kypria*, the Lesser Iliad and the other specimens of Epic literature, as separate poems, owed their origin. We know that the last line of the Iliad is but the protasis of which the first line of the Æthiopis formed the apodosis, and that the poet of the Odyssey[1] appeals to the Muses to relate to him 'also' as to others who had gone before the adventures of the Greek heroes on their return from Troy. It is plain, therefore, that some principle was adopted in cutting off one portion of the mass of Epic matter from another, in throwing it, that is to say, into the shape of a single independent poem. But a merely superficial reading will convince most people that there is a very decided difference of tone and

[1] *a.* 10. The neglect of the digamma in this line should be noted.

manner between the Iliad and the Odyssey, that the Odyssey is a much more artificial composition than the Iliad, and breathes the spirit of a more modern age. And this impression is borne out by differences in the language of the two poems. There are about 130 words found only in the Iliad, and about 120 found only in the Odyssey, and among the latter occur not only abstract nouns like σπέρμα, χρῆμα, μορφή, ἀριθμός, εὐχή, γαλήνη,[1] but words which denote a distinct advance in wealth and luxury, such as δημίουργος, δέσποινα, κοῖτος, ἤλεκτρον. The usage of certain words, too, differs in the two poems, implying that a different hand has manipulated the old traditionary materials in the two cases. Thus different epithets are employed for the same object, or, what is more significant, the same epithet is employed in different senses. Δαΐφρων and ὑλοόφρων, for instance, are 'baleful' in the Iliad, 'crafty' in the Odyssey, εὔκυκλος is used only of the shield with the meaning of 'round' in the Iliad, of the chariot with the meaning of 'well-wheeled' in the Odyssey. Similarly βουλήφορος is an epithet of princes in the Iliad, of the ἀγορά in the more demo-cratic Odyssey. So, too, the same word has different significa-tions. In the Iliad κλεῖς is 'a collar-bone'; ζωστήρ 'a warrior's belt'; λόφος, 'a neck'; ἡγεμών, 'a chief'; μῶλος, 'the moil of war'; ἔρις, 'the battle-strife'; καλέω, 'to call'; κοσμέω, 'to marshal.' In the Odyssey the same words mean 'key,' 'swine-herd's belt,' 'ridge,' 'guide,' 'struggle,' 'rivalry,' 'invite,' and 'to set huntsmen'; the accusative of ἔρις in the latter poem being the analogic ἔριν of the Attic dialect. Differences, again, appear in the use even of words like ἐξοπίσω, which always denotes *place* in the Iliad, *time* in the Odyssey, or in the expres-sion of an idea like that of the preposition 'by means of,' which is represented by ἕκητι in the Iliad, by ἰότητι in the Odyssey (and Iliad). It is, perhaps, of little moment that the later analogic comparative of φιλός, φίλτερος, is found only once in Odyssey, φιλίων· being alone employed in the Odyssey; but, on the other hand, we cannot overlook the significance of the fact that the contracted form of παρά, πάρ, occurs before the

---

[1] So οὔνομα, which frequently appears in the Odyssey, is found only twice in the Iliad (Γ 235, P 260).

letters γ, ζ, ξ, σ and τ only in the Iliad, and before κ and μ only in the Odyssey. We seem here referred to a difference of usage on the part of the poet or redactor, or whatever else we choose to term him, which points further to a difference of personality. Whether or not, however, the author of the Iliad and of the Odyssey was one and the same individual is of small consequence ; in any case he has been proved by the sure evidence of philology to have been but the inheritor of other men's labours, and, like Castrén and Lönnrott in our own age, to have worked up the materials provided by the spirit and genius of a whole nation. It was to this spirit and genius that the old Epic of Greece was due, and rightly, therefore, was its creation named Homêros, 'the fitted together.' [1]

[1] Ὅμηρος is actually used with this sense by Euripides (*Alc.* 870), who applies it to the marriage bond. The form of the name, and probably its origin also, is Ionic. The word is first found in a doubtful fragment (xxxiv.) of Hesiod. The statement of the pseudo-Herodotean Life of Homer that the word signified ' blind ' in the Cumæan dialect must be a pure fiction. G. Curtius and Angermann take a slightly different view of the original use of the word from that adopted in the text. The former says :—' Sic fere nomen Homeri esse existimaverim, ut primum poetæ inter se conjuncti et apti ὅμηροι vocati sint, ii deinde gentis sodalitio inito patronymicum Ὁμηρίδαι nomen acceperint, postea vero ex civilium gentium more eponymus quidam inventus sit Ὅμηρος, qui gentis potius quam suam personam sustineret. Nam similem sane in modum qui a cantu εὐμολποι vocati erant facti sunt Εὐμολπίδαι, Eumolpidarum autem auctor inventus est Eumolpus. Fiet igitur Homerus nobis auctor vel eponymus poetarum gentilicia communione inter se conjunctorum *Ahnherr der Sängerinnungen.*'

APPENDIX B.

ON THE DATE OF THE ODYSSEY.

IT occurs to me that I ought to say something in answer to a natural objection which may be made against the recent date assigned to the Odyssey in this volume. If this poem did not receive its present form till near 700 B.C., how is it possible to account for its vague and fabulous notions about the geography of the West? For if Syracuse and Naxos and Catana, and many other flourishing Greek cities, were founded from 735 B.C. onward, surely the fables of Polyphemus, of the oxen of the sun, of Scylla and Charybdis, and the like, must have been then already long exploded.

My answer to this objection is twofold. In the first place, recent researches have shown the geography of the Odyssey, not only as regards the West, but as regards the very home of Odysseus, to be so vague and inaccurate, that we must regard it as consciously imaginary in the poet's mind. He was no primitive bard painting facts so far as he knew them accurately, and filling in the rest from his imagination and from legend, but a deliberate romancer, who did not care to reproduce tame reality, even where he could have easily ascertained it. I know that some leading scholars, like Mr. Gladstone and Dr. Schliemann, will not agree with me, but I will merely refer the reader to the latest and ablest survey of Homeric geography in Mr. Bunbury's *Geography of the Ancients* (especially vol. i. ch. iii. § 3), where he will see my statement amply corroborated. Not even Ithaca, not even the Ionian islands, not even the neighbouring coasts are described with any approach to their real features. When Telemachus is described starting in a chariot from Pylos, and driving within two days to Sparta with his companion,[1] the poet leaves us to imagine either a smooth plain, or an easy high road along which horses can gallop. Anyone who has seen the country between the two places will know how utterly absurd this notion is. And are we to imagine any high roads at all through the gorges and defiles of Messene and of Laconia? At no period of Greek history, down to the present day was such a journey possible. It follows that we cannot infer the historical or geographical knowledge of this age from a poet who deliberately drew his pictures, even of Greece, from fancy, and not from observation.

It is therefore likely that this geographical vagueness was the result of intentional archaicising, of an affected ignorance, by the clever rhapsodist. If it had been confined to the far West, and then only, could we explain it by the antiquity of the poet and the narrow horizon of his geographical knowledge.

But even if this were not so, I could meet the objection in another way. The received dates for the foundation of the Greek colonies are all derived from Sicilian *Archæologia* of Thucydides at the opening of his sixth book. All these dates were evidently borrowed from Antiochus of Syracuse, and we need not extend to this old logographer the superstitious reverence generally accorded to every statement of Thucydides. I hope to show more fully in *Hermathena* that Dionysius probably composed his history for the purpose of glorifying his native Syracuse, then the leading city among all the western Hellenic colonies. He was prevented by the ancient tèmple of Apollo *Archegetes* at Naxos, and the customs attached to it, from asserting the greater antiquity of Syracuse to this town, but he placed his native city next, and by the smallest possible interval, and then dated all the other colonies with reference to Syracuse as really the capital of Sicily. This is manifest from Thucydides' account.

But how did Antiochus fix the date of the founding of Syracuse? Surely by no careful reasoning backward from later and clearer history, by no examination of existing records,

---

[1] γ 491, sq.

but rather by reasoning downward from an assumed date of Heracles to Archias the founder, who was the eleventh in descent from that hero. This would give 330 years from Heracles to Archias' maturity. Let us note that Pheidon of Argos was for the very same reason misdated to 747 B.C.

Starting, I believe, from this à priori determination, Antiochus seems to have reversed the natural history of Greek colonisation in the West, for the sake of glorifying Syracuse. Other legends tell of Archias helping the founder of Corcyra; they tell of his helping, on his way to Sicily, the Greek settlers in southern Italy.[1] Surely this indicates what really happened. Greek settlers first occupied Corcyra, then they pushed on to Italy, and, avoiding the barren shore north of Otranto, found rich plains about the Liris, of which Archilochus speaks (I think) as of new discoveries. Thence they found their way to Sicily. I do not believe that this latter island was colonised till after 700 B.C., and that the whole Sicilian chronology found in all our Greek histories rests on the imaginary basis laid down by Antiochus.

In order to bring my history of the Homeric question up to the present date, I here add that Kirchhoff's text of the Odyssey and his critical essays have just appeared in a new and more complete form (die homerische Odyssee, 2nd ed., Berlin, 1879). In the preface to this book Kirchhoff sums up briefly the leading points of his theory, which is here more definitely stated than in his previous essays. He holds our Odyssey to be made up (1) of the old Nostos of Odysseus,[2] composed at a very early date, complete in itself, and of the highest poetic merit, but composed when epic composition was already at its zenith, and far from its rude beginnings. (2) An early continuation of this Nostos by a later poet, but still before the first Olympiad in date. This poet sang the adventures of Odysseus after his return,[3] embodying in his work many shorter lays which we cannot now sever. That this poet was not identical with the composer of the Nostos, Kirchhoff infers with perfect confidence [4] from the fact that in poetical merit he is far beneath him. Aus diesem für

[1] Cf. Müller, FHG. i. p. 183.
[2] α–ν 184.
[3] ν 182–ψ 296.
[4] p. 496

sich allein völlig durchschlagenden Grunde ist es ganz unmöglich Identität der Verfasser anzunehmen. (3) But anyone who looks into these separately printed divisions of Kirchhoff's text will notice long passages in a smaller type. These are due to the later redaction of the poem, about Ol. 30, by a person of no poetic power, who expanded the earlier work, and in his day combined the whole with all manner of needless and disturbing interpolations.

The reader will easily see how far I am disposed to agree with this definite theory. I am unable to feel the decided inferiority of the second poet, and I see no evidence that he must have lived before 776 B.C. But in holding a conscious combination of larger unities by a poet artist in the eighth century, Kirchhoff seems to me correct. How far the redactor of the thirtieth Olympiad is necessary cannot be determined without an intricate discussion. The usual German feature of settling antiquity, and denying identity, according to subjective notions as to poetic merit, has not diminished in Kirchhoff's now long-matured views.

INDEX TO VOLUME I.

INDEX.

BIN

CLO ·

Bindseil, H., 224 (concordance of Pindar)
Bion, 419 sq.
Birds of Aristophanes, 451 sq.
Blackie, Prof. J. S.,45, 277
Blass, Dr. F., 171, 393, 404
Blaydes, 318, 442
Bloomfield, 408
Boeckh, 211, 212, 213, 224, 319
Boehme, 128
Bœotia, 96
Bœotian School of Hesiod, 26
Boissonade, 95
Bonitz, 51, 61, 62, 79
Born (trans. *Knights*), 444
Bothe, 93, 389, 448, 470
Botzon (on Sophron), 407, 408
Boyer (*Oreste* of), 357
Brandreth, 45
Brevia (or Didymic) Scholia on Homer, 41
Briggs, 418
Browning, Mr. Robert, 268, 276, 277, 329, 335, 348, 353, 361, 381, 445, 466
Browning, Mrs. (trans. *Prometheus*), 264, 277
Brumoy, 389, 470
Brunck, 192, 318
Brutus, 332
Buchanan, 328, 332
Bucolic poetry, 5, 7, 409 sq.
Bunbury, Mr. (Geography of Ancients), 523
Bupalus, the sculptor, 194
Burnouf, Émile, 11, 79, 111, 180
Butcher, Mr. (trans. *Odyssey*), 44, 45
Buttmann, 38, 42
Byron, 154

CADMEAN Letters, 11
Calcraft, J. W., 372
Calderon, 261, 263
Caligula depreciated Homer, 34
Calliergi, 418
Callimachus, 7, 94, 147, 148, 194, 195, 412, 468
Callinus, 158, 163, 191
Callistratus, 37, 388, 436, 440, 452
Calverley, Mr. C. S., 4.9
Calydon, the boar hunt of, 18
Calypso, 19
Calzabigi, 328
Camerarius, 43, 192
Campbell, Mr. L., 318, 320
Caravella, 470

VOL. I.

Carmélli (trans. Euripides), 389
Catalogue in the Iliad, 9, 25
Catalogue of Women, 18
Cavalotti, Felix (ed. Tyrtæus), 163
Centaurs, 19
Centones Homerici, 154
Cercops, 114, 116
Ceriani, M., 469
Chæremon, 396
Chalcondylas, 43, 490
Chapman, 44, 93, 121
Chapman, J. H., 419
Chappell, Mr. Wm. (*History of Music*), 158, 165, 168
Character plays, 312
Charaxus, 179
Charites of Orchomenos, 12
Charops, 14
Chateaubriand, 313
Chateaubrun, 345
Χείρωνος ὑποθῆκαι, 115
Chénier, 306
Chersias, 114
Cherubini, 333
Chian Hymn to Apollo, 25
Chilo, 201
Chionides, 423 sq.
Chios, 65
Choephori, of Æschylus, 268 sq.
Chœrile, 322
Chœrilus, (epicus) 147, (satyricus) 231, 232
Choragic monuments, 135, 246
Chorizontes, on Homer, 36-8, 68
Chorus, Greek, real character of, 258
Christopoulos, 45
Chrysippus, 33, 117
Chrysostom, Dion, 313, 380
Chrysostom, John, 440
Chrysothemis, 14
Cicero, 125, 293, 297, 303, 309, 313, 324, 332 (on the Medea), 345, 348, 357, 400, 422
Circe, 19
City editions of Homer, 29, 35
Clark, W. G., 469
Clarke, S., 43
Cleanthes, 33
Cleaver, W., 163
Cleisthenes, 26, 201
Cleobulus, 201
Cleon, 428, 429, 440, 443, 450, 451
Cleophon, 362, 429
Clitus, 339
Clonas, of Tegea, 167
Clouds, of Aristophanes, 444 sq.

M M

LONDON : PRINTED BY
SPOTTISWOODE AND CO., NEW-STREET SQUARE
AND PARLIAMENT STREET

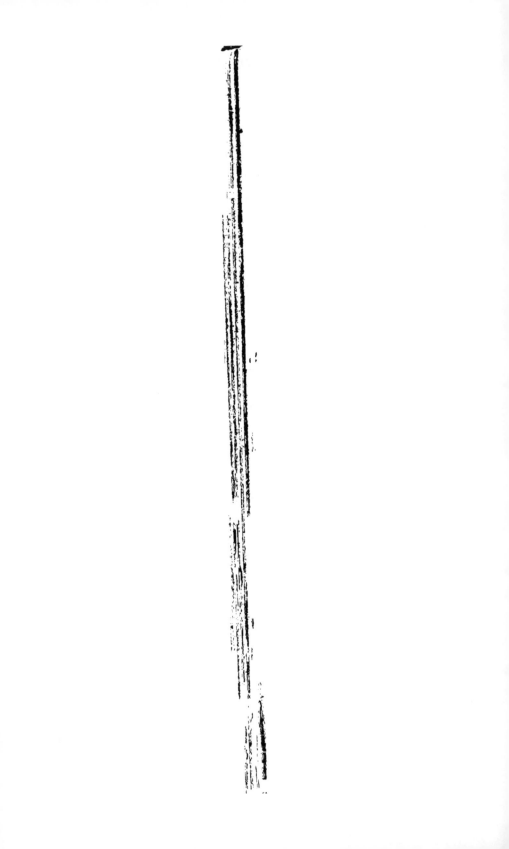

AUGUST 1887.

GENERAL LISTS OF WORKS
PUBLISHED BY
Messrs. LONGMANS, GREEN, & CO.
39 PATERNOSTER ROW, LONDON, E.C.; AND
15 EAST 16th STREET, NEW YORK.

———ooʒⁱᵒⁱᵒᵒ———

HISTORY, POLITICS, HISTORICAL MEMOIRS, &c.

Abbey's The English Church and its Bishops, 1700–1800. 2 vols. 8vo. 24s.
Abbey and Overton's English Church in the Eighteenth Century. Cr. 8vo. 7s. 6d.
Arnold's Lectures on Modern History. 8vo. 7s. 6d.
Bagwell's Ireland under the Tudors. Vols. 1 and 2. 2 vols. 8vo. 32s.
Ball's The Reformed Church of Ireland, 1537–1886. 8vo. 7s. 6d.
Boultbee's History of the Church of England, Pre-Reformation Period. 8vo. 15s.
Buckle's History of Civilisation. 3 vols. crown 8vo. 24s.
Cox's (Sir G. W.) General History of Greece. Crown 8vo. Maps, 7s. 6d.
Creighton's History of the Papacy during the Reformation. 8vo. Vols. 1 and 2,
  32s. Vols. 3 and 4, 24s.
De Tocqueville's Democracy in America. 2 vols. crown 8vo. 16s.
D'Herisson's The Black Cabinet. Crown 8vo. 7s. 6d.
Doyle's English in America : Virginia, Maryland, and the Carolinas, 8vo. 18s.
—   —   — The Puritan Colonies, 2 vols. 8vo. 36s.
Epochs of Ancient History. Edited by the Rev. Sir G. W. Cox, Bart. and C.
  Sankey, M.A. With Maps. Fcp. 8vo. price 2s. 6d. each.

Beesly's Gracchi, Marius, and Sulla.	Ihne's Rome to its Capture by the
Capes's Age of the Antonines.	Gauls.
— Early Roman Empire.	Merivale's Roman Triumvirates.
Cox's Athenian Empire.	Sankey's Spartan and Theban Supre-
— Greeks and Persians.	macies.
Curteis's Rise of the Macedonian	Smith's Rome and Carthage, the
Empire.	Punic Wars.

Epochs of Modern History. Edited by C. Colbeck, M.A. With Maps. Fcp. 8vo.
  price 2s. 6d. each.

Church's Beginning of the Middle Ages.	Longman's Frederick the Great and the Seven Years' War.
Cox's Crusades.	· Ludlow's War of American Inde-
Creighton's Age of Elizabeth.	pendence.
Gairdner's Houses of Lancaster and York.	M'Carthy's Epoch of Reform, 1830–1850.
Gardiner's Puritan Revolution.	Moberly's The Early Tudors.
— Thirty Years' War.	Morris's Age of Queen Anne.
— (Mrs.) French Revolution, 1789–1795.	— The Early Hanoverians.
Hale's Fall of the Stuarts.	Seebohm's Protestant Revolution.
Johnson's Normans in Europe.	Stubbs's The Early Plantagenets. Warburton's Edward III.

Epochs of Church History. Edited by the Rev. Mandell Creighton, M.A.
  Fcp. 8vo. price 2s. 6d. each.

Brodrick's A History of the Uni- versity of Oxford.	Perry's The Reformation in England.
Carr's The Church and the Roman Empire.	Plummer's The Church of the Early Fathers.
Overton's The Evangelical Revival in the Eighteenth Century.	Tucker's The English Church in other Lands.

₊ Other Volumes in preparation.

LONGMANS, GREEN, & CO. London and New York.

4   General Lists of Works.

Buckle's (H. T.) Miscellaneous and Posthumous Works. 2 vols. crown 8vo. 21s.
Crump's A Short Enquiry into the Formation of English Political Opinion. 8vo. 7s. 6d.
Dowell's A History of Taxation and Taxes in England. 4 vols. 8vo. 48s.
Green's (Thomas Hill) Works. (3 vols.) Vols. 1 & 2, Philosophical Works. 8vo. 16s. each.
Hume's Essays, edited by Green & Grose. 2 vols. 8vo. 28s.
— Treatise of Human Nature, edited by Green & Grose. 2 vols. 8vo. 28s.
Ladd's Elements of Physiological Psychology. 8vo. 21s.
Lang's Custom and Myth : Studies of Early Usage and Belief. Crown 8vo. 7s. 6d.
Leslie's Essays in Political and Moral Philosophy. 8vo. 10s. 6d.
Lewes's History of Philosophy. 2 vols. 8vo. 32s.
Lubbock's Origin of Civilisation. 8vo. 18s.
Macleod's Principles of Economical Philosophy. In 2 vols. Vol. 1, 8vo. 15s. Vol. 2, Part I. 12s.
— The Elements of Economics. (2 vols.) Vol. 1, cr. 8vo. 7s. 6d. Vol. 2, Part I. cr. 8vo. 7s. 6d.
— The Elements of Banking. Crown 8vo. 5s.
— The Theory and Practice of Banking. Vol. 1, 8vo. 12s. Vol. 2, 14s.
— Economics for Beginners. 8vo. 2s. 6d.
— Lectures on Credit and Banking. 8vo. 5s.
Mill's (James) Analysis of the Phenomena of the Human Mind. 2 vols. 8vo. 28s.
Mill (John Stuart) on Representative Government. Crown 8vo. 2s.
— — on Liberty. Crown 8vo. 1s. 4d.
— — Examination of Hamilton's Philosophy. 8vo. 16s.
— — Logic. Crown 8vo. 5s.
— — Principles of Political Economy. 2 vols. 8vo. 30s. People's Edition, 1 vol. crown 8vo. 5s.
— — Subjection of Women. Crown 8vo. 6s.
— — Utilitarianism. 8vo. 5s.
— — Three Essays on Religion, &c. 8vo. 5s.
Mulhall's History of Prices since 1850. Crown 8vo. 6s.
Müller's The Science of Thought. 8vo. 21s.
Sandars's Institutes of Justinian, with English Notes. 8vo. 18s.
Seebohm's English Village Community. 8vo. 16s.
Sully's Outlines of Psychology. 8vo. 12s. 6d.
— Teacher's Handbook of Psychology. Crown 8vo. 6s. 6d.
Swinburne's Picture Logic. Post 8vo. 5s.
Thompson's A System of Psychology. 2 vols. 8vo. 36s.
— The Problem of Evil. 8vo. 10s. 6d.
Thomson's Outline of Necessary Laws of Thought. Crown 8vo. 6s.
Twiss's Law of Nations in Time of War. 8vo. 21s.
— — in Time of Peace. 8vo. 15s.
Webb's The Veil of Isis. 8vo. 10s. 6d.
Whately's Elements of Logic. Crown 8vo. 4s. 6d.
— — Rhetoric. Crown 8vo. 4s. 6d.
Wylie's Labour, Leisure, and Luxury. Crown 8vo. 6s.
Zeller's History of Eclecticism in Greek Philosophy. Crown 8vo. 10s. 6d.
— Plato and the Older Academy. Crown 8vo. 18s.
— Pre-Socratic Schools. 2 vols. crown 8vo. 30s.
— Socrates and the Socratic Schools. Crown 8vo. 10s. 6d.
— Stoics, Epicureans, and Sceptics. Crown 8vo. 15s.
— Outlines of the History of Greek Philosophy. Crown 8vo. 10s. 6d.

LONGMANS, GREEN, & CO., London and New York.

MISCELLANEOUS WORKS.

A. K. H. B., The Essays and Contributions of. Crown 8vo.

Autumn Holiaays of a Country Parson. 3*s*. 6*d*.

Changed Aspects of Unchanged Truths. 3*s*. 6*d*.

Common-Place Philosopher in Town and Country. 3*s*. 6*d*.

Critical Essays of a Country Parson. 3*s*. 6*d*.

Counsel and Comfort spoken from a City Pulpit. 3*s*. 6*d*.

Graver Thoughts of a Country Parson. Three Series. 3*s*. 6*d*. each.

Landscapes, Churches, and Moralities. 3*s*. 6*d*.

Leisure Hours in Town. 3*s*. 6*d*. Lessons of Middle Age. 3*s*. 6*d*.

Our Homely Comedy ; and Tragedy. 3*s*. 6*d*.

Our Little Life. Essays Consolatory and Domestic. Two Series. 3*s*. 6*d*.

Present-day Thoughts. 3*s*. 6*d*. [each.

Recreations of a Country Parson. Three Series. 3*s*. 6*d*. each.

Seaside Musings on Sundays and Week-Days. 3*s*. 6*d*.

Sunday Afternoons in the Parish Church of a University City. 3*s*. 6*d*.

Armstrong's (Ed. J.) Essays and Sketches. Fcp. 8vo. 5*s*.

Arnold's (Dr. Thomas) Miscellaneous Works. 8vo. 7*s*. 6*d*.

Bagehot's Literary Studies, edited by Hutton. 2 vols. 8vo. 28*s*.

Beaconsfield (Lord), The Wit and Wisdom of. Crown 8vo. 1*s*. boards ; 1*s*. 6*d*. cl.

Evans's Bronze Implements of Great Britain. 8vo. 25*s*.

Farrar's Language and Languages. Crown 8vo. 6*s*.

Froude's Short Studies on Great Subjects. 4 vols. crown 8vo. 24*s*.

Lang's Letters to Dead Authors. Fcp. 8vo. 6*s*. 6*d*.

— Books and Bookmen. Crown 8vo. 6*s*. 6*d*.

Macaulay's Miscellaneous Writings. 2 vols. 8vo. 21*s*. 1 vol. crown 8vo. 4*s*. 6*d*.

— Miscellaneous Writings and Speeches. Crown 8vo. 6*s*.

— Miscellaneous Writings, Speeches, Lays of Ancient Rome, &c. Cabinet Edition. 4 vols. crown 8vo. 24*s*.

— Writings, Selections from. Crown 8vo. 6*s*.

Müller's (Max) Lectures on the Science of Language. 2 vols. crown 8vo. 16*s*.

— — Lectures on India. 8vo. 12*s*. 6*d*.

Proctor's Chance and Luck. Crown 8vo. 5*s*.

Smith (Sydney) The Wit and Wisdom of. Crown 8vo. 1*s*. boards ; 1*s*. 6*d*. cloth.

ASTRONOMY.

Herschel's Outlines of Astronomy. Square crown 8vo. 12*s*.

Proctor's Larger Star Atlas. Folio, 15*s*. or Maps only, 12*s*. 6*d*.

— New Star Atlas. Crown 8vo. 5*s*.

— Light Seience for Leisure Hours. 3 Series. Crown 8vo. 5*s*. each.

— The Moon. Crown 8vo. 6*s*.

— Other Worlds than Ours. Crown 8vo. 5*s*.

— The Sun. Crown 8vo. 14*s*.

— Studies of Venus-Transits. 8vo. 5*s*.

— Orbs Around Us. Crown 8vo. 5*s*.

— Universe of Stars. 8vo. 10*s*. 6*d*.

Webb's Celestial Objects for Common Telescopes. Crown 8vo. 9*s*.

THE 'KNOWLEDGE' LIBRARY.
Edited by RICHARD A. PROCTOR.

How to Play Whist. Crown 8vo. 5*s*.

Home Whist. 16mo. 1*s*.

The Borderland of Science. Cr. 8vo. 6*s*.

Nature Studies. Crown 8vo. 6*s*.

Leisure Readings. Crown 8vo. 6*s*.

The Stars in their Seasons. Imp. 8vo. 5*s*

Myths and Marvels of Astronomy Crown 8vo. 6*s*.

Pleasant Ways in Science. Cr. 8vo. 6*s*.

Star Primer. Crown 4to. 2*s*. 6*d*.

The Seasons Pictured. Demy 4to. 5*s*.

Strength and Happiness. Cr. 8vo. 5*s*.

Rough Ways made Smooth. Cr. 8vo. 6*s*.

The Expanse of Heaven. Cr. 8vo. 5*s*.

Our Place among Infinities. Cr. 8vo. 5*s*.

LONGMANS, GREEN, & CO., London and New York.

6 General Lists of Works.

CLASSICAL LANGUAGES AND LITERATURE.

Æschylus, The Eumenides of. Text, with Metrical English Translation, by J. F. Davies. 8vo. 7s.

Aristophanes' The Acharnians, translated by R. Y. Tyrrell. Crown 8vo. 2s. 6d.

Aristotle's The Ethics, Text and Notes, by Sir Alex. Grant, Bart. 2 vols. 8vo. 32s.

— The Nicomachean Ethics, translated by Williams, crown 8vo. 7s. 6d.

— The Politics, Books I. III. IV. (VII.) with Translation, &c. by Bolland and Lang. Crown 8vo. 7s. 6d.

Becker's *Charicles* and *Gallus*, by Metcalfe. Post 8vo. 7s. 6d. each.

Cicero's Correspondence, Text and Notes, by R. Y. Tyrrell. Vols. 1 & 2, 8vo. 12s. each.

Homer's Iliad, Homometrically translated by Cayley. 8vo. 12s. 6d.

— — Greek Text, with Verse Translation, by W. C. Green. Vol. 1, Books I.-XII. Crown 8vo. 6s.

Mahaffy's Classical Greek Literature. Crown 8vo. Vol. 1, The Poets, 7s. 6d. Vol. 2, The Prose Writers, 7s. 6d.

Plato's Parmenides, with Notes, &c. by J. Maguire. 8vo. 7s. 6d.

Virgil's Works, Latin Text, with Commentary, by Kennedy. Crown 8vo. 10s. 6d.

— Æneid, translated into English Verse, by Conington. Crown 8vo. 9s.

— — — — — — by W. J. Thornhill. Cr. 8vo. 7s.6d.

— Poems, — — — Prose, by Conington. Crown 8vo. 9s.

Witt's Myths of Hellas, translated by F. M. Younghusband. Crown 8vo. 3s. 6d.

— The Trojan War, — — Fcp. 8vo. 2s.

— The Wanderings of Ulysses, Crown 8vo. 3s. 6d.

NATURAL HISTORY, BOTANY, & GARDENING.

Allen's Flowers and their Pedigrees. Crown 8vo. Woodcuts, 5s.

Decaisne and Le Maout's General System of Botany. Imperial 8vo. 31s. 6d.

Dixon's Rural Bird Life. Crown 8vo. Illustrations, 5s.

Hartwig's Aerial World, 8vo. 10s. 6d.

— Polar World, 8vo. 10s. 6d.

— Sea and its Living Wonders. 8vo. 10s. 6d.

— Subterranean World, 8vo. 10s. 6d.

— Tropical World, 8vo. 10s. 6d.

Lindley's Treasury of Botany. 2 vols. fcp. 8vo. 12s.

Loudon's Encyclopædia of Gardening. 8vo. 21s.

— — Plants. 8vo. 42s.

Rivers's Orchard House. Crown 8vo. 5s.

— Miniature Fruit Garden. Fcp. 8vo. 4s.

Stanley's Familiar History of British Birds. Crown 8vo. 6s.

Wood's Bible Animals. With 112 Vignettes. 8vo. 10s. 6d.

— Common British Insects. Crown 8vo. 3s. 6d.

— Homes Without Hands, 8vo. 10s. 6d.

— Insects Abroad, 8vo. 10s. 6d.

— Horse and Man. 8vo. 14s.

— Insects at Home. With 700 Illustrations. 8vo. 10s. 6d.

— Out of Doors. Crown 8vo. 5s.

— Petland Revisited. Crown 8vo. 7s. 6d.

— Strange Dwellings. Crown 8vo. 5s. Popular Edition, 4to. 6d.

LONGMANS, GREEN, & CO., London and New York.

PRIZE AND PRESENTATION BOOKS.

Jameson's Sacred and Legendary Art. 6 vols. square 8vo.
Legends of the Madonna. 1 vol. 21s.
— — — Monastic Orders 1 vol. 21s.
— — — Saints and Martyrs. 2 vols. 31s. 6d.
— — — Saviour. Completed by Lady Eastlake. 2 vols. 42s.
Macaulay's Lays of Ancient Rome, illustrated by Scharf. Fcp. 4to. 10s. 6d.
The same, with *Ivry* and the *Armada*, illustrated by Weguelin. Crown 8vo. 3s. 6d.
New Testament (The) illustrated with Woodcuts after Paintings by the Early Masters. 4to. 21s.

By Dr. G. Hartwig.

Sea Monsters and Sea Birds (from 'The Sea and its Living Wonders'). With 75 Illustrations. Crown 8vo. 2s. 6d. cloth extra, gilt edges.

Denizens of the Deep (from 'The Sea and its Living Wonders'). With 117 Illustrations. Crown 8vo. 2s. 6d. cloth extra, gilt edges.

Dwellers in the Arctic Regions (from 'The Sea and its Living Wonders'). With 29 Illustrations. Crown 8vo. 2s. 6d. cloth extra, gilt edges.

Winged Life in the Tropics (from 'The Tropical World'). With 55 Illustrations. Crown 8vo. 2s. 6d. cloth extra, gilt edges.

Volcanoes and Earthquakes (from 'The Subterranean World'). With 30 Illustrations. Crown 8vo. 2s. 6d. cloth extra, gilt edges.

Wild Animals of the Tropics (from 'The Tropical World'). With 66 Illustrations. Crown 8vo. 3s. 6d. cloth extra, gilt edges.

By the Rev. J. G. Wood.

The Branch Builders (from 'Homes without Hands'). With 28 Illustrations. Crown 8vo. 2s. 6d. cloth extra, gilt edges.

Wild Animals of the Bible (from 'Bible Animals'). With 29 Illustrations. Crown 8vo. 3s. 6d. cloth extra, gilt edges.

Domestic Animals of the Bible (from 'Bible Animals'). With 23 Illustrations. Crown 8vo. 3s. 6d. cloth extra, gilt edges.

Bird Life of the Bible (from 'Bible Animals'). With 32 Illustrations. Crown 8vo. 3s. 6d. cloth extra, gilt edges.

Wonderful Nests (from 'Homes without Hands'). With 30 Illustrations. Crown 8vo. 3s. 6d. cloth extra, gilt edges.

Homes Under the Ground (from 'Homes without Hands'). With 28 Illustrations. Crown 8vo. 3s. 6d. cloth extra, gilt edges.

CHEMISTRY ENGINEERING, & GENERAL SCIENCE.

Arnott's Elements of Physics or Natural Philosophy. Crown 8vo. 12s. 6d.
Barrett's English Glees and Part-Songs: their Historical Development. Crown 8vo. 7s. 6d.
Bourne's Catechism of the Steam Engine. Crown 8vo. 7s. 6d.
— Handbook of the Steam Engine. Fcp. 8vo. 9s.
— Recent Improvements in the Steam Engine. Fcp. 8vo. 6s.
Buckton's Our Dwellings, Healthy and Unhealthy. Crown 8vo. 3s. 6d.
Clerk's The Gas Engine. With Illustrations. Crown 8vo. 7s. 6d.
Crookes's Select Methods in Chemical Analysis. 8vo. 24s.
Culley's Handbook of Practical Telegraphy. 8vo. 16s.
Fairbairn's Useful Information for Engineers. 3 vols. crown 8vo. 31s. 6d.
— Mills and Millwork. 1 vol. 8vo. 25s.
Ganot's Elementary Treatise on Physics, by Atkinson. Large crown 8vo. 15s.
— Natural Philosophy, by Atkinson. Crown 8vo. 7s. 6d.
Grove's Correlation of Physical Forces. 8vo. 15s.
Haughton's Six Lectures on Physical Geography. 8vo. 15s.

LONGMANS, GREEN, & CO., London and New York.

Helmholtz on the Sensations of Tone. Royal 8vo. 28s.

Helmholtz's Lectures on Scientific Subjects. 2 vols. crown 8vo. 7s. 6d. each.

Hudson and Gosse's The Rotifera or 'Wheel Animalcules.' With 30 Coloured Plates. 6 parts. 4to. 10s. 6d. each. Complete, 2 vols. 4to. £3. 10s.

Hullah's Lectures on the History of Modern Music. 8vo. 8s. 6d.

— Transition Period of Musical History. 8vo. 10s. 6d.

Jackson's Aid to Engineering Solution. Royal 8vo. 21s.

Jago's Inorganic Chemistry, Theoretical and Practical. Fcp. 8vo. 2s.

Jeans' Railway Problems. 8vo. 12s. 6d.

Kolbe's Short Text-Book of Inorganic Chemistry. Crown 8vo. 7s. 6d.

Lloyd's Treatise on Magnetism. 8vo. 10s. 6d.

Macalister's Zoology and Morphology of Vertebrate Animals. 8vo. 10s. 6d.

Macfarren's Lectures on Harmony. 8vo. 12s.

Miller's Elements of Chemistry, Theoretical and Practical. 3 vols. 8vo. Part I. Chemical Physics, 16s. Part II. Inorganic Chemistry, 24s. Part III. Organic Chemistry, price 31s. 6d.

Mitchell's Manual of Practical Assaying. 8vo. 31s. 6d.

Noble's Hours with a Three-inch Telescope. Crown 8vo. 4s. 6d.

Northcott's Lathes and Turning. 8vo. 18s.

Owen's Comparative Anatomy and Physiology of the Vertebrate Animals. 3 vols. 8vo. 73s. 6d.

Piesse's Art of Perfumery. Square crown 8vo. 21s.

Richardson's The Health of Nations ; Works and Life of Edwin Chadwick, C.B. 2 vols. 8vo. 28s.

— The Commonhealth ; a Series of Essays. Crown 8vo. 6s.

Schellen's Spectrum Analysis. 8vo. 31s. 6d.

Sennett's Treatise on the Marine Steam Engine. 8vo. 21s.

Smith's Air and Rain. 8vo. 24s.

Stoney's The Theory of the Stresses on Girders, &c. Royal 8vo. 36s.

Tilden's Practical Chemistry. Fcp. 8vo. 1s. 6d.

Tyndall's Faraday as a Discoverer. Crown 8vo. 3s. 6d.

— Floating Matter of the Air. Crown 8vo. 7s. 6d.

— Fragments of Science. 2 vols. post 8vo. 16s.

— Heat a Mode of Motion. Crown 8vo. 12s.

— Lectures on Light delivered in America. Crown 8vo. 5s.

— Lessons on Electricity. Crown 8vo. 2s. 6d.

— Notes on Electrical Phenomena. Crown 8vo. 1s. sewed, 1s. 6d. cloth.

— Notes of Lectures on Light. Crown 8vo. 1s. sewed, 1s. 6d. cloth.

— Sound, with Frontispiece and 203 Woodcuts. Crown 8vo. 10s. 6d.

Watts's Dictionary of Chemistry. 9 vols. medium 8vo. £15. 2s. 6d.

Wilson's Manual of Health-Science. Crown 8vo. 2s. 6d.

THEOLOGICAL AND RELIGIOUS WORKS.

Arnold's (Rev. Dr. Thomas) Sermons. 6 vols. crown 8vo. 5s. each.

Boultbee's Commentary on the 39 Articles. Crown 8vo. 6s.

Browne's (Bishop) Exposition of the 39 Articles. 8vo. 16s.

Bullinger's Critical Lexicon and Concordance to the English and Greek New Testament. Royal 8vo. 15s.

Colenso on the Pentateuch and Book of Joshua. Crown 8vo. 6s.

Conder's Handbook of the Bible. Post 8vo. 7s. 6d.

LONGMANS, GREEN, & CO., London and New York.

Conybeare & Howson's Life and Letters of St. Paul :—
Library Edition, with Maps, Plates, and Woodcuts. 2 vols. square crown 8vo. 21s.
Student's Edition, revised and condensed, with 46 Illustrations and Maps. 1 vol. crown 8vo. 7s. 6d.

Cox's (Homersham) The First Century of Christianity. 8vo. 12s.

Davidson's Introduction to the Study of the New Testament. 2 vols. 8vo. 30s.

Edersheim's Life and Times of Jesus the Messiah. 2 vols. 8vo. 24s.
— Prophecy and History in relation to the Messiah. 8vo. 12s.

Ellicott's (Bishop) Commentary on St. Paul's Epistles. 8vo. Corinthians I. 16s. Galatians, 8s. 6d. Ephesians, 8s. 6d. Pastoral Epistles, 10s. 6d. Philippians, Colossians and Philemon, 10s. 6d. Thessalonians, 7s. 6d.
— Lectures on the Life of our Lord. 8vo. 12s.

Ewald's Antiquities of Israel, translated by Solly. 8vo. 12s. 6d.
— History of Israel, translated by Carpenter & Smith. 8 vols. 8vo. Vols. 1 & 2, 24s. Vols. 3 & 4, 21s. Vol. 5, 18s. Vol. 6, 16s. Vol. 7, 21s. Vol. 8, 18s.

Hobart's Medical Language of St. Luke. 8vo. 16s.

Hopkins's Christ the Consoler. Fcp. 8vo. 2s. 6d.

Jukes's New Man and the Eternal Life. Crown 8vo. 6s.
— . Second Death and the Restitution of all Things. Crown 8vo. 3s. 6d.
— Types of Genesis. Crown 8vo. 7s. 6d.
— The Mystery of the Kingdom. Crown 8vo. 3s. 6d.

Lenormant's New Translation of the Book of Genesis. Translated into English. 8vo. 10s. 6d.

Lyra Germanica : Hymns translated by Miss Winkworth. Fcp. 8vo. 5s.

Macdonald's (G.) Unspoken Sermons. Two Series, Crown 8vo. 3s. 6d. each.
— The Miracles of our Lord. Crown 8vo. 3s. 6d.

Manning's Temporal Mission of the Holy Ghost. Crown 8vo. 8s. 6d.

Martineau's Endeavours after the Christian Life. Crown 8vo. 7s. 6d.
— Hymns of Praise and Prayer. Crown 8vo. 4s. 6d. 32mo. 1s. 6d.
— Sermons, Hours of Thought on Sacred Things. 2 vols. 7s. 6d. each.

Monsell's Spiritual Songs for Sundays and Holidays. Fcp. 8vo. 5s. 18mo. 2s.

Müller's (Max) Origin and Growth of Religion. Crown 8vo. 7s. 6d.
— — Science of Religion. Crown 8vo. 7s. 6d.

Newman's Apologia pro Vitâ Suâ. Crown 8vo. 6s.
— The Idea of a University Defined and Illustrated. Crown 8vo. 7s.
— Historical Sketches. 3 vols. crown 8vo. 6s. each.
— Discussions and Arguments on Various Subjects. Crown 8vo. 6s.
— An Essay on the Development of Christian Doctrine. Crown 8vo. 6s.
— Certain Difficulties Felt by Anglicans in Catholic Teaching Considered. Vol. 1, crown 8vo. 7s. 6d. Vol. 2, crown 8vo. 5s. 6d.
— The Via Media of the Anglican Church, Illustrated in Lectures, &c. 2 vols. crown 8vo. 6s. each
— Essays, Critical and Historical. 2 vols. crown 8vo. 12s.
— Essays on Biblical and on Ecclesiastical Miracles. Crown 8vo. 6s.
— An Essay in Aid of a Grammar of Assent. 7s. 6d.

Overton's Life in the English Church (1660-1714). 8vo. 14s.

Supernatural Religion. Complete Edition. 3 vols. 8vo. 36s.

Younghusband's The Story of Our Lord told in Simple Language for Children. Illustrated. Crown 8vo. 2s. 6d. cloth plain ; 3s. 6d. cloth extra, gilt edges.

LONGMANS, GREEN, & CO., London and New York.

TRAVELS, ADVENTURES, &c.

Baker's Eight Years in Ceylon. Crown 8vo. 5s.
— Rifle and Hound in Ceylon. Crown 8vo. 5s.
Brassey's Sunshine and Storm in the East. Library Edition, 8vo. 21s. Cabinet Edition, crown 8vo. 7s. 6d. Popular Edition, 4to. 6d.
— Voyage in the 'Sunbeam.' Library Edition, 8vo. 21s. Cabinet Edition, crown 8vo. 7s. 6d. School Edition, fcp. 8vo. 2s. Popular Edition, 4to. 6d.
— In the Trades, the Tropics, and the 'Roaring Forties.' Library Edition, 8vo. 21s. Cabinet Edition, crown 8vo. 17s. 6d. Popular Edition, 4to. 6d.
Froude's Oceana ; or, England and her Colonies. Crown 8vo. 2s. boards ; 2s. 6d. cloth.
Howitt's Visits to Remarkable Places. Crown 8vo. 7s. 6d.
Riley's Athos ; or, The Mountain of the Monks. 8vo. 21s.
Three in Norway. By Two of Them. Illustrated. Crown 8vo. 2s. boards ; 2s. 6d. cloth.

WORKS OF FICTION.

Beaconsfield's (The Earl of) Novels and Tales. Hughenden Edition, with 2 Portraits on Steel and 11 Vignettes on Wood. 11 vols. crown 8vo. £2. 2s.
Cheap Edition, 11 vols. crown 8vo. 1s. each, boards ; 1s. 6d. each, cloth.

Lothair.
Sybil.
Coningsby.
Tancred.
Venetia.
Henrietta Temple.

Contarini Fleming.
Alroy, Ixion, &c.
The Young Duke, &c.
Vivian Grey.
Endymion.

Brabourne's (Lord) Friends and Foes from Fairyland. Crown 8vo. 6s.
Caddy's (Mrs.) Through the Fields with Linnæus : a Chapter in Swedish History. 2 vols. crown 8vo. 16s.
Gilkes' Boys and Masters. Crown 8vo. 3s. 6d.
Haggard's (H. Rider) She: a History of Adventure. Crown 8vo. 6s.
— — Allan Quatermain. Illustrated. Crown 8vo. 6s.
Harte (Bret) On the Frontier. Three Stories. 16mo. 1s.
— — By Shore and Sedge. Three Stories. 16mo. 1s.
— — In the Carquinez Woods. Crown 8vo. 1s. boards ; 1s. 6d. cloth.
Lyall's (Edna) The Autobiography of a Slander. Fcp. 1s. sewed.
Melville's (Whyte) Novels. 8 vols. fcp. 8vo. 1s. each, boards ; 1s. 6d. each, cloth.

Digby Grand.
General Bounce.
Kate Coventry.
The Gladiators.

Good for Nothing.
Holmby House.
The Interpreter.
The Queen's Maries.

Molesworth's (Mrs.) Marrying and Giving in Marriage. Crown 8vo. 2s. 6d.
Novels by the Author of ' The Atelier du Lys ' :
The Atelier du Lys ; or, An Art Student in the Reign of Terror. Crown 8vo. 2s. 6d.
Mademoiselle Mori: a Tale of Modern Rome. Crown 8vo. 2s. 6d.
In the Olden Time: a Tale of the Peasant War in Germany. Crown 8vo. 2s. 6d.
Hester's Venture. Crown 8vo. 2s. 6d.
Oliphant's (Mrs.) Madam. Crown 8vo. 1s. boards ; 1s. 6d. cloth.
— — In Trust : the Story of a Lady and her Lover. Crown 8vo. 1s. boards ; 1s. 6d. cloth.

LONGMANS, GREEN, & CO., London and New York.

Payn's (James) The Luck of the Darrells. Crown 8vo. 1s. boards; 1s. 6d. cloth.
— — Thicker than Water. Crown 8vo. 1s. boards; 1s. 6d. cloth.
Reader's Fairy Prince Follow-my-Lead. Crown 8vo. 2s. 6d.
— The Ghost of Brankinshaw; and other Tales. Fcp. 8vo. 2s. 6d.
Sewell's (Miss) Stories and Tales. Crown 8vo. 1s. each, boards; 1s. 6d. cloth; 2s. 6d. cloth extra, gilt edges.

Amy Herbert. Cleve Hall.
The Earl's Daughter.
Experience of Life.
Gertrude. Ivors.

A Glimpse of the World.
Katharine Ashton.
Laneton Parsonage.
Margaret Percival. Ursula.

Stevenson's (R. L.) The Dynamiter. Fcp. 8vo. 1s. sewed; 1s. 6d. cloth.
— — Strange Case of Dr. Jekyll and Mr. Hyde. Fcp. 8vo. 1s. sewed; 1s. 6d. cloth.
Sturgis' Thraldom : a Story. Crown 8vo. 6s.
Trollope's (Anthony) Novels. Fcp. 8vo. 1s. each, boards: 1s. 6d. cloth.
The Warden | Barchester Towers.

POETRY AND THE DRAMA.

Armstrong's (Ed. J.) Poetical Works. Fcp. 8vo. 5s.
— (G. F.) Poetical Works :—
Poems, Lyrical and Dramatic. Fcp. 8vo. 6s.
Ugone : a Tragedy. Fcp. 8vo. 6s.
A Garland from Greece. Fcp. 8vo. 9s.

King Saul. Fcp. 8vo. 5s.
King David. Fcp. 8vo. 6s.
King Solomon. Fcp. 8vo. 6s.
Stories of Wicklow. Fcp. 8vo. 9s.

Bowen's Harrow Songs and other Verses. Fcp. 8vo. 2s. 6d. ; or printed on hand-made paper, 5s.
Bowdler's Family Shakespeare. Medium 8vo. 14s. 6 vols. fcp. 8vo. 21s.
Dante's Divine Comedy, translated by James Innes Minchin. Crown 8vo. 15s.
Goethe's Faust, translated by Birds. Large crown 8vo. 12s. 6d.
— — translated by Webb. 8vo. 12s. 6d.
— — edited by Selss. Crown 8vo. 5s.
Ingelow's Poems. Vols. 1 and 2, fcp. 8vo. 12s.
— Lyrical and other Poems. Fcp. 8vo. 2s. 6d. cloth, plain ; 3s. cloth, gilt edges.
Macaulay's Lays of Ancient Rome, with Ivry and the Armada. Illustrated by Weguelin. Crown 8vo. 3s. 6d. gilt edges.
The same, Popular Edition. Illustrated by Scharf. Fcp. 4to. 6d. swd., 1s. cloth.
Nesbit's Lays and Legends. Crown 8vo. 5s.
Reader's Voices from Flowerland, a Birthday Book, 2s. 6d. cloth, 3s. 6d. roan.
Southey's Poetical Works. Medium 8vo. 14s.
Stevenson's A Child's Garden of Verses. Fcp. 8vo. 5s.
Virgil's Æneid, translated by Conington. Crown 8vo. 9s.
— Poems, translated into English Prose. Crown 8vo. 9s.

AGRICULTURE, HORSES, DOGS AND CATTLE.

Fitzwygram's Horses and Stables. 8vo. 5s.
Lloyd's The Science of Agriculture. 8vo. 12s.
Loudon's Encyclopædia of Agriculture. 21s.
Steel's Diseases of the Ox, a Manual of Bovine Pathology. 8vo. 16s.

LONGMANS, GREEN, & CO., London and New York.

Stonehenge's Dog in Health and Disease. Square crown 8vo. 7*. 6d.
—   Greyhound. Square crown 8vo. 15*.
Taylor's Agricultural Note Book. Fcp. 8vo. 2*. 6d.
Ville on Artificial Manures, by Crookes. 8vo. 21*.
Youatt's Work on the Dog. 8vo. 6*.
—   — — — Horse. 8vo. 7*. 6d.

SPORTS AND PASTIMES.

The Badminton Library of Sports and Pastimes. Edited by the Duke of Beaufort
  and A. E. T. Watson. With numerous Illustrations. Cr. 8vo. 10*. 6d. each.
     Hunting, by the Duke of Beaufort, &c.
     Fishing, by H. Cholmondeley-Pennell, &c. 2 vols.
     Racing, by the Earl of Suffolk, &c.
     Shooting, by Lord Walsingham, &c. 2 vols.
     Cycling. By Viscount Bury.
         ₊ *Other Volumes in preparation.*
Campbell-Walker's Correct Card, or How to Play at Whist. Fcp. 8vo. 2*. 6d.
Ford's Theory and Practice of Archery, revised by W. Butt. 8vo. 14*.
Francis's Treatise on Fishing in all its Branches. Post 8vo. 15*.
Longman's Chess Openings. Fcp. 8vo. 2*. 6d.
Pease's The Cleveland Hounds as a Trencher-Fed Pack. Royal 8vo. 18*.
Pole's Theory of the Modern Scientific Game of Whist. Fcp. 8vo. 2*. 6d.
Proctor's How to Play Whist. Crown 8vo. 5*.
Ronalds's Fly-Fisher's Entomology. 8vo. 14*.
Verney's Chess Eccentricities. Crown 8vo. 10*. 6d.
Wilcocks's Sea-Fisherman. Post 8vo. 6*.

ENCYCLOPÆDIAS, DICTIONARIES, AND BOOKS OF REFERENCE.

Acton's Modern Cookery for Private Families. Fcp. 8vo. 4*. 6d.
Ayre's Treasury of Bible Knowledge. Fcp. 8vo. 6*.
Brande's Dictionary of Science, Literature, and Art. 3 vols. medium 8vo. 63*.
Cabinet Lawyer (The), a Popular Digest of the Laws of England. Fcp. 8vo. 9*.
Cates's Dictionary of General Biography. Medium 8vo. 28*.
Gwilt's Encyclopædia of Architecture. 8vo. 52*. 6d.
Keith Johnston's Dictionary of Geography, or General Gazetteer. 8vo. 42*.
M'Culloch's Dictionary of Commerce and Commercial Navigation. 8vo. 63*.
Maunder's Biographical Treasury. Fcp. 8vo. 6*.
  —   Historical Treasury. Fcp. 8vo. 6*.
  —   Scientific and Literary Treasury. Fcp. 8vo. 6*.
  —   Treasury of Bible Knowledge, edited by Ayre. Fcp. 8vo. 6*.
  —   Treasury of Botany, edited by Lindley & Moore. Two Parts, 12*.
  —   Treasury of Geography. Fcp. 8vo. 6*.
  —   Treasury of Knowledge and Library of Reference. Fcp. 8vo. 6*.
  —   Treasury of Natural History. Fcp 8vo. 6*.
Quain's Dictionary of Medicine. Medium 8vo. 31*. 6d., or in 2 vols. 34*.
Reeve's Cookery and Housekeeping. Crown 8vo. 7*. 6d.
Rich's Dictionary of Roman and Greek Antiquities. Crown 8vo. 7*. 6d.
Roget's Thesaurus of English Words and Phrases. Crown 8vo. 10*. 6d.
Willich's Popular Tables, by Marriott. Crown 8vo. 10*. 6d.,

LONGMANS, GREEN, & CO., London and New York.

A SELECTION

OF

EDUCATIONAL WORKS.

TEXT-BOOKS OF SCIENCE

FULLY ILLUSTRATED.

Abney's Treatise on Photography. Fcp. 8vo. 3s. 6d.
Anderson's Strength of Materials. 3s. 6d.
Armstrong's Organic Chemistry. 3s. 6d.
Ball's Elements of Astronomy. 6s.
Barry's Railway Appliances. 3s. 6d.
Bauerman's Systematic Mineralogy. 6s.
— Descriptive Mineralogy. 6s.
Bloxam and Huntington's Metals. 5s.
Glazebrook's Physical Optics. 6s.
Glazebrook and Shaw's Practical Physics. 6s.
Gore's Art of Electro-Metallurgy. 6s.
Griffin's Algebra and Trigonometry. 3s. 6d. Notes and Solutions, 3s. 6d.
Holmes's The Steam Engine. 6s.
Jenkin's Electricity and Magnetism. 3s. 6d.
Maxwell's Theory of Heat. 3s. 6d.
Merrifield's Technical Arithmetic and Mensuration. 3s. 6d. Key, 3s. 6d.
Miller's Inorganic Chemistry. 3s. 6d.
Preece and Sivewright's Telegraphy. 5s.
Rutley's Study of Rocks, a Text-Book of Petrology. 4s. 6d.
Shelley's Workshop Appliances. 4s. 6d.
Thomé's Structural and Physiological Botany. 6s.
Thorpe's Quantitative Chemical Analysis. 4s. 6d.
Thorpe and Muir's Qualitative Analysis. 3s. 6d.
Tilden's Chemical Philosophy. 3s. 6d. With Answers to Problems. 4s. 6d.
Unwin's Elements of Machine Design. 6s.
Watson's Plane and Solid Geometry. 3s. 6d.

THE GREEK LANGUAGE.

Bloomfield's College and School Greek Testament. Fcp. 8vo. 5s.
Bolland & Lang's Politics of Aristotle. Post 8vo. 7s. 6d.
Collis's Chief Tenses of the Greek Irregular Verbs. 8vo. 1s.
— Pontes Græci, Stepping-Stone to Greek Grammar. 12mo. 3s. 6d.
— Praxis Græca, Etymology. 12mo. 2s. 6d.
— Greek Verse-Book, Praxis Iambica. 12mo. 4s. 6d.
Farrar's Brief Greek Syntax and Accidence. 12mo. 4s. 6d.
— Greek Grammar Rules for Harrow School. 12mo. 1s. 6d.
Geare's Notes on Thucydides. Book I. Fcp. 8vo. 2s. 6d.
Hewitt's Greek Examination-Papers. 12mo. 1s. 6d.
Isbister's Xenophon's Anabasis, Books I. to III. with Notes. 12mo. 3s. 6d.
Jerram's Graecè Reddenda. Crown 8vo. 1s. 6d.

LONGMANS, GREEN, & CO., London and New York.

Kennedy's Greek Grammar. 12mo. 4s. 6d.
Liddell & Scott's English-Greek Lexicon. 4to. 36s.; Square 12mo. 7s. 6d.
Mahaffy's Classical Greek Literature. Crown 8vo. Poets, 7s. 6d. Prose Writers, 7s. 6d.
Morris's Greek Lessons. Square 18mo. Part I. 2s. 6d.; Part II. 1s.
Parry's Elementary Greek Grammar. 12mo. 3s. 6d.
Plato's Republic, Book I. Greek Text, English Notes by Hardy. Crown 8vo. 3s.
Sheppard and Evans's Notes on Thucydides. Crown 8vo. 7s. 6d.
Thucydides, Book IV. with Notes by Barton and Chavasse. Crown 8vo. 5s.
Valpy's Greek Delectus, improved by White. 12mo. 2s. 6d. Key, 2s. 6d.
White's Xenophon's Expedition of Cyrus, with English Notes. 12mo. 7s. 6d.
Wilkins's Manual of Greek Prose Composition. Crown 8vo. 5s. Key, 5s.
— Exercises in Greek Prose Composition. Crown 8vo. 4s. 6d. Key, 2s. 6d.
— New Greek Delectus. Crown 8vo. 3s. 6d. Key, 2s. 6d.
— Progressive Greek Delectus. 12mo. 4s. Key, 2s. 6d.
— Progressive Greek Anthology. 12mo. 5s.
— Scriptores Attici, Excerpts with English Notes. Crown 8vo. 7s. 6d.
— Speeches from Thucydides translated. Post 8vo. 6s.
Yonge's English-Greek Lexicon. 4to. 21s.; Square 12mo. 8s. 6d.

THE LATIN LANGUAGE.

Bradley's Latin Prose Exercises. 12mo. 3s. 6d. Key, 5s.
— Continuous Lessons in Latin Prose. 12mo. 5s. Key, 5s. 6d.
— Cornelius Nepos, improved by White. 12mo. 3s. 6d.
— Eutropius, improved by White. 12mo. 2s. 6d.
— Ovid's Metamorphoses, improved by White. 12mo. 4s. 6d.
— Select Fables of Phædrus, improved by White. 12mo. 2s. 6d.
Collis's Chief Tenses of Latin Irregular Verbs. 8vo. 1s.
— Pontes Latini, Stepping-Stone to Latin Grammar. 12mo. 3s. 6d.
Hewitt's Latin Examination-Papers. 12mo. 1s. 6d.
Isbister's Cæsar, Books I.-VII. 12mo. 4s.; or with Reading Lessons, 4s. 6d.
— Cæsar's Commentaries, Books I.-V. 12mo. 3s. 6d.
— First Book of Cæsar's Gallic War. 12mo. 1s. 6d.
Jerram's Latiné Reddenda. Crown 8vo. 1s. 6d.
Kennedy's Child's Latin Primer, or First Latin Lessons. 12mo. 2s.
— Child's Latin Accidence. 12mo. 1s.
— Elementary Latin Grammar. 12mo. 3s. 6d.
— Elementary Latin Reading Book, or Tirocinium Latinum. 12mo. 2s.
— Latin Prose, Palæstra Stili Latini. 12mo. 6s.
— Latin Vocabulary. 12mo. 2s. 6d.
— Subsidia Primaria, Exercise Books to the Public School Latin Primer. I. Accidence and Simple Construction, 2s. 6d. II. Syntax, 3s. 6d.
— Key to the Exercises in Subsidia Primaria, Parts I. and II. price 5s.
— Subsidia Primaria, III. the Latin Compound Sentence. 12mo. 1s.
— Curriculum Stili Latini. 12mo. 4s. 6d. Key, 7s. 6d.
— Palæstra Latina, or Second Latin Reading Book. 12mo. 5s.

LONGMANS, GREEN, & CO., London and New York.

Millington's Latin Prose Composition. Crown 8vo. 3s. 6d.
 —   Selections from Latin Prose. Crown 8vo. 2s. 6d.
Moody's Eton Latin Grammar. 12mo. 2s. 6d. The Accidence separately, 1s.
Morris's Elementa Latina. Fcp. 8vo. 1s. 6d. Key, 2s. 6d.
Parry's Origines Romanæ, from Livy, with English Notes. Crown 8vo. 4s.
The Public School Latin Primer. 12mo. 2s. 6d.
 — — — — Grammar, by Rev. Dr. Kennedy. Post 8vo. 7s. 6d.
Prendergast's Mastery Series, Manual of Latin. 12mo. 2s. 6d.
Rapier's Introduction to Composition of Latin Verse. 12mo. 3s. 6d. Key, 2s. 6d.
Sheppard and Turner's Aids to Classical Study. 12mo. 5s. Key, 6s.
Valpy's Latin Delectus, improved by White. 12mo. 2s. 6d. Key, 3s. 6d.
Virgil's Æneid, translated into English Verse by Conington. Crown 8vo. 9s.
 —   Works, edited by Kennedy. Crown 8vo. 10s. 6d.
 —   translated into English Prose by Conington. Crown 8vo. 9s.
Walford's Progressive Exercises in Latin Elegiac Verse. 12mo. 2s. 6d. Key, 5s.
White and Riddle's Large Latin-English Dictionary. 1 vol. 4to. 21s.
White's Concise Latin-Eng. Dictionary for University Students. Royal 8vo. 12s.
 —   Junior Students' Eng.-Lat. & Lat.-Eng. Dictionary. Square 12mo. 5s.
     Separately { The Latin-English Dictionary, price 3s.
         { The English-Latin Dictionary, price 3s.
Yonge's Latin Gradus. Post 8vo. 9s.; or with Appendix, 12s.

WHITE'S GRAMMAR-SCHOOL GREEK TEXTS.

Æsop (Fables) & Palæphatus (Myths). 32mo. 1s.
Euripides, Hecuba. 2s.
Homer, Iliad, Book I. 1s.
 — Odyssey, Book I. 1s.
Lucian, Select Dialogues. 1s.
Xenophon, Anabasis, Books I. III. IV. V. & VI. 1s. 6d. each ; Book II. 1s.; Book VII. 2s.

Xenophón, Book I. without Vocabulary. 3d.
St. Matthew's and St. Luke's Gospels. 2s. 6d. each.
St. Mark's and St. John's Gospels. 1s. 6d. each.
The Acts of the Apostles. 2s. 6d.
St. Paul's Epistle to the Romans. 1s. 6d.

The Four Gospels in Greek, with Greek-English Lexicon. Edited by John T. White, D.D. Oxon. Square 32mo. price 5s.

WHITE'S GRAMMAR-SCHOOL LATIN TEXTS.

Cæsar, Gallic War, Books I. & II. V. & VI. 1s. each. Book I. without Vocabulary, 3d.
Cæsar, Gallic War, Books III. & IV. 9d. each.
Cæsar, Gallic War, Book VII. 1s. 6d.
Cicero, Cato Major (Old Age). 1s. 6d.
Cicero, Lælius (Friendship). 1s. 6d.
Eutropius, Roman History, Books I. & II. 1s. Books III. & IV. 1s.
Horace,Odes,Books I. II.& IV. 1s. each.
Horace, Odes, Book III. 1s. 6d.
Horace, Epodes and Carmen Seculare. 1s.

Nepos, Miltiades, Simon, Pausanias, Aristides. 9d.
Ovid. Selections from Epistles and Fasti. 1s.
Ovid, Select Myths from Metamorphoses. 9d.
Phædrus, Select Easy Fables,
Phædrus, Fables, Books I. & II. 1s.
Sallust, Bellum Catilinarium. 1s. 6d.
Virgil, Georgics, Book IV. 1s.
Virgil, Æneid, Books I. to VI. 1s. each.
Book I. without Vocabulary, 3d.
Virgil, Æneid, Books VII. VIII. X. XI. XII. 1s. 6d. each.

LONGMANS, GREEN, & CO., London and New York.

THE FRENCH LANGUAGE.

Albités's How to Speak French. Fcp. 8vo. 5s. 6d.
— Instantaneous French Exercises. Fcp. 2s. Key, 2s.
Cassal's French Genders. Crown 8vo. 3s. 6d.
Cassal & Karcher's Graduated French Translation Book. Part I. 3s. 6d.
Part II. 5s. Key to Part I. by Professor Cassal, price 5s.
Contanseau's Practical French and English Dictionary. Post 8vo. 3s. 6d.
— Pocket French and English Dictionary. Square 18mo. 1s. 6d.
— Premières Lectures. 12mo. 2s. 6d.
— First Step in French. 12mo. 2s. 6d. Key, 3s.
— French Accidence. 12mo. 2s. 6d.
— — Grammar. 12mo. 4s. Key, 3s.
Contanseau's Middle-Class French Course. Fcp. 8vo. :—

Accidence, 8d. | French Translation-Book, 8d.
Syntax, 8d. | Easy French Delectus, 8d.
French Conversation-Book, 8d. | First French Reader, 8d.
First French Exercise-Book, 8d. | Second French Reader, 8d.
Second French Exercise-Book, 8d. | French and English Dialogues, 8d.

Contanseau's Guide to French Translation. 12mo. 3s. 6d. Key 3s. 6d.
— Prosateurs et Poètes Français. 12mo. 5s.
— Précis de la Littérature Française. 12mo. 3s. 6d.
— Abrégé de l'Histoire de France. 12mo. 2s. 6d.
Féval's Chouans et Bleus, with Notes by C. Sankey, M.A. Fcp. 8vo. 2s. 6d.
Jerram's Sentences for Translation into French. Cr. 8vo. 1s. Key, 2s. 6d.
Prendergast's Mastery Series, French. 12mo. 2s. 6d.
Souvestre's Philosophe sous les Toits, by Stiévenard. Square 18mo. 1s. 6d.
Stepping-Stone to French Pronunciation. 18mo. 1s.
Stiévenard's Lectures Françaises from Modern Authors. 12mo. 4s. 6d.
— Rules and Exercises on the French Language. 12mo. 3s. 6d.
Tarver's Eton French Grammar. 12mo. 6s. 6d.

THE GERMAN LANGUAGE.

Blackley's Practical German and English Dictionary. Post 8vo. 3s. 6d.
Buchheim's German Poetry, for Repetition. 18mo. 1s. 6d.
Collis's Card of German Irregular Verbs. 8vo. 2s.
Fischer-Fischart's Elementary German Grammar. Fcp. 8vo. 2s. 6d.
Just's German Grammar. 12mo. 1s. 6d.
— German Reading Book. 12mo. 3s. 6d.
Longman's Pocket German and English Dictionary. Square 18mo. 2s. 6d.
Naftel's Elementary German Course for Public Schools. Fcp. 8vo.

German Accidence. 9d. | German Prose Composition Book. 9d.
German Syntax. 9d. | First German Reader. 9d.
First German Exercise-Book. 9d. | Second German Reader. 9d.
Second German Exercise-Book. 9d. |

Prendergast's Mastery Series, German. 12mo. 2s. 6d.
Quick's Essentials of German. Crown 8vo. 3s. 6d.
Selss's School Edition of Goethe's Faust. Crown 8vo. 5s.
— Outline of German Literature. Crown 8vo. 4s. 6d.
Wirth's German Chit-Chat. Crown 8vo. 2s. 6d.

LONGMANS, GREEN, & CO., London and New York.

Spottiswoode & Co. Printers, New-street Square, London.

Lightning Source UK Ltd.
Milton Keynes UK
UKHW022157260219
338052UK00009B/373/P